The **Rough Guide** to

Taiwan

written and researched by

Stephen Keeling and Brice Minnigh

ROUGH
GUIDES

Contents

Taiwan's National Parks colour section following p.144

Festivals of Taiwan colour section following p.304

◄◄ Chiang Kai-shek Memorial Hall ◄ Taipei 101

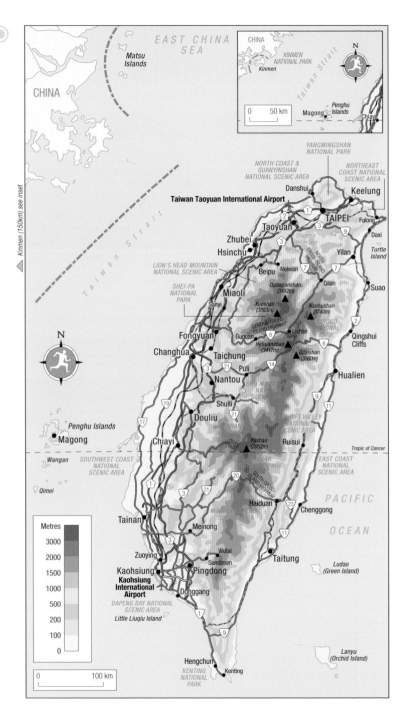

Introduction to
Taiwan

Taiwan remains largely undiscovered and seriously underrated by Western travellers, but those that make it here are in for a real treat. In the 1990s Taiwan became the first true Chinese democracy, developing a sense of civil society bewildering to its giant neighbour across the Taiwan Strait. Since then, popular culture has blossomed on the island, an eclectic mix of Chinese, Western, Japanese and indigenous influences. It has sensational food, traditional Chinese and aboriginal festivals and exuberant temples, yet the biggest surprise is Taiwan's hinterland: think towering mountains, eight national parks, a selection of alluring offshore islands and numerous hot-spring resorts.

Taiwan's perception problem stems in part from its astonishing economic success. The **Taiwan Miracle**, the island's transformation into one of the world's richest countries in less than fifty years, created images of endless manufacturing plants and overcrowded cities. The long struggle to establish a distinct political and cultural identity in the shadow of its big brother on the mainland hasn't helped – for years its rulers insisted that Taiwan was the "real China". Not any more: Taiwan has preserved much of the civilization and many of the traditions lost on the mainland, but while its political future remains uncertain, Taiwan has developed a dynamic culture all of its own.

One of the most endearing things about the island is the overwhelming **friendliness** of its people – Taiwan is one of the most welcoming countries in the world, and you are bound to encounter numerous acts of generosity or kindness throughout your travels, whether it's a taxi driver rounding down a fare, a stranger helping with directions or a family providing a bed for the night. **Eating** in Taiwan comes a close second, with a vast array of Chinese food and local delicacies on offer. Travelling around the island is relatively straightforward, though the lack of English can make things a challenge at times,

▲ Busy street, Taipei

particularly as most timetables tend to be displayed solely in Chinese. Taiwan is a relatively rich country compared to China or southeast Asia, but prices are generally lower than in most other developed nations, and the willingness of almost everyone you meet to help means it's almost impossible to get stuck.

Where to go

Most visits to Taiwan begin in **Taipei**, the capital and largest city, home to Taipei 101, the National Palace Museum and some of the island's best restaurants, bars and night markets. It's also surrounded by a host of worthy day-trips including the cable car to the teahouses of Maokong, the hot springs at **Beitou** and the volcanic peaks of **Yangmingshan National Park**. The storm-battered **North Coast and Guanyinshan National Scenic Area** is a short ride away, as is the wonderful night market in **Keelung**, the intriguing **Pingxi Branch Line Railway** and picturesque Shifen Falls. Nearby, the old mining towns of **Jinguashi** and **Jiufen** are deservedly popular for their historic streets and teahouses, while the **Northeast & Yilan Coast National Scenic Area** contains some of the most rugged coastline on the island. Southwest of Taipei, **Hsinchu** makes an excellent base for trips to **Hakka country**, the primary home of Taiwan's small but influential Hakka minority, while **Shei-Pa National Park** provides an opportunity to tackle some of Taiwan's largest and most memorable peaks. Nearby, **Taian Hot Springs** is perhaps the island's most alluring hot-spring resort.

Central Taiwan is home to some spectacular scenery, though it pays to spend a couple of days in vibrant **Taichung**, renowned for its teahouses and lively nightlife. Not far from the city, **Changhua** is noted principally for its Great Buddha Statue, and atmospheric **Lugang** is celebrated for its craftsmen and classical architecture. East of Taichung, picture-perfect **Sun Moon Lake** makes a fitting introduction to Taiwan's mighty central ranges, a place for languid lakeside walks and gorgeous views. Just outside Puli, to the north of the lake, **Chung Tai Chan Monastery** is a man-made wonder, a remarkable blend of modern architecture and Zen Buddhism. Heading south, **Chiayi** provides a staging post for the cool valleys and Tsou villages of the **Alishan National Scenic Area**. Beyond this lies **Yushan National Park** and the scintillating hike up Taiwan's highest mountain, commanding awe-inspiring, cloud-capped vistas.

South Taiwan is the most traditional part of the island, with **Tainan** making the obvious introduction to the region, a modern city crammed with historic sights, particularly temples, complemented by superb food. **Kaohsiung** is Taiwan's second city and an earthy counterweight to Taipei, its smattering of sights enhanced by a growing number of parks, outdoor cafés and bars. Nearby is the elegant monastery at **Foguangshan**, while the dramatic **Southern Cross-Island Highway** heads east across the mountains to Taitung, slicing through the northern end of **Maolin National Scenic Area**, rich in Paiwan and Rukai culture. The southern tip of Taiwan is dominated by **Kenting National Park**, with its popular beaches and surf spots.

The **east coast** is a world apart, isolated from the rest of Taiwan until very recently and still

Hot springs

With over 150 locations scattered all over the island, Taiwan has the world's second highest concentration of hot springs after Japan – many were developed commercially during the Japanese occupation and offer the same quality, scenery and therapeutic effects at a fraction of the cost. Many of the most famous springs are piped directly into hotel rooms and spa pools, where you can sample the waters via **public baths** or private tubs, but there are still places, usually in the mountains, where springs gush naturally from rocks or rivers and can be experienced for free. It's important to acquaint yourself with hot-spring etiquette before having a dip: unless the pools are mixed sex, you're expected to be naked, and you should shower before getting in.

Taiwanese food

Taiwan is celebrated for its "**little eats**" (*xiǎochī*), tasty snack food typically served in small portions at **night markets** all over the island. **Taiwanese cuisine** has its foundation in Fujianese cooking, but has been influenced by almost every other region of China, each town and village specializing in a particular dish: beef noodles in Taipei, *dānzǐ* noodles in Tainan, meatballs in Changhua, rice noodles in Hsinchu, and fish balls and milkfish in Kaohsiung – all washed down by large quantities of Taiwan Beer or *gāoliáng* liquor, the specialty of Kinmen.

home to the greatest concentration of its indigenous tribes. Most visitors make for **Taroko National Park**, with spectacular Taroko Gorge at its heart, in parts an incredibly narrow gap between lofty walls of stone. **Hualien** is the largest settlement on the east coast and makes the ideal gateway to Taroko, with plenty of opportunities to buy its famous marble, tasty dumplings and sweet-filled rice cakes. From here there are two routes south: the East Rift Valley is noted for its hot springs and rafting on the Xiuguluan River, while the coastal road twists past isolated beaches and Ami villages. Both end up at the laid-back town of **Taitung**, location of the National Museum of Prehistory and base for trips

▼ Lotus Lake, Kaohsiung

to **Ludao** (Green Island) with its exceptional outdoor springs.

Taiwan's offshore islands have their own distinctive cultures and histories. **Penghu**, in the middle of the Taiwan Strait, is an archipelago of magnificent beaches, old temples and crumbling fishing villages, a haven for windsurfing and other watersports. Just off the coast of China's Fujian province, the **Matsu Islands** provide a rare taster of traditional northern Fujian culture, as well as Taiwan's recent military history. The theme is continued on **Kinmen**, literally within sight of the now booming mainland city of Xiamen and rapidly remodelling itself as an open-air museum.

When to go

Taiwan has a subtropical monsoon **climate**, with wet, humid summers and short, relatively mild winters (though it often snows on the highest peaks). The north tends to be several degrees colder, and a lot wetter, than the tropical south. The **northeast monsoon** lasts about six months from October to late March and brings wet weather to Keelung and the northeast side of the island, while central and southern regions stay relatively dry. The **southwest monsoon** starts in May and ends in late September, primarily affecting the south. The latter part of this monsoon season is associated with **typhoons** that batter the east coast and central mountain range, with an average of two to three direct hits a year. That's not the end of the rain, however – the annual "**plum rain**" season can bring two months of rain any time between early spring and early summer, affecting the whole island.

Betel nut beauty

Betel nut, the seed of the Betel Palm (*Areca catechu*), has almost iconic status in Taiwan, where chewing it is often viewed as stereotypically Hoklo or Taiwanese behaviour. It's also big business: some estimates claim the industry nets annual revenue of around NT\$20bn. In Taiwan it's particularly popular with truck drivers, who prefer its stimulating effects to coffee: the nut is wrapped in *areca* leaf, topped with slaked lime paste and chewed without swallowing. Its most celebrated by-product is the **betel nut beauty** (*bīnláng xīshī*), scantily clad girls hired to sell the nuts from glass-encased booths on roadsides all over the island. More ominously, betel nut is a known **carcinogen**: Taiwan has one of the highest rates of mouth and throat cancer in Asia, primarily as a result of chewing the nut.

▼ Tea pickers, Lishan

In winter, the average monthly **temperature** ranges from 15 to 20°C across the island, while mid-30s are common in the summer. Temperatures in the high mountains can be substantially lower than on the plains. In general, autumn and winter are the best times to visit, though early summer (May to July) can also be pleasant at higher elevations and in the north, and the high temperatures in midsummer make watersports and beaches far more tempting at this time.

Average daily temperatures and monthly rainfall

	Jan	Feb	Mar	Apr	May	Jun	Jul	Aug	Sep	Oct	Nov	Dec
Taipei												
max/min (°C)	19/13	19/14	22/15	26/19	29/22	32/24	34/26	34/26	31/24	28/22	24/19	21/15
rainfall (mm)	87	166	180	183	259	319	248	305	275	139	86	79
Taichung												
max/min (°C)	22/12	22/13	25/16	28/19	30/22	32/24	33/25	32/25	32/24	30/21	27/18	24/14
rainfall (mm)	36	88	94	135	225	343	246	317	98	16	18	26
Kaohsiung												
max/min (°C)	23/15	24/16	27/19	28/22	30/24	32/26	32/26	32/26	31/25	30/24	27/20	25/17
rainfall (mm)	20	24	39	73	177	398	371	426	187	46	13	12
Hualien												
max/min (°C)	21/15	21/16	23/17	26/20	28/22	30/24	32/25	32/25	30/24	28/22	25/19	22/17
rainfall (mm)	72	100	87	96	195	220	177	261	344	367	171	68

things not to miss

It's not possible to see everything Taiwan has to offer in a single trip – and we don't suggest you try. What follows is a selective taste of the island's highlights: vibrant temples and monasteries, exuberant festivals, mouthwatering cuisine and spectacular landscapes. They're arranged in five colour-coded categories with a page reference to take you straight into the Guide, where you can find out more.

01 **Sun Moon Lake** Page **200** • One of the island's most relaxing retreats, with nature walks, cool breezes, calming views and a shoreline brimming with cultural interest.

02 Kinmen Page **353** •
This island is the frontline between Taiwan and China – the latter is literally a stone's throw away – and now an absorbing blend of former battlefields and well-preserved imperial Chinese monuments.

03 Hot springs
Page **159** •
Taiwan has over 150 hot springs, most set among mountainous landscapes and piped into hotel resorts, ranging from the ultra-hip to the cheap and cheerful.

04 Kenting National Park Page 278 • Studded with fine-sand beaches and rolling surf, this resort-fringed national park covers Taiwan's southern tip and is a haven of snorkelling and diving.

05 Taroko National Park
Page **299** • Taiwan's most visited national park is sliced in half by narrow, deep-cut Taroko Gorge, one of Asia's top natural wonders and an absolute must-see.

07 Lanyu (Orchid Island)
Page **328** • Inhabited almost solely by the seafaring Tao tribe, whose traditional ways of life give this lush Pacific island an almost Polynesian flavour.

06 Lugang Page **191** • Taiwan's most attractive old town, with traditional architecture, beautiful temples, tasty snack food and shops stocked with the work of the island's most accomplished craftsmen.

08 Aboriginal culture Page **395** • Taiwan's indigenous peoples, divided into fourteen officially recognized tribes and several other distinct groups, have their own vibrant cultures quite separate from the Chinese majority.

09 Tainan Page **235** • The old capital of Taiwan remains an important stronghold of Taiwanese culture, its myriad temples the perfect places to absorb its complex religious traditions.

10 Surfing Page **40** • The island's lengthy stretch of Pacific coastline has vastly underrated surfing, with countless breaks – and plenty of typhoon swell – to challenge both beginners and serious shredders.

11 Chung Tai Chan Monastery Page **212** • Nothing else quite looks like this enormous Buddhist monastery, packed with artistic gems, elegant shrines and innovative architecture.

12 Alishan National Scenic Area Page **221** • Gorgeous, rugged valleys, high mountain tea plantations and Tsou villages culminating in the misty forests of Alishan itself, home of the spectacular "sea of clouds".

13 National Palace Museum Page 81
• View the former contents of Beijing's Forbidden City in this world-famous museum, an extraordinary collection of Chinese art and historical artefacts.

14 Dajia Mazu Pilgrimage Page 188 •
One of the world's biggest festivals involves thousands of pilgrims on an animated seven-day parade circuit between the revered Mazu temples in Dajia and Xingang.

15 Matsu Islands Page 367 •
Just off the coast of China, these isolated islands are bastions of traditional Fujianese architecture, culture and cuisine, as well as being home to some awe-inspiring landscapes.

16 Cross-island highways Pages 147 & 270
• Three rough-hewn highways wind over the island's mountainous spine in the north, centre and south, making for heart-stopping, white-knuckle rides with spectacular views.

18 Climbing Yushan Page **229** • At 3952m, Yushan (Jade Mountain) is far and away northeast Asia's highest peak, but a spectacular and well-trodden trail to the summit makes it surprisingly accessible.

19 Night markets Page **29** • Taiwan's night markets are the best and cheapest places to try a selection of the island's famous "little eats".

17 East Coast National Scenic Area Page **308** • From the north's towering cliffs to the south's expansive beaches, the east coast is a feast for the eyes and is a hotbed of aboriginal cultures.

20 Taipei 101 Page **85** • At 509m, East Asia's tallest building dominates central Taipei, providing mind-blowing views of the surrounding area.

Basics

Basics

Getting there

BASICS | Getting there

Taiwan's main international gateway is Taiwan Taoyuan International Airport, located near the city of Taoyuan, about 50km southwest of the capital Taipei. The only other major international airport is at Kaohsiung, serving the country's second-largest city.

Although there are several nonstop flights to Taipei from North America and Europe, most trips will require a change of plane somewhere else in Asia – **Hong Kong** is the closest and most convenient place, with dozens of regional carriers flying into Taipei and Kaohsiung on a daily basis. Numerous nonstop flights also operate between Taiwan and mainland Chinese cities such as Beijing, Shanghai and Guangzhou.

From the UK and Ireland

There has long been a dearth of direct air connections between the **UK** and Taiwan, and the same is true when flying from **Ireland** or continental Europe. Almost all travellers coming from Europe will need to make at least one stop, with the closest and most convenient being **Hong Kong**, followed by Bangkok.

At the time of writing, the only airline with nonstop flights from **London** to Taipei was China Airlines, which flies three days a week (14hr) for about £800–900 return in peak season; they also fly to Taipei nonstop from Vienna and Frankfurt. EVA Air flies to Taipei from London via Bangkok for about the same price. From Ireland you'll save a heap of cash by taking a budget airline to London and connecting with one of the flights mentioned above.

From the US and Canada

There are several daily flights to Taiwan from North American cities on both the east and west coasts. From the **US**, direct flights leave from Los Angeles, New York, Seattle and San Francisco, with the average return fare around US$900–1200, depending on the time of year. Most nonstop flights from Canada operate out of Vancouver, but EVA Air also flies from Toronto three times a week from Can$1400.

From Australia, New Zealand and South Africa

Almost all flights between **Australia** and Taiwan have a stopover somewhere else in Asia, with **Hong Kong** the best-connected. Some of the cheapest fares to Hong Kong from Sydney are with Cathay Pacific, while the only nonstop flight between **Sydney** and Taipei (9hr) is with China Airlines (5 weekly), for about Aus$1400 return. China Airlines also flies nonstop from Brisbane three times a week for about the same price. EVA Air flies to Taipei direct from Brisbane only, twice a week.

Flights from **New Zealand** are more limited, with carriers such as Air New Zealand, Cathay Pacific and Singapore Airlines flying from Auckland to Taipei via Hong Kong for around NZ$2000.

From China

With the "three links" now open to foreigners, direct air and sea travel between Taiwan and **China** offers some intriguing travel opportunities. **Flights** between Taipei and Beijing (3hr 30min) are served by several carriers, with tickets for around US$400 return or less, but you can also reach Shanghai (just 1hr 30min), Guangzhou (2hr) and numerous other Chinese cities nonstop. The primary **sea routes** are Fuzhou to Matsu and Xiamen to Kinmen – see p.371 and p.355 respectively for details. If travelling to China from Taiwan, arrange a **Chinese visa** in Hong Kong or in your own country in advance – it's a lot of hassle to get one in Taiwan, as there are no Chinese consulates.

Airlines, agents and operators

Airlines

Air Canada ⓦ www.aircanada.com.
Air New Zealand ⓦ www.airnewzealand.com.
All Nippon Airways (ANA) ⓦ www.anaskyweb.com.
American Airlines ⓦ www.aa.com.
Asiana Airlines ⓦ www.flyasiana.com.
British Airways ⓦ www.ba.com.
Cathay Pacific ⓦ www.cathaypacific.com.
China Airlines ⓦ www.china-airlines.com.
Continental Airlines ⓦ www.continental.com.
Delta ⓦ www.delta.com.
EVA Air ⓦ www.evaair.com.
Finnair ⓦ www.finnair.com.
JAL (Japan Air Lines) ⓦ www.japanair.com.
KLM (Royal Dutch Airlines) ⓦ www.klm.com.
Korean Air ⓦ www.koreanair.com.
Lufthansa ⓦ www.lufthansa.com.
Malaysia Airlines ⓦ www.malaysia-airlines.com.
Qantas ⓦ www.qantas.com.
Royal Brunei ⓦ www.bruneiair.com.
Singapore Airlines ⓦ www.singaporeair.com.
South African Airways ⓦ www.flysaa.com.
Thai Airways ⓦ www.thaiair.com.
United Airlines ⓦ www.united.com.

Agents and operators

Absolute Asia ⓣ 1-800/736-8187, ⓦ www
.absoluteasia.com. Features several country-wide luxury tours ranging from four to nine days.
Greentours ⓣ 01298/83563, ⓦ www.greentours
.co.uk. Offers excellent eighteen-day expeditions by bus and on foot through central Taiwan and Lanyu Island, with a focus on flora and fauna, for around £3595.
Goway Travel Experiences ⓣ 1-800/387-8850 or 416/322-1034, ⓦ www.goway.com. One- to eight-day tours of all the main sights: Taipei, Taroko Gorge, Sun Moon Lake and Kenting.
Grasshopper Adventures UK ⓣ 020/8123-8144, US ⓣ 818/921-7101, ⓦ www.grasshopper adventures.com. Bicycle-tour specialist, with a variety of bike tours all over Asia including Taiwan, ranging from five to fifteen days and accompanied by experienced guides.
North South Travel UK ⓣ 01245/608 291, ⓦ www.northsouthtravel.co.uk. Friendly, competitive travel agency, offering discounted fares worldwide. Profits are used to support projects in the developing world, especially the promotion of sustainable tourism.
The Oriental Caravan ⓣ 01298/83563, ⓦ www .theorientalcaravan.com. Tour operator specializing in Japan, Tibet and Taiwan. Comprehensive tours (14 days) from £1695.
Trailfinders Australia ⓣ 1300/780-212, Republic of Ireland ⓣ 01/677-7888, UK ⓣ 0845/058 5858; ⓦ www.trailfinders.com. One of the best-informed and most efficient agents for independent travellers.
STA Travel Australia ⓣ 134 782, New Zealand ⓣ 0800/474-400, South Africa ⓣ 0861/781 781, UK ⓣ 0871/2300 040, US ⓣ 1-800/781-4040, ⓦ www .statravel.com. Worldwide specialists in independent travel; also student IDs, travel insurance, car rental, rail passes and more. Good discounts for students and under-26s.
Wings ⓣ 1-888/293-6443 or 520/320-9868, ⓦ wingsbirds.com. Specialists in birdwatching tours that cover most of Taiwan.

Getting around

Getting around in Taiwan can be ultra-convenient or infinitely frustrating, depending on where you are and what the weather is like. Efficient trains, a vast network of buses and a plethora of domestic flights are available, while ferries connect the offshore islands.

While the mountains that bisect the island make for some convoluted travel logistics, for most travellers the biggest challenge to getting around comes down to **language**.

Though signs in English – or at least in romanized script – are becoming more common, it still takes some planning to make your connections if you don't speak or

Distance chart

The figures shown on this chart represent the total distances **in kilometres** between major cities in Taiwan. They are calculated on the shortest available route by **major road**, rather than straight lines drawn on a map. For conversion, the figure **in miles** is roughly two-thirds of that given in kilometres: 8km equals 5 miles.

Changhua	Changhua								
Chiayi	66	Chiayi							
Hsinchu	103	169	Hsinchu						
Hualien	391	436	289	Hualien					
Kaohsiung	169	103	272	344	Kaohsiung				
Keelung	198	264	95	229	267	Keelung			
Taichung	19	85	84	372	188	179	Taichung		
Tainan	129	63	232	373	40	327	148	Tainan	
Taipei	173	239	70	217	342	25	154	302	Taipei
Taitung	329	262	463	88	170	403	348	199	391	Taitung

read Chinese. One of the best ways around this is to ask someone to **write down** the name of your destination in Chinese so that you can show it to clerks in bus and train stations. Likewise, it can pay to have the name of your hotel and/or the sites you wish to visit written in Chinese so you can show them to taxi drivers or people on the street if you get lost.

By rail

All major cities and towns in Taiwan are connected by the efficient Taiwan Railway Administration (TRA) network of local and express trains, though travel in Taiwan was revolutionized with the opening of the separately managed **High Speed Rail** in 2007. While regular express trains can take over five hours between Taipei and Kaohsiung, it takes just ninety minutes via the High Speed Rail (see p.22). The latter only covers major cities on the west coast however, while TRA trains run on both the **Western** and **Eastern** rail lines for about half the price of the High-Speed trains. The TRA also maintains several slower, narrow-gauge **branch lines** that mostly transport tourists inland to Jiji (see p.197), Neiwan and Pingxi (see p.139).

Updated **timetable** and fare information is listed on the *Taiwan Railway Passenger Train Timetable*, which can be found at train station information centres, as well as some convenience stores and kiosks. To check schedules online or make bookings in advance, check the TRA's website at www.railway.gov.tw.

Buying tickets

Train stations usually have separate **queues** for advance and same-day departures, as well as for cash and credit card purchases – this is usually labelled in English on the cashier's window. For shuttle journeys (see below) from main stations it's faster to use the **ticket machines** that are labelled in English. It's imperative that you **retain your ticket** when you get off the train, as you're still required to return it at the gate to exit the train station – if you lose it, you'll have to pay a fine.

There are five classes of train, from express to local services (see below). For the three fastest classes, it's often a good idea to buy your ticket **in advance** (either online or at the station), especially if you plan to travel on a weekend or public holiday, when all seats are commonly full. When no seats are available, you'll usually still be offered a ticket, but for **standing-room only**. If you do have a standing-room-only ticket but manage to find a free seat, it's acceptable to sit there until the ticket holder turns up and politely asks you to vacate.

Train classes

Note that Taiwan's penchant for different forms of pinyin is perfectly illustrated by the rail system, with station names and even

21

train classes written in a variety of styles. In this guide *Hànyǔ Pīnyīn* (see p.421–422) is the default, in line with government policy.

自強 Zìqiáng (sometimes written as *Tze-Chiang*) The fastest and most expensive, with assigned seating, a/c and, in some cases, a dining car.

莒光 Jǔguāng (sometimes written as *Chu-Kuang*). The second fastest, also with assigned seating and a/c.

復興 Fùxīng (sometimes written as *Fu-Hsing* or *Fusing*). The third fastest, also with assigned seating. Has air conditioning but is not as comfortable as the two higher classes.

區間快 "Local Express" (*qūjiān kuài*). Short- to medium-distance commuter train, which runs express. Has a/c, but there is no assigned seating

區間車 "Local Train" (*qūjiānchē*). Short- to medium-distance commuter train which stops at all stations. Has a/c, but there is no assigned seating.

Rail passes

Travellers under 30 can apply for a **Taiwan Rail Pass** (**TR Pass**) at all major train stations (you'll need a passport and student ID): five days for NT$599, seven days for NT$799 and ten days for NT$1098. If you intend to travel a lot this can be a good deal, though the catch is that the pass is only valid on non-reserved seats on *fùxīng* or commuter trains, not *zìqiáng* or High Speed Rail.

Anyone can buy the **Island-Round Rail Pass** for NT$1706, which offers up to fifteen percent discount on full *zìqiáng* fares: the pass comprises seven portions valid on all trains for fifteen days after first use (starting within sixty days of purchase).

High Speed Rail

Taiwan's superb **High Speed Rail** (台灣高鐵; *táiwān gāotiě*; @www.thsrc.com.tw) features a bullet train that has cut the travelling times between Taipei and Kaohsiung by two thirds. The train, one of the world's fastest, stops at eight stations along a 345-kilometre track travelling at an average speed of about 300kmph. Note however, that apart from Taipei, most of the specially built stations are well outside city centres and mean an additional shuttle leg for travellers looking to stay in the heart of major cities. The first eight High Speed Rail stations are: Taipei, Banqiao, Taoyuan, Hsinchu, Taichung, Chiayi, Tainan and Zuoying (Kaohsiung). Four

more stations will be added between 2012 and 2015 (Nangang, Miaoli, Changhua and Yunlin), while Kaohsiung will get it's own station sometime after that.

Sample train fares

Taipei–Kaohsiung High Speed Rail (to Zuoying); NT$1490; *zìqiáng* NT$845; *fùxīng* NT$544.
Taipei–Taichung High Speed Rail NT$700; *zìqiáng* NT$375; *fùxīng* NT$241.
Taipei–Tainan High Speed Rail NT$1350; *zìqiáng* NT$741; *fùxīng* NT$476.
Taipei–Hualien *zìqiáng* NT$441; *jǔguāng* NT$343.
Taipei–Taitung *zìqiáng* NT$786; *jǔguāng* NT$616.
Kaohsiung–Taitung *zìqiáng* NT$364; *jǔguāng* NT$280.

By bus

Buses are generally cheaper than trains, and, with the exception of the High Speed Rail, can be much faster – provided you travel when traffic is light and there are no road accidents. In addition, the best bus companies have extremely comfortable air-conditioned coaches, with big cosy **armchair-style seats**, movies and an on-board toilet. Bear in mind that the air conditioning is never turned off, so it can get quite chilly on board.

However, buses in **rural areas** are being dropped each year, as more Taiwanese tourists take to the roads in their own cars or book guided package tours. For independent travellers this makes already hard-to-reach mountain areas even more difficult to get to without your own transport.

In most cities, the main bus companies have ticket offices clustered around the train station, and their buses usually stop right outside the office. Be sure to save your ticket, as you are often required to return it to the driver before you are allowed off – if you lose it you might be asked to pay for another ticket. For more information on bus routes and recommended companies, see the relevant chapter of the guide.

Bus companies and fares

Aloha Bus ☏ 0800/043168
Free Go Bus ☏ 0800/051519
Ho-Hsin Bus ☏ 0800/002377, @www.ebus.com.tw.

Taiwan tours and the Youth Travel Card

The **Taiwan Tour Bus** programme is an umbrella for a variety of guided bus tours, usually no longer than one day, and originating in several major cities. Organized by the Tourism Bureau through local tour operators, there's a huge variety of itineraries – these can be useful for those short of time, or for visiting places difficult to reach with public transport. Prices range from NT$900 for half-day tours of Taipei to NT$1988 for day-trips to Taroko. You must reserve in advance; check ⓦwww .taiwantourbus.com.tw for more details.

If you are aged 15–30, you can also consider applying for the **Youth Travel Card** (ⓦwww.youthtravel.tw), which provides discounts at hotels, shops and sights all over the country. Apply at the airport visitor information desk on arrival (all you need is your ID – the card is free).

Kuo Kuang ☎0800/010138
Taoyuan Bus Corp ☎0800/053808
Ubus ☎0800/241560

Sample bus fares

Kaohsiung–Kenting NT$355
Taipei–Alishan NT$620
Taipei–Kaohsiung NT$520
Taipei–Sun Moon Lake NT$460
Taipei–Taichung NT$260
Taipei–Tainan NT$380

By car

In more remote areas such as the cross-island highway routes and segments of the east coast, **hiring a car** can be the most convenient way to get around. However, driving in major cities can be extremely stressful – and dangerous for inexperienced drivers – though anyone used to driving in big European and North American cities should find it manageable. Taiwanese drive on the right-hand side of the road, and the highway speed limit is 110kmph. On other roads speed limits generally range from 50 to 70kmph and police speed traps are common.

Foreign tourists renting a car in Taiwan will need to produce an **international driver's licence** and their **passport** for rentals of up to thirty days (you need a local licence for longer). **Prices** vary depending upon location, time of the week and the type of vehicle, but in general full-day rentals start from around NT$2200, and discounts of ten to fifteen percent are usually given for multiday rentals (although they're often not given during public holiday periods). Rental prices commonly include insurance, but you

may have to sign a blank credit card voucher to cover any speeding fines you may incur.

Car rental agencies in Taiwan

Car-Plus ☎0800/222-568, ⓦwww.car-plus .com.tw.
Chailease Auto Rental ☎02/2828-0033, ⓦwww.rentalcar.com.tw.
Formosa Car Rentals ☎04/2425-9831, ⓦwww.dragoncar.com.tw.
Hotai Leasing Corp ☎0800/024-550, ⓦwww.easyrent.com.tw.
Nice Rent A Car ☎02/2593-2000 or 0800/889888, ⓦwww.nicecar.com.tw.
VIP Car Rental ☎02/2713-1111, ⓦwww.vipcar.com.tw.

By scooter

The humble sc**ooter** remains the transport of choice in Taiwan, and is certainly the most convenient way to explore smaller cities and far-flung areas with little or no public transport. However, while renting a scooter is easy for Taiwanese or permanent residents, it's become increasingly difficult for foreign visitors in recent years.

The main problem is that the shops that rent the scooters are responsible for any fines you may incur on the road (which can take months to process). Most scooter shops are family operations that are not able to chase foreigners overseas to get them topay them back for these fines. Until the law is changed, most shops will insist on seeing a valid **ARC** (**Alien Resident Certificate**), proof of permanent address in Taiwan and a local licence. Few shops are aware that foreigners can legally drive a 50cc scooter with an **international driver's licence**, though as private operators they are not obliged to do business with you in any case.

Having said that, there are a few places where you can easily rent scooters – Little Liuqiu Island and Sanyi for example – by simply leaving your passport as security, and in others, you may be able to get locals to help you (this usually means your friendly homestay/hotel owner "guaranteeing" the rental). If you manage to find an amenable renter, the average scooter rental is about NT$200 per hour.

Note that **traffic accidents** – especially those involving scooters – are the leading cause of death and injury to foreigners in Taiwan. The dangers of the country's roads are apparent from the moment you arrive: vehicles of all sizes, from giant buses to cars to scooters, all aggressively jockeying for position with reckless disregard for road rules. In fact, the only practice that seems to be universally accepted is that drivers are only responsible for **what lies ahead**, and monitoring what is happening behind or to one's side is almost completely unheard of. **Drive defensively**, and allow plenty of space between yourself and any vehicles in front of you.

Cycling

The use of **bicycles** for short rides and day-trips is becoming increasingly common in many tourist destinations, with designated cycle paths cropping up all over the country. In places with such paths, bicycles – ranging from basic three-speeds (usually costing NT$100/day) to multispeed mountain bikes (typically NT$350/day) – can easily be **rented**. While these rental bicycles are generally well maintained and fine for short rides on paved paths, they're not suited to longer-distance touring, and those planning on covering longer distances should arrive with their own or buy a higher-quality bike from a shop in a major city. Respected manufacturer **Giant** (ⓦ www.giant-bicycles .com) rents bicycles for longer trips, and allows for one-way drop-offs, but you'll need to speak and read Chinese to make the

most of this service. Costs are around NT$200–300 per day for a good-quality road bike plus accessories.

While **cycle touring** is gaining popularity, this is largely (and wisely) contained to the quieter areas of the east coast as well as the more challenging cross-island highway routes over the mountains (see p.38).

By boat

There are regular **passenger ferries** to Taiwan's **outlying islands**, although in winter many services are scaled back. Ludao (Green Island) and Lanyu (Orchid Island) are easily reached by ferry in good weather, while the Taiwan Strait islands of Little Liuqiu, Kinmen, the Matsu Archipelago and the Penghu Archipelago are accessible by ferry for much of the year (see the relevant chapters for details).

By air

With High Speed Rail offering real competition on the busy west coast corridor, **flights** between the major cities in Taiwan have been dramatically cut back. Unless you're in a real hurry, flying isn't a great deal unless heading to Taiwan's **outlying islands** (particularly Kinmen, Matsu and Lanyu), when you'll save a lot of time by taking a plane.

Taipei's **Songshan Airport**, just to the north of central Taipei, operates services to many outlying islands, as well as daily flights to most major southern and eastern cities, including Hualien, Kaohsiung and Taitung. In addition, the **domestic airports** in Chiayi, Kaohsiung, Taichung and Tainan operate several domestic routes. Prices are usually set wholesale by the airlines, so there's little point in going to an agent.

Domestic airlines

Daily Air Corp ⓣ 02/2712-3995, ⓦ www.dailyair .com.tw.
Mandarin Airlines ⓣ 02/2717-1230, ⓦ www .mandarin-airlines.com.
TransAsia Airways ⓣ 02/2972-4599, ⓦ www .tna.com.tw.
Uni Air ⓣ 02/2358-3131, ⓦ www.uniair.com.tw.

Accommodation

Taiwan offers travellers a wide range of accommodation, from spartan dormitories and weathered white-tile hotels to quaint, family-run homestays and plush five-star resorts.

Few Taiwanese travel alone, so there is a severe shortage of true **single rooms** with one single bed. In most cases, the Taiwanese equivalent is a room with a **queen-sized bed** suitable for most couples – and priced accordingly. A **double room** usually has a king-sized bed and is more expensive still, while a **twin room** comes with two double beds.

Room **prices** vary considerably, depending on location, the season or time of week. While rack rates can be alarmingly high, they are only charged during **peak times**, such as weekends, public holidays and the summer school break (and even then mostly just at beach resorts and the most famous attractions). By far the most expensive time to travel in Taiwan is during **Chinese New Year**, when prices can be double the rack rates. Hotels are often full at this time, so if you plan to travel during this holiday you should try to make bookings well in advance.

Hotels

Basic **budget hotel** rooms can be had for as little as NT$600 per night at off-peak times. At this price, rooms are likely to be a bit tatty and damp, probably with cigarette burns on the furniture and a smell of stale smoke. Still, most of them will have an attached bathroom with shower, TV and phone.

Mid-range hotels usually cost NT$1000–3000, and standards generally vary in accordance with price. At the lower end, rooms are likely to resemble cleaner versions of budget hotels, often with the only difference being that they offer packets of tea and coffee in addition to cable TV. At the higher end, rooms can be quite clean and comfortable, with big bathtubs and/or shower cubicles, and breakfast is often included in the price. You're also more likely to encounter staff who can speak English.

All of the biggest cities, but especially Taipei, have international **five-star hotels** that feature giant beds with fine linen, high-speed internet connections in the rooms, business centres, fitness rooms, spa and massage services and luxury restaurants. Though discounts are sometimes offered, these hotels generally charge a minimum of NT$4000 for a standard room and prices are often twice that. Staff usually speak English.

Hot-spring hotels

Hot-spring hotels are all the rage in Taiwan, but standards vary wildly according to location. Those in resorts close to big cities

Accommodation price codes

The accommodation listed in this book has been assigned one of the following **price codes**, which represent the price of a **standard double room** (ie those with queen-sized beds, but typically not the top doubles with scenic views). Our listed prices in most cases reflect the discounts normally offered at hotels, so they are often lower than listed rack rates. Note, however, that room rates on weekends and public holidays may be higher than those listed in the guide.

❶ NT$500 and under
❷ NT$501–1000
❸ NT$1001–1500
❹ NT$1501–2000
❺ NT$2001–2500
❻ NT$2501–3000
❼ NT$3001–5000
❽ NT$5001–7000
❾ NT$7001 and over

can be expensive, often charging at least NT$6000 for rooms with **en-suite jacuzzis**, while those further afield can offer the same amenities for less than half of that price. Almost all offer **public pools**, which are free to paying guests and can be used by non-guests for what is usually a nominal fee. Many hot-spring hotels also rent rooms for shorter periods for those wishing to bathe in private without paying for overnight accommodation. Note that the quality of the spring water varies between resorts, and even between hotels at the same resort. In general, the older-looking hotels tend to be disappointing, often only having small bathtubs into which the "spring water" is piped through the tap. Meanwhile, newer – and considerably more expensive – hotels have been designed with a keener eye for aesthetics, with larger tubs made of marble or with Japanese-style wooden designs.

Homestays

So-called **"homestays"** (*mínsù*) have sprouted up all over Taiwan, particularly in rural scenic areas, where families have set up bed-and-breakfast style businesses to take advantage of mounting tourist numbers. However, the nature of these homestays varies dramatically, and many are nothing more than tiny, family-run hotels – plus, **prices** tend to be on a par with mid-range to expensive hotels. Rooms are usually in wings that adjoin the owners' houses, and breakfast, though provided, is typically not eaten with the family. However, places advertising themselves as homestays are nearly always clean and friendly, as well as exuding more character than most hotels. There are many homestays listed in the guide, but new ones are constantly opening in places such as hill resorts, so keep a lookout when you arrive. Although many aren't directly accessible by public transport, most offer **pick-up** services from the nearest train or bus station if you ring them in advance.

Hostels

These days **hostels** are just about the only accommodation in Taiwan that could accurately be described as budget. **Dormitories** can offer beds for as little as NT$350 per night, with discounts often doled out for long-term stays. Many hostels also have a few **private rooms**; though invariably small, they can be good value, with some going for as low as NT$450 a night, even in big cities – these tend to be the preferred haunts of newly arrived English teachers, who often rent them on a weekly or monthly basis, so sometimes they can be hard to find.

Most hostels in Taiwan now have affiliation with Hostelling International (ⓦwww .hihostels.com), and will provide discounts to card holders. Many hostels have laundry facilities and common cable TV rooms, while some offer shared use of their internet connections for free. Kitchens can still be found in some.

Camping

Camping is becoming increasingly popular in Taiwan, especially in national scenic and forest recreation areas. If you have your own transport and your own gear, grass spots generally go for about NT$350, while those with raised platforms usually cost about NT$500. Some campsites also offer **rentals** with eight-person tents and sleeping bags and pads provided for around NT$800 – which for groups is undoubtedly some of Taiwan's cheapest accommodation. Almost all of these types of camping areas have adjoining barbecue pits and public showers and toilets.

In **national parks** and other remote areas, camping is often your only option, though there are few designated sites and low-impact methods are recommended – **campfires** should be forsaken in favour of cooking stoves, for example. As landslips occur on mountain trails with frightening regularity, care should be taken when choosing where to pitch your tent, especially in rainy weather. The intensity of the island's rain can test the waterproofing of even the most high-end tents, so make sure yours has been fully **seam-sealed**, particularly if you'll be camping on bare earth (in which case a ground sheet is highly recommended).

Food and drink

Taiwan offers a huge variety of cuisines, from Chinese and Taiwanese food to Japanese and aboriginal dishes. Choices range from super-cheap night markets and street stalls, to wallet-draining restaurants featuring some of Asia's best chefs. In the major cities there's also plenty of Western food, from smart Italian cafés to all the familiar fast-food chains.

Taiwanese food

Taiwanese cuisine is difficult to define, and best thought of as an umbrella term for a huge variety of dishes and styles, most of which can be summarized as *xiǎochī*, or "little eats". Though these are primarily served in simple canteens or night markets, there are also plenty of restaurants specializing in Taiwanese food. Although Taiwanese cuisine is rooted in **Fujianese** cooking (from southern China), since 1949 many dishes have evolved from specialities originating in other parts of China. In addition, much of what's considered Taiwanese food, particularly cakes and desserts, was influenced by the **Japanese** during the occupation period. Being an island, Taiwan is particularly renowned for its **seafood: shellfish**, **squid** and **crab** are extremely popular, with **milkfish** a favourite in the south.

One of the classic dishes found all over Taiwan is known as *sānbēi*, "**three cups**", a sumptuous blend of soy sauce, rice wine and sesame oil, seasoned with various spices, added to meat or tofu and usually served in a clay pot. Other national staples are *lǔròufàn* (**braised pork rice**) and **oyster omelette** (*é a jiān*). **Shaved ice** ("*tsuà bīng*" in Taiwanese) **stalls** are another national institution; mounds of ice topped with fruits or traditional sweets such as red bean and sweet taro.

Local specialities

Every region, town and even village in Taiwan seems to have a speciality, eagerly dished out by local vendors. Tainan's signature dish is *dānzǎi mián*, a mixture of pork, noodles and usually egg or shrimp. **Fish balls** (*yúwán*) are most associated with

Danshui, Kaohsiung (marlin), Tainan (milkfish) and Nanfangao (mahi-mahi). **Rice noodles** (*mǐfěn*) are noted in Hsinchu, while **Sichuan beef noodles** (*niúròu mián*) is a dish primarily associated with Taipei. Steamed or deep-fried **meatballs** (*gòngwán*) are best in Changhua and Hsinchu. **Turkey rice** (*huǒ jīròufàn*) is a Chiayi innovation while Shenkeng is Taiwan's **tofu** capital. The most infamous tofu dish is *chòu dòufǔ*, or **stinky tofu**, the smell of which sickens most foreigners but tastes delicious (it's actually just tofu cubes deep-fried in pig fat). In fact Taiwan offers plenty of dishes most Westerners find revolting: good examples are pig intestines and *lǔ wèi*, a mix of tofu and various internal organs of cows or pigs, simmered in a tasty broth, and often eaten cold. Try them and you're bound to win the respect of the incredulous Taiwanese sitting next to you.

Hakka food

Hakka food, a type of Chinese cuisine associated with the Hakka people (see box, p.154), has become very popular in Taiwan, with restaurants dishing up classic favourites in all the major cities. Hakka cuisine is noted for its strong, rich flavours and salty, fatty ingredients, particularly **pork**, traditionally designed to fill hungry agricultural labourers. Favourites include *bǎntiáo* (fried noodles), bamboo shoots, braised stuffed tofu, *kèjiā máshǔ* (glutinous rice cakes rolled in peanuts) and fried pork intestines with ginger – this tastes a lot better than it sounds. One of the major culinary draws at Hakka tourist spots across the island is *léichá* (cereal tea), a tasty, thick blend of nuts and tea leaves, best experienced in Beipu.

Aboriginal food

Aboriginal food differs slightly between tribes, but the main ingredients tend to be the same. **Ginger** is a frequent ingredient in soups and tea, while the most celebrated dish is undoubtedly "**mountain pig**" (*shānzhū*) or wild boar, which is usually roasted. **Millet wine** (*xiǎo mǐjiǔ*) is mildly alcoholic and served at all times of the day, and **freshwater fish** is also a regular feature of aboriginal meals, served with mountain vegetables such as sweet potato. **Bamboo rice** (*zhútǒng fàn*), or rice cooked in bamboo tubes, is tasty but not really traditional food – rice arrived with Chinese immigrants in the seventeenth century.

Breakfast

Traditional **breakfasts** in Taiwan, particularly in the north and in the cities, follow a modified northern-Chinese style, with common items including *dòujiāng* (soybean milk), *yóutiáo* (foot-long dough fritters), *dànbǐng* (egg pancake), *mántóu* (steamed bread) and a variety of steamed buns (*bāozi*). You can usually find small hole-in-the-wall-type places or stalls serving these snacks in every neighbourhood, and while the formica tables and greasy-spoon atmosphere might be off-putting, the food is well worth a try. In south Taiwan, particularly in smaller towns, rice-based dishes are more common, and in Tainan it's not unusual to see people eat large meals of seafood and milkfish to start the day.

Starbucks has a major presence in Taiwan, and has spawned a large number of local **coffeeshop chains** such as *Dante* and *IS Coffee*, though for many Taiwanese a "Western" breakfast comprises fried egg sandwiches loaded with mayonnaise and spam, sold at an increasing number of cheap roadside stalls.

Regional Chinese cuisine

China's **regional cuisine** is well represented in restaurants all over Taiwan. The most respected northern school is **Beijing**, with its emphasis on bread, noodles, dumplings and **Beijing duck**, its most famous dish. It's rare to find places specializing in other northern styles: the handful of Shaanxi and Xinjiang restaurants are not very authentic, though **Mongolian barbecues**, where you roast your own meat and vegetables on griddles placed in the middle of the table, are deservedly popular.

Eastern-style cuisine such as **Shanghainese** food is best known for *xiǎolóngbāo* or pork dumplings, and is big business in Taiwan; the craze for 1930s-style Shanghai restaurants and food has also made its way to the island, with favourites including eel, freshwater fish with corn and pine nuts (*sōngrén yùmǐ*), yellow croaker (*huángyú*) and drunken chicken (*zuìjī*). Cuisine based on

Vegetarian food

Vegetarian food has a long history in Chinese culture and, as in China, vegetarianism in Taiwan is primarily associated with Buddhism. At the cheaper end of the scale, vegetarians will find plenty of food at **night markets**: roast corn-on-the-cob and sweet potatoes, tofu, and a huge range of fruits and nuts. Almost every city and town will have cheap **vegetarian buffets** where you can pile as many vegetables on your plate as you like – the price is calculated by weight but is rarely more than NT$100 for a large serving. The larger, more formal **restaurants** tend to be Buddhist inspired (identified by images of Buddha, Guanyin or lotus flowers on the walls). **Chinese vegetarian food** ranges from simple, fresh dishes of green vegetables to more elaborate combinations of herbs, roots and even flowers. One aspect of this might confuse foreign vegetarians however: tofu and gluten are often cooked to reproduce the textures and flavours of meat (like roast pork). Taiwanese vegetarians, including many Buddhist monks, applaud these culinary skills – eating food that tastes like meat is perfectly acceptable if it doesn't involve killing animals. It can be hard to find decent non-meat options in rural areas, where rice and local vegetables will have to suffice: note that many sauces, even on vegetables, contain shrimp or fish.

Zhejiang and Jiangsu specialities, including **Huangzhou** food, which also features delicately flavoured freshwater fish, is fairly easy to find.

Southern cuisine is best epitomized by **Cantonese** food, a global favourite with colourful and varied ingredients, but fewer spices than other schools. Often associated with lavish banquet food such as shark's fin soup, **dim sum** (*diǎnxīn*) and the ubiquitous **roast meat** stalls provide a more affordable option. **Fujianese** food is closely related to Taiwanese; "Buddha Jumps over the Wall" is probably its most lauded (and expensive) dish, a rich stew of rare seafood and meats, but the most authentic seafood dishes are found on Matsu and Kinmen.

Sichuanese food is part of the Western school, the spiciest of all Chinese cuisines, with fiery chilli and black peppercorns added to dishes such as *mápó dòufù* (a spicy meat and tofu stew), and chicken with peanuts (*gōngbǎo jīdīng*). Two Taiwanese obsessions are derivatives of Sichuan dishes: **beef noodles** (*niúròu miàn*) and **hotpot** (*huǒguō*). The latter has blossomed into a major obsession on the island, with Japanese, Cantonese, Mongolian and spicy hotpot variations; the main difference is the sauces and stock used to flavour the water. Once you've chosen the sauce, you select your raw ingredients and boil them in a gas-fired cauldron. **Hunan** food, as spicy as Sichuan food but more oily and featuring dishes such as honey ham and minced pork, is not so common and found primarily in the capital.

Japanese food

Japanese food is extremely common in Taiwan, ranging from traditional, highly expensive restaurants in hotels, to cheap, local derivatives with a decidedly Taiwanese flavour – you'll also see plenty of Japanese snacks such as *onigiri* (sticky rice wrapped in seaweed) in local convenience stores. Japanese food traditionally revolved around **rice**, but today is associated with richer fare, usually involving **seafood**: the best-known is *sashimi* or raw fish, typically served on rice to create *sushi*, which in Taiwan can be very affordable and also sold in most supermarkets. Numerous restaurants specialize in *shabu shabu* (hotpot), curry rice, *ramen*,

soba or udon noodles, *yakitori* (chicken kebabs), *tempura* (battered and deep-fried seafood and vegetables) and *teppanyaki* (stir-fried meat and vegetables).

Western and other international food

The choice of Western food, especially in the big cities, continues to improve in Taiwan, but quality varies and many restaurants produce highly localized versions of the original cuisine. Bars and pubs often serve decent staples such as burgers, sandwiches and basic Tex-Mex favourites, while hotels offer more upmarket options. In cities like Taipei and Taichung, the choice of **French**, **Italian** and **American-style** food isn't bad, with plenty of expat chefs and talented locals opening restaurants all the time – prices tend to be higher than local food however. **Korean food** is gaining popularity on the island, and tends to be a lot more authentic than southeast Asian cuisine such as **Thai**, which is usually adapted to local tastes and blander than what you'd get in Bangkok. South Asian and **Indian** food, buoyed primarily by a small but growing Pakistani and Bangladeshi expat population, is becoming more available in Taiwan, while major **fast-food chains** such as *Burger King*, *Domino's Pizza*, *KFC*, *McDonald's* and *Pizza Hut* can be found all over the country.

Where to eat

Night markets (*yèshì*) are the best places to sample local food at budget prices. They are typically NT$20–40 per dish. They are usually located along streets lined with both permanent shops and temporary stalls, though in cities such as Taipei and Tainan, a few markets have specially built premises. Some stalls open for lunch, but in general things only really get going after 5pm and start to wind down after 11pm, though many stay open till the early hours, especially at weekends. Language is not a problem – just point and get stuck in. The crowds can be suffocating at the weekends, but that's all part of the experience and probably the reason why most night markets also feature foot massage centres. Cheap local **diners** and **buffets** (*zìzhù cān*) offer similar fare, the latter an especially good idea if you want to avoid having to order in Chinese. Hygiene standards are better than they seem at these places, and it's generally safe to drink water or tea served for free on your arrival (which will have been boiled or purified).

If you fancy a stronger tipple with your food, **beerhouses** (*píjiǔ wū*) are atmospheric locations to try Taiwanese snacks such as squid, steamed peanuts with small fish, fried oysters, fresh clams and fried prawns. **Teahouses** also serve delicious food (see below).

Restaurants

Restaurants in Taiwan, as in China, tend to be set up for groups: diners sit at large, round tables in order to share the sizeable plates of food on the menu. It's quite acceptable to dine alone anywhere on the island, but with more people you'll be able to try more dishes. All the major hotels operate expensive but top-notch restaurants, their lavish buffets the best value if you want to splurge. Restaurants get going early in Taiwan, opening for lunch well before midday. Most close in the afternoons and open again at 5pm for dinner – only a handful of places do a brisk trade later in the evenings, though most will stay open till 10pm. Prices vary according to the quality of the establishment, but it's rare to pay less than NT$120 per dish, or NT$400 at smarter places.

Ordering can be difficult if there's no English menu or English-speaking staff, but unless it's exceptionally busy someone will usually be able to help. Often there will be an English menu somewhere on the premises if you ask for one, and at street stalls pointing is usually sufficient. Chopsticks are de rigueur in all Chinese-style restaurants, but larger places will have knives, forks and definitely spoons if you ask. Most restaurants will serve filtered or bottled **water** for no extra charge (other places will serve tea). Tap water is treated in Taiwan and nominally safe to drink (see opposite).

Tea and teahouses

Taiwan produces some of the world's finest **tea**, and as a result is a good place to drink and buy various strains, particularly oolong

(*wūlóng chá*, semi-fermented tea). **Lishan oolong**, grown at heights above 2200m near the town of Lishan, and **Dongding oolong**, produced around the town of Lugu in the heart of the country, are often considered the best teas in Taiwan. Relatively mild, Dongding oolong is dried for a brief period over a charcoal fire, giving it a subtle smoky flavour. Taiwan's other famous strain is **Oriental Beauty** (*dōngfāng měirén chá* or just "white oolong"), grown in Hsinchu and Miaoli counties and deriving its sweeter flavour from young leaves that have been bitten by tiny insects. This bite starts the oxidation of the leaves and adds the distinctive sweet and sour flavour. Other oolongs to look out for are Alishan "high mountain tea" (*gāoshān chá*), *tiěguānyīn* and *bāozhǒng*, the lightest and most floral of the strains (closest to green tea). Taiwan also produces small amounts of green tea (*lù chá*) and black tea (*hóng chá*), especially around Sun Moon Lake.

Teahouses are an important part of contemporary Taiwanese culture, ranging from the traditional to the ultra chic, and Taiwan is regarded as a global leader in tea innovation: its modern teashops were responsible for world-wide favourites such as **bubble tea** (*pàomò hóngchá*), and its upscale establishments have added modern twists to ancient tea ceremonies.

Visiting a teahouse

At traditional-style teahouses, after choosing your tea type, you'll be given a teapot, a flask or kettle of hot water, several smaller pots and a bag of dried tea leaves, enough for several rounds. When it comes to making tea the traditional way, Taiwan is far less rigid than Japan, but although methods do vary around the country the basic principles remain the same. The first brew washes the leaves and is poured away, while the second is drunk after a few seconds, the tea poured out of the pot into a separate container before being served into small drinking cups (get your waiter to help if you get confused). These days you can order a wide range of meals and snacks with the tea – tea-flavoured ice cream, cakes, buns and dumplings brewed in tea are often available.

Alcohol

Taiwan's tipple of choice is **beer** (*píjiŭ*), and the number one bestseller by far is **Taiwan Beer**, the brand produced by state-owned Taiwan Tobacco and Liquor Corp. The Taiwanese are immensely proud of the brew (though it's fairly average by international standards) and you'll gain much kudos by drinking it, especially in rural areas. It's sold in cheap cans and bottles in convenience stores and at food stalls, though it's rarely served in bars in the cities (especially in Taipei). Western mass-produced brands such as Budweiser, Carlsberg, San Miguel and Heineken are available in most bars and stores (along with all major Japanese brews) but a more diverse range of Irish, German, Belgian or British beers and ales is limited to a few pubs in the big cities.

Taiwan's national spirit is *gāoliáng jiŭ*, made from sorghum. **Kinmen Kaoliang Liquor** is its most celebrated incarnation, available at 38 or 58 percent proof. **Tunnel 88** is a slightly cheaper version (38 to 42 percent proof) made in Matsu. **Rice wines**, such as the **Shaoxing** variety made in Puli, tend to be too sour or sweet for Western tastes, and grape wines are slowly becoming more popular, particularly in Taipei, where the annual release of Beaujolais Nouveau has become an important event for the fashion-conscious elite. It's expensive, thanks to heavy taxation, and you'll only get a good selection in the larger or Western-oriented supermarkets and specialty stores – Australian wines are best value in regular supermarkets.

Soft drinks and water

Canned juices are sold throughout the island, and there are numerous fresh-fruit stalls. Be warned, however, that it's common to add milk, syrup and often sugar to juice drinks in Taiwan, so check before you order. Freshly pressed **sugar cane juice** is a delicious, sweet drink served by street vendors all over the country, while **papaya milk** is especially associated with Kaohsiung. Most supermarkets and convenience stores stock all the usual soft drinks, as well as fresh **milk** and a bewildering range of **soy** and **yoghurt drinks**; low-fat (or skimmed) and non-sugar versions of all of these are slowly becoming available.

Tap water in Taiwan is a potential cause of minor stomach ailments, especially for first-time visitors. Though **tap water** is considered potable in most places, it's not a good idea for travellers to drink it unless it has first been boiled – many hotels provide an electric kettle for this purpose.

The media

As the only true democracy in the Chinese-speaking world, the Taiwanese media consistently exhibit a level of openness that is almost unheard of in Asia's other Chinese societies. Since the end of martial law in 1987, when the ban on independent newspapers was lifted, there has been a rapid proliferation of print, news and entertainment media, with plenty of feisty political debate and steamy celebrity gossip. You'll need to read or speak Chinese to make the most of this, however, Otherwise you'll have to rely on a handful of English-language newspapers, magazines and websites for news and information.

Newspapers

For English-language news on Taiwan and the rest of the world, there are three **daily newspapers**, all of which have online editions: the *China Post* (⑩ www.chinapost .com.tw), the *Taipei Times* (⑩ www.taipei times.com) and *Taiwan News* (⑩ www .etaiwannews.com). The writing and editing standards of these papers are fairly high, and some of the domestic coverage can be quite incisive; however, international news is largely restricted to wire copy. All three have weekend **entertainment listings** and can be bought at bookshops, convenience stores, kiosks and business-class hotels. For deeper international news and business coverage, newspapers such as the *Wall Street Journal Asia*, the *Financial Times* and the *International Herald Tribune* can be found in five-star hotels and some news kiosks in Taipei.

Radio and television

There are more than 150 radio broadcasting companies in Taiwan, with regular domestic programming by medium-wave AM and VHF FM stations in Mandarin and other Chinese dialects, chiefly Taiwanese and Hakka. The only English-language **radio station**, International Community Radio Taipei (**ICRT**;

Ⓦwww.icrt.com.tw), broadcasts 24 hours a day at 100.7 MHz FM in northern and southern Taiwan, and 100.1 MHz FM in central Taiwan. Its broadcasts include a mix of Western pop music, news headlines, talk shows and community service segments. It also carries some BBC World Service programmes, which is otherwise unavailable in Taiwan.

Taiwanese **television** can offer travellers some interesting insights into nuances of the island's popular culture, with a host of variety and game shows, sitcoms, soap operas and films in Mandarin, Taiwanese and Hakka. Even if you don't speak Chinese, it's worth channel-surfing in your hotel room at least once, just to get a feel for what the locals watch. In terms of English-language programming, **cable TV** is available in most urban areas, offering an assortment of generally American news, movie and theme channels.

Festivals and public holidays

One of Taiwan's greatest attractions is the sheer range and depth of its festivals, all celebrated with a passion and fervour unique to the island. While the biggest ones are the traditional Chinese festivals – which double as public holidays – there is also an eclectic collection of religious festivals as well as an amazing array of time-honoured aboriginal celebrations.

The majority of cultural and religious festivals follow the **Chinese lunar calendar**. As such, the actual Gregorian calendar dates on which they are celebrated tend to fluctuate significantly each year – in our **festivals calendar** (see opposite), we have listed them under the Gregorian calendar month in which they are usually celebrated, with a note of their actual Chinese lunar calendar dates. We also specify which are **public holidays** (P), during which banks and government and private offices are closed, though many shops and restaurants remain open.

Aboriginal festivals

Though Chinese traditional and religious festivals are routinely well publicized, many **aboriginal celebrations** remain closely guarded **secrets**, and even local tourism officials are often confused about or unaware of the actual dates on which they are observed. Villages typically stage their own celebrations, and **tribal elders** usually set the dates for these in accordance with a variety of factors. Further complicating this, established dates can be changed at the last minute in the face of inauspicious omens such as the sudden illness or death of a village elder. Finally, the truly authentic aboriginal celebrations are taken very seriously, with ancient rituals performed with pinpoint precision. As such, most tribes don't want their traditions to become a spectacle for busloads of camera-toting tourists, so many – especially those along the east coast – make a concerted effort to hide their celebration dates from tourism officials. However, individual **travellers** or those in small groups are generally welcomed to events such as **harvest festivals** with open arms, often being invited to drink **local spirits** with the tribesmen. Those fortunate enough to experience these thriving cultures will learn about a side of Taiwan that most foreigners – and many Taiwanese – know precious little about, and it's well worth the effort to seek them out.

Festivals calendar

January

Foundation Day/New Year's Day Jan 1 (P). Marks the founding of the Republic of China in 1911, but also gives a nod to the beginning of the Gregorian calendar year. Offices and schools are shut, with many remaining closed on Jan 2 & 3.

January/February

Chinese New Year (*chūn jié*) Lunar Jan 1–3 (P). Taiwan's most important festival, marking the start of the Chinese year. Celebrations centre mostly on family gatherings with lavish meals; "lucky" money in small red envelopes is exchanged; fairs and public parades are held.
Qingshui Zushi's Birthday Lunar Jan 6. Commemorates the quasi-historic figure from Fujian, revered for his wisdom and munificence (see p.405). Main ceremonies at Zushi Temple in Sanxia, outside Taipei, including the ritual slaying of "God Pigs".
Jade Emperor's Birthday Lunar Jan 9. Pays tribute to the chief Taoist deity, the head of celestial government thought to mirror that of imperial China (see p.406). Main ceremonies at temples in Daxi, Taichung and Tainan.
Lantern Festival Lunar Jan 15. Marks the end of Chinese New Year festivities, but itself often lasts several days in big cities such as Taipei and Kaohsiung. Main activity is the public display of paper lanterns; in some cities, paper lanterns are launched into the sky, most famously during the Heavenly Lantern Festival in Pingxi; another popular

event is the Beehive Rockets Festival in Yanshui near Tainan, where an almost 200-year tradition of setting off fireworks has transformed into an annual free-for-all.

February

Peace Memorial Day Feb 28 (P). Instituted in 1997, and also known as "2-28 Memorial Day", it commemorates the 2-28 Incident (see History p.389).

February/March

Wenchang Dijun's Birthday Lunar Feb 3. Pays respect to the god of literature or culture, revered by students and their parents ahead of exams. Offerings of incense and wishes are written on colourful paper placed in glass jars.
Mayasvi Festival Tsou tribe celebration of warriors returning from battle, with rituals giving thanks to the god of war and the god of heaven. Hosted annually in rotation between Dabang and Tefuye villages.

March

Guanyin's Birthday Lunar Feb 19. The goddess of mercy's birthday is celebrated at Buddhist temples throughout the country, but the main place to mark the occasion is Taipei's Longshan Temple. The event is also marked at the Zizhu Temple in Neimen (near Kaohsiung), which holds a festival celebrating its 300-plus-year history as one of the most sacred sites for Taiwanese Buddhists. The festival features the island's most important annual performances of the Song Jiang Battle Array, ritualized martial performing arts depicting symbolic battles with a variety of traditional weapons, including farm tools.
Youth Day March 29. Pays tribute to the more than one hundred of Sun Yat-sen's revolutionaries who were killed in the failed Canton Uprising against the imperial Qing government on March 29, 1911. Taiwan's president officiates at a public service at the National Revolutionary Martyrs' Shrine in Taipei, and local governments hold similar ceremonies.

March/April

Queen Mother of the West's Birthday Lunar March 3. Honours the highest-ranking female deity, often portrayed as the Jade Emperor's wife (see p.406). Main festivities in Hualien (where it is celebrated on Lunar 18/7), the centre of her cult in Taiwan.
Supreme Emperor of the Dark Heaven's Birthday Lunar March 3. Pays respect to the controller of the elements, particularly fire. Worshipped at some four hundred temples throughout Taiwan.

April

Tomb Sweeping Day (*qīngmíng*) April 5 (P).
Families visit cemeteries to clean graves of relatives and pay respects to their ancestors. In Taiwan, it's celebrated on the anniversary of Chiang Kai-shek's death. "Grave cakes" are offered and paper money is burnt.

Baosheng Dadi's Birthday Lunar March 15.
Marks the birthday of Baosheng Dadi, the "Great Emperor who Preserves Life". Biggest celebration is held in Xuejia, north of Tainan.

April/May

Bunun Ear-shooting Festival Most important celebration of the Bunun tribe, traditionally a test of archery skills to mark the coming of age of the tribe's males.

Dajia Mazu Pilgrimage This eight-day, seven-night pilgrimage comprises one of the world's biggest religious festivals, with worshippers parading a caravan containing one of the island's most revered Mazu deities around a circuit before returning it to its mother temple in Dajia (see p.188). Always preceding Mazu's birthday celebration, the pilgrimage is part of the month-long Dajia Mazu Culture Festival.

Mazu's Birthday Lunar March 23. One of Taiwan's most important folk festivals, celebrating the birthday of Mazu, goddess of the sea, the island's most popular folk deity. Mazu deities are returned to their "mother temples" on this day to be blessed and increase their spiritual powers. The liveliest celebrations are held at Dajia's Zhenlan Temple (see p.188), Beigang's Chaotian Temple (see p.218) and Lugang's Tianhou Temple (see p.193).

May

Labour Day May 1 (P). Celebrates workers' rights and the eight-hour workday in line with international convention.

May/June

Cleansing Buddha Festival Lunar April 8.
Celebrates the birth of Buddha in accordance with the Mahayana school. Worshippers flock to Buddhist temples island-wide, with monasteries such as Chung Tai Chan, Foguangshan and Dharma Drum hosting legions of devotees.

Tainan City God Birthday Lunar April 20. Main festivities are held at the venerated Tainan City God Temple (see p.245).

Dragon Boat Festival (*duānwǔ jié*) Lunar May 5 (P). One of the three major Chinese holidays, featuring dragon boat races held in honour of the poet Qu Yuan who, according to legend, drowned himself in protest after being slandered by envious officials on this date in 280 BC. Races are held in most major cities with waterways – including international races in Taipei, Lugang and Keelung – but the most distinctly Taiwanese are the aboriginal-style races held in Erlong, near the east coast hot-springs resort of Jiaoxi.

June

Taipei City God Birthday Lunar May 13. Includes fireworks, elaborate dances by temple guardians and a lavish parade in which the deity is carried around the streets surrounding Taipei's City God Temple (see p.73).

July/August

Guan Di's Birthday Lunar June 24. Honours one of Taiwan's most admired deities, the red-faced patron of chivalrous warriors, misleadingly known as the god of war (see p.404). Ceremonies held island-wide, but Taipei's Xingtian Temple hosts the biggest.

Yimin Festival Lunar July. The most important annual observance of the Hakka people honours groups of Hakka militia from the late eighteenth century. The main celebration is held at the Yimin Temple in Fangliao, near Hsinchu, and is marked by offerings to ancestors, music and the ritual slaying of several dozen force-fed "God Pigs" – an increasingly controversial ceremony that is seldom witnessed by foreigners (see p.155).

August

Ami Harvest Festival One of the most colourful aboriginal celebrations, centred on dancing, singing and coming-of-age rituals for young men. Although dates vary from year to year, the most important festival of the Ami tribe is generally held in late summer, often in August. Ask at villages north of Taitung.

August/September

Ghost Month Begins (*guǐyuè*) Lunar July 1. The time when the gates of hell are opened and spirits of "hungry ghosts" haunt the living (see p.401). Daily rituals include burning of incense and paper money, while major festivals are held in Keelung, Toucheng and Hengchun at the middle and end of the month.

Ghost Festival (*yúlán jié*) Lunar July 15. Appeasement ceremonies held at temples across the island. Families offer flowers, fruit and three sacrificial offerings: chicken (or duck), pig and fish. Taiwan's most famous is the Keelung Ghost Festival, where an elaborate night parade is held before thousands of glowing "water lanterns" are released onto the Keelung River (see p.133).

Ghost Month Ends Midnight Lunar July 30. On the last day of Ghost Month, the gates of hell close and hungry ghosts return to the underworld. In the month's last hour, contests called *...qiǎng gū* – in which men race to climb tall bamboo towers to collect meat and rice dumplings – are held; the most famous is in Toucheng near Yilan, while a similar event is also staged in Hengchun in the southwest.

Thao Pestle Music Festival Held during the seventh lunar month in Itashao Village on Sun Moon Lake, members of the Thao tribe – Taiwan's smallest aboriginal group (see Contexts p.399) – pound grain into a stone mortar with bamboo pestles, creating a traditional harmony.

September

Armed Forces Day Sept 3. Honours all branches of Taiwan's military while also marking the end of China's eight-year War of Resistance against Japan. Big ceremonies at martyrs' shrines around Taiwan and military parades in the big cities.

Teachers' Day/Confucius's Birthday Sept 28. Pays tribute to teachers on the birthday of China's best-known educator and scholar, Confucius. Unique dawn ceremonies are held at Confucius temples nationwide, with the biggest at Taipei's Confucius Temple (see p.78).

September/October

Mid-Autumn Festival (*zhōngqiūjié*) Lunar Aug 15 (P). Also known as the "Moon Festival" – families gather in parks and scenic spots to admire what is regarded as the year's most luminous moon and to share moon cakes and pomeloes. Since the festival coincides with the autumn harvest, the Taiwanese also mark it by making offerings to the Earth God for a bountiful harvest.

Double Ninth Day Lunar Aug 9. Nine is a number associated with yang, or male energy, and on the ninth day of the ninth lunar month certain qualities such as male strength are celebrated through a variety of activities, including hill walking and drinking chrysanthemum wine; kite-flying is also popular. In 1966, the day also was designated as "Senior Citizens Day", and since then it has been viewed as a time to pay respects to the elderly.

October

Hualien Stone Sculpture Festival Highlights the work of local and international stone sculptors (see p.289).

Sanyi Woodcarving Festival Held in Taiwan's woodcarving capital to celebrate the craft. Includes ice sculpting and carving contests (see p.162).

National Day Oct 10 (P). Also known as "Double Tenth Day", it commemorates the Wuchang Uprising that led to the overthrow of the Qing dynasty in 1911 by revolutionaries led by Sun Yat-sen. Military and public parades and fireworks displays are held in front of the Presidential Building in Taipei.

Retrocession Day Oct 25. Marks the official end of fifty years of Japanese colonial rule over Taiwan on October 25, 1945. The national flag is flown everywhere.

November

Austronesian Culture Festival International festival of aboriginal cultures in Taitung, designed to instil pride and preserve traditions, using the example of indigenous peoples such as the Maori of New Zealand.

Rukai Black Rice Festival The Rukai tribe's major festival, named in honour of what was once their staple diet but is rarely seen today. Offerings are made for abundant harvests, and it's a traditional time for marriage proposals and weddings. The biggest ceremony is held at Duona, usually in late November, in Maolin National Scenic Area (see p.269).

Ritual of the Short Black People The most poignant expression of Saisiyat ("true people") identity, meant to appease spirits of a people the tribe are believed to have exterminated (see p.398). Major festival held every ten years, with a smaller one every other year.

Birth of Bodhidharma Lunar Oct 5. Honours the legendary Buddhist monk, also known as the Tripitaka Dharma Master, traditionally credited as the founder of the meditative Chan – or Zen as it's known in Japan and the West – school of Buddhism (see p.402). Rites performed at the Chung Tai Chan Monastery near Puli (see p.209).

Sun Yat-sen's Birthday Nov 12 (P). Marks the birthday of Sun Yat-sen, founder of the Republic of China and the Chinese Nationalist Party who is commonly known as the father of modern China.

Qingshan's Birthday Lunar Oct 22. Celebrates the birthday of the King of Qingshan (Green Mountain), who is believed to ward off pestilence and dispense justice in the underworld. Ceremonies held at Taipei's ornate Qingshan Temple (see p.72).

December

Puyuma Ear-shooting Festival Celebration of the Puyuma tribe, traditionally a test of archery skills. Rituals held near Zhiben, to the south of Taitung.

Constitution Day Dec 25. Commemorates the passage of the Constitution of the Republic of China on December 25, 1946. The national flag is flown throughout the country, but these days Christmas is celebrated.

Outdoor activities and adventure sports

One look at a relief map of Taiwan shows you its huge adventure sports potential; bisected by northeast Asia's highest mountains and with the rushing rivers and sheer cliffs of the east coast, this hidden paradise of outdoor pursuits is starting to attract more adventurous travellers from Asia and the rest of the world. As well as a haven for trekkers and mountaineers, the island also offers excellent conditions for a range of activities, from mountain biking and kayaking to paragliding and surfing, with many grassroots operators springing up to meet the needs of travellers.

Hiking and trekking

Contrary to the widely held assumption that Taiwan is one giant industrial wasteland, most of the island is, in fact, rugged wilderness that offers some of Asia's most amazing **hiking** and **trekking** possibilities. With an extensive network of national parks, scenic areas and forest reserves – all of which are laced with trails – the hardest part for most hikers is deciding where to start. There also are eighteen **forest recreation areas** in Taiwan, and while the trails in some of them have suffered extensive typhoon damage, others boast well-marked paths, some of which have English signage. For more on these areas, visit the Forestry Bureau's website: ⓦ www1.forest.gov.tw.

A monumental effort is under way to link up many of Taiwan's major trails into an island-wide, north-to-south interlocking network known as the **National Trail System** – which could someday make it possible for hikers to traverse the entire length of Taiwan. However, the series of typhoons that strikes the island each summer inevitably wipes out various sections of trail, often taking years to rebuild, so the prospect of a completely unified network is perhaps an overly optimistic undertaking. For more detail on the trails that will make up the system, visit ⓦ trail.forest.gov.tw.

Mountain climbing

With 258 mountains over 3000m and the **highest peaks** in northeast Asia (excluding some of the volcanoes on northeastern Russia's Kamchatka peninsula), you'd think

Taiwan would be a mountaineering hotspot, but most of its stunning peaks are only tackled by a few climbers each year. Many of the trails are cut straight into the mountainsides and are thus extremely prone to dangerous **landslips** – especially during spring and summer rain – but apart from this most of the main routes up major peaks pose few technical challenges. Despite this, **mountain permits are** required for almost all of them (see box opposite).

By far the most famous peak is **Yushan** (Jade Mountain), which at 3952m is northeast Asia's highest. Ironically, it's one of the most accessible, thanks to a well-built, scrupulously maintained trail and one of Taiwan's most often-used mountain shelters. In good weather, reasonably fit climbers can ascend Yushan and its surrounding peaks without much difficulty (see p.230).

Taiwan's second-highest peak, the 3886m **Xueshan** (Snow Mountain), makes for a beautiful climb that often yields awe-inspiring vistas of the mountains of Shei-Pa National Park and nearby Taroko National Park. During winter, Xueshan and the surrounding mountains that make up the so-called Holy Ridge live up to its name, often remaining covered in snow for months. The main trail to the summit is usually in excellent nick, and though the climb is steeper than that for Yushan, there are two mountain shelters that can help break up the journey (see p.166).

The favourite of almost every serious Taiwanese climber is **Nanhushan**, also known as "Nanhu Dashan". Tucked away in the far northwest corner of Taroko

Mountain permits

One of the main reasons why relatively few foreigners climb Taiwan's tallest peaks – and as a result miss out on one of the island's most extraordinary features – is the astounding level of misinformation regarding **mountain permits**. Taiwanese and foreign expats alike talk about them as if they're next to impossible to obtain, and even some official sources insist the only way foreigners can climb major peaks is to join one of the regular weekend climbing excursions arranged by **outdoor shops** in major cities, especially Taipei. While these shops will take care of the permit paperwork and can cut out most of the logistical planning – attractive options for non-Chinese speakers with limited time – the downside is that you'll be shunted into a large **group** of complete strangers of varying experience and abilities, and you won't be allowed to stray from them for the entire journey. In addition, most foreigners will find that the group pace is ridiculously slow, and the noise levels are so high that you're almost guaranteed not to spot any wildlife; a better option are expat-run companies such as **Barking Deer Adventures**, which organize smaller groups (see below).

In fact, it's relatively straightforward to **arrange your own permits**, the process for which is continually being simplified for travellers. No longer is it necessary to hire a local **guide** for walks up the main mountains, although it's still advised for peaks that require technical climbing skills, as well as for multiday treks across remote stretches of the parks. The minimum-person rule also has been abolished, and it's possible for individual climbers to obtain **solo permits**, although park officials might be reluctant to issue these for more dangerous mountains, or during periods of heavy rain or snow.

In all cases, the easiest way to apply is **in person** at the headquarters of the relevant park, as this allows you to thoroughly explain your plan to conservation section officials. It also enables them to suss out your prior experience and climbing ability as well as inspect your kit. And while they're under no obligation to do so, park officials will sometimes prepare your permit more quickly if you apply in person.

Applications

There are two kinds of permits: the standard **national park entry permit** (入園; *rùyuán*) and the **police permit** or **mountain entry permit** (入山; *rùshān*). Both are free. The latter is normally easy to obtain in person just before you start hiking, usually at the police station or checkpoint closest to the trail – you'll need an application form, three copies of your hiking itinerary and one copy of your passport and park entry permit.

Park permits take more time. If you aren't able to apply in person, the best way for foreigners to apply for the park permit is by completing the **application form on line** and printing out the permit yourself. The form must be received by the park seven to thirty days before the planned start of your climb. The Yushan National Park (ⓦwww.ysnp.gov.tw), Shei-Pa National Park (ⓦwww.spnp.gov.tw) and Taroko National Park (ⓦwww.taroko.gov.tw) **websites** have the application process clearly mapped out in English – the Shei-Pa and Taroko sites have example forms to download, and a copy of the mountain permit application form.

In addition to providing your personal details, you'll need to briefly outline your proposed **itinerary**, including the expected date and time of your start and where you plan to spend each night: for **mountain cabins**, the park will reserve spaces for you, though you must bring your own sleeping bag and foam or air mattress. Once approved, officials will either fax or email the permit to you.

National Park, this gorgeous 3742m peak has been climbed by precious few foreigners (see p.307).

If you don't want to plan your own climb, try Tainan-based **Barking Deer Adventures** (☎0938/337-710, ⓦwww.barking-deer.com), which specializes in small-scale, personalized tours of all the major national parks – they will also arrange permits for DIY trips for a small fee.

Mountain biking

Given its hilly terrain and extensive trail network, Taiwan has some of the world's top **mountain biking**, rivalling the best of North America and southern Europe. Heart-stopping downhill courses, technical rock gardens, jumps, berms and super-fast single track: the island has it all, and much is easily accessible from cities such as Taipei and Taichung. If you're an avid trail rider and plan to visit Taiwan for any length of time, it's worth bringing your bike with you (rental bikes tend not to be suitable for mountain biking; see p.24). Check the archived website of the **Formosan Fat Tire Association** (ⓦwww.formosanfattire.com) for details of bike shops such as **Alan's Mountain Bike** in Taipei (ⓦwww.alansmountainbike .com.tw) – these are the best places to hook up with local riders and join organized rides.

Cycle touring

Another two-wheeled activity for which Taiwan is well suited is **bicycle touring**, as the dramatic "cross-island" roads that wind their way across the central mountain ranges offer remarkable alpine scenery and an honest cycling challenge to boot. The **Southern Cross-Island Highway**, which at its highest point cuts through part of Yushan National Park, is highly recommended, though during heavy rains there can be dangerous rockslides and caution is essential on the road's many blind curves. The **Northern Cross-Island Highway** is also an extremely rewarding route, as are the amazingly scenic **central cross-island routes**. Although the highway that runs along the east coast from Taipei to Taitung is a tempting option, the road is choked with giant gravel trucks and runs through several long, dark tunnels, making for a very harrowing ride. To see much of the island's best mountain and coastal scenery in one long ride, try a route that combines one of the central cross-island routes with the southern one: start at Sun Moon Lake or Puli and head north past Wushe until you reach Dayuling, then turn east and ride through the Taroko Gorge until you come out at Highway 9; go south to Hualien and follow Highway 9 through the East Rift Valley to just before Haiduan, then head west over the Southern Cross-Island Highway (see p.270). When the road finally spills out at Laonong, you could carry on cycling south into the Maolin National Scenic Area.

Whitewater raftingand kayaking

Taiwan's steep mountains combined with typically heavy spring and summer rains often make for solid whitewater raftingand kayaking conditions. Though many streams are too steep and technical for all but the most experienced kayakers, a few of the island's rivers are well known for **whitewater rafting**. By far the most popular – and one of the safest – is the **Xiuguluan River**, which at 104km is eastern Taiwan's longest. The main 24km run begins in Ruisui, about midway between Hualien and Taitung on the East Rift Valley's Highway 9, and cuts through a gorge in the Coastal Mountain Range to finish at the Changhong Bridge just before the Pacific estuary at Dagangkou (see p.309). For rafting and canyoning tours, contact **Green Island Adventures**, which organizes two-day packages from NT$4500 (ⓦwww .greenislandadventures.com). Bear in mind that if you have rafted on more challenging rivers such as those in North America, you might find the Taiwanese approach is over-cautious, with operators using support rafts and speedboats, leading to a less exciting experience.

If you prefer to negotiate your white water in a **kayak**, there are several other less-commercialized rivers. Some kayakers put in at the headwaters of Taipei County's **Nanshi River** at Fushan and paddle all the way down to Wulai, an elevation loss of about 200m. Another appealing option is the **Beigang River** in Nantou County's Huisun Forest, which has a fast-but-short stretch of rapids. Contact **Paddle Around International** (ⓦwww.kayak.com.tw; Chinese only) or the **Aruba Outdoor School** (ⓦenaruba .blogspot.com) for lessons and tours.

Paragliding

The exhilarating sport of **paragliding** is gaining enormous popularity in Taiwan, with a steady stream of fledgling pilots joining a dedicated community of die-hard expats and Taiwanese. Having said that, it's not a great place for **beginners** – clubs are unlicensed and unregulated and flying sites can be tough for first-timers. Assuming you've done your initial training elsewhere, there are around six well-known flying sites scattered across the island, each with its own prime season, making it possible for local pilots to fly pretty much year round. Two places vie for honours as Taiwan's top paragliding spot: Luye Gaotai, in the East Rift Valley near Taitung, and the Saijia Aviation Park in Pingdong County, not far from Kaohsiung. The **Saijia Aviation Park** was the first in Taiwan to open to paragliding and has the largest landing and best thermalling potential; sadly, it was officially closed in 2004 after a fatal accident involving a tandem passenger. At the time of writing the private landowner was allowing flying to take place for a fee, but check with the Maolin Scenic Area for the latest (see p.266).

Luye Gaotai, which generally has better conditions in summer, has two specialized take-off sites with rubber running-track surfaces and is the site of an international competition that attracts some of the world's most talented pilots. Along the northeast coast are some other popular paragliding sites, such as **Feicuiwan** (Green Bay) near Keelung, as well as **Yilan** and **Hualien**. Taiwan's best English-language website on paragliding is at ⓦwww.wingstaiwan.com.

Diving and snorkelling

Taiwan's **scuba-diving** and **snorkelling** spots are not nearly as famous as those of southeast Asia, but a few of them compete. The top spots are **Kenting National Park**, Little Liuqiu Island, the Penghu Islands, and the superb Pacific islands of **Ludao** and **Lanyu**. However, while the Kenting area has numerous dive shops that offer scuba trips, most of the other spots have less reliable operators, and if you want to undertake serious dives in these areas it's best to arrange them in advance through one of the many scuba companies in major cities such as Taipei: **Green Island Adventures** is a good place to start (ⓦwww.greenisland-adventures.com).

Some operators offer reasonably priced **scuba courses**, with basic open-water certification available for as little as NT$5000. If you know you'll be travelling to one or more of these islands, it's a good idea to bring your own **mask** and **snorkel**; fins are not essential, but in some places **neoprene boots** are necessary to keep from cutting your feet on the coral as you wade out. If you don't have your own kit with you, it's worth asking snorkelling shop owners if you can rent just the mask, snorkel and boots for a discounted rate and make your own way to the reef. In summer, there is little need for a wetsuit in Taiwan's warm tropical waters, and, though some shop owners may tell you that a wetsuit is needed to protect you from jellyfish, in most cases this is not necessary.

As for **marine wildlife**, the Pacific islands of Ludao and Lanyu are veritable treasure troves of tropical fish and dolphins, and sightings of sea turtles and magnificent striped sea snakes are possible even while snorkelling (see p.328). Advanced scuba divers can see giant schools of **hammerhead sharks** off the southern tip of Ludao from January to March of each year. For more information, visit the Green Island Adventures website.

Windsurfing

Taiwan is well known for its **windsurfing**, and the **Penghu Islands** (see p.339) are widely considered one of the world's top windsurfing spots. Given the islands' unique flatness, the northeast monsoon winds that whip across the strait are especially powerful here with wind speeds of up to 50 and sometimes even 60 knots possible in winter. And the horseshoe-like shape of the Penghu Archipelago generates a venturi effect that squeezes every bit of the wind pressure, making it a spectacular place for slalom sailing, chop hopping and just pure speed.

While Penghu is packed with Taiwanese tourists in summer, due to the fierce winter winds it's practically deserted from October to March, save for the growing number of world-class windsurfers who are making the islands part of their annual circuit. Visit Ⓦwww .penghuwindsurf.idv.tw for organized tours.

Surfing

Although Taiwan's **surf** is not of the same calibre and consistency as the likes of Hawaii, Indonesia or Sri Lanka, anyone who has surfed the island on a good day will tell you that it can be nothing short of inspiring. Rideable waves can be found from tip to toe of Taiwan, but in general those that travel across the Pacific to crash against the eastern coastline are the ones to look out for – especially in the days preceding a **typhoon**. There are spots suited to all levels, from sandy beach breaks swarming with beginners to reef breaks that only the experienced should attempt. For advanced surfers, crowds aren't a major problem, as the only really big waves are at the vanguard of typhoons or during the winter when you'll need a wetsuit, especially in the north.

While there are some **surf shops** near the most popular beaches, these rent mostly longboards and only sell basics such as baggies, rash vests and wax, so bring your own board and back-up supplies if you're planning any serious surfing. The beaches best kitted out for travellers looking to surf are **Daxi** on the northeast coast (see p.144) and Nanwan and Jialeshui near the island's southern tip (see p.281), as both **board rental** and **accommodation** are possible. But most of the best breaks are near the tiny farming hamlets north of Taitung, where the local scene is of farmers in straw hats rather than surfers in flip-flops. To surf these, you'll need your own board, private transport, loads of time to scout out the coastline and plenty of experience navigating reef. One of the easiest to find is the **Donghe River mouth** – if you can catch it when there is solid groundswell from a typhoon you'll be smoking some heavy river-mouth barrels (see p.312). Some of the best surfing info on Taiwan can be found on the blog at Ⓦwww .bluebirdboarding.com/gazza.htm, but you should also check out Sammy Hawkins site at Ⓦwww.taiwansurftours.com/fudog.

Culture and etiquette

Mainstream Taiwanese culture is a curious combination of traditional Chinese practices, modern commercialism and technological ingenuity, capped off with a palpable Japanese flavour left over from decades of colonial rule. Those expecting stereotypical "Chinese" experiences akin to what can be had in mainland China or even Hong Kong are likely to be surprised and enchanted by the striking behavioural differences between the Taiwanese and their fellow Chinese neighbours.

For starters, Taiwanese people are unquestionably some of the friendliest in Asia, if not the entire world, and most foreign visitors are impressed by the often staggering level of **hospitality** from the moment they arrive.

If you're invited to someone's home, it's a good idea to bring a **gift**, usually something simple such as flowers, a tin of biscuits or cookies, or a box of chocolates. Before entering someone's home, always remember first to remove your **shoes**, even if your host initially says it's not necessary.

Facing up to face

As in many parts of Asia, the concept of "**face**", the grey area between politeness and public pride, is an omnipresent reality in Taiwan, but foreigners who are by nature thoughtful and sensitive to others are not likely to encounter serious problems. Many

Taiwanese have travelled, studied or worked overseas and are somewhat accustomed to behaviour that could be categorized as "Western". As such, many Taiwanese, particularly in urban areas, are extremely accommodating of foreigners and often grant them general amnesty from the Taiwanese nuances of face.

The best working rule is to avoid behaving in a way that causes someone to be embarrassed in front of others, or in front of you. Pointing out other people's mistakes or shortcomings, especially in public, is rarely appreciated and will usually precipitate the proverbial "loss of face". Losing one's **temper** in public and openly expressing anger is a sure-fire way to lose face, both for yourself, and the recipients of your outburst, and sometimes even for those in the near vicinity. Not only are such public displays of emotion likely to cause profound embarrassment, they often will convince others that you are uncivilized and undeserving of further attention or assistance. This doesn't mean that Taiwanese people don't get angry, but rather that there is a general belief in the virtue of self-control when dealing with others.

When Taiwanese are embarrassed or upset, they often will **smile** or giggle nervously, which can be confusing or even annoying for the uninitiated foreigner. Understand that such smiles or laughter are in fact expressions of apology rather than amusement, and try to respond with a smile of your own.

Physical gestures and greetings

Visitors to Taiwan and many other Asian countries will notice that most people beckon to each other with their palms facing down, waving towards the ground, and travellers are well advised to emulate this – calling people towards you by rolling your fingers back with your palms up is widely considered to be crudely suggestive, particularly when a man is motioning towards a woman.

Although in Chinese tradition **shaking hands** was not the usual manner of greeting, Taiwanese men now commonly practise this custom, particularly in business circles. However, powerful or overly enthusiastic handshakes are considered aggressive and can cause considerable bewilderment. Men and women generally don't shake hands upon meeting, opting instead for slight nods of deference, although this is changing and urban businesswomen are increasingly likely to offer their hands when meeting foreigners.

Business cards

Exchanging **business cards** (*míngpiàn* in Mandarin) is a Taiwanese obsession, even between people with no business intentions, and name cards with contact details can be very useful for any foreigner planning to spend time in Taiwan. Printing of business cards in Taiwan is cheap and quick; sophistication and detail are not essential, with your telephone, email address and preferably your **name in Chinese characters** being sufficient.

When exchanging business cards, gifts or tokens of esteem, presenting them with **both hands** tells your counterpart that you are offering them unreservedly, as a wholehearted expression of yourself. To the contrary, passing business cards with one hand or flipping them across tables is uniformly viewed as uncultivated, flippant and even disrespectful. When receiving another's business card it's considered respectful to read their name and title and, when appropriate, to praise them for their position on the career ladder. Avoid immediately putting cards in your wallet or pockets – even if you're only trying to secure them, such action is likely to be interpreted as a sign of uninterest. Also, **writing** on business cards – especially in red ink, which is typically reserved for letters of protest or angry remarks – is still a major faux pas in Taiwan. This should only be done when you need to jot down essential information, such as a mobile phone or hotel room number, and have nothing else to write on. Even then it's best to first apologize and ask permission.

Superstition

One of the most fascinating features of Taiwan, and one that never ceases to amaze even the longest-term of foreign expatriates, is how some of the most ancient of Chinese **superstition** has survived – and even thrives – in one of the world's most technologically advanced societies. This seeming paradox pervades everyday life in Taiwan and is visible through countless actions, from the hip young computer salesman making elaborate offerings at a makeshift shrine in front of his trendy downtown Taipei shop to the practising female geneticist praying fervently to a fertility god for the blessing of a son.

While most of the places of ancient lore are in mainland China, many of the traditional practices no longer exist there, stamped out during decades of Maoist revisionism and replaced primarily with conspicuous consumerism. And though traditional southern Chinese beliefs such as those of the Cantonese have survived in places such as Hong Kong and Macau, nowhere are age-old Chinese superstitions – mostly Fujianese – more a part of everyday life than in Taiwan (see p.401 for more on Taiwanese belief).

Bad omens

For the visitor, one of the most obvious aspects of this is the widespread belief in **bad omens**, and the lengths to which many Taiwanese will go to avoid them. Comments or jokes that imply **death** or disaster are almost certain to elicit visible cringes from those within earshot and can make some people decidedly edgy. For example, a seemingly innocuous statement such as "she's going to get herself killed walking in front of all that traffic," can imply in the minds of many Taiwanese that this will actually happen. This is not to say that warning people to be careful is taboo, but rather to not follow up such a warning with a statement of what could happen if it's not heeded.

Actions that imply the notion that something untoward could happen are also widely avoided in Taiwan, which helps to explain why so many Taiwanese refuse to write **last wills** out of fear that such action could precipitate their own demise. Giving someone a **handkerchief** as a gift, for example, is not recommended as it implies that the recipient may soon have reason to cry. Likewise, things that are symbolic of death, such as **white flowers** – requisite at funerals – are to be avoided. If you want to give someone flowers, it's best to choose other colours.

Even words or phrases that remind people of death can cause offence, with the most obvious of these being mispronunciations of the Chinese word for "four," (*sì*) which said in the wrong tone can mean "to die" (*sǐ*). Giving **clocks** as gifts also is unthinkable, as the Mandarin phrase "to give a clock" (*sòngzhōng*) sounds the same as that for "to attend a funeral".

Swimming

Another fairly common Taiwanese fear that in part can be chalked up to superstition is that of **deep water**. Many Taiwanese are unwilling to venture into water that is deeper than their heads, and most public swimming pools are no more than chest deep. Although this can be partially attributed to poor Taiwanese swimming standards – generally much lower than those of most Western countries – for some it has more to do with the fear that discontented ghosts lurking beneath the surface could possess them, as their bodies are believed to be particularly vulnerable while submerged in water. During the seventh lunar month, which usually lands in August, many Taiwanese – especially older ones – will avoid the sea altogether. However, this belief is far less common among the young and is quickly dying out.

Travel essentials

Costs

Taiwan is one of Asia's most developed countries, and, as such, is a more expensive place to travel than say Thailand or Vietnam. Still, you'll find it considerably cheaper than Hong Kong, Japan or South Korea, and there are plenty of ways for inventive travellers to keep their costs to a manageable level.

While staying in Taipei can be challenging for backpackers on a tight budget, once you get outside the capital you'll find that prices typically run the gamut of budgets, from backpacker to mid-range to luxury traveller. **Accommodation** ranges from as little as NT$400 (US$12/£8/€10) for a hostel dorm bed to NT$8000 (US$250/£163/€190) for a double in a business hotel, while **food** can cost as little as NT$30 (US$0.90/£0.60/€0.70) for basic street food such as noodles to easily more than NT$1000 (US$30/£20/€24) for a meal in a semi-posh sit-down restaurant. By staying in basic doubles and keeping mostly to ordinary, working-class Chinese places to eat, most budget-conscious travellers should be able to keep their costs to around NT$1500 (US$45/£30/€36) per day, perhaps a bit more when undertaking long train, bus or boat journeys.

Admission prices to most museums and tourist sights are usually quite reasonable; government-run venues are typically very cheap, while the cost of privately operated attractions varies wildly. Though discounts for museums and public performances are usually given to senior citizens and students, most travellers are unlikely to fit in the second category as foreign student cards are generally not recognized. However, foreigners who are genuinely in Taiwan to study Mandarin on a full-time basis can qualify for **student cards** that will be honoured throughout the country.

Crime and personal safety

For the vast majority of foreign travellers and residents, Taiwan is an exceptionally safe place, and foreigners are seldom witnesses to – much less victims of – crime. By far the biggest threat to personal safety in Taiwan is traffic accidents, especially those involving scooters and motorcycles (see p.24), and foreigners should employ extreme caution while out on the roads.

All **drugs** including marijuana are strictly illegal, and simple possession can lead to jail time and almost certain expulsion from the country. Police **raids** on clubs are common, especially in Taipei and Taichung, and in a few cases the police have taken all revellers to the station for urine tests.

Police departments in most big cities have **foreign affairs sections** that are normally staffed with English-speaking officers.

Customs

You're allowed to **import** into Taiwan up to 200 cigarettes or 25 cigars, and a one-litre bottle of liquor. Adults can bring in goods valued up to NT$20,000, and the duty-free allowance is up to NT$6000. It's prohibited to import gambling articles, fruits, live animals, non-canned meat products and toy pistols, and **drug trafficking** can be punishable by death.

Electricity

Taiwan's electric current is 110V AC, the same as the US and Canada, and the wall

Emergency numbers

The national number for police is ☏110, while the island-wide number for **general emergencies** such as fire or ambulance services is ☏119.

sockets are made for standard American two-pin flat plugs. Unless they're dual voltage (most cellphones, cameras, MP3 players and laptops are), all Australian, British, European, Irish, New Zealand and South African appliances (as well as those from Hong Kong and mainland China) will need a voltage transformer as well as a plug adapter (hair-dryers are the most common problem for travellers).

Entry requirements

Nationals of the UK, Ireland, US, Canada, Australia, New Zealand and South Africa do not require a visa for stays of up to thirty days. This **visa-free period** is for travel only – working is not permitted – and it cannot be extended under any circumstances. Citizens of these countries must have a passport valid for at least six months from the date of entry, a return or onward air ticket and no criminal record. For longer stays and other nationalities you can check information on various visa requirements at the Taiwanese legation in your home country, or on the BoCA **website**: ⓦ www.boca.gov.tw. The site also outlines the procedures for changes of visa status, such as from student to resident.

Embassies and consulates

Due to the pressures of the "**One China Policy**" only 23 states have full diplomatic relations with Taiwan under its official name Republic of China (see p.393 for the full list). These states have proper embassies in Taipei, and likewise Taiwan has full missions in their capitals under the ROC name. Most other countries are represented in Taipei by a "trade and cultural" or "commerce and industry" office. Despite such names, however, these offices provide the same services as all other embassies and consulates.

Similarly, Taiwan is represented in most countries by **consular, information and trade offices**, but adding to the confusion is the fact that most don't have "Taiwan" or "Republic of China" in their names; caving in to pressure from the PRC, most countries insist that something such as "Taipei" is used instead.

Taiwanese foreign legations

Australia Taipei Economic & Cultural Office ⓦ www.teco.org.au; Unit 8, 40 Blackall St, Barton, ACT 2600, Canberra (℡ 02/6120 2000); Level 46, 80 Collins St, Melbourne, VIC 3000 (℡ 03/9650 8611); Suite 1902, Level 19, MLC Centre, King St, Sydney, NSW 2000 (℡ 02/9223 3233).

Canada Taipei Economic & Cultural Office ⓦ www .taiwan-canada.org; 45 O'Connor St, Suite 1960, World Exchange Plaza, Ottawa, Ontario K1P 1A4 (℡ 613/231 5080); 151 Yonge St, Suite 1202, Toronto, Ontario M5C 2W7 (℡ 416/369-9030); #2008 Cathedral Place, 925 West Georgia St, Vancouver, BC V6C 3L2 (℡ 604/689-4111, ⓦ www .taiwan-vancouver.org).

Hong Kong Kwang Hwa Information and Culture Centre, 40/F, One Pacific Place, 88 Queensway (℡ 852/2523 5555).

Ireland Taipei Representative Office, 8 Lower Hatch St, Dublin 2 (℡ 01/678 5413, ⓦ www .roc-taiwan.org/IE).

New Zealand Taipei Economic & Cultural Office. Level 21, 105 The Terrace, Wellington (℡ 04/473-6474); Level 18, 120 Albert St, Auckland (℡ 09/303-3903, ⓦ www.roc-taiwan.org/NZ).

Singapore Taipei Representative Office, 460 Alexandra Rd, 23-00 PSA Bldg 119963 (℡ 65/6278 6511, ⓦ www.roc-taiwan.org/SG).

South Africa Taipei Liaison Office ⓦ www .roc-taiwan.org/ZA; 1147 Schoeman St, Hatfield, Pretoria (℡ 012/430 6071); 1004, 10/F, Main Tower, Standard Bank Centre, Hertzog Blvd, Foreshore, Cape Town (℡ 021/418 1188).

UK Taipei Representative Office ⓦ www.roc-taiwan .org/uk; 50 Grosvenor Gardens, London SW1W OEB, England (℡ 020/7881 2650); 1 Melville St, Edinburgh EH3 7PE, Scotland (℡ 0131/220-6886).

US Taipei Economic & Cultural Representative Office ⓦ www.roc-taiwan.org/US; 4201 Wisconsin Ave, NW, Washington DC 20016 (℡ 202/895-1800); Two Prudential Plaza, 180 North Stetson Ave, Suite 5701, Chicago, IL 60601 (℡ 312/616-0100); 3731 Wilshire Blvd, Suite 780, Los Angeles, CA 90010 (℡ 213/389-1158); 1 East 42nd St, 4/F, New York, NY 10017 (℡ 212/486-0088); other offices in Atlanta, Boston, Guam, Houston, Kansas, Miami, San Francisco and Seattle.

Gay and lesbian travellers

Despite the traditional underpinnings of Taiwanese society, **homosexuality** is no longer considered taboo and the general public view of gays and lesbians is far more progressive than that of most of its Asian neighbours. Though pockets of prejudice remain, public acceptance of homosexuality has grown markedly since the lifting of martial law in 1987, and there are now thriving gay communities in big cities such as Taipei, Kaohsiung and Taichung. The country's **legal stance** towards homosexuals is widely considered the most advanced in Asia, with gays and lesbians enjoying most of the same freedoms as heterosexuals: there is no law against sodomy, and homosexual behaviour between consenting adults over the age of 16 in private is legal. In 2003, the government proposed legislation that would legalize same-sex marriages and allow homosexual couples to adopt children (it's since been stalled thanks to opposition in the legislature).

Much of this public enlightenment has been the result of a concerted drive by Taiwan's homosexual community, which boasts more than thirty gay and lesbian organizations. The country's first **gay pride festival** was held in 1997 at the 2-28 Peace Park, a popular night-time cruising spot for gay men, and what was hailed as the first gay rights parade in the Chinese-speaking world was held in Taipei in 2003. Around 25,000 people attended the **Taiwan Pride** parade in 2009, making it the largest LGBT event in Asia. It usually takes place in Taipei at the end of October (Ⓦwww.twpride.info).

Indeed, Taipei has become a magnet for overseas gay tourists, elevating the city's status from the gay capital of Taiwan to a top gay destination for all of Asia. While the capital undoubtedly has the most sophisticated **gay scene**, with numerous bars, clubs and saunas specifically catering to gays and lesbians, such venues are springing up in other major cities and same-sex couples are commonly seen in mainstream social establishments as well. Given this openness, gay and lesbian travellers should easily find places to hang out: some of the best-known venues in Taipei (see p.97) have information on gay clubs in other cities and often can provide you with their business cards. For current information on gay life in Taiwan check out Ⓦwww .utopia-asia.com/tipstaiw.htm or Ⓦwww .outintaiwan.com.

Health

As one of Asia's most highly developed destinations, Taiwan on the whole doesn't present many significant health risks for foreign travellers and residents – most visitors will find that using the same precautions they exercise in their home countries will be more than enough to keep them healthy during their stays and the worst you'll face is stomach upsets, dehydration and heat stroke. Medical facilities in the big cities are of a high standard, although English-language abilities vary so if you don't speak Chinese you may need the help of someone who does.

There are **pharmacies** in all Taiwanese towns, and most of them are of a high standard and offer a similar range of products to those in Western countries. Near the prescription windows there are sometimes counters offering treatment advice for a variety of ailments, but usually little if any English is spoken at these. In emergencies, you may wind up having to play a slightly embarrassing game of charades, acting out your ailment and pointing to the affected area – in such cases, the Taiwanese are invariably earnest and will try to help you without showing the faintest trace of amusement. Most pharmacies have a wide range of antibiotics.

There are **public health clinics** in most towns, and they generally are of a reasonable standard and can offer diagnoses and provide medication for most non-emergency conditions. Seeing a doctor at public clinics or hospitals is not expensive (NT$300–400), but you'll be expected to **pay first** and then make the claim to your insurance company later. Private clinics in Taipei (see p.104), where most staff will speak English, can be much more expensive: expect to pay NT$1200 or more just to see a doctor.

For emergencies and serious illnesses, you should go to a **hospital** – all major towns have them, although if you have time, you should try to get to a major city as their hospitals are usually of a higher quality and there is a greater likelihood that English will be spoken. The best hospitals are in **Taipei**, but Kaohsiung, Taichung, Tainan, Taitung, Chiayi and Hualien all have adequate hospitals. At these, you'll also be expected to pay on the spot for treatment and make your own insurance claim later.

Dengue fever

There is no malaria in Taiwan, but **dengue fever** – a mosquito-borne viral disease whose symptoms are similar to malaria – has been a resurgent problem in recent years, in both rural areas and cities. There have been cases of dengue all over Taiwan, but over the past two decades it has been more common in the south, particularly in Kaohsiung and Pingdong counties. Outbreaks tend to occur after summer rains, when pools of standing water stagnate, creating breeding grounds for the *aedes aegypti*. The peak period is June to September, but increasingly cases are occurring earlier in the year as temperatures get warmer.

There is no vaccine, nor are there any prophylactics against the disease, so the only way to prevent it is to avoid being bitten by mosquitoes. The *aedes aegypti* mosquitoes that transmit dengue bite day and night, so you should use insect-avoidance measures at all times. Also known as "break bone fever", the onset of the disease is characterized by severe joint pain that gives way to high fever, sweating and pounding headaches. Some people may also develop a rash over their torso and limbs. There's no cure, but bed rest is recommended while the symptoms run their course, and paracetamol can help the headache. The symptoms usually subside after several days of rest, but they can return intermittently over the next several weeks. Although dengue is not life-threatening to adults, a more virulent strain called **dengue haemorrhagic fever** primarily affects young children and can be dangerous for infants.

SARS and "bird flu"

In 2003, Taiwan had the world's third-highest number of confirmed cases (346) of the potentially lethal **SARS** (Severe Acute Respiratory Syndrome) virus. It also had the fourth-highest number of deaths, at 37, according to World Health Organisation figures (many of the infected were hospital workers). There have been no confirmed cases of SARS in Taiwan since June 2003.

Outbreaks of **avian influenza**, an infectious disease of birds caused by type A flu strains, have continued however. Although the so-called "bird flu" usually only infects birds and pigs, the number of humans being infected with a mutated form of the virus has been rising, especially in countries such as China and Vietnam, and there also have been cases in Taiwan. Most travellers aren't at much risk of bird flu, unless they visit commercial or backyard poultry farms or markets selling live birds such as chickens, geese, ducks, pigeons and wild waterfowl.

The **H1N1 Virus** (so-called "swine flu") pandemic in 2009 also affected Taiwan, with around forty people dying of the illness by mid-2010, but far fewer than in many Western countries.

Since the SARS outbreak, the practice of wearing **surgical masks** when suffering from colds and flu has become much more common in Taiwan.

Medical resources for travellers

Australia, New Zealand and South Africa

Travellers' Medical and Vaccination Centre ☎ 1300/658 844, ⓦ www.tmvc.com.au. Lists travel clinics in Australia, New Zealand and South Africa.

UK and Ireland

Hospital for Tropical Diseases Travel Clinic ☎ 0845/155 5000 or ☎ 020/7387 4411, ⓦ www .thehtd.org.
MASTA (Medical Advisory Service for Travellers Abroad) ☎ 0113/238 7575, ⓦ www .masta-travel-health.com
Tropical Medical Bureau Republic of Ireland ☎ 1850/487 674, ⓦ www.tmb.ie.

US and Canada

Canadian Society for International Health ⓦ www.csih.org. Extensive list of travel health centres.
CDC ☎ 1-877-394-8747, ⓦ www.cdc.gov/travel. Official US government travel health site.
International Society for Travel Medicine ☎ 1-770-736-7060, ⓦ www.istm.org. Has a full list of travel health clinics.

Insurance

It's essential to take out an insurance policy before travelling to Taiwan, as much to cover against theft and loss or damage to property as for illness and accidental injury. A typical **travel insurance policy** usually provides cover for the loss of baggage, tickets and – up to a certain limit – cash or cheques, as well as cancellation or curtailment of your journey. Most of them exclude injuries caused by so-called **dangerous sports** unless an extra premium is paid, and it's crucial to ensure that any borderline activities you're likely to engage in are covered. In Taiwan, this can mean cycling, mountain biking (trail riding), paragliding, river tracing, rock climbing, scuba diving, surfing (especially during storms), white-water rafting, windsurfing and even trekking. Given the likelihood that you'll find yourself driving or riding on the back of a motorcycle or **scooter** while travelling round Taiwan – especially if you plan to visit any offshore islands – you should make sure this activity is covered as well. If you need to **make a claim**, you should keep receipts for medicines and medical treatment, including copies of signed medical reports clearly stating the diagnosis and prescribed treatment, in English if possible. In the event you have anything stolen, you'll need to visit the nearest police station and file a report for **stolen property**. Although this can be complicated in small towns where little English is spoken, police stations in the biggest cities usually have somebody on hand who can speak some English.

Finally, if your trip to Taiwan is part of a longer, multi-country journey, make sure that your policy covers Taiwan in the first place: some insurers will not provide coverage for Taiwan due to perceptions of military-political risk.

Internet

Taiwan is one of the world's biggest users of the **internet**, although most surfing is done via home computers and laptops, so internet cafés are not as common as might be expected. If you're travelling with your laptop and have cash to splash out on mid-range to business-class hotels, then getting a high-speed connection in your room shouldn't be a problem, although five-star hotels often charge formidable amounts for this service.

In the more touristy bits of Taiwan, there are usually **internet cafés**. However, in most places – even in the big cities – you may be forced to enter the grisly world of the Taiwanese **computer game centre**. At these, you are likely to find a high-speed internet connection but you'll have to endure the background noises of automatic gunfire and enough secondhand cigarette smoke to make the Marlboro Man suffocate. **Prices** vary among computer game centres, but in general most charge about NT$25–30 per hour (double this in Taipei) and usually offer discounts for multiple-hour use.

Another option, though one that takes some planning, is to visit a **local library**. Internet access at these is usually free for a specified period of time (typically about an hour), but you might have to queue up for a terminal so it's best to turn up early in the day to put your name on the waiting list.

Living in Taiwan

Taiwan has long attracted foreigners to work or study. **Teaching English** is by far the most common form of employment, though in recent years the trend seems to be reversing, apparently due to a decrease in demand for English lessons. Though it's certainly harder to make a decent living teaching in Taiwan these days, there are still plenty of jobs for the determined. Unlike places such as Hong Kong and Singapore, where teachers with English accents are preferred, in Taiwan it is the **North American accent** that is almost universally desired, so Americans and Canadians comprise the majority of teachers. However, there are plenty of teachers from countries such as the UK, Ireland, Australia, New Zealand and South Africa, and if English is your first language it shouldn't be too hard to land a job.

Although it's possible to source jobs from your home country before you leave, it can be difficult to determine the legitimacy of the company from overseas and most teachers recommend that you simply pick the place where you most want to live and turn up to look for work – most towns and cities have English-language schools. In general, the best times to look are towards the end of summer and just after the Lunar New Year.

It's possible to teach a wide variety of **age groups** in Taiwan, from kindergarteners singing English songs to businessmen looking to refine their formal English skills. However, probably the most plentiful job opportunities are with the ubiquitous **bushiban** (after-hours cram schools, mostly for teenagers). While these night-time language centres are a major employer of English teachers, many foreigners have found teaching overworked and exhausted high-school kids to be depressing.

Qualifications, work visas and pay

To teach legally, you must have a **bachelor's degree** or the equivalent from an accredited university in an English-speaking country. It's not imperative to have **TESL** (Teaching English as a Second Language) or **TEFL** (Teaching English as a Foreign Language) certification, but it will bolster your credentials and make your job easier and more rewarding – in some cases it might also put you into a higher pay bracket.

Once you've found work and signed a contract, your school will apply for your **work visa**, which will qualify you for an **Alien Resident Certificate** (ARC) and basic health insurance. However, Australians and New Zealanders aged 18 to 30 are eligible to apply for a **working holiday visa** that allows them to engage in part-time work while they travel for up to one year. Canadians aged 18 to 35 can also apply for one-year visas (US$100) through the aegis of the Youth Mobility Program. Contact the Taiwan representative offices in your country for more details (see p.44).

Many schools pay on a monthly basis, so you may have to wait for your first payment and should come with enough money to live on for at least one month (at least NT$40,000). How much you get paid will depend on the number of hours you work per week and the hourly rate. Most jobs pay NT$600–700 per hour, with the amount of hours worked anywhere from fourteen to thirty; figure on earning NT$40,000 to NT$60,000 per month. Many teachers supplement their incomes – and try to dodge taxes – by taking side jobs that pay cash under the table, such as **private tutoring**. However, in the unlikely event that you are caught doing this, you are almost certain to be kicked out of the country.

The cost of a room in a pre-furnished **shared flat** varies widely, but in general they range from NT$5000–12,000 per month in the big cities; one-bedroom apartments will be N$8000–15,000, and over NT$20,000 per month in Taipei.

Useful websites

The following **websites** have job listings, flats for rent and regularly updated information on issues affecting English teachers in Taiwan: Ⓦ www.tealit.com; Ⓦ www.forumosa.com. Another useful site with information for English teachers around the world, including Taiwan job postings, is Ⓦ www.daveseslcafe.com.

Mail

Taiwan's **postal service**, the state-owned **Chunghwa Post**, is speedy and reliable, offering a range of services that are user-friendly even if you don't speak Chinese. **Post offices** are located in all cities, towns and most villages, though **opening hours** vary in accordance with their size – expect most to be open from about 8am until 5pm Monday to Friday and about 8.30am to 12pm on Saturday. In small villages, offices are usually open from about 8am to 3.30pm on weekdays, and closed at weekends, while main branches in the biggest cities have much longer hours, often from 8am to 8pm on weekdays and 8.30am to 4.30pm on Saturday. **Stamps** can be bought at post offices, convenience stores and even on line at Ⓦ www.post.gov.tw, where you also can find a list of prices, branch addresses and opening hours.

Mailboxes come in two colours: the red box is where you post overseas mail (in the left-hand slot) and Taiwan express mail (in the right-hand slot). Green boxes are for domestic surface mail (left) and local city mail (right).

Poste restante services are available at the main post offices of the large cities. Letters should be addressed to GPO Poste Restante, together with the city name – be sure to use the romanization for city names that is used in this book. They'll keep mail for fifteen days for free before they start adding daily charges.

Money

Taiwan's currency is the **New Taiwan Dollar** (NT$) or *xīntáibì*, although it's usually referred to by the generic Mandarin terms **yuán** or **kuài**. Notes come in denominations of NT$100, 200, 500, 1000 and 2000, while coins come in units of NT$0.5 (rare), 1, 5, 10, 20 and 50. You may also come across old cent coins (*fēn*), but these have become outmoded and prices are always quoted in dollar amounts. The **exchange rate** has been fairly steady at around NT$32–34 to the US dollar for a number of years now; at the time of writing it was NT$50 to the pound and NT$41 to the euro. You can check current exchange rates at ⓦ www .xe.com. Note that foreign currencies will almost never be accepted in Taiwan.

Almost all cities and towns have **ATMs** from which travellers can withdraw funds using bank **debit** or **credit cards** – this is by far the most convenient and safe method of obtaining cash for daily expenses. Though some ATMs are only for domestic bank account holders, many of them support international systems such as Accel, Cirrus, Interlink, Plus and Star (always check for the correct logo). The most common ATMs – and the most useful to foreigners – are those of **Chinatrust Commercial Bank**, which allow cash advances from major credit cards and can be found in **7-Eleven convenience stores** throughout the country. Other banks with ATMs that recognize international debit or credit cards are **Bank of Taiwan** and **International Commercial Bank of China** (ICBC). Citibank and HSBC also have branches in Taiwan's five biggest cities. Most **hotels** accept credit card payment, with Visa and MasterCard the most widely accepted. American Express and Diners Club also are fairly commonly recognized, though this is more the case in the big cities. Stores in most cities will accept credit card payment, although in many rural areas this is not possible.

Private moneychangers are rare in Taiwan, and if you need to exchange foreign currency you'll probably have to do so in a bank – in most towns, Bank of Taiwan will have a **foreign exchange counter**, and branches are usually centrally located. The most widely accepted currency for exchange in Taiwan is **US dollars**, followed by Japanese yen, **British pounds** and **Hong Kong dollars**.

Travellers' cheques are becoming increasingly outmoded in Taiwan and are probably more trouble than they're worth if the island is your only destination. Those cut in US dollars are the easiest to cash.

Phones

Domestic calls are easily made from private and public telephones; the latter come in two types: coin and card. Though there are still a few **coin booths** around, most of them only take NT$1, NT$5 and NT$10 coins, and with local calls costing NT$2 for up to two minutes (NT$6 for two-minute calls to mobile phones) you need a stack of coins to make it worth your while. Far more common these days are **card phones** (prepaid **phone cards** can be bought in convenience stores), and the ones marked with yellow can be used for both domestic and international calls. You also can make an overseas direct-dial call by first keying in ☎002, followed by the country code, area code and number. It's possible to call via an **international operator** on ☎100, but this is very expensive. English **directory assistance** is

Calling home from Taiwan

Note that the initial zero is omitted from the area code when dialling the UK, Ireland, Australia and New Zealand from abroad.

Australia 002 + 61 + area code
Ireland 002 + 353 + area code
New Zealand 002 + 64 + area code
UK 002 + 44 + area code
US and Canada 002 + 1 + area code

Country code ☎886
Taipei ☎02
Kaohsiung ☎07
Kinmen ☎0823
Matsu Islands ☎0836
Miaoli ☎037
Nantou ☎049
Pingdong, Little Lioucicu Island ☎08
Taichung, Changhua ☎04
Tainan, Penghu Islands ☎06
Taitung, Ludao, Lanyu ☎089
Taoyuan, Hsinchu, Yilan, Hualien ☎03
Yunlin, Chiayi ☎05

on ☎106 and costs NT$10 per call. For domestic calls, there is no need to dial the area code when making calls within the same area code.

Mobile phones

Your **mobile phone** may already be compatible with the Taiwanese network, which is GSM 900MHz/1800MHz (visitors from North America should ensure their phones are GSM/Triband and have the appropriate MHz capabilities).

Buying a SIM card

Assuming you bring your GSM phone with you to Taiwan, you'll save on roaming charges by purchasing a local GSM-standard **SIM card**, which gives you a new number for use within Taiwan, and allows you to **pay-as-you-go** (for longer stays it's even cheaper to sign a contract and pay monthly). **Regulations** seem to change frequently, so the best strategy is to visit a mobile service provider store on arrival. Chunghwa Telecom, FarEasTone and Taiwan Cellular are the biggest service providers, and all have desks at **Taiwan Taoyuan International Airport** (most close by 9pm). These stores can also **rent you a handset**. If you miss the airport desks and can't find one of their stores elsewhere (usually located in most cities), **7-Eleven** and hypermarket chain **Carrefour** also sell SIM cards through their MVNO (mobile virtual network operator) agreements with FarEas-Tone and Chunghwa respectively. However,

not all 7-Elevens seem to offer this service (especially outside Taipei); find a branch of Carrefour, or look for a 7-Eleven where one of the clerks speaks English – as long as it's not busy, they'll usually be happy to walk you through the process.

Getting a SIM card can be tough for non-residents, as mobile providers usually insist on an ARC card number, work permit or local driver's licence; if you have an **international driver's licence** or at least two pieces of photo ID (some will accept your regular driving licence), that should suffice. You could also ask a local friend to provide these details for you (though they will be called by the phone company to verify). In addition to the ID, the application involves filling out a form and providing a photocopy of your passport. SIM cards (with air-time) can be bought for as little as NT$600, and your new Taiwan number is usually activated within 24 hours. Taiwanese SIM cards allow you to receive incoming calls for free; you're only charged for the calls you make.

Smoking

Lung cancer has long been a leading cause of death in Taiwan, and in 2009 the government implemented some of the most stringent **anti-smoking laws** in Asia. Smoking is banned in all indoor public places, including transport systems, hotels, shopping malls, restaurants and bars, though the latter can get round this if they have open-air areas or smoking rooms with independent ventilation, completely separated from the non-smoking sections (bars that open after 9pm are also exempt). Plans have been slated to ban smoking while driving and even walking on the street.

Studying Chinese

Foreigners have been coming to Taiwan to learn Chinese for decades, with many claiming that Taipei is the best place in the world to study **Mandarin** as the version spoken here is far more intelligible than the heavily accented drawls of the Beijing dialect, for example. Be aware, however, that if you study in central or southern Taiwan – places where the Taiwanese dialect is commonly spoken – you are likely to hear highly corrupted forms of Mandarin in your daily activities, and this can seriously complicate the learning process.

Chinese language schools

Taipei

China Language Institute 2/F, 51 Tianmu N Rd (☎02/2872-7127, ⓦwww.china-language.org).
Chinese Culture University Mandarin Learning Center Room 406, 4/F, 231 Jianguo S Rd Sec 2 (☎02/2700-5858, ⓦmlc.sce.pccu.edu.tw).
International Chinese Language Program National Taiwan University, 170 Xinhai Rd Sec 2, Daan (☎02/2363-9123, ⓦiclp.ntu.edu.tw).
Mandarin Training Center National Taiwan Normal University, 162 Heping E Rd Sec 1 (☎02/7734-5130, ⓦwww.mtc.ntnu.edu.tw).
Taipei Language Institute 4/F, Taipei Roosevelt Center, 50 Roosevelt Rd Sec 3 (☎02/2367-8228, ⓦwww.tli.com.tw).

Taichung

Chinese Language Center at Donghai University 181 Taizhonggang Rd Sec 3 (☎04/2359-0121, ⓦwww.thu.edu.tw).
Fengchia University's Language Center 100 Wenhua Rd, Xitun (☎04/2451-7250, ⓦwww.fcu.edu.tw).
National Chunghsing University 250 Guoguang Rd (☎04/22873181, ⓦwww.nchu.edu.tw).
Taipei Language Institute Taichung Center 9/F-14, 50 Yizhong St, North District (☎04/2225-4681, ⓦwww.tli.com.tw).

Time

Taiwan is eight hours ahead of GMT throughout the year, the same as Beijing, Hong Kong, Macau and Singapore. Daylight-saving time is not observed.

Tipping

On the whole, **tipping** at restaurants, bars and in taxis is not expected, although this is changing slowly in big-city districts. When you're travelling round the country you'll rarely be expected to tip, except perhaps in the occasional Western-oriental establishment, particularly those run by North American expats. Even then, many of these will levy a ten-percent **service charge** on your bill, obviating the need for any further gratuity. In some areas, such as Taipei's university district, you may receive a bill pointing out that a ten-percent service charge is not included, indicating that some sort of tip is expected.

Tourist information

Taiwan's Tourism Bureau (ⓦwww.go2taiwan.net) operates a number of **overseas branches** (see below), with offices in Australia and the US offering basic leaflets on Taiwan's best-known attractions. There also are tourism offices scattered across Asia, with those in Hong Kong and Singapore offering the best range of English-language materials.

In Taiwan itself, reliable English information is a pretty mixed bag, especially considering the formidable number of **tourist information centres** around the island. Most of the material is simply translated directly from the original Chinese version, with literal interpretations that are more likely to leave tourists revelling in their literary merit than their usefulness. The most useful information sources are the **visitor centres** of the national parks and scenic areas, which often have educational overviews with English labelling and free pamphlets. Published under the auspices of the tourism bureau, the glossy bi-monthly *Travel in Taiwan* (ⓦwww.tit.com.tw) contains features on a variety of travel destinations and is worth seeking out. The free publication, which has **calendars of events** throughout the country, is available in many tourist information centres.

Useful phone numbers

24-hour toll-free travel information ☎0800/011-765
English-language directory assistance ☎106
Time ☎117
Tourist information hotline ☎02/2717-3737
Weather information ☎166

Taiwanese tourist offices abroad

Hong Kong Taiwan Visitors Association, Room 904, 9/F, Nan Fung Tower, 173 Des Voeux Rd, Central (☎852/2581-0933).
US Taiwan Visitors Association ⓦwww.go2taiwan.net; The Wilshire Colonnade Building, Suite 780, 3731 Wilshire Blvd, Los Angeles, CA 90010 (☎213/389-1158); 1 East 42nd St, 9/F, New York, NY 10017 (☎212/867-1632); 555 Montgomery St, Suite 505, San Francisco, CA 94111 (☎415/989-8677).

Travel advisories

Australian Department of Foreign Affairs
Ⓦwww.smartraveller.gov.au.
British Foreign & Commonwealth Office
Ⓦwww.fco.gov.uk.
Canadian Department of Foreign Affairs
Ⓦwww.voyage.gc.ca.
Irish Department of Foreign Affairs
Ⓦforeignaffairs.gov.ie.
New Zealand Ministry of Foreign Affairs
Ⓦwww.mfat.govt.nz.
South Africa Department of Foreign Affairs
Ⓦwww.dfa.gov.za.
US Department of State Ⓦtravel.state.gov.

Travellers with disabilities

Taiwan is making progress when it comes to accessible tourism, though overall the country remains woefully unequipped to accommodate travellers with **disabilities**. A good place to start is the **Eden Social Welfare Foundation** (☎02/2578-4515, Ⓦengweb.eden.org.tw), which specializes in helping people with disabilities in Taiwan. Eden operates a network of wheelchair-accessible buses – if you don't speak Chinese, someone at the foundation should be able to help you hook up with these. You should also get in touch with the **Taiwan Access for All Association** (☎02/2620-9944, Ⓦtwaccess4all.wordpress.com), which has a special focus on accessible tourism; they can arrange hotels, transport, wheelchair rentals, assistants and organize excellent nature tours and day-trips all over the island, with English-speakers on hand as guides.

All stations and trains on the **Taipei MRT** (subway) are handicap-accessible, with special restrooms, ramps, elevators, extra-wide ticket gates and designated wheelchair areas on the trains. The **Kaohsiung MRT** has similar facilities. Most of the bigger hotels in Taipei can comfortably accommodate disabled travellers – *Sherwood*, *Fullerton* and *Grand Hyatt* among them. Major sights in Taipei shouldn't provide too many hassles: the National Palace Museum has handicapped-accessible restrooms and elevators, and getting around Taipei 101 and the Chiang Kai-shek Memorial is relatively straightforward.

However, most city streets and sidewalks pose formidable challenges, with consistently uneven pavements, steep inclines, steps and few access ramps to be found. Most of the older buildings remain frustratingly inaccessible for those with walking disabilities, and beyond Taipei, travelling will be tough going without the help of the above organizations.

Women travellers

Taiwan is an extremely safe country, and most **women travellers** here are unlikely to attract any special attention other than that usually paid to most foreign visitors. Still, it's always a good idea to be cautious when walking at night or through unlit areas such as underground tunnels, and, if possible, to take a friend with you. Late-night assaults on women by their **taxi drivers** are very rare but occasionally happen, and you should be attentive if you take a taxi at night by yourself. You'll minimize the possibility of being harassed if the driver knows he is accountable – calling for a cab and taking down the vehicle number is good practice, or if you hail one on the street you might visibly jot down the driver's name and vehicle number. Also, if you are carrying a mobile phone, make sure it's visible to the driver.

Guide

Guide

Taipei and around

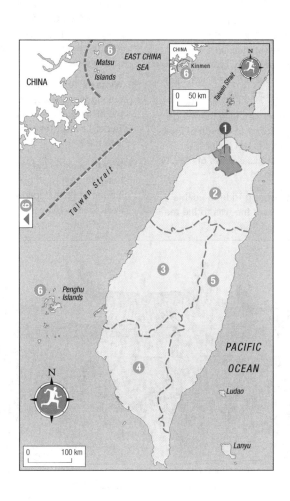

CHAPTER 1 # Highlights

* **Baoan Temple** Other religious sites get more tourists, but this temple is a work of art, packed with intricate carvings and exceptional craftsmanship. See p.78

* **National Palace Museum** One of the world's greatest museums with an extraordinary collection of Chinese art and historical artefacts. See p.80

* **Taipei 101** Take the world's fastest lift to the top of East Asia's tallest building for spectacular views of the city. See p.85

* **Maokong** Ride the cable car over the hills to the tea plantations of Maokong, home to alluring teahouses open long into the night. See p.86

* **Shilin Night Market** Taipei's largest and most popular night market, with a vast array of cheap Taiwanese food, clothes stalls and foot massage parlours. See p.90

* **Wistaria Teahouse** Sip oolong tea and absorb the historical ambience at Taipei's oldest teahouse. See p.90

* **Beitou** Soak up the hot-spring baths in one of Taiwan's oldest Japanese spas. See p.105

▲ Baoan Temple

Taipei and around

T aiwan's political and financial heart, **TAIPEI** (台北; *táiběi*) is one of the most densely inhabited cities on earth. Surrounded by mountains at the northern tip of the island, the capital is a melee of motor scooters, markets, skyscrapers and temples, with almost three million people packed into the Taipei Basin. Don't be put off by first impressions: much of its architecture is shabby and unattractive, the result of slapdash construction in the early years of Kuomintang (KMT) rule, primarily to accommodate almost one million new arrivals from China in 1949. The KMT government (and many residents) regarded Taipei as a temporary home, a base from which to launch the recovery of the mainland. Not anymore – Taipei's newest buildings are smart, stylish and built to last, and it's the most international place on the island.

Though you could spend months here and still not absorb all the city has to offer, a week is usually enough to get a decent taster. Many tourists come solely to visit the mind-blowing **National Palace Museum**, but they risk missing out on a host of other attractions. Tour the **Presidential Building**, **National Taiwan Museum** and **Chiang Kai-shek Memorial Hall** to grapple with Taiwan's complex history, while **Longshan Temple** is the best introduction to its religious traditions. Further north, **Dihua Street** is packed with traditional stores, while **Baoan Temple** is one of the country's most elegant shrines, and the **Shunyi Museum of Formosan Aborigines** is an excellent introduction to Taiwan's indigenous peoples. East Taipei offers a change of pace and scenery, with **Xinyi** district a showcase of gleaming office towers and glitzy shopping malls, all of them overshadowed by cloud-scraping **Taipei 101**. Eating in Taipei is always memorable, with a huge choice of exceptional **restaurants**, **teahouses** and some of Taiwan's best **night markets**, while a vast range of department stores, specialist shops and antique stalls makes **shopping** in the city just as rewarding. To the north, **Yangmingshan National Park** and **Beitou** are where the best hikes and hot springs are located, while **Maokong** and **Wulai** to the south provide a taster of Taiwan's wilder hinterland.

Some history

People have lived in the Taipei Basin for thousands of years, but the modern city is an amalgamation of several villages brought together little over a century ago. The region's original inhabitants were the indigenous people known as the **Ketagalan** (see p.396), but the Qing government in Beijing, having assumed control of Taiwan in 1683, granted farmer **Chen Lai-zhang** (from Quanzhou in Fujian), the first official licence to settle the Taipei area in 1709. More immigrants

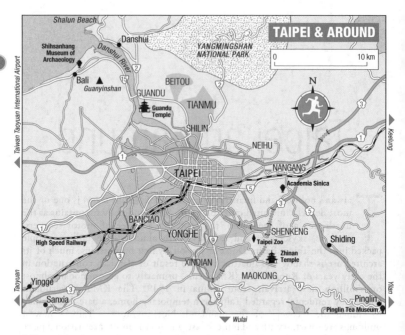

followed, leading to the creation of **Bangka**, Taipei's first Chinese settlement and today's Wanhua district. In 1853, new arrivals from Tongan in Fujian clashed with more established settlers from Zhangzhou in what's known as the **Ding-Xia Feud**. The fight left 38 dead and led to the establishment of **Dadaocheng** (today's Datong) by the aggrieved Tongans.

Taipei (literally "North Taiwan") Prefecture was created in 1875. The location of the city (initially refered to as "Chengnei" or city centre) was carefully chosen midway between Bangka and Dadaocheng so as not to provoke the rival clans. Construction of the city walls began in 1879, but, hampered by lack of funds, they weren't complete until 1884, marking the official **founding of the city**. When Taiwan was upgraded to a province of China in 1885, first governor **Liu Mingchuan** was already living in Taipei, but Dadun (modern Taichung), was chosen as the provincial capital. Liu started to develop Taipei regardless, building schools, establishing Taiwan's first railway and commissioning a British architect to construct the first bridge over the Danshui River in 1888. Taipei was finally made **provincial capital** of Taiwan in 1894, on the eve of the **Japanese occupation** a few months later. The Japanese era (1895–1945) saw the emergence of modern Taipei – many of the capital's finest buildings were constructed in the first half of the twentieth century, and with the destruction of the city walls between 1900 and 1904, Bangka and Dadaocheng were gradually absorbed.

In February 1947, the **2–28 Incident** began here (see p.389) and in 1949 Taipei became the **capital of the Republic of China**, its population swollen by an influx of mainland Chinese – by 1967 it had topped 1.5 million. These days being Taipei mayor is one of the nation's top jobs; President **Ma Ying-jeou** and former presidents Lee Tung-hui and Chen Shui-bian all held the post.

Arrival and information

Most visitors' first experience of Taipei is the traffic-choked ride along the expressway from the **airport**, a distant 50km from the city centre. By 2013 a high-speed express train should whisk passengers to Taipei Station in just 35 minutes. Until then, it's best to allow at least an hour for the road journey. From elsewhere in Taiwan, arriving at the domestic airport or train station is far more convenient.

By air

All **international flights** to Taipei arrive at **Taiwan Taoyuan Internatonal Airport** (臺灣桃園國際航空站; *táiwān táoyuán guójì hángkōngzhàn*; ⓦwww .taoyuanairport.gov.tw), near Taoyuan, southwest of the capital. Terminal one's **Tourist Service Center** (daily 7.30am–11.30pm; ☎03/398-2194) is on the right as you exit immigration. In terminal two the Tourist Service Center (daily 7.30am–11.30pm; ☎03/398-3341) is located in the middle of the arrivals area, while ATMs and exchange counters are available in both terminals.

Several **bus** companies offer services into the city from both terminals, with **bus stations** clearly signposted in each arrival hall. Airbus is the most comfortable and offers two popular loop routes: the West Line (daily 6am–1am; every 30min; NT$90) covers all the major hotels in West Taipei between the *Grand Hotel* and *Sheraton* (two minutes from the *Taipei Hostel*), while the East Line (daily 5.50am–12.15am; every 20min; NT$145) ends up at the *Grand Hyatt* in Xinyi. Both routes pass a couple of MRT stations – just tell the ticket seller where you want to go and they will identify the closest stop. Kuo Kuang operates a service to Taipei Station (daily 5.40am–midnight; every 15min; NT$125) and Songshan Airport (daily 6.45am–midnight; every 20min; NT$125). You can also buy tickets here for buses to **Taichung** (NT$220) and **Taoyuan High-Speed Rail Station** (6.20am–10.15pm; NT$30), just 6km away, providing a fast service to all points south. **Taxis** are available at both terminals 24 hours a day. All taxis use the meter but heading into the city a fifty-percent surcharge is incurred – expect to pay NT$1200–1400. Heading back, you should be able to arrange a pick-up for just NT$1000 (cheaper than flagging down a taxi) – ask your hotel.

Domestic flights arrive at **Songshan Airport** (松山機場; *sōngshān jīchǎng*; ⓦwww.tsa.gov.tw), conveniently located at the top of Dunhua Road on the edge of downtown Taipei. Facilities include a post office, bank, 24-hour lockers, ATM machines and **visitor information centre** (daily 8am–8pm; ☎02/2546-4741). The **metro station** (see p.90) and local bus stop are just outside the terminal, but it's less than NT$200 by taxi to most destinations in central Taipei.

By train and bus

High Speed Rail (HSR) **trains** from points south terminate at **Taipei Station** (台北車站; *táiběi chēzhàn*). All other trains (TRA) also stop here, though services from the south usually end up at **Songshan** (松山; *sōngshān*) in the eastern part of the city near the domestic airport, while those from the east coast head for the southwestern suburb of **Shulin** (樹林; *shùlín*). To transfer to the MRT network, save time by following the signs on the platform to the special MRT transfer exits rather than walking up to the main concourse. Taxis line up at the station entrance and there's a **visitor information centre** (daily 8am–8pm; ☎02/2312-3256) on the west side of the main ticket hall. Most **buses** arrive at the new **Taipei Bus Station** (臺北轉運站; *táiběi zhuǎnyùnzhàn*) opposite the train station (see "Moving on", p.103).

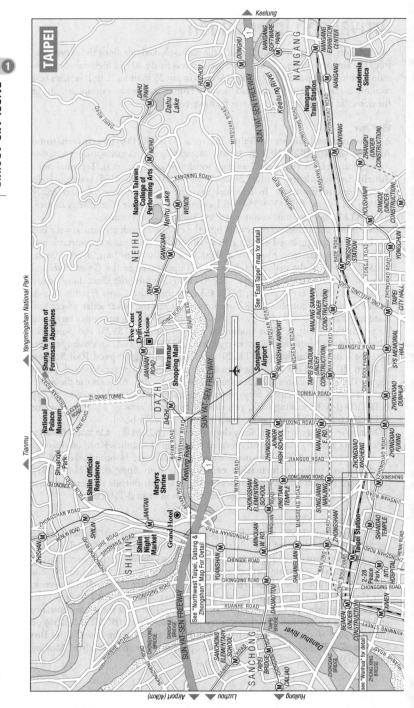

▲ Keelung

TAIPEI

NANGANG
NANGANG SOFTWARE PARK
YANGANG EXHIBITION CENTER

Academia Sinica

Nangang Train Station

SUN YAT-SEN FREEWAY

Keelung River

NANGANG ROAD

ZHANGPU (UNDER CONSTRUCTION)

SONGDE (UNDER CONSTRUCTION)

HOUSHANPI

YONGCHUN

M TAIPEI CITY HALL

SYS MEMORIAL HALL

SONGSHAN STATION

BADE ROAD

GUANGFU ROAD

ZHONGXIAO DUNHUA

ZHONGXIAO FUXING

ZHONGXIAO XINSHENG

XINSHENG

SHANDAO TEMPLE

Taipei Station

2-28 Peace Park

NTU HOSPITAL

XIMEN

BEIMEN (UNDER CONSTRUCTION)

KUNMING STREET

See "East Taipei" map for detail

NANJING SANMIN (UNDER CONSTRUCTION)

Songshan Airport

SONGSHAN AIRPORT

TAIPEI STADIUM (UNDER CONSTRUCTION)

DONHUA ROAD

FUXING ROAD

NANJING E. RD.

JIANGUO ROAD

NANJING

SONGJIANG NANJING

SONGJIANG ROAD

YINGTIAN TEMPLE

ZHONGSHAN JUNIOR HIGH SCHOOL

ZHONGSHAN ELEMENTARY SCHOOL

MINSHENG ROAD

MINQUAN

MINZU ROAD

ZHONGSHAN

NAN-JING

CIVIC BOULEVARD

CHANGDE ROAD

CHONGQING ROAD

HUANHE ROAD

DAQIAOTOU

YUANSHAN

SHUANGLIAN

NEIHU

National Taiwan College of Performing Arts

Neihu Lake

NEIHU

WENDE

KANGNING ROAD

GANGQIAN

XIHU

DAZHI

DAZHI

Five Cent Driftwood House

Miramar Shopping Mall

JIANNAN ROAD

DIHUA BLVD.

BIHE BLVD.

ZI-QIANG TUNNEL

BEIAN ROAD

MINGSHUI ROAD

Keelung River

Martyrs Shrine

JIANTAN

Grand Hotel

Shilin Night Market

SHILIN

ZHISHAN

WENLIN ROAD

JIHE ROAD

SISHANG ROAD

ZHONGSHAN ROAD

ZHONGSHAN N. RD.

CHENGDE ROAD

CHONGQING ROAD

DAHU PARK

Dahu Lake

DAHU ROAD

MINQUAN ROAD

DONGHU

SUN YAT-SEN FREEWAY

National Palace Museum

ZHISHAN ROAD

Shuanqxi Park

Shilin Official Residence

TILIN ROAD

ZHONGSHAN RD.

GUOGUANG ROAD

LINXI ROAD

▲ Tianmu

▲ Yangmingshan National Park

See "Northwest Taipei, Datong & Zhongshan" Map For Detail

SANCHONG ELEMENTARY SCHOOL

SANCHONG

CHONGQING BRIDGE

DANSHUI BRIDGE

TAIPEI BRIDGE

Danshui River

HUANHE ROAD

ZHONGXING BRIDGE

CAILIAO

SANHE ROAD

SUN YAT-SEN FREEWAY

see "Wanhua" for detail

HUANHE ROAD

ZHONG XING BRIDGE

▼ Hulong

▼ Luzhou

▼ Airport (40km)

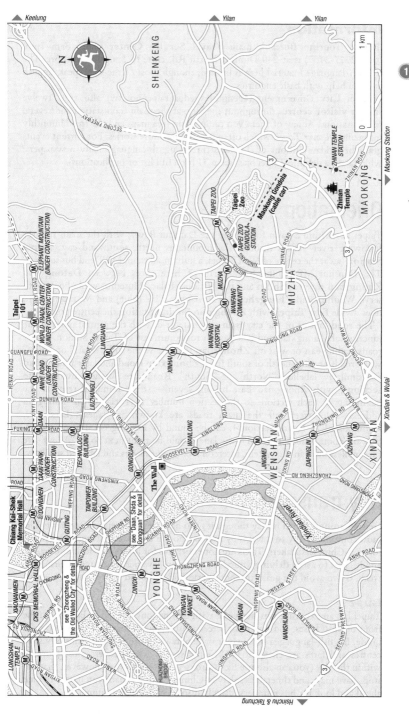

Information

Taiwan Tourism Bureau's main **Travel Service Center** (daily 8am–7pm, ☎02/2717-3737) is at 240 Dunhua North Rd, close to Songshan Airport. The English-language material here is limited, though most of the staff speak English and can help with basic enquiries.

Taipei City Government (Ⓦenglish.tpedoit.taipei.gov.tw) also runs twelve smaller **visitor centres** throughout the city, at the main train station and several MRT stations. At any of them you can pick up free maps and the free bimonthly magazine *Discover Taipei*, which often has useful feature stories. For current events grab the Friday editions of Taiwan's three English-language daily newspapers, which have a definite Taipei bias (see p.31 for a full list of publications).

Orientation

Taipei lies within a basin formed by the Danshui River, with the main suburbs following river valleys through the mountains north, south and east. **Taipei Station** lies at the centre of West Taipei, a hub for all train, MRT and bus services. The Danshui MRT Line (red) north of here slices between **Datong** and **Zhongshan** towards **Shilin** and the National Palace Museum, while lines south serve **Wanhua** and **Zhongzheng**. The Bannan Line (blue) and Muzha (brown) lines divide **East Taipei**, with **Zhongxiao Fuxing Station** the centre point.

The **road layout** of the city is an elaborate grid, with the central point at the junction of Zhongxiao and Zhongshan roads just east of Taipei Station. Major roads leading east or west off **Zhongshan Road** have the suffix "East" or "West" while roads heading north or south from **Zhongxiao Road** and later **Bade Road** are similarly labelled "North" or "South". Roads are further divided into **sections**, with Zhongxiao East having seven – street numbers reset at the beginning of each section, so the section number is crucial when finding an address. Side streets off the main roads are known as "lanes": Lane 180, Zhongxiao East Road, Section 4, can be found by locating no. 180 on section four of Zhongxiao East Road – the lane should be right next to it. "Alleys" are the smallest units in the system, interconnecting with lanes and labelled similarly.

City transport

Getting around Taipei is easy though it's too big to explore entirely on foot. The most convenient way to travel is by **metro**, though **buses** are getting easier to use for non-Chinese-speakers. **Taxis** are not expensive for journeys within the centre, and it's best to avoid **driving** yourself unless you have nerves of steel. During the week, try to avoid the peak rush hour periods (8–9am and 5.30–7pm).

Buses

Taipei has an extensive **bus network** with destinations marked in English on the front of most buses, and electronic screens displaying the name of each stop once inside. English-language route maps can be obtained from MRT stations or visitor centres and fares are cheap at NT$15 per sector, which covers most journeys within the city (you can also use EasyCard, see opposite). Note, however, that bus stops have maps and timetables solely in Chinese, which means you'll have to plan ahead and look for bus numbers (usually displayed as Western numerals).

Metro

Taipei Metro, also known as the **MRT** ("Mass Rapid Transit"; @english.trtc .com.tw), is by far the best way to get around. The system comprises several colour-coded lines, with numerous new routes and extensions under construction – it's easy to pick up **maps** from stations. Services operate at short intervals from 6am to midnight every day and are efficient, clean and fast. Single-trip **tokens** cost NT$20–65 depending on distance travelled and can be purchased from ticket offices or machines in the stations. You can also buy a one-day, unlimited travel card for NT$200 (including a NT$50 refundable deposit), though if you're planning to stay longer than a week it's a good idea to buy an **EasyCard**. This costs NT$500 (including a NT$100 refundable deposit) and can also be used on buses in the city and surrounding area – it's easy to top it up with coins, notes or credit cards via machines located in all MRT stations. In addition, the **TaipeiPass** (NT$180/one day; NT$310/two days; NT$440/three days; NT$700/five days) can save you money if you intend to do a lot of travelling in the city (it allows for unlimited rides on bus and subway).

Taxis

Taxis are plentiful within the city centre: the initial fare is NT$70 and is good for the first 1.5km, after which it's NT$5 for each additional 300m. After 11pm, an extra twenty percent is charged automatically and carrying luggage incurs another NT$10 fee. The meter is always used, the only exception being trips to the airport, which are often negotiated in advance.

Cycling

With the government promoting **cycling** as a "greener" way to get around, you might be tempted to tour the city by bike, though despite the growing number of bike lanes, riding Taipei's traffic-soaked streets remains unappealing and fairly dangerous. Riding along dedicated paths can be fun; the **You Bike** public rental system (@www.youbike.com.tw) offers bikes at eleven locations, mostly in East Taipei. You must become a member to use the system; the first thirty minutes of each rental is **free**, and then it's NT$10 for each additional fifteen minutes (NT$3000 credit card deposit required). For other **bike rental shops**, see p.104.

Accommodation

Taipei has a plentiful supply of mid-range and luxury **hotels** scattered all over the city, with hefty discounts available year round (see p.25) – however, beware of major trade shows such as Computex (May/June), which can lead to a shortage of rooms. Budget accommodation is also easy to find, with Taipei the only city in Taiwan that offers a decent choice of **hostels**. Most of the cheap accommodation is concentrated in the old city centre, but in recent years a new crop of hostels has emerged in **Shida**, near the major universities and plenty of nightlife.

With a bigger budget, where you stay will largely depend on your priorities: **Zhongzheng** and the area around the train station is the best base for getting around and convenient if arriving by bus or train, but **Zhongshan** is where you'll find most of the mid-range hotels and several five-stars. This district is not quite as convenient for transport, but there's plenty to eat and Zhongshan Road is one of the city's more leafy (and upmarket) thoroughfares. **Wanhua** and **Datong** are historic neighbourhoods, good for temples and traditional food, but with less choice when it comes to hotels and a long way from the nearest nightlife.

East Taipei, which includes Songshan, Xinyi and most of Daan district is where the majority of luxury hotels are located – this is the modern financial and commercial heart of the city as well as the location of its trendier restaurants and bars, and beds are priced accordingly. Note that all the hotels listed have broadband connections in rooms unless otherwise stated.

Zhongzheng

See map, p.67.

Forte Orange Business Hotel (Guanqian) 福泰桔子商務 (館前) (*fútài jiézi shāngwù lǚguǎn, guǎnqián*) 22 Guanqian St ⊕02/2381-1155, ⓦwww.forte-hotel.net; MRT: Taipei Main Station. Great value and great location near the station, with compact, practical rooms, chic bathroom (with glass walls), a clothes rack (no wardrobe) and plenty of English-language cable TV channels via the flat-screen TV. Breakfast vouchers provided for nearby *Dante Coffee*. ❺

Hotel 73 新尚旅店 (*xīnshàng lǚdiàn*) 73 Xinyi Rd Sec 2 ⊕02/2395-9009, ⓦwww.hotel73.com; MRT: Dongmen. Sleek boutique hotel with a modern but minimalist artsy theme: think simple colours, large flat-screen TV and bold murals ranging from 1980s space invader figures to a forest of red fir trees behind the bed. Light fittings are futuristic and the bathrooms feature lots of glass screens. ❼

🏃 **Hotel Eight Zone** 八方美學商旅 (*bāfāng měixué shānglǚ*) 8 Jinshan S Rd Sec 1 ⊕02/2358-3500, ⓦwww.hotel8zone.com; MRT: Zhongxiao Xinsheng. Plush boutique with stylish, individually decorated rooms, just a 5min walk from Zhongxiao Xinsheng MRT. There's a cool lounge bar, 24hr coffee and tea, free wi-fi, 42in plasma TVs, and jacuzzi tub and rainforest shower in the bathroom. ❼

🏃 **Just Sleep Ximending** 捷絲旅西門町 (*jiésīlǚ xīméndīng*) 41 Zhonghua Rd Sec 1 ⊕02/2370-9000, ⓦwww.justsleep.com.tw; MRT: Ximen. This budget boutique lies on the boundary between Wanhua's bustling Ximending and the old city, with 150 simple but stylish rooms; spaces are small, but intelligently designed so that it doesn't seem cramped. Each room comes with wi-fi and satellite TV, breakfast voucher and fridge. There's another decent branch at 117 Linsen N Rd. ❻

Keyman's Hotel 懷寧旅店 (*huáiníng lǚdiàn*) 1 Huaining St ⊕02/2311-4811, ⓦwww.keymans .com.tw; MRT: Taipei Main Station. Close to the junction with Zhongxiao Road and convenient for the main station, this is popular with travellers and a great budget option with decent discounts. Rooms are smallish and old-fashioned, but comfy and clean facing a pleasant inner atrium – a real contrast to the bustle outside. ❹

Sheraton Taipei 台北喜來登大飯店 (*táiběi xǐláidēng dàfàndiàn*) 12 Zhongxiao E Rd Sec 1 ⊕02/2321-5511, ⓦwww.sheraton-taipei.com; MRT: Shandao Temple. This five-star is a showcase for contemporary Asian design; standard rooms are a little small however. Highlights include the soaring inner atrium with the *Kitchen 12* buffet at its base, outdoor eighteenth-floor pool and hip lobby lounge bar. ❽

Taipei K-Mall Traveller's Hostel
台北自助旅行家 (*táiběi zìzhù lǚxíngjiā*); (also known as *Holo Family House*). 22/F, 50 Zhongxiao W Rd Sec 1 ⊕02/2331-7272; MRT: Taipei Main Station. Smart hostel with spotless dorms and family rooms, free internet (four computers and wi-fi), breakfast, lockers and 24hr front desk. Conveniently located opposite the station, in the K Mall building next to Shin Kong Tower – take the elevator from the main entrance. Dorm beds NT$690, and single rooms NT$790 (shared bathrooms).

Yo Xing Regency 友星大飯店 (*yǒuxīng dàfàndiàn*) 11 Heping W Rd Sec 1 ⊕02/2394-3121, ⓦyoxing.ffh-tpe.com; MRT: Guting. Convenient location close to Guting MRT Station (exit 8), featuring modern rooms with raised wooden floors and brightly tiled bathrooms. Extras include free shuttle bus to Xinyi, Songshan Airport and the train station (8am–8pm), free internet and free breakfast. ❹

Shida

See map, p.88.

Cat's Pajamas 貓的睡衣青年之家 (*māo de shuìyī qīngnián zhījiā*) 1/F, 10-1 Lane 62, Taishun St ⊕0966/410410, ⓦwww.tcphostel.com; MRT: Taipower Building. Another modern, friendly hostel, close to Taipower Building MRT Station and the nightlife in Shida. Expect clean, newly furbished dorms and facilities, free internet, washer/dryer and plenty of advice from your English-speaking hosts (including learning Chinese and teaching English). Dorm beds NT$460, private rooms from NT$800. Cash only. ❷

Chocolate Box Backpackers 2/F, 11-1 Pucheng St ⊕02/2364-5848, ⓦwww.chocolatebox -backpackers.com; MRT: Guting. Located a short walk from Guting MRT Station, this newish hostel is one of the most popular in town, for good reason:

the property is spotless, modern and a cool place to just hang out; there's free internet, lockers and washing machine, TV and kitchen. Six-to-eight bed dorms are just NT$500–550 (including an all-female option), while comfy doubles are NT$1300. **❸**

Eight Elephants Hostel 八隻大象青年之家 (*bā zhī dàxiàng qīngnián zhījiā*) 1/F, 6 Alley 4, Lane 48, Jinjiang St ☏09/6848-4614, ⓦwww.eehostel.com; MRT: Guting. Cosy hostel in Taiwan's university district, handy for Guting MRT Station. Kitchen, a/c, washing machine, free internet all included. Spotless dorm beds are NT$490, single-bed rooms NT$1030 and doubles/twins NT$1560. **❹**

Wanhua

See map, p.71.

Chun Shai Han She Hotel 君帥函舍商務旅店 (*jūnshuài hánshèshāngwù lǚdiàn*) 4/F, 68 Chengdu Rd ☏02/2371-8812; MRT: Ximen. One of Taipei's most appealing hotels, a short walk from Ximen MRT Station. Rooms are tastefully decorated in classical Chinese style with wooden furniture and gold-painted carvings on the walls. The entrance is actually on Lane 76 off Chengdu Road: look for the "Hotel" sign in between *Taipei Milk King* and the *Olympia Bakery*. **❻**

Ferrary Hotel 華麗大飯店 (*huálì dàfàndiàn*) 41 Kangding Rd ☏02/23818111, ⓦwww.f-hotel.com.tw; MRT: Ximen. Pleasant hotel offering excellent value for money in the heart of Wanhua, with clean, modern rooms and a host of amenities: breakfast in an attractive restaurant overlooking the street, free internet access and DIY laundry, plus a small gym. **❹**

Royal Castle Hotel 成都大飯店 (*chéngdū dàfàndiàn*) 115 Chengdu Rd ☏02/2383-1123, ⓦwww.royalcastle-tpe.com.tw; MRT: Ximen. Cosy hotel, a short walk from busy Ximending. Rooms have smart new beds and Chinese-style dark wood furnishings – it's worth paying slightly more for the bigger rooms though. Free internet. **❹**

Datong

See map, p.74.

City Suites 城市商旅 (*chéngshì shānglǚ*) 69 Nanjing W Rd ☏02/2550-7722, ⓦwww.citysuites.com.tw; MRT: Zhongshan/Taipei Main Station. Set in one of Taipei's oldest neighbourhoods, this five-star boutique is excellent value; rooms feature a blend of wood, marble and soothing beige tones, topped off with flat-screen TVs, DVD players and wireless internet. **❼**

Dongwu Hotel 東吳飯店 (*dōngwú fàndiàn*) 238 Yanping N Rd Sec 2 ☏02/2557-1261, ⓦwww.dongwu-hotel.com; MRT: Daqiaotou. Business

hotel situated in an interesting part of Datong opposite the Ci Sheng Temple, providing useful maps and information on local attractions and cheap eats. Rooms are modern and comfortable, with satellite TV and free wi-fi. **❺**

Zhongshan

See map, p.74.

Ambience Hotel 喜瑞飯店 (*xǐruì fàndiàn*) 64 Changan E Rd Sec 1, ☏02/2541-0077, ⓦwww.ambiencehotel.com.tw; MRT: Songjiang Nanjing. One of Taipei's newest designer hotels, with rooms decked out with sleek Philippe Starck and Ferruccio Laviani furniture, flat-screen TVs and a striking all-white colour scheme. **❼**

Dandy Hotel Tianjin 丹迪旅店天津店 (*dāndí lǚdiàn tiānjīn diàn*) 70 Tianjin St ☏02/2541-5788, ⓦwww.dandyhotel.com.tw; MRT: Zhongshan. Stylish business hotel, close to Zhongshan MRT Station. Thirty rooms with an all-white and blond wood Scandinavian-like colour scheme, with flat-screen TVs and wi-fi. Free washers/dryers and breakfast is included. There's another branch at 33 Xinyi Rd Sec 3. **❼**

Grand Formosa Regent 晶華酒店 (*jīnghuá jiǔdiàn*) 3 Lane 39, Zhongshan N Rd Sec 2 ☏02/2523-8000, ⓦwww.grandformosa.com.tw; MRT: Zhongshan. Taipei institution, serving as a frenetic hub for banquets, weddings and family get-togethers. Rooms are comfortable if standard five-star fare, but the views are impressive and the rooftop pool is a good place to escape the crowds. **❽**

Grand Hotel 圓山大飯店 (*yuánshān dàfàndiàn*) 1 Zhongshan N Rd Sec 4 ☏02/2886-8888, ⓦwww.grand-hotel.org; MRT: Yuanshan. The Imperial-style architecture and Chinese decor definitely have character, though the spacious rooms are a little worn for a five-star and the spectacular views are only available from deluxe rooms and above. The historic *Yuan Yuan Teahouse*, still serving Madam Chiang's favourite red-bean cake, adds ambience, but check if internet is included – otherwise it's NT$500/24hr. The inconvenient location is mitigated by the free shuttle bus to Yuanshan MRT station. **❼**

Guest House Taiwanmex 2/F, 18-1, Lane 18, Nanjing W Rd ☏02/5552-9798 or 0800/060-468, ⓦwww.taiwanmex.com; MRT: Zhongshan. Tiny but relatively new, spotlessly clean rooms managed by an extremely friendly Mexican/Taiwanese couple. The second-floor dorms are NT$450 while private en-suite doubles at nearby *Taiwanmex 2* cost around NT$1000. *Taiwanmex 3* is the newest section, with four-bed dorms at NT$450 per person (bathrooms and flat-screen TVs included). Extras include free a/c, internet and laundry. Convenient location right next to

Zhongshan MRT Station (exit 1), in an area with plenty of appealing coffee shops and cafés. **②**

Happy Family Hostel 2/F, 2 Lane 56, Zhongshan N Rd Sec 1 ☎02/2581-0716, ⊛happyfamily .tripod.com; MRT: Taipei Main Station. Backpacker institution, with clean, if rather ageing, rooms close to the main station. Owner John Lee is a fount of information and there's a small balcony and free washing machine on the top floor. Dorm beds NT$400 (a/c free), singles NT$500–600 (NT$50 extra for a/c). **②**

Hsuan Mei Hotel 宣美商務飯店 (*xuānměi shāngwù fàndiàn*) 52 Jianguo N Rd Sec 1 ☎02/8771-3066 ⊛www .hsuanmeihotel.com; MRT: Songjiang Nanjing. Stylish hotel with a mix of contemporary and Asian design; standard rooms come with DVD player, shower, spa and wireless internet. Discounts make this one of Taipei's best bargains but though the central location is handy for buses and taxis, it's a bit of a hike to the MRT (a free shuttle bus can drop you off within the city). **⑥**

Landis Taipei Hotel 台北亞都麗緻大飯店 (*táiběi yǎdūulìzhì dàfàndiàn*) 41 Minquan E Rd Sec 2 ☎02/2597-1234, ⊛taipei .landishotelsresorts.com; MRT: Zhongshan Elementary School. Taipei's classiest hotel, its elegant Art Deco theme reflected in the lobby and luxurious rooms, all with LCD TVs. The posh French restaurants are a nice bonus: try *La Brasserie* for an aperitif and *Paris 1930* for dinner. There's a gym and spa but no pool. **⑧**

Taipei House International Youth Hostel 台北 之家 (*táiběi zhījiā*) Rm 110,1 293 Songjiang Rd ☎02/2503-5819 or 0952/212312, ⊛www .taipeiyh.com; MRT: Xingtian Temple. One of Taipei's cleanest and most comfortable hostels, with free washing machine, dryer and internet. IYHF members pay NT$550 for dorms and NT$1380–1880 for private rooms, otherwise it's NT$60 extra – you can join the IYHF on arrival (NT$700).

East Taipei

See map, p.84.

Charming City Hotel 香城大飯店 (*xiāngchéng dàfàndiàn*) 295 Xinyi Rd Sec 4 ☎02/2562-1962 or 0800/021-112, ⊛www.city-hotel.com.tw; MRT: Anhe Road (from 2012) This friendly hotel is the best deal in Xinyi, with a vast array of rooms and prices. Ignore the garish lobby with its mix of Asian and baroque decor – rooms are extremely stylish, with flat-screen TVs, DVD players and designer furniture. Pay a little more for the spa and jacuzzi tubs. **⑤**

Delight Hotel 大來飯店 (*dàlái fàndiàn*) 432 Changchun Rd ☎02/2716-0011, ⊛www .delighthotel.com.tw; MRT: Nanjing E Road. Smart business hotel and one of the best bargains in the city, a short walk from the MRT station. Chinese art lines the corridors, and rooms have been decorated in a swish, contemporary style. Free internet and LCD TVs. **⑥**

Far Eastern Plaza Hotel 遠東國際大飯店 (*yuǎndōng guó jì dàfàndiàn*) 201 Dunhua S Rd Sec 2 ☎02/2378-8888, ⊛www.feph.com.tw; MRT: Technology Building. Taipei's tallest and one of its most luxurious hotels, close to the bars on Anhe Rd. Rooms have the best views in the city though the real highlight is the fabulous 43rd-floor pool. Free internet. **⑨**

Grand Hyatt Taipei 台北君悦大飯店 (*táiběi jūnyuè dàfàndiàn*) 2 Songshou Rd ☎02/2720-1234, ⊛www.taipei.hyatt.com; MRT: World Trade Center (from 2012). Gargantuan five-star with vast, marble-clad lobby and 856 luxurious rooms in the heart of Xinyi's business district. Taipei's biggest outdoor pool area and a spread of upmarket, trendy restaurants make nice extras, but you'll pay NT$693 per day to use the internet. **⑧**

Hotel Éclat 台北怡亨酒店 (*táiběi yíhēng jiǔdiàn*) 370 Dunhua S Rd Sec 1 ☎02/2784-8888, ⊛eclathotels.com; MRT: Daan. Small luxury hotel littered with expensive European art – perfect for a romantic getaway and serious splurge. The beds are extra soft, and there's free wi-fi, Starck chairs, Bang & Olufsen CD player and an LCD TV in the bathroom so you can watch whilst enjoying the rainforest shower. **⑧**

Les Suites Taipei 台北商旅 (慶城) (*táiběi shānglǚ, qìngchéng*) 12 Qingcheng St ☎02/8712-7688, ⊛www.suitetpe .com; MRT: Nanjing E Road. Taipei's top boutique hotel, close to the MRT, with a sleek, contemporary Asian design and plenty of clever touches; a lounge offering free hot drinks and biscuits throughout the day; a 24hr computer room; and a bamboo-fringed garden for breakfast. Rooms feature modern Chinese art and canopy beds, with Japanese baths in superiors. **⑧**

Tango Xinyi 台北柯旅天閣-信義館 (*táiběi kēlǚ tiāngé – xìnyì guǎn*) 297 Zhongxiao E Rd Sec 5 ☎02/2528-8000, ⊛www.tango-hotels .com; MRT: Yongchun. One of three slick chain boutique hotels in Taipei, with this one close to an MRT Station and all the action in Xinyi. The stylish, contemporary rooms come with DVD and flat-screen TVs, whirlpool tubs and use of the heath club. Breakfast is usually included. The Nanshi branch at 3 Nanjing W Rd is also worth considering. **⑦**

The City

Taipei is modern Taiwan at its most dynamic, the fusion of ancient Chinese tradition, state-of-the-art technology and contemporary pop culture more pronounced here than anywhere else on the island. The frenetic energy of the streets is part of the attraction, but there's a surprising array of fascinating sights tucked away between the concrete and neon.

Start exploring in **Zhongzheng** district, the city's historic and political core. **Gongguan** and **Shida** further south are lively student areas, containing plenty of cheap bars and restaurants. To the west and sandwiched against the Danshui River, the districts of **Wanhua** and **Datong** are the city's oldest neighbourhoods, home to Taipei's dwindling stock of ramshackle wooden houses and early twentieth-century facades. **Zhongshan** is a more affluent district with a smattering of sights, while **East Taipei**, including Songshan, Xinyi and parts of Daan district, is the city's modern business centre, chiefly noted for its department stores and restaurants, as well as Taipei 101. **Nangang** lies further east, while **Shilin**, which contains the National Palace Museum, lies north of the Keelung River. The appealing teahouses and temples of **Maokong** lie to the south in Wenshan.

Zhongzheng

Renamed to commemorate Chiang Kai-shek in 1990, **Zhongzheng** (中正; *zhōngzhèng*) district is where Taipei was born in the 1880s. Today the old walled

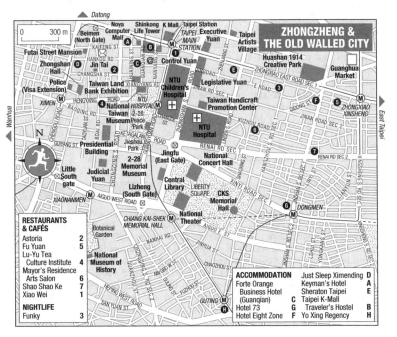

city lies just south of Taipei Main Station and still contains most of Taiwan's government offices. Further south are the National Museum of History and Chiang Kai-shek Memorial Hall, one of Taipei's most famous landmarks. The area is easily accessed by MRT, though distances are not great and it's possible to walk between the main sites.

The old walled city

Little remains of Liu Mingchuan's **old walled city** (城內; *chéngnèi*) today, as the walls and most of the early buildings were demolished by the Japanese after 1895. Indeed, it's the Japanese period that gives the area much of its historic character, most evident in its numerous government offices and the particularly distinctive **Presidential Building** southwest of **2-28 Peace Park**, another colonial legacy. Today's Zhongxiao, Zhongshan, Aiguo and Zhonghua roads follow the line of the old walls.

Taiwan Storyland

Just south of the main train station on Zhongxiao Road is the K Mall, worth a quick visit for **Taiwan Storyland** (台灣故事館; *táiwān gùshìguǎn*; daily 10.30am–11pm; NT$200, children $130), a slightly kitsch but absorbing reconstruction of a Taiwanese neighbourhood, circa 1965. It's located in the basement, and includes several stores, restaurants and snack stalls.

National Taiwan Museum

The building you'll see heading south at the end of Guanqian Road from K Mall is the beautifully restored **National Taiwan Museum** (國立臺灣博物館; *guólì táiwān bówùguǎn*; Tues–Sun 10am–5pm, last entry 4.30pm; NT$20; Ⓦ www.ntm .gov.tw). The museum was completed in 1915 to house artefacts dug up by Japanese archeologists, and today the museum is one of Taipei's finest colonial buildings, with a Neoclassical facade and 32 Corinthian columns flanking a magnificent whitewashed lobby.

Despite containing four floors of exhibition rooms, only a small part of its huge collection can be displayed at one time, mostly through temporary exhibits in the basement and on the first and third floors (these almost always have English labelling). The only permanent displays are on the second floor, with a marginally interesting area dedicated to Taiwan's animals and plants, and the far more absorbing original collection of **aboriginal artefacts**. Highlights include some rare *píngpǔ* finds, such as tools and wood carvings, as well as a small **prehistoric area** containing a remarkable ensemble of Neolithic pottery and tools, many from the Beinan site (see p.319), and a replica of the skull of **Tsochen Man**, unearthed in Tainan County and estimated to be between 20,000 and 30,000 years old. At the time of writing this section had only basic labelling in English.

The city gates

The old city originally had five gates but only four remain today, the West Gate being destroyed by the Japanese. Five minutes, walk west of Taipei Station along Zhongxiao Road stands Taipei's modest **North Gate** (北門; *běimén*), the only example of the original south Fujian style of the gates, though its location in the middle of a roundabout overshadowed by a concrete overpass is hardly picturesque. The **Zhongxi Gate** (重熙門; *chóngxīménxīmén*; Little South Gate), **Lizheng Gate** (麗正門; *lízhèngmén*; South Gate) and **Jingfu Gate** (景福門; *jǐngfúmén*; East Gate) were substantially altered in 1966 as part of a restoration programme and now reflect Chiang Kai-shek's penchant for northern Chinese architecture.

Your ticket also includes entry to the **Taiwan Land Bank Exhibition Hall** (25 Xiangyang Rd; same hours) across the street, another Neoclassical gem completed in 1933 for Nippon Kangyo Bank. It served as the Land Bank after World War II, and its huge two-storey vault has been converted into a cramped but illuminating exhibit on the building's history. The big crowd-pleaser here, though, is the **Evolution Hall**, with its array of giant dinosaur skeletons, T-Rex and two-storey sauropods among them. English is used throughout, and you can grab a coffee at the *Dino Café* terrace upstairs.

2-28 Peace Park

Behind the museum, **2-28 Peace Park** (二二八和平公園; *èrèrbā hépínggōngyuán*; daily 10am–5pm; free) was created by the Japanese in 1899 and known as Taipei Park or New Park until 1997. It was renamed by former Taipei mayor Chen Shui-bian to commemorate the tragic massacre that began on 28 February 1947 (see p.389). The park featured heavily in Pai Hsien-yung's groundbreaking novel *Crystal Boys*, which highlights the struggles of Taipei's gay community in the 1960s, but today it's a popular place for locals to stroll, have lunch and take photos. It contains several Qing dynasty and Japanese-era relics, though many of the latter have been torn down over the years, most notably Governor-General Kodama Gentaro's statue, destroyed to make way for the spire-like **2-28 Monument** in the centre of the park.

In the southeast corner of the park, the former home of Japan's colonial Taipei Broadcasting Bureau has been converted into the **2-28 Memorial Museum** (二二八紀念館; *èrèrbā jìniànguǎn*; Tues–Sun 10am–5pm; NT$20; free on Wed), a fascinating if sobering place to learn about the 2-28 Incident and subsequent struggle for democracy in Taiwan. Apart from an informative video with English subtitles, the rest of the museum's extensive displays are frustratingly labelled in Chinese only so it's best to visit midweek, when there are fewer visitors, and ask for an English-speaking guide (free). The first-floor exhibits provide the historical context of the incident, starting with the Japanese occupation, while the second floor recounts the major events of the massacre and subsequent "White Terror".

The Presidential Building

Leave the park at the southern entrance, then turn right on Ketagalan Boulevard and walk towards the imposing redbrick facade of the **Presidential Building** (總統府; *zǒngtǒngfǔ*; Mon–Fri 9am–12pm; free; ☎02/2312-0760; Ⓦwww .president.gov.tw), its 60m tower for years the highest point in the city. The president and vice-president still work here and security is understandably tight: the entrance is at the back of the building at Boai and Baoqing roads, where you must show some form of photo ID (passport preferably). English-speaking guides are provided free of charge – it's not possible to tour the place without one and many exhibits have Chinese-only captions.

Constructed between 1912 and 1919 by the Japanese to mimic British imperial architecture, the building served as the office of Japanese governor-generals until 1945, assuming the function of Taiwan's presidential office from 1949. The first-floor rooms are arranged around two inner gardens that form the Chinese character for "sun" (日) when viewed from above (also the first character for "Japan"). Here you'll find an informative exhibit on all nineteen Japanese governor-generals, including the fourth governor, the **Kodama Gentaro** – the Taiwanese used to say "his spit is law," a fairly vivid indication that colonial rule wasn't all green tea and sushi at the time. The building also contains exhibits on Taiwan's five post-Japanese-era presidents, the history of the site itself, a basic history of the island and temporary art displays.

On eight or so Saturdays and Sundays throughout the year the building has an "**open house**" (usually 8am–4pm; free), which means you get to see some of the other areas (including the impressive Entrance Hall and Presidential Reception Room), wander around the first floor independently and take photographs (forbidden on weekdays).

Chiang Kai-shek Memorial Hall

Ten minutes' walk from the southern end of 2-28 Peace Park is one of Taipei's grandest sights, the collection of monumental architecture surrounding **Chiang Kai-shek Memorial Hall** (中正紀念堂; *zhōngzhèng jìniàntáng*; daily 9am–6pm; free; Ⓦ www.cksmh.gov.tw). It doesn't seem to matter that all this was completed in the 1980s – these buildings are some of the largest examples of classical Chinese architecture anywhere in the world.

Built as a shrine to commemorate the man that – admire him or loathe him – did more to create modern Taiwan than any other, the memorial hall sits at the centre of a grand plaza (known as "**Liberty Square**" since the DPP renamed it in 2007), its striking 70m octagonal roof designed to resemble the Temple of Heaven in Beijing and covered with blue glazed tiles. Start by climbing the 89 granite stairs to the main hall, which contains a giant bronze statue of the Generalissimo under an elegant red cypress wood ceiling; though it seems a bit like a mausoleum, Chiang isn't buried inside. Inscribed onto the marble wall behind the statue are the three pillars of Chiang's political thought, loosely adapted from Sun Yat-sen's "Three Principles of the People": Science (科學; *kēxué*), Democracy (民主; *mínzhǔ*) and Ethics (倫理; *lúnlǐ*). The hourly **changing of the guard** here is an elaborate ceremony that takes around ten minutes. Downstairs at ground level you'll find a series of renovated art galleries and a special section of exhibition rooms that tell the story of Chiang's life through photographs, paintings and personal effects, all labelled in English, though you might tire of the predictably flattering commentary. His two shiny Cadillacs are also on display. Don't miss the gift shop either, where Chiang's image – rather like Mao's in China – now adorns designer T-shirts, bags and trendy cards.

The magnificent classical Chinese buildings at the other end of the plaza form the "National Chiang Kai-shek Cultural Center" (daily noon–8pm; ☎ 02/339-39831, Ⓦ www.ntch.edu.tw), Taiwan's premier performing arts venue, and comprise the **National Theater** (國家戲劇院; *guójiā xìjùyuàn*; closest to the MRT station exit) and the **National Concert Hall** (國家音樂廳; *guójiā yīnyuètīng*).

National Museum of History

A fifteen-minute walk west along Nanhai Road from the CKS Memorial MRT Station, the **National Museum of History** (國立歷史博物館; *guólì lìshǐ bówùguǎn*; Tues–Sun 10am–6pm; NT$30; Ⓦ www.nmh.gov.tw) was founded in 1955, the third in a series of ageing Ming and Qing dynasty replica buildings along this stretch of road. The bulk of its collection, largely comprising artefacts from central China, was transferred from the Henan Museum back on the mainland in 1949. If you've already been to the National Palace Museum, you might feel it's a waste of time coming here, but it's much smaller and easier to absorb – the extensive collection of **Shang and Zhou dynasty bronzes** is particularly impressive and the temporary exhibits usually have a Taiwanese focus, with a bias towards painting and calligraphy. If you're still not impressed, grab a coffee at the second-floor *Pavilion of Tranquillity*, which commands a picture-perfect location overlooking the lily pond in the **Taipei Botanical Garden** (台北植物園; *táiběi zhíwùyuán*; daily 4am–10pm; free) behind the museum.

Wanhua

Wanhua (萬華; *wànhúa*) district, bounded by Zhongzheng to the east and the Danshui River to the west, is the oldest part of the city. Founded by immigrants from China in the early eighteenth century, the village was gradually absorbed by newly created Taipei in the 1890s. Originally known as **Bangka** or Manka in Taiwanese (from the Ketagalan word for "canoe"), its name was changed by the Japanese in 1920: the new characters read "Manka" in Japanese but "Wanhua" in Chinese. It's best explored on foot – some of the city's most famous temples and markets remain squashed between modern apartment blocks and to the north, **Ximending** is one of Taipei's funkier neighbourhoods.

Longshan Temple

The most important of Wanhua's "big three" temples (the others being Qingshui and Qingshan), **Longshan Temple** (龍山寺; *lóngshān sì*; daily 6am–10pm) is the ideal place to soak up Taiwan's vibrant religious traditions. Located a block north of Longshan Temple MRT Station across Mangka Park, the temple was established in 1738 (making it Taipei's oldest), renovated 1919–1924 and partially rebuilt after US bombing destroyed much of the complex during World War II. It's principally a Buddhist temple dedicated to the Bodhisattva **Guanyin**, but there are more than a hundred deities worshipped here, mostly from the Taoist pantheon.

The main entrance on Guangzhou Street borders a pleasant courtyard, replete with artificial waterfall on the right-hand side. Before entering the temple proper, take a look at the two dragon pillars outside the **Front Hall**, the only bronze pair in Taiwan. Once inside you'll see prayer tables and worshippers facing the **Main Hall** in the centre where Guanyin is enshrined – the principal image of the goddess has proved virtually indestructible over the years, surviving local conflicts, earthquakes and even

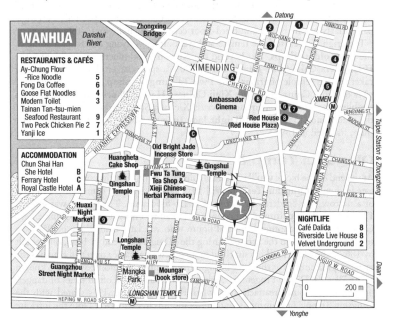

the US bombing. Note the two gold censers (incense burners) in front of the hall, with their vivid cast images of "silly barbarians lifting a corner of the temple", supposedly eighteenth-century depictions of the Dutch. This is the busiest part of the temple, but the deity-packed **Rear Hall** also receives a steady stream of visitors. The goddess Mazu is worshipped in the centre and fringed by *guāngmíng* lights, each representing a donation made in the hope of attracting good fortune. To the far right is a separate shrine dedicated to the gods of literature, primarily Wenchang Dijun in the middle, patronized by students and anxious parents at examination time. Guan Di occupies the shrine on the far left and in front of this in a side hall is a newer altar dedicated to the Matchmaker, a sort of Chinese cupid (see p.407).

Turn left on exiting the temple and you'll see the entrance to Lane 224 or **Herb Alley** (青草巷; *qīngcǎo xiàng*), a narrow, L-shaped street crammed with 100-year-old stalls selling aloe vera, sweet basil and a variety of Chinese herbs and roots including "white-horse dung" – you'll probably smell it before you see it. Retrace your steps and pass Longshan Temple in the other direction to Xiyuan Road: beyond this point **Guangzhou Street Night Market** gets going from around 5pm and connects to the venerable **Huaxi Tourist Night Market**, also known as Snake Alley (see p.89).

Qingshan Temple

Keep walking a couple of blocks north on Xiyuan Road and you'll reach Guiyang Street. Turn left, and you should see the narrow facade of **Qingshan Temple** (青山宮; *qīngshāngōng*; daily 5.30am–9.30pm) ahead on the left. Established in 1854 by immigrants from Quanzhou, it's dedicated to General Zhang, a quasi-historical figure from China's Three Kingdoms period, also known as "King of Qingshan" and a popular administrator. Admirers began to worship him after his death, and in time he was credited with special powers of protection – he was also the deity favoured by tea merchants in the area. Qingshan is enshrined amidst an elaborate gold altar in the **Main Hall**; beyond here the **Rear Hall** houses various deities, but don't miss the temple's gold-painted **carvings**, particularly on the beams and third-floor ceiling which are incredibly ornate.

Turn right on leaving the temple and walk along Guiyang Street, past some of the area's **oldest shops**. Just beyond the Xiyuan Road junction at no. 200 is the **Huanghefa Cake Shop** established in 1909, a specialist producer of bright-red cakes used as temple offerings. The **Fwu Ta Tung Teashop** at no. 196 sells aged *pǔ ěr* tea from China, while the **Xieji Chinese Herbal Pharmacy** at no. 186 was established over eighty years ago. Across Xichang Street and on the other side of the road at no. 153, the **Old Bright Jade Incense Store** is another atmospheric shop, founded in 1897.

Qingshui Temple

At the end of the block you'll reach Kangding Road; on the other side is a traditional gate leading to **Qingshui Temple** (清水巖; *qīngshuǐyán*; daily 6am–9pm) at the end of a narrow lane bordered by a row of cheap food stalls. The temple was built in 1787 by immigrants from Anxi county in Fujian and is dedicated to Chinese hero Chen Zhao-ying, another historical figure who was later deified (see p.405). The temple was burned to the ground during the "Ding-Xia" Feud in 1853, but rebuilt by 1867 – the **Main Hall** has survived more or less intact since then and contains the seven original images of the deity brought from China. The most powerful is known as the "Penglai Divine Progenitor", whose nose is said to fall off in times of danger, only to miraculously reattach itself when the coast is clear. He's shared with the Qingshui Temple in Danshui, spending six months in each place. Note the intricate artwork inside, particularly on the roof beams. It's a short walk north from here along Changsha Street to Zhonghua Road and Ximen MRT Station.

Ximending

Forming the northern section of Wanhua, **Ximending** (西門町; *xīméndīng*) is a grid of narrow streets squashed into a triangle formed by Chengdu and Zhonghua roads with the Danshui River. Named after the long-gone West Gate and now a trendy shopping district accessible from Ximen MRT station, this is where Taipei's teenagers come to have fun – at weekends it's packed with Mandopop fans checking out wannabe performers, and wearing the latest fads. Just south of the main Ximen plaza at 10 Chengdu Rd is the **Red House** (西門红樓; *xīmén hónglóu*; Tues–Thurs & Sun 11am–9.30pm, Fri & Sat 11am–10pm; free; ☏02/2311-9380), an attractive old market building completed in 1908 and now housing a series of boutiques, a teahouse, a theatre, the *Riverside Live House* and a small exhibition on the history of the site.

A short walk north (on the other side of Zhonghua Rd), the **Futai Street Mansion** (撫臺街洋樓; *fǔtáijiē yánglóu*; Tues–Sun 10am–5pm; NT$20), at 26 Yanping South Rd, serves as an easily absorbed history museum for the old walled city (which you've just crossed back into). The beautifully restored Japanese commercial building was constructed in 1910, and the displays inside include a decent section on Liu Mingchuan (p.386) as well as a cool e-book of city history that flips pages (in English) when you wave your hand.

Datong

Taipei's second oldest neighbourhood after Wanhua, **Datong** (大同; *dàtóng*) lines the Danshui River north of Ximending. The district evolved from two villages; north of Minquan Road, **Dalongtong** was established in the early eighteenth century while to the south **Dadaocheng** was created in 1853 by refugees from Wanhua. The latter flourished in the 1870s as tea exports boomed and foreign companies established bases on the wharf. Today it's a enticing place to wander, its narrow lanes littered with historic buildings, traditional shops and temples.

Dihua Street

Historic **Dihua Street** (迪化街; *díhuà jiē*) cuts through the southern half of Datong, crammed with photogenic shophouses built in Chinese Baroque style, many dating from the 1920s; at Chinese New Year the street expands into an open-air emporium for traditional gifts and snacks. Start exploring at the Nanjing Road end, thirty minutes' walk east of Zhongshan MRT Station (or NT$90 by taxi). North of here, the road is lined with silk and cloth stores, followed by Traditional Chinese Medicine, herbs and dried-food sellers. Just beyond Yun-Lo Market and Yongchang Street, on the right, the **Xiahai City God Temple** (霞海城隍廟; *xiáhǎi chénghuáng miào*; daily 6am–8pm) at no. 61 may be small but it's one of Taipei's most venerated places of worship. The temple was completed in 1859 by Tongan migrants to replace the one destroyed in Wanhua six years earlier – the main City God statue had been brought to Taiwan from its hometown in China in 1821. The main shrine contains the revered City God image and his officials, but it's also the most popular place in Taipei to make offerings to the "**Matchmaker**", represented by a 43cm-high image of an old man with a long beard in front and to the left of the main altar. Praying to this Chinese cupid is

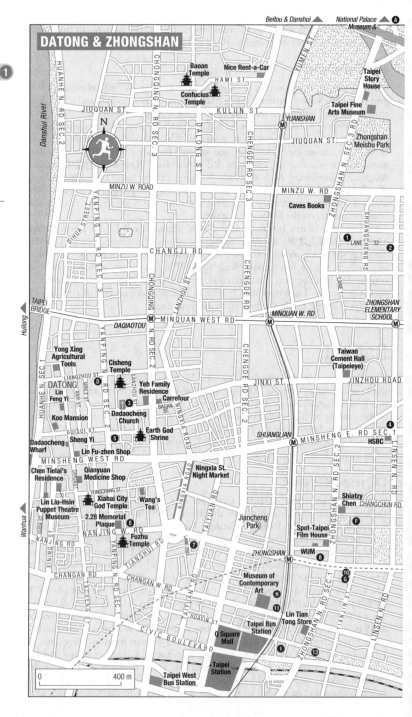

Beitou & Danshui ▲   National Palace ▲ Ⓐ
Museum &

DATONG & ZHONGSHAN

HUANHE N. RD SEC. 2

CHONGQING N. RD SEC. 3

DALONG ST.

CHENGDE RD SEC. 3

YUMEN ST.

Baoan Temple

Nice Rent-a-Car

HAMI ST.

Confucius Temple

Taipei Story House

JIUQUAN ST.   KULUN ST.

Taipei Fine Arts Museum

Ⓜ YUANSHAN

Zhongshan Meishu Park

JIUQUAN ST.

ZHONGSHAN N. SEC. 3 RD

SHUANGCHENG RD

MINZU W. ROAD

MINZU W. RD

Caves Books

YANPING N. RD SEC. 2

DIHUA STREET

CHONGQING N. RD SEC. 2

LANZHOU ST.

CHANGJI RD

CHENGDE RD

LANE 32

❶   ❷
LANE 1

ZHONGSHAN ELEMENTARY SCHOOL

TAIPEI BRIDGE

Hullong ▲

YANPING N. RD SEC. 3

HUANHE N. RD SEC. 1

Ⓜ DAQIAOTOU

MINQUAN WEST RD

Ⓜ MINQUAN W. RD

CHENGDE RD SEC. 2

Ⓜ

Yong Xing Agricultural Tools

DATONG

Cisheng Temple

LIANGZHOU ST.

MINLE ST.

ANXI ST.

GANZHOU ST.

Lin Feng Yi

Ⓓ

Yeh Family Residence

❸   Carrefour

JINXI ST.

JINZHOU ROAD

Taiwan Cement Hall (Taipeieye)

Koo Mansion

Dadaocheng Church

BAOAN ST.

NINGXIA ROAD

Ⓜ SHUANGLIAN   MINSHENG E. RD SEC. 1

❹

ZHONGSHAN N. RD SEC. 2

LINSEN N. RD

GUISUI ST.

Sheng Yi   ❺

Earth God Shrine

HSBC

Dadaocheng Wharf

Lin Fu-zhen Shop

MINSHENG WEST RD

Wanhua ▲

Chen Tielai's Residence

Qianyuan Medicine Shop

Ningxia St. Night Market

NINGXIA RD

TAIYUAN RD

Shiatzy Chen   CHANGCHUN RD

Ⓕ

YONGCHANG ST.

DIHUA ST.

Lin Liu-Hsin Puppet Theatre Museum

Xiahai City God Temple

Wang's Tea

Jiancheng Park

Spot-Taipei Film House

2.28 Memorial Plaque   Ⓔ

NANJING W. RD

WUM   ❽

GUDE ST.

NANJING RD

YANPING N. RD

Fuzhu Temple

TIANSHUI RD

LANE 25❼

Ⓜ ZHONGSHAN

❿ Ⓖ

JINXIN ST.

CHANGAN RD

CHANGAN W. RD

Museum of Contemporary Art   Ⓗ

ZHONGSHAN N. RD SEC. 1

TIANJIN ST.

NANJING E. RD

LINSEN N. RD

TAIYUAN RD

HUAYIN ST.

❶❶

Lin Tian Tong Store

CIVIC BOULEVARD

Q Square Mall

Taipei Bus Station

Ⓘ   ❶❸

N

0   400 m

Taipei West Bus Station

Taipei Station

74

ACCOMMODATION

Ambience Hotel	K
City Suites	E
Dandy Hotel Tianjin	G
Dongwu Hotel	D
Grand Formosa Regent	F
Grand Hotel	A
Guest House Taiwanmex	H
Happy Family Hostel	I
Hsuan Mei Hotel	J
Landis Taipei Hotel	B
Taipei House International Youth Hostel	C

RESTAURANTS & CAFÉS

Celestial Restaurant	8
Cha for Tea	9
Kiki Restaurant Kiki	14
Kitchen Pucci	8
Le Petite Cuisine Brasserie by JQ	12
Peng Yuan	4
Seoul Korean Barbeque	13
Si Hai Soybean Milk Store	11
Tian Xiang Huwei Hot Pot	10
Tien Hsiang Lo	B
Xia Er Zui	3
Xiao Xiang Ting	7
Yi Men Wang Noodles	5

NIGHTLIFE

Brass Monkey	6
Front Page Sports Bar	2
Jurassic Restaurant	15
My Place	1

believed to result in finding your ideal partner in less than six months – the temple claims that 9316 couples got married in 2008 alone, thanks to his help. Should this tempt you, leaflets in English explain how you can make an offering. The side hall to the right of the main shrine contains Guanyin (nearest the entrance), the City God's wife next door (make-up is a common offering here) and at the end, an altar commemorating the 38 men (the *yì yǒng gōng*) killed saving the City God in the Ding-Xia Feud of 1853. The City God's birthday on Lunar May 13 (usually in June) is one of Taipei's biggest religious **festivals** involving fireworks, parades and traditional performances over several days.

Just north of the temple is the traditional **Qianyuan Medicine Shop** at no. 71 (乾元行; *qiányuán háng*), established in the nineteenth century and renowned for its powerful remedies. At Minsheng Road, turn left and walk two blocks (past Xining Rd) to Guide Street; it's the narrow lane on the left just before Huanhe Road and **Dadaocheng Wharf** (大稻埕碼頭; *dàdàochéng mǎtóu*), the place to catch ferries upriver on the **Blue Highway** (see box below). Guide Street ran along the quayside in the nineteenth century, facing the Danshui River and home to Taipei's affluent tea merchants – you can still see the raised foundations that protected them from flooding. The best-preserved house is tea tycoon **Chen Tian-lai's residence** at no. 73 (also known as the Jinji Teashop), a grand three-storey mansion dating from 1920 and still privately owned. Continue walking down Guide and take the first left (Lane 86) back to Xining North Road: across the road and a little to the north is the **Lin Liu-Hsin Puppet Theatre Museum** (林柳新紀念偶戲博物館; *línliǔ xīn jìniàn ǒuxì bówùguǎn*; Tues–Sun 10am–5pm; NT$120; ☏02/2552-9079, ⊛www.taipeipuppet.com) at no. 79. Housed in an atmospheric shophouse, the museum contains three floors of exhibits devoted to Taiwanese and Asian puppetry. The theatre next door hosts traditional puppet shows most Saturdays at 2 or 3pm (NT$200), but check the website to confirm.

Return to Minsheng Road and turn right: on the corner of Minsheng and Dihua Street at no. 105 is the store founded by **Lin Fu-zhen** (林復振商行; *lín fùzhèn shāngháng*), the merchant leader of the Tongan refugees in 1853 and still owned by his family, though the building is not the original. Heading north again along Dihua, animal lovers might want to skip **Sheng Yi** (勝益食品; *shèngyì shípǐn*) at

---

Blue Highway – white elephant?

One of Ma Ying-jeou's ambitious schemes to develop tourism in Taipei, the **Blue Highway** (藍色公路; *lánsè gōnglù*) has struggled to take off since it launched in 2004. A ferry route connecting **Dadaocheng Wharf** with **Guandu**, **Bali** (p.114), **Danshui** (p.110) and **Fisherman's Wharf** (see p.113) lower down the Danshui River (as well as a smaller service along the Keelung River), it's part of an optimistic plan to integrate ferry services, bicycle routes and tourist destinations around the north coast. Though it's not one of the world's most photogenic boat rides, it's an appealing alternative to the MRT for the journey downriver, with pleasant views of the mountains on either side. Tourist literature tends to promote the scheme as a scheduled ferry service, but at the time of writing boats were still not operating on a regular basis: most boats are rented by groups or run special cruises on weekdays. Normal services do usually run on Sat & Sun, at 10am, noon, 2pm and 4pm, but always check ahead. Tickets are NT$150 for Guandu to Dadaocheng (one-way), and a further NT$110 on to Bali/Danshui or NT$160 to Fisherman's Wharf. If you can speak Chinese, call the companies that run the boats for the latest timetables and fares (Haloha Shipping ☏02/2558-5519, ⊛www.uuboat.com.tw; CH Shipping ☏02/2618-2226, ⊛www.chshipping.com.tw; SeaSky ☏02/2618-6348, ⊛www.seasky.com.tw), or check at any visitor information centre.

no. 144 on the other side of the street – it has one of the largest displays of **shark's fin** you're ever likely to see on dry land. At Guisui Street turn left and walk one block to narrow Lane 303 on the right: up here on the right (no. 9) is the lavish 1920 **Koo Family Salt Hall**, home of the Lugang-based tycoon (see p.191), now a kindergarten. Back on Dihua, check out **Lin Feng Yi**'s (林豐益; *línfēngyì*) bamboo crafts and cypress wood tubs at no. 214, while beyond Liangzhou Street, there's **Yong Xing Agricultural Tools** (永興農具店; *yǒngxīng nóngjùdiàn*), a traditional ironmonger and wood store at no. 288.

Cisheng Temple and around

Two blocks east of Dihua Street, just south of Liangzhou Street on Yanping Road, is a traditional arch leading to Lane 225 and **Cisheng Temple** (慈聖宮; *císhènggōng*; daily 6am–8pm). Dedicated to Mazu, the temple dates from the 1860s when it was established on the riverbank by immigrants fleeing Wanhua to the south – it was moved to this location in 1914. Today it's a quiet, unassuming place, chiefly notable for its atmospheric forecourt lined with Indian laurel trees and excellent seafood stalls, filled with local workers and mahjong players at lunchtime. Have a peek inside, then walk around the back of the temple, along narrow Lane 52 to Ganzhou Street. Turn right here and you'll see **Dadaocheng Church** (大稻程教堂; *dàdàochéng jiāotáng*), at no. 40 on the right, built in 1915 to replace the original established by Canadian missionary George Mackay (see p.113), but destroyed during the Japanese invasion. Its red brickwork has been immaculately restored (with a massive extension on the back), but there's little to see inside.

Keep walking south to Guisui Street where you'll see an excellent example of a neighbourhood **Earth God shrine**, or *tǔdì gōng miào* (see p.405). Completed in 1914, this one is usually quite active – in addition to a steady stream of worshippers you'll see a motley collection of old boys playing dominoes or sipping beer outside most afternoons. Turn right here and walk along Guisui Street to Yanping Road. Continue south on Yanping, past Minsheng Road, to Lane 61 and turn left: keep bearing straight ahead beyond a small junction (it's now Lane 64) and less than 50m on the right is **Wang's Tea** (有記名茶; *yǒujì míngchá*; Mon–Sat 9am–8.30pm), at no. 26. Housed in a beautifully restored building, this teashop was first established in Fujian, China, in the 1880s and opened here after the family fled the mainland in 1949 – you can sample quality Taiwanese tea inside.

Museum of Contemporary Art

The **Museum of Contemporary Art** (台北當代藝術館; *táiběi dāngdài yìshùguǎn*; Tues–Sun 10am–6pm; NT$50; Ⓦ www.mocataipei.org.tw) at 39 Changan West Rd is an innovative modern art gallery, housed in one of the most attractive Japanese-era buildings in the city. Constructed in the 1920s and 1930s, it served as an elementary school and Taipei's City Hall before opening in 2001. The thought-provoking temporary exhibitions here feature international but primarily Taiwanese artists and include contemporary painting, installation art, sculpture, photography, video and film. Be warned, however, MOCA sometimes closes for up to two weeks in between exhibitions. The museum is a short walk from Zhongshan MRT Station.

Dalongtong

The northwest corner of Datong occupies the site of the eighteenth-century village of **Dalongtong** (大龍峒; *dàlóngtóng*), once famed as the home of scholars, though little remains of it today apart from two of the city's most alluring temples. Both are signposted and a short walk from Yuanshan MRT Station.

Confucius Temple

Taipei's **Confucius Temple** (孔廟; *kǒngmiào*; Tues–Sat 8.30am–9pm, Sun 8.30am–5pm; ⓦwww.ct.taipei.gov.tw) at 275 Dalong St is best known for hosting the world's most authentic annual celebration of Confucius's **birthday** on September 28 (see *Festivals of Taiwan* colour section). Though the great teacher is still revered in Taiwan, he's not associated with any of the daily rituals that make other temples so colourful, and on other days it's relatively peaceful. Built in South Fujianese style but laid out according to the original Confucius temple in Qufu (in China's Shandong province), the oldest buildings were constructed between 1927 and 1939.

Enter via the **Hong Gate** on Dalong Street, which leads into a garden with Minglun Hall on your left and the **Li Gate** just ahead; walk through this to get to the front of the main temple complex. The first building on your left is the ceremonial **Lingxing Gate**, while beyond this the **Yi Gate** fronts the central stone courtyard and **Dacheng Hall**, the most important part of the temple. Note the decorated cylinders on the hall's roof, symbolizing the bamboo containers used to hide Confucian classics during the Qin Emperor's fanatical "Burning of the Books" in 213 BC. The hall is typically bare inside: it contains a single tablet commemorating Confucius in the centre, and sixteen others for the Four Sages (including Mencius) and the Twelve Wise Men, all Confucian disciples, as well as various musical instruments used in ceremonies. The black tablet hanging from the beam above the shrine was written by Chiang Kai-shek and says "education for all". The courtyard is ringed by the **East and West Rooms**, containing the memorial tablets of 154 other Confucian disciples and scholars, and a small office (daily 8.30am–5.30pm) on the right where you can pick up English leaflets, while the **Chongsheng Shrine** at the back of the complex houses tablets venerating the first five generations of Confucius's ancestors.

Baoan Temple

Baoan Temple (保安宮; *bǎoān gōng*; daily 6am–10pm; ⓦwww.baoan.org.tw), a few metres north of the Confucius Temple on Hami Street (and signposted from Yuanshan MRT Station), is Taipei's most beautiful shrine. Though there are many deities enshrined here, the principal figure is Baosheng Dadi, regarded as a god of medicine or healing (see p.406). Tradition maintains that immigrants from Tongan began worshipping here in 1742 and a simple shrine was completed in 1760, but the first official temple was constructed between 1805 and 1830. The temple won a UNESCO conservation award in 2003 in recognition of the incredible restoration work completed in the 1990s.

Before you go in, check out the painted wall carving inside the East Gate to the right of the Entrance Hall – it features Chinese hero Yue Fei having the words "Serve Your Country" being carved onto his back by his patriotic mother. Once inside you'll see the **Main Hall** across the courtyard, packed with numerous images of Baosheng and surrounded by statues of the **36 celestial officials**, carved between 1829 and 1834 and exceptionally rare pieces of temple art. Hard to spot, but there are slight differences between the left and right sides of the hall, a result of the rivalry between the two master craftsmen hired for the restoration of 1917. You won't miss the seven eye-catching **murals** that adorn the outer walls of the hall however – they depict various Chinese legends and were completed in 1973. The **Drum Tower** on the left (west) side of the courtyard houses a shrine to the Birth Goddess, while the **Bell Tower** on the opposite side is a shrine to Mazu. Shennong Dadi, the god of agriculture, is worshipped in the **Rear Hall**. The **Baosheng Cultural Festival** is usually held April to May and comprises several weeks of traditional performances to celebrate **Baosheng's birthday** (Lunar March 15), including an extensive programme of Chinese opera and music in the evenings. The birthday is marked by a solemn ceremony in the temple, while a boisterous parade usually takes place the day before.

Zhongshan

Bounded by Fuxing Road in the east and maple-lined Zhongshan Road in the west, one of the city's more pleasant thoroughfares, **Zhongshan** (中山; *zhōngshān*) is a lively modern district covering much of the northern part of central Taipei. Though there's plenty to see, especially in its northern half, Zhongshan is primarily a collection of residential neighbourhoods, shopping streets and offices with no discernible centre, its sights spread out and often best combined with attractions in other areas; Taipei's excellent **Fine Arts Museum** is close to Yuanshan MRT station and the temples in Dalongtong (see p.77), while the **Su Ho Memorial Paper Culture Foundation** lies much further south, best approached from Songjiang Nanjing MRT Station.

Taipei Fine Arts Museum

If you only have time for one art gallery in Taipei, make it the **Taipei Fine Arts Museum** (台北美術館; *táiběi měishùguǎn*; Tues–Sun 9.30am–5.30pm, Sat closes 8.30pm; NT$30; ☎02/2595-7656, ⓦwww.tfam.museum) at 181 Zhongshan N Rd Sec 3, a short walk across the park from Yuanshan MRT Station. Its four floors primarily showcase modern Taiwanese art – though exhibitions change every few months, they usually include pieces from the museum's extensive and important permanent collection. This includes Chen Cheng-po's nostalgic *Street Scene on a Summer Day* and Liao Chi-chun's colourful oil painting *Courtyard with Banana Trees*, as well as work by Li Chi-mao, Lee Chun-shan and Yu Cheng-yao (see p.410). Next door, the **Taipei Story House** (台北故事館; *táiběi gùshìguǎn*; Tues–Sun 10am–6pm; NT$30; ⓦwww.storyhouse.com.tw) was built in 1914 as an opulent private mansion, and is now a venue for art exhibitions and performances of *nanguan* music, as well as containing an elegant **teahouse**.

Lin An Tai Historical Home

Set on the northern edge of Xinsheng Park, around 750m east of the Fine Arts Museum, the **Lin An Tai Historical Home** (林安泰古厝; *línāntài gǔcuò*; Tues–Sat 9am–9pm, Sun 9am–5pm; free) is Taipei's oldest residential building. It was built by wealthy merchant Lin Hui-gong in 1783–85 and moved here from its original location in Daan district in 1983, to avoid destruction during a road-building project. The house is a pristine example of southern Fujian-style architecture from the Qing dynasty, though apart from a few pieces of furniture there's not much to see inside – the historic atmosphere is reduced further by the roar of jets coming into land at Songshan Airport, and the highway overpass at the back. You can walk here from the Fine Arts Museum, but it can be dangerous crossing Xinsheng Road and it's best to take a taxi.

Xingtian Temple

Set on the corner of Minquan and Songjiang Roads, **Xingtian Temple** (行天宮; *xíngtiān gōng*; daily 3.30am–11pm) was built in classical Chinese style in 1968, and is a fascinating place to observe **traditional rituals**. Dedicated to Guan Di, represented by a large statue in the **Main Hall**, the main attraction for locals is the smorgasbord of spiritual services on offer; these include *píng ān dài* (a charm worn around the neck), *shōuhún* (spiritual healing) and *shōujīng* (fortune telling by drawing lots). Most temples offer the latter, but here believers have a choice of one hundred readings dating back over eight hundred years, compared to the usual 64 (for more on this and Guan Di see p.404). Volunteers, often English-speaking and wearing blue robes (*dào yī*), are on hand to answer questions. The temple is a short walk from Xingtian Temple MRT station.

Su Ho Memorial Paper Culture Foundation

A short walk from Songjian Nanjing MRT Station, the **Su Ho Memorial Paper Culture Foundation** (樹火紀念紙文化基金會; *shùhuǒ jìniànzhǐ wénhuà jījīnhuì*; Mon–Sat 9.30am–4.30pm; NT$100; ⓦ www.suhopaper.org.tw), at 68 Changan East Rd, is one of Taipei's few craft-based museums, offering a welcome break between temples and department stores, and the chance to make your own traditional Chinese paper.

Crammed into this four-storey shophouse are tastefully presented displays on **paper making** and Taiwan's paper industry, a mini paper mill and a decent gift shop – though most of the labels are in Chinese, there's an informative English audio-guide included in the entry price. The paper-making sessions can be a lot of fun; they start at 2pm on Saturdays (NT$180; no booking required), though if your visit coincides with private tour groups on other days you're welcome to join in.

National Palace Museum and around

The district of Shilin (士林; *shìlín*), north of the Keelung River, is noted principally for being the home of Taipei's biggest **night market** (see p.90) and the **National Palace Museum**, one of the world's finest collections of Chinese art and historical artefacts. It's obviously one of the city's highlights and needs several hours to do it justice, though there are a couple of other sights near Shilin MRT Station to keep you occupied for a day or so. The northern part of Shilin contains **Tianmu** (天母; *tiānmǔ*), an affluent suburb favoured by many expat residents and packed with shops and restaurants, but with nothing much to see for visitors.

National Palace Museum

The **National Palace Museum** (國立故宮博物院; *guólì gùgōng bówùyuàn*; Mon–Fri & Sun 9am–5pm, Sat 9am–8.30pm; NT$160, free Sat 5–8.30pm; ⓦ www .npm.gov.tw) is the most famous attraction in Taiwan, pulling in over two million visitors a year with its unparalleled collection of **Chinese art**, a priceless treasure trove going back five thousand years. The museum also owns hundreds of documents, pieces of furniture, rare books and official decrees issued by the Imperial Chinese government, as well as masses of everyday items that provide a fascinating insight into life at court. Very little of this has to do with Taiwan of course – the contents are a legacy of Chiang Kai-shek's retreat from China in 1949, when the former Imperial art collection was shipped, crate by crate, across the Taiwan Straits. While the Forbidden City in Beijing (also known as the Palace Museum) has more items, the finest pieces ended up in Taipei, becoming a contentious and often heated political issue between the two countries. Note that parts of the museum can be utterly swamped by tour groups throughout the day; your best chance of avoiding the crowds is **late on Saturday evenings**.

To get here, take the MRT to Shilin Station and look for the Zhongzheng Road exit: at the end of the plaza bus #304, R30 and minibuses 18 and 19 pass the museum in around ten minutes (NT$15); R30 goes straight to the main entrance (you can also take this back). Next door to the museum, the **Zhishan Garden** (至善園; *zhìshànyuán*; also "Chih-Shan Garden"; Tues–Sun 7am–7pm; NT$20 or free with museum ticket) is a pleasant reproduction of a classical Song dynasty garden, best enjoyed in spring when the flowers are in bloom.

Some history

While the museum continues to expand (mostly from donations), at its core remains the priceless collection of art and artefacts once owned by the Chinese emperors. The **Imperial collection** was formally established in the reign of the first Song dynasty emperor, Taizu (960–975), who seized the artwork owned by rulers he had defeated in battle; his brother and successor, Taizong (976–997), expanded the hoard considerably, commissioning new pieces and collecting ceramics, artwork and statuary from all over China. This very private collection ended up in Beijing's Forbidden City, and it wasn't until the last emperor **Pu Yi** was forced to leave in 1924 that it was opened to the public: it became the **National Palace Museum** one year later. After the Japanese invaded Manchuria, its precious contents were carted around the country by the Nationalist government, on and off, for almost sixteen years, but by 1949 defeat at the hands of the Communists looked certain. During one, tense night in February of that year, most of the collection was packed into crates and shipped from Nanjing to Taiwan, just weeks before the city fell. It's worth noting, however, that although the most valuable pieces were spirited across the Taiwan Strait, much was left behind. The retreat was meant to be temporary, and it took another fifteen years before the authorities, resigned to the status quo, decided to unpack the boxes and build a museum in 1965.

China, where many see the removal of the collection as looting, would love to see it returned to the mainland. There's little chance of that happening any time soon: most Taiwanese point to the destruction of artwork during China's **Cultural Revolution** in the late 1960s and claim that they have worked hard to protect important treasures that might otherwise have been lost. Meanwhile, as Taiwan gradually sees itself as part of a wider East Asian community, a new branch of the museum to be opened near Chiayi in 2012 will centre on **Asian art**, and emphasize the foreign traditions that have influenced Chinese culture.

The collection

The museum's collection of over 654,500 pieces is still too large for everything to be displayed at the same time, but thanks to the completion of a major renovation project in 2006, more can be exhibited than ever before. The museum is arranged thematically, but galleries tend to be grouped in chronological order: start on the third floor and work down. The daily tours in English (free) at 10am and 3pm offer a more digestible introduction to the main exhibits, while the *Sanxitang Tea Room* on the fourth floor is the best place to take a break.

Early China: the third floor

The third floor charts the beginnings of Chinese civilization in the Neolithic period, through to the end of the Han dynasty in 220 AD. The museum's remarkable ensemble of Neolithic artefacts (gallery 303) primarily comprises early pottery and exquisite **jade** pieces – at this time jade was believed to be a medium for spirits, and as such was given special reverence.

The real highlights, however, are the collection of stunning **bronzes** from the Shang and Zhou dynasties (1600–221 BC; gallery 305), principally ritual vessels owned by the wealthy. Typical pieces include the cauldron-like *dǐng*, and sets of cast bronze bells (zhōng), which had a ceremonial function. The most celebrated exhibit is the **San P'an Basin** dating from the late Western Zhou dynasty (700–900 BC), a ritual water vessel with an invaluable 350-character inscription inside. Another illustrious piece, the **Maogong Ding** (*máogōng dǐng*), named after the Duke of Mao and engraved with five hundred characters from the Zhou Dynasty, has its own special gallery to the side (301). The innovative, multimedia **Mystery of Bronzes** exhibition (gallery 300) is an enlightening introduction to the relatively advanced technologies of the era.

The **Qin and Han dynasties** (221 BC–220 AD; gallery 307) were the last to use ritual jades and bronzes, represented by the highly ornate *zūn*, or wine vessel. The gallery also contains some rare glazed ware, used by the rich, and "grey pottery", often used by commoners to store burial goods.

The third floor also contains temporary exhibit galleries (304 and 306) as well as the "**Dazzling Gems of the Collection**" gallery (308), which features a selection of the museum's most famous pieces: you'll probably have to wait to get in. The biggest crowd-pleaser of all has its own room (302), the exceptional *Jadeite Cabbage with Insects*, a delicate Qing dynasty jade carving made to look like bok choy.

Han to Qing dynasty: the second floor

The second floor covers the flowering of Chinese civilization from the end of the Han to the Qing dynasty (221–1911). Here the range of artwork, media and materials expands dramatically from porcelain and ceramics, to fine art, jewellery and sculpture. The museum's rare collection of silk-screen **painting** and **calligraphy** (West Wing galleries) is truly magnificent, beginning with masterpieces from the **Song dynasty** (960–1279), when landscape watercolour painting was reaching its zenith: highlights include Fan K'uan's *Travellers Among Mountains and Streams*, the lyrical *Storied Mountains and Dense Forests* by Chu-jan and *Early Spring* by Guo Xi (note that paintings are usually on display for no longer than three months at a time to prevent light damage). The museum also has an extensive collection of Ming and Qing dynasty artwork.

China's golden age, the **Tang dynasty** (618–907), is best represented by the first **ceramics** gallery (201). The era is one of the few in Chinese history when plump women were considered attractive: the earthenware figures of suitably curvaceous court ladies are indicative of the period. Porcelain and ceramics also flourished in the **Song dynasty** (960–1279). Don't miss the rare *rǔ yáo* ceramic *Narcissus Basin* in bluish-green glaze (gallery 205), a container dating from Northern Song dynasty.

The **Ming dynasty** (1368–1644) galleries (205 and 207) feature the best of China's porcelain and ceramics, much of it from the famous kilns at Jingdezhen. The intricate *Doucai Cup with Chickens* and *Blue-and-white Flat Vase with Figures* are considered the most accomplished pieces from the early part of the era (gallery 205).

The **Qing dynasty** (1644–1911) collections (galleries 209 and 211) contain a staggering number of artworks from elaborate *cloisonné* and high-quality porcelain to ornate jade and stone carvings (note that some of the most spectacular **olive stone carvings** are usually on display in gallery 304).

The first floor

The first floor has permanent galleries dedicated to **Qing dynasty furniture** (108), a vast array of **religious sculptural art** (101) and arts from the Qing Imperial collection (mostly intricate **curio boxes**; 106). Galleries 103 and 104 show rotating exhibits from the **rare books** and documents departments.

Shung Ye Museum of Formosan Aborigines

The **Shung Ye Museum of Formosan Aborigines** (順益台灣原住民博物館; *shūnyì táiwān yuánzhùmín bówùguǎn*; Tues–Sun 9am–5pm, closed Jan 20–Feb 20; NT$150; ⓦwww.museum.org.tw), 100m up Zhishan Road from the Palace

Museum, is one of Taipei's most appealing museums, providing a thorough introduction to Taiwan's indigenous population (see p.395). As of 2010 there were fourteen formally recognized tribes, though the museum focuses on the nine most prominent: the Ami, Atayal, Bunun, Paiwan, Puyuma, Rukai, Saisiyat, Tao and Cou (Tsou). The collection isn't particularly large, but it's well presented in English and Chinese, and videos covering the origins and current social situation of the various tribes on the **first floor** are excellent – just make sure you avoid school parties and tour groups because you'll miss most of the commentary. The **basement** is the most intriguing part of the museum, highlighting festivals, myths and rituals, with a special area dedicated to head-hunting and a selection of ceremonial weapons.

Shilin Official Residence

Just to the east of Shilin MRT Station, a short walk along Fulin Road, the **Shilin Official Residence** (士林官邸; *shìlín guāndǐ*; Mon–Fri 8am–5pm, Sat & Sun 8am–7pm; free) was the most important of **Chiang Kai-shek**'s fifteen former estates. The problem is that the actual "official residence" isn't open to the public – all you can see are the lush **gardens** (famed for their roses and plum blossoms), the **Victoria Chapel** where the Chiangs prayed and a brief glimpse of the main house through iron gates and drooping palms. When (or if) the Chiang family agrees to open the house, it's likely to become one of Taipei's most popular attractions – the gardens are a major draw for mainland Chinese tour groups, so visit early if you want a tranquil experience.

National Revolutionary Martyrs' Shrine

Just over 1km east of Jiantan MRT Station, not far from the Keelung River, the **National Revolutionary Martyrs' Shrine** (忠烈祠; *zhōngliècí*; daily 9am–5pm; free) is the largest of similar memorials all over Taiwan, dedicated to more than 300,000 civilians and soldiers killed in struggles with the Qing dynasty, the Japanese and the Communists. It's also another reminder of Taiwan's official status as Republic of China – most of the people honoured here died on the mainland. The main gate sits on Beian Road, but you have to trudge across a vast plaza from here to get to the grand collection of buildings known as the Sanctuary. Completed in 1969 to resemble the Taihedian in Beijing's Forbidden City, the **Main Shrine** contains a central tablet that commemorates all those who died – Taiwanese visitors usually bow here. Note the painting of Sun Yat-sen to the left. Individual tablets are enshrined in the **Civilian Martyrs' Shrine** on the right side of the complex, or the **Military Martyrs' Shrine** on the left, the whole thing encircled by a walkway lined with paintings and boards describing every military campaign fought by the Nationalists. The **colour guard ceremonies** (daily 8.50am and 5pm) or failing that, the hourly **changing of the guard**, are extremely elaborate affairs, lasting more than fifteen minutes and highly photogenic. It's a bit awkward to get here – Red Bus #5 from Yuanshan MRT Station is one of several services that stop outside, or it's a ten-minute walk from the *Grand Hotel*.

East Taipei

East Taipei, comprising Songshan, Xinyi, most of Daan and the suburban district of Nangang, is the modern commercial heart of the city. Best known for Taipei's premier **shopping malls** and its most hip **restaurants** and **nightlife**, it also has a handful of worthwhile sights tucked in between the office towers.

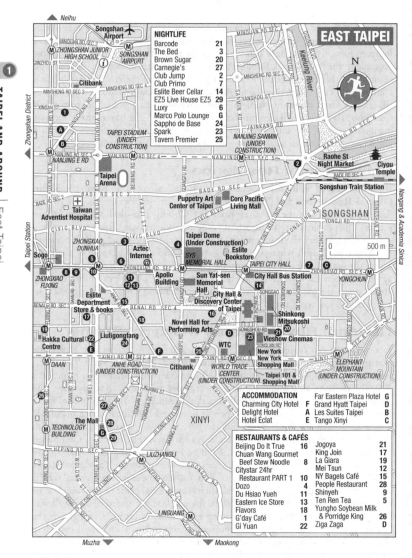

EAST TAIPEI

N

▲ Neihu

Songshan Airport

Zhongshan District

Taipei Station

Nangang & Academia Sinica

NIGHTLIFE	
Barcode	21
The Bed	3
Brown Sugar	20
Carnegie's	27
Club Jump	2
Club Primo	7
Eslite Beer Cellar	14
EZ5 Live House EZ5	29
Luxy	6
Marco Polo Lounge	G
Sappho de Base	24
Spark	23
Tavern Premier	25

Songshan Junior High School
Citibank
Taipei Stadium (Under Construction)
Nanjing E Rd
Taipei Arena
Taiwan Adventist Hospital
Raohe St Night Market
Ciyou Temple
Songshan Train Station
SONGSHAN
Puppetry Art Center of Taipei
Core Pacific Living Mall
Zhongxiao Dunhua
Taipei Dome (Under Construction)
Eslite Bookstore
Sogo
Aztec Internet
SYS Memorial Hall
Taipei City Hall
Zhongxiao Fuxing
Apollo Building
Sun Yat-sen Memorial Hall
City Hall Bus Station
Eslite Department Store & books
City Hall & Discovery Center of Taipei
Shinkong Mitsukoshi
Hakka Cultural Centre
Liuligongfang
Novel Hall for Performing Arts
Vieshow Cinemas
WTC
New York New York Shopping Mall
Daan
Anhe Road (Under Construction)
Citibank
World Trade Center (Under Construction)
Taipei 101 & Shopping Mall
Elephant Mountain (Under Construction)
The Mall
Technology Building
Xinyi
Liuzhangli
Linguang

0 ——— 500 m

ACCOMMODATION		
Charming City Hotel	F	Far Eastern Plaza Hotel G
Delight Hotel	A	Grand Hyatt Taipei D
Hotel Éclat	E	Les Suites Taipei B
		Tango Xinyi C

RESTAURANTS & CAFÉS			
Beijing Do It True	16	Jogoya	21
Chuan Wang Gourmet		King Join	17
Beef Stew Noodle	8	La Giara	19
Citystar 24hr		Mei Tsun	12
Restaurant PART 1	10	NY Bagels Café	15
Dozo	4	People Restaurant	28
Du Hsiao Yueh	11	Shinyeh	9
Eastern Ice Store	13	Ten Ren Tea	5
Flavors	18	Yungho Soybean Milk	
G'day Café	1	& Porridge King	26
Gi Yuan	22	Ziga Zaga	D

▲ Muzha ▼ ▼ Maokong

Xinyi

Central **Xinyi** (信義; *xìnyì*) is sandwiched between Zhongxiao and Xinyi roads, bounded to the west by Keelung Road and to the east by mountains. It's a former wasteland that as little as twenty years ago was covered in sugar cane. Today it's plastered with **shopping malls**, modern residential blocks and office towers, including one of the world's tallest, **Taipei 101**, and the **International Convention Center**, venue for some of Asia's biggest trade shows.

A short walk from Taipei City Hall MRT Station, the **Discovery Center of Taipei** (台北探索館; *táiběi tànsuǒguǎn*; Tues–Sun 9am–5pm; free), the city's de facto history museum, is an excellent place to start a tour of the area. It's located within **City Hall** and contains several floors of high-tech displays focusing on Taipei's history and culture – each district is covered in turn. For the **Puppetry Art Center of Taipei**, see p.99.

Taipei 101

Looming over Xinyi, and indeed the whole of Taipei, **Taipei 101** (台北一零一; *táiběi yīlíngyī*) became the world's tallest building on completion in 2003 – it was overtaken by Dubai's Burj Khalifa (828m) in 2009. Designed by Taiwanese architect C.Y. Lee to resemble a stalk of bamboo, it is 508m (and 101 floors) tall. The entrance is on the fifth floor of the shopping mall on Xinyi Road (see p.101), where the world's fastest elevators shoot to the top in just 37 seconds. Up on the 89th floor, the indoor **observatory** (daily 9am–10pm, last entry 9.15pm; NT$400) provides unparalleled views of the city and the surrounding mountains, while you'll get a hair-raising perspective from the outdoor gallery on the 91st floor. A free audio-guide provides commentary on the views, but don't miss the massive steel-plated **damper** in the centre, which at 660 tonnes is the world's largest and helps stabilize the building in case of typhoons. Free **shuttle buses** travel between 101 and Taipei City Hall MRT (daily 11am–9pm).

National Dr Sun Yat-sen Memorial Hall

Grandly located in a small park on the western edge of Xinyi, a short walk from City Hall, the **National Dr Sun Yat-sen Memorial Hall** (國立國父紀念館; *guólì guófù jìniànguǎn*; daily 9am–7pm, art galleries close at 5pm; free; Wwww .yatsen.gov.tw), is a striking postmodern recreation of a classical Chinese palace, with concrete pillars and bright yellow roof. It was completed in 1972 to preserve the memory of the founder of the Republic of China, and what's now referred to, in all seriousness, as "Sunology".

A giant bronze statue of Sun Yat-sen guards the main entrance, and here you can witness another solemn **changing of the guard** ceremony (daily, on the hour), often mobbed by mainland Chinese tourists – Sun is eulogized on both sides of the Taiwan Strait. On either side of the statue are rooms documenting Sun's life and his relationship with Taiwan (with English labelling), though you'll see scant mention of his influential wife, Soong Qing-ling, who sided with the Communists after his death and died in Shanghai in 1981. The rest of the building contains several **galleries** that showcase Taiwanese art, while the **History Room** on the third floor focuses on the history of the building and has an informative English video. SYS Memorial Hall is the closest MRT station.

Sun Yat-sen: father of the nation?

Sun Yat-sen (1866–1925) made just three brief visits to Taiwan: in 1900, 1913 (for a day) and 1918 (when he was turned away at Keelung harbour). Despite growing apathy among younger generations, he is still officially regarded as the **father of modern China** on both sides of the Taiwan Strait; every town in Taiwan (and China) has a "Zhongshan" Road or building, recalling Sun's preferred Chinese name, and his mausoleum in Nanjing is a pilgrimage site for all Chinese. Sun's popularity stems from his crucial role in the overthrow of the Qing dynasty in 1911, and the formation of the Republic of China. He was also one of the founders of the Kuomintang (KMT) or Nationalist party in 1912. In Taiwan, many pro-independence politicians object to his title as "founding father" (used in school textbooks) for the obvious reason that he had little to do with the island, but while Taiwan remains the "Republic of China" they have little hope of changing his formal status.

Academia Sinica

The district of **Nangang** (南港; *nángǎng*), east of Xinyi, is home to **Academia Sinica** (中央研究院; *zhōngyāng yánjiùyuàn*; ⓦ www.sinica.edu.tw), one of Taipei's less-visited treasures. Founded in 1928 as China's foremost academic research institute, the Academia relocated to Taiwan with the Nationalists in 1949 and today the main campus is at 128 Academia Rd, with a couple of fine museums clustered at the southern end. To get here take the MRT to Kunyang, look for exit 4 and cross Zhongxiao Road to the bus stop on the other side. Bus #212, #270 or Blue #25 pass the campus in about ten minutes.

The Academia's **Museum of the Institute of History and Philology** (歷史文物陳列館; *lìshǐ wénwù chénlièguǎn*; Wed & Sat 9.30am–4.30pm; free) is a remarkable treasure-trove of Chinese archeological finds, excavated by the institute in the 1930s. It's not huge, but the collection is magnificently presented. Among the most important artefacts are the **"wooden slips"** (tablets inscribed with Chinese characters), dating from the Han dynasty (206 BC–220 AD) and found at frontier fortresses in Gansu province. Inscribed with everything from official orders to the letters of ordinary soldiers, they provide a unique insight into everyday life in China two thousand years ago. The museum's display of **Shang and Zhou dynasty bronzes** is equally impressive and beautifully laid out. Next door, the **Museum of the Institute of Ethnology** (民族學研究所博物館; *mínzúxué yánjiùsuǒ bówùguǎn*; same hours; free) houses an interesting collection of artefacts from Taiwan's indigenous tribes and China's minority groups – explanations are in Chinese only.

Maokong

The valley south of Taipei is known as **MAOKONG** (貓空; *māokōng*), one of Taiwan's oldest tea-growing areas and beloved for its teahouses, temples and romantic night views of the city. Production of **Tiěguānyīn** (a high-quality, semi-fermented oolong tea), began here in the 1880s, though **Bāozhǒng** (another type of oolong) is just as prevalent. In both cases production is relatively small and it's the "tea tourism" that brings in the cash today. In 2007 the 4km **Maokong Gondola** (貓空纜車; *māokōng lǎnchē*) linked Maokong and Zhinan Temple with Taipei Zoo, further boosting visitor numbers. It's definitely the most appealing way to get there, with gasp-inducing views of the jungle-smothered slopes and city beyond. The base station is a short walk from Taipei Zoo MRT Station, with cars running daily 9am–9pm: grab a "queue ticket" first, and enter when your time is called. You can use your EasyCard to pay, or buy tickets at machines inside the station (NT$50 to Maokong, M$40 to Zhinan Temple and N$30 between the temple and Maokong). Make sure you grab a **map** first at the **visitor centre** (same hours; ☏ 2/8661-7627). Be warned; the wait for a ride can be as much as three hours at peak periods, so get there early or check the electronic screens at Zhongxiao Fuxing MRT Station before you go.

Zhinan Temple

The second gondola stop (after Taipei Zoo South) is **Zhinan Temple** (指南宮; *zhǐnán gōng*; daily 4am–8.30pm), one of Taiwan's most important religious centres. Established in 1891, it blends Confucian, Taoist and Buddhist practices and features five main halls dedicated to a mixture of gods.

Follow the path from the gondola station, and the **Lingxiao Shrine** is the first temple you come to. It's also the most impressive architecturally, with several swirling levels and a multitude of gods inside (the Jade Emperor is on the top floor while the "Three Pure Ones" reside on the first floor).

Walk down the hill under the covered walkway and you'll come to the most important part of Zhinan, the **Chunyang Shrine** or **Original Hall**. This contains the chief deity, and the biggest draw for pilgrims, **Lu Dong-bin**, one of the "Eight Immortals" and a patron of barbers, though like many gods he's supposed to grant good health and general prosperity to all his believers. There's one exception: legend has it that Lu was rejected by the only female member of the Eight Immortals, Ho Hsien-ku, and driven by jealousy, he's been an incorrigible flirt ever since, making it bad luck for couples to visit the temple.

Before the cable car, the traditional way down (and up) from Zhinan was via the stone stairs in front of the Chungyang Shrine: the first section ends a short way down the mountain at a small Earth God shrine – turn right and follow the stone pathway, lined with Japanese stone lanterns, 900m to Lane 33, a short walk from Zhinan Road and the bus stop on the edge of Muzha. There are supposed to be 1185 or 1192 steps, depending on where you start counting.

The biggest shrine, and the stupa you can see all over the valley, is the much quieter **Daxiong Hall**, a short walk to the right (facing the Original Hall). This is a Buddhist temple, with gold statues of Sakyamuni Buddha, Amitabha and the Medicine Buddha in the main hall. You can walk back to the gondola station via the very steep road behind Daxiong Hall.

Maokong teahouses

The final gondola station (at 299m) is **Maokong** itself, where you'll find a small group of snack stalls. From here, everything is well marked in English, with teahouses divided into three colour-coded zones. Minibuses 10 and 15 (daily 6am–midnight; NT$15) zip between destinations every twenty to thirty minutes if you don't fancy walking, though unless it's unusually hot the lanes make for a pleasant stroll through small tea plantations. Maokong's **teahouses** are predominantly scattered on this south side of the valley. Pots of tea usually start at NT$250 and can last most of the afternoon depending on how many people are in your group – expect to pay a cover charge of around NT$70 per person at the better places. The closest place to the station is *Yuanxuyuan* (緣續緣; *yúanxùyúan*;

daily noon–2am; ☎02/2936-7089) at no. 16 on Lane 38 (Yellow 11), with a cosy, classical Chinese interior – its wooden booths overlook the valley and are set around an indoor fishpond bridged by stepping stones. Take the right-hand fork at the junction – the teahouse is 50m on the right, marked by a "moongate" or round entrance. The cover charge is NT$120 per person till 6pm, then NT$150 thereafter; teas range from NT$$300 to 350, with snacks from NT$80–100 (English menu available).

If you take the left-hand fork back at the junction, you'll eventually pass **Tian En Temple** (天恩宮; *tiānēn gōng*) a good example of an I-kuan Tao shrine (see p.401), and the red-brick **Taipei Tea Promotion Center** (台北市茶推廣中心; *táiběi shìchá tuīguǎng zhōngxīn*; daily 9am–4.30pm; free) at 8, Lane 40 (1.2km from the gondola station), which houses a small exhibition on the history of the area, and the tea-making process (plus free tea). Continue walking for around 400m (turn right on exiting the centre) to reach *Yaoyue Teahouse* at 6 Lane 40 (邀月茶坊; *yāoyùe cháfǎng*; 24hr; ☎02/2939-2025), one of the best teahouses in Maokong with rustic wooden pavilions and a series of outdoor terraces overlooking tea and bamboo plantations. The entrance is marked by a Chinese gate flanked by lanterns on the left side of the road. Service charges vary according to the time of day (NT$70–120), with teas extra (NT$220–NT$360); English menu available.

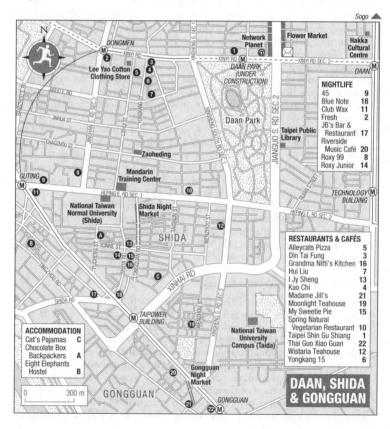

Eating

Taipei is one of the world's greatest showcases for **Chinese cuisine**. Be adventurous; many places have English menus or at least photographs of food, and where one dish is the main feature, pointing will usually suffice. In addition to a vast array of **restaurants**, the city's **teahouses** (*cháguǎn*) are atmospheric places to eat light meals and sip Chinese-style tea. For a cheaper, more local experience try Taipei's vibrant **night markets** (*yèshì*) is which offer a bewildering range of dishes and excellent value for money. Another budget favourite is the **"Taiwan Buffets"** (自助餐; *zìzhù cān*) you'll see in every neighbourhood – these canteen-style places allow you to pile up as much food on your tray as you like, with each dish incurring a small charge (it's rarely more than NT$120 for a huge plateful). In the summer make for a **shaved ice** stall (*bào bīng* or more commonly "*tsua bing*" in Taiwanese) – the sweet, tasty toppings make sumptuous desserts. If it's too hot, almost every department store has an air-conditioned **food court** in the basement, with the biggest under Taipei 101.

Night markets and food streets

Night markets are a quintessential part of the Taipei food experience, offering a vast range of cheap *xiǎochī* or "little eats". You'll rarely pay more than NT$25–60 per order. It's also worth exploring some of Taipei's "food streets": **Yongkang Street** (see Daan map, opposite; Dongmen MRT Station) south of Xinyi Road has a huge range of restaurants, from Chinese dumpling stores to Vietnamese and German cafés, while the alleys between **Linsen** and **Tianjin roads**, north of Changan and south of Nanjing Road (see Datong & Zhongshan map pp.74–75), are packed with authentic **Japanese** restaurants, about fifteen minutes' walk from Zhongshan MRT Station. **"Korean Street"** is Zhongxing Street in Yonghe (see Taipei map pp.60–61), lined with Korean restaurants, food stores and (mostly) Korean clothes shops. Take exit 1 from the Dingxi MRT Station.

Gongguan Night Market 公館夜市 (*gōngguǎn yèshì*) Gongguan MRT Station. Food stalls cram the lanes between Roosevelt and Tingzhou roads south and north of the MRT station. Note the queues at 193 Tingzhou Rd Sec 3 – this nameless stall, known as *Gongguan Red Bean Pastry* (daily 4.30–10.30pm), serves Japanese-style sweet cakes stuffed with red bean paste (*hóngdòu bīng*) and custard (*nǎiyóu bīng*) for NT$25. The other must-try is *Lan's Steamed Sandwiches* (藍家割包; *lánjiā gēbāo*; NT$45) at 3 Alley 8, Lane 316, Roosevelt Rd Sec 3.

Guangzhou Street Night Market 廣州街夜市 (*guǎngzhōujiē yèshì*) Longshan Temple MRT Station. Traditional outdoor market, with the best stalls on the junction with Wuzhou Street: *Memory Aiyu Ice* (懷念愛玉冰; *huáiniàn àiyù bīng*) serves cooling "aiyu" jelly drinks (*àiyù bīng*; NT$35), made from the seeds of a fig-like fruit, while *Ding Ji Tempura* (頂級甜不辣; *dǐngjí tiánbúlà*) on the other side offers Taiwanese-style squid *tiánbúlà* "tempura" (NT$40–55).

Huaxi Street Tourist Night Market 華西街夜市 (*huáxījiē yèshì*) Between Guangzhou St and Guiyang St; Longshan Temple MRT Station. This covered pedestrian-only street is half food and half CDs, bags, foot massages and jewellery. Try the juicy pork *gēbāo* at *Yuanfang Steamed Sandwiches* (源芳割包; *yuánfāng gēbāo*; NT$30; closed Wed). The street is traditionally famous for snake dishes (it's also known as "Snake Alley") and gruesome "snake shows" where the snakes are fed, toyed with and slit open – try no. 49 and 53.

Raohe Street Night Market 饒河街夜市 (*ráohéjiē yèshì*) Songshan Station; Songshan MRT Station (from 2013). Try the delicious charcoal-baked Fuzhou beef pepper pies (*hújiāobǐng*; NT$40) from *Fuzhou Shizu Pepper Buns* (福州世祖胡椒餅; *fúzhōu shìzǔ hújiāobǐng*) near no. 249; *Dongfa Oyster Noodles* (東發號蚵仔麵線; *dōngfā hàoézǐ miànxiàn*) at no. 94 (oyster noodles NT$50); and *Chen Dong Medicinal Spareribs* (陳董藥燉排骨; *chéndǒng yàodùn páigǔ*; mutton and ribs simmered in medicinal herbs for NT$70).

Shida Night Market 師大路夜市 (*shīdàlù yèshì*) Taipower Building MRT Station. An eclectic mix of fried chicken, crepes, burritos, Chinese, Indian and Thai influences; most of the stalls and restaurants line Longquan St parallel to Shida Road from Lane 50 to Heping Rd. *Lantern Hot Stew* (燈籠加熱滷味; *dēnglóng jiārè lǔwèi*) at no. 52 is the place to try *lǔ wèi*: select meat and vegetables first, then wait while they're boiled in a tasty broth (big plates NT$130).

Shilin Night Market 士林夜市 (*shìlín yèshì*) Opposite Jiantan MRT Station. The city's biggest and oldest night market (dating from 1910), and because the main "food square" is located in a large covered building it's generally weatherproof. Try the *dàpíngbāo xiǎopíng* (NT$35) at *Shilin Old Little Roll in Big Roll Shop* (士林老字號大餅包小餅; *shìlín lǎozìhào dàbǐngbāo xiǎobǐng*) and Shilin sausage at *shengji* (昇記士林大香腸; *shēngjì shìlín dàxiāngcháng*; NT$50). The market also occupies the narrow lanes between Wenlin and Dadong rds just to the north, selling mostly clothes but peppered with snack stalls.

Teahouses

Taipei's numerous **teahouses** are ideal places to sample Taiwan's celebrated infusions. **Wenzhou Street**, north of Gongguan MRT Station, has the most variety, but there are plenty of decent alternatives scattered all over the city.

Cha for Tea 喫茶趣 (*chīcháqù*) 152 Fuxing N Rd ☎02/2719-9900; MRT: Nanjing E Road (see map pp.74–75). One of Taiwan's most popular teahouse chains, this branch is an easy introduction to the island's fine teas – a pot here will cost NT$160–350, with an incredible spread of snacks and dishes on the English menu (sets from NT$385). Daily 7.30am–11pm.

Hui Liu 回留 (*huíliú*) 9 Lane 31, Yongkang St ☎02/2392-6707, ✆huiliu.info; MRT: Dongmen (see map, p.88). Tranquil and elegant teahouse located on the corner of Yongkang Park, with wooden tables and beautiful handicrafts. Organic specialities include *Tiěguānyīn*, *Bāozhǒng* and wild Pu-Er tea, and there's an excellent vegetarian menu – avoid meal times if you just want to drink (around NT$380 per pot). Daily 11.30am–10pm.

Lu-Yu Tea Culture Institute 陸羽茶藝中心 (*lùyǔ cháyì zhōngxīn*) 3/F, 62–64 Hengyang Road ☎02/2331-6636, ✉luyutea@ms59.hinet.net; MRT: Ximen (see map, p.67). Best place to see tea ceremonies and tea masters at work, with classes held a couple of times a week, though it's best to call ahead (Chinese only). In the same building is a branch of *Cha for Tea* (3/F) and *Ten Ren Tea* (1/F). Daily 9am–10pm.

Moonlight Teahouse 玥飲軒 (*yuèyǐnxuān*) 80 Wenzhou St ☎02/8369-3963; MRT: Taipower Building (see map, p.88). Atmospheric, Chinese traditional-style teahouse with cosy wooden booths and tables, some arranged around goldfish tanks. Pots of tea from NT$200 (no English menu) and Chinese dishes for NT$160–380. Daily noon–midnight.

Ten Ren Tea 天仁集團 (*tiānrén jítúan*) 174 Zhongxiao E Rd Sec 3; MRT: Zhongxiao Dunhua (see map, p.84). Founded in 1953, this is one of the largest and most respected tea manufacturers in Asia, with stores all over the island. This branch, just off Dunhua Road, also doubles as a simple café with a take-away counter and a few chairs and tables inside to sample the formidable range of teas (from NT$60 a cup). Daily 9am–10.30pm.

Wistaria Teahouse 紫藤廬 (*zǐténglú*) 1 Lane 16, Xinsheng S Rd Sec 3, ☎02/2363-7375; MRT: Taipower Building (see map, p.88). Taipei's most historic Japanese-era teahouse, best known for being the meeting place of artists and political dissidents post-1949, and where much of the movie *Eat Drink Man Woman* was shot. Sip tea (NT$250–350) in the main room with simple wooden tables and chairs, or try the Japanese rooms with tatami mats further back. Daily 10am–11pm.

Restaurants

The capital's **Chinese restaurants** run the gamut of almost every regional cuisine from Beijing duck and spicy Sichuan dishes to Cantonese *dim sum* (*diǎnxīn* in Mandarin) and of course Taiwanese specialities (see p.27). Taipei also has more **Japanese** restaurants than any city outside Japan, while **Western** options, though still a bit hit-and-miss, have mushroomed in recent years – all the major fast food chains from *McDonalds* to *Pizza Hut* are well represented if you get really desperate. Luxury hotels are the best places to splurge, and usually cater to all tastes – **buffets** here are incredibly elaborate affairs, with gargantuan piles of food and correspondingly high prices.

All the restaurants listed below have English menus and are open 11.30am–2.30pm, and around 5–10pm, unless stated otherwise. It's rarely worth making a reservation unless you're eating on a Friday or Saturday night in one of the more upmarket places.

Zhongzheng

See map pp.67.

Astoria 明星咖啡廳 (*míngxīng kāfēitīng*) 2/F, 5 Wuchang St Sec 1 ☏02/2381-5589; MRT: Ximen. Charming Western-style café established by émigré Russians in 1949 with decent coffee, cakes and light meals (NT$250–350 per dish). It was the closest thing Taipei had to a literary salon in the 1950s – some of the famous regulars that once dined here include writers Huang Chun-ming and Pai Hsien-yung. Daily 10am–9.30pm.

Fu Yuan 馥園餐廳 (*fùyúan cāntīng*) 17 Linyi St ☏02/2321-0279; MRT: Zhongxiao Xinsheng. One of Taipei's best restaurants, serving a range of high-quality Chinese, Italian and Japanese cuisine. It's worth the high prices (set lunch from NT$880, dinner NT$1800) for the innovative dishes that include "foie gras with herbal tea sauce", and for the building itself, which is an elegant reproduction of a Ming dynasty teahouse. Daily 11.30am–2.30pm & 5.30–10pm.

Mayor's Residence Arts Salon 官邸藝文沙龍 (*guāndǐ yìwén shālóng*) 46 Xuzhou Rd (no English signs) ☏02/2396-9398; MRT: Shandao Temple. This gallery and café has one of the most atmospheric settings in the city: a beautifully restored Japanese-style wooden house, once the home of Taipei's mayors. Serves up Western-style breakfasts (from NT$190), coffee or smoothies (NT$150), light pasta dishes (NT$240) and lunch specials (NT$330). English menus. Daily 9am–11pm.

Shao Shao Ke 勺勺客 (*sháosháokè*) 15 Lane 41, Renai Rd Sec 2 (at Jinshan Rd) ☏02/2351-7148; MRT: Dongmen. Laid-back Shanxi-style restaurant with succulent lamb kebabs, and soup with unleavened bread (*pào mò*, from NT$160): break the bread into chunks before the soup is served. The graffiti-covered stucco walls are supposed to resemble a cave dwelling, but it's more like a student diner. Daily 11.30am–2.30pm & 5.30–10.20pm.

Xiao Wei 小魏 (*xiǎowèi*) 3/F, 13 Gongyuan Rd ☏02/2371-8427; MRT: Taipei Main Station. Venerable Sichuan restaurant with a reputation for quality despite the very plain decor inside. Favourite orders include fiery *mápó dòufǔ* (spicy mince with eggplant and tofu) and the stir-fried chilli shrimp (NT$150–350 per dish). There are no English signs – just take the lift up to the third floor. Daily 11.30am–10pm.

Wanhua

See map, p.71. MRT: Ximen (unless stated otherwise).

Ay-Chung Flour-Rice Noodle 阿宗麵線 (*ā zōng miànxiàn*) 8 Ermei St ☏02/2388-8808, ⊛www.ay-chung.com. A Taipei institution, this stall has been serving sumptuous rice noodles in delicious soup (NT$55) since 1975 – the added slices of pig intestine may not be to everyone's taste but this is the best bowl of noodles in the city. Take away or eat standing up. Mon–Thurs 11am–10.30pm, Fri–Sun 11am–11pm.

Fong Da Coffee 蜂大珈琲 (*fēngdà kāfēi*) 42 Chengdu Rd ☏02/2371-9577. Cosy coffe shop close to Ximen MRT, established in 1956 and always busy. Antiquated machinery grinds and roasts fresh coffee near the entrance. Daily 8am–10.30pm.

Goose Flat Noodles 鴨肉扁土鵝專賣店 (*yāròu biǎntǔé zhuānmàidiàn*) 98-2 Zhonghua Rd Sec 1 ☏02/2371-3918. Cheap, no-nonsense local diner serving delicious goose noodles in soup (NT$50) and plates of sliced goose meat (NT$70). Daily 9.30am–10.30pm.

Modern Toilet 便所主題餐厅 (*biànsuǒ zhǔtí cāntīng*) 2/F, 7 Lane 50, Xining S Rd ☏02/2311-8822, ⊛www.moderntoilet.com.tw. The food served here is an unexceptional mix of Chinese and "Western" dishes, but being served your spaghetti (NT$200) or hot pot (NT$250) in a fake toilet bowl, and ice cream (NT$100) that looks like poo in a "squat" toilet will either amuse or sicken you; the restaurant's slogan is "Shit or food?" (seriously). You have been warned. Mon–Fri 11.30am–10pm, Sat & Sun 11am–10.30pm.

Tainan Tan-tsu-mien Seafood Restaurant 台南擔仔麵 (*táinán dānzǐmiàn*) 31 Huaxi St ☏02/2308-1123, ⊛www.seafoodtaipei.com.tw; MRT: Longshan Temple. Taipei's seafood pioneer, this elegant but oddly incongruous Baroque dining room is set in the heart of Snake Alley. Select which fresh fish, crab or prawns you want to eat, then grab a table inside – the signature *dānzǐ miàn* (minced pork noodles, NT$50) makes a tasty snack. Daily 11.30am–2.30pm & 5–10.30pm (closes between lunch and dinner).

Two Peck Chicken Pie 2派克脆皮雞排 (*èr pàikè cuìpí jīpái*) Red House courtyard, just off Chengdu Rd, Ximending. This fried chicken chain has become a major fad in recent years, with tiny takeaway counters all over Taiwan. The main event (*jī pái*) is a crispy delight, but you can also munch on a variety of deep-fried snacks: squid (*yóu yú kuài*), chips (*dìguā*) and, everyone's favourite, fried pigs' blood cake (*zhūxiěgāo*) for NT$20–50 per order. Daily 11am–11pm.

Yanji Ice 楊記冰店 (*yángjì bīngdiàn*) 38 Hankou Rd Sec 2. This traditional, no-nonsense *tsuàbīng* shop in Ximending serves shaved ice with delicious, authentic toppings such as thick taro, peanuts and corn: huge bowls cost NT$50. Daily noon–10pm.

Datong
See map pp.74–75.

Si Hai Soybean Milk Store 四海豆漿店 (*sìhǎi dòujiāngdiàn*) 29 Changan W Rd; MRT: Zhongshan. Part of a chain created in 1968 by one of the owners of the original soybean store in Yonghe (see box, p.86), "Four Seas" still knocks out excellent soybean and traditional snacks (NT$16–25), with seating area at the back. Daily 5.30am–10pm.

Xia Er Zui 呷二嘴 (*xiá èr zuǐ*) 34 Ganzhou St ☎02/2557-0780; MRT: Daqiaotou. This place has been cooking up old-fashioned shaved ice bowls (think jelly, beans and cold noodles) and various kinds of dumplings since 1954 (NT$30–35). Daily 9am–5.30pm.

Xiao Xiang Ting 小巷亭 (*xiǎoxiàngtíng*) 8 Lane 250, Nanjing W Rd ☎02/2558-7258; MRT: Zhongshan. This is a fun, cheap place to eat: you'll see the stalls from Nanjing Road (it's the unmarked, narrow alley beyond Lane 162). You can grab some Japanese sushi, dumplings and rolls (NT$50–100) at the stalls and eat them at the outside eating area nearby, or sit inside the small sushi place at no. 8. Daily 11.30am–9.30pm.

Yi Men Wang Noodles 意麵王 (*yìmiànwáng*) 204 Guisui St ☎02/2553-0538; MRT: Daqiaotou. This small local diner has been cooking up cheap beef noodles for over fifty years (NT$40–50) and makes a handy pit-stop in historic Datong. Daily 10.30am–9pm.

Zhongshan
See map pp.74–75.

Celestial Restaurant 天廚菜館 (*tiānchú càiguǎn*) 3/F, 1 Nanjing W Rd ☎02/2563-2380; MRT: Zhongshan. The best-value Beijing duck in Taipei (NT$900, plus NT$200 for soup), though the "duck cake" (duck wrapped in pancake) is cheaper (NT$450) for small groups and there's plenty of other dishes on the menu. Look for the *Royal Inn Taipei* entrance and take the lift up (it's only marked in Chinese). Daily 11am–2pm & 5–9pm.

Kiki Restaurant Kiki餐廳 (*kiki cāntīng*) 28 Fuxing S Rd Sec 1 ☎02/2752-2781; MRT: Zhongxiao Fuxing. Trendy Sichuan restaurant with bright, contemporary decor and an extensive menu providing spiciness ratings (1–4) for each dish; think spicy braised bean curd and stir-fried chicken with chilli (NT$180–300). Daily 11.50am–3pm & 5.15–11pm (10pm Sun).

Kitchen Pucci 葡吉小廚 (*pújí xiǎochú*) 1 Nanjing W Rd ☎02/2563-2787; MRT: Zhongshan. Modern, trendy snack bar serving up Shanghai food, tapas style; think juicy *xiǎolóngbāo* (steamed dumplings; NT$180 for 12) and *dāoxiāo miàn* (thick knife-shaved noodles; NT$80), all made in the small kichen area at the front. Mon–Fri 11am–9.30pm, Sat & Sun 11am–10pm.

Le Petite Cuisine Brasserie by JQ *Evergreen Laurel Hotel* 2/F, 63 Songjiang Rd ☎02/2509-0332; MRT: Songjiang Nanjing. Exquisite French food and five-star service mark this stylish hotel restaurant owned by Justin Quek, the respected Singaporean chef. Lavish set dinner menus from NT$3080, with cheaper set lunches from NT$850. Daily 6.30–10am, noon–2pm & 6–10pm.

Peng Yuan 彭園 (*péngyuán*) 2/F, 380 Linsen N Rd ☎02/2551-9157; MRT: Shuanglian. Named after founder and celebrated chef Peng Chang Gui (who is said to have invented "General Tso's Chicken" or *zuǒzōngtáng jī*; NT$180), this banquet-style restaurant specializes in fiery Hunan cuisine. "Peng's Tofu" (*péngjiā dòufǔ*; NT$180), served with pork and chillies, is a must order, though everything else is excellent (most dishes NT$180–360). Daily 11.30–2pm & 5–9.30pm.

Seoul Korean Barbeque 漢城餐廳 (*hànchéng cāntīng*) 4 Lane 33, Zhongshan N Rd Sec 1 ☎02/2511-2326; MRT: Taipei Main Station. Ageing but atmospheric Korean diner, specializing in succulent barbecued meat (*bulgogi*) and decorated in classical style. Prices are reasonable with dishes of meat from NT$200. Daily 11.30am–2pm & 5–10pm.

Shinyeh 欣葉台菜本店 (*xīnyè táicài běndiàn*) 34 Shuangcheng St ☎02/2596-3255; MRT: Zhongshan Elementary School; 2/F, 112 Zhongxiao E Rd Sec 4 ☎02/2752-9299; MRT: Zhongxiao Fuxing. Celebrated Taiwanese restaurant chain; the Shuangcheng branch is the original while the outlet at Zhongxiao Road is newer and slightly more upmarket. The food is outstanding – expect to pay NT$100–200 for noodles or rice and NT$200–400 for a main dish. Specialities include fried oyster omelette, pumpkin congee and pork knuckle. Daily 11.30am–9.30pm.

Tian Xiang Huwei Hot Pot 天香回味 (*tiānxiāng huíwèi*) 2/F, 16 Nanjing E Rd Sec 1 ☎02/2511-7275; MRT: Zhongshan. Popular *málà* (spicy hotpot) restaurant, Mongolian style. There's no English but the menu has pictures and it's basically a case of choosing which meat (NT$160–300) and vegetables (less than NT$100) to stick in the pot. Special "medicinal" pots (tastier than they sound) are NT$380. Daily 11.30am–2am.

Tien Hsiang Lo 天香樓 (*tiānxiānglóu*) B1, *Landis Hotel*, 41 Minquan E Rd Sec 2 ☎02/2597-1234; MRT: Zhongshan Elementary School. One of Taipei's most elegant restaurants, blending modern and classical design and offering an extensive menu of Hangzhou-style food including fried shrimps with *Lóngjǐng* tea leaves, drunken chicken and West Lake-style steamed fish. A la carte dishes start at around NT$300, with set menus from NT$1280. Daily noon–2.30pm & 6–10pm.

Daan (with Shida and Gongguan)

See map, p.88.

Alleycats Pizza B1, Lishui St ☎02/2321-8949, ⓦwww.alleycatspizza.com; MRT: Dongmen. The best pizza in town, impressing even NYC afionci-ados with their gooey mozzarella, crispy crust and refined toppings (such as goat's cheese, Italian chorizo and artichoke). Large (12 inch) from NT$280–NT$480. Check the website for other branches. Reservations advised. Mon–Thurs 5–11pm, Fri–Sun 5pm–2am.

Din Tai Fung 鼎泰豐 (*dǐngtàifēng*) 194 Xinyi Rd Sec 2 ☎02/2321-8928, ⓦwww.dintaifung .com.tw; MRT: Dongmen. This Taiwan institution has been serving up sumptuous dumplings for thirty years, though its Shanghai-style food is a little over-hyped. It's still worth trying the legendary steamed pork dumplings (*xiǎolóngbāo*) – which at NT$180 for ten are not bad value. The original site is on Xinyi Road (Mon–Fri 10am–9pm, Sat & Sun 9am–9pm) but there's a smarter branch at 218 Zhongxiao E Rd Sec 4 (Mon–Fri 10–2.30pm & 4–10pm, Sat & Sun 10–10pm; ☎02/2721-7890): enter via Lane 216 (MRT: Zhongxiao Dunhua). Be prepared to wait at both.

🏃 **Five Cent Driftwood House 伍角船板** (*wǔjiǎo chuánbǎn*) 8 Lane 32, Neihu Rd Sec 1 ☎02/8501-1472 (see map pp.60–61). Close to Jiannan Road MRT Station and the Miramar Mall, this bizarre-looking restaurant is worth making the trek across the river into Neihu. The whole thing is made out of scraps of wood and metal, with a broadly aboriginal theme and wildly ornate sculptures, while the food is rustic Taiwanese, with plenty of vegetarian options and their famous

mochi for dessert (mains NT$300–$500). Daily 11 am–2 pm & 5–9 pm.

🏃 **Grandma Nitti's Kitchen** 8 Lane 93, Shida Rd. MRT: Taipower Building. Great-value Western diner attracting crowds of expats, students and young professionals. The all-day breakfast is first-rate, and the burritos, sandwiches and pasta dishes on offer make perfect brunch material (NT$180–280). Check out the rooftop terrace. Mon–Fri 9am–11pm, Sat & Sun 10am–11pm. Minimum charge NT$100.

I Jy Sheng 一之軒 (*yīzhīxuān*) 53 Shida Rd ☎02/2362-0425; MRT: Taipower Building. Popular bakery with Asian-style breads and twelve scrumptious flavours of *máshǔ* (glutinous rice cakes); they also do frozen versions (try the maple walnut). Daily 7am–11.30pm.

Kao Chi (Gaoji) 高記 (*gāojì*) 5 Yongkang St; ☎02/2341-9984; MRT: Dongmen; also 150 Fuxing S Rd Sec 1 ☎02/2751-9393; MRT: Zhongxiao Dunhua. A worthy alternative to *Din Tai Fung* just around the corner, with a wide selection of Shanghai-style food (drunken chicken, chicken soup and fried pork buns; NT$200–400) and steamed pork dumplings that are just as tasty (NT$180). Daily 9.30am–10.30pm.

Madame Jill's 翠薪越南餐廳 (*cuìxīn yuènán cāntīng*) 11 Lane 24, Tingzhou Rd Sec 3; MRT: Gongguan. Taipei's best Vietnamese restaurant, tucked away in the heart of Gongguan and knocking out cheap but mouthwatering favourites such as spring rolls, *pho*, curry chicken and spicy coconut beef with French bread (dishes from NT$120).

My Sweetie Pie 3 Lane 93, Shida Rd ☎02/3365-3448; MRT: Taipower Building. Cutesy American bakery from the folks across the road at *Grandma Nitti's*, specializing in all those luscious favour-ites: apple pies, cheesecake, bread pudding and choc chip cookies (cakes NT$80–100). Daily 11am–midnight.

🏃 **Taipei Shin Gu Shiang 臺北新故鄉** (*táiběi xīngùxiāng*) 37 Xinyi Rd Sec 3 ☎02/2754-0023; MRT: Daan Park. The most atmospheric restaurant in downtown Taipei, located inside a rustic wooden hall just off Xinyi Road. There's no menu – the staff bring out a selection of dishes and as much delicious pork oil rice as you can eat for NT$200 per person. The decor recalls Taiwan of the 1950s and 60s and old pop songs play in the background. Daily 6pm–midnight.

Thai Guo Xiao Guan 泰國小館 (*tàiguó xiāoguǎn*) 219 Tingzhou St Sec 3 ☎02/2367-0739; MRT: Gongguan. There are many Thai restaurants in Taipei, but few are as authentic or cheap as this Thai-owned student hangout in Gongguan. Most dishes are NT$100–200, but with no English menu you'll have to point at the photos. Daily 11am–10pm.

Yongkang 15 永康15 (*yǒngkāng shíwǔ*) 15 Yongkang St; MRT: Dongmen. This shaved-ice (*tsua bing*) stall opened in June 2010 in the spot once occupied by legendary *Ice Monster* (which tragically closed earlier that year). It's not quite as good as the old place and it's pricey, but the fruit is high-quality and the mountainous plate of mango shaved ice (NT$160) is still superb.

East Taipei
See map, p.84.

Beijing Do It True 北京都一處 (*běijīng dūyīcù*) 506 Renai Rd ☎02/2720-6417; MRT: SYS Memorial Hall. Cheerful Beijing-style restaurant, best known for its Chinese sesame buns served with sliced pork, fried "jumbo" dumplings and Beijing Style Hotpot (NT$200–400). It's named after an old restaurant in Beijing, feted by Emperor Qianlong. Daily 11am–2pm & 5–9pm.

Chuan Wang Gourmet Beef Stew Noodle 饌王精品牛肉麵 (*zhuàn wáng jīngpǐn niúròu miàn*) 2/F, 94 Zhongxiao E Rd Sec 4; ☎02/2711-0388 MRT: Zhongxiao Fuxing. Voted Taipei's best beef noodle restaurant, the eponymous dish is simply delicious (NT$150-200). Daily 11am–9pm.

Citystar 24hr Restaurant PART 1 京星港式飲茶 (*jīngxīng gǎngshì yǐnchá*) 2/F, 216 Dunhua S Rd Sec 1 ☎02/2741-2625; MRT: Zhongxiao Dunhua. Respectable *dim sum* restaurant that stays fairly busy all night, with a convenient location on the corner of Dunhua and Zhongxiao roads. Good-value Cantonese food at NT$100–300 per dish. Open 24hr.

Dozo 102 Guangfu S Rd ☎02/2778-1135, ⊛www.dozoizakaya.com; MRT: SYS Memorial Hall. Hip Japanese *izakaya* bar-restaurant with live Japanese drummers every night, a large, open-plan area, sunken tables and dark, minimalist decor. Offers a variety of Japanese sushi, rice, noodles and meat dishes from NT$150–300, and giant two or four-litre towers of Orion Okinawa draft beer. Mon–Thurs & Sun 6pm–2am, Fri & Sat 6pm–3am.

Du Hsiao Yueh 度小月擔仔麵 (*dùxiǎoyuè dànzǐmiàn*) 12 Alley 8, Lane 216, Zhongxiao E Rd Sec 4 ☎02/2773-1244; MRT: Zhongxiao Dunhua. This restaurant is a branch of the revered Tainan noodle maker established over one hundred years ago (see p.249). Deservedly popular, the *dànzǐ* noodles (NT$60 for a bowl) are a must-order. The decor is sleek, contemporary Chinese; the chef cooks over charcoal-fired pots near the entrance. There's another branch at 9-1 Yongkang St (☎02/3393-1325; see map, p.88). Mon–Sat 11.30am–11pm, Sun 11.30am–9.30pm.

Eastern Ice Store 東區粉圓 (*dōngqū fěnyuán*) 38 Lane 216, Zhongxiao E Rd Sec 4; MRT: Zhongxiao Dunhua. The best place in East Taipei for shaved ice (*tsuàbīng*), with a small seating area and a choice of four toppings for NT$50. Daily 11am–11pm.

Vegetarian restaurants

Vegetarians are well catered for in Taipei, with numerous local diners serving Buddhist-inspired or cheap, buffet-style vegetarian food. For ambience it's hard to beat *King Join* (京兆尹; *jīngzhàoyǐn*; daily 10am–10pm; ☎02/2701-3225; MRT: Zhongxiao Dunhua) at 18 Siwei Rd, just off Renai Circle in East Taipei, which has an extensive English menu of northern Chinese-style vegetarian dumplings, noodles, main dishes and desserts from NT$100. The lacquered redwood furniture and gold Chinese lions and lanterns are slightly kitsch, but certainly add character.

The vegan chain known as *Loving Hut* (愛家國際餐飲; *àijiā guójì cānyǐn*; ⊛www.lovinghut.com) has several reliable restaurants in Taipei, including those at 44 Huaining St (☎02/2311-9399) in Zhongzheng, 303 Changchun St (☎02/2518-9518) in Zhongshan, and 6, Alley 1, Lane 217, Zhongxiao E Rd Sec 3 in Daan (☎02/2771-1365). Expect a wide-range of dishes from wild rice stew and soy steaks to pumpkin noodles and blueberry bagels.

Spring Natural Vegetarian Restaurant (春天素食餐廳; *chūntiān sùshí cāntīng*) at 3/F, 177 Heping E Rd Sec 1 (daily 11.45am–9pm; ☎02/2393-0288; MRT: Guting) in the Shida area (see map, p.88) is a brighter, more contemporary buffet restaurant with a massive selection (11.45am–2pm: NT$500; 2.30–4.30pm: NT$350; 5.45–9pm: NT$600). Note that *Hui Liu* (p.90) also has excellent organic vegetarian food.

Flavors 瑞典餐館 (*Flavors ruìdiǎn cānguǎn*) 13, Alley 26, Lane 300, Renai Rd Sec 4 ☎02/2709-6525, ⊛www.flavors.com.tw; MRT: Anhe Road (from end 2012). One of the most popular upscale Western restaurants in Taipei, for good reason. For starters, it's Swedish, which is extremely unusual in Asia, and the food is exquisite. The choice is huge, but meatballs with lingonberry jam are excellent, the bread is home-made and the apple pie a crumbly masterpiece, perhaps the best in Asia (tasting menus NT$1100/700). Lunch by reservation only. Tues–Fri 6–10.30pm, Sat & Sun noon–2.30pm & 6–10.30pm.

G'day Café 晴西餐廳 (*qíngxī cāntīng*) 180 Xingan St ☎02/2717-5927; MRT: Nanjing E Road. Small and homely diner with a decent selection of Western comfort food on the edge of Songshan district, popular with expats and locals alike. Mexican favourites like burritos, burgers, sandwiches, some basic Asian dishes and as much coffee as you can drink, all reasonably priced at NT$150–200. Mon–Sat 10am–10pm, Sun 10am–5pm.

Gi Yuan 驥園 (*jì yúan*) 324 Dunhua S Rd Sec 1; ☎02/2708-3110 MRT: Anhe Rd (from end 2012). Sichuan restaurant with signature stone-pot chicken soup, a delicious broth made from three chickens simmered for over twelve hours and added to various meats and vegetables: one pot is good for four people (from NT$2160). Daily 11.30am–2pm & 5.30–9pm.

Jogoya 上閣屋 (*shànggéwū*) 3/F, 22 Songshou Rd (Neo Mall) ☎02/2720-5555; MRT: World Trade Center (from 2012). Modern restaurant with huge buffet of Japanese food including sushi, tempura and teppanyaki, with Chinese favourites such as dumplings thrown in. The free wine, draft Tsingtao beer and Movenpick ice cream are welcome extras. The price ranges NT$598–758 (plus 10 percent) depending on the time of day. Daily 11.30am–12.30pm.

La Giara 義大利餐廳 (*yìdàlì cāntīng*) 2/F, 352 Fuxing S Rd Sec 1 ☎02/2705-0345, ⊛www.lagiara.com.tw; MRT: Daan. One of Taipei's most elegant Italian restaurants, with chic, modern decor and an extensive menu: the strong Sicilian element reflects the origin of the two owners. Set lunches are around NT$550, with home-made pastas and pizzas from NT$450 and mains NT$920. Daily noon–2.30pm & 6–11.30pm.

Mei Tsun 梅村 (*méicūn*) 6 Lane 216, Alley 32, Zhongxiao E Rd Sec 4; MRT: Zhongxiao Dunhua. If you fancy gorging on Japanese food, this is the place to do it: for NT$428 on weekdays and NT$468 on weekends you can order as much sushi and tempura as you can handle. No English menus – point to the photos instead. Located just off Guangfu Road.

NY Bagels Café 147 Renai Rd Sec 4 ☎02/2752-1669; MRT: Zhongxiao Dunhua. The best place to satisfy cravings for a traditional NYC breakfast. Bagels start at NT$58, with cream cheeses (including walnut, fruit and bacon flavours) from NT$28, but there are also lunch specials like burgers and lasagna (from NT$200) and decent breakfast sets (NT$79). Even better, it's open 24hr and has spawned several branches all over the city.

People Restaurant 人間 (*rénjiān*) B1, 191 Anhe Rd Sec 2 ☎02/2735-2288; MRT: Technology Building/Anhe Road from 2012. One of the capital's hippest restaurants, the shiny, sleek interior here has a lounge-bar atmosphere while the menu comprises small plates of Chinese fusion cuisine (from NT$220) and plenty of cocktails. A light-sensor opens the huge bronze doors, activated by putting your hand into the stone lantern outside. Daily 11.45am–2am.

Taipei 101 Shopping Mall 45 Shifu Rd; MRT: World Trade Center (from 2012). The fourth floor of Taipei's smartest mall is a cavernous atrium ringed by hip, contemporary restaurants: *iR China* offers a fusion of Yunnan and Sichuan cuisine, while *Wasabi* (☎02/8101-8166) is a stylish, modern Japanese diner (lunch buffet NT$648, NT$800 for dinner). The food court in the basement is one of the city's best, and very cheap. Restaurants usually open 11.30am–3pm & 5–10pm.

Yungho Soybean Milk & Porridge King 永和豆漿大王 (*yǒnghé dòujiāng dàwáng*) 102 Fuxing S Rd Sec 2 ☎02/2703-5051; MRT: Daan. A 10min walk south of Daan MRT Station, this no-nonsense local diner has been in business for over forty years, selling a variety of buns, spring rolls, egg pancakes, noodles and soybean milk from NT$25. Open 24hr.

Ziga Zaga 2/F Grand Hyatt Taipei, 2 Songshou Rd ☎02/2720-1200; MRT: World Trade Center (from 2012). Taipei's swankiest Italian restaurant serving pasta and pizza (NT$500–600), and main dishes from NT$800. Turns into a club and bar after 9.30pm with live music, DJs and cocktails. Tues 6pm–1am, Wed & Thurs 11.30am–2pm & 6pm–1am, Fri & Sat 11.30am–2pm & 6pm–2am, Sun 11.30am–2pm.

Drinking and nightlife

In recent years **nightlife** in Taipei has expanded from a small cluster of mainly expat pubs and local beerhouses to a variety of lounge bars and a decent selection of live music venues. Taipei's nightclubs have also taken off in a big way – though the situation is constantly changing, the scene here is as good as any in Asia, regularly attracting top DJs from Japan, North America and Europe.

Bars

Taipei's bars and clubs are scattered throughout the city in much the same way as everything else, but there are enough clusters to allow some stumbling around on foot. For years the area around **Shuangcheng Street** north of Minquan Road (in Zhongshan district), was considered the centre of Taipei nightlife, particularly for foreigners. US soldiers on R&R frequented the area until the late 1970s and it's still known as the **"Combat Zone"** today. Though it's packed with over twenty pubs it's decidedly tired compared to more hip parts of the city and tends to be frequented by an older crowd. The university districts of **Shida** and **Gongguan** in the southwestern half of the city are funkier hunting grounds for cheaper pubs and clubs, while upscale **East Taipei** is where you'll find many of Taipei's top lounge bars and clubs.

Shida

See map pp.88.

45 酒吧 (*45jiǔbā*) 45 Heping E Rd Sec 1 ☎02/2321-2140; MRT: Guting. Student-favourite pub, with two floors accessed via a narrow stairway from street level, close to Guting MRT Station, popular with expats and locals. Snack food and beers from NT$130. Daily 4pm–4am.

JB's Bar & Restaurant 傑比士英國餐館 (*jiébǐshì yīngguó cānguǎn*) 148 Shida Rd ☎02/2364-8222; MRT: Taipower Building. English-style pub serving excellent food including fish and chips (NT$499) and a huge all-day breakfast. The bar upstairs serves fine English draught beers (Abbot Ale and Ruddles). Mon–Thurs & Sun 11.30am–1.30am, Fri–Sat 11.30am–3am.

Roxy Junior 1 Lane 80, Shida Rd ☎02/2366-1799; MRT: Taipower Building. Another popular pub with students and expats in the heart of busy Shida, with a selection of reasonably priced spirits and beers (NT$160) plus comfy sofas; there are pool tables in the basement. Open 24hr.

Zhongshan

See map pp.74–75.

Brass Monkey 銅猴子 (*tónghóuzi*) 166 Fuxing N Rd ☎02/2547-5050, ⓦwww.brassmonkeytaipei .com; MRT: Nanjing R Rd. Popular pub close to Nanjing E Road MRT Station with quality beers on tap and large servings of Western food on the menu. Big-screen TV means it's a popular expat venue for major sports events (and Thurs is Ladies'

Night). Mon–Thurs 4pm–1am, Thurs 5pm–4am, Fri & Sat 5pm–2am.

Front Page Sports Bar 長虹酒吧 (*chánghóng jiǔbā*) Imperial Hotel, 600 Linsen N Rd ☎02/2596-5111; MRT: Zhongshan Elementary School. Popular hotel bar with local businessmen and drinkers heading into the Zone: it feels a bit like a comfortable gentleman's club during the day, reverting to sports bar at night with giant TV screen. Taiwan Beer on tap for NT$110. Daily 11am–midnight.

Jurassic Restaurant 印地安侏儸紀餐廳 (*yìndìān zhūluójì cāntīng*) 196 Bade Rd Sec 2 ☎02/2741-0550; MRT: Zhongxiao Fuxing. Classic beerhouse with a cave-like interior, complete with mock dinosaur skeletons. Live music, extensive menu of Chinese comfort food (*sānbēi* from NT$450) and seven-litre San Miguel beer kegs for NT$1000. Mon–Thurs & Sun 5.30pm–2am, Fri & Sat 5.30pm–3am.

My Place 3-1 Lane 32, Shuangcheng St ☎02/2592-8122; MRT: Zhongshan Elementary School. Closest thing the Zone has to an institution, this British-style pub is one of the oldest in the area, opening in 1975. Daily 4pm–3am, till 4am at the weekends.

East Taipei

See map, p.84.

Barcode 5/F, 22 Songshou Rd ☎02/2725-3520; MRT: Taipei City Hall. Definitely a hangout for beautiful people, with funky interiors and sublime cocktails (from NT$400) – the best reason to visit. Daily 8pm–3am.

Gay nightlife

Taipei has come a long way since the dark old days depicted in Pai Hsien-yung's *Crystal Boys* (see p.416) and the city has a thriving gay community. *Funky* (℡02/2394-2162; daily 8pm–2am, Sat & Sun till 4am; NT$300–450; MRT: Shandao Temple) at B1, 10 Hangzhou S Rd Sec 1 is the oldest gay bar in town with a mix of music and young, fashionable clientele; *Fresh* at 2/F, 7 Jinshan S Rd Sec 2 (℡02/2358-7701, ⓦwww.fresh-taipei.com; Mon–Thurs & Sun 9pm–3am, Fri–Sat 9pm–5am; cover NT$300–350; MRT: Dongmen) has two lounge bars, a cosy garden and one club level which gets busy at the weekends: look for the red door leading to a narrow staircase. *Café Dalida* (daily 5pm–3am; ℡02/2370-7833; usually free; MRT: Ximen) in Ximending's Red House Plaza, 51 Lane 10, Chengdu Road, is another hot spot, while *Club Jump* at 8 Keelung Rd Sec 1 (Fri 11pm–5am, Sat 11pm–6am; ℡02/2756-0055, ⓦclub-jump.com; MRT: Songshan) is one of the newer, lavish dance clubs. *Luxy* (see p.98) is also a major player in the LGBT scene.

The Bed 水煙館 (*shuǐyānguǎn*) 29 Alley 35, Lane 181, Zhongxiao E Rd Sec 4 ℡02/2711-3733; MRT: Zhongxiao Dunhua. Lounge bar with dark corners, comfy sofas, divans and a couple of beds to relax on amidst the vaguely Indochinese decor: if the Vietnamese snacks and cocktails aren't enough, for around NT$500 you can puff on a *shisha* (water pipe filled with fruit-flavoured tobacco). Daily 6pm–2am.

Brown Sugar 黑糖餐廳 (*hēitáng cāntīng*) 101 Songren Rd ℡02/8780-1110, ⓦwww.brownsugarlive.com; MRT: Taipei City Hall. This jazz club and restaurant has a regular programme of international acts from 9.30pm, reverting to a trendy nightclub after 1am. Packed at weekends, with a big cocktails and drinks list, it's tucked away behind the Capital Center: walk down the alley at the end of Songshou Road. Daily noon–3am (4am weekends).

Carnegie's 卡奈基餐廳 (*kǎnàijī cāntīng*) 100 Anhe Rd Sec 2 ℡02/2325-4433, ⓦwww.carnegies.net; MRT: Anhe Road (from 2012). Big expat favourite (the original is in Hong Kong) and the place to come for dancing on tables and general drunken mayhem. It's also one of the best places for English pub food (NT$360–460), including all-day breakfasts, plus alfresco dining in the summer. Daily 11.30am–2am (5am weekends).

Eslite Beer Cellar 金色三麥 (*jīnsè sānmài*) B1, 11 Songgao Rd ℡02/8789-5911, ⓦwww.lebledor.com.tw; MRT: Taipei City Hall. Enjoy this outpost of Taipei's only microbrew pub (there's another one in the Miramar Mall) – try the stout and pale ales, though the beer fruit slushies are thirst quenching in summer. Mon–Thurs & Sun 11am–midnight, Fri & Sat 11am–1am.

Marco Polo Lounge 38/F *Far Eastern Plaza Hotel*, 201 Dunhua S Rd ℡02/2376-3156; MRT: Anhe Road (from 2012). It's hard to beat the stunning views from this hotel cocktail bar, right across the city to Taipei 101. The drinks are pretty good, too. Daily 11.30am–1am.

Tavern Premier 運動主題餐廳 (*yùndòngzhǔtí cāntīng*) 415 Xinyi Rd Sec 4 ℡02/8780-0892; MRT: World Trade Center (from 2012). An incredible amount of TV screens of all sizes packed into this amiable pub makes it a prime spot for viewing international sports events, but the pub grub (from NT$360) and beers (such as Abbot Ale for NT$240 and Hoegaarden for NT$260) are also pretty good. Daily noon–4am.

Live music

Taipei's **live music** scene continues to evolve, with a growing number of venues hosting everything from local rock bands and Mando-pop to international jazz and blues acts. For larger venues and concerts see p.99.

Blue Note 藍調台北 (*lántiáo táiběi*) 4/F, 171 Roosevelt Rd Sec 3 ℡02/2362-2333; MRT: Taipower Building. This pioneer jazz club, established in 1974, is a little hard to find but well worth the effort for the cosy venue and quality live jazz (entry usually around NT$350 and includes one drink). The entrance is on Shida Rd: look for the first doorway on the left after Roosevelt Rd and take the lift up. Daily 7pm–2am.

EZ5 Live House EZ5音樂餐廳 (EZ5 *yīnyuè cāntīng*) 211 Anhe Rd Sec 2 ℡02/2738-3995; MRT: Technology Building. Hosts up-and-coming

Mando-pop singers backed by a live band every night, anything from syrupy love ballads and rock to funky R&B. Daily 7pm–1.30am.

Riverside Music Café 河岸留言 (*héàn liúyán*) 2 Lane 244, Roosevelt Rd Sec 3 ⊤02/2368-7310; MRT: Gongguan. Live rock and jazz venue just off Roosevelt Rd. Shows start from 9.30pm most days (cover charge NT$300 or NT$350 at weekends with one drink), though it tends to be quiet at other times. Wed–Sat 7pm–2am.

Sappho de Base 莎芙 (*shāfú*) B1, 1 Lane 102, Anhe Rd Sec 1 ⊤02/2700-5411, ⓦwww .sappho102.biz; MRT: Anhe Rd from 2012. Hip live jazz and blues venue, with dancefloor, bar snacks and cocktails. Cover NT$300–350. Tues–Thurs 9pm–3am, Fri & Sat 9pm–4.30am.

Velvet Underground 地下絲絨搖滾餐廳 (*dìxià sīróng yáogǔn cāntīng*) aka *VU Live*

House, Eslite, B1, 77 Wuchang St Sec 2, ⊤02/2314-1868; MRT: Ximen. No-frills venue in Ximending with an eclectic roster than can include hip-hop, reggae and electronica in addition to the usual indie bands. Cover from NT$350. Daily 7pm–3am.

The Wall 這牆音樂藝文展演空間 (*zhèqiáng yīnyuè yìwénzhǎnyǎn kōngjiān*) B1, 200 Roosevelt Rd Sec 4 ⓦwww.the-wall.com.tw; MRT: Gongguan. Taipei's best live rock venue with acts playing most nights from 8pm (opens as a record store during the day), though it can close early once the music stops – check the website for times. Located just off the busy Roosevelt and Keelung Rd junction, next to a cinema entrance. Admission NT$300–500. Tues–Sun: shop 3–11pm, bar 8pm–2am; bands 8–11pm.

Clubs

Taipei has a dynamic club scene, with its biggest **nightclubs** regularly hosting global DJ icons. Hardcore clubbers will appreciate the multi-room venues, but there are also several disco-type places more popular with students where a round of drinks won't break the bank.

Club Primo 2/F, 297 Zhongxiao E Rd Sec 5 ⊤0958/783838, ⓦwww.clubprimo.com; MRT: Yongchun. Very glamorous LA-like club, with plenty of luxurious couches, sunken tables, hip-hop and R&B – get there early to ensure you get in without a VIP card (possible as long as there's room). Wed–Sat 10.30pm–4.30am.

Club Wax B1, 67 Roosevelt Rd Sec 2 ⊤02/3365-3041; MRT: Guting. Fun club popular with students and expats, packed most weekends and all you can drink for NT$600 (men) and NT$350 (women) – just hold on to your glass and they'll keep filling it up. Wed–Sat 9pm–2am or 6am weekends.

Luxy 5/F, 201 Zhongxiao E Rd Sec 4 ⓦwww .luxy-taipei.com; MRT: Zhongxiao Dunhua. Still the trendsetter in the heart of Daan, with two separate dancefloors and a big cocktail list (and NT$20 lockers). Resident DJs offer plenty of hip-hop and tough competition to the big names that fly in

every weekend – check the website for details (NT$500–1200 cover). Wed 9pm–4am, Thurs 9pm–3am, Fri & Sat 9pm–5am.

Roxy 99 B1, 218 Jinshan Rd Sec 2, ⊤02/2351-5970 ⓦwww.roxy.com.tw; MRT: Guting. The place to come for unpretentious drinking and dancing, with a good mix of expats and locals. The drinks are cheap, and the music ranges from hip-hop and house to rock and pop. Wed 8pm–3am, Fri & Sat 10pm–7am.

Spark B1, Taipei 101 Shopping Mall, 45 Shifu Rd ⊤02/8101-8662, ⓦwww.spark101.com.tw; MRT: World Trade Center (from 2012). *Spark* has become one of the city's top clubs since opening in 2009, its powerful sound system an erstwhile successor to the now defunct *Ministry of Sound*. LCD screens, glowing floors and multicoloured ceilings enhance the experience. Cover usually NT$800. Sun–Tues, Thurs 10pm–3am, Wed (Ladies' Night) 10pm–4am, Fri & Sat 10pm–5am.

Entertainment and the arts

Taipei has an incredibly vibrant **cultural life**, with a daily feast of exhibitions, shows, gigs, plays and traditional performances. Performance groups such as **U-Theatre**, **Cloud Gate** and **Han-Tang Yuefu** (see p.411), all based in the city, are world class. The best way to buy **tickets** is to approach the venue directly or visit one of the ERA ticket offices located in Eslite or Kingstone bookstores. You can also download an

English order form from ERA's Chinese website (W www.ticket.com.tw; scroll down to the end of the page).

Chinese opera

Taipei is one of the world's best places to see various styles of **Chinese opera** – it's not unusual to have ten or more productions running each month in various locations. An easily digested taster is provided by **TaipeiEYE** (臺北戲棚; *táiběi xìpéng*; Fri–Sat 8–10pm; NT$880; T 02/2568-2677, W www.taipeieye.com), held on the third floor of the Taiwan Cement Hall, at 113 Zhongshan N Rd Sec 2. Featuring various acts from aboriginal song and dance to Chinese puppetry and opera, it's firmly targeted at tourists but the standard is high – many of Taiwan's premier troupes play here.

The students at the **National Taiwan College of Performing Arts** (國立臺灣戲曲學校; *guólì táiwān xìqǔ xuéxiào*; NT$400; T 02/2796-2666, W edu.tcpa .edu.tw) at 177 Neihu Rd Sec 2 also perform from a varied repertoire Monday and Thursdays at 10am, comprising thirty minutes of acrobatics, a tour of the Jin-ju Opera Museum upstairs, a video introducing Chinese opera and a 35-minute performance taken from a Beijing opera (with English subtitles).

Puppetry

The **Puppetry Art Center** (2/F, 99 Civic Blvd Sec 5; Tues–Sat 10am–5pm; NT$50; W www.pact.org.tw), next to Core Pacific City, is a lavish tribute to Chinese puppetry in Taiwan, though sadly there are no labels in English (this may be rectified in the future). Traditional **puppet shows** are held most weekends at the **Lin Liu-Hsin Puppet Theatre Museum** in Datong (p.76) and occasionally at TaipeiEYE (p.99).

You can also check out the **See-Join Hand Puppet Theater Restaurant** at 2/F, 46 Yitong St, just south of Nanjing E Road Section 2 (T 02/2506-7447, W www .see-join.com.tw), where performances are combined with traditional Taiwanese snacks and beer, served as you watch. Shows (NT$400, not including food) run every day 7.30–8.30pm (arrive by 6pm), but you must reserve in advance.

Concert venues

Western classical and Chinese music, especially *nanguan* (see p.411) is usually performed somewhere in Taipei year round and the standards are generally high – prices vary from show to show (see opposite for information about tickets). The **National Concert Hall** (國家音樂廳; *guó jiā yīnyuètīng*; T 02/2343-1587, W www.ntch.edu.tw) in Chiang Kai-shek Memorial Plaza on Zhongshan Road is where Taiwan's premier orchestra, the National Chinese Orchestra, regularly performs Chinese classical music. At other times expect to hear a wide range of jazz or Western classical music. The **Novel Hall for Performing Arts** (新舞臺; *xīnwǔtái*) in Xinyi at 3 Songshou Rd (T 02/2722-4302) is one of the city's newest and plushest venues, with a varied programme of Chinese opera, theatre and classical and choral music. It can be hard to find the entrance – look for the white Chinatrust building and walk round the back. In contrast, **Zhongshan Hall** (中山堂; *zhōngshān táng*; T 02/2381-3137, W www.csh.taipei.gov.tw), near Ximending at 98 Yanping S Rd, is Taipei's oldest concert hall, completed in 1936 (the Japanese in Taiwan surrendered here in 1945), and a venue for traditional Chinese or classical music. The futuristic **Taipei Arena** (台北小巨蛋; *táiběi xiǎojùdàn*; T 02/2578-3536) at 10 Nanjing E Rd Sec 4 hosts major pop concerts by the likes of Jay Chou, Disney on Ice and Cirque du Soleil productions, as well as sporting events. Also hosting larger shows is **Legacy Taipei**, inside Huashan 1914 Creative Park (see p.100).

Cinemas

Taipei is loaded with cinemas, most of them packed at the weekends. All the major Hollywood movies arrive in Taiwan soon after their US release dates and are rarely dubbed into Chinese: **Ximending** is where you'll find the older and larger screens – check times in local English newspapers. The one with the biggest screen is the **Ambassador** (國賓電影院; *guóbīn diànyǐngyuàn*; ℡02/2361-1223; NT$280) at 88 Chengdu Rd and Kunming Street.

Vieshow Cinemas, 20 Songshou Rd (威秀影城; *wēixiù yǐngchéng*; ℡02/8780-5566; NT$250–300), is a huge multiplex cinema in Xinyi and one of the most popular places in town. **Ta Chien Cinema** (大千電影院; *dàqiān diànyǐngyuàn*; ℡02/8770-6565; NT$400, NT$360 for restaurant or hotel guests) in basement 2 of the *Westin Hotel*, 133 Nanjing E Rd Sec 3, is Taipei's luxury cinema, with comfy two-seater sofas from which you can order snacks and drinks from the hotel menu. For art films try the **SPOT-Taipei Film House** (光點台北電影主題館; *guāngdiàn táiběi diànyǐng zhǔtíguǎn*; ℡02/2511-7786, Ⓦwww.spot.org.tw; NT$220) at 18 Zhongshan N Rd Sec 2, which screens several movies daily (local and international) and is located within the tastefully restored former US consulate built in 1926. It also houses a bookshop, café and bar with terrace (daily 11am–midnight).

Art galleries

Contemporary and classical **art** is booming in Taipei, with numerous galleries, museums and shops displaying everything from traditional Chinese paintings to installation art and glass sculpture. The **Apollo Building** at 218-220 Zhongxiao E Rd Sec 4 has five tower blocks containing several galleries (the Apollo, Imavision and East galleries are the most established). Most shops are open from 10.30am to 6.30pm. To catch up on some of Taiwan's art and music festivals, as well as its alternative art trends, visit the **Huashan 1914 Creative Park** (華山1914創意文化園區; *huáshān 1914 chuàngyì wénhuà yúanqū*; daily 10am–11pm, some galleries close at 6pm; ℡02/2358-1914, Ⓦwww.huashan1914.com) at 1 Bade Road. It occupies the grounds of the old Taipei Winery, a ten-minute walk from Zhongxiao Xinsheng MRT Station. The more intimate **Taipei Artists Village** (台北國際藝術村; *táiběi guójì yìshùcūn*; ℡02/3393-7377; daily 10am–6pm) at 7 Beiping Rd is close to the main station: the first-floor galleries are open to the public while artists in residence occupy the higher floors.

Shopping

Taipei is packed with huge **shopping malls**, most of them upmarket affairs located in East Taipei, while **traditional shops** tend to be in the older, western parts of the city. In addition to night markets (see p.89) and the shops listed below, **Ximending** (see p.73) is the place to check out Taipei street fashion. Elsewhere, the weekend **Jade Market** is a definite highlight, while **Guanghua Market** is computer-geek heaven.

Department stores and shopping malls

Eslite 誠品書店 (*chéngpǐn shūdiàn*) 245 Dunhua S Rd Sec 1; MRT: Zhongxiao Dunhua. Stylish department store packed with boutiques and housing Eslite Bookstore (2/F; 24hr), which has a decent English-language selection.

The Mall 遠企購物中心 (*yuǎnqì gòuwùzhōngxīn*) 203 Dunhua S Rd Sec 2; MRT: Anhe Road (from 2012). This upmarket shopping centre next to the *Far Eastern Hotel* contains the Rich Jade jewellery collection on 1/F; Shiatzy Chen on 4/F, and Liuligongfang, Bamboola bamboo gift boxes and cups, Tittot glassware and the Franz Collection's award-winning porcelain designs on the fifth floor. There's a City supermarket in the basement. Mon–Thurs & Sun 11am–9.30pm, Fri & Sat 11am–10pm.

Miramar Entertainment Park 美麗華百樂園 (*měilìhuá bǎilèyuán*) 20 Jingye 3rd Rd; MRT: Jiannan Road. This shopping centre in Dazhi, just north of the Keelung River, is crammed with all sorts of shops, as well as Asia's largest IMAX cinema screen and its second largest Ferris wheel (with two full-glass cars) at NT$200 per ride at weekends, and NT$150 weekdays. Daily 11am–midnight.

Sogo 太平洋百貨 (*tàipíng yáng bǎihuò*) 45 Zhongxiao E Rd Sec 4; MRT: Zhongxiao Fuxing. Posh Japanese department store selling just about anything, from designer clothes to steel woks. Daily 11am–9.30pm.

Taipei 101 Shopping Mall 台北101購物中心 (*táiběi 101 gòuwùzhōngxīn*) 45 Shifu Rd; MRT: World Trade Center (from 2012). Taipei's smartest mall, jammed with boutiques and designer stores, restaurants (p.95) and bookshops (p.102). The basement contains Taipei's largest food court and *Jason's Market Place* (daily 10am–10pm) the best supermarket for imported food. Mon–Fri 11am–10pm, Sat & Sun 10am–11pm.

Clothes

EB Shoes 小格格鞋坊 (*xiǎogégé xiéfāng*) 96 Xining S Rd; MRT: Ximen. This small shop is the home of beautifully hand-crafted Chinese-style shoes and slippers, not far from Ximen MRT (NT$400–700). Daily 10am–10pm.

Lee Yao Cotton Clothing Store 李堯棉衣店 (*lǐyáo miányī diàn*) 2 Lishui St; MRT: Dongmen. Designer boutique popular with expats, specializing in traditional Chinese clothes with vivid floral designs. Prices range from NT$1000 to NT$10,000 (no English signs). Daily 11.30am–9.30pm.

Shiatzy Chen 夏姿服飾 (*xiàzī fúshì*) 49 Zhongxiao N Rd Sec 2; MRT: Zhongshan. Flagship store of Taiwan's top designer, famous for making chinoiserie and the *cheongsam* hip. Daily 10am–7pm.

Small Garden Embroidered Shoes 小花園 (*xiǎohuāyuán*) 70 Ermei St; MRT: Ximen. Venerable old store with roots in 1930s Shanghai, specializing in handmade embroidered shoes in classical Ming and Qing dynasty style. Daily noon–6pm.

Wufenpu Garment Wholesale Area 五分埔商圈 (*wǔfēnpǔ shāngquān*) Between Zhongxiao E Rd Sec 5 and Songren E Rd/Zhongpo N Rd; MRT: Houshanpi and Songshan. Discount clothes market, choked with everything from brand-name designers (or at least good copies of them) to absolute kitsch, as well as a variety of accessories. Daily 9am–9pm.

WUM 1 Lane 16, Zhongshan N Rd Sec 2; MRT: Zhongshan. Two shiny metallic floors full of chic, women's fashion in Stephane Dou and Changlee Yugin's boutique. Daily 10am–7pm.

Antiques, arts and crafts

Taipei has several craft centres firmly targeted at tourists, though prices and quality aren't bad and they are the most convenient way to stock up on gifts and souvenirs. If you're a serious buyer, the **antique shops** around Jianguo Road between Renai and Xinyi make fascinating browsing, with **Lane 291** lined with posh stores full of jewellery, paintings, carvings, and statues (many are closed Mondays). Heping East Road Section 1, east of Guting MRT Station, is home to traditional Chinese **calligraphy equipment stores**: the shops at no. 77 and 123 are the best.

The Jianguo Flower Market (建國假日花市; *jiànguó jiàrì huāshì*) in the other direction highlights Taiwan's impressive range of semi-tropical flora. Both are open Sat & Sun from 8am till around 6pm. **Jianguo Jade Market** 建國假日玉市 (*jiànguó jiàrì yùshì*) Under the Jianguo Elevated Freeway, between Renai and Jinan roads; MRT: Zhongxiao Xinsheng. Massive selection of jade jewellery, carvings and other antique stalls.

Lin Tian Tong Store 林田桶電 (*líntiántǒng diàn*) 108 Zhongshan N Rd Sec 1; MRT: Zhongshan/Taipei Main Station. Established in 1928 and specializing in Japanese-style tubs, basins and flowerpots made from *hinoki* cypress wood. The scarcity of such wood in Taiwan today accounts for the high prices, but even if you're not buying it's worth a quick look.

Liuligongfang 琉璃工坊 (*liúligōngfǎng*) 346 Dunhua S Rd Sec 1 ☎02/2701-3165; MRT: Anhe

Road (from 2012). Upmarket glass sculpture studio, founded by movie star Loretta Yang in 1987. There are also showrooms in most shopping malls. Daily 9.30am–8pm.

Taiwan Handicraft Promotion Center
台灣手工業推廣中心 (*táiwān shǒugōngyè tuīguǎngzhōngxīn*) 1 Xuzhou St; MRT: NTU Hospital. The best place for standard Chinese arts and crafts, including jewellery, porcelain, tea, fans,

cloisonné enamelware and even traditional clothing. Daily 9am–5.30pm.

Zaoheding 昭和町 (*zhāohédīng*) 60 Yongkang St; MRT: Guting. Compact warehouse packed with cheap antique stalls selling everything from old books and statues to pieces of furniture. This section of Yongkang St is lined with antique shops – things get going at around 2pm and wind down after 8pm (officially closing at 10pm).

Cameras, computers and electrical equipment

Taipei's **"camera street"** covers Hankou Street Section 1 and the section of Boai Road south of Kaifeng Street – here you'll find all the latest in high-tech photographic equipment. **Jin Tai** (金泰; *jīntai*; 10am–6pm) at 60 Boai Rd is the oldest repair shop in town: craftsman Lin Wen Ji is reputed to be able to fix anything (charges start at NT$600). Taipei is a great place to pick up computer hardware at reasonable prices, though English is rarely spoken by sales assistants (or used in manuals) and systems may not always be compatible with your home country. Try **Guanghua Market** (光華商場; *guānghuá shāngchǎng*; daily 10am–9pm), on Civic Boulevard near Xinsheng North Road and MRT Zhongxiao Xinsheng Station, for computer parts, games and accessories, or the **NOVA Computer Mall** at 2 Guanqian Rd (daily 11am–10pm), on the corner of Zhongxiao Road.

Books

Page One (首頁文化; *shǒuyè wénhuà*; Mon–Fri 11am–10pm, Sat & Sun 10am–11pm; ☎02/8101-8282) on the fourth floor of Taipei 101 Shopping Mall, 45 Shifu Road, Xinyi, is the best English-language bookshop in town, with a huge selection of novels and reference books. **Caves Books** (敦煌外文書籍網; *dūnhuáng wàiwén shūjíwǎng*; Mon–Sat 10.30am–9pm, Sun 10.30am–7pm; ☎02/2599-1169) at 54-3 Zhongshan N Rd Sec 3 at Minzu Road is smaller but also has a good selection of China and Taiwan-related books, as well as reference/teaching materials. **Moungar** (莽葛拾遺; *mǎnggě shíyí*) at 4 Lane 154, Guangzhou Street (on Mangka Park) sells old CDs and a small selection of secondhand English books, in a converted Chinese shophouse close to Longshan Temple. There's a smaller version, **Dixiajie** (地下階; *dìxiàjiē*) at 11-4 Yongkang St.

Eslite on Dunhua Road is open 24 hours (see p.100), and has branches all over the city – there's a big one in Xinyi at 11 Songgao Rd (daily 10am–2am).

Listings

Airlines All Nippon Airways (ANA), 3/F, 129 Zhongshan N Rd Sec 2 (☎02/2521-1989); Asiana Airlines, 9/F, 101 Nanjing E Rd Sec 2 (☎02/2581-4000); Cathay Pacific Airways/Dragonair, 12/F, 129 Minsheng E Rd Sec 3 (☎02/2715-2333); China Airlines, 131 Nanjing E Rd Sec 3 (☎02/2715-1212); Continental Airlines (☎02/2712-0131); EVA Air, 117 Changan E Rd Sec 2 (☎02/2501-1999); Far Eastern Air Transport 5 Alley 123, Lane 405, Dunhua N Rd (☎02/2712-1555); Mandarin Airlines (☎02/2717-1230); Philippine Airlines, 11/F, 139 Songjiang Rd (☎02/2506-7383 or 02/2506-7255); Singapore Airlines, 148 Songjiang Rd (☎02/2551-6655); Thai International, 7/F, 308 Bade Rd Sec 2 (☎02/2509-6899); TransAsia Airways, 9/F, 139 Zhengzhou Rd (☎02/2972-4599); Uni Air 117 Changan E Rd Sec 2 (☎02/2518-2626); United Airlines 12/F, 2 Renai Rd Sec 4 (☎02/2325-8868).

Moving on from Taipei

Taipei has connections to just about everywhere in Taiwan, though it's best to buy tickets in advance if you're planning to travel at the weekend, when transport is jammed with locals pouring out of the city.

By air

Buses to the **international airport** (臺灣桃園國際航空站; *táiwān táoyuán guójì hángkōngzhàn*) are plentiful (see p.59). Taxi drivers rarely use the meter – if you negotiate you should get them to take you for NT$1200 or less, but your hotel should be able to arrange a pick-up for NT$1000. You can buy tickets for **domestic flights** by simply rolling up to one of the airline desks at **Songshan Airport** (松山機場; *sōngshān jīchǎng*) an hour before departure, though it's obviously safer to reserve a seat in advance. From Taipei there are regular flights to every major destination in Taiwan – see Listings (opposite) for airline details.

By train

Taipei Station (台北車站; *táiběi chēzhàn*) is at the heart of Taiwan's rail system with services to all major cities: southbound trains follow the **Western Line** to Hsinchu (NT$180), Taichung (NT$375) and Kaohsiung (NT$845) while "northbound" services go to Keelung (NT$43) or travel the **Eastern Line** to Hualien (NT$441) and Taitung (NT$786). **High Speed Rail** services also depart from here; Hsinchu (NT$290; 33min), Taichung (NT$700; 50min–1hr); Tainan (NT$1350; 1hr 45min); Zuoying (Kaohsiung; NT$1490; 1hr 30min–2hr). You can buy tickets from machines with cash or credit cards, or from dedicated windows.

The station is relatively easy to navigate for non-Chinese speakers: there are ticket windows in the main hall, though it's usually faster to use the ticket machines that are labelled in English (there are separate machines for local and express services). If you're travelling to the station by metro you can beat the queues by following signs to the "TRA Transfer Area" before you exit the MRT station.

By bus

Most buses operate from **Taipei Bus Station** (臺北轉運站; *táiběi zhuǎnyùnzhàn*) on Civic Boulevard, part of the Q Square mall complex opposite the train station: companies such as Ubus run frequent 24hour services to all the major cities on the west coast, while KML (Kamalan Bus) runs several times a day to **Jiaoxi** (NT$70), **Yilan** (NT$90) and **Luodong** (NT$90). Kuo Kuang runs buses to **Miaoli** and **Hsinchu** from here, but its other services operate from the smaller **Taipei West Bus Station** (台北西車站; *táiběi xīchēzhàn*) at Zhongxiao and Chongqing roads: buses to **Jinshan** (every 15–20min; 5.40am–11pm; NT$120), **Dharma Drum Mountain** (hourly; 6.15am– 9.15pm; NT$135) and the **airport** (every 15–20min; 4.30am–11.20pm; NT$125) run from **Terminal A**, while buses to **Taichung** (NT$260), **Tainan** (NT$360) and **Kaohsiung** (NT$520) depart from adjacent **Terminal B**. There are also less frequent buses to **Puli/ Sun Moon Lake** (NT$460), and **Alishan** (Fri & Sat: 8.45pm March–Oct; 9.45pm Nov– Feb; NT$620; 6hr). Both terminals are a short walk west of the train station via the underground **Station Front Metro Mall**, which also connects to the MRT station.

The new **Taipei City Hall Bus Station** (市府轉運站; *shìfǔ zhuǎnyùnzhàn*) in Xinyi, at the intersection of Zhongxiao E Road and Keelung Road, offers commuter bus services to Taoyuan, Hsinchu and Yilan.

Banks Most banks will exchange foreign currency, while Chinatrust and Cathay Trust ATMs take Cirrus, Mastercard, Plus or Visa cards (not Maestro) – ATMs are also available in most 7-Elevens, MRT stations and some McDonalds. HSBC has ATMs at 167 Nanjing E Rd Sec 2; 6 Zhongxiao W Rd Sec 1; 2 Fuxing S Rd Sec 1; 372 Linsen N Rd; 185 Zhongshan N Rd Sec 2; 70 Nanjing E Rd Sec 3; and 8 Xinyi Rd Sec 5. Citibank has ATMs at 1 Fuxing N Rd; 8 Xiangyang Rd; 376 Dunhua Rd Sec 1; 101 Nanjing E Rd Sec 2; and 460 Xinyi Rd Sec 4.

Baseball Until the Taipei Dome on the corner of Guangfu South Rd and Zhongxiao East Rd is completed (probably in 2012/2013), Taiwan's national sport will be played at Xinzhuang Stadium (新莊棒球場; *xīnzhuāng bàngqiúchǎng*) in the western suburbs (take a taxi from Xinpu MRT Station) and Tianmu Baseball Stadium (天母棒球場; *tiānmǔ bàngqiúchǎng*). Around 23–27 games are held in both stadiums from March to October. The national CPBL league had just four teams sponsored by corporations in 2010 – they rotate matches between cities island-wide so there is no Taipei team as such, though Brother Elephants are nominally based in the city. Admission is NT$300 (reserved seats) or NT$250 open grandstand. Check the Chinese Professional Baseball League site at ⓦ www.cpbl.com.tw.

Bike rental Bike rental kiosks (usually operated by Giant), along official Riverside Bikeways (Bali, Daodacheng Wharf, Dajia, Muzha, Jingfu Bridge) allow you to rent bikes from one place and return them at any other affiliated kiosk or store (daily 8am–noon & 2–5.30pm; around NT$15–60/hr or NT$350 per day). You need ID, and may have to leave a deposit. You can pick up a free map showing the cycle paths and the bike rental locations from MRT stations. See also p.63 for the You Bike public rental scheme.

Car rental It is possible to rent cars in Taipei, though driving in the city can be intimidating for the inexperienced. See p.23 for a full list of companies.

Chinese language schools See p.51.

Consulates Australia, 27–28/F, President Int'l Building, 9-11 Songgao Rd (☎02/8725-4100, ⓦ www.australia.org.tw); Canada, 5–6/F, Hua-Hsin Building, 1 Songzhi Rd, Xinyi (☎02/2544-3000, ⓦ canada.org.tw); Philippines, 11/F, 176 Changchun Rd (☎02/2508-1719, ⓦ www.meco .ph/contact.html); New Zealand, Rm 2501, 25/F, International Trade Building, 333 Keelung Rd Sec 1 (visa section ☎02/2757-7060); South Africa, Suite 1301, 13/F, 205 Dunhua N Rd (☎02/2715-3251); UK, 26/F President Int'l Building, 9-11 Songgao Rd, (☎02/8758-2088, ⓦ ukintaiwan.fco.gov.uk/en); US, American Institute in Taiwan, 7, Lane 134, Xinyi Rd Sec 3 (☎02/2162-2000, ⓦ www.ait.org.tw).

Emergencies ☎110.

Hospitals and clinics Most hotels will be able to help with treatment or doctors if you feel sick, and most downtown hospitals have staff that can usually speak English. The Taiwan Adventist Hospital at 424 Bade Rd Sec 2 (☎02/2771-8151) has a special clinic for foreigners with English-speaking staff towards the back of the main building known as the Priority Care Center (☎02/2776-2651) – it's NT$1000 for a walk-in registration and doctors are on duty Mon–Thurs 9–11.30am and 2–4.30pm, and 9–11.30am on Fri and Sun.

Information ☎0800/024-1111. English directory services ☎106.

Internet access Most hotels have wi-fi or internet access, while Xinyi is covered by WLAN, the outdoor wireless internet system using pre-paid HiNet cards, which you can buy at Chunghwa Telecom service centres (ⓦ wlan.mytaipei.tw/ english/qa.html). If you don't have a computer there are plenty of internet cafés scattered around the city: American Pie e-café 4/F, 8 Nanyang St (24hr; NT$30/hr); Aztec, 235 Zhongxiao E Rd Sec 4, B1, 60 Zhongxiao E Rd Sec 4 and 2/F 206 Nanjing E Rd Sec 2 (24hr; NT$60 first hour, NT$0.8/min thereafter); Nova Computer Arcade, 2 Guanqian Rd (free internet terminals on 3/F); ha2, B1, 119 Minsheng E Rd Sec 2 (24hr; NT$50/hr); Network Planet 75 Xinyi Rd Sec 3 (24hr; NT$30/hr).

Left luggage Taipei Station has coin-operated lockers tucked away in the basement, with rates starting at NT$20 for three hours for a small backpack-sized locker and NT$50–100 for larger spaces. The maximum storage time is 72hr. Songshan Airport lockers are NT$40–80 for 12hr (maximum six days).

Pharmacies Taipei is littered with Traditional Chinese Medicine stores, but conventional Western non-prescription remedies (and toiletries) can be purchased in Watsons stores all over the city: try the branch next to Sogo on the junction of Zhongxiao and Fuxing rds, or in Taipei 101 Shopping Mall.

Post office The main Post Office is at 114 Zhongxiao W Rd Sec 1 and Boai Rd (Mon–Fri 7.30am–9pm, Sat 8.30am–4.30pm, Sun 8.30am–noon). There is a post restante service at window 12.

Scooter rental Local firms are reluctant to rent scooters to foreigners in Taipei, though Bike Farm (☎0926/283-300, ⓦ www.bikefarm.net) is owned by an English expat and offers one-daily rentals for NT$500 and monthly rentals from NT$2200–2600, including all servicing (there's no shop, they bring the bike to you). You'll need a passport and a NT$7000 deposit.

Travel agents Edison Travel Service at 4/F, 190 Songjiang Rd has English-speaking staff (☎02/2563-5313, ⓦ www.edison.com.tw) and operates Taipei tours. The most popular local agent for cheap air tickets and packages is Eztravel with its main office at 258 Dunhua N Rd (☎02/4066-6777), but the cheapest deals are reserved for local residents.

Around Taipei

The mountains and river valleys that surround the capital are loaded with attractions, making for an enticing series of day-trips or short breaks. Beitou's **hot-spring spas** are some of Taiwan's best, while hikers should find plenty to keep them busy in **Yangmingshan National Park**. The old port towns of **Danshui** and **Bali** contain a smattering of historical sights, while **Wulai** and the towns to the southeast offer a taster of the island's mountainous interior. **Yingge** is a must-see for anyone with an interest in ceramics, and the temple at **Sanxia** is one of Taiwan's most beautiful.

Note that in 2010 all the major museums listed below were free of charge, to celebate the creation of the new municipality of **Xinbei City 新北市** (*xīnběishì*) out of the old Taipei County – it's not clear what the future policy will be, so previous charges are included here for reference.

Beitou

The northern Taipei district of **BEITOU** (北投; *běitóu*) nestles in the shadow of Yangmingshan, twenty minutes from downtown by MRT. The name derives from "*Patauw*" or "home of witches" in the Ketagalan language, an allusion to the area's bubbling sulphur carbonate **hot springs**. Osaka merchant **Hirada Gengo** opened Beitou's first hot-spring inn in 1896, and during the Japanese occupation it became one of the island's most prominent resorts. The Japanese were particularly attracted to **hokutolite**, a mineral-laden stone formed by the springs, and bathers still come here to enjoy its therapeutic qualities. Most visitors come for the day, taking a dip in one of the many spas in the area (as in much of Taiwan, you can't actually bathe in the hot springs at source – water is piped into spa pools and hotels), but it's also worth exploring a smattering of sights recalling Taiwan's Japanese past.

Beitou is on the Danshui MRT line, easily accessible from central Taipei. There's not much to see around the main station however, and it's best to take the branch line to **Xinbeitou** (新北投; *xīnběitóu* or "New Beitou"), a few minutes away and closer to the main hotels and spas. By 2012, the controversy-plagued Beitou Cable Car Link Project (北投空中纜車; *běitóu kōngzhōng lǎnchē*) may finally link Xinbeitou with Yangmingshan National Park.

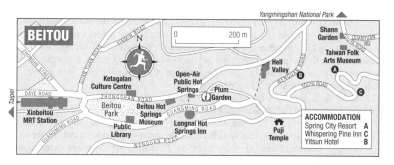

Accommodation and spas

Beitou's hot-spring water is piped into **spas** all over the valley, many doubling as attractive **hotels**. Unless you're a real hot-spring fan it's usually not worth staying the night, as most places offer affordable day rates for their spa facilities. The places listed below are special options, but you'll see plenty of perfectly decent modern hotels as you walk along Beitou Park. You'll normally be allowed to stay in the "public" pools (typically including sauna, steam room and a variety of hot and cold spring pools) as long as you like, and during the week you'll have them mostly to yourself. Private rooms with sunken baths are often available at the best spas, but these are pricey – at least NT$1500–3000 per hour.

Longnai Hot Springs Inn 龍乃湯 (*lóng nǎi tāng*) 244 Guangming Rd. Founded in 1907 and the oldest of Beitou's traditional Japanese bathhouses (there are no rooms here despite the name), this is a no-nonsense affair where you just strip off and get into the fairly basic separate male and female indoor stone baths (NT$90/hr). Look for the white shack-like hut below the Open-Air Hot Springs. Daily 6.30am–9pm.

Open-Air Hot Springs 公共露天溫泉 (*gōnggòng lùtiān wēnquán*) 6 Zhongshan Rd. Also known as the Millennium Hot Springs, this is the cheapest outdoor spa in Beitou (NT$40), featuring several mixed-sex pools that close for cleaning at regular intervals through the day (wear your swim suit). Nice location on the banks of the creek, but it can get crowded, especially at weekends. Coin-operated lockers available. Daily 5.30–7.30am, 8–10am, 10.30am–1pm, 1.30–4pm, 4.30–7pm & 7.30–10pm.

Spring City Resort 春天酒店 (*chūntiān jiǔdiàn*) 18 Youya Rd ☎02/2897-5555, ⓦwww .springresort.tw. Located high on the hills above

Beitou and regarded as its top resort, this modern five-star hotel offers stylish private bathhouses open 24hr (NT$600/hr per person), while you can access the shared outdoor spa (nine different pools) for NT$800 for the day (9am–10pm). ❽

Whispering Pine Inn 吟松阁閣旅社 (*yínsōnggé lǚshè*) 21 Youya Rd ☎02/2895-1531. Established in 1934, this Japanese-era inn has wooden floors and goldfish ponds, creating an authentic and remarkably serene atmosphere. It's showing its age and expensive considering, so it's not for everyone; you're paying for the historic atmosphere. There's no TV or internet, though each room comes with original stone hot-spring bath and there are indoor men's and women's public baths. ❼

Yitsun Hotel 逸邨大飯店 (*yìzun dàfàndiàn*) 140 Wenquan Rd ☎02/2891-2121. The last of Beitou's three historic Japanese inns (dating from 1901), set in a quiet location above the creek with charming, if a little basic accommodation. The stone bathing pools here are particularly attractive – the men-only pool is larger and open to non-guests (NT$300/hr). ❻

Beitou Park

From **Xinbeitou** MRT station, head straight up Zhongshan Road on the north side of **Beitou Park** (北投公園; *běitóu gōngyuán*), a swath of green that follows sulphuric Beitou Creek up the valley. Two hundred metres on the left is the **Ketagalan Culture Center** (凱達格蘭文化館; *kǎidágélán wénhuàguǎn*; Tues–Sun 9am–5pm; free; ☎02/2898-6500), which was established as a focus for the indigenous community in Taipei (there are around thirteen thousand aboriginal residents registered in the city). It has a shop on the first floor, and two floors of exhibits which provide a decent introduction to Taiwan's fourteen aboriginal tribes with sculptures, everyday artefacts like smoking pipes, costumes and videos, with a particularly good section on the *píngpǔ* tribes (see p.395); labelling is in Chinese and English.

A short walk further along Zhongshan Road is the beautiful and eco-friendly **public library** (台北市立圖書館北投分館; *táiběishì lìtúshūguǎn běitóu fēnguǎn*; Mon & Sun 9am–5pm, Tues–Sat 8.30am–9pm; ☎02/2897-7682), reputed to be Taiwan's greenest structure (the wooden building creates solar power and conserves rainwater). Beyond here on the right is **Beitou Hot Springs Museum** (北投溫泉博物館; *běitóu wēnquán bówùguǎn*; Tues–Sun 9am–5pm; free;

02/2893-9981), housed in the attractively restored public bathhouse built in 1913, complete with stained-glass windows and original bathing pool in the basement. It's the best place to learn about the history of the area. Beyond the museum take the right-hand fork in Zhongshan Road: just past the Open-Air Hot Springs you'll see the **Plum Garden** 梅庭 (*méitíng*; Tues–Sun 9am–5pm; free; 02/2897-2647) at no. 6, the latest of Beitou's Japanese-style mansions to be restored. It was built as a private residence in the 1930s, but its principal purpose today is to act as official Beitou **visitor information centre** and memorial to revered scholar and calligrapher Yu Youren, who spent summers here between 1949 and 1964.

Hell Valley and Puji Temple

Another 200m or so along Zhongshan Road you'll see a lane on the left leading to the **Thermal Valley**, traditionally known as **Hell Valley** (地熱谷; *dìrègǔ*; daily 9am–5pm; free). It's essentially a huge pool of bubbling spring water that feeds Beitou Creek, especially impressive in winter months when it's shrouded in billowing clouds of steam. The lake is fenced off for safety reasons (the average temperature is 70°C). Continue up the main street and turn left at Wenquan Road: not far on the right you'll see stone steps (take the right-hand fork) leading up to **Puji Temple** (普濟寺; *pǔjì sì*; daily 8am–7pm), a typically elegant Japanese Buddhist shrine, now rare in Taiwan. Built between 1905 and 1916, today it's dedicated to Guanyin.

Taiwan Folk Arts Museum

Continuing on Wenquan Road beyond the temple, bear left at the next junction then turn right up Youya Road: it's a twenty-minute walk up the valley from here to the **Taiwan Folk Arts Museum** (北投文物館; *běitóu wénwùguǎn*; Tues–Sun 10am–5.30pm; NT$120; 02/2891-2318), another gorgeous Japanese-style structure and teahouse at no. 32. The building started life in 1921 as the *Jiashan Hotel*, but its tranquil wooden corridors and rooms feel more akin to a temple. The permanent exhibit explains the building's history, while revolving displays show everything from Taiwanese aboriginal artefacts to textiles, clothing and handicrafts from minority groups in mainland China. The exhibits are always visually stimulating, but you'll get more out of this (and the roster of cultural events held here) if you speak and read Chinese.

Next door, at 34 Youya Rd, **Shann Garden** (禪園; *chányuán*; Mon–Fri 11.30am–2.30pm & 5.30–9.30pm, Sat & Sun 11.30am–3pm & 5.30–10pm; 02/2896-5700) comprises a Mongolian barbecue restaurant and Japanese-style **teahouse**, both with grand views of Beitou below – sipping tea on tatami mats here is the perfect way to end an afternoon. It was originally a Japanese hotel, and later was where warlord **Zhang Xueliang** (instigator of China's Xian Incident) was held under house arrest between 1949 and 1990. Buses #230 and S25 head back to Beitou from the road outside – you can also take #230 on to Yangmingshan (below).

Yangmingshan National Park

A comfortable day-trip from Taipei, **Yangmingshan National Park** (陽明山國家公園; *yángmíngshān guójiāgōngyúan*; www.ymsnp.gov.tw) sits on a geological fault line sprinkled with dormant **volcanoes**, **hot-spring spas** and well-marked **hiking trails**. The highlight is the climb up **Mount Qixing**, the park's highest peak, but it also contains important historical sights – Chiang Kai-shek built his first and last homes in Taiwan here. Minibuses race between the main attractions making it unusually accessible to non-hikers, so try to avoid visiting at weekends and during holidays, especially in the spring and summer flower-viewing seasons, when the park is at its busiest.

Exploring the park

Buses from Jiantan MRT (see p.110) terminate at the park **bus station** (just beyond 7-Eleven and *Starbucks*), close to several hotels with hot-spring spas. This is also where the **park shuttle bus #108** (daily 7am–5.30pm) departs every twenty to thirty minutes on weekdays, and every ten minutes at weekends, providing a loop service to all the main points of interest for NT$15 per trip or NT$60 for unlimited rides (buy tickets from the bus station office). The first stop is the main park **visitor centre** (Tues–Fri 9am–4.30pm, Sat–Sun 8.30am–4.30pm; ☏02/2861-3601), which is also a surprisingly steep fifteen-minute hike, 700m from the bus station – the sidewalk path goes all the way so there's no need to follow the road. The centre contains several exhibition rooms and provides free information, but it's best to buy one of the more detailed maps from the shop if you intend to do a lot of hiking. Though you may still see some *tōngyòng pīnyīn* signage in the park, *hànyǔ pīnyīn* is used as default here.

Mount Qixing (Mt Cising)

The energetic climb to the top of **Mount Qixing** (七星山; *qīxīngshān*; 1120m) takes about two hours from the visitor centre (2.4km) – the path is well marked and paved most of the way, though it gets steep in places and it can get cool and cloudy on top. On a clear day, the views across the Taipei Basin and the sea to the north are spectacular. On top you'll grasp why the park area used to be known as "Grass Mountain" (*cǎoshān*) – the windswept peaks are covered in thick silver-grass. The park was later renamed in honour of the Ming dynasty philosopher Wang Yang-ming. From the peak you have a choice of routes down: the western path to Xiaoyoukeng (1.65km) is more dramatic, lined with yellow sulphurous rocks and steaming vents, while the eastern trail leads to Lengshuikeng (1.9km).

Yangmingshuwu

The second shuttle bus stop is **Yangmingshuwu** (陽明書屋; *yángmíngshūwū*; Tues–Sun 9am–1.30pm; NT$50), the best-preserved of Chiang Kai-shek's fifteen former homes in Taiwan. From the bus stop it's a ten-minute walk down the hill to the **visitor centre** (Tues–Sun 9am–4.30pm; ☏02/2861-1444) where you pick up a guide: tours take around one hour though you'll have to call ahead to ensure English-speakers are on hand. From here it's another short walk to the house itself, once surrounded by five hundred armed guards and several tanks.

Originally known as the *Chung Hsing Guesthouse*, it was built in 1970 as a luxury hotel where the Generalissimo could host foreign dignitaries. Instead, it became the last home of the ailing president after Taiwan's withdrawal from the UN saw official visits dwindle. Inside it's an odd mix of classical Chinese decor, 1970s Western design (check out Madam Chiang's pink-tiled bathroom) and extreme security: the basement was bolstered by reinforced concrete to resist air attacks, with a series of escape tunnels leading to the gardens and beyond. The contents of the house – furniture, personal items – are authentic reproductions, including a small collection of Madam Chiang's own paintings.

Yangming Park

Twenty minutes' walk downhill from Yangmingshuwu (follow signs to the "Flower Clock") is **Yangming Park** (陽明公園; *yángmíng gōngyúan*), a popular subsection of the national park often packed out with tourists. The main attraction is **flowers**: in spring the gardens here are crammed with cherry blossoms and azaleas. Walk across the car park and follow the road for around 500m back towards the bus station and you'll come to the Gate of Yangming Park: just beyond here on the right is narrow Hudi Road which leads to a Japanese-style house dubbed the **Grass Mountain Chateau** (草山行館; *cǎoshān xíngguǎn*), Chiang Kai-shek's first home in Taiwan. In 2003 it was turned into a series of **art galleries** and a **café**, but tragically the whole place was burnt to the ground (in suspicious circumstances) in 2007. After a meticulous restoration, it's slated to reopen by early 2011 (ask at the visitor centre).

Zhuzihu to Juansi Waterfall

Bus stop number three is **Zhuzihu** (竹子湖; *zhúzihú*), a dried-up lake now ringed with vegetable and flower farms, and best visited in December, when the **calla lilies** are in bloom. Follow the signs along the road from the bus stop and you'll reach a junction in around 300m: this is the 3–4km loop road that circles the area, dotted with rustic **teahouses** and **restaurants**.

Mount Datun (大屯山; *dàtúnshān*; 1092m), the park's third highest peak, is accessible from the fourth bus stop, (confusingly labelled "Mount Cising"); from here it's a 1.5km scenic hike along Bailaka Road to the Anbu Trail car park, and another 1.5km up to the top.

The fifth bus stop is **Xiaoyoukeng** (小油坑; *xiǎoyóukēng*), which features a huge and highly photogenic sulphuric steam vent eating into the side of Mount Qixing.

Stop number six is **Lengshuikeng** (冷水坑; *lěngshuǐkēng*), where you'll find free hot-spring baths (see below), and "**Milk Lake**" (*niúnǎihú*) with its unusual greenish-white sulphur surface. The bus stops in front of the hot springs first, makes a small loop to Qingtiangang and returns to Lengshuikeng to stop outside its small visitor centre.

Qingtiangang (擎天崗; *qíngtiāngāng*) is a wide, open plateau noted for its silvergrass and herd of cattle: there's a short but pleasant loop trail here as well as access to the more challenging **Jinbaoli Trail** (金包里步道; *jīnbāolǐ bùdào*; also known as Fisherman's Old Trail). The latter actually starts at the **Juansi Waterfall** (涓絲瀑布; *juānsī pùbù*) bus stop a few kilometres south of Lengshuikeng, and meanders its way 7km north to the small village of **Dingbayan** (頂八煙; *dǐngbāyān*) on Highway 2 – it's an enjoyable hike that can take half a day, but you'll have to catch the infrequent Taipei–Jinshan bus back from here or walk for another hour or so to Jinshan (p.110). From the waterfall stop, the shuttle bus completes the loop and ends up back at the bus station. Note that Xiaoyoukeng, Lengshuikeng and Qingtiangang have small visitor centres and basic shops on site – opening times are similar to the main visitor centre.

Hot springs

The park's acidic sulphur **hot springs** are some of the most famous in Taiwan. A cluster of **hotels** near the park bus station allows day-guests to use their spa facilities for a fee, though staying the night isn't good value. If you're feeling adventurous try the **free public pools** at Lengshuikeng (opposite the first Lengshuikeng shuttle bus stop; daily 9am–5pm) – simply walk in and strip off (you're expected to be naked), leaving clothes on the shelves by the pool (men and women are separate). The place to splurge is the ⚑ *Landis Resort* (陽明山中國麗緻大飯店; *yángmíngshān zhōngguó lìzhì dàfàndiàn*; ☏02/2861-6661, ⓦ www .landisresort.com.tw; ❾), 237 Gerzhi Road, Yangmingshan's most luxurious hotel. Day-guests can use the spa pools, spring-water swimming pool and gym (7am–10pm; NT\$999–1099; private rooms NT\$1500–1750 for 2hr). Taipei buses stop outside, or it's a twenty-minute walk from Yangmingshan bus station.

Practicalities

The fastest way to Yangmingshan is to take the MRT to Jiantan and catch Red #5 bus (daily 6am–12.15am), or #260 (daily 5.10am–10.30pm) on Wenlin Road just outside the station; buses depart every seven to thirteen minutes. From Beitou, #230 also rattles up the hill (daily 6am–10.10pm) and #9 (daily 5.20am–10pm) goes all the way to Zhuzihu (all buses are NT$15). Royal Bus (T02/8295-7022) runs a handy **Taipei to Jinshan** service straight across the park; catch these from the Government Insurance Building stop near the junction of Gongguan and Qingdao West roads in Taipei (NT$130 to Jinshan), or near the park bus station (Taipei NT$40; Jinshan NT$100). Buses run from 6.20am to 6.30pm weekdays, every hour from 7am, and 7am–6pm weekends, every half-hour.

Beyond the hotels and a couple of local diners near the bus station, **eating options** are limited in the park, so stock up at 7-Eleven if you want to snack.

Around Yangmingshan

If you have more time, it's worth exploring a couple of places on the way back from the national park, both easily accessible from the main bus route into Taipei. The **Hwa Kang Museum** (華岡博物館; *huágāng bówùguǎn*; Mon–Fri 9am–4pm; free; T02/2861-0511) is located within the Chinese Culture University, just over 2km south of the park bus station. The museum's collection comprises almost fifty thousand historical artefacts from China and Taiwan, though only a fraction is displayed at one time. Highlights include work by painters **Zhang Da-qian** and **Pu Xin-yu**, prehistoric pottery and jade from the Beinan site (see p.319) and an original Tao canoe from Lanyu. The museum is located in the Hsiao Fong Memorial Building, a ten-minute walk along Aifu 2nd Street and Huagang Road from the university bus stop (#260) – Red #5 goes all the way into the campus. It's the first building on the left as you enter the university: the museum is on the left side. You can walk back into Taipei from here via **Tianmu Water Pipe Trail** (天母水管步道; *tiānmǔ shuǐguǎn bùdào*), which is clearly signposted on Aifu 3rd Street, not far from the main road. It's around 2km to the start of Zhongshan Road Section 7, where you can take bus #220 into the city.

Further south along the main bus route is **Lin Yutang House** (林語堂故居; *línyǔtáng gùjū*; Tues–Sun 9am–5pm; NT$30; T02/2861-3003;) at 141 Yangde Road Section 2, a small but atmospheric monument to one of China's greatest writers. Lin had a peripatetic career that saw him live in the West for many years, and in 1937 he topped the *New York Times* bestseller list for a year with *The Importance of Living*. He spent the last ten years of his life in this house, dying in 1976 – he's buried in the garden. Lin's fame has faded somewhat, but the house is certainly special and commands a magnificent viewpoint over Taipei. Bus #260 and Red #5 stop outside.

Danshui

Set on the northern bank of the Danshui River, 20km north of Taipei, the old port town of **DANSHUI** (淡水; *dànshuǐ*) is hugely popular with local day-trippers and tourists from the south. The chief draw is the food – at the weekends you'll see thousands of Taiwanese trawling up and down its wharves and old streets eagerly stuffing themselves with local specialities and enjoying carnival games. Danshui has plenty more to offer however: it's packed with historical attractions that include **Fort San Domingo** and a small but fascinating collection of sights associated with Canadian missionary **George Leslie Mackay**.

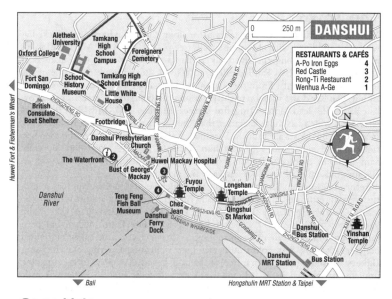

DANSHUI

0   250 m

RESTAURANTS & CAFÉS
A-Po Iron Eggs	4
Red Castle	3
Rong-Ti Restaurant	2
Wenhua A-Ge	1

Some history

Danshui means "fresh water", and it is thought to have been the name given to the area by early Chinese seafarers. The settlement was established around **Fort Santo Domingo** (known as "Fort San Domingo" today), built by the Spanish in 1628 and later occupied by the Dutch (see p.383). By 1662 the Dutch had been driven off the island, the village growing slowly as more Chinese immigrants started to arrive in the eighteenth century. Danshui boomed after the Treaty of Beijing opened up the port to foreign trade in 1860 – **Robert Swinhoe**, the first British vice-consul, arrived a year later and a customs office was in operation by 1862 (the treaty stipulated that Chinese Customs should be administered by British officers). *Hongs* such as Jardine Matheson were soon busy exporting oolong and *Bāozhǒng* **tea**, but Danshui's downfall was its lack of a deepwater harbour – from 1906 it began to lose precedence to Keelung and by the 1920s had become a relative backwater. Today, in addition to a healthy tourist trade, Danshui is the home to two universities and growing numbers of Taipei commuters.

Arrival and information

Danshui is the last station on the Danshui MRT line, just 35 minutes from Taipei Station, making it an easy day-trip from the capital. There's little point in staying the night here, but it is a convenient starting point for trips to the **north coast** (see p.126). **Ferries** run from the wharf a short walk from the MRT station to Bali every ten to fifteen minutes (daily 7am–8pm, weekends till 9pm; NT$20; 10min) and Fisherman's Wharf every fifteen to twenty minutes (daily 7am–8pm; NT$50; 15–20min). Buy tickets from the booths on the wharf before boarding (you can use EasyCard for the Bali ferry).

Danshui's **visitor information centre** (Mon–Fri 11am–5pm, Sat & Sun 10am–6pm; ⊕02/2629-6464) is located in the **Rong-Ti Waterfront restaurant** (see p.114) near the end of the wharf area, under a shady banyan tree.

111

The Town

Most of the action in Danshui takes place along the **old wharf area**, packed at weekends and lined with cheap food stalls (see p.114). From the MRT station it's possible to walk along the riverbank as far as the old British Consulate Boat Shelter, just below Fort San Domingo, or take the inland route past some of the town's historical sights. From the station, turn left along Zhongzheng Road, pass Zhongshan Road and walk on to the junction with Gongming Street. The narrow lane opposite leads into **Qingshui Street Market** (清水街市場; *qīngshuǐjiē shìchǎng*), which has more character than the wharf area and features some tasty snack food, but closes after lunch. Turning left along Qingshui Street and then first right should take you to **Longshan Temple** (龍山寺; *lóngshān sì*; daily 5am–8.30pm), a peaceful Buddhist shrine to Guanyin dating from 1858, with an elegant gold statue of the Bodhisattva in the main hall.

Return to Qingshui Street and turn right: when you reach the main road ahead, turn left to return to Zhongzheng Road. Turn right here and a short walk on the left is *Sanxiecheng Bakery* at no. 81 (三協成餅舖; *sānxiéchéng bǐngpù*; daily 9am–9pm; ℡02/2621-2177), better known as **"Chez Jean"**, which has been producing Chinese-style cakes since 1935 – their hefty sesame cakes and famed *dōngguā ròubǐng* ("wax gourd meat pies"), are delicious. The tiny **Sanxiechong Bakery Museum** (same hours; free) at the back has small displays of cake-making implements labelled in French and German, and some English leaflets. A little further on the other side of the road at no. 200 you'll see **Fuyou Temple** (福佑宮; *fúyòu gōng*; daily 5am–9pm), completed in 1796, making it Danshui's oldest and important because of the historic inscriptions on its columns and steles. The temple is dedicated to Mazu, which is not surprising given its proximity to the wharf. Opposite at no. 117 is the **Teng Feng Fish Ball Museum** (登峰魚丸博物館; *dēngfēng yúwán bówùguǎn*; Mon–Fri 10.30am–9pm, Sat & Sun 10.30am–10pm; free; ℡02/2629-3312), another quirky Danshui attraction, opened by one of the town's most popular fish-ball makers. More local snacks are on offer just beyond here at no. 135 – *A-Po Iron Eggs* (阿婆鐵蛋; *ā pó tiědàn*) is a good place to buy Danshui's famous "iron eggs" (*tiě dàn*; NT$100 for six large ones), while opposite is Lane 14 leading to the *Red Castle* (see p.114).

Memorials to George Mackay

A little further along Zhongzheng Road is the junction with Jensi Street and the bust of **George Mackay** (see box, opposite), complete with gigantic beard. This lies opposite the narrow, unmarked lane known as **Mackay Street** (*mǎjiē jiē*) leading to the white stone **Huwei Mackay Hospital** (滬尾偕醫館; *hùwěi jiēīguǎn*; Tues–Fri 11am–6pm, Sat & Sun 11am–9pm; free), which he opened in 1897. Today it houses a small exhibition on the great man (Chinese labels only), as well as *Mackay Coffee* café. Next door, the current **Danshui Presbyterian Church** (淡水長老教會; *dànshuǐ zhǎnglǎo jiāohuì*) was built in 1933 on the site of the chapel Mackay established in 1890. It still attracts a sizeable congregation and is only open on Sundays.

Keep walking and turn right at the junction ahead, then follow the road uphill, over the footbridge and straight up to Zhenli Street at Wenhua Elementary School. Turn right here and you'll see *Wenhua A-Ge* (see p.114), while to the left is the **Little White House** (小白宮; *xiǎo báigōng*; Tues–Sun 9.30am–6pm; NT$40) built between 1869 and 1876. Serving as Danshui's British-run custom house before becoming a Japanese clubhouse in 1900, the chalk-white colonial bungalow has been immaculately refurbished, though the rooms are a little bare – the exhibits inside do provide plenty of history and background on the site however, with English labelling. A little further ahead is the entrance to **Tamkang High School** (淡江中學; *dànjiāng zhōngxué*; Mon–Sat 8am–4.30pm, Sun 1–5pm; free), which includes several Mackay-related

George Mackay (1844–1901)

Canadian missionary **George Leslie Mackay** is still fondly remembered in Taiwan for his pioneering work in the fields of education and medicine (he's famous for the somewhat gruesome achievement of having extracted over 21,000 teeth), as well as his primary task of establishing the Presbyterian Church in northern Taiwan. Born in Oxford, Ontario in 1844, he came to Taiwan in 1871, and after a brief stint in Kaohsiung arrived in Danshui in 1872. In 1878, Mackay married a local woman and settled in Danshui, which remained his home until he died in 1901. Although there was considerable resistance to his early proselytizing efforts (vividly described in his 1895 memoir *From Far Formosa*), he gathered a sufficient number of disciples to build north Taiwan's first church here in 1882, as well as a boys' school (Oxford College) – his educational legacy continues at Tamkang High School.

sights, notably his **grave** at the far end of the campus amidst those of his immediate family. Behind this is the **Foreigners' Cemetery** (1867–1974), testimony to the town's early colonial history. Just inside the school entrance, on the left, is the **School History Museum** with displays on Mackay's life labelled in English. Mackay's original boys' school (the precursor of Tamkang) was known as **Oxford College** (牛津學堂; *niújīnxuétáng*; daily 9am–4pm; free) and you can still visit the humble building (used 1882–1901) just inside the campus of Aletheia University, a bit further along Zhenli Road. Construction was funded by the concerned residents of Mackay's hometown in Oxford, Ontario after they found out he'd been teaching students under a banyan tree. The restored interior is more like a gallery than a museum, displaying old photos associated with Mackay, Canadian cultural exchanges over the years and the school itself. From here the road swings left, and leads downhill to Fort San Domingo.

Fort San Domingo to Fisherman's Wharf

Touted as Danshui's premier historic site, **Fort San Domingo** (紅毛城; *hóngmáo chéng*; Tues–Sun 9.30am–10pm; NT$60), known as "Fort of the Red-haired Barbarians" in Chinese, comprises two separate buildings. Walking up the slope from the main entrance, you'll arrive at the **fort** itself, though nothing remains of the **Spanish** original built 1636–38, a stone replacement for the wooden stockade they'd established in 1628. The current structure is a mixture of the **Dutch** fortifications completed in 1644 and renovations (including the portico and red paint job) made after 1867 when it became the permanent **British Consulate**, leased from the Chinese government. You can explore some of the rooms inside, all well labelled in English. The redbrick **consular residence** next to the fort (built in 1891) is a typical example of the colonial-style architecture of the time, with a couple of rooms furnished in reasonably authentic Victorian decor, and more exhibits related to the site. The Brits maintained a presence here until 1971.

Leaving the fort, turn right along Zhongzheng Road and in around ten minutes you should reach the turning leading to **Huwei Fort** (滬尾砲臺; *hùwěi pàotái*; Tues–Sun 9am–5pm; NT$25). Built by a German architect in 1886 for the Qing government, Huwei Fort never saw action – today it's a pristine example of a sizeable nineteenth-century gun fortification, though there's not much to do other than wander the main courtyard and clamber on the walls. The vaults inside contain a small exhibition on the French invasion of Dansui during the **Sino–French War** in 1884.

It's a boring two-kilometre walk from here to **Fisherman's Wharf** (漁人碼頭; *yúrén mǎtóu*), at the mouth of the river, but there are also buses that ply up and down the main road from the MRT station. Restaurants and shops surround the new marina and it's a prime sunset-viewing location, but otherwise not that interesting. Catch the **ferry** back to the old wharf area (NT$50).

Eating

Danshui is famous throughout Taiwan for its delicious snack **food**. Favourites include **fish crisps** (*yú sū*) sold in packets all over town (NT$50–100), "**iron eggs**" (*tiě dàn*, chicken or dove eggs boiled until they shrink, harden, and turn black; NT$10 each) and **fish ball soup** (*yúwán tāng*). **Gongming Street** runs parallel to the riverside from the station and is packed with snack stalls.

Keep walking along the waterfront and you'll eventually end up at *Rong-Ti Restaurant* (榕堤水灣餐廳; *róngtí shuǐwān cāntīng*; Mon–Fri 11.30am–11pm, Sat & Sun 11.30am–1am), part of the Waterfront complex and a stylish place to eat or just sip drinks overlooking the river. It's reminiscent of a posh beach resort, with thatched *palapas*, designer sofas and wicker chairs, and serves mainly Western-style dishes (NT$200–300).

🍴 *Red Castle* (達觀樓; *dáguānlóu*) at 6 Lane 2, Sanmin St (accessible via the 106 steps at the end of Lane 14 off Zhongzheng Road), is one of the highlights of the town. Built by British merchants in 1899 in colonial style reminiscent of the consular residence, today it houses a Chinese restaurant and *Red 3 Café* (Mon–Fri noon–2.30pm & 5.30–9pm, Sat & Sun noon–9pm) on the third floor with one of the best views in Danshui, especially at sunset. For lunch, try *Wenhua A-Ge* (文化阿給; *wénhuà ā-gěi*; daily 9.30am–6.30pm) at 6-4 Zhenli St, near the Little White House, which has been cooking up sumptuous *ā-gěi* (tofu packets stuffed with vermicelli noodles, fried and smothered in rich, seafood sauce, NT$35) for over one hundred years. Order at the counter, then take your bowl to the seating area at the back.

Bali and around

It's a short ferry ride from Danshui to **BALI** (八里; *bālǐ*), a fast-developing suburb of Taipei on the left bank of the Danshui River. Bali was a thriving port in the eighteenth century, but after its wharves began to silt up in the 1840s business moved to the other side of the river. Today the riverbank is being developed into a series of parks and attractions dubbed **Shore-Community-Museum** (水岸 · 社區 · 博物館; *shuǐàn-shèqū-bówùguǎn*) by local authorities, but the real highlight is the **Shihsanhang Museum of Archaeology**, 3.55km further along the coast. The town itself is an unattractive mix of light industry and residential development, but the magical views of Yangmingshan across the river more than compensate.

Arriving by boat, you'll disembark at **Bali Old Wharf Street** (八里渡船頭老街; *bālǐ dùchuántóu lǎojiē*), a smaller version of Danshui's promenade of snack stalls and carnival games. From here you can walk up the narrow lane opposite the ferry quay to Zhonghua Road and catch the R13 bus, or alternatively hire a bike and **cycle** the 4km to the museum. This is not a bad idea if you have time – the route is well marked and bikes can be hired from the shop close to where the ferry docks (NT$60/hr; ID required).

Shihsanhang Museum of Archaeology

Tucked away behind the pot-shaped domes of the local water treatment plant, the **Shihsanhang Museum of Archaeology** (十三行博物館; *shísānháng bówùguǎn*; April–Oct Tues–Fri 9.30am–6pm, Sat & Sun 9.30am–7pm; Nov–March Tues–Fri 9.30am–5pm, Sat & Sun 9.30am–6pm; free; ☏02/2619-1313; ⓦwww.sshm.tpc.gov.tw) displays a remarkable collection of archeological finds dating from 200 to 1500 AD. The building itself has won several awards, while the actual dig site now lies within the treatment plant, and a small area of this is open to the public. The finds are particularly significant because it's the only prehistoric site in Taiwan to show evidence of **iron smelting** and, in addition, **Tang dynasty coins** suggest the community traded with merchants from China. Perhaps the most intriguing object on display is the mysterious **anthropomorphic jar**, one of the few prehistoric artefacts ever found in Taiwan depicting a human face. The collection isn't huge but it's still impressive – it even includes **jade earrings** that experts believe were already 1000-year-old antiques when acquired by the people at Shihsanhang. The museum also highlights the archeological process that lies behind the discoveries, including excavation techniques and how, crucially, the experts made their assumptions. The Shihsanhang site was abandoned five hundred years ago and its inhabitants remain a mystery – the logical conclusion that they were the ancestors of the Ketagalan, the aboriginal tribe that occupied the area when Dutch and Chinese settlers arrived in the seventeenth century, is still debated. Most of the displays have English labels.

Practicalities

To reach Bali from **Taipei** take the MRT to Guandu Station and switch to the frequent R13 **bus**, just outside exit 1 (NT$15), which swings past the wharf area and then the museum in around twenty minutes. There's plenty of places **to eat** around the wharf: delicious fried squid and crab is a specialty. Located opposite the ferry pier at 22 Duchuantou St, the speciality at *She Family Peacock Clam King* (佘家孔雀蛤大王總店; *shéjiā kǒngquègé dàwáng zǒngdiàn*; daily 10am–9pm; ☎02/2610-3103) is not clams, but large stir-fried green **mussels** (*kǒngquègé*; NT$200) garnished with basil, making them look (sort of) like peacocks.

Look out also for people waiting in front of ⏧ *Double Sister Donut* (姊妹雙胞胎; *jiěmèi shuāngbāotāi*; daily 9am till they sell out) at 25 Duchuantou St (the lane leading up to the main road); this stall is justly famed for its gut-busting fried donuts; try the taro flavour (from NT$15).

Guanyinshan

Dominating the skyline above Bali, **Guanyinshan** (觀音山; *guānyīnshān*; 612m) is the only part of the North Coast and Guanyinshan National Scenic Area (see p.126) south of the Danshui River. It's the closest thing the Taipei region has to a holy mountain, supposedly resembling Bodhisattva Guanyin in repose and littered with numerous temples dedicated to the Buddhist deity. Hundreds of temples in Taiwan have been constructed with andesite rock (known as Guanyin Stone) from the mountain over the years, but quarrying is now restricted – these days it's better known for bird-watching, particularly for hawks and eagles between March and May, and the panoramic views of the Taipei Basin from the top.

Hiking trails crisscross the mountain, but the easiest way to climb the main peak is to start from **Lingyun Temple** (凌雲禪寺; *língyún chán sì*) on the south side and end up in Bali, where there are plenty of places to eat and you can catch the ferry back to Danshui. From Lingyun Temple it's 2km to the top via a well-signposted stone path that passes the larger **Lingyun Chan** (**Zen**) **Temple** (凌雲禪寺; *língyúnchán sì*), built in 1882 but now looking a bit like a car park – its 11m statue of Guanyin in the main hall is one of Taiwan's largest. More rewarding is the **Guanyinshan visitor centre** (觀音山游遊客中心; *guānyīnshān yóukè zhōngxīn*; daily 9am–5pm; free; ☎02/2292-8888), which has friendly English-speaking guides, an exhibition room and video presentations on the mountain's volcanic origins, temples and history. The centre is another 1km along the road from Lingyun Temple, or an energetic 1.1km detour from the main trail down a steep path – you'll have to walk back the same way to reach the peak.

The summit of Guanyinshan is known as **"Tough Man Peak"** (硬漢嶺; *yìnghànlǐng*) to encourage the scores of young army recruits that once trained here. It's actually 609m high, but the Yinghan Monument on top adds another 3m. From here it's 4.6km straight down to Bali Wharf along similarly well-marked paths and lanes – you should emerge on the main Bali highway where you turn left and walk a further 600m to the narrow lane leading to the wharf on the right.

Practicalities

To reach the southern slopes of Guanyinshan, take Sanchong **bus #1205** from Tacheng Street in Taipei, just north of Zhongxiao Road and the North Gate in Zhongzheng district. Buses depart from 6.40am daily (every 40–50min; 1hr; NT$48). The final stop is Lingyun Temple – going the other way buses depart at similar intervals until 6.10pm. Bring food with you.

Yingge

Just 20km south of the capital, the historic town of **YINGGE** (鶯歌; *yīnggē*) is best known today as Taiwan's premier **ceramics** manufacturing centre, overflowing with over eight hundred ceramic shops and factories.

The industry was founded by a Fujian immigrant called **Wu An** – legend has it that he recognized the quality of the local soil in 1805 and invited his relatives to join him in a pottery-making venture. The Wu family dominated production thereafter, until the Jianshan Ceramic Cooperative broke their monopoly in 1921 and the Japanese introduced modern kilns in the 1930s. Yingge boomed in the postwar period but like many traditional industries in Taiwan, declined in the 1980s, with tourism and the art trade keeping the dollars flowing today.

Fifteen minutes' walk from the train station, **Yingge Ceramics Museum** at 200 Wenhua Road (鶯歌陶瓷博物館; *yīnggē táocí bówùguǎn*; Tues–Fri 9.30am–5pm, Sat & Sun 9.30am–6pm; NT$100; ☎02/8677-2727, ⊛www.ceramics.tpc.gov.tw) tells you everything you'd ever want to know about Yingge's history and ceramics in general, with an additional exhibition on future prospects and the use of ceramics in advanced technology – everything has bilingual labels. To **get here** from the station, turn right after leaving the turnstiles, following the signs to "Wunhua Road", then turn right again when you exit the station – keep walking till you reach a crossroads. Turn left here (it's still Wenhua Road) and the museum is beyond the garage on the right-hand side.

Leaving the museum, head back to the crossroads and continue under the railway bridge, taking the first left up a gentle slope: this is Jianshanpu Road, otherwise known as **Yingge Old Street** (鶯歌老街; *yīnggē lǎojiē*) and the birthplace of Yingge ceramics, though you won't see any old buildings here. Despite the palm trees and paved road it's just a modern strip of pottery shops and snack stalls. Nevertheless, it is one of the best places in Taiwan to stock up on ceramics.

Practicalities

Getting to Yingge is easy: take any **train** heading south from Taipei Station (NT$40) – the only trains that don't stop are the express services. Moving on to **Sanxia**, the **bus** from Taoyuan stops at the station's Wenhua Road exit (every 15–20min daily 6.10am–10.30pm; NT$26) and takes ten minutes, but you can also catch Taipei Bus #702 from the stop close to the ceramics museum further along Wenhua Road. **Taxis** to Sanxia from Yingge station cost around NT$200.

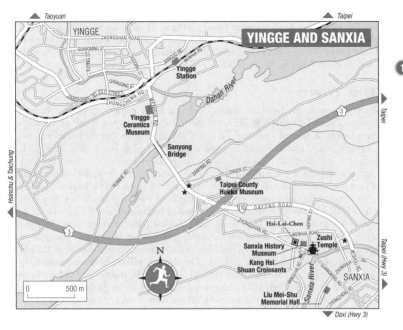

Sanxia

Three kilometres south of Yingge across the Dahan River, **SANXIA** (三峽; *sānxiá*) is the home of one of Taiwan's most striking temples, a stylish museum and an atmospheric old street. In the nineteenth century the town emerged as an important distribution centre for camphor and tea along the banks of the Sanxia River, later developing its own cloth-dyeing industry. By the 1970s these trades were in decline, and though agriculture is still an important part of the local economy, tourism has provided a much-needed boost.

Before you reach Sanxia proper, it's worth stopping at the **Taipei County Hakka Museum** (台北縣客家文化園區; *táiběi xiàn kèjiā wénhuà yuán qū*; Tues–Fri 9am–5pm, Sat & Sun 9am–6pm; free), located on the outskirts of town: if you're taking the bus from Yingge get off just after the Dahan Bridge and turn left down Longen Street – the museum is five minutes away. The museum is really a lavish Hakka (see p.154) cultural centre, with one very creative gallery blending multi-media installations with glass-cased exhibits, and a couple of temporary exhibition rooms. It's best to visit at the weekends, when the **performance centre** hosts various dramas, dancing and singing shows in the Hakka language. To get into town from here, you'll have to walk back to the bus stop or flag down a taxi.

Arrival

Sanxia is close enough to Yingge to walk but don't try it – there's no footpath on Sanying Bridge. **Buses** from Yingge or Taipei should drop you on Fuxing or Wenhua roads just north of the Sanxia River, from where it's a short walk to the temple and Old Street.

Sanxia is also easy to reach from **Taipei**: take the MRT to **Yongning Station**, take exit 4 and catch one of the frequent #275, #705, #706, #812, #916 and #922 buses to Sanxia (NT$15; EasyCard accepted). All buses are marked in

English and take around fifteen to twenty minutes. If you have more time, you can also connect with buses to **Daxi** (p.144) in Sanxia – catch bus #9103 from Wenhua Road (every 30min; NT$42; 25–30min). Heading back to Taipei from Sanxia, you can catch buses on Wenhua Road.

The Town

Tucked away in the heart of Sanxia, and facing the river in front of Changfu Bridge, **Zushi Temple** (祖師廟; *zǔshī miào*; daily 4am–11pm) is one of Taiwan's most beautiful. It's not far from "old street" (Minquan Street) at the end of narrow Changfu Street, and dedicated to popular deity Qingshui (see p.405). Though it lacks the grandeur and scale of larger temples, its lavish decor and intricate craftsmanship make this a unique showcase for temple art – for many connoisseurs it's the finest on the island. Though the temple dates from 1769 it has been rebuilt three times – the most recent renovation began in 1947 and is still ongoing. The **Main Hall** housing Qingshui's image is flanked by shrines to the Moon Goddess (*tàiyīn niángniáng*) on the left (West) and Sun God (*tàiyáng xīngjūn*) on the right (East). The key here is attention to detail: the temple beams are plastered in intricate carvings covered in real gold foil and it's one of the few shrines in Taiwan to use **bronze sculptures** throughout. The **dragon pillars** here are particularly ornate: there are supposed to be an incredible 156 inside, though not all have been completed – the six pillars in the central courtyard are regarded as the finest examples. If you're in Taiwan around Chinese New Year, try and visit on Lunar January 6 – the **festival** marking Qingshui's birthday is particularly colourful.

Minquan Street lies 50m behind the temple, and south of here this becomes Sanxia's pedestrianzied "**old street**" with most of the more than one hundred redbrick shop fronts dating from the late nineteenth century. The Chinese Baroque architecture on display is extremely photogenic, but the street is lined shops selling mostly kitsch gifts and snacks. Retrace your steps north and turn left at Zhongshan Road: the **Sanxia History Museum** (三峽鎮歷史博物館; *sānxiázhèn lìshǐ bówùguǎn*; daily 9am–5pm; free) is at no. 18, located in a 72-year-old shophouse. The museum provides an interesting introduction to the town's history, though it's only worth a visit if you can read Chinese.

Eating

The latest slightly bizarre **food** fad to hit Sanxia is the "**croissant**" (*jīnniújué*) – Taiwan-style of course. These are more like buttery rolls shaped like cow horns than the Parisian version, and are available stuffed with a variety of fillings like red bean, plum and peanut (NT$22–25).The main purveyor of croissants (complete with servers wearing cow-horn hats), with branches on "old street" and all over town, is *Kang Hsi Shuan Croissants* (康喜軒金牛角; *kāngxǐxuān jīniújiǎo*). Otherwise *Hsi-Lai-Chen* (喜徕珍古井餐廳; *xǐláizhēn gǔjǐng cāntīng*; daily 11am–9pm; ☎02/8671-1798) at 40 Zhongshan Rd is the most atmospheric

Getting to Wulai

To get to Wulai from Taipei, head for **Xindian MRT Station** (final stop on the green line) and turn right at the main exit to the bus stop just outside. **Bus #1601** to Wulai (marked in English) passes every twenty minutes (daily 5.30am–9.30pm; 30min; NT$40 or EasyCard plus NT$25). **Taxis** are a bit of a rip-off unless you have a group: they charge NT$600 from Xindian; once in Wulai it's NT$240 to the cable car and NT$360 to Neidong.

restaurant in central Sanxia. It occupies an old shophouse and serves excellent green tea and light meals (NT$90 for a small pot).

Wulai

Lying in a valley 25km south of Taipei, **WULAI** (烏來; *wūlái*) is another popular day-trip from the capital, offering magnificent mountain scenery and northern Taiwan's highest **waterfall**. It's also a traditional home of the **Atayal** tribe, though the mixture of kitsch stores and dance shows on offer are aimed squarely at tourists. The **museum** is definitely worth a visit though, and a short walk beyond the tourist carnival lie quiet valleys and rivers offering some beautiful **hikes** and genuine Atayal villages. Wulai is also one of three popular **hot-spring** areas near Taipei (with Beitou and Yangmingshan), though the main difference here is that it doesn't have that rotten egg smell. "Wulai" loosely translates as "hot spring", and comes from the Atayal word *urai* meaning poisonous.

Hot springs and accommodation

Hot springs are big business in Wulai, and most spas double as hotels – the cheapest places line Wulai "old street", but these often have only indoor baths. *Xiaochuanyuan Hot Springs* at 32 Wulai Old St (小川園溫泉; *xiǎochuānyuán wēnquán*; ☏02/2661-6222) has older, tiled indoor pools for men and women, but it's not bad for a soak (daily 8am–midnight; NT$300). The free **public hot springs** by the river (see p.120) are mixed and open-air so you'll need a swim suit, while for unabashed luxury the *Spring Park Urai Spa & Resort* at 3, Yanti Village (春秋烏來; *chūnqiū wūlái*; ☏02/2661-6555, ⓦ www .springparkhotel.com.tw; ❾) is hard to beat, with Japanese-inspired rooms and private spas overlooking the river. **Day-guests** can pay NT$1200 for one hour in a private bathhouse with a view (for two people), or NT$1000 per day (8am–midnight) for use of the lavish pools. The bus passes the hotel about 500m before the terminus.

▲ *Taipei*

WULAI

0   200 m

Ⓐ

Bus Terminus

Wulai Village

● Wulai Atayal Museum
● ①
Ⓑ

Lake Old St

Tonghou River

Public Hot Spring Pools

Railway Station ●②

Wenshan Street

Nanshi River

Wulai Log Cart

N

ACCOMMODATION
Spring Park Urai Spa & Resort   A
Xiaochuanyuan Hot Springs   B

Puru Rd (Flowers' Walk)

Railway Terminus

WULAI SPECIAL SCENIC AREA

Cable Car Station

Wulai Log Cart Museum

●③

ⓘ ● Wulai Falls

▲ *Doll Valley*

Cable Car Station

Yunsian Dreamland
Ⓐ

RESTAURANTS & CAFÉS
Aboriginal Restaurant   3
Helen Coffee   2
Taiya Popo Restaurant   1
Yun Hsien Resort   4

119

Wulai Old Street

The bus from Taipei terminates right in front of **Wulai Village** – cross the bridge over the Tonghou River ahead to run the gauntlet of tourist shops, snack stalls and gift stores on **Wulai "old street"** (烏來老街; *wūlái lǎojiē*). This is where most of Wulai's cheaper accommodation and spas are located, while the **Wulai Atayal Museum** (烏來泰雅博物館; *wūlái tàiyǎ bówùguǎn*; Tues–Fri 9.30am–5pm, Sat–Sun 9.30am–6pm; NT$50) is an absorbing introduction to the valley and the people that once dominated the area. Its three floors focus on the history, architecture and culture of the tribe, with explanations in English. Highlights include a collection of huge curved Atayal hunting knives and a description of "*tuxan*", the Atayal system of spiritual belief.

At the end of the main street you'll come to a second bridge over the wider **Nanshi River**, from where Wulai's **public hot-spring pools** (free) are clearly visible on the far right bank – the pools are carved into the rocks along the riverside and tend to get very busy.

Wulai Special Scenic Area

From the Nanshi bridge you can walk 1.6km to the falls and the **Wulai Special Scenic Area** (烏來風景特定區 烏來瀑布; *wūlái fēngjǐng tèdìngqū*) in around twenty minutes, or take the five-minute trip on the **Wulai Log Cart** (烏來台車; *wūlái táichē*; daily 8am–5pm; NT$50 one-way), a miniature train located up the flight of steps next to *Helen Coffee*. Tiny trains holding up to twenty people run every few minutes along old tram tracks, built by Japanese forestry companies in the 1920s. If you are walking, the road is rarely crowded – after passing a row of hotels and spas it rises along the side of a deep and preciptious gorge smothered in jungle (this section has been dubbed "**Lovers' Walk**"). Just after you first spot the falls you'll come to the train terminus and the second tourist village – the view of **Wulai Falls** (烏來瀑布; *wūlái pùbù*) on the far bank is certainly picturesque, and at 80m it's northern Taiwan's highest, but it's best seen during the rainy season. By 2011 the **Wulai Log Cart Museum** (烏來台車博物館; *wūlái táichē bówùguǎn*) should be open overlooking the river, a smart new gallery highlighting the history of the track and the area.

The *Aboriginal Restaurant* at 12 Pubu Rd (原住民美食餐廳; *yuánzhùmín měishí cāntīng*; marked in Chinese only) hosts lively **dance performances** upstairs twice a day (10.40am & 2pm; NT$350; ☏02/2661-6551) – tickets can be purchased from the booth near the stone steps. The **cable car** station (daily 8.30am–10pm; NT$220 return), a short walk up the steps, glides across the river to **Yunsian Dreamland** (雲仙樂園; *yúnxiān lèyuán*; daily 8.30am–10pm; entry with cable car ticket) on top of the waterfall – an odd and rather faded mixture of theme park rides and gardens firmly targeted at families, tour groups and dating couples. The *Yun Hsien Resort* (☏02/2661-6383, ⓦwww.yun-hsien.com.tw; ❼) on site is expensive, but once the day-trippers leave it becomes a tranquil retreat: come midweek and all you'll hear are the sounds of running water and the mountain forest.

You'll find Wulai's **visitor information centre** (daily 8.30am–5pm; ☏02/2661-635), beyond the cable car station back on the village side, but it only stocks basic information.

Doll Valley

Walk a few minutes upstream from the falls and you'll leave most of the tourists behind. Scenic **Doll Valley** (娃娃谷; *wáwágǔ*) is a pleasant hour-long hike from here, along the edge of an increasingly wild and lush gorge. The name has nothing to do with dolls; one theory is that it's a corruption of the original

Chinese name "Frog Valley" – the Chinese characters for Doll Valley are very similar. Follow the main road along the Nanshi River for about twenty minutes from Wulai Falls until you reach the pedestrian suspension bridge and cross to the other side – from here the path follows the left bank of the river through **Xinxian** village, to another road and eventually the car park in front of **Neidong National Forest Recreation Area** (內洞國家森林遊樂區; *nèidòng guójiā sēnlín yóulè qū*; daily 8am–5pm; NT$80). Once you've paid the entrance fee, the path passes the **Xinxian Falls** (信賢瀑布; *xìnxián pùbù*) on the right bank, before continuing past a dam and on to the mouth of **Doll Valley** itself, containing the middle and upper **Neidong Falls** (內洞瀑布; *nèidòng pùbù*) in a gorge off the main river. It's become a popular spot for swimming in recent years, but during the week it shouldn't be too busy. From here it's possible to follow paths further up the valley to the top of the falls, though you have to return to Wulai via the same route.

Eating and drinking

Beyond the hotel restaurants, the most convenient **food** options are located in the two tourist areas. On Wulai "old street", the Atayal-run *Taiya Popo Restaurant* (泰雅婆婆美食店; *tàiyǎ pópó měishídiàn*; ☏0939/1866-246) at no. 14 (marked "Tayan Aboriginal Shop" in English), with its bamboo decor, is one of the better places to eat, though all the restaurants nearby serve up the same dishes: rice stuffed into bamboo tubes (*zhútǒnggfàn*; NT$50–70), fried or barbecued "mountain pig" (*shānzhū*; NT$100), fried fish and shrimp (NT$100), millet cakes (*mua-ji*; NT$100/box) and lots of green vegetables, all nominally aboriginal fare and very tasty.

Helen Coffee at 1 Lane 86, Wenquan Rd, on the other side of the Nanshi bridge (daily 8am–5pm; ☏02/2661-6392), has a lovely terrace overlooking the river, with coffee and tea from NT$90.

Southeast of Taipei

Taiwan's mountainous interior begins just beyond Taipei's southern suburbs, making the valleys southeast of the capital the easiest way to get a sense of its rural hinterland. **Shenkeng** is a short bus ride from city and best known for its **tofu** dishes, while the village of **Pinglin** is further south, surrounded by picturesque tea plantations and hiking trails.

Shenkeng

The old town of **SHENKENG** (深坑; *shēnkēng*) is an excellent place to gorge on Taiwanese delicacies. It's easy to get here by bus: #660 and #251 stop on the opposite side of Muzha Road from the Muzha MRT Station between around 5.30am and 10.30pm and take ten to fifteen minutes (NT$15). Most of the action takes place along "**old street**", close to the bus stop and marked by a 100-year-old banyan tree at its entrance. The street does have a few old buildings and storefronts, but it's principally noted for its gift shops and especially for its food. The chief specialty here is **tofu**, served up in a bewildering number of ways from huge vats of stewed tofu (*hóngshāo dòufǔ*) to tofu ice cream (*dòufǔ bīngqílín*). There are plenty of restaurants to choose from – no. 138–140 is one of the better options but they're all pretty good. Bamboo shoots (*lù zhúsǔn*) are another specialty.

Pinglin

The small town of **PINGLIN** (坪林; *pínglín*) feels a million miles from Taipei, even with a steady trickle of tour buses rattling along its main street. In fact, it's only 20km from the edge of the city via the new Taipei–Yilan Highway. Located at the bottom of the Beishi River valley it makes a good day-trip but is also the centre of an attractive region of hiking trails and smaller sights that really require your own transport (or bike) to explore fully. Pinglin is famous principally for its tea, much of which is **Bāozhǒng** oolong – you can see acres of tea bushes lining the hills that surround the town.

The **Pinglin Tea Museum** (坪林茶葉博物館; *pínglín cháyè bówùguǎn*; Tues–Fri 9am-5pm, Sat & Sun 8am–6pm; NT$100; ☎02/2665-6035) is the town's main attraction and a good introduction to everything connected with tea in Taiwan. From the bus station keep walking along the street and you'll see the museum on the other side of the river. For cheaper tea and food (fried **freshwater shrimps** and **fish** are the specialities here) head back to the main street where there is a huge choice of restaurants lining the roadside – most main dishes cost between NT$50 and NT$80.

Unless new services start to use the highway, Pinglin will continue to be a long and winding hour-and-a-half ride from Taipei: **bus #1602** is operated by the Xindian bus company from the stop outside the Government Insurance Building on Gongyuan Road (take exit 8 from Taipei Main Station MRT). It's faster to catch the same bus outside Xindian MRT Station (NT$96); turn right at the main exit and the bus stop is just ahead on the main road.

The **He Huan Campground** (合歡露營渡假山莊; *héhuān lùyíng dùjià shānzhuāng*; ☎02/26656424) at 5-1 Shuide Village is a twenty-minute walk along the south side of the river from the tea museum, and bikes can be hired for NT$80 per hour from here – Pinglin's **cycling trails** are worth exploring if you have time. There are also plenty of homestays in the area – ask at the museum.

Travel details

Buses

Taipei to: Jinshan (daily; 1hr); Kaohsiung (frequent; 5hr 30min); Keelung (frequent; 1hr); Lugang (8 daily; 3hr 30min); Pingxi (hourly; 40min); Puli (10 daily; 3hr); Sanxia (frequent; 40min); Sun Moon Lake (10 daily; 4hr); Taichung (frequent; 2hr); Tainan (frequent; 4hr 30min); Taiwan Taoyuan International Airport (daily; 45min–1hr); Wulai (daily; 40min); Yeliu (40min).
Danshui to: Baishawan (hourly; 20min); Jinshan (hourly; 1hr); Shimen (hourly; 40min).

Flights

Songshan Airport to: Chiayi (10 daily; 45min); Hengchun (3 daily; 1hr 10min); Hualien (13 daily; 35min); Kaohsiung (40 daily; 50min); Kinmen (17 daily; 1hr); Magong (20 daily, 45min); Matsu (Nangan, 9 daily; 50min; Beigan, 3 daily; 50min); Pingdong (3 daily; 1hr); Taichung (5 daily; 35min); Tainan (15 daily; 45min); Taitung (7 daily; 50min).

Trains

Taipei Station to: Changhua (18 express daily; 2hr 20min); Chiayi (High Speed every 30min; 1hr 40min); Fulong (9 express daily; 1hr 5min); Hsinchu (High Speed every 30min; 34min); Hualien (14 express daily; 2hr 50min); Kaohsiung (High Speed every 30min; 1hr 30min–2hr); Keelung (frequent; 40min); Sanyi (6 daily; 2hr 20min); Taichung (High Speed every 30min; 50min–1hr 5min); Tainan (High Speed every 30min; 1hr 48min); Taitung (6 express daily; 5hr); Yilan (17 express daily; 1hr 30min); Yingge (frequent; 25min).

North Taiwan

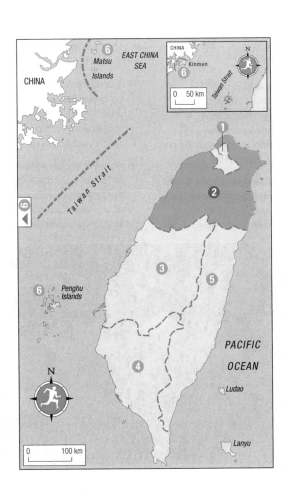

EAST CHINA SEA

CHINA

Matsu Islands

CHINA

Kinmen

Taiwan Strait

N

0   50 km

Taiwan Strait

PACIFIC

OCEAN

Penghu Islands

N

Ludao

Lanyu

0   100 km

CHAPTER 2 # Highlights

* **Yeliu Geopark** View the geological oddities peppering this jagged outcrop on the north coast. See p.130

* **Keelung Night Market** One of the island's best night markets, rich in seafood, tasty rice noodles and mouthwatering fruit ice stalls. See p.134

* **Jinguashi** Explore the narrow hillside streets of this old mining town, or hike up Mount Keelung for spectacular views of the north coast. See p.138

* **Northeast and Yilan Coast National Scenic Area** Some of Taiwan's most dramatic coastline is contained within this scenic area, with cliff-top trails, picturesque beaches and a top-notch surfing destination. See p.142

* **Hakka culture** Beipu and Shengxing are enchanting places to absorb Hakka culture, feast on excellent food and enjoy some *léichá* or "cereal tea". See p.154

* **Taian Hot Springs** Soak up one of Taiwan's most attractive hot-spring resorts, tucked away in the hills of Miaoli county. See p.159

* **Shei-Pa National Park** Home to Taiwan's second-highest mountain, Xueshan, the apex of an extraordinary massif of tantalizing peaks. See p.164

▲ Worshippers at a Hakka festival near Hsinchu

North Taiwan

N orth Taiwan is the most scenically varied part of the country. Wild terrain, fierce indigenous tribes and even wilder weather terrified early settlers, making it one of the last parts of the island to be colonized by the Chinese. In 1949 the region was swamped by a huge influx of refugees from China, and today its jam-packed cities contain more Mandarin-speaking "mainlanders" and their descendants than anywhere else in Taiwan, providing a high proportion of Kuomintang (KMT; see p.389) support.

The region encompasses Hsinchu, Miaoli, Taoyuan, Taipei and Yilan counties, part of a densely populated **urban corridor** stretching from Keelung on the northeast coast to the fast-expanding cities of Taoyuan and Zhongli further west. Proximity to the capital makes the whole area highly accessible and much of it can be visited as a series of extended day-trips. Beyond this urban core lies a **dramatic coastline**, one of the north's most appealing features: the **North Coast and Guanyinshan National Scenic Area** and, further south, the **Northeast and Yilan Coast National Scenic Area** offer spectacular scenery and some decent beaches. Between the two areas, the port city of **Keelung** is set in a strategic harbour surrounded by ruined fortresses and is home to Taiwan's best night market, as well as its biggest annual Ghost Festival. Inland, the **Pingxi Branch Rail Line** winds its way through a lush mountain valley, past scenic **Shifen Falls** and **Pingxi** itself, home of Taiwan's most magical event, the release of hundreds of "heavenly lanterns" during the **Lantern Festival**. Nearby, the once booming mining towns of **Jiufen** and **Jinguashi** have been reinvented as tourist attractions, sporting atmospheric teahouses, snack stalls and museums.

Heading south, Hsinchu and Miaoli counties form the **Hakka heartland** of Taiwan, with **Beipu** providing ample opportunity to experience Hakka food and culture, and **Sanyi**, renowned as the country's foremost woodcarving centre. But beyond all of this, and never far from view, lies an untamed interior of giant peaks and isolated valleys, home to the awe-inspiring **Shei-Pa National Park** and **Taian Hot Springs**, a tranquil spa retreat surrounded by great hiking country and Atayal tribal villages. With more time and preferably your own transport, you can traverse the winding **Northern Cross-Island Highway**, connecting the historic streets of Daxi with Yilan on the east coast. **Yilan county** contains a handful of worthwhile stops, especially the plunging **Wufongqi Waterfalls**.

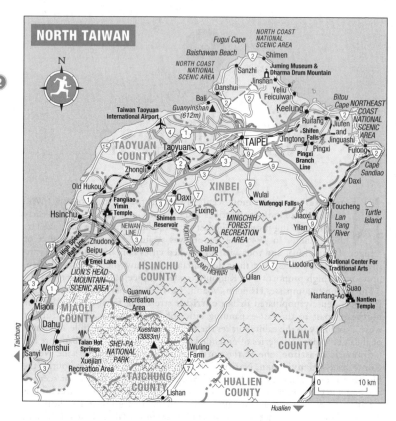

North Coast and Guanyinshan National Scenic Area

Taiwan's rugged coastline between Danshui (see p.110) and Keelung falls within the **North Coast and Guanyinshan National Scenic Area** (北海岸及觀音山國家風景區; *běihǎiàn jí guānyīn guójiāfēngjǐngqū*), easily accessible from Taipei and a popular destination for day-trips (Guanyinshan itself is covered on p.115). The northeast corner has the best scenery, with highlights including the **Dharma Drum Mountain** monastery, **Yeliu Geopark's** fascinating rock formations and the entrancing modern sculptures at the **Juming Museum**.

Sanzhi

The first major stop north of Danshui is the small agricultural town of **SANZHI** (三芝; *sānzhī*) a tea- and rice-growing area best explored with your own transport. The **Sanzhi Visitor Center** (三芝遊客中心; *sānzhī yóukè zhōngxīn*; daily 9am–5pm; ℡02/8635-3640) is 2km east of the town and home to a couple of enlightening museums, both with English labelling. The first recounts the history of the area and includes a section on the north coast's earliest inhabitants, the Ketagalan (see p.396), while the **Gallery of Famous Sons** commemorates the town's most respected former residents, in particular **Lee Teng-hui**, Taiwan's first democratically elected president (see p.392). Across the park at the back of the centre is the **Yuanxing Residence** (源興居, *yuánxīngjū*) , the traditional three-sided home where Lee was born. You can usually peek inside the simple central room (daily 9am–5pm), but the rest of the house remains private. Most buses stop on Provincial Highway 2 on the western side of town – to avoid a long take a taxi from Danshui.

Baishawan

BAISHAWAN (白沙灣; *báishāwān*) is a popular beach destination, just twenty minutes north of Danshui by bus and 3km from Sanzhi (NT$23). It's free, has the finest sand on the north coast and from May to September is home to regular beach parties featuring top-notch DJs. **Summer Aquarian** (Ⓦ www.summer-aquarian .com; NT$500–800) is the biggest, a slick annual event held at various beaches along the coast. There's not much point visiting during the cooler months, however, although the main scenic area **visitor centre** (daily 9am–5pm; Ⓣ 02/26364503, Ⓦ www.northguan-nsa.gov.tw) is at its northern end. Buses stop next to the row of shops and snack stalls on the road behind the beach.

Fugui Cape

The next major stop after Baishawan, **Fugui Cape** (富貴角; *fùguìjué*) is Taiwan's most northerly point, a rugged headland topped by a stumpy 14m lighthouse. The nearest bus stop is on the main road, a few minutes' walk from **Fuji Fishing Harbour** (富基漁港; *fùjī yúgǎng*), a compact and ramshackle dock crammed with fishing boats. A lively fish market (daily 10am–8pm) hugs the quayside, and there's a row of popular **seafood restaurants** nearby. The cape is a short walk from the back of the harbour, along the rocky coastline. The **lighthouse** 富貴角燈塔 *fùguìjué dēngtǎ* was built in 1949 and is off limits, as is the military radar station nearby, but the trail offers wide ocean views and a chance to gaze at the cape itself, a battered jumble of rocks below the headland often littered with driftwood.

Shimen

Another 4km beyond Fugui Cape, **SHIMEN** (石門; *shímén*) is Taiwan's most northerly village and a convenient lunch stop. The main street is lined with stalls selling the local specialty, *ròuzòng* (rice dumplings with chicken and mushroom, wrapped in bamboo leaves; NT$20–25); the best place to sample them is *Liu Family Rouzong* (劉家肉粽; *liújiā ròuzòng*) at 30 Zhongyang Rd (Ⓣ 02/2638-1088),

---

Getting around the north coast

From Taipei, take the MRT to **Danshui** (p.110) where **buses** ply Provincial Highway 2 to Keelung (#1262; daily 5.50am–8.30pm; every 20–30min; NT$171), stopping at all the main sights including Sanzhi (NT$34), Baishawan (NT$53), Shimen (NT$67), Jinshan (NT$107) and Yeliu (NT$125), while another service, stopping at the same places, terminates at Jinshan (#1267; every 30min; daily 5.40am–9.30pm). You can use your EasyCard on these buses.

There's also the #1815 Kuo Kuang bus from **Taipei West Bus Station** to *Jinshan Youth Activity Center* (daily 5.40am–10.40pm; every 10–20min; NT$125), which stops at Yeliu (NT$96) and Jinshan (NT$120); some of these buses terminate at Dharma Drum Mountain (NT$135), so check before you get on (see p.103). See p.134 for connections from Keelung.

with its special minced radish recipe. On the eastern side of Shimen lies the topographic feature that gave the village its name ("Stone Gate"), the **Shimen Cave** (石門洞; *shímén dòng*) a naturally eroded stone arch, just off the beach.

Just under 4km east of the village, the **Temple of Eighteen Lords** (十八王公廟 *shíbā wánggōng miào*; daily, 24hr) is a tiny shrine swathed in gold leaf and surrounded by a throng of small stalls and trinket sellers. It's a short walk from the bus stop on the main road, behind the highway bridge. Despite its size, this is one of the most popular temples on the north coast – not least because worshipping here is supposed to bring good luck when it comes to gambling or playing the lottery. Several legends are associated with the site, the official one being that the shrine was established in the late Qing dynasty to commemorate the faithful **dog** (the eighteenth "lord") of one of seventeen fishermen drowned at sea. When the bodies of the men were washed ashore near Shimen, the dog was miraculously still alive, but, overcome with grief, it threw itself into its master's tomb as a sign of loyalty.

The **tomb** representing the eighteen is to the left side of the main hall, lined with cigarettes placed here for the fishermen's spirits to smoke, but to get a piece of the money-making action you'll need to get your hands on one of two bronze dog statues guarding them; touch the dog's mouth for general good luck, its feet for great wealth and the head to ensure your children grow up extra smart. Note that this tomb is a recently built reproduction – the real one is behind the shrine in the basement.

Jinshan and around

JINSHAN (金山; *jīnshān*), 12km south of Shimen (bus NT$40), is the largest town on the north coast and a good place to grab lunch or take a dip in one of its numerous hot-spring resorts. The town sits behind a small promontory that divides its two popular but unexceptional beaches. Running parallel to the east of the main thoroughfare, Zhongshan Road, is Jinshan's "old street", also known as **Jinbaoli Street** (金包裡老街; *jīnbāolǐ lǎojiē*) to commemorate the Ketagalan name for the area, and once the site of a busy riverside dock. Few old buildings remain, but it's a pleasant place to browse (the town is noted for its traditional cakes, wooden shoes and baked sweet potatoes and yams). The Traditional Medicine store at no. 26, and rice shop at no. 28 are its best examples of early twentieth-century architecture.

At the southern end of Jinbaoli Street is **Cihu Temple** (慈護宮; *cíhùgōng*; daily 5am–9pm), established in 1809 and dedicated to Mazu – it's the biggest temple on the north coast, containing a plethora of statues and one central gold-faced image of the main deity. The temple faces Minsheng Road, and turning left here takes you towards the beach – hail a cab or catch any bus that's heading this way if you don't fancy the 1.2-km walk over the hill. The road forks a short distance ahead; the left-hand road passes the **Jinshan Visitor Center** (金山遊客中心; *jīnshān yóukè zhōngxīn*; daily 9am–5pm; ☎02/2492-2016), which can provide local maps. At the end of this road is **New Jinshan Beach** (新金山海水浴場; *xīnjīnshān hǎishuǐyùchǎng*; June–Sept daily 8am–6pm; NT$100), managed by the *Jinshan Youth Activity Center* (金山青年活動中心; *jīnshān qīngnián huódòng zhōngxīn*; see opposite). The beach is no tropical paradise however, with Mandopop blaring out of strategically-placed speakers, and crowds of students enjoying various activities in midsummer, but the massive **public hot-spring pools** (Tues–Fri 7am–10.30pm, Sat & Sun 7am–10pm), are reasonably priced at NT$250 (NT$300 weekends and holidays).

The right-hand fork along Minsheng Road leads to Shuiwei Fishing Port (水尾 漁港; *shuǐwěi yúgǎng*) on the south side of the promontory, and **Old Jinshan Beach** or Jiatou Xialiao Beach (加投下寮海灘; *jiātóu xiàliáo hǎitān*), which is free, but often littered with flotsam. The best thing here is the *San Francisco Governor Hot Spring Resort* at 196 Minsheng Rd (舊金山總督溫泉; *jiùjīnshān zǒngdū wēnquán*; daily 9am–midnight, ☏02/2408-2628), housed in a grey Japanese-era building built in 1938. The second-floor **restaurant** (daily 11am–10pm) is a decent place to have lunch, while the attractive outdoor pools cost NT$500 (there's no accommodation).

Practicalities

Buses from Danshui and Keelung stop on Zhongshan Road in the centre of town, while bus #1815 from Taipei terminates just outside the large grey reception building of *Jinshan Youth Activity Center* near the beach (☏02/2498-1190, ⓦchinshan.cyh.org.tw; ❼). The centre offers a range of chalet accommodation, all clean and fairly spacious. **Camping** (tent provided) costs NT$800, or NT$500 with your own tent, while hot meals are available in the reception building.

The local specialty is **duck noodles**; you'll find them served in the bustling forecourt of **Guangan Temple** (廣安宮; *guǎngāngōng*; daily 9am–7.30pm), halfway along Jinbaoli Street (no. 104). Plates of duck, with special plum sauce and fresh ginger, as well as fried prawns, noodles and bamboo shoots cost NT$60 to NT$120. Grab your food, then head to the three numbered eating areas further down the street. The stalls nearby serve up plenty of snacks: bags of sweet-potato cubes (in caramelized sugar; NT$50), potato crisps (from NT$80) and bags of crispy sesame balls (*málǎo*; NT$100) – try *Lion Grove* at 92 Jinbaoli St (獅子林餅舖; *shīzilín bǐngpù*).

Dharma Drum Mountain

Beautifully located in the hills above Jinshan, around 3km from the centre of town, **Dharma Drum Mountain** (法鼓山; *fǎgǔshān*; daily 8am–4pm; free; ⓦwww .ddm.org.tw) is an absorbing Buddhist educational complex and monastery with extensive gardens. Established in 1989 by respected monk and scholar Master Sheng Yen, it is Taiwan's newest Chan (Zen) Buddhist foundation. Visitors are welcome but it's best to email in advance if you require a **guided tour** in English (free).

From the main entrance, make your way up the hill to the Reception Hall where you'll find an information desk, gift shop and enthusiastic English-speaking volunteers. From here, you can walk across to the adjacent Main Building: the third floor contains the **Founding History Memorial Hall**, which uses a suitably futuristic blend of Buddhist relics and modern technology to recount the history of Buddhism and the life of Master Sheng Yen, while the Glories of Dharma Drum Mountain on the next floor up is a vast but rather hagiographical portrait of the founder and scenes from his life. Another highlight is the **Great Buddha Hall** in the main temple of the complex, with its imposing bronze images of Sakyamuni Buddha (centre), the Medicine Buddha (right) and Amitabha Buddha (left), backed by ornate canopies carved by Japanese craftsmen.

Commuter **buses** #829 and #828 connect the main entrance (a short walk from the Reception Hall) with Jinshan (NT$15) in the early mornings, departing from the latter at 8am, 8.35am, 9.15am and 9.55am, and returning at 7.45am, 8.20am, 9am and 9.40am. More usefully, there's a direct bus (#1815; 6.15am–9.15pm, 7 daily Mon–Fri, 13 daily Sat & Sun; 1hr 30min; NT$135) from Taipei West Bus Station. A taxi from Jinshan should cost NT$200.

Juming Museum

One of the highlights of the north coast, the **Juming Museum** (朱銘美術館; *zhūmíng měishùguǎn*; Tues–Sun 10am–6pm, Nov–April closes at 5pm; NT$250; ☏02/2498-9940, ⓦwww.juming.org.tw) lies over the ridge behind Dharma

Drum Mountain. Opened in 1999 by Ju Ming, Taiwan's most celebrated sculptor, it's more a sculpture park than a museum, with most exhibits displayed around a series of landscaped gardens and ponds – it's obviously best to visit on a fine day.

From the museum **service centre**, walk down through a gallery of paintings (including Andy Warhol's "Mao Tse-Tung") to the outdoor area. The first installations on display are usually taken from Ju Ming's **Living World Series**: anything from life-size parachutists cast in bronze to stainless steel swimmers (exhibits rotate). The real highlight however, is the sculptor's most famous work: thirty giant pieces of his extraordinary **Taichi Series**, a collection of huge, chunky figures created in the late 1970s and early 1980s. The abstract, faceless bronze forms manage to convey intense movement and the controlled energy of the Chinese martial art without resorting to minute detail. The museum's pyramid-shaped **Main Building** (closes 15min before the rest of the site) is where much of Ju Ming's early Nativist woodcarvings are displayed, along with work from Yu Yu Yang, his teacher; notable pieces include *Girl Playing with Sand*, created in 1961 using Ju Ming's wife as a model, and *In One Heart*, a vivid carving of a buffalo pulling a cart weighed down with logs. English-language documentaries about the sculptor are screened here throughout the day.

Special **buses** (Tues–Fri 10.30am & 2pm, returning 1.40pm & 5pm; Sat & Sun 10.30am, 12.30pm & 2pm, returning 1.40pm, 3.40pm & 5pm; free) run to the museum from Jinshan Township Office. **Taxis** from Jinshan should cost around NT$250. You can walk to Dharma Drum Mountain from here, though it's around 2km by road – ask staff to point out the short cut or call a taxi.

Tomb of Teresa Teng

Hugging the slopes above the Juming Museum, **Jinbaoshan Cemetery** (金寶山陵園; *jīnbǎoshānlíngyuán*; daily; 24hr) has become a pilgrimage site for music fans from all over the world, as the last resting place of **Teresa Teng** (*Dèng Lìjūn* in Chinese), one of the most famous Chinese pop singers of all time – she died tragically in 1995, after an asthma attack at the age of 43. Her tomb is often littered with flowers, while her memorial garden features a life-size statue and a giant electronic keyboard that can be "played" by stepping on the keys. Her ten most famous hits (including *Will You Come Back Again*) echo around the site on permanent loop.

Yeliu

Just to the north of the fishing village of **YELIU** (野柳; *yěliǔ*) lies **Yeliu Geopark** (野柳地質公園; *yěliǔ dìzhì gōngyuán*; daily 8am–6pm, Oct–April closes 5pm; NT$50; ☎02/2492-2016, ⓦwww.ylgeopark.org.tw), home to a series of bizarre geological formations. The park lies on Yeliu Cape and commands stunning views across the bay to Jinshan and Yangmingshan beyond – hike to the end of the headland and you'll usually have the place to yourself. Unique rock formations litter the cape, the result of years of weathering and seismic activity – the small **visitor centre** at the entrance shows twelve-minute English videos on the geology of the area. From here, well-marked trails lead along the 1.7km headland past all of the most famous formations: rocks that resemble tofu and ginger, the unique and mystifying candle rocks and the ubiquitous mushroom rocks, the most famous of which is the **Queen's Head** (女王頭; *nǚwángtóu*) – the original has become so weathered there's a fibre-glass replica.

Buses from Jinshan (NT$23) and Keelung (NT$47) stop on the main highway just outside the village – walk along the road to the right of the harbour, past the seafood restaurants till you reach the Geopark, a few minutes further on the left.

Keelung

The port city of **KEELUNG** (基隆; *jīlóng*), sandwiched between verdant mountains and northern Taiwan's best natural harbour, is a strategic location that has been fought over by foreign powers since the seventeenth century. Though it's a typically modern Taiwanese city, home to around 400,000 people, its setting is picturesque and there's plenty to see: numerous **fortresses**, a legacy of the city's violent past, the **Fairy Cave**, one of Taiwan's most atmospheric shrines, an easy-to-navigate **night market** and the country's largest and most illuminating **Ghost Festival**, held every August.

Some history

The **Spanish** first established an outpost on **Heping Island** near Keelung in 1626, when the area was inhabited by the **Ketagalan**, who called it "Kelang". In 1642 the Dutch kicked out the Spaniards after a bloody siege, but they abandoned their last stronghold in Taiwan in 1668. Chinese immigrants began to arrive in large numbers in 1723 and the town became an important **port** in the nineteenth century, making it a regular target for foreign powers; during the 1841 Opium War a British squadron shelled the harbour, while in the Sino-French War the city was occupied by the French for eight months. The harbour was almost completely destroyed by Allied bombing at the end of World War II, and the postwar years saw a gradual rebuilding of its facilities – it's now Taiwan's second-biggest container port after Kaohsiung.

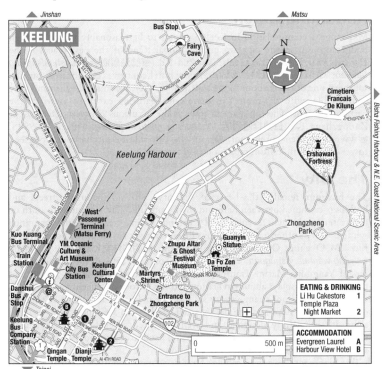

Arrival and information

Regular local train services from Taipei (40min; NT$43) arrive at the **train station**, conveniently located at the southwestern corner of the harbour. The main **bus stations** are all nearby. Keelung's useful **tourist information centre** (Mon–Fri 8.30am–5.30pm, Sat–Sun 9am–4pm; ☎02/2428-7664, ⓦtour.klcg .gov.tw) is on your right as you exit the train station and stocks plenty of English-language material – staff here can help with bus information and hotels. Chinatrust Commercial Bank has **ATMs** conveniently located in the train station and most 7-Elevens in town. Note that Keelung **street signs** are gradually being converted to *hànyǔ pīnyīn*, but you are likely to see some written in *tōngyòng* till at least 2012.

City transport

Central Keelung is best explored on foot, but to see everything you'll save time by using **local buses**. The **city bus station** is to the left of the train station as you exit. Bus #101 trundles along Zhongzheng Road beneath Ershawan Fortress, then on to Heping Island (every 10–12min; 5.50am–11.20pm); #103 goes to Bisha Fishing Harbour and Badouzi Seashore Park (every 10–12min; 5.50am–10.36pm); and #301 goes along the northern side of the harbour to Fairy Cave and Baimiwang Fort (every 20–25min; 5.50am–11.20pm). Buses cost NT$15 per journey – use your **EasyCard** (p.63) or make sure you have change. Taxis are available from the train station, but negotiate the fare in advance.

Accommodation

Mid-range accommodation in Keelung tends to be reasonably priced, though budget options in the city are unexceptional. One of the best places is the *Harbour View Hotel*, 108 Xiao (Siao) 2nd Rd (華帥海景飯店; *huáshuài hǎijǐng fàndiàn*; ☎02/2422-3131, ⓦharborview.hotel.com.tw; ❹), located on the southern side of the harbour in the centre of the city. Rooms are stylish and very comfortable, with the more expensive ones featuring excellent views of the harbour at night. The top place in town is the luxurious *Evergreen Laurel*, 62-1 Zhongzheng Rd (長榮桂冠酒店; *chángróng guìguàn jiǔdiàn*; ☎02/2427-9988, ⓦwww.evergreen-hotels.com; ❼), on the east side of the harbour, its green tower clearly visible from most points in the city.

The City

The **harbour** remains the heart of the city, with all the main streets and buildings crammed between here and the mountains. The vibrant area south of the waterfront is where you'll find Keelung's shops, temples and restaurants, while the city's other main attractions lie either east or west of the port. Start at the **YM Oceanic Culture & Art Museum** (陽明海洋文化藝術館; *yángmíng hǎiyáng wénhuà yìshùguǎn*; Tues–Sun 9am–5pm; NT$50), in the old headquarters of Yangming Marine Transport Corp, just opposite the station. The second floor contains displays about navigation and the history of ancient vessels, while the other exhibitions change every six months and focus on a range of subjects connected with ships and the ocean, particularly with a Chinese or Taiwanese slant. It's beautifully designed and well presented: everything is labelled in English and there is an army of volunteers on hand to answer queries, though the video presentations are aimed more at children.

Two blocks southeast lies Keelung's busiest and most important place of worship, the **Qingan Temple** (慶安宮; *qìngān gōng*; daily 6am–10pm) – walk down Xiao

(Siao) 2nd Road from the harbour, turn left along Zhong 2nd Road and you'll see the temple courtyard on the right, lined with food stalls. Dedicated to Mazu, the temple was established in 1780 with the most recent renovation completed in 1999. In addition to numerous ancient Mazu deities (with gold, black and brown faces), check out the shrine to five gods of wealth on the second floor of the Rear Hall, to the right. You're supposed to put a few coins into the box to get the gods' attention, the idea being you need to "invest" to enlist their help in becoming rich.

Turn right when you exit the main gate and it's a couple more blocks to Keelung's best-known shrine, **Dianji Temple** (奠濟宮; *diànjì gōng*; daily 7am–10pm) on Ren 3rd Road, at the heart of the Temple Night Market (see p.134). Established in 1875 on the site of an older shrine to the Water God, the main hall dates from 1923 and is dedicated to the Sage King Kaizhang (*kāizhāng shèngwáng*) – his main image sits in the central shrine. The other main deity here is Marshal Tian Du (*tiándū yuánshuài*), symbolized by a statue on the second floor of the Rear Hall, an historical figure from the Tang dynasty and a patron of *xīpí* music, a branch of *běiguǎn* (traditional "northern" music).

Zhongzheng Park

Perched on the hills lining the east side of the harbour, the 22m white **Guanyin Statue** in **Zhongzheng Park** (中正公園; *zhōngzhèng gōngyuán*; 24hr) is the symbol of Keelung, and a good place to get a panoramic view of the city. The entrance to the park is on Xin 2nd Road, five minutes' walk east of the city's bulky Cultural Centre – the main trail passes several shrines and temples on the way up, skirting around the Martyrs' Shrine on the lower slopes and emerging at the **Zhupu Altar** (主普壇; *zhǔpǔtán*), the grand *pudu* (spirit offering) shrine which is the focus of Keelung's Ghost Festival. The shrine was completed in 1976 and is only opened during Ghost Month, when offerings and rituals made here are supposed to appease the "hungry ghosts" that are thought to wander the earth at this time (see "Festivals", p.32) – the rest of the year it's worth visiting the **Keelung Midsummer Ghost Festival Museum** (中元祭典文物館; *zhōngyuán jìdiǎn wénwùguǎn*; Tues–Sun 9am–5pm; free) on the first floor, a small but informative exhibition about the festival, with labels in English. It's a short walk up the final stretch of hill to the Guanyin Statue from here – built on a scenic spot facing the sea, it's now part of the unremarkable **Da Fo Zen Temple** (大佛禪院; *dàfó chányuàn*) complex, built in 1969.

From the snack stalls at the back of the temple it's a twenty-minute walk along the road (take a left turn at the first junction), past assorted ex-military hardware, to **Ershawan Fortress** (二砂灣砲台; *èrshāwān pàotái*; 24hr; free) dating from 1840 but rebuilt several times. This is Keelung's largest and best-preserved fortress, though it's little more than a series of hefty gun emplacements – the path loops around the main battlements and barrack areas behind, passing a few old tombs and a line of steep steps leading to the original gate further down the slope. This has the words 海門天險 (*hǎimén tiānxiǎn*) inscribed on the front, which roughly translates as "Dangerous Sea-Gate". From here you can walk down the hill to Zhongzheng Road along the harbour and catch a bus back to the station.

One of Keelung's more unusual sites is a few metres north along Zhongzheng Road on the left, just before the junction with Zhengfeng Street. The French Cemetery, or **Cimetière Français de Kilung** (法國公墓; *fǎguó gōngmù*; 24hr) is all that remains of the graves of over six hundred French soldiers killed during their occupation of the town in 1884–85. Estimates suggest that only 270 died as a result of fighting – the majority succumbed to diseases such as malaria, cholera and dysentery. Only a few of the original tombstones remain on the far right; the

Moving on from Keelung

Heading south to Kaohsiung, there are only a couple of express **trains** per day and it's easier to take one of the frequent local trains to Taipei (NT$43) and transfer. Get off at Badu to pick up services down the east coast. The Keelung Bus Company stop, located across Zhong 1st Road from the train station, is the place to catch regular **bus** services: bus #1022 to Yeliu (NT$47) and Jinshan (NT$64); bus #1013 to Jiufen (NT$45) and Jinguashi (NT$53); and bus #1052 to Fulong (NT$122) and the Northeast Coast National Scenic Area. All buses have their destinations marked in English on the front.

Long-distance services and buses to Taipei (NT$55) leave from the Kuo Kuang Bus Station just behind the information centre. For the North Coast Scenic Area buses (daily 6.15am–8.10pm; every 20–40min), walk through the Kuo Kuang station to the right and along Xiao 4th Road to the bus stop (no English). Bus #1262 (daily 6.15am–8.10pm) stops at all the main sights along the north coast: Yeliu (NT$47), Jinshan (NT$64), Shimen (NT$104) and Danshui (NT$171).

You'll also find fast buses (daily 6am–10pm; every 30–60min) to Jiaoxi (NT$95), Yilan (NT$125) and Luodong (NT$150) here. **Taxis** to Jinshan should cost a maximum NT$400, less to Yeliu.

Ferries to Matsu (with onward connections to Fuzhou, China) and Xiamen, China, depart from the **West Passenger Terminal**, a short walk north of the train and bus stations, on the northern side of the harbour – buy tickets from the second floor (see p.370 for more on travelling to Matsu).

main stone monument was erected in 1954 when the French government transferred the graves of two senior officers who had died in Penghu to the cemetery. The two pillar monuments on site were erected by the Japanese.

Fairy Cave

On the other side of the harbour, ten minutes by bus from the train station, the **Fairy Cave** (仙洞巖; *xiāndòngyán*; daily 6am–6pm) is actually a series of Buddhist shrines carved into the limestone caves facing Keelung container port – the wall carvings provide the illusion of great antiquity, unusual in Taiwan, though the temple dates from the relatively recent Qing dynasty. The cave contains four shrines; the first is dedicated to Milefo (see p.403), while the second cavern features an altar to Guanyin. Behind this, the main hall contains the three principal images of Buddha. To the left of the second cavern, a narrow passage through the rock takes you to another incense-filled shrine with a small stone effigy of Guanyin. The passage is very tight and may require some crawling.

Eating

Keelung's **Temple Plaza Night Market** (廟口夜市; *miàokǒu yèshì*; Ⓦ www.miaokow.org) on Ren 3rd Road, between Ai 3rd Road and Ai 4th Road, is one of Taiwan's culinary highlights and by far the best **place to eat** in the city. The market dates from the late Japanese occupation era and fronts Dianji Temple; each stall advertises its main dishes in English, and it's open 24 hours. The ice and fruit stalls are refreshing in summer, and the thick soups, meatballs, oyster omelettes, curry rice and rice-flour noodles (*mǐfěn*) are especially recommended. *Ding Bian Cuo* (鼎邊趖; *dīngbiānsuǒ*) at no. 25-1 and 27-3 inside the temple courtyard is one of the oldest and most celebrated stalls, serving thick rice noodles in a mixed seafood broth (NT$20–50). Not far from the market, venerable *Li Hu Cakestore*, 90 Ren 3rd Rd (李鵠餅店; *lǐhú bǐngdiàn*; daily 9am–9.30pm; no English signs;

T 02/2422-3007), has been baking delicious crumbly pastries with a variety of sweet fillings since 1882: the most popular are pineapple (*fènglísū*) and green bean (*lǜdòubǐng*; NT$22 each, boxes for NT$280).

Jiufen and Jinguashi

The historic gold mining town of **Jiufen**, an easy day-trip from Taipei or Keelung, occupies a stunning hillside location with fine views of the northeast coast. It's justifiably renowned for its tasty **snack food** and atmospheric **teahouses**, though despite the hype, the town itself is architecturally fairly typical and not especially attractive. From Jiufen, the road runs 2km over the Mount Keelung ridge to **Jinguashi**, fast becoming a major tourist destination in its own right and far more interesting. Most of the town's mining-related attractions have been absorbed into the **Gold Ecological Park**, an ambitious project that combines restored Japanese buildings with old mining tunnels and ruined temples.

Some history

Gold was discovered in the Keelung River in 1889, and in 1896 the Japanese began intensive mining in the area, dividing the land split by Mount Keelung between two government-run companies named after the officers in command: the concession operated by **Tanaka Group** became Jinguashi, while **Fujita Group** developed Jiufen. The gold ore on the Jiufen side was less pure and in 1899 the Japanese began to lease the concession to local entrepreneur **Yen Yun-nien** who founded the Taiyang Mining Corp in 1920 and began sub-leasing smaller chunks of land to Chinese prospectors. As a consequence, Jiufen developed haphazardly as a series of independent claims, gaining a reputation as a get-rich-quick town, or **Little Hong Kong**, in the 1930s.

Taiyang ceased all operations in Jiufen in 1971, and though artists started to settle here in the early 1980s, the good times seemed to be over – **Hou Hsiao-hsien's** 1989 movie *City of Sadness*, in large part shot in a then atmospheric Jiufen, changed all that. The film was the first to make reference (very indirectly) to the 2-28 Incident (see p.389) and won the Golden Lion at the Venice Film Festival. Overnight the town became a must-see attraction, creating the tourist carnival that still exists today. One of its admirers is Hayao Miyazaki, who used Jiufen as inspiration for the village in his Japanese anime hit *Spirited Away* (2001).

In contrast, the Japanese maintained direct control over Jinguashi until 1945, the town developing in an orderly, pragmatic fashion. Its silver and especially **copper** deposits, discovered in 1905, became far more important than gold – by the 1930s

---

Getting to Jiufen and Jinguashi

From **Taipei**, the fastest option to both towns is to take a train to **Ruifang** (NT$80), then switch to one of the regular **buses** to Jinguashi, which first stop at Jiufen (both NT$15; EasyCard accepted). Buses are marked in English, take around fifteen minutes and depart from the opposite side of the road from Ruifang station's main (west) exit. Bus #1013 leaves **Keelung** (outside the train station) every fifteen minutes (daily 6am–9pm) and takes around 30–40min to reach Ruifang (NT$29), Jiufen (NT$45) and Jinguashi (NT$53), while bus #1016 starts at **Taipei** West Bus Station (over 1hr; Jiufen NT$87; Jinguashi NT$95). Buses between Jiufen and Jinguashi are NT$15. **Taxis** from Ruifang station operate under a fixed-rate system: NT$180 to Jiufen and NT$240 to Jinguashi.

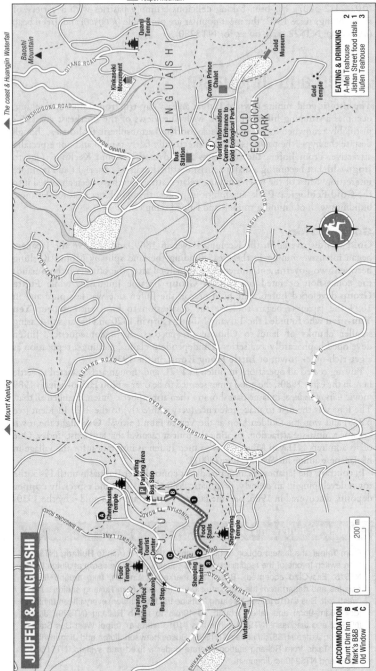

JIUFEN & JINGUASHI

Teapot Mountain ▲

▲ The coast & Huangjin Waterfall

▲ Mount Keelung

▲ Ruifang & Taipei

Baoshi Mountain ▲

Quanji Temple

Kinkaseki Monument

QITANG ROAD

JINSHUIGONG ROAD

WUHAO ROAD

Crown Prince Chalet

Bus Station

Tourist Information Centre & Entrance to Gold Ecological Park

Gold Museum

JINGUASHI

GOLD ECOLOGICAL PARK

JINGUANG ROAD

SHANTI ROAD

JINGUANG ROAD

MAIN ROAD

RUISHUIGONG ROAD

N

Gold Temple

JIUFEN

JIU BINGGONG ROAD

JINGGUAGWEI LANE

Chenghuang Temple

Keting Parking Area
P Bus Stop

QINGTIAN ROAD

Jiufen Tourist Center
i

SHUQI ROAD

Food Stalls

Shengming Temple

JISHAN STREET

Shenping Theatre

Fude Temple

Taiyang Mining Office

Bafankeng
Bus Stop

JIANSHAN STREET

QICHE ROAD

Wudankeng

SHIKAN LANE

0   200 m

ACCOMMODATION
Chunt Dint Inn   B
Mark's B&B   A
Old Window   C

EATING & DRINKING
A-Mei Teahouse   2
Jishan Street food stalls 1
Jiufen Teahouse   3

136

the town was home to around 80,000 people with the hills honeycombed by a staggering 600km of tunnels. Mining finally ceased in 1987 when debts bankrupted the state-owned Taiwan Metal Mining Company – there's still gold in the hills but it's become too expensive to extract commercially.

Information and accommodation

The **Jiufen Tourist Center** (九份遊客中心; *jiǔfèn yóukè zhōngxīn*; Mon–Fri 9am–5pm, Sat & Sun 9am–6pm; ☎02/2406-3270) at 89 Qiche Rd (the main road towards the lower end of the town), has a small but informative exhibition and English-language brochures.

Jiufen has plenty of **accommodation**, and Qingpian Road (輕便路; *qīngbiànlù*) in particular is lined with simple hotels and homestays. *Chiu Chunt Dint Inn* (九重町客棧; *jiǔchóngdīng kèzhàn*; ☎02/2496-7680; ❹) at 29 Jishan St is a stylish, centrally located place with a traditional theme, while *Old Window* at 294-2 Qingpian Rd (古窗; *gǔchuāng*; ☎02/2406-2289; ❻) is a modern homestay with a fashionable rooftop teahouse. One of the cheapest places is *Mark's B&B* (馬克村莊; *mǎkè cūnzhuāng*; ☎02/2497-2889; ❹), just off the main road at 86 Qiche Rd – the rooms are basic, but some have superb views.

Jiufen

The narrow backstreets of **JIUFEN** (九份; *jiǔfèn*) are generally vehicle-free and, away from the busier areas, local life proceeds remarkably undisturbed. Most visitors get off the bus adjacent to the Keting Parking Area at the top end of town, proceeding downhill straight into **Jishan Street** (基山街; *jīshān jiē*) to gorge on its vast array of **snacks** (see below). However, if you fancy some exercise before tucking in, it's not far up the road to the trailhead for **Mount Keelung** (基隆山; *jīlóngshān*). On a fine day the short but steep hike to the summit (588m) offers a spectacular panorama of both Jiufen and Jinguashi (allow 30min for an easy hike up).

Back in town, if you keep walking along Jinshan Street you'll eventually reach Jiufen's most picturesque corner, **Shuqi Road** (豎崎路; *shùqí lù*), actually a series of stone steps slicing through the middle of town and lined with teahouses and old buildings. Walk downhill to the junction with Qingpian Road, turn left along the road and you'll eventually come to a small square in front of the entrance to **Wufankeng** (五番坑; *wǔfānkēng*) or No. 5 Mine, an evocative relic of Jiufen's mining days – it's locked up but you can still peer through the bars. Retrace your steps to Shuqi Road and a short walk in the other direction along Qingpian you'll see gaudy **Chenghuang Temple** (城隍廟; *chénghuáng miào*), housing Jiufen's City God. Continuing downhill, back on Shuqi Road, you'll end up at a junction on the main road, with the bus stop on the opposite side.

Eating and drinking

Sampling the famous snacks on **Jishan Street** is an essential part of any visit to Jiufen: favourites include fish balls in soup (*yúwán*) at *Chuantong Yuwan* (九份張記傳統魚丸 *jiǔfèn zhāngjì chuántǒng yúwán*; NT$25) at no. 23; translucent meatballs flavoured with red wine (*bah-oân* in Taiwanese) at *Jinzhi* (九份金枝紅糟肉圓; *jiǔfèn jīnzhī hóngzāo ròuyuán*; NT$40) at no. 112; and *Grandma Lai's Taro Dumpling* (賴阿婆芋圓; *làiāpó yùyuán*) at no. 143 for taro balls.

There are also plenty of **teahouses**, and the ⚑ *Jiufen Teahouse* (九份茶坊; *jiǔfèn cháfāng*; ☎02/2496-9056 at 142 Jishan St), close to Shuqi Road, is one of the highlights – make sure you get a wooden booth with a view. There's a NT$100 charge per person, in addition to the price of a tea set (NT$400–900) but the ambience, views and service makes up for the cost. The tea (in 40g bags), warmed on charcoal, lasts for

Prisoner of war camps in Taiwan

Thailand's "death railway" is notorious in the English-speaking world (in part thanks to the film *Bridge on the River Kwai*), but few people are aware that the Japanese operated at least fifteen POW camps in Taiwan during World War II. More than 4300 men were incarcerated on the island, most of them British or Commonwealth troops captured in Hong Kong or Singapore, Dutch from Indonesia and Americans from the Philippines. Life was as brutal for the POWs here as anywhere else in Asia, with each camp revolving around a system of forced labour: in Camp No. 1, also known as **Kinkaseki** (金瓜石戰俘營; *jīnguāshí zhànfúyíng*) and the biggest, prisoners were forced to work in the Japanese copper mine in appalling conditions, while those at **Taichu Camp** (Camp No. 2), near Taichung, worked on a massive flood channel – many died from starvation, disease and ill-treatment. The camps were largely forgotten after the war, but thanks to a long campaign by former prisoners and expats living in Taiwan, a memorial was erected at the Kinkaseki site in 1997, and in 1999 the Taiwan POW Camps Memorial Society was formed to research all POW camps on the island (ⓦwww.powtaiwan.org). Several plaques have since been erected all over Taiwan, and a short memorial service takes place at Kinkaseki every year around November 11.

hours – you can take the leftovers home. The *A-Mei Teahouse* (阿妹茶酒館; *āmèi chájiǔguǎn*) at 20 Shixia Lane (above 121 Shuqi Rd), on the right as you descend the steps below Jishan Street, is a multistorey Chinese palace with black wood and red lanterns. This place featured heavily in *City of Sadness* – a faded board showing the Chinese characters for the film marks the steps up to the entrance and is a favourite photo spot for Taiwanese tourists. The *Xiao Shanghai* teahouse across the street at no. 35 also claims a connection with the movie, though this seems to be more tenuous.

Jinguashi

Nestling in a small valley, just over the hill from Jiufen, **JINGUASHI** (金瓜石; *jīnguāshí*) has only a handful of inhabitants and plenty of atmospheric alleys and streets to explore. Much of the old village is preserved within the absorbing **Gold Ecological Park**, an industrial heritage area that covers the western half of the valley.

Buses terminate on the eastern side of the valley at **Quanji Temple** (勸濟堂; *quànjì táng*). Rebuilt in 1933 based on an 1896 original, the temple is noted principally for its bronze statue of Guan Di, which at 35m is one of the tallest in Asia. Steps to the right of the temple lead to the trailhead for **Teapot Mountain** (茶壺山; *cháhú shān*; 580m) which really does look like a teapot if you're standing in the right place. It's a steep 2km climb to the summit along a stone path, with a rope-assisted scramble across the scree at the top, from where the views are magnificent. Back at the temple, the lane to the left leads 200m up to an abandoned smoke tunnel and Baoshi Mountain, which is just a lookout over the valley and "**Yingyang Sea**" (陰陽海; *yīnyánghǎi*) below – the iron ore in the river here has stained the water yellow, creating a two-tone effect in the bay. Further down the valley the remains of the old **copper refinery** (十三遺層; *shísān yícéng* or "Thirteen Levels" in Chinese) make for a dramatic post-industrial landscape: the three serpent-like pipelines running up the mountainside are the world's longest smoke vents, all now abandoned, while the **Huangjin Waterfall** (黃金瀑布; *huángjīn pùbù* or "Golden Falls") nearby also gets its name from the iron and copper deposits in the river. At weekends, shuttle buses pass the falls (NT$15), otherwise it's a long walk down. Back at Quanji Temple, steps lead downhill to a narrow lane: turn right here and you'll come to a quiet park containing the **Kinkaseki Monument** and the remnants of a Japanese prisoner of war camp. A small **memorial** marks the area where 1135 Allied POWs were incarcerated between November 1942 and March 1945 – the camp was known simply as "Prisoner of War Camp No. 1" or "Kinkaseki", the Japanese name for Jinguashi. From here you can wander through the town, across the river and up to the Gold Ecological Park via **Old Qitang Alley**, or follow the trail from Quanji Temple.

Gold Ecological Park

Occupying the slopes on the western side of Jinguashi, the **Gold Ecological Park** (黃金博物園區; *huángjīn bówùyúan qū*; Tues–Fri 9.30am–5pm, Sat & Sun 9.30am–6pm; NT$100) is a mixture of museums and restored mining buildings, most dating from the Japanese period. The park's **tourist information centre** (遊客服務中心; *yóukè fúwù zhōngxīn*) is located at the entrance, and from here well-marked walkways lead to all the main sights. The principal trail leads past a row of food stalls to the **Environment Educational Center** (環境館; *huánjìngguǎn*) containing exhibits about the geology and ecology of the area, and a short introductory film. Behind here you'll find the **Crown Prince Chalet** (金瓜石太子賓館; *jīnguāshí tàizǐbīnguǎn*), a distinctively Japanese guesthouse built in 1922 for Prince Hirohito's state visit the following year, though in the end he never made it up the mountain. Just before the Gold Museum, the **Benshan Fifth Tunnel** (本山五坑; *běnshān wǔkēng*) is a 180m section of renovated mine complete with wax exhibits – you have to join a tour to go inside (Tues–Fri 9.30am, 1.30pm, 3.30am; Sat–Sun 9.30am, 10.30am, 1.30am, 3.30pm, 4.30pm; NT$50). From here it's a short but steep walk up to the ruined **Gold Temple** (黃金神社; *huángjīn shénshè*), a Japanese Shinto shrine built in 1933 and later destroyed by fire.

Housed in the former Taiwan Metal Mining Company building at the end of the old rail track beyond the Benshan Tunnel, the **Gold Museum** (黃金館; *huángjīnguǎn*) focuses on the area's mining history. The highlight for many tourists is the chance to touch the **world's largest gold bar**, located on the second floor; at 220kg, it was worth over US$8.5m in late 2010. There is also a small exhibition in the museum dedicated to the Kinkaseki POW camp (see box opposite).

Pingxi Branch Rail Line

Just south of Jiufen, the scenic **PINGXI BRANCH RAIL LINE** (平溪支線; *píngxī zhīxiàn*) makes another rewarding day-trip from Taipei, winding its way almost 13km up the Keelung River valley to the atmospheric village of

---

Exploring the Pingxi Branch Rail Line

The **branch line** starts at **Ruifang** (瑞芳; *ruìfāng*; connected by express trains to Taipei, 45min; or frequent buses from Jiufen), runs along the main line for 8km to Sandiaoling and then breaks off and follows the valley. You can buy an all-day Pingxi Line pass at Ruifang Station for NT$54, or pay per journey – the maximum is NT$30 for the Ruifang to Jingtong trip (trips between Jingtong, Shifen and Pingxi are just NT$15). Trains depart at irregular but fairly frequent intervals from early morning to 11pm: the last train leaves Jingtong at 10pm. An alternative from Taipei is to take the **#1076 bus**, which connects Muzha with Jingtong and Pingxi village (40min; NT$45), and join the train from there. The bus departs from the opposite side of Muzha Road from Muzha MRT Station at 7.15am, 8.20am, 9.45am, 11am, 12.20pm and thereafter at irregular intervals until 10.40pm. The last bus leaves Pingxi for Muzha at 11.30pm.

Jingtong and passing through the old mining communities of Pingxi and Shifen. For much of the twentieth century this was the heart of Taiwan's **coal industry**, and, though the mines have all now closed, you'll find several reminders of its industrial past scattered around the valley. These days however, it's the mountain scenery, **hiking trails** and **waterfalls** that attract most of the tourists. The valley is also the location for one of Taiwan's most captivating **lantern festivals**.

Houtong

The virtually abandoned mining village of **HOUTONG** (猴硐; *hóutóng*), 4.55km and five minutes down the track from Ruifang (first stop), is the latest Taiwanese post-industrial site to get the tourism treatment, its eerie old buildings and pits being transformed into the **Houtong Coal Mine Ecological Park** (猴硐煤礦博物園區; *hóutóng méikuàng bówùyuánqū*). You can wander the area for free, stopping in at the museum (English labels) and **visitor centre** (daily 9am–5pm; ☎02/2497-4143) for maps and information (limited English). Highlights include the half-ruined Coal Preparation Plant, built in 1920, the Main Pit (gradually being restored) and the remnants of the Houtong Shrine. Rather bizarrely, Houtong is also known as "Cat Village", thanks to the hordes of feral moggies that thrive here (cat tours are offered in Chinese).

Shifen

From Ruifang, the village of **SHIFEN** (十分; *shífèn*) is the fourth stop on the Pingxi Line, swamped at the weekends by tourists that come primarily to gawp at its celebrated **waterfall**. The falls are back towards Ruifang, on the eastern side of Shifen, but the village is also a good place to see and launch "heavenly lanterns" (see Festivals of Taiwan). Try **Grandma's Flying Lanterns** (阿媽的天燈; *āmāde tiāndēng*; daily 9am–9pm; ☎02/2495-8422) at 109 Shifen St. The **Coal Mine Museum** (台灣煤礦博物館; *táiwān méikuàng bówùguǎn*; daily 9.30am–5pm; NT\$200; ☎02/2495-8680) is also a worthy detour en route to the falls; follow the tracks through the centre of the village, then the road as it bears left, and you'll pass the entrance a short walk ahead. The museum is actually the abandoned New Pingxi Coal Mine and processing plant, the whole thing eerily frozen in time from the day the miners stopped working in 1997. The site has two parts: the entrance stands beside the old processing plant and from here a trail follows a conveyor belt, still littered with coal, up a slope and to the end of a narrow-gauge rail line. It's a bone-shaking, painfully slow 1km ride from here to the second area at the mine head, a collection of exhibition rooms (Chinese labels only) and the **mineshaft** itself, the most interesting part of the site (you can walk 100m into the mountain).

Continue walking along the lane in front of the museum entrance and you'll eventually hit the main road: take the lower fork across the river (past the "Shifen Scenic Area" sign) to the **visitor centre** (daily 8am–5.30pm; ☎02/2495-8409), which has maps, information and a small café. **Shifen Waterfall** (十分瀑布; *shífèn pùbù*; daily 7.30am–6pm; NT\$80) is another fifteen minutes from here along a trail that starts at the back of the building and crosses the river twice before rejoining the rail tracks. En route you'll pass **Eyeglass Hole Waterfall** (眼鏡洞瀑布; *yǎnjìngdòng pùbù*), named after the two hollows that have been eroded into the rock behind it. The main falls are 15m high and 30m wide, not quite Niagara, but impressive nonetheless, and wonderfully photogenic, especially in full flood.

Pingxi

PINGXI (平溪; *píngxī*) is the seventh stop and one of the valley's most atmospheric villages, though there's not much to see unless you visit during the **Lantern Festival** (Jan or Feb) – the village (along with Shifen) is home to one of Taiwan's most enchanting spectacles, the release of hundreds of "heavenly lanterns", or *tiāndēng* (see Festivals of Taiwan). At other times you can buy and launch individual lanterns (NT$80–100) from shops that line the main road towards Jingtong – try no. 67 or 68. Narrow **Pingxi Old Street** (平溪老街; *píngxī lǎojiē*), a short walk from the station via Zhonghua Street, is a good place to eat: try the *Pingxi Taro Ball Shop* (平溪芋圓店; *píngxī yùyuándiàn*) at no. 23, near the junction with Zhonghua (bowl of taro dessert NT$60) or *Honggui Noodles* (紅龜麵店; *hóngguī miàndiàn*), at 1 Gonghua St, just off "old street" (noodles and braised tofu NT$35; daily 8am–6pm).

Pingxi is also surrounded by tantalizing **hiking trails**. Walk through the village and across the river to the main road – turn left here and in a few metres you should pass a signposted trail on the right leading to **Putuo Mountain** (普陀山; *pǔtuóshān*; 450m) and **Xiaozi Mountain** (孝子山; *xiàozǐshān*; 360m), both just 1km away (allow 2hr round-trip). The summit of the latter is one of the most dramatic on the island; a steep tower of rock scaled by steel ladders – the views are impressive, but don't try the climb on a wet day.

Jingtong

The old mining village of **JINGTONG** (菁桐; *jīngtóng*) is another reminder of the valley's industrial past – mining ceased here in 1987. It's the final stop on the line or a 1.3km walk from Pingxi, along the road that follows the tracks. The small wooden **train station**, built in 1931 by the Japanese, lies on narrow "**old street**": to the left, the **Jingtong Mine Museum** (菁桐礦業生活館; *jīngtóng kuàngyè shēnghuóguǎn*; daily 9.30am–5pm; free; ℡02/2495-2749) displays information about the area and the mine, though there are no English labels, while in the other direction the street is lined with small shops and snack stalls, including *Yang's Chicken Roll* (楊家雞捲; *yángjiā jījuǎn*) at no. 127. You'll also notice hundreds of small bamboo wind chimes (*zhútǒng fēnglíng*) hanging all over the place, inscribed with messages; the practice is supposedly in memory of two local lovers and is popular with young couples who hang them up for luck – you can write your own one for NT$30.

"Old street" ends a few metres beyond at the main road overlooking the bridge – turn right here, taking the lane that leads down to the river, to the Tai Yang Clubhouse, also known as the **Crown Prince Hotel** (太子賓館; *tàizǐbīnguǎn*) a few metres below. This Japanese-style guesthouse was built in 1922 for Crown Prince Hirohito's visit the following year and is being restored – it should be open by the end of 2011. Keep walking around the hotel and cross the river: turn immediately right then left up an alley and you'll see the *Palace Tea House* (皇宮茶坊; *huánggōng cháfāng*; Wed–Sun 10.30am–9pm) on the right, another Japanese-era building now functioning as an attractive restaurant. The tranquil interior offers a choice of tables with tatami mats or chairs – you can order tea (NT$250–500 per pot) or light meals, though there are no English menus (or signs).

Back in the village, the area above and behind the station is dominated by the **Coal Mine Memorial Park** (24hr; free) the remains of the Shidi Mine that closed in 1979. A path on the other side of the tracks leads first to the derelict coal preparation plant, topped by a small café, and, further up the hill, the ruins of the mine-head buildings and the main tunnel, sealed by an iron-bar gate.

Northeast and Yilan Coast National Scenic Area

The **Northeast and Yilan Coast National Scenic Area** (東北角暨宜蘭海岸國家風景區; *dōngběijiǎo jì yílán hǎiàn guójiā fēngjǐngqū*) incorporates some of Taiwan's most spectacular coastal scenery, stretching 102.5km from Nanya, just east of Jiufen, to Suao. Accessible by bus or train, the area can be covered as a series of lengthy day-trips from Taipei or Keelung, though **Fulong**, with its attractive **beach**, is a gateway to the region (and home to the Scenic Area **visitor centre**) and a more convenient base for longer stays. Highlights include the network of **hiking trails** between Bitou Cape and Longdong and the surfing hotspot of **Daxi**. To the south, the towns of **Jiaoxi** and **Luodong** (just outside the Scenic Area proper) are worthy detours before heading on Hualien (p.289).

Bitou to Aodi

BITOU (鼻頭; *bítóu*) is a small fishing community that lies at the trailhead to **Bitou Cape** (鼻頭角; *bítuójiǎo*), a rugged outcrop of layered sandstone and one of Taiwan's most scenic pieces of coastline. From Keelung (30–40min), get off the bus before the tunnel on the edge of the village. From here there's a choice of two **hiking trails**. The **Lighthouse Trail** (1.2km) starts across the bridge over the road, but for the best views head back into the village for the **Ridge Valley Trail** (1.1km), which starts on the right side of the harbour near the temple. All the trails are well marked in English – the latter rises steeply over the top of the cape to join the main trail on the southern side. There's a small lighthouse at the end, but it's the magnificent views that make the hike worthwhile. From the lighthouse, follow the **Coastal Trail** (0.8km) along the seashore, passing a cluster of bizarre geological formations to **Longdong Bay Park** (龍洞灣公園; *lóngdòngwān gōngyuán*; June–Oct Mon–Fri 8am–5pm, Sat & Sun 7am–6pm; NT$100; ☎02/2490-3639), a series of sea-fed swimming pools next to the main road. From here it's another 2km around the bay to Longdong village – the stone pools here are abalone farms. Longdong's popular **rock climbing** area is a further 1.5km around the next cape, the 30m sandstone cliffs packed with climbers at the weekends. The start of the trail to **Longdong Coastal Park** is clearly marked back in the village, climbing 100m above the cliffs and providing several stunning viewpoints. The trail ends at the main road and a bus stop. The busy town of **AODI** (澳底; *àodǐ*) is a further 4km down the

---

Getting around the Northeast and Yilan Coast National Scenic Area

The northern section of the Scenic Area is accessible by **bus**: the easiest option is to catch #1052 from Keelung to Fulong (daily 5.21am–9.44pm; every 30–60min; NT$122), which stops at Bitou (NT$66), Longdong (NT$72) and Aodi (NT$96). Catch it at the Keelung Bus stop, opposite the train station (see p.132) – the bus should be marked in English.

Fulong is also accessible from Taipei by frequent **express trains** (1hr 5min; NT$130). Trains continue south from here to Daxi (local only; NT$19), Jiaoxi (NT$46; NT$71 express), Luodong (NT$72; NT$112 express) and Hualien (NT$138; NT$315 express). For destinations south of Fulong you can also pick up daily **Kuo Kuang buses** from Taipei: these stop outside the 7-Eleven in Fulong (near the train station) at 10am, 11am, noon, 4pm, 7.30pm and 10pm, before passing all the major attractions as far south as Luodong.

road, a largely unattractive fishing port famous for its wholesale fish market (daily 5–9am) and the **seafood restaurants** that line its main street.

Fulong

Just under 6km south of Aodi, **FULONG** (福隆; *fúlóng*) has one of north Taiwan's best **beaches**, with heaps of fine sand surrounded by a ring of lush mountains. It's also the most convenient place to stay on the northeast coast, and famous in Taiwan for its **lunchboxes** or *biàndāng*, typically grilled pork or fish with a boiled egg, several types of vegetables and rice. You can buy these for around NT$60 on the train station platform or at shops such as *Xiangye* (鄉野; *xiāngyě*; daily 7am–7pm) just to the left outside the entrance. Since 1999 Fulong has also been home to the **Ho-Hai-Yan Rock Festival** (Ⓦ www.hohaiyan.com), held every July over three days, and primarily featuring bands from Taiwan and Japan – it's free and attracts up to 500,000 people.

Arrival and information

Keelung buses (see p.134) terminate in the car park facing the main **Northeast Coast Scenic Area Visitor Center** (九份遊客中心; *jiǔfèn yóukè zhōngxīn*; daily 9am–5pm; Ⓣ 02/2499-1115, Ⓦ www.necoast-nsa.gov.tw). To get there from the **train station**, walk to the main road and turn left – you'll see the centre across the car park on your right. There's plenty of information available and several exhibition rooms inside.

Accommodation

There are a few cheap but nondescript **hotels** (❷) on the main road near the station, but 500m to the north the sprawling *Longmen Campsite* (龍門露營區; *lóngmén lùyíng qū*; Ⓣ 02/2499-1791, Ⓦ www.lonmen.tw; NT$70 entry), 100 Xinglong St, is better value and the biggest **campsite** in Taiwan. It costs NT$800 per night for tents for four people (NT$1000 for the drive-in area). If you bring your own tent, you pay NT$150 less. Chalet-type rooms are also available from NT$2300 for two. There are showers, a swimming pool (NT$60) and a small shop on site. Parking is NT$20 for a scooter and NT$50–100 for cars. Bike rental costs NT$80 per hour.

Fulong Beach

The main entrance to **Fulong Beach** (福隆海水浴場; *fúlóng hǎishuǐ yùchǎng*) is just beyond the visitor centre at the northern end of the village, a long spit of sand across the Shuangxi River: it's officially open June to October when there's a charge of NT$100, though approach the beach via the southern end of the village and you'll find a free section. The sand is fine, but tends to get covered in flotsam in the winter when it's not cleaned. While **swimming** is Fulong Beach's main draw, it sometimes gets waves suitable for **surfing**. You can **rent** surfboards (NT$550/day) and bodyboards (NT$300/day) at the **Being Surf Shop** (地球人戶外休閒家; *diqiúrén hùwài xiūxiánjīa*; Ⓣ 02/2499-1372 or mobile Ⓣ 0919/575372, Ⓦ www.dollar-fulong.com.tw), close to the train station entrance at 16 Fulong St Owner Dollar Huang speaks English and can also sort out accommodation (from NT$1680); he's usually open daily 9am–5pm in the summer, but call ahead at other times.

Bike trails

For a change of scene, rent **bicycles** (NT$100/day) from the shops outside the train station; the bike paths around Fulong are well marked in English. The **Caoling Tunnel Bikeway** (舊草嶺自行車隧道; *jiùcǎolǐng zìxíngchē suìdào*) is the most popular, a 5km ride taking in the old 2km railway tunnel and ending with stupendous views of Turtle Island at the **Shicheng Scenic Area** (石城觀景區; *shíchéng guānjǐngqū*) and coffee shop.

In the other direction, the Longmen–Yanliao Bikeway (龍門鹽寮自行車道; *lóngmén yánliáo zìxíngchēdào*) runs 4km across the Longmen Suspension Bridge over the Shuangxi River and through the dunes, north to **Yanliao Beach Park** (鹽寮海濱公園; *yánliáo hǎibīn gōngyuán*; daily 9am–6pm; NT$90, NT$60 in winter) – bikes must be left at the entrance. This beautiful beach is part of Taiwan's longest continuous stretch of sand (3km) and is the spot where the **Japanese invasion** force landed in May 1895 – a stone monument commemorates those that died resisting the occupation, while information boards labelled in English and Chinese detail the main events of the initial invasion. By the end of 2011 a 16km bike lane along Provincial Highway 2 (the coast road) will link the two bikeways, creating a 26km loop.

Caoling Historic Trail

The **Caoling Historic Trail** (草嶺古道; *cǎolǐng gǔdào*) is a 9.7km path that cuts across the hills between Fulong and Dali – it's a beautiful walk with mesmerizing views of the ocean at its southern end, and is easily covered in half a day. The trail incorporates the only remaining section of a stone trail, built in 1807 by Taiwan's first settlers, to link Danshui with Yilan; the most historic sight en route is the **Tiger Tablet**, a stone flamboyantly engraved with the Chinese character for "Tiger". The story goes that military official Liu Ming-deng made the carving in 1867 in allusion to the mythical powers tigers have to control powerful winds: you'll probably see why this is appropriate when you reach the head of the pass nearby.

The trail can be tackled in either direction, though the steepest climb is the 2.8km between Dali and the pass – the route climbs more smoothly from Fulong, which also has more convenient rail connections. A new four-kilometre route links Fulong to the head of the main trail; from **Fulong Station** walk to the main road and turn left – you'll see the first sign about 150m further along directing you back under the tracks. In **DALI** (大里; *dàlǐ*), the trail ends at the back of the surprisingly large **Tiangong Temple** (天公廟; *tiāngōngmiào*), dedicated to the Jade Emperor and a popular pilgrimage site. Just next door the **Dali Visitor Centre** (大里遊客中心; *dàlǐ yóukè zhōngxīn*; daily 9am–5pm; ☎03/978-0727) houses decent exhibitions on the area and particularly its Ketagalan inhabitants, but only in Chinese. Dali train station is a short walk along the main road.

Daxi

Four kilometres south of Dali, **DAXI** (大溪; *dàxī*) is a once tranquil town that is quickly being transformed into Taiwan's premier **surf centre**. Daxi is widely considered to have the most consistent beach break in northern Taiwan, and the waves on the edge of town in **Honeymoon Bay** (蜜月灣; *mìyùewān*) hold great appeal for experienced and novice surfers alike, with typically hollow faces yet enough power and speed to lend themselves to shortboards and quick take-offs. Although Daxi can be surfed year-round, the biggest waves occur in **winter** – particularly in March – when faces of up to three metres can be had, though the water is cold at this time and you'll definitely need a wetsuit.

Cross the street after you exit the **train station**; the surf shops are about 100m to the left, while the beach is about 500m down the road to the right. Apart from the popular option of bringing your own tent and camping on the beach, **accommodation** is limited to the rooms available at the town's three **surf shops**

Taiwan's National Parks

Since the 1970s, Taiwan has established eight national parks to protect its considerable natural and historic treasures, though only seven are easily accessible (the Dongsha Marine National Park covers remote islands in the South China Sea). They encompass territory within Taiwan's mountainous interior, along the east and west coasts and even among the Taiwan Strait islands. Inside the parks you'll find some of the country's most spectacular sights, from soaring cliffs and alpine mountains to aboriginal villages and well-preserved Chinese architecture.

Mountains

With 258 peaks rising above 3000m, Taiwan is one of the most mountainous places on earth. Most of the highest mountains are within national parks, with **Yushan National Park** boasting the tallest of them all: **Yushan** (Jade Mountain), which at 3952m is the loftiest peak in northeast Asia. Despite its daunting height, Yushan can be accessed via a well-maintained trail, making it an extremely popular and worthwhile climb. While Yushan receives most of the fanfare, mountain-choked **Shei-Pa National Park** comes a close second, with 51 peaks over 3000m. Though many of these are off limits, the 3886m **Xueshan** (Snow Mountain) and adjacent **Holy Ridge** can be scaled with some advance planning. And while **Taroko National Park** is best known for its magnificent gorge, its towering western hinterlands are teeming with challenging climbs such as **Qilaishan** and **Nanhushan**.

Sunset in Yushan National Park ▲

Beautiful beach in Kenting National Park ▼

Beaches

Though Taiwan is surrounded on all sides by beaches, few are as protected as the sandy shores of **Kenting National Park**, where shimmering **sand dunes** often stretch hundreds of metres from the sea. Set against turquoise waters – highlighted by well-preserved offshore coral reef – these dunes are atmospheric places to watch sunrises and sunsets. While several of Kenting's beaches have uniquely high percentages of calcium carbonate and have been made off limits to visitors in order to protect them, there are still plenty of beaches open to the public for sunbathing and swimming. Among the most popular are **Xiaowan**, in Kenting Town, and the beautiful white-sand beach at **Baisha**, on the park's western fringe.

Historic preservation

Taiwan is keen to protect its rich historic and cultural heritage, with **Kinmen National Park** established to preserve its imperial Chinese monuments and hybrid Chinese-European architecture. Having been shelled by mainland China for decades, Kinmen also bears the scars of war, and several battlefield memorials and museums have been erected to honour the fallen. Important archaeological sites are scattered across the island, some of them under national park protection. Among the most significant is a 700-year-old settlement of stone slab houses, believed to have belonged to the **South Paiwan aboriginal civilization**, which is being excavated in Kenting National Park.

▲ Pavilion in Kinmen National Park

▼ Taroko Gorge from above

The top three

While the primary function of Taiwan's national parks is the protection and conservation of precious natural resources and historic sites, they also are intended to serve as educational and recreational areas, and some attract droves of visitors each year. The most visited is **Taroko National Park**, with its awe-inspiring **Taroko Gorge** drawing increasing numbers of domestic and foreign tourists each year. With its steep cliffs and smooth marble walls, the 20km gorge offers truly world-class scenery. Enveloping the island's southern tip – and ringed by beautiful golden-sand beaches – **Kenting National Park** also packs in the crowds, especially during summer, but its warm tropical climate means it's a pleasant place to visit year-round. With low-elevation mountains laced with hiking trails – most within walking distance of Taipei's city centre – **Yangmingshan National Park** continues to be the favoured stomping ground of the capital's residents.

Ecological protection zones

All of Taiwan's national parks have **ecological protection zones** designed to preserve threatened species of flora and fauna. Among the best-known is the zone protecting the endangered **Formosan Landlocked Salmon** in Shei-Pa National Park, which also has a zone to protect the Taiwan **Sassafras tree**. Kenting National Park has several protection zones, some sheltering ancient coral beds, others shielding pristine beaches from human degradation. Kinmen hosts more migratory birds than any other place in Taiwan, and its **Shuangli Wetlands Area** has been set aside to protect them. **Yangmingshan** is a hotbed of post-volcanic activity, and some of its areas with fumaroles and volcanic fissures are protected zones.

Yangmingshan National Park ▲

Relief depicting an Atayal village ▼

Aboriginal areas

With many of Taiwan's indigenous inhabitants long relegated to the island's mountainous interior, pockets of the highlands remain strongholds of **traditional aboriginal culture** and fall within the boundaries of various national parks. Though the parks' strict conservationist laws are at odds with time-honoured aboriginal **hunting practices** – still a source of tension in some areas – poaching of protected species is on the wane. The most celebrated aboriginal hunters are the **Atayal tribe**, some of whom still live in parts of Shei-Pa and Taroko national parks, and the **Bunun tribe**, who inhabit the fringes of Yushan National Park. In the north of Kenting National Park, broad swaths of land are occupied – and even farmed – by members of the **Paiwan tribe**.

> ## Surf Daxi
>
> **Jeff's Surf Shop**, 100 Binhai Rd Sec 5 (衝浪俱樂部; *"Jeff's" chōnglàng jùlèbù*; ☎03/978-1781, ⓦwww.jeffsurf.com.tw), is run by Jeff Sun, one of Taiwan's seminal surfers, and offers an excellent two-day/one-night surfing package for NT$3500, including meals and board rentals (accommodation consists of mattresses on the floor). Next door, the **Spider Surf Club**, 96 Binhai Rd Sec 5 (台灣蜘蛛衝浪俱樂部; *táiwān zhīzhū chōnglàng jùlèbù*; ☎03/978 1321, ⓦwww.spidersurfing.com), is popular with young surfers who spend weekends in the cheap but dingy basement air-conditioned dorm (NT$300 per bed; NT$250 in winter). Their two-day/one-night surfing costs NT$3000, and the club's website has limited English information on daily conditions.

(see box above). These spartan lodgings can fill up quickly on summer weekends, so if you're planning to come at this time reservations are highly recommended. Two of the three offer surfing packages that include accommodation, meals, lessons and board rentals; if you just want to hire a board expect to pay around NT$600 per day. Daxi's best **place to eat** is *Dou-Dou* (荳荳; *dòudòu*; ☎03/978-1147), a few hundred metres past the surf shops, on the same side of the road, serving up simple Chinese and Western dishes all day long. The house specialities are the delicious fried pork dumplings (*guōtiē*) and fried turnip cakes (*luóbǔgāo*). The fresh coffee is excellent.

Leo Ocean Resort

Around 4km south of Daxi, the 🏯 **Leo Ocean Resort**, 36 Binhai Rd Sec 4 (理歐海洋溫泉渡假中心; *lǐōu hǎiyáng wēnquán dùjiǎzhōngxīn*; ☎03/978-0782, ⓦwww.leogroup.com.tw; ❻), is an exclusive **hotel** that doubles as an unusual **museum** (daily 9am–6pm; NT$180). A mix of contemporary and southern Fujian-style architecture, the museum takes up the two basement floors and displays a portion of the six thousand Chinese **stone lions** collected by owner John Kao over more than thirty years – the oldest piece is from Shanxi and is over three 3000 years old.

The main attraction here, however, is the **view**: watching the sunrise over Turtle Island, just across the water, is a captivating experience, assuming you can get up early enough to see it. The hotel's attractive gardens border the rocky shoreline and are a good place to relax, though during weekdays the main road next to the hotel roars with traffic.

Jiaoxi

Some 20km south of Daxi, the inland resort town of **JIAOXI** (礁溪; *jiāoxī*) is best known for its **hot springs** and the spectacular **waterfalls** just outside the city. Buses drop you on Jiaoxi Road, a short walk from the train station on Wenquan Road. You can pick up taxis at the latter for the 5km ride (NT$140) to the **Wufengqi Falls** (五峰旗瀑布; *wǔfēngqí pùbù*), among the most impressive in Taiwan. If you have time, you can walk through town (via Deyang Road) and up Wufeng Road, but only the last section is pleasant and there's always a lot of traffic.

The falls consist of three separate cascades, with the upper two thin threads of water plummeting dramatically over sheer, moss-smothered bluffs at least 30m high – the first falls are the highest and most spectacular. A paved pathway leads some 550m to the top, but it's a steep climb. Just before the trailhead is a line of **food stalls** selling an assortment of snacks and drinks, usually including the area's famed crop of **kumquats** (*jīnzǎo*; NT$50/bag). Make sure you take your taxi driver's number if you want a ride back.

Practicalities

Getting here from Daxi is easiest by train, while Taipei is just over an hour by bus thanks to the Xueshan Tunnel and Highway 5; Kamalan **buses** (NT$104) run frequently from Taipei Bus Station.

Jiaoxi's bicarbonate hot-spring water is clear and odourless, and is piped into the dozens of **spa hotels** in town. One of those with the most elaborate public bathing complexes is the *Chuan Tang Hotel* (泉湯旅館; *quántāng lǚguǎn*; ☎03/988-0606; ❺) at 218 Zhongshan Rd Sec 2, the first hotel on the right after you exit the train station (the sign just says "Hotel" in English). Non-guests can use its several bathing pools with massage showers for NT$250 (open 24hr). For a bit more luxury, opt for the *Guan Xiang Four Seasons* (冠翔四季溫泉會館; *guànxiáng sìjì wēnquán huìguǎn*; ☎03/987-5599, ⓦwww.hotspring-hotel.com.tw; ❽) – non-guests can use the lavish spa facilities for NT$500 (daily 8am–10pm).

In addition to kumquats, Jiaoxi is best known for its **spring onion pancakes** (*cōngyóubǐng*). Try them at the much-loved stall at 128 Jiaoxi Rd Sec 4 (礁溪蔥油餅; *jiāoxī cōngyóubǐng*), deep-fried with a choice of three different sauces and an egg topping (daily 9am–6.30pm; NT$25).

Luodong

Around 10km and a short bus or train ride south of Jaoxi is the humdrum town of **LUODONG** (羅東; *luódōng*), known primarily for the **National Center for Traditional Arts** (國立傳統藝術中心; *guólì chuántǒng yìshù zhōngxīn*; daily 9am–6pm; NT$150; ☎03/970-5815, ⓦwww.ncfta.gov.tw), located 7km east of the train station. The privately run centre puts on daily **performances** of Chinese opera, folk dance and acrobatics, and there's a **Folk Art Boulevard** lined with shops selling expensive handmade crafts such as wooden slippers, tea sets, glassware, candles, finger puppets, fans and jewellery. The interesting **exhibition hall** (Mon noon–6pm, Tues–Sun 9am–9pm) has in-depth explanations of many traditional arts, including those of various aboriginal tribes. The complex also includes a coffee shop and convenience store, as well as a couple of snack bars.

The centre is located at 268 Wubin Rd Sec 2, just off Provincial Highway 2, making it convenient if you've got your own transport (it's about 32km from Daxi). Alternatively, **taxis** from Luodong train station cost NT$250 one-way; remember to book one for the return journey as you can't count on catching one from outside the centre and there is no public transport.

Practicalities

Kamalan **buses** run to Luodong (NT$136) frequently from Taipei Bus Station. The city is a convenient place to **spend the night**, with a solid option being the *Hua-Wang Business Hotel* (華王商務旅館; *huáwáng shāngwù lǚguǎn*; ☎03/954-4155; ❹) at 41 Zhongzheng N Rd, which is spotlessly clean and excellent value, with comfortable beds and cable TV. To get there, walk a few hundred metres down Gongzheng Road, from the station, until you reach Zhongzheng North Road; turn right, and it's about 200m further on your left. The **Minsheng Market** (民生市場; *mínshēng shìchǎng*), along the second street to your left coming down Gongzheng Road from the train station, is a lively **night market** known for its cooked lamb stalls and iced desserts.

Northern Cross-Island Highway

The **Northern Cross-Island Highway** (北部橫貫公路; *běibù héngguàn guānglù*; Provincial Highway 7) is one of three spectacular routes that cross the mountainous interior of Taiwan, connecting the western plains with the east coast. The northern route starts in **Daxi**, around 35km south of Taipei, and follows the Dahan River before crossing the lofty Xueshan range and joining the main Yilan to Lishan road at **Qilan**, 120km away in Yilan county.

Daxi

The official starting point for the Northern Cross-Island Highway is the historic town of **DAXI** (大溪; *dàxī*), worth a pit-stop for its two old streets lined with ornate Chinese baroque architecture (this Daxi is not to be confused with the east-coast surfing centre; see p.144). From the bus station, **Zhongyang Road** (中央路; *zhōngyāng lù*) is to the left of the main entrance, crammed with small stores and a daily wet market in the mornings. Walk north (right) up here to the end and you should hit **Heping Road** (和平路; *hépíng lù*), Daxi's gorgeous "old street", crammed with craft stores, teashops and restaurants. The elaborate facades on display are some of the best preserved in Taiwan, most dating from the grand redevelopment of the town that began in 1912, the finely carved arches and beams etched with the names of the trading companies that once operated here. Many of the stores sell Daxi's most celebrated snack, **preserved tofu** (*dòugān*), which is usually flavoured and much tastier than it sounds – *Hwang Ryh Shiang* (黃日香; *huáng rì xiāng*) at 56 Heping Rd is one of the oldest and most popular tofu sellers (daily 7am–8pm; NT$30–100/bag).

The "Culture Resort of the Jiang's"

From Daxi, Provincial Highway 7 runs southeast to the village of **CIHU** (慈湖; *cíhú*), centre of what Taoyuan county has dubbed the "**Culture Resort of the Jiang's**" (兩蔣文化園區; *liǎngjiǎng wénhuà yuánqū*), a collection of several sights associated with the Chiang family. Since his death in 1976 (see p.390), the influence of Chiang Kai-shek has faded – here at least his reputation has been rehabilitated and jazzed up with fancy marketing which has transformed the old dictator's image into a fashion concept, much like that of his old foe Mao Zedong. In 1988, Chiang's son, Chiang Ching-kuo, was buried at the **Daxi Mausoluem** (大溪陵寢; *dàxī língqǐn*; daily 8am–5pm; free), built in 1962 as an office of the president and the first site you'll hit coming from Daxi itself. Opposite is the **Daxi Visitor Center** (大溪遊客中心; *dàxī yóukè zhōngxīn*; daily 8am–5pm; ⊤03/388-4437), 1268 Fuxing Rd Sec 1

Transport on the Northern Cross-Island Highway

You'll need your own transport to complete the whole route as buses only travel as far as Shangbaling. **Bus** #9103 (daily 6am–9.30pm; roughly every 30min; N$65, exact change required) connects Daxi (via Sanxia; see p.117) with Taipei's **Yongning MRT Station** (*yǒngníng zhàn*) in around 45 minutes (take exit 1 at Yongning and the bus stop is straight ahead; buses marked in English). From Daxi Bus Station you can catch regular onward services to Cihu (N$23) and hourly buses to Fuxing (6.40am–9.45pm; NT$56) and Little Wulai (NT$81). Buses to Baling (N$158) depart at 6.20am, 7.20am and 3pm; buses to Shangbaling (NT$160) via Baling at 9.50am and 1.30pm. **Taxis** are supposed to use the meter – reckon on NT$160 to Cihu from Daxi Bus Station, and at least NT$500 to Baling.

(Highway 7), which has a small exhibition about Ching-kuo and his Russian-born wife. From here you can walk along the pleasant 2km Touliao Eco-walking Trail to Cihu along the Caoling Creek, past Niujiaonanpi Lake and through the **Cihu Sculpture Memorial Park** (慈湖紀念雕塑公園; *cíhú jìniàn diāosù gōngyuán*) − a vast collection of Chiang Kai-shek statues "donated" (ie torn down) from other parts of Taiwan. Across the park bridge you'll find the **Cihu Visitor Center**, 1097 Fuxing Rd Sec 1 (慈湖遊客中心; *cíhú yóukè zhōngxīn*; daily 8am–5pm; ☏03/388-3552), with a small exhibition highlighting Chiang's career in China and Taiwan, and at the end of another trail (past Cihu or "Lake Kindness" itself), **Cihu Mausoleum** (慈湖陵寢; *cíhú língqǐn*; daily 8am–5pm; free), where the great man is buried − this was one of his many summerhouses, built in 1959 because it reminded him of his childhood home in China. Plans to move both men closer to Taipei seem to have been shelved; in any case, the idea was always to rebury them in China after reunification. **Buses** pass close to both mausoleum sites (see box, p.147).

Fuxing

Around 18km south of Daxi, the small town of **Fuxing** (復興; *fùxìng*) is the best place to stay on the highway: the *Youth Activity Center* (復興青年活動中心; *fùxìng qīngnián huódòng zhōngxīn*; ☏03/382-2276, ⓦfuhsing.cyh.org.tw; ⑦) at 1 Zhongshan Rd, operated by China Youth Corp, occupies a superb location overlooking an arm of **Shimen Reservoir** (石門水庫; *shímén shuǐkù*), best appreciated from the sun deck of the restaurant on site. The centre was the location of another of Chiang Kai-shek's summer retreats, though the current building is a modern construction. The rooms are simple but comfortable (with space for four people), all en suite with TVs, breakfast and magnificent views from the more expensive rooms on the top floor. Japanese-style tatami rooms are cheaper (⑩). Fuxing is the first stop on the highway with an obvious **Atayal** influence; cheap eats are available along the main street close to the *Youth Activity Center*.

Fuxing to Qilan

From Fuxing, the highway follows a series of gorges created by the Dahan River deep into the Xueshan range, with the scenery becoming increasingly wild and rugged. Around four kilometres from Fuxing, the **Xiao Wulai Special Scenic Area** (小烏來風景區; *xiǎowūlái fēngjǐngqū*; daily 8.30am–4.30pm; free; NT$100 parking) contains the 50m **Little Wulai Falls** (小烏來瀑布; *xiǎowūlái pùbù*), Taiwan's most picturesque waterfall. You can walk down to the river in front of the falls from the main road near the tollbooth via a steep path − if you drive down to the car park near the river, the trails lead to a variety of attractions and viewpoints above the falls. The site lies 2km off the main highway: only a handful of **buses** connect the falls to Daxi and Fuxing each morning.

South of here the highway becomes narrower, ending up as a winding, single-track road. Buses (see opposite) go as far as the village of **Baling** (巴陵; *bālíng*), at the bottom of the valley and lined with several basic places to eat, and on to the Atayal settlement of **Shangbaling** (上巴陵; *shàngbālíng*), a further 200m up the mountain on a side road. The village is perched on a narrow ridge, often shrouded in mist, and has a single street lined with cheap restaurants and places to stay if you get stuck (be sure to try the fresh honey peaches or *shuǐmìtáo* here). The village is on the road to **Lalashan Forest Reserve** (拉拉山國有林自然保護區; *lālāshān guóyǒu línzìrán bǎohùqū*; daily 7am–6pm; NT$100; ☏03/394-6061), also known as Daguanshan, an incredibly atmospheric reserve of giant cypress trees or "God Trees" (*shénmù*), 1550m up in the mountains and 12.5km from the main highway. The small visitor centre (daily 9am–6pm) here marks the start of a 3.7-km trail around 22 of the biggest trees and viewpoints. The trees survived undiscovered during the period of intense logging initiated by the Japanese – most are between 500 and an astonishing 2800 years old, with the tallest topping out at 55m. There's no public transport to Lalashan.

Back on the main highway, the route climbs to its highest point (1250m) near the **Mingchi Forest Recreation Area** (明池國家森林遊樂區; *míngchí guójiā sēnlín yóulèqū*; daily 6.30am–5pm; NT$120), a tranquil alpine-like mountain retreat (free of tour buses), set around a small lake. The *Mingchi Mountain Hostel* (明池山莊; *míngchí shānzhuāng*; ☎03/989-4104; ❼) is a relatively expensive resort hotel near the visitor centre, but also contains an attractive restaurant and café. The area was once a lumber station and is surrounded by more giant hardwoods and "God Trees". Beyond Mingchi, the road drops steeply for 17km through thickly wooded slopes to another forest reserve at **Qilan** (棲蘭; *qílán*) and the end of the highway: turn left for Yilan, Luodong (see p.146) and the east coast, and right for Lishan (see p.214) and the Wuling Recreation Area (see p.164).

Hsinchu

Just 86km and 34 minutes from Taipei by High Speed Rail, **HSINCHU** (新竹; *xīnzhú*) is one of the wealthiest cities in Taiwan, largely as a result of the huge revenues generated by the **Science Park** on its southeastern border. Yet tucked away in the centre are remnants of one of north Taiwan's oldest cities, with plenty to offer casual visitors: **temples** and **traditional food stalls** reflect the city's historic roots while the absorbing **Glass Museum** is testimony to its central role in Taiwan's glass industry. It's also the gateway to the heart of Taiwan's **Hakka country**, centred on the town of Beipu.

Arrival, information and city transport

Hsinchu **train station**, built in 1913 and Taiwan's oldest, is at the southern end of the city, a short walk from East Gate. You'll find **lockers** just outside (NT$20/3hr; maximum 6 days). All the major **bus** stations are nearby along Zhonghua Road. Hsinchu's **High Speed Rail Station** (☎03/612-1000) is 11km east of the city at 6 Gaotie 7th Road in Zhubei, linked to the centre of Hsinchu by **free shuttle bus** (every 20–30min; daily 7.15am–11.50pm); the bus stops at Baida Church and terminates at "Dongmen Market", which means Zhongzheng Rd near the Hsinchu Municipal Image Museum. You can also take a bus from the HSR station direct to the Science Park.

You won't find many **internet cafés** in walking distance of the train station these days: Qi Yan Cheng (奇岩城; *qíyánchéng*) at 327 Zhonghua Rd Sec 2 (open 24hr) is cheap at NT$15 per hour and fairly reliable. **ATMs** and banks are plentiful throughout the city: Citibank has a branch at 321 Beida Rd (☎03/522-6617), on the north side of downtown.

The best place for **information** and help in English is the **Hsinchu Foreigner Assistance Center** (新竹地區外國人協助中心; *xīnzhú dìqū wàiguórén xiézhù zhōngxīn*; Mon–Fri 8am–noon & 1–5pm; ☎03/522-9525 or 0800/024-111, ⒲foreigner.hccg.gov.tw/en) at 107 Zhongyang Rd (see map, p.150).

City buses depart from several different stops around the train station; they are marked in English and Chinese and cost NT$15 per sector, though you are unlikely to need them for sightseeing within the city. **Taxis** are plentiful in the centre of town (the meter starts at NT$100). Like Taipei, most streets in Hsinchu are clearly marked in *hànyǔ pīnyīn*.

EATING & DRINKING

An Zhi Ju	3
Black Cat Pastry	2
Curry Fans	6
Da Jie Tea House	5
Double Stars Tempura	10
Golden Mountain	11
Hsinfuzhen	9
Liquid	4
Pumpkin	7
Red	8
T.J's Lounge Bar	7
Ya Rou Hsu	1

HSINCHU

N

250 m

0

Taipei Road

Minzu Road

Minzu Road

Minsheng Road

Windance Shopping Mall (Warner Village Cinema)

Zhongyang Road

Sanmin Road

Zhongzheng Rd Sec 2

Guangfu Rd Sec 2

Bade Road

Zhongxing Rd

Stadium

Hsinchu Glass Museum

Vision Hall

Hsinchu Park and Zoo

Confucius Temple

Qi Yan Cheng ②

Dongmen Street

Zhonghua Rd Sec 2

Train Station

Jinhua Street

D O N G D A   R O A D

Renai Street

Wenhua Street

Qinshui Park

Hsinchu Art Gallery

Old City Moat

Ⓒ

⑦⑧

Ⓓ

East Gate

Hsinchu Municipal Image Museum

Sogo Department Store

North Bus Station

South Bus Station

Performance Hall

Cultural Centre

Beida Church

Ⓐ

Fuhou Street

Hsinchu City Hall

High Speed Rail Bus Stop

ⓘ

Earth God Temple

Dongning Temple

Ⓔ

Eslite Bookstore

Minzu Road

Kuo Kuang Bus Staion

Yanyi Road

Jinshi Mansion & Zheng Family Shrine

①

②

③

⑤

Xing Chun

Changhe Temple

Guoda

Beimen Street

Zhangan Street

Police Station

Hsinchu Assistance Foreigner Center

Pinghe St

Dongmen St

Chenghuang Temple

⑨

Far Eastern Department Store

Nanmen Street

Wuchang Street

Linsen Road

Zhongshan Road

▼ Taichung

ACCOMMODATION

Ambassador Hotel	B
East City Hotel	D
Howard Plaza Hotel	A
Shin Yuan Park Hotel	E
Sol Hotel	C

150

Accommodation

Hsinchu has several luxury **hotels** catering to business travellers, but it's still possible to find good discounts on websites.

Ambassador Hotel 新竹國賓大飯店 (*xīnzhú guóbīn dàfàndiàn*) 188 Zhonghua Rd Sec 2 ℡03/515-1666, ⓦ www.ambassadorhotel.com.tw. Hsinchu's top five-star hotel and consequently host to a steady stream of business visitors, it occupies the 9th–24th floors of the city's tallest building, above the Shinkong Mitsukoshi department store. Rooms are modern, stylish and very comfortable, with extras including an indoor swimming pool and excellent restaurants such as *Prego* on site. ❽

East City Hotel 東城大旅館 (*dōngchéng dàlǚguǎn*) 1 Lane 5, Fuhou St ℡03/522-2648. Decent budget option in an excellent location, near the old moat and a row of cool restaurants and bars – the entrance is just behind the *Garden 3 Restaurant*. Rooms are basic but adequate. ❷

Howard Plaza Hotel 福華大飯店 (*fúhuá dàfàndiàn*) 178 Zhongzheng Rd ℡03/528-2323, ⓦ www.howard-hotels.com.tw. Five-star hotel

with a stylish contemporary design. The rooms have modern Asian decor and are equipped with comfy armchairs, CD players and large bathtubs with mini TVs. ❼

Shin Yuan Park Hotel 新苑庭園大飯店 (*xīnyùantíngyuán dàfàndiàn*) 11 Datong Rd ℡03/522-6868, ⓦ www.shinyuan-hotel.com.tw. Comfortable mid-range option, not far from the East Gate and the train station. Rooms are relatively spacious, with bright but outdated blond wood decor. ❹

Sol Hotel 迎曦大飯店 (*yíngxī dàfàndiàn*) 10 Wenhua St ℡03/534-7266, ⓦ www.solhotel .com.tw. A plush five-star, with flat-screen TVs, free wi-fi and buffet breakfast included. The spacious rooms fuse modern Asian style, with plenty of workspace for the bus-loads of Japanese business men who stay here. Slightly better value than the other top hotels. ❼

The City

Hsinchu has a compact centre, easily explored on foot. The **East Gate** (東門; *dōngmén*), a short walk north from the train station along Zhongzheng Road, the city's main commercial street, is its most distinctive landmark. The gate was completed in 1829 and is the only remnant of the old city walls. A couple of blocks north of here, the **old city moat** has been transformed into a flower-filled park between Linsen Road and Zhongyang Road, where it merges into Qinshui Park; it's an attractive place to wander, especially at night, lined with coffee shops, stores and restaurants. The **old town** lies west of the moat, and still contains a smattering of historic sights and temples.

Just north of the East Gate at 65 Zhongzheng Rd, **Hsinchu Municipal Image Museum** (文化局影像博物館; *wénhuàjú yǐngxiàng bówùguǎn*; Wed–Sun 9am–noon, 1.30–5pm, 6.30–9pm; NT$20) occupies an old cinema built in 1933. The actual museum is very small, comprising a couple of exhibition rooms behind the Movie Hall. You can take a peek inside the latter, but it's more interesting to watch one of the old Taiwanese films screened here (usually from 7pm Wed–Sun). The museum ticket includes entry to the film playing that day.

Retrace your steps to the East Gate and turn right along Dongmen Street; at the junction with Zhongshan Road is Hsinchu's most important place of worship, **Chenghuang Temple** 城隍廟 (*chénghuáng miào*; daily 4.30am–10.30pm), surrounded by food stalls and attended by a constant stream of visitors. The stalls form the city's best **night market** (see p.153) and add to the boisterous atmosphere – during festivals locals like to eat here while traditional opera is performed in the courtyard. Built in 1748, much of the temple's current beauty stems from the restoration of 1924: look out for the iron abacus and lurid depictions of hell on the walls, a warning to would-be criminals. The large black-faced City God image in the **Main Hall** is said to be the most senior in Taiwan, while the City God's wife and two sons are worshipped in the Rear Hall.

Hsinchu Science Park

Hsinchu Science Park (新竹科學園區; *xīnzhú kēxué yuánqū*; ☏03/577-3311, ⓦwww.sipa.gov.tw) is the engine driving Taiwan's high-tech revolution, attracting more foreign visitors than any other place on the island. These are all business people of course, not tourists – government-funded tax breaks, cheap rents and infrastructure investment have attracted over 440 technology companies, making this Taiwan's "Silicon Valley". The park generated around NT$883.5bn in total sales in 2009, and acts as a model for schemes all over Asia, but there's not much to see for tourists. If you fancy a look anyway take bus #1 or #31 to the "Science Park" Stop, and then take the Green Line Shuttle Bus to the Science Park Life Hub; the hub acts as an information centre containing cafés and a small exhibition room on the fourth floor.

Beimen Street

North of Chenghuang Temple, **Beimen Street** (北門街; *běimén jiē*) is the city's most atmospheric thoroughfare and its earliest commercial street, lined with old shops, restaurants and teahouses.

Don't miss the old puppet store, **Guoda** (國達民俗藝品; *guódá mínsú yìpǐn*) at no. 109, and just beyond Beida Road, on the right, **Xing Chun** (杏春; *xìngchūn*), a traditional Chinese Medicine shop at no. 156. Opposite sits **Changhe Temple** (長和宮; *chánghé gōng*; daily 3.30am–10pm), Hsinchu's "outer" Mazu temple. Built in 1742 next to a long-silted-over wharf, the nickname refers to its position just outside the old city walls. Mazu is enshrined in the **Main Hall**, flanked by Wenchang Dijun on the left and Guan Di on the right. The Rear Hall is dedicated to Guanyin, while the attached shrine to the right of the Main Hall is known as **Shuixian Temple** (水仙宮; *shuǐxiān gōng*) and dedicated to the Water God or the Great Yu, mythical founder of the Xia dynasty (2205–1766 BC), China's first. It's a short walk north of here to the end of Beimen Street, past a row of dilapidated but charming Qing dynasty buildings; the two best maintained are the **Jinshi Mansion** (進士第; *jìnshìdì*) at no. 163, which was built in 1838 for Zheng Yong-Xi (who became the first Taiwanese *jìnshì*, or official, in 1810), and the **Zheng Family Shrine** (鄭氏家廟; *zhèngshì jīamiào*) at no. 175 (completed in 1853), both closed to the public.

Hsinchu Park

The cluster of attractions centred on **Hsinchu Park** (新竹公園; *xīnzhú gōngyuán*) southeast of the station, tends to attract more tourists than the old town, though only the Glass Museum has much appeal. To walk there, take the underpass to the right of the train station (opposite Sogo), then turn right and immediately left upon exiting the tunnel. Walk across the car park to Nanda Road and turn left to Dongda Road, where you should see the garish main entrance to the park ahead on the right. The entrance leads to the **Hsinchu Zoo** (新竹市立動物園; *xīnzhú shìlì dòngwùyuán*; Tues–Sun 8.30am–5pm; NT$10; ⓦzoo.e-tobe.com/eng) that occupies most of the park, but unless you like zoos or have kids in tow it's not particularly exciting. More worthwhile is the **Hsinchu Municipal Glass Museum** (玻璃工藝館; *bōlígōngyìguǎn*; Wed–Sun 9–5pm; NT$20; ⓦglassmuseum .cca.gov.tw) to the left of the entrance, an innovative mixture of glass art exhibitions and permanent displays on the history and use of glass. There are few English labels however; the most interesting installations are the reinforced glass bridge on the second floor, and the **Jail of Glass** on the first floor with its glass walls, bars and even a glass toilet.

Eating

Eating in Hsinchu is lots of fun as the city is renowned for its culinary specialities: pork meatballs in soup (*gòngwántāng*), rice noodles (*mǐfēn*) and stuffed meatballs (*ròyuán*), especially at the **food stalls** in and around Chenghuang Temple and along Beimen Street.

An Zhi Ju 安之居 (*ān zhī jū*) 200 Beimen St ☏03/525-8750. One of Hsinchu's most alluring teahouses, set inside an attractive Qing dynasty shophouse, with a series of atmospheric wooden booths. Pots of tea start at NT$90. Daily noon–3am.

Black Cat Pastry 黑貓包 (*hēimāo bāo*) 187 Beimen St. Small take-away selling delicious smoked buns (*hēimāo bāo*) crammed with juicy stewed pork (NT$20), much tastier than the average Taiwanese *ròubāo*. Daily 11am–midnight.

Chenghuang Temple Night Market 75 Zhongshan Rd (inside the temple courtyard). Stalls to try include *Wang Ji E-a Jian* (王記蚵仔煎; *wángjì é zǐjiān*) which faces the main hall and specializes in oyster omelettes; just opposite, *A Cheng Hao* (阿城號; *āchénghào*) does noodles and pork meatballs from NT$35. Outside on Dongmen St, *Guo Run Bing* (郭潤餅; *guōrùnbǐng*) sells delicious *rùnbǐng* (spring rolls stuffed with pork and mushroom; NT$40). Daily 8am–11pm.

Curry Fans 咖哩番 (*kālǐfān*) 13 Sanmin Rd Sec 2 ☏03/531-3372. As you might expect, this place cooks up curry in a variety of styles (NT$180), inspired by Indonesia, Thailand, India and Japan. English menu and English-speaking owner. Daily 11.30am–2pm & 5–9pm.

Da Jie Tea House 大街茶酒館 (*dàjiē chájiǔguǎn*) 168 Beimen St ☏03/526-6466. Foreign-owned late-night café and bar, set inside a cool old shophouse with great ambience, wooden tables and assorted antique bric-a-brac. Daily 5pm–5am.

Double Stars Tempura 星甜不辣 (*xīngtiánbúlà*) 42 Datong Rd. No-frills local diner a short walk from the East Gate, serving one of the most delicious dishes in Taiwan: a selection of boiled fish balls and tofu topped in a thick, satay-like sauce (*tiánbúlà*; NT$45 for a small bowl). Daily 11am–11.30pm.

Golden Mountain 金山面藝術生活館 (*jīnshānmiàn yìshù shēnghuóguǎn*) 13 Jinshan 13th St ☏03/563-6296. Hsinchu's most captivating restaurant, beautifully designed in the style of a Tang dynasty palace, with a variety of tasteful wooden rooms arranged around tranquil fish pools. The extensive menu ranges from

Moving on from Hsinchu

Hsinchu is on the main western rail line with regular express services to Taipei (NT$180), Taichung (NT$198), Tainan (NT$561) and Kaohsiung (NT$668). Hsinchu Bus Company's **North Bus Station** is on Zhonghua Road opposite Sogo with infrequent services to Xinpu or "Shinpu" (新埔; *xīnpǔ*; for Yimin Temple; 9 daily; 6.50am–6.50pm; NT$46). For Zhudong (竹東; *zhúdōng*; for Beipu; 6.10am–10.35pm; every 10–20 min; NT$46) head to the **South Bus Station**, just to the left of the train station. Buses also depart for Taipei (NT$130) and Taichung (NT$150) from here. You'll need to change buses in Zhudong for Beipu and Lion's Head Mountain.

All the **long-distance bus stations** are clustered around the South Bus Station: Kuo Kuang and How Tai are among the companies offering services to Taipei, Taichung and points further south. There are no direct buses to Taiwan Taoyuan International Airport; take a bus to Zhubei and change there, or go via the High Speed Rail to Taoyuan station, which has shuttle bus connections to the airport.

High Speed Rail

Hsinchu's **High Speed Rail Station** is linked to the city by **free shuttle bus** (daily 6.05am–10.45pm; every 20–30min), which departs from Zhongzheng Road, north of East Gate and Lane 96 ("Dongmen Market"). Given that the shuttle bus takes at least thirty minutes (plus waiting times at either end), if you're heading to the centres of Taipei (35min; NT$245) or Taichung (25min; NT$345), taking the regular express train isn't much slower. Tainan is 1hr 10min and NT$1060, Zuoying (Kaohsiung) 1hr 25min and NT$1200.

Cantonese dishes (NT$120–450) to Taiwanese tea (from NT$250), the only downside being its distant location on the other side of the Science Park. Taxis should cost about NT$250 from the station. Daily 10am–midnight.

Hsinfuzhen 新復珍 (*xīnfùzhēn*) 6 Beimen St. Opposite Chenghuang Temple, this venerable cake-maker was established in 1898 and is famous for its deep-fried *zhúqiàn bǐng* (or "chu chan") meat cakes (NT$30), a pastry filled with

tasty blend of onion and pork, and sprinkled with sesame seeds – the sweet/sour combination is perfectly balanced. English labels. Daily 9.30am–9pm.

Ya Rou Hsu 鴨肉許 (*yāròu xǔ*) 212 Zhongzheng Rd. One of Hsinchu's most famous local diners, serving duck noodles and plates of roast duck for over forty years (from NT$45); the secret is the mouthwatering special sauce. Lots of imitators in Hsinchu, but this is the best. Daily 11am–4am.

Nightlife

Hsinchu once had a small but lively foreign **pub scene**, fuelled by a sizeable expat population; since 2009 most of these have closed. Instead you'll find numerous bars downtown that cater to more local tastes: karaoke, TVs, plenty of Taiwanese snacks and a limited selection of bottled beers and cocktails. Few open before 7pm, and most close well into the early hours. A good place to start is Minzu Road, Lane 33, which is crammed with bars such as *Red* (no. 50), *TJ's Lounge Bar* and *Pumpkin* (no. 45). *Liquid* at 128 Sanmin Rd (daily 7pm–3am; ☎03/533-8774) is Hsinchu's best lounge bar, with a classy interior featuring comfy sofas and chilled-out music to accompany the cocktails. Regular DJ nights at the weekends make it more like a club.

Hakka country

Stretching southeast from Hsinchu, **Hsinchu country** is home to large numbers of **Hakka** people: though the ethnic group accounts for roughly fifteen percent of Taiwan's population, eighty percent of Hsinchu claims Hakka ancestry. **Beipu** is

The Hakka

Known as *kèjiārén* in Chinese ("guest families", or *hak-kâ ngin* in the Hakka language), the **Hakka** (客家人) are an ethnic sub-group of the Han Chinese family, with their own language, customs and traditions. Originally from the northern Chinese provinces of Henan and Shanxi, Hakka people began coming to Taiwan in the seventeenth century and have since developed a particularly strong identity. At first, Hakka migrants settled in Taipei county and along the western plains, but by the nineteenth century they had moved to the areas in which they predominate today: the mountainous parts of Taoyuan, Hsinchu and Miaoli counties, and in the Kaohsiung-Pingdong area. Though few Hakka are farmers today, they're still regarded as hard workers and have a reputation for producing some of the island's top **scholars** and **writers**: famous Hakka people include ex-president Lee Teng-hui, Soong Mei-ling (Chiang Kai-shek's wife) and film director Hou Hsiao-hsien. Mainland Chinese leaders Sun Yat-sen and Deng Xiaoping were also Hakka.

Hakka people subscribe to the same **religious beliefs** as other Chinese groups in Taiwan, but they also have their own special gods and festivals. The worship of the **Yimin** (義民; *yìmín*; mostly in north Taiwan) is unique to Taiwan (see p.155) while the island also has around 145 temples dedicated to the **Three Mountain Kings** (三山國王; *sānshān guówáng*), protective spirits of the Hakka and a tradition that came from Guangdong.

The **Council for Hakka Affairs** was created by the government in 2001 to help preserve Hakka culture on the island, and to ensure its language survives: there are several dialects spoken in Taiwan, with *sìxiàn* being the most important, and the one you'll hear on train announcements. **Hakka TV** (客家電視台; *kèjiā diànshìtái*), a 24-hour station, has been on air since 2003.

God Pigs

One of the most controversial of Taiwan's traditional religious practices is the rearing of "**God Pigs**" (神豬; *shénzhū*) – unfortunate hogs that are fed to grotesque size, often so large they can no longer walk. The pigs are used as offerings to the gods – it's a particularly Hakka custom, used mostly at the Yimin Festival when literally hundreds are sacrificed. Pigs are killed the day before, by knife, and the carcass stretched over a metal cage so that it looks disturbingly similar in size to a small bus. It doesn't take much imagination to work out why animal rights activists get upset about this: cases of force-feeding, alleged ill-treatment and the relatively simplistic method of slaughter have led to increased calls for a ban over the years. Hakka groups say that it's a traditional part of their culture and that the pigs are well cared for. While it's true that the tradition of offering pigs goes back to the 1830s, the official "contest" to see who has the biggest and intensive, modern factory methods are relatively new; many pigs are actually bought by Hakka families at the end of the fattening process (which can take two years) when they already sport monstrous proportions.

the most famous Hakka town in north Taiwan, while the **Yimin Temple** near Xinpu is the centre of Hakka religious life on the island.

Fangliao Yimin Temple

The **Fangliao Yimin Temple** (枋寮義民廟; *fāngliáo yìmín miào*; daily 6am–9pm) at 360 Yimen Rd Sec 3 (County Road 17), around 10km northeast of Hsinchu (just outside Zhubei), is the original and most important *yìmín* temple in Taiwan, serving as the spiritual centre for the Hakka community on the island. The temple commemorates the Hakka militia killed during the Lin Shuangwen Rebellion of 1786–88: legend has it that the oxen pulling the cart laden with dead soldiers stopped at this site and refused to move any further. The bodies of almost two hundred militiamen were buried here as a result, and you can still see the vast **burial mound** at the rear of the temple. A shrine was built on the site soon afterwards. The **auxiliary burial mound** to the right of the original contains the bodies of over a hundred Hakka volunteers killed fighting during the Dai Chao-chun Rebellion (1862–65). All the dead warriors are venerated as gods (*yìmín* means "righteous people"), symbolized by the wooden tablets at the main altar.

There are three major **temple festivals** each year: the **Spring Festival** before Tomb Sweeping Day on April 5, the **Autumn Festival** at the end of October or beginning of November, and the most important, the **Yimin Festival** on Lunar July 20 – this is one of the few religious festivals to have originated wholly in Taiwan and features the infamous "God Pigs" (see box above). Xinpu **buses** pass the temple (see p.153) with the last bus back to Hsinchu leaving at around 6pm.

Beipu

Lying around 20km southeast of Hsinchu, just north of the Lion's Head Mountain Scenic Area, the small town of **BEIPU** (北埔; *běipǔ*) is the centre of Hakka culture in north Taiwan, the counterpart of Meinong in the south (see p.268). Though it's a bit touristy these days, the compact area of old buildings and teahouses around Citian Temple has plenty of rustic charm, and it makes an easy excursion from Hsinchu or even Taipei.

Beipu's tiny bus station is on Zhongzheng Road (中正路; *zhōngzhèng lù*), a short walk from the old part of town. Walk a few metres to Nanxing Street (南星街; *nánxīngjiē*) and turn right, passing some good places to try *léichá*

> ## Léichá
>
> Beipu is the best place in Taiwan to sample *léichá* (擂茶), or **"ground tea"**, a popular Hakka drink with origins in ancient China. Its modern incarnation is one hundred percent contemporary Taiwan however; a green tea mixed with a paste of peanuts, sesame, pumpkin and sunflower seeds. It's delicious and very filling (it's sometimes called "cereal tea"), but the twist is that you get to prepare it yourself. DIY sessions are offered at most of the teashops in town, and in general you are expected to at least have a go, the staff sometimes reluctant to pitch in. After a few minutes you'll understand why; the raw ingredients are placed into a ceramic bowl and must be pounded into an oily paste with a giant wooden pestle, a process which takes a strong arm, or preferably, several. The tea is usually served with Hakka-style *muaji* (*máshǔ* in Mandarin), sticky rice rolled in ground peanuts.

(see box, above), and on to the next junction with **"old street"** (aka Beipu Street; 北埔街; *běipǔjiē*), thick with touristy shops and food stalls. The shop on the corner is **Lung Yuan Pastry Store** (隆源餅行; *lóngyuán bǐngháng*; Mon–Fri 9am–6pm), established in 1871 and maker of tasty sweet potato and taro cakes (around NT$150/box). Turn left here and head towards **Citian Temple** (慈天宮; *cítiān gōng*; daily 5am–9pm) at the end of "old street", established in 1830 and the town's main centre of worship. The Main Hall is dedicated to Guanyin, flanked by tablets on the right representing the *sānguān dàdì* (Three Great Emperor-Officials) and on the left, the *sānshān guówáng* (Three Mountain Kings), all Hakka favourites.

Beipu's oldest and most appealing buildings are crammed into a relatively small area around the temple, a mixture of traditional red- and mud brick Chinese houses, well worth exploring. To the south, the **Zhongshu Tang** (忠恕堂; *zhōngshùtáng*) built in 1922, is a charming Qing dynasty house with an unusual Baroque facade (it was being renovated at the time of writing). Many of these houses are linked to the wealthy **Jiang family** – patriarch Jiang Xiou-nuan built the grand **A-Hsin Jiang Residence** (姜阿新宅; *jiāng āxīn zhái*) in the 1940s just to the north of the temple on Miaoqian Street (廟前街; *miàoqiánjiē*) in a blend of Western and Japanese styles. Like most of the buildings here, it's still privately owned and closed to the public. Beyond here, on the corner of Zhongzheng Road is the traditional building known as **Jinguangfu** (金廣福; *jīnguǎngfú*), the old meeting hall built in the 1830s, and opposite, **Tianshui Tang** (天水堂; *tiānshuǐtáng*), a huge Chinese mansion still occupied by the Jiang family. Zhongzheng Road becomes a narrow alley east of here, containing some of the town's most atmospheric **teahouses**.

Practicalities

The easiest way to get to Beipu is catch a **bus** to Zhudong (竹東; *zhúdōng*) from Hsinchu (see p.153) and take one of several onward services to Beipu from the Zhudong bus station (15min; NT$23). Buses run from around 6am to 8.30pm in both directions, every twenty to thirty minutes.

Almost every **teahouse** and **restaurant** in Beipu serves classic **Hakka food**. To sample the special local tea, try the *Fanpokeng Tavern* (番婆坑客棧; *fānpókēng kèzhàn*) at 35 Old Street, an attractive old teahouse with red-tiled floors, wooden tables and decorated with Chinese antiques. Beipu's most atmospheric teahouse is at the eastern end of Zhongzheng Road, where it becomes very narrow; *The Well* (水井; *shuǐjǐng*) at no. 1 is a tranquil Qing dynasty building, with stone walls, wooden ceilings and rustic tables and chairs. Tea, coffee and light meals are available from NT$150.

Lion's Head Mountain Scenic Area

The Buddhist temples of the **Lion's Head Mountain Scenic Area** (獅頭山國家風景區; *shītóushān guójiā fēngjǐngqū*) have been attracting pilgrims since the Qing dynasty. The area is shaped like a rectangle, with an area of 242 square kilometres divided between Miaoli and Hsinchu counties. Its most accessible **hiking trails** and **temples** are clustered around **Lion's Head Mountain** (*shītóushān*) itself, in the northern half of the area, and along the Zhonggang River Valley just to the south. The region is also the home of the **Saisiyat** people (see p.398). The suggested route below can be completed with a combination of buses and hiking – it's possible to see everything in a fairly long day, but there are a few places to break the journey. The other main section worth checking out is **Emei Lake**, dominated by the immense **statue of Maitreya Buddha**, one of Taiwan's highlights.

Lion's Head Mountain and around

There are a couple of easy hikes near the Lion's Head Mountain Visitor Center, where buses terminate (see box below): the 1.7km **Tengping Historic Trail** (藤坪古道; *téngpíng gǔdào*) is a lush, forested path rich in bird life which takes around an hour to complete, while a few metres further along the main road takes you to the signposted path to **Shuilian Cave** (水濂洞; *shuǐliándòng*), noted for its waterfall. Moving on from the visitor centre, your best option is to hike the **Lion's Head Mountain Historic Trail** (獅山古道; *shīshān gǔdào*), which starts nearby; the **trail was closed** after heavy rain at the time of research, so check at the visitor centre before starting out. It's a scenic, 4km path over the hills to Quanhua Temple, lined with stone slabs and weaving past eleven temples, as well as smaller shrines, statues and calligraphy inscribed onto the rocks. Many of the temples are carved into the limestone cliffs, but most of the original buildings were destroyed during the Hsinchu earthquake of 1935, and what you see today are faithful reproductions. The path and main sites are well marked in English. At Wangyue Pavilion (望月亭; *wàngyuè tíng*) not far from **Yuanguang Temple** (元光寺; *yuán guāng sì*) about 2.5km from the visitor centre, a trail spur leads 700m to the summit of **Lion's Head Mountain** (492m), with sweeping views of the valley from the top (the peak vaguely resembles a lion's head).

From the pavilion the trail drops steeply into the Zhonggang River Valley for 1km to **Quanhua Temple** (勸化堂; *quànhuà táng*; daily 6am–8pm), a spectacular cluster of classical-style temples and halls perched on the hillside, its tiered structure providing a wonderful close-up perspective of the elaborate, dragon-covered roofs and beams. The temple was established in 1900 as the only nominally Taoist place of worship on the mountain, primarily dedicated to the Jade Emperor and Guan Di, but, in true Taiwanese style, there are also shrines to Confucius and Sakyamuni

---

Getting to Lion's Head Mountain

The Scenic Area is a short drive south of Hsinchu, but if you're taking public transport you'll need to change bus in Zhudong (竹東; *zhúdōng*). **Buses** to the Scenic Area via Emei (35–40min; NT$46) depart from Zhudong bus station five times a day: 7.30am, 9am, 12.20pm, 2pm and 4.45pm. Buses return to Zhudong at 8.30am, 9.50am, 1.30pm, 2.45pm and 5.35pm. To get to Zhudong, take a bus from Hsinchu (see p.153). Buses from Zhudong arrive a short walk from the **Lion's Head Mountain Visitor Centre** (daily 8.30am–5.30pm; ℡03/580-9296, ⊛www.trimt-nsa.gov.tw), in the northern part of the Scenic Area, around 6km south of the village of Emei. English-language materials and an informative video are available, but the exhibits here are labelled in Chinese only.

Buddha. It's a beautiful location, and a good place for lunch: the canteen serves superb **vegetarian meals** for just NT$60 (breakfast 6.30–8.30am; lunch 11.50am–1.30pm; dinner 5.30–7.30pm). The temple runs a hotel opposite the canteen, the *Shishan Dalou* (獅山大樓; *shīshān dàlóu*; ☎037/822-563; ❷), which offers slightly faded but clean rooms, all en suite with TVs. The real highlight, however, are the balconies, which all have fine views of the valley below, especially beautiful in February when the cherry blossom flowers.

Moving on from the temple, follow the trail five minutes further down the slope (ignore the car park and link road on the left) to the main road (County Route 124), where you should be able to pick up a **bus** to Nanzhuang, around 4.5km to the south (usually every 30min).

Nanzhuang

Midway up the Zhonggang River valley and 10.5km from the main visitor centre, **NANZHUANG** (南庄; *nánzhuāng*) is a small, atmospheric Hakka village that once was a major coal-mining and logging centre. Today it mostly caters to tourists, with well-preserved Japanese-era wooden houses, an official "old street" and the small but helpful **Nanzhuang Visitor Center** (南庄旅遊服務中心; *nánzhuāng lǚyóu fúwù zhōngxīn*; daily 8.30am–5.30pm; ☎037/824-570) at 151 Zhongzheng Rd. It also has an excellent hot-springs spa blessed with odourless sodium bicarbonate spring water. The **East River Spa Resort Garden** (東江溫泉休閒花園; *dōngjiāng wēnquán xiūxián huāyuán*; Mon–Fri 10am–8pm, Sat 9am–10pm, Sun 9am–8pm; ☎037/825-285; NT$350 for outdoor pools) is the perfect place to end the day, with a series of landscaped outdoor pools designed with a blend of Hakka, Japanese and Western styles, and rustic private baths lined with rocks overlooking the Donghe River (NT$1000/hr; includes snacks and use of outdoor pools all day). The spa is surrounded on all sides by mountains, the only downside being the quarry nearby which generates a lot of traffic during the week. The spa is 1.5km from Nanzhuang, off Route 124 – if you don't fancy the walk, a taxi should be NT$60, but during the week the spa should be able to pick you up if you call ahead.

Practicalities

To avoid retracing your steps, take a bus from Nanzhuang to Zhunan (竹南; *zhúnán*; 1hr; NT$65), on the main train line south of Hsinchu. The last bus leaves Nanzhuang at 7.30pm.

Nanzhuang has plenty of **hotels** and **homestays**, but few decent budget options. *Yu He Yuan* (玉荷園; *yùhéyuán*; ☎037/825-800; ❻), 238-1 Zhongzheng Rd at the northern end of the village, is a modern homestay arranged around an attractive lotus pond with spotless, marble-floored rooms and bathrooms – the cosy pinewood rooms in the loghouse across the garden are about the same price. *Lao Jin Long* (老金龍; *lǎojīnlong*; 10am–8pm, closed Tues and weekdays 2–5pm) serves excellent **Hakka food**, with set meals from NT$490 – these typically include local trout, as well as classic pork and bamboo dishes. The 40-year-old restaurant is at 1 Minzu St, near the junction with Zhongzheng Road at the southern end of the village.

Emei Lake

Emei Lake (峨眉湖; *éméi hú*) occupies the far northwestern corner of the Scenic Area and contains a couple of islands in its centre. Despite the tourist hype, it's not big or especially beautiful and the main reason to come here is to wonder at the 72m-high bronze **Maitreya Buddha Statue** (彌勒大佛; *mílèdàfó*) on one of the islands. In 2001, the World Maitreya Great Tao Organization began construction of the statue – said to be the tallest of its kind in the world – and the gigantic

Maitreya Monastery (聖地建築; *shèngdì jiànzhú*) that will accommodate both monks and nuns when completed around 2014 (the site is already open to visitors). Known as *mílèfó*, Maitreya Buddha is the chubby, smiling incarnation of Buddha popular throughout Taiwan (see p.402).

To get to Emei Lake by public transport, you'll have first to take a **bus** to **Toufen** (頭份; *tóufèn*), a few kilometres east of Zhunan, and accessible by bus from Hsinchu or a direct Kuo Kuang service from Taipei. Buses depart from Toufen every thirty minutes and take around 35 minutes (NT$40).

Taian Hot Springs

Straddling the Wenshui River just to the south of Lion's Head Mountain Scenic Area, **TAIAN HOT SPRINGS** (泰安溫泉區; *tàiān wēnquánqū*) is one of Taiwan's most attractive resorts, offering visitors an enticing combination of **hill walks** and rejuvenating **hot springs**. It's no longer a tranquil haven however, with plenty of tour buses and large groups enjoying a range of outdoor activites. As a result, hotels tend to be pricey, but don't be put off: all are open for public bathing, so you don't have to stay overnight to enjoy the waters, and the area rarely feels crowded, especially on weekdays.

Note that from the May "plum rains" and onwards through the summer typhoon season, the trails can become washed-out gullies and are extremely difficult to negotiate.

Arrival and information

Miaoli Route 62 winds for 12km alongside the Wenshui River before reaching the main hot-springs village of **Jinshui** (錦水; *jǐnshuǐ*). The *Tenglong Hot Spring Villa* (see p.160) is the best place to get information about trail conditions (someone usually speaks English); the safety of the trails varies widely depending on the weather, so it's a good idea to ask here before setting out. There are no **ATMs** in Jinshui, so be sure to take enough cash – if you're stuck, there's a Chinatrust Commercial Bank ATM in the 7-Eleven back at the junction of highways 3 and 62. If you're planning to do some hiking in Taian, you could also stock up on some trail snacks at the 7-Eleven, as there is only one **shop** (8am–10pm) in Jinshui (at the *Tenglong Hot Spring Villa*) and it's a bit pricey.

Accommodation and hot springs

Though plush hot-spring **hotels** and **homestays** line much of Miaoli Route 62, **Jinshui** has the best range, all within easy walking distance of the main trails. Most

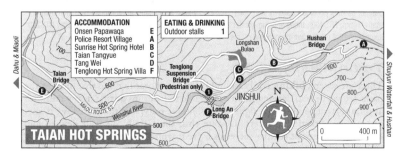

Getting to Taian

Getting here without your own transport is tough. One relatively easy option is to **rent a scooter** in Sanyi (about a one-hour ride away; see p.162). By public transport, you'll need to take a train to **Miaoli** (苗栗; *miáolǐ*); from Miaoli train station walk straight ahead about 50m to the bus station on your right and catch one of the **buses** that leave for **Dahu** (大湖; *dàhú*) roughly two to three times an hour (1hr).

There are just two local buses a day from Dahu on to Taian Hot Springs (Mon–Fri only), but the schedule is erratic, so you're better off trying to get a **taxi** from Dahu (NT$400) or at the village of **Wenshui** (汶水; *wènshuǐ*; bus from Miaoli NT$65), around fifty minutes from Miaoli. If you plan to stay at one of the Taian hotels, they can help you arrange taxis from Dahu or Wenshui. Alternatively, get off the Miaoli bus 1km south of Wenshui on Provincial Highway 3, at the junction with **Miaoli Route 62** (the stop is known as "*fǎyúnsì*", 法雲寺, but the busy 7-Eleven here is the main landmark). From here you can walk up Route 62, 200m or so, to the **Shei-Pa National Park Headquarters** (p.164), then either hitch a ride to Taian or get staff to call a taxi for you.

are expensive, but you should be able to snag better discounts on weekdays. Hotels tend to have a **public bathing area**, usually gender-segregated nude pools open late into the evening.

Onsen Papawaqa 泰安觀止 (*tàiān guānzhǐ*) 58 Yuandun (Route 62, km 10.5) ☏037/941-777, ⓦwww.papawaqa.com.tw. A stylish blend of concrete and bamboo, overlooking the river 1km or so before the main village. Use of mixed and segregated pools and outdoor spa is NT$400–450 (daily 8am–10pm), private villas from NT$2000 (for 2hr). ❽

Police Resort Village 警光山莊 (*jǐngguāng shānzhuāng*) ☏037/941-175. Convenient place to soak after a hike (though not to stay), just beyond the car park at the very end of Miaoli Route 62. Formerly the Japanese-era officers' club, it now caters mostly to Taiwanese policemen, but foreigners are welcome to soak in the segregated nude pools, the area's cheapest (daily 7am–noon & 1–9pm, opens at 8am in winter; NT$100).

Sunrise Hot Spring Hotel 日出溫泉渡假飯店 (*rìchū wēnquán dùjiàfàndiàn*) 34 Henglong Shan ☏037/941-988. Stylish rooms with attached stone-slab bathing tubs. The lavish communal outdoor bathing pools are open to the public (8am–10pm; NT$400); those seeking greater luxury can rent private two-person spa rooms

(NT$1000/1hr). About 1km further up the road from Tenglong. ❽

Taian Tangyue 泰安湯悦溫泉會館 (*tàiān tāngyuè wēnquán huìguǎn*) 45 Henglong Shan ☏037/941-941. Posh, tranquil hotel with fabulous rooms and facilities, if you can afford it; traditional wooden tubs on pinewood terraces, private stone hot-spring pools, a vast indoor spa and haute cuisine await. Hot springs only NT$400 – well worth it. ❽

Tang Wei 湯唯溫泉民宿 (*tāngwéi wēnquán mínsù*) 72-2 Henglong Shan ☏037/941-885, ⓦwww.tangwei.com.tw. Modern Euro-style chalet right on the river, offering a range of private spa villas for non-guests (NT$900–2000/2hr), or public pools for NT$200 (NT$250 weekends). Spa open to non-guests Mon–Fri 6–10pm and 2–10.30pm weekends. ❽

Tenglong Hot Spring Villa 騰龍溫泉山莊 (*ténglóng wēnquán shānzhuāng*) 5 Henglong Shan ☏037/941-002. Sprawling resort, with spacious doubles in A-frame wooden bungalows plus a small campsite for those with their own tents (NT$300/tent). Hot-spring pools only NT$200 (daily 6.30am–10pm). ❻

Taian hiking trails

There are several **hiking trails** around Jinshui, but bear in mind that most of the paths are very steep, leaving them vulnerable to landslips during heavy rains. It's also important to note that signs are in Chinese only, and there are few, if any, distance or direction markers. Despite this, most trails are well defined and invariably flagged at regular intervals by red, white and yellow **ribbons** left by hiking clubs from all over Taiwan; be sure to ask locals about the latest trail conditions before setting out.

Shuiyun Waterfall

The area's easiest hike – though one not to be attempted in rainy weather – is to the **Shuiyun Waterfall** (水雲瀑布; *shuǐyún pùbù*), a shimmering cascade hidden behind a bend along the Wenshui River. Most of the trail follows the northern side of the river, which remains dry for much of the year but is prone to flash floods in rainy weather.

The route begins at the car park at the end of Miaoli Route 62 (2km beyond the village). Here, the pavement ends and a landscaped gravel trail continues for another kilometre or so before it reaches the **Shuiyun Suspension Bridge** (水雲吊橋; *shuǐyún diàoqiáo*), which you must cross in order to reach the trail proper. After crossing the bridge, climb the wooden steps for a couple of hundred metres until the trail enters the forest and splits into two directions (with signs in Chinese): the left-hand fork leads to the top of Hushan (see below), while the right-hand path drops down to the river trail to the falls. Take the right-hand trail for about 50m until you reach another sign pointing to the left; follow this path for a few minutes until you reach a rocky outcrop along the riverbank. If you look closely at the rock's edge you'll find a rope you can use to lower yourself to the riverbed. From here, keep to the left side of the river to reach the Shuiyun Waterfall, about 1.5km upstream: the easiest line to follow is marked by **bamboo poles** stuck deep into the ground and crested with red flags. If the river level is really low, it's possible to walk up to the base of the waterfall, where there is a clear pool, ideal for a refreshing swim. Allow yourself at least ninety minutes to make the return trip from the car park.

Hushan

The steep path to the top of triangular **Hushan** (虎山; *hǔshān*; 1492m) is the area's most challenging and rewarding hike. Though the trail is well built, the upper portion has precious few switchbacks and slices straight up the mountainside, with sturdy **ropes** anchored to trees along the way for support. The ascent is strenuous and suitable only for fairly fit and experienced hill walkers. From the left-hand fork beyond the Shuiyun Suspension Bridge (see above), the trail winds through a cool, shaded forest before cutting sharply up to the top of Hushan (flagged with **ribbons**). Close to the top, the trail crosses the rocky riverbed that can fill up rapidly in the rainy season, and you must walk up the riverbed itself for about 100m before reconnecting with the trail; here it's essential to look for the trail ribbons tied to overhanging tree branches in order to keep to the path. On clear days, the **views** from the top of Hushan can be thrilling, especially looking across the valley to the majestic peaks of **Shei-Pa National Park**. From the car park at the end of Route 62, allow yourself three to four hours for the return hike.

Eating and drinking

Apart from the hotel restaurants, which tend to be pricey and uninteresting, the only **places to eat** in Jinshui Village are the lively **outdoor stalls** (露天小吃店; *lùtiān xiǎochīdiàn*) clustered on the north side of the suspension footbridge. These establishments dish up delicious local food, including nominal aboriginal dishes such as **roasted mountain pig** (*kǎoshānzhū*; NT$100) and grilled pork sausages. If you want to stick to the basics the owners can quickly whip up steaming plates of fried rice and noodles (NT$60–100). These restaurants are popular with locals, especially **Atayal tribespeople** from nearby Longshan Buluo (龍山部落; *lóngshān bùluò*). The best of the hotel restaurants is at *Tenglong Hot Spring Villa* (see opposite), which serves up decent Chinese and Hakka dishes (daily noon–2pm & 6–8pm).

Sanyi

Tucked away in the south of Miaoli County, **SANYI** (三義; *sānyì*) is Taiwan's **woodcarving** centre, some fifty minutes from Hsinchu by train – trains from Taipei take two-and-a-half hours, making day-trips possible (Taichung is also just 30min away). Apart from the **Sanyi Wood Sculpture Museum**, the town's main attractions are its numerous woodcarving (*mùdiāo*) shops, selling a vast range of work from religious icons to kitsch souvenirs squarely aimed at the tourist trade. Nearby **Shengxing** offers some beautiful hiking, historic Hakka teahouses and the photogenic ruin of Longteng Bridge. The village is halfway along a 16km loop of old rail line between Sanyi and Houli (后里; *hòulǐ*), abandoned in the 1990s; the stretch between Sanyi and Shengxing should be reopened as a tourist train route by the end of 2011 (for more information, ask at the visitor information centres in Taipei or Taichung – see p.62 & p.175 respectively).

Arrival and orientation

Sanyi's **train station** is inconveniently located at the far northern end of town, just off the main street, Zhongzheng Road (Provincial Highway 13). The built-up area south of the station is the original and fairly unattractive town centre, while most of the woodcarving shops lie a further 2km to the south, where Zhongzheng Road is known as **Shuimei Street**. The sculpture museum sits on the hillside above here in a small collection of modern buildings known as **Guangsheng**. **Shengxing** is quite separate from all this, tucked away in the hills to the southeast and halfway along the abandoned rail tracks. The area is too spread out to see everything on foot, and unless you visit during a festival (when a **minibus** usually shuttles between all the main sights), you'll have to rent a **scooter**. Jian Guang (建光; *jiānguāng*; Mon–Fri 8am–6pm, Sat & Sun 7.30am–6pm; ☎037/871-879; no English signs and little English spoken) at 162-2 Zhongzheng Rd, opposite the station, is pretty relaxed about renting to foreigners; all you need is a driving licence, though with no ARC (see p.23) you'll need to leave your passport with them. Rates are around NT$150 for two hours (125cc), and NT$50 per hour thereafter, or around NT$400 for the day (you won't need more than NT$70 for petrol). **Taxis** charge NT$200 to Shengxing (one-way), so unless you have all day to walk, the scooter is better value.

The Town

Heading south along Zhongzheng Road from the train station, there's not much to see in the main part of Sanyi; turn left on County Route 130, then first right beyond the rail tracks on Miaoli Route 49 towards Shengxing. Just ahead you'll see signs (in Chinese) to the **Sanyi Duck Factory** (三義一ㄚ箱寶; *sānyì yā xiāngbǎo*; Mon–Fri 9am–5pm, Sat & Sun 9am–6pm; ☎037/872-076) at 176 Chonghe Rd, just off the main road. Local carvers sell a wide-range of multi-coloured wooden ducks, birds and animals here, and from NT$200 to NT$1000 (depending on size) you can paint your own model in a warehouse next door – the whole process takes about two hours. If you can't wait for Shengxing, a great place **to eat** in Sanyi is *Lai Xinkui Noodles* (賴新魁麵館; *làixīnkuímiànguǎn*) at 170 Zhongzheng Rd (☎037/872-600), with big bowls of steaming *bǎntiáo* noodles from NT$60.

Shengxing

Rejoin Route 49 after the duck shop and follow the signs 3km to the attractive Hakka village of **Shengxing** (勝興; *shèngxīng*), particularly appealing in the spring when the area's distinctive white **tung flowers** (*tónghuā*) are in bloom. Shengxing was once an important transport hub for the **camphor oil** industry, but a new tunnel meant main-line trains bypassed the village in the late 1990s. Today the tourist industry is booming, which means weekends and holidays turn the place into a bit of carnival, surrounded by car parks; plans to revive the rail line to Sanyi station will no doubt intensify this, so visit on a weekday if possible.

The **old station**, completed in 1911 and once Taiwan's highest main-line stop at 402m, is a picturesque wooden building at the bottom of the narrow main street. The road back up the hill is lined with teahouses and stores serving Hakka food, snacks and souvenirs.

Suitably refreshed, you can ride or walk to **Longteng Broken Bridge** (龍騰斷橋; *lóngténg duànqiáo*), just under 6km to the southeast. The hike along the old rail tracks is very pleasant, and mostly level – head south through the 726m tunnel near Shengxing station. The bridge is a redbrick viaduct that collapsed during the Hsinchu earthquake of 1935, now a romantic ruin, overgrown with weeds and bushes and surrounded by lush, wooded hills. Assuming you have a scooter, you can loop back to Sanyi from here via Miaoli Route 51, which rejoins Provincial Highway 13 at the southern and more interesting end of town.

Eating

Shengxing is teeming with snack stalls and restaurants, especially at the weekends, but the village's oldest **restaurant** is the atmospheric *Shengxing Inn* (勝興客棧; *shèngxīng kèzhàn*; daily 9am–8pm; meals from 10.30am; ☎037/873-883) at 72 Lane 14, on the right just up the slope from the station. The cosy wooden dining room was strengthened with red bricks taken from the Longteng Bridge after the earthquake. Recommended Hakka dishes include the bamboo and pork dish (NT$230 small, NT$280 big), special tofu (NT$150/200) and the succulent duck or *zhīsù yāròu* (NT$150/200). *Léichá* (see box, p.156) costs NT$100 per person (DIY), or NT$250 for a bowl made for you. Menus are in Chinese only, but the owner's wife speaks English.

Also good is *Shanzhong Chuan Qi* (山中傳奇; *shānzhōng chuánqí*; Mon-Fri 10am–9pm, Sat & Sun 9am–10pm), a café (Chinese signs only) set on a series of wooden terraces on the slopes across the tracks. *Léichá* costs NT$260 (for two) and coffee NT$150; you can try your hand at making cups at a potter's wheel for NT$350. Menus are in Chinese, but someone usually speaks English.

Shuimei Street and Sanyi Wood Sculpture Museum

Re-entering the southern end of Sanyi on Highway 13 you'll find yourself on **Shuimei Street** (水美雕刻街; *shuǐměi diāokèjiē*) the town's main commercial woodcarving area. It's crammed with over two hundred shops stretching for almost 1km, and is a good place to browse for gifts – though the most visually striking pieces are often big and expensive, there's plenty of smaller, more affordable artwork on display.

At the end of the strip, turn left at County Route 130 and follow the signs to the **Sanyi Wood Sculpture Museum** (三義木雕博物館; *sānyì mùdiāo bówùguǎn*; Tues–Sun 9am–5pm; NT$80), a modern building at the end of a small strip of woodcarving shops, many doubling as teahouses and cafés. This is **Guangsheng Village** (廣聲新城; *guǎngshēng xīnchéng*), purpose-built to accommodate Taiwan's finest wood sculptors, in order to pool their artistic (and tourist-attracting) synergies – it's also the focus of the month-long Sanyi Woodcarving

Festival, usually held between August and October. The museum houses a small exhibition on the history of woodcarving and a collection of absorbing sculptures on the higher floors, but most of the explanations are in Chinese only. If you're walking, the museum is clearly signposted in English off Zhongzheng Road, 2.7km from the station.

Shei-Pa National Park

An unapologetically rugged reserve of pristine mountain peaks and raging rivers, **SHEI-PA NATIONAL PARK** (雪霸國家公園; *xuěbà guójiā gōngyuán*) is one of Asia's most untouched expanses of wilderness. Stretching across almost 770 square kilometres of the magnificent **Xueshan range**, Taiwan's third-largest national park is studded with stunning peaks, 51 of them higher than 3000m – putting them on a par with most of the European Alps. The park's highest peak is the range's namesake: **Xueshan** (Snow Mountain), which at 3886m is the second-tallest mountain in northeast Asia. Despite its lofty height, it's one of the island's most accessible and rewarding climbs, with an extremely well-maintained trail that is typically open for most of the year. This path is also a grandiose gateway to the park's other mountain highlights, such as the precipitous **Holy Ridge** that extends north from Xueshan to the 3492m **Dabajianshan**, whose distinctive pyramid shape has made it one of the country's most celebrated peaks.

Seasonal conditions vary, but in general the **best time** for climbing in Shei-Pa is October to December and late February to April. The May rains and the frequent typhoons that hit the island from June to September can cause severe damage to the trails, making landslips a concern. Though winters are cold and the main peaks are usually covered with **snow** from late December to mid-February, for experienced climbers with proper gear and crampons this can be the most rewarding time to visit.

Information

The **Shei-Pa National Park Headquarters** (雪霸國家公園管理處; *xuěbà guójiā gōngyuán guǎnlǐchù*) and its **visitor centre** (daily 9am–5pm; ℡037/996-100, Ⓦwww.spnp.gov.tw) are rather inconveniently located along Miaoli Route 62 just off Provincial Highway 3, about 2km from the town of Wenshui on the way to the Taian Hot Springs (see p.159). The visitor centre has two exhibition halls that give an excellent bilingual overview of the park's most notable attractions and show films (Tues–Sun). On most days **English-speaking staff** are on hand and can provide you with park **maps** as well as more detailed topographical maps (Chinese only) of trails in the Xueshan area. Those wishing to climb mountains within the park can apply here for national park entry permits, although you must submit your application seven working days before the proposed start date of your climb (see p.37).

Wuling Recreation Area

The only section of Shei-Pa accessible by public transport, the **WULING RECREATION AREA** (武陵遊樂區; *wǔlíng yóulèqū*) is the base for Xueshan climbs and is a worthwhile destination in its own right. Commonly known as **Wuling Farm** (武陵農場; *wǔlíng nóngchǎng*), the area was established as an **orchard** in 1963 by retired KMT soldiers, and still draws domestic tourists looking to buy freshly plucked peaches, pears and apples.

Getting to Wuling

Driving to Wuling (via the Xueshan Tunnel) takes around three hours from Taipei. The simplest way to reach Wuling by public transport is to take one of the two daily Kuo-Kuang **buses** (7am & 12.40pm; 2hr 45min; NT$337) that run from the east-coast city of **Yilan** (宜蘭; *yílán*). These buses stop in Wuling before heading on to **Lishan** (梨山; *líshān*; see p.214). Yilan is 1hr 5min to 1hr 20min from Taipei by express train; Yilan's bus station is 150m left of the train station.

Heading back, buses depart from Lishan for Wuling and Yilan at 8.30am and 1.30pm, stopping at Wuling at around 9.10am and 2.10pm, but get to the bus stop well in advance just in case. At Lishan (which is 29km south of Wuling), you can catch a bus to **Taroko Gorge** and **Hualien** (see p.289).

From **Taichung** (台中; *táizhōng*; see p.173), a bus departs daily for Lishan (8am; NT$561), arriving around 2pm, from the Fengyuan bus station (豐原客運; *fēngyuán kèyùn*). Onward services for Wuling leave Lishan at 4.50pm (NT$74). Heading back, buses leave Wuling at 6.30am, and Lishan at 8am. The bus stops at Puli on the way at around 11.20am, where you change for for **Sun Moon Lake** (see p.200). It's imperative you **check all current departure times** (with the local tourist office if you don't speak Chinese) before making plans, as mountain bus routes are especially liable to change.

Before you enter the Recreation Area you'll be required to pay an entrance fee (Mon–Fri N$130, Sat & Sun NT$160); the **tollgate** is shortly after the turnoff into Wuling from Provincial Highway 7A. Many tourists drive up the main road, stopping at various orchards along the way to pick fruit, until they reach the **Wuling Suspension Bridge** (武陵吊橋; *wǔlíng diàoqiáo*). It's possible to walk the entire distance, but it's about 10km each way so make sure you have enough time for the return journey. Beyond the suspension bridge the road leads to one of the area's best-known hikes, to **Taoshan Waterfall** (桃山瀑布; *táoshān pùbù*). The 4km walk climbs about 450m before reaching the 50m-high cascade; allow two to three hours for the return journey.

Practicalities

Just behind the bus stop is a **shop** (9am–5pm) with basic supplies such as instant noodles, nuts, dried fruit and bottled water. Next to the shop is the **Wuling Visitor Center** (武陵遊客中心; *wǔlíng yóukè zhōngxīn*; Tues–Sun 9am–4.30pm; ☏04/2590-1350, ⓦwww.wuling-farm.com.tw), where you can get a basic map of the Wuling Farm area. The **main road** through the Recreation Area is paved and heads north from the tollgate, with everything of interest lying just off it.

Wuling has a few comfortable if slightly pricey **hotels**, all within walking distance of the visitor centre. The best value is the *Wuling Guest House* (武陵國民賓館; *wǔlíng guómín bīnguǎn*; ☏04/2590-1259, ⓦwww.wuling-farm.com.tw; ❼), which has large doubles with cable TV as well as two- and four-person cabins; a Chinese-style buffet breakfast is included in the room rate (otherwise NT$150), and the **restaurant** near the hotel lobby serves lunch and dinner (NT$350 per person). The on-site *Maple Forest Café* (daily 12.30–4.30pm & 6.30–10.30pm) offers snacks and drinks. There is also a **campsite** (NT$400 with own tent or NT$900 for raised-platform tent with mattress for four people; ☏04/2590-1265, see website above) near the Xueshan trailhead.

A posher, more expensive option is the *Hoya Resort Hotel* (武陵富野渡假村; *wǔlíng fùyě dùjiǎcūn*; ☏04/2590-1399; ❾), on a hill to the left of the road after you enter the recreation area. This package-style resort includes breakfast and dinner buffets in its room rates, but the restaurant is for guests only.

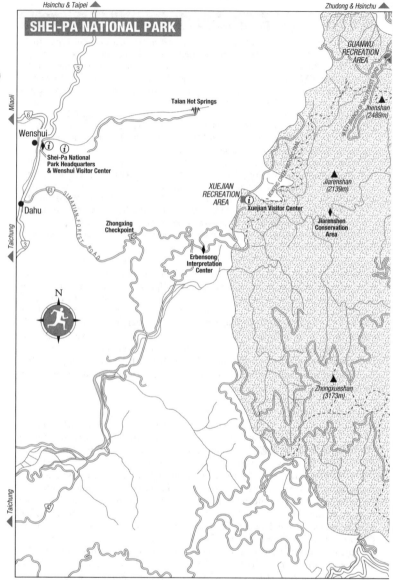

SHEI-PA NATIONAL PARK

GUANWU
RECREATION
AREA

Taian Hot Springs

Jhenshan
(2489m)

Wenshui

Shei-Pa National
Park Headquarters
& Wenshui Visitor Center

Jiarenshan
(2139m)

XUEJIAN
RECREATION
AREA

Xuejian Visitor Center

Dahu

Jiarenshen
Conservation
Area

Zhongxing
Checkpoint

Erbensong
Interpretation
Center

N

Zhongxueshan
(3173m)

SIMAKAN FOREST ROAD

WEST BRANCH OF DAHU FOREST ROAD

BEIKENG CREEK HISTORICAL TRAIL

Xueshan

The 3886m-high **Xueshan** (雪山; *xuěshān*) is one of Asia's most scintillating climbs, and though it takes a modicum of planning it's well worth the effort. An exceptionally fit walker could make the nearly 22km journey from the trailhead to the peak and back in one long day, but most climbers choose to take their time and spend a night in the 369 Cabin (free). For experienced climbers with more

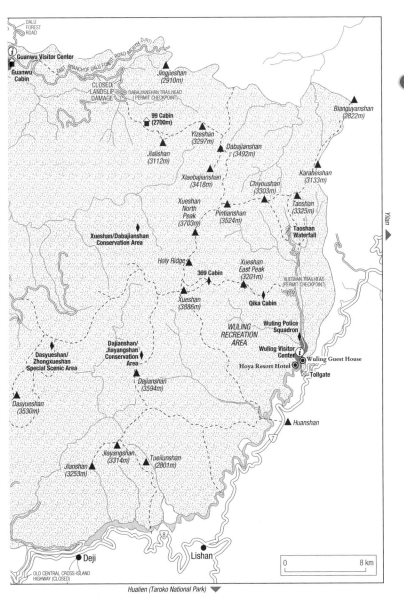

Hualien (Taroko National Park) ▼

time and their own camping equipment, this trail can be the gateway to a two- to three-day circuit over the hair-raising **Holy Ridge** and on to **Dabajianshan** – without question one of Taiwan's top treks.

You'll need to arrange a **national park entry permit** (入園; *rùyuán*; apply in advance) and **police permit** or **mountain entry permit** (入山; *rùshān*; handed out by local police stations on the spot) to make any of these climbs;

see Basics, p.37, for details about the permit system. The Shei-Pa **website** also has the application process clearly mapped out in English. Though applications for the park entry permit are technically supposed to be received **seven to thirty working days** before the proposed start date of your climb, in practice they are often approved within a few days, and if you turn up to the park headquarters to apply in person (foreigners are allowed to do this), the staff are likely to prepare your permit much more quickly. Alternatively, **Barking Deer Adventures** (☏0938/337-710, ⓦwww.barking-deer.com) can do all the work for you (for around NT$2500).

Getting to the trailhead

Before you begin your climb, you must pick up your **mountain entry permit** at the **Wuling Police Squadron** (武陵警察小隊; *wǔlíng jǐngchá xiǎoduì*; ☏04/2590-1117), a few hundred metres north along the main road from the visitor centre, on the left-hand side. You'll need an application form (from the Shei-Pa website), three copies of your hiking itinerary, and one copy of your passport and park entry permit. The rangers are also likely to inspect your kit to ensure that you have the necessary **equipment**. It's best to arrive the day before you're scheduled to set out to allow plenty of time to check in and to arrange **transport** to the trailhead. It's a 7km walk along the main road from the visitor centre to the trailhead, and, though the scenery is pleasant, the walk adds considerable time and distance to the climb and could make it a challenge for some hikers to make it to the 369 Cabin by nightfall. If the rangers are free, they might offer to drop you off at the trailhead the following morning; otherwise, you'll have to arrange a shuttle and pick-up with your hotel.

The climb

From the Xueshan trailhead (雪山登山口; *xuěshān dēngshānkǒu*), it's 2km to the **Qika Cabin** (七卡山莊; *qīkǎ shānzhuāng*; 2463m), which has pit toilets and a nearby tap with a fresh water supply. From here it's a steep 5km climb, mostly up stone steps, to the 369 Cabin – allow between two to five hours depending on your fitness. Once you reach Xueshan's **East Peak** (雪山東峰; *xuěshān dōngfēng*; 3201m), the trail becomes more gradual and gives good views directly west across the valley to the Holy Ridge. About 1km further is the **369 Cabin** (三六九山莊; *sānliùjiǔ shānzhuāng*), which overlooks a giant valley and a vast plain to the north, making for an ideal place to relax and soak up the scenery – in late afternoon clouds often roll into the valley, creating the spectacular **"sea of clouds"** phenomenon. There are no designated sleeping spaces, so you're free to grab whatever bunk you fancy. Near the cabin are pit toilets and a tap with fresh water – a convenient place to replenish your **drinking water**, as there are no other reliable sources between here and the summit.

Many climbers set their alarms for as early as 3am to ensure they can cover the remaining 3.9km to **Xueshan Main Peak** (雪山主峰; *xuěshān zhǔfēng*) before dawn, and indeed watching the sun rise here, over a pinkish-blue sea of clouds below, is an ethereal experience. However, the summit can be phenomenal at any time of day, and if there is a large crowd getting up early for the sunrise it's worth sleeping in and heading to the top a bit later, when you can have it all to yourself. Average walkers should be able to complete this stage in two to three hours. It's important to try to reach the top by midday to allow yourself plenty of time for the descent to the trailhead, which can take anywhere from four to five hours.

From Xueshan's Main Peak it's also possible to set out across the **Holy Ridge** (聖稜線; *shèng léngxiàn*) from where you can carry on north to **Dabajianshan** (p.169) or head east to **Taoshan** and back down to the Wuling Recreation Area.

However, the Holy Ridge is precarious in places and there are some steep fixed-rope sections, so it's really only suited to more experienced climbers. It's essential to ask the park rangers in Wuling about the latest trail conditions and the weather forecast – the ridge is highly exposed and lightning is a real danger here.

Guanwu Recreation Area

The **Guanwu Recreation Area** (觀霧遊樂區; *guānwùyóulèqū*; free) reopened in July 2009 after successive typhoons had closed the area for five years. At around 2000m in elevation, the area is cool and densely vegetated, with one of Taiwan's most humbling old-growth forests and the island's only **Sassafras Conservation Area**. If wilderness walks are what you're after, it's well worth the effort to get here; in addition to having the safest trail to **Dabajianshan** (permits required), it offers several shorter **hikes** that on clear days can yield splendid vistas of the park's highest mountains – especially those along the Holy Ridge.

To get to Guanwu you'll need to have your own transport. The area is around 60km southeast of Hsinchu via County Route 122 and the winding **Dalu Forest Road** (allow 2hr by car). At the 15km point you'll pass the Yuanshan Checkpoint (雲山檢查哨; *yúnshān jiǎncháshào*), where you need to get your mountain entry permit (free). **Guanwu Visitor Center** (觀霧遊客中心; *guānwù yóukè zhōngxīn*; Tues–Sun 9am–4.30pm; ☎037/276-300), just inside the park entrance at the 26km mark, is where you should enquire about trail conditions. The nearby **Guanwu Cabin** (觀霧山莊; *guānwù shānzhuāng*; ☎03/521-8853), originally built for loggers, has been transformed into a **restaurant** serving basic meals (no accommodation). Just below the cabin is the beginning of the 1.5km trail to the **Guanwu Waterfall** (觀霧瀑布; *guānwù pùbù*), which drops delicately down a near-vertical 30m rock face.

Dabajianshan

For most hikers, the journey to spectacular **Dabajianshan** (大霸尖山; *dàbàjiānshān*) takes a minimum three days, with two overnight stays in the **99 Cabin** (九九山莊; *jiǔjiǔ shānzhuāng*; NT$200/night – pay at Guanwu Visitor Center); reservations for the cabin will be included in your permit. To reach the original **trailhead** (at 1750m) from the visitor centre, you'll need to hike around 20km of the generally flat east branch of the earthen Dalu Forest Road (vehicles may be able to traverse this section in future – check in advance). The climb to the cabin, which sits at about 2700m, is fairly steep, and most walkers stop here for the night, rising well before dawn for the slog to the summit. However, as Dabajianshan has sheer faces on all sides, it's not possible to go to the very top: though the park installed **metal railings** on one side to make the ascent possible, a couple of climbers fell off and they had to be closed. Most walkers return to the 99 Cabin and spend a second night there before hiking down to the road the next morning. Barking Deer can arrange the whole trip for NT$2500 (see opposite).

Xuejian Recreation Area

The remote **Xuejian Recreation Area** (雪見遊樂區; *xuějiàn yóulèqū*; free) on the park's western side is a one-and-a-half-hour drive from the park headquarters in Wenshui (see p.164), inaccessible without a car or scooter; the sense of isolation and pristine wilderness here makes this an exceptional adventure. You'll have to drive or hitch down Miaoli Route 61 (aka **Simaxian Forest Road**; 司馬限林道因道路; *sīmǎxiàn líndàoyīn dàolù*) from **Dahu** (大湖; *dàhú*), just south of the park headquarters near Wenshui. Around 6km from Dahu, you need to pick up mountain entry permits (free; see p.37) at the Zhongxing Checkpoint (中興檢查哨; *zhōngxīng jiǎncháshào*). You can also drive up from Taichung via Zhuolan on Taichung Route 47.

After around 21km from Dahu the forest road passes the **Erbensong Interpretation Center** (二本松解説站; *èrběnsōng jiěshuōzhàn*; Tues–Sun 9am–4.30pm), showcasing traditional **Atayal** artefacts. Another 8.5km along is the **Xuejian Visitor Centre** (雪見遊客中心; *xuějiàn yóukè zhōngxīn*; Tues–Sun 9am–4.30pm; ⊕037/962-166) staffed by English-speaking interpreters, with information on local hiking trails.

Travel details

Buses

With so many services operating in the region, most bus frequencies have not been included.
Daxi (Northern Cross-Island Highway) to: Baling (5 daily; 1hr 30min); Cihu (20min); Fuxing (40min); Little Wulai Falls (4 daily; 45min); Shangbaling (2 daily; 2hr).
Fulong to: Bitou (30min); Daxi (coast; 35min); Keelung (1hr); Leo Ocean Resort (40min); Toucheng (45min).
Hsinchu to: Taichung (1hr); Taipei (1hr); Yimin Temple (10 daily; 30min); Zhudong (40min).
Jinshan to: Baishawan (40min); Danshui (1hr); Dharma Drum Mountain (10min); Keelung (30min); Shimen (20min); Taipei (1hr); Yeliu (10min).
Keelung to: Bitou (30–40min); Danshui (1hr 30min); Fulong (1hr); Jinguashi (40min); Jinshan (30min); Jiufen (30min); Taipei (1hr); Yeliu (20min).
Miaoli to: Sanyi (30min); Wenshui (hourly; 50min).
Pingxi to: Jingtong (5min); Taipei (40min).
Ruifang to: Jinguashi (20min); Jiufen (15min).
Sanyi to: Miaoli (30min).
Toufen to: Emei Lake (35min); Hsinchu (20min); Taipei (1hr 20min).
Wuling Farm to: Lishan (2 daily; 15–20min); Luodong (2 daily); Yilan (2 daily; 2hr 45min).
Yilan to: Lishan (2 daily; 3hr); Wuling Farm (2 daily; 2hr 45min).
Zhudong to: Beipu (15min); Lion's Head Mountain (5 daily; 40min).
Zhunan to: Nanzhuang (1hr).

Ferries

Keelung to: Matsu (daily; 8hr).

Flights

Taiwan Taoyuan International Airport near Taoyuan and **Songshan Airport** in Taipei serve as the regional airports (see p000).

Trains

Fulong to: Dali (15 daily; 15min); Daxi (coast; 15 daily; 10min); Jiaoxi (7 express daily; 25min); Ruifang (7 express daily; 25min); Taipei (10 express daily; 1hr 5min).
Hsinchu to: Sanyi (18 daily; 50min); Taichung (15 express daily; 1hr); Taipei (frequent high-speed trains daily; 32min; 16 express daily; 1hr 5min); Zhudong (14 daily; 25min);
Keelung to: Hsinchu (2 express daily; 1hr 35min); Taichung (2 express daily; 2hr 30min); Taipei (frequent; 40min).
Luodong to: Jiaoxi (16 express daily; 15min); Taipei (18 express daily; 1hr 50min); Yilan (16 express daily; 10min).
Miaoli to: Sanyi (14 daily; 35min); Taipei (12 express daily; 1hr 30min).
Ruifang to: Jingtong (14 daily; 45min); Pingxi (14 daily; 40min); Shihfen (14 daily; 30min); Taipei (16 express daily; 45min).
Sanyi to: Hsinchu (18 daily; 50min); Taichung (18 daily; 40min); Taipei (3 express daily; 2hr 15min).
Yilan to: Taipei (18 express daily; 1hr 40min).
Zhunan to: Hsinchu (14 express daily; 15min); Taichung (10 express daily; 50min); Taipei (14 express daily; 1hr 25min).

Central Taiwan

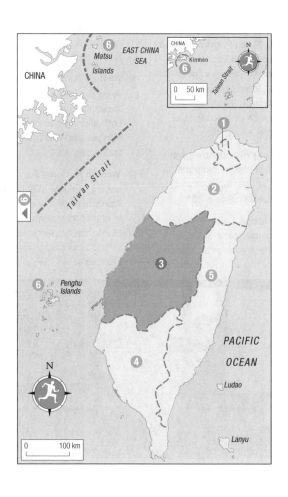

CHAPTER 3 # Highlights

* **921 Earthquake Museum** Informative and poignant memorial to the devastating quake that hit Taiwan in 1999, with high-tech exhibits built around the hauntingly stark ruins of a junior high school. See p.183

* **Dajia Mazu Pilgrimage** The annual Mazu Pilgrimage to celebrate Taiwan's "patron saint" is an exuberant celebration involving hundreds of thousands of people. See p.188

* **Lugang** Historic town with bags of charm, old streets, craft shops, temples and tasty "little eats". See p.191

* **Sun Moon Lake** The ancestral home of Taiwan's smallest aboriginal tribe, the Thao, this tranquil lake offers some of the most gorgeous scenery in the country. See p.200

* **Chung Tai Chan Monastery** Taiwan's largest Buddhist temple complex is an incredible blend of modern engineering and dazzling traditional craftsmanship. See p.212

* **Alishan National Scenic Area** Explore a lush, mountainous region sprinkled with alluring homestays, Tsou villages and pristine hiking trails. See p.221

* **Yushan National Park** The ascent of Yushan, northeast Asia's highest mountain, is one of the country's highlights, a spectacular hike through the clouds with mind-blowing views. See p.229

▲ View of Sun Moon Lake

Central Taiwan

B ounded by the densely populated cities of the north, and the lush tropical plains of the south, **central Taiwan** is a region principally defined by mountains: the mighty central ranges contain a vast array of tantalizing landscapes, from the mesmerizing beauty of **Sun Moon Lake** to the awe-inspiring peak of **Yushan**, northeast Asia's tallest mountain.

Taichung is one of the most dynamic cities in the country and gateway to the region, noted for its innovative teahouses and vibrant nightlife. To the south, the flat river plains sandwiched between the hills and the sea are rich in traditional Chinese culture; worship of Taoist deity Mazu, known as Goddess of the Sea and often regarded as the country's patron saint, is more intense here than any other part of Taiwan. The towns of **Beigang** and **Dajia** are home to the most important Mazu temples on the island, and the annual Dajia Mazu Pilgrimage is Taiwan's largest religious festival. **Lugang** is one of Taiwan's oldest towns, a living museum of master craftsmen, narrow streets and temples, while the **Great Buddha Statue** in Changhua is one of Asia's biggest. The geographical centre of the island, Puli, is home to the mind-boggling **Chung Tai Chan Monastery**, a staggering monument to contemporary architecture and Zen Buddhist philosophy.

Further south, the narrow valleys and traditional Tsou villages of **Alishan National Scenic Area** lie to the east of Chiayi, an area best explored on foot or with your own transport. The Scenic Area's appeal is compounded by an array of attractive and highly individual homestays, while aboriginal culture is particularly strong here. Alishan borders the **Yushan National Park**, offering a more challenging hiking experience, though the stunning path up its main peak is tackled by hundreds of visitors every year.

This chapter covers Changhua, Chiayi, Nantou, Taichung and Yunlin counties, and though **getting around** the coastal plains is straightforward given the profusion of north–south transport links, accessing remote parts of the interior can be tricky without your own transport. Buses connect the most popular destinations with the main cities, however, and distances are not huge.

Taichung

Sprawled over the flat coastal plains west of the mountains, **TAICHUNG** (台中; *táizhōng*) is Taiwan's third-largest city, the unofficial capital of central Taiwan and an important transport hub for the region. It's also regarded as the country's most attractive place to live: the climate is drier, the air less polluted, housing cheaper, and the streets greener and less crowded than Taipei or Kaohsiung. Taiwanese **tea**

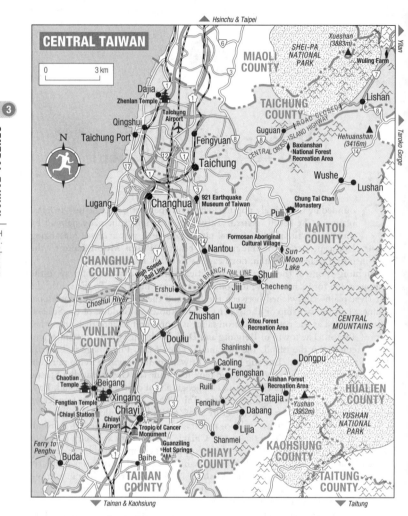

culture is particularly developed here; the city's appealing mix of elegant classical teahouses and stylish contemporary cafés are the perfect setting for a varied range of teas. Taichung's old centre still contains attractive remnants of its Japanese colonial past and a smattering of unusual **temples**, while in the modern western half of the city, I.M. Pei's **Luce Memorial Chapel** is a striking piece of modern architecture and the **National Taiwan Museum of Fine Arts** is a world-class contemporary art gallery. Beyond the suburbs, the chief attractions are **Dajia** and its famous **Mazu Pilgrimage**, and the **921 Earthquake Museum**.

Some history

Taichung traces its origins to a military post and village known as **Datun**, established in 1733 on the site of today's Taichung Park, but the modern city is an amalgam of several places, explaining why its oldest buildings and temples appear to be scattered all over the city – the western district of Nantun grew up around another army camp, founded in 1721 on the site of a farm that was built sixteen years earlier, and was absorbed by Taichung in 1950. Datun was briefly the **capital of Taiwan** after the island became a province of China in 1885, but local infrastructure was poor and Taipei, which was provisional capital, assumed the official role in 1894. After the Japanese occupied Taiwan in 1895 the city's name was changed to Taichung, or "Central Taiwan" and development began in earnest, with Englishman William Barton hired to design the new road layout for the city. The economy boomed in the 1970s and 1980s, with manufacturing and particularly shoe making leading the way, and by the 1990s the commercial centre of the city had drifted west towards Taichung Port (Taiwan's third largest). The city's population topped the million mark in 2003 (the current population of the metropolitan area is around 2.3 million).

Arrival and information

Taichung Airport (台中航空站; *táizhōng hángkōngzhàn*; Ⓦ www.tca.gov.tw) is a tedious 20km northwest of the city centre, near the village of Xishi (西勢; *xīshì*): to get into the city, take a taxi (around NT$500) or Taichung Bus #6115 (NT$20). Taichung is almost midway on the **western train line** between Taipei and Kaohsiung, and the **train station** (台中火車站; *táizhōng huǒchēzhàn*) sits in the old centre of the city, close to all local and long-distance **bus** stations (see box, p.187) – taxis are also plentiful. Lockers outside the train station cost NT$20–50 per three hours (maximum 6 days). If you plan on staying in western Taichung, note that most inter-city buses stop along Taizhonggang Road before terminating near the train station.

Taichung's helpful **visitor information centre** (台中火車站旅遊服務中心; *táizhōng huǒchēzhàn lǚyóu fúwù zhōngxīn*; daily 9am–6pm Ⓣ 04/2221-2126, Ⓦ english.tccg.gov.tw) sits near the main exit of the train station – staff usually speak English.

High Speed Rail Station

The **High-Speed Rail Station** (高鐵台中站; *gāotiě táizhōngzhàn*; Ⓣ 04/3601-5000) is located at 8 Zhanqu 2nd Rd, **Wuri** (烏日; *wūrì*), 7km southwest of the city centre. Once here you can take the **free shuttle bus** into the city (daily 7.35am–12.10am, every 15–20min; 50min), which terminates at Taichung Park, via Sogo, or cough up NT$15–23 for a local train; these depart regularly from the connecting Xinwuri Station (新烏日車站; *xīnwūrì chēzhàn*) and are generally much faster into the old centre (15min to the main train station). There are also buses to **Sun Moon Lake** (see p.187) and plenty of **taxis** (Ⓣ 0809/005-006); it's NT$200–250 into the city and around NT$900–1000 to Sun Moon Lake (1hr). Assuming you have an international driver's licence, you can also **rent cars** outside the station (see p.188).

Orientation

Taichung covers a vast area, divided into eight districts, but it's easier to think of the city as having two distinct parts. The **old centre**, comprising Central, East, South and parts of North and West districts, lies around the train station in the eastern half of the city and is home to many government offices, shops, cheap hotels and traditional food stalls. In contrast, the modern city comprises **Beitun** to the north and sprawling **Nantun**, **Xitun**, and **West** districts beyond **Wuquan Road** (五權路; *wǔquán lù*) – this contains the business centre and most of Taichung's international food and nightlife. **Taizhonggang Road** (台中港路; *táizhōnggǎng lù*) is the main east–west thoroughfare connecting the two parts of the city and providing a route to the freeway, Donghai University and the harbour beyond (24km). The road starts at the train station and is known as **Zhongzheng Road** (中正路; *zhōngzhèng lù*) as far as Wuquan Road.

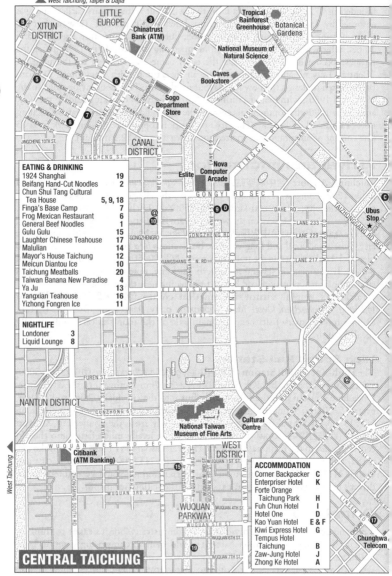

EATING & DRINKING

1924 Shanghai	19
Beifang Hand-Cut Noodles	2
Chun Shui Tang Cultural Tea House	5, 9, 18
Finga's Base Camp	7
Frog Mexican Restaurant	6
General Beef Noodles	1
Gulu Gulu	15
Laughter Chinese Teahouse	17
Malulian	14
Mayor's House Taichung	12
Meicun Diantou Ice	10
Taichung Meatballs	20
Taiwan Banana New Paradise	4
Ya Ju	13
Yangxian Teahouse	16
Yizhong Fongren Ice	11

NIGHTLIFE

Londoner	3
Liquid Lounge	8

ACCOMMODATION

Corner Backpacker	C
Enterpriser Hotel	K
Forte Orange Taichung Park	H
Fuh Chun Hotel	I
Hotel One	D
Kao Yuan Hotel	E & F
Kiwi Express Hotel	G
Tempus Hotel Taichung	B
Zaw-Jung Hotel	J
Zhong Ke Hotel	A

CENTRAL TAICHUNG

City transport

The main **city bus station** (台中汽車站; *táizhōng qìchēzhàn*) is just opposite the main entrance to the train station: numerous buses ply Taizhonggang Road from here (including #6106, #88 and #6147). Most **buses** display destinations in English (and have stop announcements in English), but timetables and maps at bus stops are provided solely in Chinese – most journeys should cost the standard

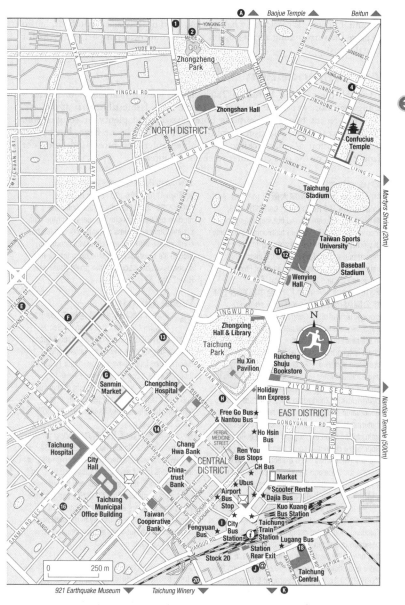

❶ YONGXING ST.
❷
Zhongzheng Park
YUDE RD.
YINGCAI RD.

Zhongshan Hall

NORTH DISTRICT

❹

Confucius Temple

JINNAN RD.

JINXIN ST.
YUCAI N. ST.

Taichung Stadium

DIANTAI ST.

Taiwan Sports University

Baseball Stadium

❶❷

Wenying Hall

JINGWU RD.

N

❶ ❷ ❸

Zhongxing Hall & Library

Taichung Park

Hu Xin Pavilion

Ruicheng Shuju Bookstore

ZIYOU RD. SEC. 3

Sanmin Market

Chengching Hospital

❶❸

Holiday Inn Express

Free Go Bus ★ & Nantou Bus

EAST DISTRICT

GONGYUAN E. RD.

★ Ho Hsin Bus

Taichung Hospital

City Hall

❶❹

Chang Hwa Bank

China-trust Bank

HERBAL MEDICINE STREET

Ren You Bus Stops

★ CH Bus

NANJING RD.

Market

CENTRAL DISTRICT

Taichung Municipal Office Building

Taiwan Cooperative Bank

Fengyuan Bus ★

❶

★ Ubus

Airport Bus Stop

City Bus Station

Scooter Rental

★ Dajia Bus

Kuo Kuang Bus Station

Taichung Train Station

Lugang Bus ❶❽

Stock 20

Station Rear Exit

Taichung Central

❷❶

0 250 m

single-sector fare of NT$20. In addition, there are six so-called TTJ buses ("Taichung Traffic Jam Bus"; daily 6am–10pm; every 10–15min), which were free in 2010 (the scheme may be extended) – get maps and the latest from the visitor centre at the train station. The **Taichung Metro** (TMRT) is finally under construction, scheduled for completion in 2015.

Taxis are not a bad way to get around – the meter starts at NT$85 and you'll usually pay less than NT$250 for trips across the central part of the city. **Driving**

around Taichung is particularly hair-raising, even by Taiwanese standards, but to explore the surrounding area it's useful to have your own transport (see p.188 for rental firms).

Accommodation

As usual, the cheapest **hotels** in Taichung are located near the train station – things get more expensive in the western and more fashionable parts of the city, where a recent boom in boutique hotels has created plenty of competition. There's a reasonable selection of mid-range hotels to choose from, but budget accommodation is sadly lacking. Most hotels offer free broadband access for laptop users, or use of a computer to check the internet.

Old centre

Enterpriser Hotel 企業家大飯店 (*qìyèjiā dàfàndiàn*) 160 Heping St ☎04/2220-7733, ⓦwww.gohotel.com.tw. Old but well-maintained rooms with cable TV, decent bathrooms and plenty of workspace – free wi-fi, computer in lobby and decent buffet breakfast included. A short walk behind the station (one block south of Fuxing, between Lide and Dayong sreets). ❹

Forte Orange Taichung Park 台中福泰桔子商旅公園店 (*táizhōng fútài jiézi shānglǚ gōngyuándiàn*) 17 Gongyuan Rd ☎04/2226-2323, ⓦwww.forte-hotel.net. Overlooking the park in the heart of the old centre, this spanking new chain hotel offers comfy, well-equipped rooms with breakfast included. Friendly English-speaking staff and excellent rates on-line. ❹

Fuh Chun Hotel 富春大飯店 (*fùchūn dàfàndiàn*) 1 Zhongshan Rd ☎04/2228-3181. Good-value budget hotel that's redubbed itself an "Internet Hotel", conveniently located opposite the train station in an old, slightly shabby building. Rooms are clean and come with TVs and wi-fi, but are otherwise what you'd expect, basic and a bit worn – the price and friendliness of the staff make it just about worthwhile for short stays. ❷

🏃 **Kao Yuan Hotel** 高苑旅館 (*gāoyuàn lǚguǎn*) 444 Zhongshan Rd ☎04/2229-8755. Cosy, modern business hotel in central Taichung. Rooms are compact but attractively designed in a smart, contemporary style, making this one of the best deals in town. There's a slightly older and cheaper branch at 392 Zhongzheng Rd (☎04/2226-1566; ❻), just around the corner. ❻

Kiwi Express Hotel 台中奇異果快捷旅店 (*táizhōng qíyìguǒ kuàijié lǚdiàn*) 253 Zhongzheng Rd ☎04/2229-4466, ⓦkiwi.hotel .com.tw. Excellent-value hotel, on the edge of downtown, with bright, compact all-white modern rooms enhanced with contemporary Asian murals on the walls. Free internet and a funky dining area for the ample breakfast buffet of Chinese and Western food (included). ❹

Zaw-Jung Hotel 瑞君商務旅館 (*ruìjūn shāngwù lǚguǎn*) 100 Fuxing Rd Sec 4 ☎04/2223-5838. Friendly budget hotel, set in a modern building opposite the rear exit of the train station. Standard rooms are simply decorated but comfortable, with TVs and clean wooden floors, though it's worth paying a little extra for the more spacious doubles. Look for the green "Business Hotel" sign. ❸

West district

🏃 **Corner Backpacker** 背包旅店 (*bèibāo lǚdiàn*) 85 Rixin St, at Xitun Rd Sec 1 ☎0973/331-020, ⓦwww.cornerbackpacker.com. Newish, bright hostel in central Taichung, with clean shared bathrooms, free wi-fi and TV in the lobby. There's a two- to six-people room for NT$1100–2700, depending on night of the week and how many people, and two dorms (male/female) where beds are NT$490 and NT$540 (Fri & Sat). Cash only.

Hotel One 台中亞緻大飯店 (*táizhōng yǎzhì dàfàndiàn*) 532 Yingcai Rd ☎04/2303-1234, ⓦwww.hotelone.com.tw. New luxury high-rise, set in the city's tallest skyscraper (designed by Kohn Pedersen Fox), with rooms designed for business; huge work stations with 37in flat-screen TVs, free wi-fi, iPod adapters and links to printers. The rooms are otherwise extremely plush, with neat, contemporary furnishings and top-notch service. Look for discounts on line. ❾

Xitun

Hung's Mansion Hotel 台中商旅 (*táizhōng shānglǚ*) 177 Taizhonggang Rd Sec 2 ☎04/2255-6688, ⓦwww.hungsmansion.com. One of Taichung's flashiest boutique hotels, right out on the edge of the city, perfect for exploring the outskirts or for onward travel. The spacious rooms come with giant 42in flat-screen TV, DVD players and bathrooms equipped with funky Japanese technology (think automatic toilets and massage showers). ❽

Tempus Hotel Taichung 永豐棧酒店 (*yǒngfēngzhàn jiǔdiàn*) 9 Taizhonggang Rd Sec 2 ☏04/2326-8008, ⊛www.tempus.com.tw. The former *Landis* is still Taichung's most elegant luxury hotel, smack in the heart of the busy western half of the city. Rooms are stylishly decked out with natural wood and designer furnishings, the bathrooms swathed in marble. Facilities include access to the Mandara Life Club, a lavish spa and pool, as well as a couple of swanky restaurants. ❼

Nantun

Tango Taichung 柯旅天閣台中 (*kēlǚ tiāngé táizhōng*) 525 Dadun Rd ☏04/2320-0000, ⊛www.tango-hotels.com. Ultra hip boutique chain (the suites have jacuzzis with huge TVs), a bit far from the old centre but worth

the taxi fare; even the standard rooms are very stylish, there's a cool health club and spa, the staff all speak English, a big Western breakfast buffet is included and there are plenty of shops/restaurants in the area. The only gripe – the gym is only open 3–10.30pm.

Beitun

Zhong Ke Hotel 中科大飯店 (*zhōngkē dàfàndiàn*) 256 Chongde Rd Sec 2 ☏04/22465599, ⊛www.zkhotel.com.tw. Modern hotel, with wi-fi and business centre for those without a computer. Rooms are cosy, stylish and very good value – the catch is the inconvenient location in the northern part of the city, close to the Folklore Park, but it's a relatively easy taxi ride the old centre. ❺

The City

Taichung is a modern city, but there are plenty of sights tucked away between all the development, especially in the **old centre**, best explored on foot. The attractions in west Taichung are much more spread out, and will require travelling by bus or taxi.

The old centre

The shabby **old centre** (中區; *zhōngqū*) around Taichung main train station is a bit the worse for wear, but still offers an absorbing glimpse of Taichung's traditional shopping streets and food stalls, as well as its finest **Japanese colonial buildings**. Start by heading to the south side of the train station, itself an attractive building completed in 1917, to **Stock 20** (台中二十號倉庫; *táizhōng èrshí hào cāngkù*; Tues–Fri 10am–6pm, Sat & Sun 10am–7pm; free), an innovative art centre converted from old train warehouses. Inside you'll find a café and main gallery open to the public, while up to eight artists in residence utilize the workshops on site. Take the underpass under the station (right as you exit) and turn right when you emerge – the gallery is a few metres ahead along the tracks.

Back at the station, walk north along Zhongzheng Road, past the canal on Luchuan Street, and turn left into narrow **Electronic Street** (電子街; *diànzijiē*), a pedestrianized alley crammed with Filipino, Thai and Indonesian stalls, and numerous electronic and computer stores beyond Zhongshan Road – it tends to get going after midday. Running parallel just to the north, **Jiguang Street** (激光街; *jīguāngjiē*) is the longest pedestrianized thoroughfare in the city (though plenty of scooters zip down it), lined with clothes shops and snack stalls. Walk west down either of these streets to Minquan Road and turn right, continuing north to the junction with Shifu Road. On the north side is Taichung's **City Hall** (台中市政府; *táizhōng shìzhèngfǔ*), completed by the Japanese in 1913. A typically meticulous imitation of Second Empire architecture, with white stone, mansard roof and striking Ionic column facade, it initially served as the Taichung regional administration office. The elegant white building on the other side of the road is the city's most stately colonial legacy. Built in 1911 with a handsome Neoclassical portico and domed roof, this was the original City Hall or **Taichung Municipal Office Building**, (台中市役所; *táizhōng shìyìsuǒ*; Tues–Sun 1–9pm; free) 97 Minquan Rd, now operating as an attractive gallery for temporary art and history exhibitions.

Head back down Minquan Road to Ziyou Road and turn left – from Minzu Road onward this becomes Taichung's **cake street** (see p.184). Walk a few blocks and turn right along Chenggong Road, continue south past Jiguang Street and take the first left down **Herbal Medicine Street** (草藥街; *cǎoyàojiē*; Lane 90), actually a series of narrow alleys lined with Traditional Medicine stores. The subtle aromas and torpid atmosphere here make it more redolent of old Taichung than anywhere else in the city. The alleys form a small cross, with *Chen Bai Cao Diàn* (陳百草店; *chén bǎicǎodiàn*; no. 12) at the central axis selling refreshing **iced herbal tea** (*bǎicǎochá*; daily 8am–6.30pm; NT$15). At Guangfu Road turn left, walk back onto Ziyou Road and turn right towards **Taichung Park** (台中公園; *táizhōng gōngyuán*), a block to the east. Created by the Japanese in 1903 on the site of the eighteenth-century fort of Datun, it's a universe away from modern Taichung and the location of the unlikely city symbol, the twin-peaked **Hu Xin Pavilion** (湖心亭; *húxīntíng*) in the middle of the lake. Built in 1908 to commemorate the completion of the north–south rail line, it makes a welcome retreat from the sun on sweltering afternoons.

Nantian Temple

Taichung's East District has little in the way of sights, but **Nantian Temple** (南天宮; *nántiān gōng*; daily 6.30am–10pm), just under 1km east of Taichung Park on Ziyou Road, is certainly photogenic. Dedicated to Guan Di, the Main Hall is fairly typical, but it's backed by a huge (48m) and slightly garish statue of the general, seated above a tiger and swathed in colourful robes. Stroking his beard – he's also known as the "Beautiful Whiskered One" – his posture is meant to convey great wisdom, as well as the loyalty and bravery symbolized by his bright red face and hands, his most distinctive features. You can climb up to the sixth floor, just below the statue, to take a closer look. Bus #33 from the city bus station stops close to the temple.

North District

Old Taichung spills over into **North District** (北區; *běiqū*) the home of several significant temples. A few blocks north of Taichung Park at 30 Shuangshi Rd Sec 2, Taichung's **Confucius Temple** (孔廟; *kǒngmiào*; Tues–Sun 9am–5pm; bus #40, 41, 63) makes up in scale what it lacks in history. Taiwan's second-largest Confucian temple, it was completed in 1976, and, as a result, it's in relatively pristine condition – it's built in the style of the Northern Song dynasty and is a massive, palatial structure. The ceremonial entrance is the **Lingxing Gate** on Lixing Road, but this only opens for the president – everyone else enters via the modest **"Gate of Perceiving Virtue"** on Shuangshi Road. The Dacheng Gate on your left leads to the central **Dacheng Hall**, a magnificent structure that contains a single tablet commemorating Confucius. Next door on Lixing Road, the sombre **Martyrs' Shrine** (忠烈祠; *zhōngliècí*; Sat & Sun 9am–5pm; free) was a shrine for Japanese soldiers until 1945; it's now a memorial for those that died fighting for the Republic of China.

Fifteen minutes' walk north, **Baojue Temple** (寶覺寺; *bǎojuésì*; daily 8am–5pm; bus #88 or red bus #55) at 140 Jianxing Rd, is one of Taichung's most popular – tourists come to gape at the 27m-high gold-painted statue of *mílêfó* (the chubby Maitreya Buddha) to the far right of the compound. The temple was built in 1928 and the main hall in the centre (now enclosed within a huge modern structure) actually honours Sakyamuni Buddha. Japanese tourists tend to congregate around the small pavilion and stele to the left, next to the remembrance hall; some Taiwanese fought for Japan in World War II, and this is where many of them were interred after being killed overseas. The calligraphy on the stele is an epitaph written by former president Lee Teng-hui – Lee's brother was killed fighting for the Japanese and is enshrined at the Yasukuni Shrine in Tokyo.

Further west, the gargantuan **National Museum of Natural Science** (國立自然科學博物館; *guólì zìrán kēxué bówùguǎn*; Tues–Sun 9am–5pm, no entry after 4.30pm; NT$100; ℡04/2322-6940, ⓦwww.nmns.edu.tw; bus #27, 35, 70, 71, 88), is Taichung's top attraction, at least for Taiwanese tourists, but it's primarily targeted at children and there isn't much labelled in English. The **National Botanical Gardens** (國立植物園; *guólì zhíwùyuán*; daily 9am–10pm; free), behind the main complex, is a pleasant place to relax, while the striking **Tropical Rainforest Greenhouse** (熱帶雨林溫室; *rèdài yǔlín wēnshì*; Tues–Sun 9am–5pm; NT$20) has become a city landmark with its 31m-high steel and glass exterior and lush rainforest inside, complete with simulated rainfall.

National Taiwan Museum of Fine Arts

Essential for anyone with even a vague interest in Taiwanese and Chinese art, the **National Taiwan Museum of Fine Arts** (國立台灣美術館; *guólì táiwān měishùguǎn*; Tues–Fri 9am–5pm, Sat & Sun 9am–6pm; free; ℡04/2372-3552, ⓦwww.ntmofa.gov.tw), at 2 Wuquan W Rd Sec 1 in West district, contains a beautiful series of galleries displaying a wide range of both Taiwanese and international work. Most of the exhibits change every few months and tend to have English explanations, though the permanent gallery introducing the history of Taiwanese art on the first floor is presented solely in Chinese. To get to the museum take yellow bus #56 or bus #71 from the city bus station or Renyou bus #89 from Luchuan East Street.

Nantun District

Modern **Nantun District** (南屯; *nántún*) covers a vast swath of southwest Taichung, but its roots go back to the late seventeenth century. It's here, not the centre, that you'll find the city's oldest place of worship, **Wanhe Temple** (萬和宮; *wànhégōng*; daily 5.30am–10pm; yellow bus #56 or bus #75), at 51 Wanhe Road Section 1. The current structure, which comprises three main halls and is dedicated to Mazu, was begun in 1726 on the site of a shrine built in 1683, but has been renovated many times – the intricate *koji* (*jiāozhǐtáo*) figurines set into the walls are particularly vivid here.

Behind Wanhe Temple, **Wenchang Temple** (文昌公廟; *wénchānggōng miào*; daily 5.30am–10pm) is the modern sister temple of an older shrine in Beitun. This version has two storeys and is dedicated not only to Wenchang Dijun (the "Emperor of Passing Exams"), but also Guan Di and Sakyamuni Buddha, and is popular with students for obvious reasons. The box in front of the main altar is stuffed with photocopies of test applications and ID cards.

A short walk north, the area around the junction of Nantun and Wanhe roads is known as **Nantun Old Street** 南屯老街; (*nántún lǎojiē*), lined with old shophouses and a couple of cheap food stalls.

Xitun District

Xitun District (西屯區; *xītún qū*) covers a massive chunk of northwest Taichung, its main attraction the elegant **Luce Memorial Chapel** (路思義教堂; *lùsīyì jiàotáng*) within the grounds of **Tunghai University** (東海大學; *dōnghǎi dàxué*), around 9km from the train station at 181 Taizhinggang Rd Sec 3. Designed by lauded architect I.M. Pei, it's a breathtaking piece of engineering: completed in 1963 and named after the American missionary Henry Winters Luce, its graceful tent-like structure resembles an inverted ship's hull, or more appropriately, praying hands. It still functions as the university chapel and tends to be locked up

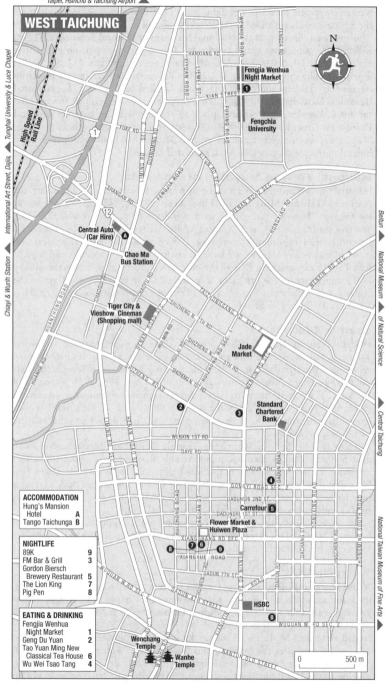

Taipei, Hsinchu & Taichung Airport ▲

WEST TAICHUNG

N

HANXIANG RD

Fengjia Wenhua
Night Market ❶

Fengchia
University

International Art Street, Dajia, ▲ Tunghai University & Luce Chapel ▲

High Speed Rail Line

FUKE RD

Chiayi & Wurih Station ▲

Central Auto ❹
(Car Hire)

Chao Ma
Bus Station

Tiger City &
Vieshow Cinemas
(Shopping mall)

Jade
Market

❷

❸

Standard
Chartered
Bank

WENXIN 1ST RD
DAYE RD

DADUN 4TH ST

GONGYI ROAD ❹

DADUNSHI 2ND ST
DADUNSHI 1ST ST.

Carrefour ❺

ACCOMMODATION
Hung's Mansion
   Hotel   A
Tango Taichunga   B

Flower Market &
Huiwen Plaza

XIANGSHANG RD SEC
❽ ❼❻ ❾
XIANGXUE ROAD

NIGHTLIFE
89K   9
FM Bar & Grill   3
Gordon Biersch
   Brewery Restaurant 5
The Lion King   7
Pig Pen   8

DADUN 7TH ST.

HSBC

❽

EATING & DRINKING
Fengjia Wenhua
   Night Market   1
Geng Du Yuan   2
Tao Yuan Ming New
   Classical Tea House   6
Wu Wei Tsao Tang   4

Wenchang
Temple

Wanhe
Temple

NANTUN OLD STREET

0   500 m

Beitun ▲

National Museum ▲

of Natural Science ▲

Central Taichung ▲

National Taiwan Museum of Fine Arts ▲

on weekdays. The university grounds are also worth exploring if you have time, as this is probably the most attractive campus in Taiwan, with Tang dynasty themed buildings, and the main avenues lined with Phoenix trees and blossoms. **Buses** to the university are plentiful: #88, #106 and #6106 run from the city bus station, and there's a free shuttle from the High-Speed Rail Station. Another 2.5km west from the university, **International Art Street** (國際藝術街坊; *guójì yìshù jiēfāng*) is an appealing place to spend an afternoon, with a range of small boutiques, craft shops, cheap clothes stores, teashops, furniture emporiums and art studios. It's beyond Tunghai University and accessible via the same buses: turn right off Taizhonggang Road on Guojie Street – the entrance is next to the first 7-Eleven on the left.

The 921 Earthquake Museum of Taiwan

Located near the small town of Wufeng (霧峰; *wùfēng*) in the village of Kengkou (坑口; *kēngkǒu*), roughly 14km south of Taichung train station, the **921 Earthquake Museum of Taiwan** (九二一地震教育園區; *jiǔèryī dìzhèn jiàoyùyuánqū*; Tues–Sun 9am–5pm; NT$30; Ⓦwww.921emt.edu.tw) is a vivid, if sobering, introduction to the damage and destruction wrought by the massive earthquake of 1999, particularly in this part of the country. Though it has attracted a fair amount of criticism from people who say it ignores the controversial aspects of the 921 earthquake (such as substandard construction), it's extremely informative and very moving.

The museum is centred on the former site of **Guangfu Junior High School** – most of the school collapsed during the quake and pictures of its mangled running track were some of the most visually shocking images in the days afterwards (it was mercifully empty at the time). The ruined school buildings form the outdoor area of the museum; on both sides of this are two futuristic exhibition halls packed with interactive displays labelled in English and Chinese; the **Chelungpu Fault Gallery**, which crosses the actual fault line – a clearly visible ridge created by the quake that cuts across the running track; and the **Earthquake Image Gallery** featuring a selection of audio-visual images of the quake and its aftermath, climaxing in hourly shows in a huge theatre.

The 921 Earthquake

All over Taiwan, but particularly in the central part of the country, you'll hear about the **921 Earthquake** (九二一大地震; *jiǔèryī dàdìzhèn*): the epithet refers to the 7.3-magnitude quake that ripped across the island at 1.47am on September 21, 1999, killing 2455 people, injuring more than 8000 and destroying 50,652 buildings. It's also known as the **Chi-Chi Earthquake** – the epicentre is beneath the town of Jiji, 12.5km west of Sun Moon Lake. In fact, many of the casualties in Nantou county occurred during an aftershock five days later that measured 6.7 on the Richter scale, flattening buildings weakened on September 21.

Despite the heroic efforts of rescue services in the days after the disaster, the government was criticized in some places for its slow response. Though it established the **921 Earthquake Post-disaster Recovery Commission** to oversee around NT$106bn in funding to help affected areas, many building contractors responsible for illegal construction – blamed for many of the deaths – have never been prosecuted.

Earthquakes are a problem in Taiwan because the island sits on a fault line between the Eurasian and Philippine tectonic plates, causing almost constant seismic activity, though 75 percent of all quakes occur in the sparsely populated eastern half of the island. When western Taiwan is affected, the results can be catastrophic, though most buildings today can easily absorb all but the strongest tremors.

You can take bus #6107 to Kengkou from the city bus station in Taichung, but there are only two a day. It's easier to take a Nantou-bound bus from the Fengyuan bus station (these depart every 30min or so), but you need to make sure it's via Zhongxing (中興新村; *zhōngxīng xīncūn*); tell the driver you want to get off at **Guangfu Xingcun** (光復新村站; *guāngfù xīncūn zhàn*), from where it's a short walk to the museum.

Eating

Taichung is an excellent place to gorge on both Taiwanese and international food. Traditional places tend to be focused in the old centre, with the plusher, more cosmopolitan options in the west: trawl the **Art Museum Parkway** (美術綠園道; *měishù lùyuándào*; aka Wuquan Parkway) for a good selection, or the **Canal District** (河堤區; *hétíqū*) south of Taizhonggang Road. Taichung's night markets offer a good introduction to the local specialities – the most convenient are **Zhongxiao Night Market** (忠孝夜市; *zhōngxiào yèshì*) on Zhongxiao Road between Taizhong and Guoguang roads south of the train station, and **Zhonghua Road Night Market** (中華夜市; *zhōnghuá yèshì*) further north (mostly seafood stalls – pick your dinner then sit down while they cook it; NT$40–60). For a more eclectic range of traditional and Western snack food, popular with students, try the stalls crammed along **Yizhong Street** (一中街; *yīzhōngjiē*) between Taiping Road and Yucai Street (open from late morning).

Travellers with a penchant for something sweeter won't be disappointed, with Ziyou Road (自由路; *zìyóulù*) between Zhongzheng and Minquan roads crammed with cakeshops selling **suncakes** (*tàiyáng bǐng*), flat, crumbly pastries filled with sweet wheatgerm, honey or taro paste (NT$20–30). The venerable *Taiyang Tang Bakery* (太陽堂餅店; *tàiyángtáng bǐngdiàn*) at 23 Ziyou Rd Sec 2 is one of the oldest (boxes only, from NT$150).

Old centre

Malulian 瑪露連 (*mǎlùlián*) 133 Zhongzheng Rd ☎04/2228-8359. The best shaved-ice stall in the old centre, with a covered outdoor eating area and good selection of fresh, tasty toppings (three with each order), such as creamy taro, almond pudding, red bean and various fruits (NT$50). Tues–Sat 10.30am–9pm, Sun 10.30am–7pm.

Taichung Meatballs 台中肉丸 (*táizhōng ròuwán*) 529 Fuxing Rd Sec 3 ☎04/2226-4409. This no-nonsense local diner has been serving deep-fried meatballs since the 1930s. The main event comes in small bowls (NT$35) and has a gooey, sticky texture – its translucent skin is made of a taro and rice mixture filled with pork and bamboo shoots and topped with a delicious sweet and sour sauce. Daily 10.30am–6.30pm.

Ya Ju 雅居健康素館 (*yǎjū jiànkāng sùguǎn*) 39 Gongyuan Rd ☎04/2226-5505. Modern and spotlessly clean Buddhist-inspired vegetarian restaurant with round wooden tables and calligraphy on the walls. The menu offers a decent selection of Chinese food, but there's no English menu – use the photos instead (NT$150–300/dish). Daily 11am–2pm & 5.30pm–9pm.

North District

Beifang Hand-Cut Noodles 北方館 (*běifāngguǎn*) 154 Meide St ☎04/2235-8632. Popular local lunch stop for traditional "knife-cut" noodles, thicker than the normal version, deliciously flavoured with big chunks of beef (NT$100). It's located on the north side of Zhongzheng Park – turn right off Xueshi Rd before the junction with Jianxing Rd. No English. Daily 11am–2pm & 5–8pm.

General Beef Noodles 將軍牛肉大王 (*jiāng jūn niúròu dàwáng*) 158 Xueshi Rd ☎04/2230-5918. The chef at this cheap and cheerful canteen has won culinary awards for his version of the Taichung classic, beef noodles (NT$80–100) – it's definitely one of the best. Not far from Baojue Temple. No English. Daily 11am–2pm & 4pm–10pm.

Mayor's House Taichung 台中市長公館 (*táizhōng shìcháng gōngguǎn*) 125 Shuangshi Rd Sec 1 ☎04/2223-3723. Two-storey colonial house, once the mayor's residence, and now a pleasant café and art gallery. It's a useful pit-stop on the way to the Confucius Temple – grab a coffee or ice cream and relax in the garden or second-floor balcony. Light meals NT$100–200. Daily 11am–9.30pm.

Taiwan Banana New Paradise 香蕉新樂園 (*xiāng jiāo xīn lèyúan*) 111 Shuangshi Rd Sec 2 ☎04/2231-7890. An old train carriage marks the entrance to this kitsch-but-fun Taiwanese restaurant, approved as a "local museum" by the National Palace Museum in Taipei. Inside, tables are scattered along a reproduction of a 1930s street evoking old Taichung, the walls decorated in memorabilia (main dishes NT$180–300, *dim sum* NT$60, drinks NT$50). Daily 11am–2am.

Yizhong Fongren Ice 一中豐仁冰 (*yīzhōng fēngrén bīng*) 1 Yucai St, at Shuangshi Rd. Popular with students, this small shaved-ice stall offers mouthwatering combinations of plum ice shavings, kidney beans and ice cream (NT$30). Daily 10am–8.30pm.

West district

1924 Shanghai 新月梧桐 (*xīnyùe wútóng*) 95 Wuquan W 3rd St ☎04/2378-3181. One of Wuquan Parkway's many stylish, themed restaurants, with a focus on Shanghai and Jiangsu food – try the coddle pork (a bit like a stew), eel and various tofu dishes (most dishes NT$180–280). The atmospheric interior recalls fashionable Shanghai of the 1920s and 30s, with old posters, wooden tables and antiques. Daily 10am–10pm (main courses served 11.30am–2.30pm & 5.30–9pm).

Finga's Base Camp 風格 (*fēnggé*) 61 Zhongming S Rd ☎04/2327-7750. Western deli and café, on the edge of the Canal District – the sandwiches (NT$160–210), salads (from NT$100) and Mexican food (from NT$160 for nachos to around NT$260 for mains) are the closest you'll get to the real thing this side of the Pacific. Breakfast from NT$110. Mon–Fri 10am–10pm, Sat & Sun 8am–10pm.

Frog Mexican Restaurant 青蛙的店 (*qīngwādediàn*) 105 Huamei W St Sec 1 ☎04/2321-1197 🌐www.frogpub.com. Mexican restaurant doubling as popular bar, with a prime location in the heart of the Canal District. Relaxed café-style interior, with Taiwan Beer (NT$180) and Heineken (NT$200) on tap and tacos from NT$100 (mains NT$200–300). Daily 10am–2am.

Gulu Gulu 咕嚕咕嚕音樂餐廳 (*gūlūgūlū yīnyùe cāntīng*) 2 Lane 13, Wuquan W 4th St ☎04/2378-3128. Fun restaurant set inside a colonial-era house, owned by a Paiwan singer and serving authentic indigenous Taiwanese food. Try the grilled mountain pig (boar) with spicy boar-skin chips (barbecued outside), or set meals (average NT$280–380) and millet wine. Chinese menu only. Daily 10am–2pm & 5pm–12.30am.

Meicun Diantou Ice 美村點頭冰 (*měicūn diǎntóu bīng*) 176 Meicun Rd Sec 1 ☎04/2301-2526. Best shaved-ice shop in this part of town, with lavish piles of fruit and ice topped with condensed milk and coconut syrup – try the fresh mango, taro or "diantou ice" with three types of seasonal fruit (NT$60). Daily midday–11pm.

Xitun

Fengjia Wenhua Night Market 逢甲文華夜市 (*féngjiā wénhuá yèshì*) It's a long way from downtown, but narrow Wenhua Rd in front of Fengchia University is host to one of Taichung's best night markets. Stalls to look out for include *Grandma's Tea-boiled Eggs* (阿婆茶叶蛋; *āpócháyèdàn*; NT$10) at 85 Wenhua Rd, and *Richuan Octopus Balls* (日船章魚小丸子; *rìchuán zhāngyúxiǎo wánzi*; NT$35) at 69 Wenhua Rd. Daily 6pm–1.30am.

Teahouses

Taichung is a city of **teahouses**, home to Taiwan's most successful teahouse chains and its most innovative drinks: **bubble tea** (*pàomò hóngchá*), a frothy black tea, was created around 1983, and **pearl milk tea** (*zhēnzhū nǎichá*) in 1987 (milky tea with large chewy tapioca balls in the bottom), both served hot or cold and extremely sweet. Legend has it that bubble tea was created at the *Yangxian Teahouse* (see p.186) by accident, and that pearl milk tea was introduced by the same shop after the owner's mother mixed gelatine balls from her market stall with leftover tea. These days the names tend to get blurred somewhat, both associated with the tapioca "pearls", while a vast range of traditional **Chinese**, **fruit** and **flower teas** accompany the original favourites.

Chun Shui Tang Cultural Tea House 春水堂人文茶館 (*chūnshuǐtáng rénwén cháguǎn*) 17 Lane 155, Gongyi Rd ☎04/2302-8530; 9 Dadun 19th St (at Jingming 1st St) ☎04/2327-3647; 186 Fuxing Rd Sec 4 (inside Taichung Central) ☎04/2227-2712. This modern chain has several branches in its home town – the above are the most convenient options. Credited with bringing bubble tea and pearl milk tea to a wider world, its English menus outline the huge number of drinks available (NT$100–140), and the perfect tea accompaniment, brown sugar cake (NT$45). Daily 8.30am–11pm.

Geng Du Yuan 耕讀園書香茶坊 (*gēngdúyuán shūxiāng cháfāng*) 109 Shizheng Rd
☎04/2251-8388; 520 Chongde 9th Rd
☎04/2422-4099. Another Taichung chain, its design based on classical Suzhou gardens with tatami mats, fishponds, waterfalls, bridges and cosy tea rooms; pots of oolong start at NT$200, snacks from NT$60. Daily 10am–2am.

🏃 **Laughter Chinese Teahouse** 悲歡歲月 人文茶館 (*bēihuān suìyuè rénwén cháguǎn*) 29 Daquan St ☎04/2371-1984. Exquisite teahouse set in a tiny wooden Japanese house, with tatami mats, screen doors and Japanese decor. Features a range of special infusions including white hair oolong, sweet osmanthus honey, green and mountain teas (NT$450 per pot), with light Chinese meals from NT$300. Daily 11am–10pm.

Tao Yuan Ming New Classical Tea House 陶園 茗新古典茶水空間 (*táoyuánmíng xīngǔdiǎn cháshuǐ kōngjiān*) 179 Xiangshang Rd Sec 2 ☎04/2387-6188. One of the city's most alluring teahouses, a blend of classical Chinese wooden pavilions and fishponds with contemporary stone and concrete design. Drinks and pots of quality teas range from NT$130 to NT$288, with plenty of snacks on the menu. Opposite the Flower Market in Nantun, and close to the *Pig Pen*. No English menus (NT$100 minimum charge). Daily 10am–1am.

🏃 **Wu Wei Tsao Tang** 無為草堂 (*wúwéi cǎotáng*) 106 Gongyi Rd ☎04/2329-6707. Taichung's most atmospheric classical teahouse, surrounded by trees and beautifully arranged around a traditional fishpond, with wooden corridors lined with Chinese art. Teapots for one start at NT$150, NT$350 for larger groups. Daily 10am–1am.

Yangxian Teahouse 楊賢茶館 (*yángxián cháguǎn*) 30 Siwei Rd ☎04/2229-7991. The place where bubble tea was invented, this pleasant teahouse became the first *Chun Shui Tang* chain store and retains much of its original character – the blue tablet above the entrance says "Spring Water Hall", (also *Chun Shui Tang*) written in ancient Chinese script. Daily 8am–11pm.

Nightlife

Weekends in Taichung can be raucous all-night affairs, with a host of **pubs**, sophisticated **lounge bars** and hip **nightclubs**. Most of the action takes place on the west side of town in the Canal district or further afield, so if you really want to check out the scene you're going to have to take taxis. Taichung's eye-popping **Fulfillment Amphitheater** (台中市圓滿戶外劇場; ☎04/2372-7311, ⓦfa.tccgc .gov.tw) at 289 Wenxin Rd Sec 1 is the premier venue for concerts; check the website or the visitor centre for upcoming events.

89K 21 Daguan Rd ☎04/2381-8240. Ex-pub turned nightclub and live music venue with a vaguely American West theme (think cowhides and Confederate flags). It's mostly rock Fri & Sat nights (with jam night every Thurs). Open from 7pm, cover Fri & Sat from N$250 (usually free beer). Near the *Pig Pen* (see opposite) in Xitun. Daily 8pm–4am.

FM Bar & Grill 2/F, 1 Shizheng N 1st Rd ☎04/2251-4500. Longstanding Taichung favourite, *FM* moved into plush new digs in 2010, on the second floor of the Le Free mall. Lots of Western-style food (burgers NT$300), BBQ Pork Ribs (NT$400/half rack, NT$750/full) and a decent spread of drinks (Boddington's, Hoegaarden and Stella on tap). Daily 6pm–2am.

Gordon Biersch Brewery Restaurant 533 Dadun Rd ☎04/2310-7678. Congenial micro-brewery and restaurant, serving hand-crafted German and Czech-style lagers (NT$170) and hearty pub food such as pizzas, burgers and tacos (from NT$370). Mon–Fri 11.30am–midnight, Sat & Sun 10am–midnight.

The Lion King 獅子王 (*shīziwáng*) 38 Dachuan St (just off Daguan Rd) ☎04/2387-6789. Cavernous club with second-floor balcony, packed most nights with DJs spinning a good mix of house and serious hip-hop. Cover charge is usually NT$300. Next door to the *Pig Pen*, but tends to keep going longer and more popular with a younger local crowd. Wed–Sat 8.30pm–4 or 5am (Ladies Night Thurs).

Liquid Lounge 液態西餐廳 (*yìtài xīcāntīng*) 98 Zhongming S Rd ☎04/3601-9980. Fashionable lounge bar and restaurant, with stylish, softly lit interiors and plenty of comfy sofas and chairs. In-house DJs supply a mellow blend of ambient and lounge music most nights, while the tempo picks up at the weekends when it becomes more like a club. Sun–Thurs 6.30pm–3am, Fri & Sat 6.30pm–4am.

Londoner 倫敦公園 (*lúndūn gōngyuán*) 143 Huamei W St Sec 1 ☎04/2314-6919. Bright, modern pub in the Canal district, with a small first-floor bar and spacious second floor with pool table, sofas and giant TV for sports events. Also serves decent food like fish and chips and burgers, with Old Speckled Hen and Stella on tap. Mon 8am–3pm, Tues–Sun 8am–3pm & 7pm–late. **Pig Pen** 犁棧 (*lízhàn*) 41 Daguan Rd ☏04/2383-3666. Once a Brit-themed pub and

Taichung institution, this popular spot operates more like a nightclub these days – it's not really a pub any more and doesn't get going till 10pm most nights, though there're usually live bands at 7pm on Wed, Fri & Sat. Cover NT$120, Fri & Sat NT$500 (latter price includes two beers).

Listings

Airlines Cathay Pacific Airways, Room A, 8/F, 239 Minquan Rd ☏02/2715-2333 (Taipei number); China Airlines, 15/F, 160 Taizhonggang Rd Sec 1 ☏04/2320-4718/4719; EVA Air, Building A, 7-14/F, 20 Dalong Rd ☏04/2329-9566; Mandarin Airlines ☏04/2615-5088.
Banks There are plenty of banks and ATMs throughout the city, and most 7-Elevens have

Chinatrust ATMs: Citibank, 242 Zhongming S Rd ☏04/2372-6601 & 428 Taizhonggang Rd Sec 1 ☏04/2313-1861; HSBC, 218 Wenxin Rd Sec 1 ☏04/2471-2626.
Bookshops Caves Books (daily 10am–10pm) is at 12 Guanqian Rd, with a decent English-language section on the second floor and heaps of ESL material. Established in 1912, Taiwan's oldest

Moving on from Taichung

Taichung Airport hosts domestic services to Magong, Hualien, Nangan (Matsu) and Kinmen, as well as a growing number of flights to mainland China and southeast Asian destinations. For the airport, take a taxi or bus #6115 (only 6 daily) from Luchuan East Street, a short walk from the station (turn left off Zhongzheng Road). **Trains** to Taipei (NT$375), Kaohsiung (NT$470) and all stations in between depart throughout the day from the main station. Free shuttle buses (daily 5.35am–10.10pm) run from Taichung Park to the **High-Speed Rail Station** in Wuri (you can also take local trains from the station). From here trains to Taipei (NT$565) take just 1 hour, or 50 minutes if you catch a direct train. Services to Kaohsiung (NT$670) take 1 hour or 45 minutes.

Buses

There are two principal areas to catch **long-distance buses** in Taichung: the **Chao Ma area** (朝馬; *cháomǎ*) near the freeway and, more conveniently for most travellers, the streets around the main train station. Most companies have stations along Jianguo Road or Shuangshi Road. The Kuo Kuang bus station is immediately to the right of the train station, with regular hourly services to **Taipei** (NT$260), **Taiwan Taoyuan International Airport** (NT$220), **Tainan** (NT$170), **Chiayi** (NT$165) and **Kaohsiung** (NT$300); opposite on Jianguo Road are the Ubus and CH Bus stations, with a similar line-up of destinations and prices. North of Chenggong Road on the right as you walk from the train station are regular buses for **Dajia** (NT$100). On Shuangshi Road, first up on the left is the CH Bus Station for **Puli** (NT$125), followed by Ho Hsin (☏04/2227-7279) further along, which has frequent minibus (15–30min) departures to **Lugang** (NT$85) as well as Taipei (NT$120–199), Tainan (NT$80–110) and Kaohsiung (NT$250). The Lugang buses go along Taizhonggang Road and stop at Sogo and Chao Ma before going direct to Lugang. North of Gongyuan Road you'll find Changhua Bus, Free Go Bus, Nantou Bus and Yuanlin Bus; Nantou Bus offers the most reliable service to **Sun Moon Lake** (NT$188), via Puli (NT$120), though Renyou Bus also runs several buses a day to Sun Moon Lake from Luchuan East Street. Direct buses to **Beigang** (NT$220) depart the City Bus Station opposite the train station.

Turn left when you exit the train station, and the Fengyuan Bus Station is south on Jianguo Road; catch buses here for Dajia (NT$105), the **921 Earthquake Museum** (see p.183) and **Wuling** (8am only; NT$561; 6hr).

bookshop is Ruicheng Shuju (瑞成書局; *ruìchéng shūjú*) at 4-33 Shuangshi Rd Sec 1 opposite Taichung Park, though the current shop is modern, and a good place to buy gifts and stationery (daily 10am–10pm).

Car rental Car Plus (daily 8.30am–8.30pm; ☎0800/222-568 or 04/3601-5775, Ⓦwww.car-plus.com.tw) or Easy-Rent (☎0800/024-550, Ⓦwww.easyrent.com.tw) are both at the High Speed Rail Station.

Cinema Vieshow Cinemas (威秀影城; *wēixiù yǐngchéng*; Ⓦwww.vscinemas.com.tw) has two locations: in Taichung Central at 186 Fuxing Rd Sec 4, and Tiger City at 120 Henan Rd Sec 3 (tickets NT$260).

Cultural centres The Cultural Centre (文化中心; *wénhuà zhōngxīn*; Tues–Sun 9am–9pm; free; Ⓦwww.tccgc.gov.tw), at 600 Yingcai Rd, has a periodical reading room with English-language magazines, and several exhibition halls, the focus primarily on local, contemporary painters, though there are also rooms dedicated to traditional porcelain, pottery and jade. The abandoned warehouses and factory buildings of the former Taichung Winery (台中酒廠; *táizhōng jiǔchǎng*) at 362 Fuxing Rd Sec 3, south of the station, are being developed into an atmospheric contemporary art centre and museum (daily 10am–6pm).

Cycle rental You can rent bicycles at the east side of Taiyuan train station (太原火車站; *tàiyuán huǒchēzhàn*; Mon–Fri noon–10pm, Sat & Sun 8am–10pm; NT$80–150/hr) in Beitun district.

Hospital The biggest hospital in town is China Medical University Hospital (中國醫藥大學; *zhōngguó yīyào dàxué*; ☎04/2205-2121) at 2 Yude Rd, off Xueshi Rd in North district.

Mazu Holy Pilgrimage

The annual eight-day **Mazu Holy Pilgrimage** from **Zhenlan Temple** (鎮瀾宮; *zhènlángōng*) in **Dajia** (大甲; *dàjiǎ*) to **Fengtian Temple** (奉天宮; *fèngtiāngōng*) in **Xingang** (新港; *xīngǎng*) has become one of the greatest and perhaps most bizarre of all Taiwan's religious festivals. The event has become a veritable media circus, attracting ambitious politicians and even street gangs who in the past have ended up fighting over who "protects" the goddess during the procession.

The pilgrimage traces its origins to the early nineteenth century, when Taiwanese pilgrims would cross the Taiwan Strait to the Mazu "mother temple" in Meizhou in Fujian every twelve years. The practice was suspended after the Japanese occupation in 1895 but cattle herders are believed to have restarted the pilgrimage in the 1910s, making the more permissible journey to **Chaotian Temple** in Beigang, long regarded as Taiwan's most senior Mazu temple. In 1987 however, after Meizhou officials assured Dajia that its Mazu statue was equally sacred, Beigang was snubbed with a new annual pilgrimage route to what was considered a "sister" temple in Xingang, 5km east.

The core **procession** comprises a series of palanquins that ferry Mazu and other senior Taoist deities 300km through rice fields and small villages, the roads lined with believers who kneel to allow Mazu's palanquin to pass over them for luck. Stops are made at smaller "branch" temples to enhance the power of local deities, and a constant stream of free drinks and food is handed out to the pilgrims trudging along behind. If you want to experience the mayhem you'll need to plan ahead – the best locations to watch the procession are in Dajia itself when it leaves town and returns eight days later, or in Xingang at the end of the third day when the town becomes a massive carnival of parades and traditional performers. The statue remains in Xingang for a day of celebrations (confusingly termed "Mazu's birthday", though the official birthday is Lunar March 23) before embarking on its four-day journey back to Dajia. Unfortunately, it's hard to know when the parade will start until a few weeks before: the day of departure is determined by a special cast of "throwing blocks", on the eve of the Lantern Festival (usually in January or February). The parade itself usually takes place in **April** in the period leading up to Mazu's official birthday (see Ⓦmazu.taichung.gov.tw for the schedule; Chinese only). Dajia Bus Company runs minibuses from Taichung train station (on the corner of Jianguo and Chenggong Roads) to Dajia (NT$100) throughout the day, but you can also pick them up on Taizhonggang Road.

Internet access Most hotels have internet, and most internet cafés are open 24hr. E Square Internet at 114 Fuxing Rd Sec 4 is not far from the train station (NT$35 for 3hr; NT$55 for 5hr; NT$85 for 8hr); the Far East Tone counter in basement 1 of the Nova Computer Arcade at 508 Yingcai Rd has two free terminals (it shuts at 10pm).

Language courses Taichung is a popular place to learn Chinese. Taipei Language Institute Taichung Center at 50 Yizhong St (ⓣ04/2225-4681, ⓦwww .tli.com.tw) is a decent private school with a variety of classes and prices. The more established schools are attached to the major universities: the city's largest public university is National Chunghsing University (ⓣ04/2287-3181; ⓦwww.nchu.edu.tw); apply six weeks in advance for courses at Fengchia University's Language Center (ⓣ04/2451-7250, ⓦwww.fcu.edu.tw); and the Chinese Language Center at Tunghai University is also very good (ⓣ04/2359-0259, ⓦwww.thu.edu.tw).

Pharmacies Watson's has branches at 88–90 Jiguang St in the old centre (daily 10am–11pm; ⓣ04/2223-9369) and 17 Zhongzheng Rd (daily 9.30am–11pm; ⓣ04/2227-3218).

Post The main post office is at 86 Minquan Rd (Mon–Fri 7.30am–9pm, Sat 8.30am–4.30pm, Sun 8.30am–midday).

Scooter rental Companies generally do not rent to overseas travellers. Foreigners living in Taiwan can rent scooters at Huan Qi (環球租車; huánqiúzūchē; ⓣ04/2223-9073; NT$250–800/ day) at 156 Xinming St, to the right of the train station as you exit, but you'll need a driving licence and your ARC card.

Shopping Try Hui Wen Plaza (惠文廣場; huìwén guǎngchǎng), off Huiwen Rd in Nantun and inside the Flower Market, for antiques (Tues–Sun 10am–9pm); Tianjin Road (天津成衣街; tiānjīn chéngyī jiē; North district, east of Daya Rd as far as the canal), for cheap clothes and accessories; and Taichung Jade Market (台中玉珮市場; táizhōng yùpèi shìchǎng; Fri–Sun 10am–6pm) on the corner of Taizhonggang and Wenxin roads.

Travel agent Whose Travel are English-speaking travel agents that can handle all sorts of international and domestic itineraries: 3/F, 106 Huamei W St Sec 1 (above the *Frog*, see p.185) ⓣ04/2326-5191, ⓦwww.whosetravel.com).

Changhua

Just 16km southwest of Taichung, **CHANGHUA** (彰化; *zhānghuà*) is best known the **Great Buddha Statue** that overlooks the city centre from its lofty perch atop **Baguashan**. But while this is certainly Changhua's most remarkable attraction, the city has many other charms, from imaginative **culinary specialities** to its engrossing temples. Most of the noteworthy sights are within easy walking distance of the train station, making the city an easy stopover on your way south.

Arrival and information

Regular **express trains** from Taipei and Kaohsiung stop at Changhua train station at the western edge of downtown. Changhua **High-Speed Rail** Station is expected to open in 2015, but until then Taichung will be the nearest stop. From **Taichung** it's only fifteen to twenty minutes by local train (NT$27) to Changhua. Ho Hsin, Kuo Kuang and Ubus all have regular **express bus** services from Taipei to Changhua's **bus station**, conveniently located across Zhongzheng Road from the train station. From here, Changhua Bus has frequent **buses** to neighbouring **Lugang** (30min; NT$47), but you'll need to look out for the Chinese charcters on the front (鹿港). You'll find a handy **visitor centre** (Mon–Fri 9am–5pm, Sat & Sun 8am–6pm; ⓣ04/728-5750) inside the train station, with friendly, English-speaking staff but not much in the way of English brochures. Note that at the time of writing Changhua was still using *tōngyòng pīnyīn* for its road signs.

Accommodation

There is a handful of **hotels** within walking distance of the train station; just to the right as you exit is the *Taiwan Hotel* (台灣大飯店; ⓣ04/722-4681; ❸) at 48 Zhongzheng Rd Sec 2, with clean, spacious rooms and a convenient location. A

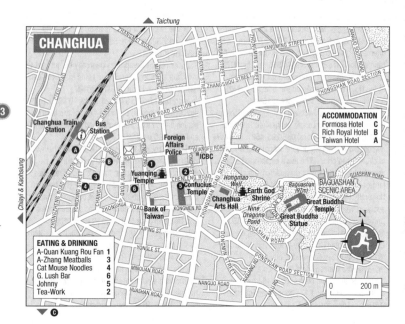

CHANGHUA

Chiayi & Kaohsiung

ACCOMMODATION
Formosa Hotel C
Rich Royal Hotel B
Taiwan Hotel A

Changhua Train Station
Bus Station
Foreign Affairs Police
ICBC
Yuanqing Temple
Confucius Temple
Changhua Arts Hall
Bank of Taiwan
Hongmao Well
Earth God Shrine
Nine Dragons Pond
Baguashan (97m)
BAGUASHAN SCENIC AREA
Great Buddha Temple
Great Buddha Statue
GUASHAN ROAD

N

0   200 m

EATING & DRINKING
A-Quan Kuang Rou Fan   1
A-Zhang Meatballs   3
Cat Mouse Noodles   4
G. Lush Bar   6
Johnny   5
Tea-Work   2

few minutes' walk southeast of the train station, at 97 Changan St, is the garish *Rich Royal Hotel* (富皇大飯店; *fùhuáng dàfàndiàn*; ☏04/723-7117; ❸), with slightly ageing theme rooms that are nevertheless good value. About 2km south of the train station, at 668 Zhongzheng Rd Sec 2, is the more luxurious *Formosa Hotel* (全台大飯店; *quántái dàfàndiàn*; ☏04/725-3017; ❺), which has plush doubles and a range of amenities. Room rates include breakfast, use of the hotel's fitness room, internet access and free bicycle use (up to 3hr).

The City

With Changhua's main sights packed in the middle of town, between the train station and Baguashan to the east, a walk down narrow Chenleng Road – just southeast of the train station – will take you near most of them. As you head east on Chenleng, at the intersection with Minsheng Road is the ornate **Yuanqing Temple** (元清觀; *yuánqīngguān*) originally built in 1763 and dedicated primarily to worship of the chief Taoist deity, the **Jade Emperor**. Turn right on Minsheng and to your left you'll see the stately **Confucius Temple** (孔廟; *kǒngmiào*; daily 8am–5.30pm), one of the oldest in Taiwan. First built in 1726, this ageing complex is a quiet haven in the heart of the city, its symmetrical layout of halls and courtyards emblematic of a classical Confucian temple. Flanking the entrance to the main **Dacheng Hall** is a pair of stone columns, beautifully carved with dragon motifs (English signage inside).

Head east along Kongmen Road from here and cross busy Zhongshan Road to see what remains of the 300-year-old **Hongmao Well** (紅毛井; *hóngmáojǐng*), one of the few surviving Dutch-built wells in Taiwan. The well's crumbling stone base has been cemented over and covered by a clear glass shelter for protection, making it difficult to imagine its original incarnation. Immediately behind the well is a tiny **Earth God Shrine** (土地公; *tǔdìgōng*) that gets much more attention from locals than the well itself.

Baguashan

Rising majestically on the city's eastern fringe is the 92m **Baguashan** (八卦山; *bāguàshān*; open 24hr), from the top of which its crowning glory – the **Great Buddha Statue** (大佛像; *dàfóxiàng*) – keeps a constant vigil over the town. To get there, keep walking along Kongmen beyond Zhongshan and follow the signs. Towering 22m above its brightly coloured lotus-flower base, the statue has become one of Taiwan's most recognizable landmarks since its construction in 1961. It is made entirely of reinforced concrete and has a hollow, six-storey interior; you can go inside to check out the **dioramas** depicting the stages of Buddha's life. Behind the statue to the east is the three-storey Great Buddha Temple, the top floor of which is a superb place to watch the sun set over the Great Buddha's shoulders. Still further east is the tranquil **Baguashan Scenic Area** (八卦山風景區; *bāguàshān fēngjǐngqū*), interspersed with short walkways leading to pavilions and city overlooks.

Eating and drinking

Changhua is a culinary adventure in its own right, known for its **three treasures**: meatballs (*bâh-wán* in Taiwanese), "cat-mouse noodles" (*niau-qī mi* in Taiwanese) and *lūròufàn* (stewed pork rice). The **meatballs** are served in a translucent coating made of glutinous rice and filled with ingredients such as pork, shredded bamboo, mushrooms, egg yolk and, in some cases, pig's liver. The best place to try them is *A-Zhang Meatballs* (阿璋肉圓; *āzhāng ròuyuán*; daily 8am–7pm; NT$30–35; ☏04/722-9517), 144 Changan St, at the intersection of Chenleng Road. About 100m north of here, at 223 Chenleng Rd, is *Cat Mouse Noodles* (貓鼠麵; *māoshǔmiàn*; daily 10am–7pm; NT$40; ☏04/726-8376), so named because the restaurant's founder was said by his friends to have mouse-like mannerisms (and the Taiwanese word for "mouse" sounds like the Mandarin word for "cat"). Apart from the noodles' novel name, they are noted for the refreshingly non-oily **soup** in which they are served.

Lūròufàn (or *kuàngròufàn* as it's known here) can be found throughout the city, but one lauded place to try it is *A Quan Kuang Rou Fan* (阿泉爌肉飯; *āquán kuàngròufàn*; daily 7am–1.30pm; ☏04/728-1979), a small stall at 216 Chenggong Rd (here the pork comes in one big piece, with a thick rind; NT$40). None of the places listed above features any English (or *pīnyīn*).

For a sit-down meal, try *Tea-Work* (人水私房; *rénshuǐ sīfáng*; ☏04/727-7588), a lovely old Japanese-era house converted into an attractive teahouse at 53 Yongfu St, near Chenleng Road. Small plates (tempura, shrimp rolls) start at NT$60.

As for **nightlife**, there is a string of pubs on Chenleng Road, though little happens mid-week and nothing much opens till 7pm. Try *G. Lush Bar* (daily 5pm–2am), 135 Chenleng Rd, or, beyond Minsheng Rd, *Johnny* at 65 Chenleng Rd is considerably quieter.

Lugang

One of Taiwan's oldest port towns, **LUGANG** (鹿港; *lùgǎng*) has preserved much of its architectural and cultural heritage, largely thanks to the efforts of its famously conservative inhabitants. Lugang's historic **temples** are wonderfully atmospheric, but much of the town's fame derives from its tasty **snacks** and traditional **handicrafts**, created by the greatest concentration of master craftsmen in the country. But while the town is eulogized in Taiwan as the epitome of classical China, its appeal tends to be exaggerated – the historic centre is relatively small, and it's surrounded by urban development that's classic modern Taiwan. Adjust your expectations accordingly and Lugang can still make a fascinating day-trip from Changhua or Taichung. Thanks to the gradual silting up of its harbour, one of the oddest things about Lugang today is that the Lugang River is a long walk from the old part of town, and the sea is now several kilometres away.

Some history

Lugang means "**Deer Harbour**," an allusion to the herds of deer that once roamed the Changhua plains, now long since hunted to extinction. Settlers from Fujian established the town in the early seventeenth century, and it became Taiwan's

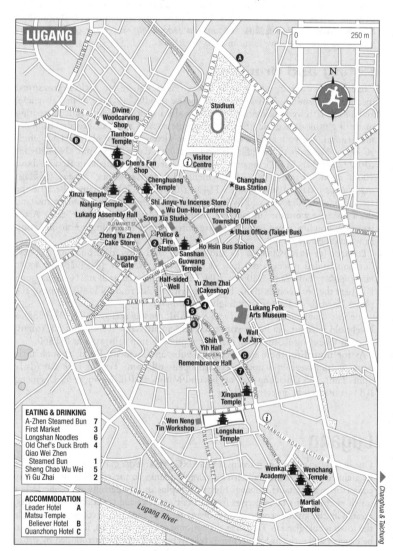

LUGANG

0   250 m

N

Divine Woodcarving Shop
Tianhou Temple
Chen's Fan Shop
Stadium
Visitor Centre
Changhua Bus Station
Chenghuang Temple
Xinzu Temple
Nanjing Temple
Lukang Assembly Hall
Shi Jinyu-Yu Incense Store
Wu Dun-Hou Lantern Shop
Song Xia Studio
Township Office
Zheng Yu Zhen Cake Store
Police & Fire Station
Ho Hsin Bus Station
Ubus Office (Taipei Bus)
Lugang Gate
Sanshan Guowang Temple
Half-sided Well
Yu Zhen Zhai (Cakeshop)
Lukang Folk Arts Museum
Wall of Jars
Shih Yih Hall
Remembrance Hall
Xingan Temple
Wen Neng Tin Workshop
Longshan Temple
Wenkai Academy
Wenchang Temple
Martial Temple

OLD MARKET ST (PUTOU ST)

Changhua & Taichung

EATING & DRINKING
A-Zhen Steamed Bun	7
First Market	3
Longshan Noodles	6
Old Chef's Duck Broth	4
Qiao Wei Zhen Steamed Bun	1
Sheng Chao Wu Wei	5
Yi Gu Zhai	2

ACCOMMODATION
Leader Hotel	A
Matsu Temple Believer Hotel	B
Quanzhong Hotel	C

second largest after Tainan for most of the 1700s. Lugang's decline began in the late nineteenth century as the harbour began to silt up and by 1895 it was closed to major shipping: the town rapidly became a conservative backwater in the years that followed, avoiding the modernization engulfing the rest of the island until the late 1970s, when tourism gave the economy a much needed boost.

Arrival and information

Frequent **buses** from **Changhua** (NT$47) terminate at the small bus station on Fuxing Road (just north of Minquan Road), but it's better to get off on Zhongshan Road. Minibuses from **Taichung** (every 15–30min; NT$85) also travel along Zhongshan Road before terminating at 208 Minquan Rd at the Ho Hsin bus station, while buses from **Taipei** (NT$350) end up at the Ubus office a bit further along the same street. Lugang currently has two **visitor centres** (daily 9am–5pm; ⓦwww.lukang.gov.tw), packed full of information (though not much in English): the north area is covered at 488 Fuxing Rd (ⓣ04/784-1263) and the south area at 2 Qingyun Rd (ⓣ04/775-0830). **ATM** and banking facilities for non-Taiwan residents are limited in town, so make sure you bring enough cash.

Lugang had just got round to adding *tōngyòng pīnyīn* road signs when the KMT reverted to *hànyǔ* in 2008; we've adhered to the latter here, but it may be some time before street signs are changed.

Accommodation

Accommodation in Lugang is limited, though during the week it's easy to find rooms. The best option is the *Matsu Temple Believer Hotel* (天后宮香客大樓; *tiānhòugōng xiāngkè dàlóu*; ⓣ04/775-2508; ❸), the pristine modern building just north of Tianhou Temple at 475 Zhongshan Rd, with comfortable but basic rooms. The cheapest place is the faded *Quanzhong Hotel* (全忠旅社; *quánzhōng lǚshè*; look for the "Hotel" sign; ⓣ04/777-2640; ❷) at 104 Zhongshan Rd, while the only luxury hotel in town is the comfortable but rather sterile *Leader Hotel* (立德鹿港會館; *lìdé lùgǎng huìguǎn*; ⓣ04/778-6699, ⓦleader-lukang.hotel.com.tw; ❼), 588 Zhongzheng Rd, ten minutes' walk from Tianhou Temple.

The Town

Lugang is a large, modern town, but the historic centre is a thin wedge bordering **Zhongshan Road** from **Tianhou Temple** in the north to **Wenkai Academy** in the south. All the main points of interest can be reached as part of a long circular walk, though if you have time it can be a rewarding place to just wander.

Tianhou Temple

Established in 1591, **Tianhou Temple** (天后宮; *tiānhòu gōng*; daily 6am–10pm), at the northern end of Zhongshan Road (no. 430), is one of the oldest temples in Taiwan, though the first stone temple here was completed in 1647 and the current buildings are a result of renovations completed in 1936.

Much of the temple has a palpably archaic feel, and its intricate **stone carvings**, original woodwork and religious artefacts make it one of the country's most authentic. Before you go in, take a look at the gold-painted carvings of foreigners on the beams on either side of the main gate: the cherubic faces and clogs are supposed to be wicked Dutch colonizers. The **Main Hall** inside houses the chief Mazu deity (known as the "black-faced goddess" after being exposed to incense smoke for centuries), said to be one of six original statues from the Mazu mother temple in Meizhou in Fujian, brought to Taiwan by admiral **Shi Lang** in 1683. It's the smallest

In 1985 the Ministry of Education established the **Folk Art Heritage Awards**, also known as "Living Heritage Awards", to recognize the country's top craftsmen: the first winner was from Lugang, and the town has had six "folk arts masters", more than any other in Taiwan. **Chen Wanneng** (1942–) won the award in 1988 for his ornate **tin sculptures**. Traditional pieces can be seen at his shop at 635 Zhanglu Rd Sec 7 (T04/777-7847), while you can also view his work at the **Wan Neng Tin Workshop** (萬能錫舖; *wànnéng xípū*; usually daily 9am–5pm, but call ahead; T04/778-2877) at 81 Longshan St, opposite Longshan Temple. **Li Songlin** (1907–1998) was the first winner in 1985 and regarded as the greatest master of them all, primarily in woodcarving. Many of his works can be seen in Lugang's temples, but if you call in advance (Chinese only) you can view his exquisite sculptures in **Song Xia Studio**, home of his son Li Binggui, at 28 Putou St (Old Market St; T04/777-2448). **Shi Zhenyang** (1946–) is another talented woodcarver of the Quanzhou school who won the award in 1992, while **Shi Zihe** (1935–) is also a woodcarver, winning the award in 1994. You can see the master at work in his **Divine Woodcarving Shop** (施自和佛店; *shīzìhé fódiàn*; T04/777-450) at 655 Fuxing Rd. **Wu Qingbo** (1931–) is a fifth-generation woodcarver and award winner in 1987, famous principally for religious statues. **Wu Dun-hou** (1925–) is a celebrated creator of traditional lanterns who won the award in 1988, and his **Wu Dun-hou Lantern Shop** (吳敦厚燈舖; *wúdūnhòu dēngpù*); daily 9am–noon & 2–10pm; T04/777-6680) at 310 Zhongshan Rd is a popular place to buy beautifully crafted Chinese lanterns.

statue in the main shrine, honoured by several imperial tablets from various emperors hanging from the beams above. The altar through the doorway on the right honours Jing Zhu Gong, a local land god, while the Birth Goddess is worshipped on the left side – this arrangement is repeated in all Lugang's major temples.

Old Market Street

Turn left when you exit the Tianhou Temple and walk south along Zhongshan Road: turn right at the first junction and a little further along Wenkai Road on the left is Lugang's official Mazu shrine, established by imperial decree in 1788 and known today as **Xinzu Temple** (新組宮; *xīnzǔgōng*; daily 7am–8pm). The series of narrow lanes that lead south from the temple's main entrance are collectively known as **Old Market Street** (古市街; *gǔshì jiē*) and form what is undoubtedly Lugang's most atmospheric neighbourhood. The initial stretch is Putou Street (*pǔtóu jiē*); first on your left down here is **Nanjing Temple** at no. 74 (南京宮; *nánjīnggōng*), dedicated to Guan Di and dating from 1784, followed by **Lukang Assembly Hall** at no. 72 (鹿港公會堂; *lùgǎng gōnghuìtáng*), built in 1928 and now home to the **Lukang Art and Culture Centre** (鹿港藝文館; *lùgǎng yìwénguǎn*; Tues–Sun 9am–5pm; free). Inside is a modest collection of permanent and temporary Chinese paintings, calligraphy and sculptures. Beyond this the street is lined with beautifully preserved Qing dynasty buildings, many converted into touristy shops and cafés, but several still functioning as homes and workshops, giving the street an authentic edge. Lugang's **cakeshops** and bakeries are renowned for their sweet specialities, and the *Zheng Yu Zhen Cake Store* (鄭玉珍餅舖; *zhèngyùzhēn bǐngpù*; T04/778-8656) at no. 23, managed by the fourth generation of the Zheng family, is a good place to sample them (boxes from NT$60) – the first Zheng was head chef at *Yu Zhen Zhai* (see p.196). The final section south of here is Yaolin Street (*yáolín jiē*). The diminutive **Half-Sided Well** (半邊井; *bànbiān jǐng*) at no. 12, tucked away on the east side not far from Minquan Road has an interesting history – built so that the public could share the spring water bubbling up inside one of Lugang's richer homes, it's testimony to the munificence of the town's former elites.

Nine-Turns Lane

At Minquan Road cross over and continue south: barring a few twists and turns (turn left at the T-junction), you should end up at Daming Road and First Market (a great place to eat, see p.196). Turn left and follow Daming round to Minzu Road, and where Minzu shoots off to the right, look for a narrow lane opposite (at around 183 Minzu Road). This becomes **Nine-Turns Lane** (九曲巷; *jiǔqūxiàng*). Named after the ninth month, September, tourists are told that its thin, crooked alleyways were designed to confuse pirates and protect against the chill winds prevalent at this time of year, but most scholars believe it simply ran behind houses that stood, unevenly, along Lugang's harbour front. There's not a lot to see but it's one of the town's more appealing areas, especially the intriguing passageway that crosses the lane further south known as **Shih Yih Hall** (十宜樓; *shíyílóu*) where Lugang's literati would, as the English sign explains, "recite poetry and partake in alcoholic revelry". The lane ends on Xinsheng Road but it's possible to follow redbrick alleys south from here, past the elaborate round window of the **Remembrance Hall** (意樓; *yìlóu*), and **Xingan Temple** (興安宮; *xīngāngōng*), Lugang's first Mazu shrine, before eventually reaching Sanmin Road near Longshan Temple.

Longshan Temple and around

Longshan Temple (龍山寺; *lóngshān sì*; daily 5am–9.30pm) is one of the most famous Buddhist temples in Taiwan, though its sobriquet of "Taiwan's Forbidden City" is a little misleading. What it lacks in size it makes up for in artistic beauty however, especially with its exquisite dragon pillars and **woodcarvings** – check out the amazing eight trigram windows in the **main entrance hall** and the roof beams above. The temple is principally dedicated to Guanyin and traces its origins to a shrine founded in 1653 – it was moved to the current site in 1786 when the area was outside the town and much quieter.

The temple was flattened by the 921 Earthquake (see box, p.183), triggering a massive restoration project that ended in 2009; everything was meticulously replaced exactly the way it was before the quake, exceptional artwork as well as faded paintwork. The **Main Hall** holds the most revered images of Guanyin in the centre, and you can also have a peek at the **Rear Hall**, dedicated to several Buddhist bodhisatvas.

Before you move on, visit the **Wan Neng Tin Workshop** (萬能錫鋪; *wànnéng xípù*), opposite the main temple entrance on Longshan Street (see box opposite). Walk back to Sanmin Road, then right to Zhongshan Road: if you've still got some energy left, there is a cluster of Qing dynasty buildings a block further south. **Wenkai Academy** (文開書院; *wénkāi shūyuàn*) was once a school (now preserved as a monument), completed in 1827 and serving as the focus not only for young scholars but also Lugang's famed literati for much of the subsequent 150 years. Next door the **Wenchang Temple** (文祠; *wéncí*) or "Civil Shrine" dates from 1811 and is dedicated to the god of literature, Wenchang Dijun, while finally, separated by the **Tiger Well**, is the **Martial Temple** (武廟; *wǔmiào*), completed the same year and dedicated to Guan Di. The main buildings are open 6am–9pm daily.

North along Zhongshan Road

It's a long walk back to Tianhou Temple from the southern end of **Zhongshan Road** (中山路; *zhōngshān lù*) but the street has plenty of character, lined with early twentieth-century shophouses, many still home to traditional stores and master craftsmen (see box opposite). North of Sanmin Road, the main attraction is

Lukang Folk Arts Museum (鹿港民俗文物館; *lùgǎng mínsú wénwùguǎn*; daily 9am–5pm; NT$130; ☎04/777-2019, ⓦwww.lukangarts.org.tw): ignore the first sign on the right and instead walk to the next narrow lane, by the side of a police station at no. 108, and turn right here. This alley takes you past the "**wall of jars**", old wine jars used to build courtyard walls, and on to a bigger road – the museum is the huge Baroque mansion on the left. Completed in 1920, it was the home of the mighty **Koo family**, one of Taiwan's richest and most influential. Though it contains a fascinating collection of artwork and everyday artefacts from the Qing and early Japanese period, most of the objects reflect the lives of the very wealthy and, one presumes, the Koos themselves. Patriarch **Koo Xian-Rong** established Lugang's salt industry in the 1890s and his son **Koo Chen-Fu** (1917–2005) was involved in landmark China negotiations in the 1990s. The family still wields considerable economic clout, controlling giants such as Taiwan Cement and Chinatrust Commercial Bank.

Return to Zhongshan Road and head north to Minzu Road, where you'll see the venerable cakeshop **Yu Zhen Zhai** (玉珍齋; *yùzhēnzhāi*; daily 8am–11pm; ☎04/777-3672) on the corner at 168 Minzu Rd, home of phoenix eye cake (*fènghuáng yǎngāo*), phoenix egg cake (*fènghuáng sū*) and the comparatively prosaic green bean cake (*lǜdòugāo*; NT$35) since its founding in 1877 by Fujianese immigrant Zheng Cui.

North of Minzu Road lies the town's modern commercial heart, but keep walking beyond Minquan Road and you'll find the **Wu Dun-hou Lantern Shop** (吳敦厚燈舖; *wúdūnhòu dēngpù*; see box, p.194) at no. 310, next to the main police station. A short walk north on the left, at no. 327-1 is the aged **Shi Jinyu Incense Store** (施金玉香舖; *shī jīnyù xiāngpù*; daily 8am–7.30pm), founded in 1756 and now owned by the seventh generation of proprietors. Not far from here on the other side of the road at no. 366 is **Chenghuang Temple** (城隍廟; *chénghuáng miào*; daily 6am–9pm), housing Lugang's City God, a small single-hall structure with a large abacus hanging above the main entrance.

The next major junction south of Tianhou Temple completes the loop: turn right here along Lucao Road, and the second shop on the left, 400-1 Zhongshan Rd, is **Chen's Fan Shop** (陳朝宗手工扇; *chén cháozōng shǒugōngshàn*; generally 9am–5pm daily), home to exquisite, hand-painted Chinese fans. Chen Chao-zong has received many awards, though he's not yet an official "Living Treasure".

Eating

Lugang specializes in *xiǎochī* or "little eats": favourites include **oyster omelettes** (*é a jiān*; NT$50) and "**shrimp monkeys**" (*xiāhóuzi*; mud shrimp fried with basil; plates for around NT$100) – though you'll need a vivid imagination to see the monkey; both are available at the snack stalls and restaurants in front of Tianhou Temple. Try the bakeries around here for **ox-tongue biscuits** (*niúshébǐng*; NT$10) a sweet flat pastry that tastes nothing like tongue, though it vaguely resembles one.

Tea, coffee and delicious **rice powder tea** (*miànchá*; NT$40) can be sampled at *Yi Gu Zhai* (怡古齋; *yígǔzhāi*) at 6 Putou St (Old Market St), an atmospheric café in a narrow shophouse with wooden benches and Qing dynasty decor – it's a thick, sweet drink best sampled cold. **First Market** (第一市場; *dìyī shìchǎng*) on Minzu Road also has food stalls open from 6am till around 9pm. The most popular include *Old Chef's Duck Broth* (老師傅鴨肉羹; *lǎoshīfù yāròugēng*; NT$40) at no. 159; *Sheng Chao Wu Wei* (生炒五味; *shēngchǎo wǔwèi*) at no. 171, named after its main dish, a broth of shrimp, cuttlefish, pork, mushrooms and bamboo shoots (NT$30); and, around the corner at no. 193, *Longshan Noodles* (龍山麵線糊; *lóngshān miàn xiànhú*), cooking up delicious vermicelli noodles with pork and dried shrimp (NT$25). *A Zhen Steamed Bun* (阿振肉包; *ā zhèn ròubāo*; daily 9am–7pm; ☎04/777-2754) at 73 Zhongshan Rd produces delicious **pork buns** (*ròubāo*; NT$15) with mushrooms, while *Qiao Wei Zhen Steamed Bun* (巧味珍包子店; *qiǎowèizhēn bāozidiàn*; daily 7am–9.30pm; ☎04/776-9448), just south of Tianhou Temple at 406 Zhongshan Rd, also serves up tasty steamed savoury buns (NT$15), founded by one of Zhen's former staff.

Jiji Branch Rail Line

The **JIJI BRANCH RAIL LINE** (集集線鐵道; *jíjíxiàn tiědào*) beginning southeast of Changhua and stretching 29.5km to an old depot near Sun Moon Lake, is one of the country's four **narrow–gauge railways** that have been preserved for tourists. It chugs its way through tranquil countryside, stopping at a handful of **historic towns** that offer glimpses of a Taiwan that is fast disappearing. Much of the area is linked by easily navigable **bike paths** and dotted with a growing number of family-run **homestays**, many in restored traditional homes.

First opened in 1922 by the occupying Japanese to transport construction materials to Sun Moon Lake, the railway begins in the quaint town of **Ershui** – about thirty minutes by train from Changhua – and runs west through **Jiji** and **Shuili** before terminating in the rustic old village of **Checheng**, just south of Sun Moon Lake.

Ershui

The railway's official starting point, the town of **ERSHUI** (二水; *èrshuǐ*) holds considerable allure, with bucolic surroundings and a **bike path** that winds through several kilometres of farmland, much of it **betel nut plantations**. The paved route – meant to be for cyclists only but also used by cautious local motorists – passes a number of folk shrines and some wonderfully well-preserved traditional houses. To get to the beginning of the bicycle path, turn right after you exit the train station and walk about 200m until you reach the railway crossing to your right; cross the tracks and the path begins immediately to your right. **Bicycles** can be rented (NT$100 per day) from the shop just outside the train station.

The other main attraction is the **Fongbo Trail** (豐柏山步道; *fēngbóshān bùdào*), which starts at **Fongbo Square** (豐柏廣場; *fēngbó guǎngchǎng*), essentially a car park about 2.5km from the train station. It takes around twenty minutes to walk here using hand-drawn maps from the visitor centre (see p.198)

Exploring the Jiji line

The Jiji Branch Rail Line begins at the town of **Ershui** on the **western rail line**, roughly halfway between Changhua and Chiayi, but most trains actually start in **Taichung** (台中; *tái zhōng*; Ershui NT$73, Jiji NT$103). **Tickets** can be bought at stations or on the train itself: by 2011 there should special **multiple-stop tickets** (from NT$80) available at stations on the line, but you can also buy single tickets. Note that **Shuili** and the railway's western terminus at **Checheng** are both connected to nearby **Sun Moon Lake** by a free shuttle bus (see p.201). **Bicycles** can be rented at several places along the line (NT$100/day), and **bike paths** run along the railway – especially appealing from Jiji onwards.

but you can also take a **taxi** (N$100). From the car park, a path leads through the **Taiwan Macaque Protection Area** (台灣獼猴保護區; *táiwān míhóu bǎohù qū*), home to an estimated three hundred of the eponymous energetic, bluish-grey-haired **monkeys**. Feeding them is strictly prohibited, though plenty of visitors ignore this rule, and as a result the monkeys can be a touch aggressive; keep your distance and keep food well hidden. The best time to see them is 10am–noon or 2–3pm. The path climbs gently for about 2km up the **Songbo Ridge** (松柏嶺; *sōngbó lǐng*), at the top of which await fine views and the **Shoutian Temple** (受天宮; *shòutiān gōng*), dedicated to Taoist deity Supreme Emperor of the Dark Heaven (*xuántiān shàngdì*); the large exterior makes for an impressive sight from a distance.

Practicalities

Ershui's tiny but helpful **visitor centre** (Mon–Fri 9am–5pm, Sat & Sun 8am–5pm; ☏04/879-8129), just outside the station on the right, is usually manned by English speakers and has English hand-drawn maps of the town. There is a Chinatrust Commercial Bank **ATM** that accepts international credit cards in the 7-Eleven at 10 Guangwen Rd, about 200m from the train station, on the left.

The most famous place **to eat** in town is *Fire-Burning Noodles* (火燒麵; *huǒshāo miàn*) at 724 Yuanji Rd Sec 3 (keep walking from the 7-Eleven and it's around the corner on the left). The name refers to the fiery wok used to fry the main dish – a sumptuous plate of fried pork noodles costs just NT$35.

Jiji

The tourist-friendly town of **JIJI** (集集; *jíjí*) is the fourth stop on the line (20km and NT$31 from Ershui), its rustic charms drawing droves of visitors searching for remnants of the Japanese colonial era. The most intact of these is **Jiji Station** itself (集集火車站; *jíjí huǒchēzhàn*). Built in 1933, it was badly damaged in the 921 Earthquake and was completely rebuilt; the same red-cypress beams and planks were used (although the main pillars were reinforced with steel), and its black-glazed roof tiles were replaced with those retrieved from other Japanese-era buildings in the area.

Most of Jiji's attractions are accessible via a series of **bike paths** (ranging 1.55–2.9km and forming a loop around the town), clearly marked with metal signs in the shape of a bicycle (maps available at the visitor centre). Barely a kilometre along the main path, across the road to the left from the station, is tiny **Junshi Park** (軍史公園; *jūnshǐ gōngyuán*; 24hr; free), an outdoor museum filled with an array of military equipment, including tanks, anti-aircraft artillery launchers, a cargo plane and a fighter jet. A few hundred metres further on you'll see an ornamental Chinese archway to the right, beyond which lies the historic **Mingxin Academy** (明新書院; *míngxīn shūyuàn*; daily 7am–9pm; free), a Confucian school and shrine founded in 1882 and moved to its present location in 1902.

One of the most fascinating sights along the main bike path loop is the **Wuchang Temple** (武昌宮; *wǔchāng gōng*), which ironically rose to prominence after collapsing in the 921 Earthquake. The symmetrical fashion of its collapse is intriguing – its lower walls gave way, yet its ornate, multi-tiered roof remains almost completely intact, down to the guardian statues that now watch over the ruins.

Practicalities

Jiji's large **visitor centre** (集集旅客服務中心; *jíjí lǔkèfúwù zhōngxīn*; Mon–Fri 8am–5pm, Sat & Sun 8.30–5.30pm; ☏049/276-4625; Chinese maps only, but English spoken) is a short walk from the station at 162 Minsheng Rd, opposite the

7-Eleven. Free wi-fi is available here, but otherwise there's nowhere to use the **internet**. Several shops across the street from the train station rent **bicycles** (NT$50–100/day), and **scooters** (from NT$200/hr). At the time of writing it was easy for non-Taiwan residents to rent scooters at any of these shops, but bring your passport. The **ATM** at Taiwan Cooperative Bank, 174 Minsheng Rd, takes international cards.

The closest **accommodation** option to the train station is the rather institutional *JiJi Hotel* (集集大飯店; *jíjí dàfàndiàn*; ☏049/276-0778; ❸) at 113 Minsheng Road (turn left from the station), with basic but bright and clean doubles. Further afield but with more amenities is the plush *Mountain, Fish, Water* (山魚水渡假飯店; *shānyúshuǐ dùjiǎ fàndiàn*; ☏049/276-1000; ❼) at 205 Chenggong Road. The spacious rooms come with big, comfortable beds, flat-screen TVs and a slick modern Chinese design; rates include a buffet breakfast and use of the complex's **swimming pool** and spa facilities. Jiji's signature culinary specialty is its **stinky tofu** (*chòu dòufǔ*), prized for its taste, freshness and firm texture, despite its notorious aroma (caused by the oil used to fry it). The best-known place to try it is *Grandma's Stinky Tofu* (阿婆臭豆腐; *āpó chòu dòufǔ*; daily from 3pm until they run out; Chinese only), a no-frills canteen at 7 Zhibin St, a small alley just across Minsheng Road from the *JiJi Hotel*. For more than forty years it has served only two items: *chòu dòufǔ* (NT$45) topped with lightly stir-fried cabbage, and steaming bowls of dried duck's blood soup (NT$25). You'll find plenty of **snack stalls** around the station, including *Laowu Pig's Foot King* (老五豬腳大王; *lǎowǔ zhūjiǎo dàwáng*; daily 7am–7pm, Wed from 2pm; ☏049/276-0034) at 285 Minquan Road, where trotters are fried and stewed in soy sauce, apples and plums.

Shuili

The next stop and biggest town on the rail line, 7.3km from Jiji, is **SHUILI** (水里; *shuǐlǐ*; NT$41 from Ershui, NT$23 from Jiji). It's best known for the 1927 **Shueli Snake Kiln**, (水里蛇窯; *shuǐlǐ shéyáo*; daily 8am–5.30pm; NT$150; ☏49/277-0967) at 41 Dingkan Lane on the outskirts of town, though there's not much to see beyond the world's largest vase (6.6m) and the giant kiln itself, unless you fancy buying or making some pottery (from NT$280). Take a Puli-bound bus from the train station.

The town is also home to the **Yushan National Park Headquarters** and its main visitor centre, (玉山國家公園管理處; *yùshān guójiā gōngyuán guǎnlǐchù*; daily 9am–4.30pm; ☏049/2773121; ⓦwww.ysnp.gov.tw), 300 Zhongshan Rd Sec 1, where you can get excellent English-language park **maps**. To get to the headquarters, walk straight down Minsheng Road from the train station for about 500m until you reach a big intersection next to the river; turn right here and walk another 500m to the next intersection – cross the bridge to the left and you'll see the large, white headquarters building on the right.

Shuili's main **bus station** is to the left after you exit the train station, directly across the street from the 7-Eleven on Minquan Road. From here, buses leave for the mountain hot-springs town of **Dongpu** (6am, 8am, 8.50am, 11.10am, 1pm, 2.30pm, 4pm & 5.10pm; 1hr 10min; NT$115). For **Sun Moon Lake** (daily 6am–6pm; 30min; NT$56) and **Puli** (1hr; NT$107), keep walking along the road to the Green Transit bus station. At 117 Minquan Rd (just to the right as you exit the station), shared taxis go to Taichung for only NT$180 (☏049/277-3976). Free shuttle buses to Checheng, the Snake Kiln and **Sun Moon Lake** run from the main bus station on major holidays.

There is a Chinatrust Commercial Bank **ATM** that accepts international credit cards inside the 7-Eleven just outside the train station.

Checcheng

Just over 2km from Shuili, the rail line terminates at the handsome wooden station at **CHECHENG** (車埕; *chēchéng*; NT$44 from Ershui, NT$23 from Shuili), rebuilt with precious cypress wood after the 921 Earthquake destroyed the old building and most of the village. Originally developed by the Japanese as a **logging centre**, the first timber factory was built in 1933, but by the 1970s the business had virtually collapsed. Since 2000 the village has been sensitively redeveloped as an eco-friendly tourist centre within the Sun Moon Lake Scenic Area (see below), backed by a stunning ridge of mountains.

The dual focus of the village today is the **Lumber Pond**, ringed by attractively restored timber buildings, and **The Grove** (林班道; *línbāndào*; Mon–Fri 10am–6pm, Sat & Sun 9am–7pm), a shopping mall containing places to eat, the Lohas Warehouse (樂活倉庫; *lèhuó cāngkù*), selling sustainable products, and the **Experience Factory** (體驗工廠; *tǐyàn gōngchǎng*) where NT$160 gets you a DIY session (a bit like an IKEA kit) to build a Finnish spruce wood stool.

Nearby, the **Checheng Wood Museum** (車埕木業展示館; *chēchéng mùyè zhǎnshìguǎn*; Mon–Fri 9am–5.30pm, Sat & Sun 9am–6pm; NT$40; ☏049/287-1793) is housed in a huge cypress wooden shed over the old timber workings, with carvings, exhibits on the history of the village and a slowly developing Railway Park, with old steam engines from the early twentieth century. You can also check out the **Checheng Winery** (車埕酒莊; *chēchéng jiǔzhuāng*; daily 9am–5.30am; free; ☏049/287-0399), a small local producer of plum wines at 118 Minquan Lane – wander through the distillery vats to the tasting room upstairs, where free samples are handed out in the hopes you'll buy one of the surprisingly tasty bottles (from NT$299).

Practicalities

The useful **Checheng visitor centre** is in the centre of the village at 36 Minquan St (daily 9am–5pm; ☏049/277-2982). Free shuttle buses from Checheng via Shuili to **Sun Moon Lake** run on major holidays. By 2016 a 4.72km **cable car** should link Checheng with Sun Moon Lake (12–15min), at Xiangshan (向山; *xiàngshān*; 4km from Shuishe), but in the meantime **taxis** to Sun Moon Lake are NT$500–600.

Staying in the village is popular at the weekends, but it's fairly tranquil during the week. Try the *Che Cheng Chateau* at 118 Minquan Lane (☏049/287-0399), above the Winery, which is a bit old but offers four, clean en-suite rooms (❸) with local TV, and Japanese-style rooms for two (❷), four (NT$2000) and six (NT$2700) with shared bath – breakfast is included. The *Cedar Tea House* (木茶房; *mùcháfáng*; Mon–Fri 10am–6pm, Sat & Sun 10am–6.30pm), 105 Minquan Lane, is the best place for tea, coffee and light snacks.

Sun Moon Lake

Hemmed in by lush tiers of mountains in the heart of Taiwan, **SUN MOON LAKE** (日月潭; *rìyuè tán*) is the island's largest freshwater body, its calm, emerald-green waters creating some of the country's most mesmerizing landscapes. The lake's name is inspired by its distinctive shape, with a rounded main section likened to the sun and a narrow western fringe compared to a crescent moon. Encircling it all is a 33km road, dotted with fascinating **temples** and picturesque **pavilions**, each offering a unique perspective on the waters below, while the **cable car** provides a stupendous panorama of the whole lake.

Given its abundant beauty, Sun Moon Lake attracts large crowds throughout the year (it's a prime draw for mainland tourists), especially at weekends when hotel rates skyrocket – weekdays, particularly in winter, are the best time to visit.

Swimming in the lake is allowed on only one day each year, when at least ten thousand yellow-capped Taiwanese take to the waters for the annual **Sun Moon Lake Swimming Carnival**, a 3km cross-lake race that takes place around the Mid-Autumn Festival, usually in September. The lake is also the ancestral home of the **Thao** (pronounced "Shao", meaning "people"), Taiwan's smallest officially recognized aboriginal tribe (see p.399).

Some history

Until the early twentieth century, the lake was a shallow marsh called **Shuishalian**. In 1919 the Japanese started work on a **dam** for hydroelectric power, finally flooding the area in 1934 – and destroying the last traditional Thao community that had clung to the slopes of pyramid-shaped **Lalu Island** in the marsh's centre. Those inhabitants were forced to move to the lake's south side, into a village that today is known as Itashao. After 1950 **Chiang Kai-shek** made the lake his favoured summer retreat, spurring further development that continued into the 1970s. In 1999, the 921 Earthquake severely damaged much of the lakeside infrastructure, levelling hotels and restaurants and rendering some hiking trails temporarily impassable. However, the tourist villages on the lake's northern and southern shores were gradually rebuilt and have long surpassed their former grandeur.

Arrival and information

All **buses** to Sun Moon Lake terminate at the bus station next to the visitor centre at **Shuishe**, on the lake's northwest side; if you don't have your own transport this is the best place to base yourself. In addition to onward transport links, it has the widest selection of hotels and restaurants and the **Shuishe Visitor Center** (水社遊客中心; *shuǐshè yóukè zhōngxīn*; daily 9am–5.30pm; ℡049/285-5668, ⓦwww.sunmoonlake.gov.tw) at 163 Zhongshan Rd, where you can get maps, hire bikes, buy boat tickets and see a short English-language film about the area. On the lake's southeast side is **Itashao**, which has some very

---

Getting to Sun Moon Lake

Sun Moon Lake is easily accessed by **bus**. There are frequent buses daily from **Taichung Station** (1hr 30min) with Ren You Bus (仁友客運; *rényǒu kèyùn*; N$200; 8am, 10.10am, 12.30pm & 3pm) and Nantou Bus (南投客運; *nántóu kèyùn*; NT$188; 2–3/hr 7.25am–10.25pm); the latter also stops at the **Taichung High-Speed Rail Station** (20min from downtown), and most buses also run through **Puli** (1hr 10min from Taichung). The 7.50am, 8.50am, 9.50am and 3.50pm departures also stop at the **Formosan Aboriginal Culture Village** (connected to Sun Moon Lake by cable car; see p.207). From **Puli** (daily 6am–6pm; 30min; NT$56), there are also hourly Green Transit (豐榮客運; *fēngróng kèyùn*) services to Shuishe; the same bus runs on from Shuishe to **Shuili** (NT$51). **Free shuttle buses** run between Checheng, Shuili and Shuishe on major holidays.

From **Taipei** (3hr 30min; NT$440–480), Kuo Kuang runs direct buses at 7am, 8.20am, 10am, 3pm and 5pm; returning buses depart 7.40am, 9.20am, 11.20am, 1.20pm, 2.20pm and 4.20pm.

To travel between Sun Moon Lake and **Alishan** (see p.221), take a bus to Shuili and switch to the Jiji Rail Line (hourly; p.197) – at Ershui you can catch trains to **Chiayi** (2/hr; 45min), from where there are buses to Alishan.

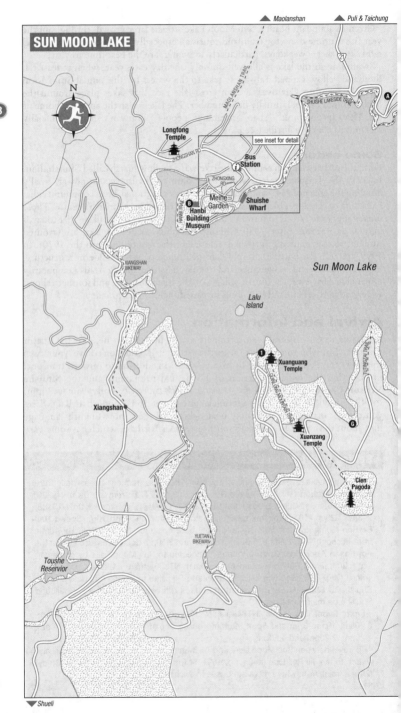

SUN MOON LAKE

▲ Maolanshan   ▲ Puli & Taichung

N

MAOLANSHAN TRAIL

SHUISHE LAKESIDE TRAIL

A

Longfong
Temple

ZHONGSHAN RD

see inset for detail

Bus
Station
i

ZHONGXING
RD

B
Hanbi
Building
Museum

Meihe
Garden

Shuishe
Wharf

HANBI TRAIL

XIANGSHAN
BIKEWAY

21

Sun Moon Lake

Lalu
Island

Xiangshan

1

Xuanguang
Temple

QINGLONGSHAN TRAIL

YUTINGZAI TRAIL

G

Xuanzang
Temple

Cien
Pagoda

YUETAN
BIKEWAY

Toushe
Reservoir

21

▼ Shueli

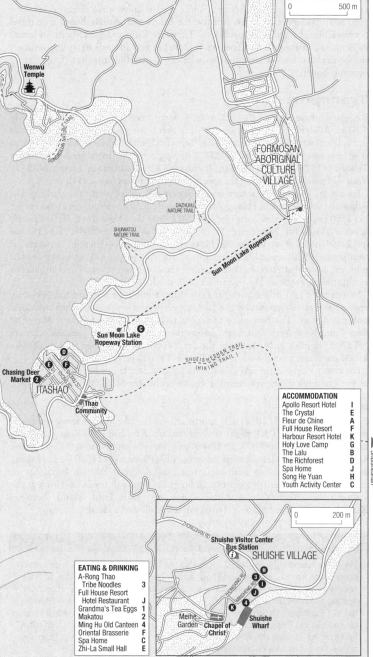

0   500 m

Wenwu Temple

SONGBOLUN NATURE TRAIL

FORMOSAN ABORIGINAL CULTURE VILLAGE

DAZHUHU NATURE TRAIL

SHUWATOU NATURE TRAIL

Sun Moon Lake Ropeway

Sun Moon Lake Ropeway Station ©

SHUEISHESHAN TRAIL (HIKING TRAIL)

Chasing Deer Market ②

ITASHAO

Thao Community

▶ Shuisheshan

ACCOMMODATION

Apollo Resort Hotel	I
The Crystal	E
Fleur de Chine	A
Full House Resort	F
Harbour Resort Hotel	K
Holy Love Camp	G
The Lalu	B
The Richforest	D
Spa Home	J
Song He Yuan	H
Youth Activity Center	C

0   200 m

ZHONGSHAN RD

Shuishe Visitor Center Bus Station 🛈

SHUISHE VILLAGE

ZHONGXING RD

Ⓗ

③ 🛈

Ⓙ

EATING & DRINKING

A-Rong Thao Tribe Noodles	3
Full House Resort Hotel Restaurant	J
Grandma's Tea Eggs	1
Makatou	2
Ming Hu Old Canteen	4
Oriental Brasserie	F
Spa Home	C
Zhi-La Small Hall	E

Meihe Garden   Chapel of Christ

Ⓚ ④

Shuishe Wharf

pleasant hotels and restaurants and is adjacent to the main **Thao community** and the trailhead for Shuisheshan. While it's less convenient if you don't have your own transport, you can still use the **boats** and **shuttle buses** that travel between Shuishe and Itashao villages. There are Chinatrust **ATMs** in 7-Elevens in Shuishe and Itashao, and **free wi-fi** (24hr) in and around the visitor centre – the centre also has two computers where you use the **internet** (free) during opening hours.

Transport

Regular **shuttle buses** (℡049/298-4031) leave from Shuishe bus station (daily 9.30am–5.30pm; Sat & Sun also 7.30am every 30min), stopping at the major sights (clockwise) as far as Xuanguang Temple (30min) before making the return trip; you can buy a day-pass (NT$80) or single tickets (from Shuishe: Wenwu Temple NT$24; cable car NT$26; Itashao NT$28; Xuanguang Temple NT$45). Your day pass is also valid on the special **Puli tour buses** (see p.211).

Foreigners can rent **scooters** on Zhongxing Road opposite the parking lot, below the visitor centre; Huang Zhi Chen (daily 8.30am–6pm) rents scooters for NT$150 per hour (third hour free) and NT$500 a day. Next door, Helio Electric Scooter (Mon–Fri 9am–6pm, Sat & Sun 8.30am–6pm; ℡049/220-1163 or 0912/191-667, ⓦwww.taiwanhelio.com.tw) offers eco-friendly scooters at similar rates, with several branches around the lake so you can exchange models with exhausted batteries. In both cases, if you don't have a local (Taiwan) licence you'll still get a scooter but you won't be insured.

You can also rent **bikes**, with the entire loop around the lake (around 30km) an enjoyable way to experience the lake, especially on weekdays, when vehicular traffic is lighter. The best place to rent is Giant (daily except Thurs: May–Oct 6am–7pm; Nov–April 7am–6pm), below the visitor centre; the cheapest bikes are NT$200 per hour or NT$800 for the day. Mountain bikes range from NT$500–$1000 per hour (second hour NT$200) to NT$1600 per day.

For closer views of the lake, **rowboats** for two people can be rented at the end of the Zhongxing car park, near the visitor centre, for NT$200 per hour.

Ferries

Ferries (℡049/285-5118) usually shuttle around the lake in a clockwise direction, from Shuishe Wharf (水社碼頭; *shuǐshè mǎtóu*), to Itashao Pier, Xuanguang Pier and back again (Mon–Fri 9.20am–4.50pm, every 45min; Sat & Sun 8.50am–4.50pm, every 30min). Each segment costs NT$100, or it's NT$300 for a complete loop (discounts are often available). You can take your bike on board for an additional NT$50 per trip, but not all boats have enough room, so check at the visitor centre first. Note that the ferries only skirt **Lalu Island** (between Xuanguang and Shuishe); only Thao people are allowed to land.

Lalu Island

Tiny **Lalu Island** (拉魯島; *lālǔdǎo*), just off the lake's southern shore is the most sacred site of the indigenous **Thao** people, who believe the spirits of their ancestors dwell there. For decades, the island served the purposes of tourism, hosting a shrine containing Taiwan's largest **Matchmaker** statue (see p.406). After the 921 Earthquake, there was considerable political pressure for the island to be returned to the Thao, and in 2000 it was renamed Lalu in accordance with tribal tradition. Its shores are now protected, and only the few remaining Thao are allowed to set foot on it – tourist boats generally circle the island.

Accommodation

Sun Moon Lake has a range of **accommodation**, though the trend is definitely heading upmarket – some of Taiwan's most expensive hotels are here. The most appealing places in Shuishe face the lake along Minsheng Road, near Shuishe Wharf. All of these have lake-view rooms with balconies. **Room rates** rise dramatically during summer, as well as at weekends and public holidays, making it especially expensive to visit at these times.

Shuishe

Apollo Resort Hotel 鴻賓休閒渡假旅棧 (*hóngbīn xiūxián dùjiǎ lǚzhàn*) 3 Minsheng Rd ☏049/285-5381. An attractive lakeside hotel, with friendly staff, spotlessly clean rooms and small balconies affording some of the finest lake and mountain views. ❻

Harbour Resort Hotel 碼頭休閒大飯店 (*mǎtóu xiūxián dàfàndiàn*) 113 Zhongshan Rd ☏049/285-5143. Next to the wharf entrance, *Harbour Resort* has bright, jazzed-up balcony rooms with great lake views. ❼

The Lalu 涵碧樓 (*hánbì lóu*) 142 Zhongxing Rd ☏049/285-5311, ⊛www.thelalu.com.tw. Unabashedly devoted to pure indulgence, with rack rates ranging from NT$13,800 for a one-bedroom suite to NT$65,000 for the presidential suite. All suites have large living and bathing areas, with twenty-square-metre balconies commanding superb lake views, and wood and stone interiors whose soft tones blend with the lake's natural colours. There's an "infinity pool", whose waters seem to spill straight into the lake, a spa, where you can soak in flower-petal-filled perfumed baths or have a massage, plus a fitness room, teahouse and three restaurants. ❾

Song He Yuan 松鶴園飯店 (*sōnghèyuán fàndiàn*) 137 Zhongshan Rd ☏049/285-6547. Clean, comfortable and spacious doubles just off the main drag, with kettle, tiled floors and local TV; Chinese breakfast included, plus toast. Favourite with foreigners on a budget – bargain and you'll usually get a discount (singles for as low as NT$600–800), though rates are NT$600 higher at the weekends. ❸

Spa Home 飯店 (*Spa Home fàndiàn*) 95 Zhongshan Rd ☏049/285-5166, ⊛www.spahome.com.tw. Near the junction of Zhongshan and Minsheng roads, this lakefront boutique has sleek, stylish doubles dressed up with black beech wood furnishings. Rooms facing the lake have balconies, but the hotel's highlight is its spa. Rates include breakfast. ❼

Itashao

The Crystal 晶澤會館 (*jīngzé huìguǎn*) 3 Shuishlian St ☏049/285-0097, ⊛www.thecrystal.com.tw. Plush boutique right on the waterfront near

Itashao Pier, with just twenty luxurious rooms with balconies overlooking the lake and huge bath tubs. Rates include dinner and breakfast. ❾

Full House Resort 富豪群渡假民宿 (*fùháoqún dùjiǎ mínsù*) 8 Shuixiu St ☏049/285-0307, ⊛www.fhsml.idv.tw. In a three-storey timber building fronted by a peaceful garden café, *Full House* has a slightly offbeat charm, its halls and cabin interiors decorated with portraits painted by the owner's wife. ❺

The Richforest 儷山林哲園會館 (*lìshānlín zhéyuán huìguǎn*) 31 Shuixiu St ☏049/285-0000. Eclipsed by newer and more luxurious places, the former *Lingo's* was once the lake's top hotel, a huge chalet-like complex with gorgeous lake-view rooms and Canadian maple-wood interiors; check the room first, as some have yet to be renovated. Amenities include a swimming pool, sauna, fitness room, pool tables and even a mahjong room. ❽

Other lakeside spots

Fleur de Chine 雲品酒店 (*yúnpǐn jiǔdiàn*) 23 Zhongzheng Rd ☏049/285-6788. Incredibly plush lakeside retreat, with a choice of lakeside or mountain views, all with French windows, private balcony and a natural hot spring bathtub. LCD TVs, DVD players, free wi-fi and fluffy bathrobes included. ❾

Holy Love Camp 聖愛營地 (*shèngài yíngdì*) 261-10 Zhongzheng Rd (Hwy-21A km 9.5) ☏049/285-0202 or 04/2205-9715. This rustic lakeside retreat, tucked in a secluded cove a few kilometres northwest of Itashao Village, is a haven of water sports in summer, with canoeing, pedal-boating and windsurfing the main activities. The camp is accessed via a steep trail off the main road at around km 9.5, but the path is hard to spot and there is no parking, so call in advance to arrange a boat pick-up in Shuishe or Itashao. Single or multi-night packages including pick-up, meals and dorm-room accommodation must be made by phone. Dog lovers only (they keep a colony). ❷

Youth Activity Center 青年活動中心 (*qīngnián huádòng zhōngxīn*) 101 Zhongzheng Rd ☏049/285-0070, ⊛sun.cyh.org.tw. A few kilometres northeast of Itashao, just off the main road around the lake, this hotel is popular with school groups and can be very noisy at times. However, its large, clean rooms – some Japanese-style – are great value (book on-line), especially for groups, and the centre rents fair-quality bicycles (NT$200/day). ❸

Shuishe

The booming commercial centre of Sun Moon Lake is **Shuishe** (水社; *shuǐshè*), and beyond the wharf, hotels and serene lake views are several noteworthy sights. The set of stone steps just west of the Shueishe Wharf climb to the **Meihe Garden** (梅荷園; *méihé yuán*), a covered viewpoint, while further up is the **Chapel of Christ** (耶穌堂; *yēsū táng*; daily 9am–5pm), built in the 1970s for the exclusive use of Chiang Kai-shek and his wife. Their private residence (known as the "Hanbi Building") then occupied the hilltop just west of here, where *The Lalu* hotel now stands. Near *The Lalu*'s main entrance is the **Hanbi Building Museum** (涵碧樓博物館; *hánbìlóu bówùguǎn*; daily 8am–5pm; free), with a fascinating collection of black-and-white photos of Chiang and a host of foreign luminaries who visited him at his lake retreat. There are also old photos of the lake that predate the dam's construction, giving a glimpse of what the triangular-shaped Lalu Island looked like before it was mostly submerged.

Back at the hill's base, leading west from the Meihe Garden, is the gentle **Hanbi Trail** (涵碧步道; *hánbì bùdào*) which makes a 1.5km loop of the shoreline surrounding the hill.

Around 1km further west of Shuishe along Provincial Highway 21 is the **Longfong Temple** (龍鳳廟; *lóngfèng miào*; daily 8am–5pm; ☎049/285-6818), best known for the **Matchmaker** statue that sits in a separate shrine just outside the entrance. The statue – Taiwan's largest Matchmaker (see p.406) image – was originally placed on Lalu Island in a small shrine built in the 1960s, and was a fashionable place for group weddings on National Day. After the 921 Earthquake, however, it was removed from the island and taken to its less contentious location. It's still extremely popular with Taiwanese couples. Near here is the beginning of the **Maolanshan Trail** (貓蘭山步道; *māolánshān bùdào*), actually a 3km paved road that winds up the mountainside, through lovely terraces of Assam black tea bushes, to a **weather observatory** (氣象站; *qìxiàngzhàn*) that the Japanese built on the mountaintop in 1940.

Around the lake

Heading around 3.3km east (clockwise) from Shuishe along Provincial Highway 21, the first major attraction (5min by bus) is the imposing **Wenwu Temple** (文武廟; *wénwǔ miào*; open 24hr; ☎049/285-5122), perched on a hill overlooking the lake's northeastern shore. The temple is dedicated primarily to learning and is popular with students who come here to pray during important examinations. In the Rear Hall is a statue commemorating **Confucius**, in front of which is a table covered by candle jars filled with red-paper wishes written by students. The temple's other highly venerated deity is **Guan Di** (the red-faced one in the Main Hall). The last **shuttle bus** to Itashao departs at 5.35pm, while the last bus back to Shuishe leaves at 6.21pm.

Sun Moon Lake Ropeway

Another 5.5km from Wenwu Temple is the lake's newest (and wildly popular) attraction, the **Sun Moon Lake Ropeway** (日月潭纜車; *rìyuètán lǎnchē*; daily 10.30am–4pm; NT$300 one-way). The Swiss Doppelmayr cable car glides across Bujishan to the Formosan Aboriginal Cultural Village, a 1.8km journey that takes around ten minutes (most people come back the same way). Even if the theme park doesn't interest you, it's worth taking the ride for the gasp-inducing views over the lake (it tops out at 1044m on Bujishan), trumped only by the seven-hour hike up Shuisheshan (see below). You'll need to get a queue ticket first, then line up to pay at the appointed time – arrive early or late in the day to avoid a lengthy wait.

The cable car terminates at the southern entrance to the **Formosan Aboriginal Culture Village** (九族文化村; *jiŭzú wénhuàcūn*; ☎049/289-5361, ⓦwww.nine .com.tw; NT$100 or NT$700 with return cable car ticket), a touristy showcase for Taiwan's primary aboriginal tribes, in addition to housing a theme park and European-style garden. Despite the rather artificial feel, the grounds are wooded and pleasant, it can be a lot of fun for kids and the park is certainly an earnest attempt to preserve aboriginal culture – one third of employees are aborigines. Note that the park sometimes closes when it reaches its maximum of twenty thousand people.

Back at the ropeway station on the lake you can walk along the lakeside trail (750m) to Itashao, or take the free **shuttle bus**; the last one departs at 5.42pm, while the last bus back to Shuishe is 6.14pm.

Itashao

On the lake's southern fringe is **Itashao** (伊達邵; *yīdáshào*) the area's second-biggest tourist centre (Yuchi – 魚池 or *yúchí* – is the township, not the village name), which thrives mostly on the dying remnants of Thao culture, with numerous shops selling traditional Thao handicrafts and items associated with the tribe's folklore. This is a good place to grab **lunch**, however (see p.209) and you can get a lively but Sinicized forty-minute Thao **song and dance show** at the Chasing Deer Market (逐鹿商集; *zhúlù shāngjí*; 11.20am, 2.20pm, 6.20pm; free) at the end of Itathao Street. The main village is now eighty percent ethnic Chinese, and the dwindling Thao population of about six hundred remains largely segregated, tucked away behind the tourist shops in a collection of corrugated iron huts. This **makeshift settlement** was set up to house the Thao who had lost their homes in the 921 Earthquake, and there still has been no agreement on where a permanent Thao village should be located. Today the only way to be sure of meeting true Thao people is to wander around this deprived area, and though the people you'll meet will be friendly you might find the experience a bit voyeuristic. Just behind the settlement is the beginning of the Shuisheshan Trail. Note that the last **ferries** back to Shuishe (via Xuanguang) depart 5.05pm weekdays and 5.10pm weekends; the last **shuttle bus** is 6.12pm.

Shuisheshan Trail

For hikers, the highlight of any visit to Sun Moon Lake is the challenging 5.6km climb to the top of **Shuisheshan** (水社山; *shuǐshèshān*; 2059m), by far the area's tallest mountain, the summit of which provides dizzying **panoramas** of the lake and its environs. The **Shuisheshan Trail** (水社山步道; *shuǐshèshān bùdào*) winds its way up two mountains, first crossing over the densely forested **Bujishan** (卜吉山; *bǔjíshān*), and is really only suited for experienced, fit hikers – the mostly dirt path is very steep in places, and the return journey should take most reasonably conditioned walkers around seven hours (you can always take the cable car instead). There are few trail signs in English, but most of the way is flagged with **coloured ribbons** and a **rope** tied to tree branches and bamboo poles. The hike should only be attempted in clear weather, and it's a good idea to ask about trail conditions in the Shuishe visitor centre before you set out.

The **trail** starts at the edge of the Thao settlement behind Itashao, and is marked by a large stone monument inscribed with the word "Thao" in English. It begins with wide stone steps that lead several hundred metres to a fork with a Chinese sign: from here you can go left or right, as this first part of the trail is a loop. After a gruelling hike through bamboo groves, hardwood forest and thick rhododendron bushes you must shimmy over a series of big **quartz boulders** to reach the top, from where you can see the entire lake and a wide flood plain beyond, as well as the nearby city of Puli.

Xuanzang Temple and Xuanguang Temple

Heading northwest around 3.5km around the lake from Itashao, the first sight of note is **Xuanzang Temple** (玄奘寺; *xuánzàng sì*; daily 7.30am–5pm; ℡049/285-0220), named after **Xuan Zang** – China's most famous monk – whose travels in India formed the basis of the classic tale *Journey to the West*. The temple was built to house precious **relics** that many Buddhists believe are among Asia's most sacred. These relics are enshrined in two miniature gold pagodas in the temple's main hall, with the jewel-encrusted middle pagoda holding several tiny, hardened kernels that some believe came from the ashes of **Buddha** himself. The small pagoda on the right contains what is claimed to be a **sliver** from Xuan Zang's skull – the sliver is said to have been looted from Nanjing by the Japanese and taken to a temple in Saitama prefecture. In 1955 the fragment was returned to Chiang Kai-shek's government, and in 1958 it was moved into the newly built **Xuanguang Temple** (玄光寺; *xuánguāng sì*; daily 7.30am–5.30pm; ℡049/285-0325), closer to the lakeshore. This temple, 2.5km northwest of the Xuanzang Temple, was soon deemed too small, and the relic was transferred to its present location in 1965. You can **hike** between the two temples and the Ci En Pagoda (see below) via the 2.5km **Qinglong Trail** (青龍山步道; *qīnglóngshān bùdào*). Be sure to visit *Grandma's Tea Eggs* (see opposite) when exploring Xuanguang Temple, and remember that the last **ferry** back to Shuishe departs 5.20pm weekdays and 5.30pm weekends; the last **shuttle bus** is 6pm.

Ci En Pagoda

Crowning the hill behind the Xuanzang Temple is the nine-tiered **Ci En Pagoda** (慈恩塔; *cíēntǎ*; open 24hr), which Chiang Kai-shek had built in memory of his mother in 1971. One of the lake's major landmarks, the pagoda is accessed via a 700m paved pathway and commands outstanding views. The 46m-high pagoda's base is at an elevation of 954m, making the top exactly 1000m above sea level. From this point, one can look down on the Xuanzang Temple, Lalu Island and across the lake to *The Lalu* hotel, all three of which are on the same axis – most auspicious for *feng shui* believers. Ringing the **giant bell** that hangs inside the top of the pagoda is considered requisite for Taiwanese tourists.

Eating and drinking

There are plenty of **restaurants** in Shuishe and Itashao, many of them serving standard Chinese fare. Individual travellers would do better to head straight to Shuishe's Minsheng Road, where there are a few small establishments with basics such as fried rice and noodles, or Itashao's Yiyong Street (義勇街; *yìyǒngjiē*), packed with snack stalls serving sausage, roast quail and other aboriginal favourites. There is a dearth of pubs or bars in both villages, so for a **drink** your best bet is to order a beer in one of the restaurants, or grab a bottle from 7-Eleven and enjoy the lakeside scenery (totally legal).

Shuishe

A-Rong Thao Tribe Noodles 阿榮邵族麵店 (*āróng shàozú miàndiàn*) 18 Minsheng St ℡049/285-6876. Delicious bowls of "Thao-Tribe Noodles" for NT$80, served with wild boar meat and *cicōng* leaves, a mountain herb (not really aboriginal, but tasty nonetheless). Daily 11am–3pm & 5–8pm.

Ming Hu Old Canteen 明湖老餐廳 (*mínghú lǎocāntīng*) 15 Minsheng St ☏049/285-5182. This unassuming place serves up tasty Chinese staples such as fried rice and noodles (NT$80–150), and its friendly staff can speak some English. Daily 11am–2pm & 5–9pm.

Oriental Brasserie 東方餐廳 (*dōngfāng cāntīng*) 142 Zhongxing Rd ☏049/285-5311. One of *The Lalu*'s major restaurants, the *Oriental* is open to non-guests and features pricey contemporary Western cuisine throughout the week (mains from NT$800). Its lunch sets (from NT$900; 11.30am–2.30pm) are popular. Daily 7am–11pm.

Spa Home 餐廳 (*Spa Home cāntīng*) 95 Zhongshan Rd ☏049/285-5166. More upmarket than the places on Minsheng Rd, this restaurant has a big balcony with good lake views and specializes in Italian dishes and Japanese hot pot, with delicious handmade pastries and cocktails (NT$200 minimum). Daily 7–9.30am & 11am–8pm.

Itashao and around

Full House Resort Hotel Restaurant 富豪群渡假民宿餐廳 (*fùháoqún dùjiǎ mínsù cāntīng*) 8 Shuixiu St ☏049/285-0307. This trendy establishment prides itself on Chinese-Western fusion dishes made completely from local and seasonal ingredients (pork stew, lamb or beef sets from NT$220). Coffee/tea and snacks from NT$150. Guests can eat in the first-floor restaurant or the garden café. Daily 8am–10pm.

Grandma's Tea Eggs 阿婆茶葉蛋 (*āpó cháyèdàn*) Xuanguang Temple. These "Sun Moon Lake Eggs" (NT$10), hugely famous in Taiwan, are stewed in tea and mushrooms for 24hr and are the most popular snack at Sun Moon Lake – queues regularly form beneath Xuanguang Temple (on the waterfront) and they sell around thirty thousand daily. Daily 9.30am–5.30pm or till sold out.

Makatou 瑪蓋旦 (*mǎgàidàn*) 39 Itathao St ☏049/285-0523. Grab a table by the water and order from a menu of local "Thao" fare, which is tasty even if it's not necessarily authentic: delicious wild boar, chilli fish, bamboo shoots and millet wine (NT$150 for big dish). No English menus, just photos.

Zhi-La Small Hall 支蠟小館 (*zhīlà xiǎoguǎn*) 87 Yiyong Rd ☏049/285-0095. No-frills place that serves delicious fried shrimp and fish from upwards of NT$70. Daily 9am–8pm.

Puli and around

Located in the heart of Taiwan and surrounded by mountains, sprawling **PULI** (埔里; *pǔlǐ*) is an easy day-trip from Sun Moon Lake, and lies at the start of the spectacular road to Wushe and **Hehuanshan**. The best reason to visit is the mind-blowing **Chung Tai Chan Monastery** on the outskirts of town, one of Taiwan's most remarkable sights. With more time and, preferably, your own transport, Puli offers an assortment of secular attractions associated with traditional manufacturing and crafts that have flourished here for decades. Much of this is linked to the quality of the local water and surrounding natural resources – the town once produced eighty percent of Taiwan's **lacquer** and was the centre of a flourishing **paper** trade; it is still the home of Taiwan's most famous **Chinese wines**. Puli was also the birthplace of glamorous 1960s film star Chang Mei-yao – perhaps the real reason why tourist literature claims the town is famous for "water, wine, weather and women".

Accommodation

There's plenty of choice in Puli when it comes to accommodation, but it's mostly mid- to top-range **hotels** in the centre of town, and newer **homestays** on the fringes – many of these tend to be upscale resorts rather than typical B&Bs.

Cheng Pao Hotel 鎮寶大飯店 (*zhènbǎo dàfàndiàn*) 299 Zhongxiao Rd ☏049/290-3333. The best hotel in town with comfortable rooms and a decent pool and gym, about a 20min walk from the bus station. Forty percent discounts are common during the week. ❼

Song Yuan Mountain Villa 松園山莊 (*sōngyuán shānzhuāng*) 15-9 Neipu Rd ☏049/299-3098. Located just north of the Geographic Centre Monument off Highway 14, this mini resort has spa pools, and Japanese-style bedrooms in wooden chalets. It's a bit out

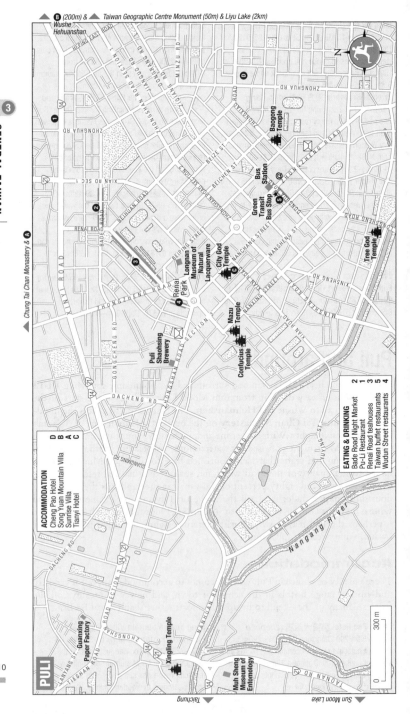

PULI

▲ Chung Tai Chan Monastery & Ⓐ

▲ Ⓑ (200m) & ▲ Taiwan Geographic Centre Monument (50m) & Liyu Lake (2km)
Wushe
Hehuanshan

N

HEPING EAST ROAD

DONGPING RD

MINZU RD

ZHONGHUA RD

Baogong
Temple

ZHONGHUA RD

ZHONGHUA RD

ZHONGSHAN ROAD SECTION 1

DONGRONG RD

XIAN RD SECT 1

BEIHUAN ROAD

BADE ROAD

RENAI ROAD

BEIZE ST

BEICHEN ST

ZHONGSHAN ROAD SECTION 2

Bus
Station

Green
Transit
Bus Stop

DONGSHENG ROAD

BEIPING STREET

Longnan
Museum of
Natural
Lacquerware

Renai
Park

City God
Temple

NANCHANG STREET

NANSHENG ST

DONGHUA ROAD

LINYI ROAD

ZHONGZHENG ROAD

GONGCHENG RD

ZHONGZHENG ROAD SECTION 2

Mazu
Temple

XINSHENG ST

XINSHENG RD

MINSHENG ROAD

Puli
Shaoshing
Brewery

Confucius
Temple

NANXING STREET

XIAN ROAD

NANAN ROAD

DACHENG RD

Tree God
Temple

台14

台14

DACHENG ROAD SECTION 3

ZHONGSHAN ROAD SECTION 3

DUANNING RD

YULU ST

Nangang River

NANHUAN RD

▼ Taichung

GONGSHAN ROAD

LANTANG ST

Guanxing
Paper Factory

台21

Xingling
Temple

Muh Sheng
Museum of
Entomology

TAONAN RD

NANHUAN RD

TIESHAN ROAD

▼ Sun Moon Lake

ACCOMMODATION
Cheng Pao Hotel   D
Song Yuan Mountain Villa   B
Sunrise Villa   A
Tianyi Hotel   C

EATING & DRINKING
Bade Road Night Market   2
Pu-Li Restaurant   1
Renai Road teahouses   3
Taiwan buffet restaurants   5
Wudun Street restaurants   4

0   300 m

Puli is only accessible by bus, all of which stop at the bus station in the centre of town on Zhongzheng Road. Green Transit buses (daily 6am–6pm) to Puli run from Shuili (NT$107; 1hr) via **Sun Moon Lake**, and from Shuishe (N$56; 30min) to the Puli bus station every hour.

Several companies have frequent services from **Taichung**: CH Bus on Shuangshi Road runs buses for NT$125, while Nantou Bus offers a reliable service to Sun Moon Lake (NT$188) via Puli (NT$120).

To move on to **Lishan** (see p.214) and **Wuling Farm** (p.164) there is only one daily bus, which starts in Taichung and stops at Puli at around 10.45am (arriving Lishan at 2pm); **Wushe** is otherwise serviced by hourly buses from Puli. If you miss the through bus, to reach Hehuanshan and beyond you'll need to use your own transport, hitch (generally safe) or hire a taxi (NT$3000 to Lishan).

Up to March 2011 there were hourly colour-coded "**Puli Round-the-town Tourist Buses**" in operation (NT$80 for day-pass); the green line took in the Muh Sheng Museum, Puli Brewery and Puli Paper Factory, while the blue line stopped at Chung Tai Chan Monastery, Puli Brewery, the Geographic Center of Taiwan monument and Liyu Lake; check at the Shuishe Visitor Center at Sun Moon Lake (see p.200) or any other visitor centre to see if the service has been continued.

Taxis will charge NT$150–200 for most journeys in Puli. In practice it's best to negotiate a rate for at least half a day (assuming you speak Chinese), if you're serious about seeing everything (NT$3000/day for four people), though the special tour buses (see above) are much better value. It's difficult to rent **scooters** in Puli if you are not a Taiwan resident.

of the way but the free bicycles are a definite bonus and the owners will pick you up from the bus station if you call in advance (English spoken). ❼
Sunrise Villa 眉溪曉莊 (*méixī xiǎozhuāng*) 2-5 Shoucheng Rd ☎049/299-3038. Upscale homestay just outside Puli, surrounded by paddy fields and a small stream. Rooms are tastefully decorated with views across the plain, and breakfast is served in a bright sunroom – the only

problem is its relative isolation, since you'll need your own transport to get here. ❻ Discounts of 25 percent during the week. ❺
Tianyi Hotel 天一大飯店 (*tiānyī dàfàndiàn*) 89 Xian Rd Sec 1 ☎049/299-8100. Centrally located budget hotel with English-speaking staff. Rooms are old and a bit faded but come with TV and are comfortable enough, though the liberal use of white tiles all over the place is reminiscent of a public convenience. ❷

The Town

Most of Puli's attractions are located in the north or northwestern corners of town, a long way from the bus station and traditional centre along **Zhongzheng Road**. Tucked away on the western edge of downtown Puli, the **Longnan Museum of Natural Lacquer Ware**(龍南天然漆博物館; *lóngnán tiānránqī bówùguǎn*; daily 9am–5pm; free; ☎49/298-2076; ⓦwww.longnan.us), 211 Beiping Street, is the only remaining enterprise in Taiwan making traditional lacquers, so durable the owners claim they'll last for a thousand years. It contains a small display area with a variety of lacquered artefacts, including a 2500-year-old cup, and a shop that sells excellent gifts, but is more popular with groups for its DIY sessions.

A short walk west of the Longnan Museum, the **Puli Shaohsing Brewery** (埔里紹興酒廠; *pǔlǐ shàoxīng jiǔchǎng*; daily 8am–5pm; free), 219 Zhongshan Rd Sec 3, is the home of the **Puli Winery Corp**, producer of the famous **Shaohsing** wine, originally from the town of the same name in Zhejiang, China. It's one of Puli's most popular attractions and often crawling with tourists stocking up on all manner of wine-related products, from Shaohsing ice cream and cake to Shaohsing sausage, sold on the first floor of the main building. Mildly intoxicating foods apart, there's not a lot to see here: the second floor contains exhibits on the winery and the devastation wrought by the 921 Earthquake, but there are few labels in English.

Located on the western fringes of Puli, at the end of Zhongshan Road, **Guangxing Paper Factory** (廣興紙寮; *guǎngxīng zhǐliáo*; daily 8.30–5.30pm; free; T049/291-3037), 310 Tieshan Rd, is an attractive series of open-air workshops where you can observe the laborious process of making paper by hand. Paper goods are sold in the small gift shop on site and there's an exhibition room at the back, but otherwise it's primarily set up for frequent DIY sessions held by school groups; individuals can have a go for NT$350 (you get to keep the paper you make).

A bit further out of town, just off the main highway to Taichung, the **Muh Sheng Museum of Entomology** (木生昆蟲博物館; *mùshēng kūnchóng bówùguǎn*; daily 8am–5.30pm; NT$120; T049/291-3311), 6-2 Nancun Rd, is a curious relic of Puli's once highly lucrative butterfly trade. The museum was established by **Yu Mu Sen** (1903–74) who started working for the Japanese as a butterfly catcher in 1919, and contains two floors packed with an assortment of live and dead butterflies, huge moths, insects, frogs and scorpions. Before you reach the main building you can walk through a greenhouse thick with **Bird-winged Butterflies**, Taiwan's largest species and still endangered in the wild.

The **Taiwan Geographic Center Monument** (台灣地理中心碑; *táiwān dìlǐ zhōngxīnbēi*) sits 2.5km northeast of the town centre on the outskirts of Puli, at the junction of Zhongshan and Xinyi roads. The monument, inscribed with the lines "clear water, clear mountain", written by ex-president Chiang Ching-kuo in 1979, lies in a park at the foot of **Hutoushan** (虎頭山; *hǔtóushān*; 555m), but the actual centre point of Taiwan is on the top of the hill, a short but steep walk along the path behind this – a plaque up here marks the spot first identified by the Japanese in 1906.

From here you can continue walking to tranquil **Liyu Lake** (鯉魚潭; *lǐyútán*; allow 1hr) though you'll have to get a special blue tour bus back into town (9.45am, 11.45am, 2.45pm & 4.45pm; NT$80) or get one of the overpriced lake hotels to call a taxi (NT$250–300).

Eating

The usual range of cheap Taiwanese snacks is available at the **Bade Road Night Market** (八德夜市; *bādé yèshì*), just north of the centre, and at the **Third Market** between Donghua and Nansheng roads, a few minutes south of the bus station: Donghua Road is also lined with cheap "Taiwan buffet" diners. Renai Road is a good place to find **teahouses** and better restaurants, while **Wudun Street** just north of Renai Park is another strip of decent local eateries.

The best place to eat in town is the *Pu-Li Restaurant* (金都餐廳; *jīndū cāntīng*; T049/299-5096), 236 Xinyi Rd, north of the centre, worth a visit to experience Puli's "flower cuisine": dishes such as osmanthus flowers with shrimps, rose-petal salad and deep-fried wild ginger flowers. Justly renowned for its lavish banquets, simple sets for two start at NT$660, but it's best experienced Chinese-style, in a big group (from NT$1320 for four).

Chung Tai Chan Monastery

Just a few kilometres north of Puli, the **Chung Tai Chan Monastery** (中台禪寺; *zhōngtái chán sì*; daily 8am–5.30pm; free; T049/293-0215, F049/293-0836, W www.ctworld.org.tw) is one of the world's most lavish modern monuments to

Chan Buddhism, fusing ancient tradition with contemporary building techniques. Designed by C.Y. Lee (the architect of Taipei 101; see p.85), at an estimated cost of US$110m, the monastery is worth half a day of exploring. You'll need to reserve a tour (1hr 30min) three to seven days in advance by downloading the reservation form on the website and then faxing it to the number listed. After faxing, phone the Reception Office at ☎049/293-0215 immediately for confirmation. At the time of writing, special **blue tour buses** were running to the monastery from Puli bus station at 8am, 10am, 1pm, 3pm and 5pm (NT$80 day-pass). Otherwise a taxi from the centre of Puli should cost around NT$200.

Chan is better known as "Zen" in the West, though you'll see few signs of the more austere Japanese version of the practice here. Chung Tai founder **Grand Master Wei Chueh** began a life of simple meditation in the 1970s in the mountains of Taipei County, and established Chung Tai Chan Monastery in 1987. Today he is head of **Chung Tai World**, a Buddhist order that includes several monasteries and over eighty meditation centres located throughout Taiwan and the world.

The monastery

The monastery complex is dominated by the massive central building with its 37 floors, and surrounded by a series of ancillary halls and statues. The 150m central tower is its most distinctive feature, flanked by two sloping dormitory wings and topped by an ornate gold pearl, set on gilded lotus leaves.

From the entrance, it's a short walk to the main building and the **Hall of Heavenly Kings**, with its impressive 12m-high guardians and colourful Milefo (the chubby, smiling incarnaton of Buddha; see p.403). They protect the **Great Majesty Hall** where Sakyamuni Buddha is enshrined – this incarnation represents the historical Buddha and the virtue of liberation, carved from Indian red granite. To the right is **Sangharana Hall**, where in typically eclectic Taiwan style, Taoist deity Guan Di is enshrined as temple protector, while to the left you'll find a statue of Indian monk Bodhidharma (or Damo, the 28th Buddhist patriarch and founder of the Chan school) in the **Patriarch Hall**, along with the inscribed religious lineage of the temple's founder, Wei Chueh. To go further you'll need to have arranged a guide in advance – this is highly recommended.

The fifth floor contains the **Great Magnificence Hall**, housing a graceful statue of the Rocana Buddha, crafted from white jade and positioned on a gold-covered thousand lotus platform. This incarnation represents the virtue of wisdom. From here it's customary to walk up to the ninth floor via a series of inclined corridors, eventually leading to the **Great Enlightenment Hall**. Everything here is brilliant white: the ceramic glass walls and floor, the doors, ceiling and even the statue of the Vairocana Buddha, which represents the spiritual or "dharma" body.

The sixteenth floor is usually as far as most tours go: the **Hall of 10,000 Buddhas** contains a seven-storey teak wood pagoda, facing Puli through two giant windows. The walls of the hall are decorated with twenty thousand tiny copper Buddha statues. From here you can descend down the pilgrims' staircase, or if you're lucky, continue up into the sacred higher levels of the monastery – this will depend on the mood of your guide. The 31st floor is the **Sutra Treasury Pavilion**, containing the monastery's most valuable texts and decorated with soft jade carvings, while the very top, the 37th floor, is known as the **Mani Pearl**. The shell is made of titanium, but the interior of the ball is a simple shrine finished in wood containing a small Buddha statue and is rarely open to visitors.

Even if you haven't booked a tour you can visit the impressive **Chung Tai Museum** (daily 9.30am–5.30pm, closed second and fourth Mon of each month;

NT$100) and its extensive collection of modern and ancient **artwork** on the first floor – particularly noted are the ancient stone carvings, many "liberated" from China over the years.

On to Hehuanshan and Lishan

With the original **Central Cross-Island Highway** closed indefinitely since the 921 Earthquake, Provincial Highway 14 from Puli is the only link between central Taiwan and the east coast. It's a spectacular, winding road through the clouds, and one of Asia's highest, passing the 3000m mark at its uppermost point. Only a few **buses** connect Puli and Lishan (see p.211), so having your own transport makes a huge difference here.

From Puli, the road follows the Mei River valley to **Wushe** (霧社; *wùshè*), an Atayal village and location of the infamous "incident" of 1930 (see p.388), though only a small monument in the centre marks the tragedy. Wushe is the best place to eat this side of the mountains (or fill up on petrol). A few kilometres before Wushe, a narrow side road leads around 25km to **Aowanda National Forest Recreation Area** (奧萬大國家森林遊樂區; *àowàndà guójiā sēnlín yóulè qū*; daily 8am–5pm; NT$200 weekends & holidays, otherwise NT$150; ☎049/297-4511), one of Taiwan's most isolated and atmospheric forest parks, but considering the hassle in getting here (you have to drive back the same way), only worthwhile December to January when the leaves of its magnificent maple trees change colour. Another spur road from Wushe leads to **Lushan Hot Springs** (廬山溫泉; *lúshān wēnquán*), a pleasant resort area nestled in the upper valley with plenty of hotels, odourless, acidic sodium carbonate waters (40–90°C) and outdoor public pools at the spring source.

From Wushe, Highway 14 rises steeply into the mountains, past Wanda Reservoir and, at 1750m, **Qingjing Farm** (清境農場; *qīngjìng nóngchǎng*; daily 8am–5pm; ☎049/280-2222, ⓦwww.cingjing.gov.tw; NT$100), one of the most popular of Taiwan's veterans' farms, and covered with fruit orchards, cattle fields and flower gardens. The road here is lined with pricey "European-style" **homestays** (like alpine chalets) and restaurants taking advantage of the stunning views across the valley, but beyond the farm the road narrows dramatically. The final stretch to **Hehuanshan National Forest Recreation Area** (合歡山森林遊樂區; *héhuānshān sēnlín yóulè qū*), on the western edge of **Taroko National Park**, is the most scenic: the road snakes between the main or western (3416m) and eastern peaks (3421m) of Hehuanshan, the former easily climbed in a couple of hours from the road. The car park opposite the eastern peak is the best place in Taiwan to see snow during the winter, and often very busy. From here the road cuts across the mountains to **Dayuling** where it forks to Taroko Gorge (see p.299) or Lishan and Shei-Pa National Park (see p.164).

Lishan

Perched on the southeastern fringe of Shei-Pa National Park, the tiny village of **LISHAN** (梨山; *líshān*) is a superb place for an overnight stop: an idyllic mountain community of apple and pear growers surrounded by picturesque **tea plantations**. The best place to stay in Lishan is *Swallow Castle* (飛燕城堡渡假飯店; *fēiyàn chéngbǎo dùjià fàndiàn*; ☎04/2598-9577; ⑤) at 46 Minzu St. Although the rooms are a bit ostentatious, the splendid **mountain views** from the windows are more than enough to divert your attention from the tacky decor. Breakfast and dinner are available in the hotel's restaurant, and there also are some simple **Chinese food stalls** across the street where you can get basic rice and noodle dishes. Just up the hill behind the **fruit market** in the centre of Lishan is a small **visitor centre** (daily

8.30am–5.30pm; ☎04/2598-1331), which has **Chinese maps** of the area and also can provide the latest information on bus times. There are three **buses** daily (8.30am, 1.30pm & 4.50pm; NT$74) from Lishan to Wuling Farm, 29km to the north (see p.164).

Chiayi

Backed by the tantalizing peaks of Taiwan's mighty central mountain ranges, **CHIAYI** (嘉義; *jiāyì*) is the gateway to the Alishan National Scenic Area and Yushan National Park, as well as one of the country's most famous Mazu temples at Beigang. Just north of the Tropic of Cancer, it also marks the beginning of Taiwan's tropical south and, as one of the island's earliest cities, has plenty of historic temples and lively markets tucked in between the usual neon and concrete.

Some history

Immigrant farmers from Fujian established the first settlement in the area in 1621, though the city formally dates its creation from 1704 when the county government was moved here and the first wooden city walls were constructed. The area was originally called **Chu-lô-san** in Taiwanese, a transliteration of *Tirosen*, a **Hoanya** word (one of the *pingpu* tribes; see p.396). Following the Lin Shuangwen Rebellion of 1787–89, Emperor Qianlong renamed the town Chiayi, an honorific title meaning "praising them for their loyalty" to reward the inhabitants

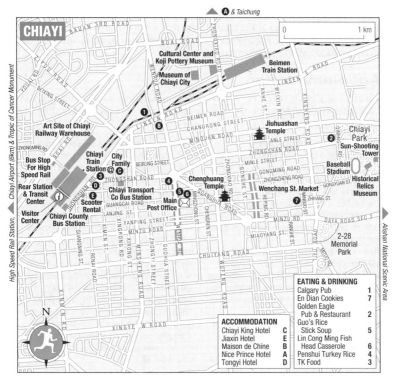

for resisting the rebels. During the Japanese occupation, it gained the more creative epithet "**city of painting**" when masters such as Wu Meiling and Chen Cheng-po spearheaded the first **Nativist** art movement. With a population of around 270,000 Chiayi is now the largest city and commercial centre of Chiayi county, though the county government is located in **Taibao** (太保; *tàibǎo*), 15km to the west.

Arrival and information

Chiayi Airport (嘉義航空站; *jiāyì hángkōng zhàn*) is just over 6km south of the city near the village of Shuishang – it's best to take a taxi into the centre (around NT$300). Chiayi's **train station** (嘉義火車站; *jiāyì huǒchēzhàn*) is on the western side of the city centre at 528 Zhongshan Rd – all the major **bus stations** are nearby (see p.219). Lockers at the station cost NT$20–50 for six hours.

Chiayi's **High-Speed Rail Station** (高鐵嘉義站; *gāotiě jiāyì zhàn*) is inconveniently located in Taibao at 168 Gaotie W Rd; free shuttle **buses** ("BRT") run into the city centre (daily 6am–11.40; every 20min), stopping at the back of the train station (where you need to get off if you are heading for **Alishan**; see p.221), running along Chuiyang Road (and Wenhua Road) and terminating at Chiayi Park. The journey takes around 25 minutes. Note that you can take normal pay buses from the High Speed Rail Station direct to Beigang (see p.219) and Budai (for the **Penghu** ferry; p.339).

Taxis are abundant in the city centre; the meter starts at NT$100, with trips to Chiayi Park around NT$150 from the station (locals tend to negotiate rates at around NT$100 per trip). See p.218 about renting **scooters**. There is a **visitor information centre** (daily 8am–5pm; ☎05/225-6649, ⓦwww.cyhg.gov.tw) with brochures and maps at the train station, to the left just after the exit (English spoken). Chiayi is slowly introducing *hànyǔ pīnyīn* street signs, though you are likely to see *tōngyòng* and other systems still in use.

Accommodation

Chiayi has a wide range of **accommodation** catering both to budget and business travellers. Most of the budget options are near the train station on Zhongzheng Road.

Chiayi King Hotel 嘉義皇爵大飯店
(*jiāyì huángjué dàfàndiàn*) 234 Xinrong Rd ☎05/223-3411. Solid mid-range choice; despite the dour exterior, rooms are jazzed up with comfy beds, stylish bathrooms, flat-screen TVs and free wi-fi. Decent breakfast included, though mainland Chinese tour groups use this hotel, so time your appearance accordingly if you want a quiet one. ➍

Jiaxin Hotel 嘉新大飯店 (*jiāxīn dàfàndiàn*) 687 Zhongzheng Rd ☎05/222-2280. Simple but adequate budget hotel not far from the station, with ageing but reasonably clean rooms – all come with TVs and hand-held showers, though the cheapest rooms are very small. ➋

Maison de Chine 兆品酒店 (*zhàopǐn jiǔdiàn*) 257 Wenhua Rd ☎05/229-3998, ⓦchiayi .maisondechinehotel.com. Central Chiayi's best hotel (the former *Chinatrust Hotel*), set in an

anonymous white modern building in the centre of town. Comfortable, five-star rooms with business centre, fitness room and free shuttle bus to the airport; also has decent Cantonese *dim sum* restaurant. ➐

Nice Prince Hotel 耐斯王子大飯店 (*nàisī wángzi dàfàndiàn*) 600 Zhongxiao Rd ☎05/277-1999, ⓦwww.niceprince.com.tw. Chiayi's poshest hotel is great for a splurge, but isn't particularly convenient for downtown. Rooms are dressed in slightly unusual but warm dark green colours, with an aboriginal theme, and there are flat-screen TVs and some decent Japanese restaurants. ➐

Tongyi Hotel 統一大飯店 (*tǒngyī dàfàndiàn*) 720 Zhongzheng Rd ☎05/225-2685. Opposite the *Jiaxin Hotel*, cleaner and a bit smarter than some of the other budget hotels in the area, with newly renovated rooms and decent showers, but still rather basic. ➋

The City

Chiayi's commercial heart lies along Zhongshan Road east of the train station, but the older parts of the city lie further to the southeast. The city's most popular shrine is **Chenghuang Temple** (城隍廟; *chénghuáng miào*; daily 5am–9.30pm), on Wufong Road between Guangcai Street and Guanghua Road, around 1.5km from the station. Established in 1715 to worship Chiayi's City God, the current buildings date from 1940. The most valuable object inside the **Main Hall** is the plaque above the central altar that reads "Protector of Taiwan and the Ocean", awarded to the temple by Emperor Guangxu in 1887. Take a look at the ceiling – the woodcarvings here and the dragon pillars are exquisite, and the *koji* pottery figures set into the walls (behind glass) are equally renowned.

Another 1.5km east, at the end of Zhongshan Road, **Chiayi Park** (嘉義公園; *jiāyì gōngyuán*) is the city's largest green space. The eastern part of the park was once a Japanese Shinto shrine built in 1943 – two of its elegant cypress-wood temple buildings have been preserved and now function as the **Chiayi Historical Relics Museum** (嘉義市史蹟資料館; *jiāyìshì shǐjī zīliàoguǎn*; Tues–Sun 9am–noon & 1.30–5pm; free), which documents various aspects of Chiayi's history – although there is a small English leaflet available, the exhibits are labelled in Chinese only. The 62m high **Sun-Shooting Tower** (射日塔; *shèrìtǎ*; Wed–Sun 9am–9pm; NT$50), just beyond here, offers panoramic views of the city.

Back towards the train station and north of Zhongshan Road, at 455 Minquan Rd, is the **Jiuhuashan Temple** (九華山地藏庵; *jiǔhuáshān dìzàngān*), dedicated to **Dizang Wang**, confusingly known as the King of Hell (see p.407). Established in 1697, the current structure was restored in the 1970s. The temple's most unusual feature is its **seven-storey pagoda** above the main hall – take the elevator up to the top (free), for another fine panorama of the old city (you can walk down).

North of the station

Twenty minutes' walk northeast of the train station, along Linsen West Road and across the rail lines, the **Museum of Chiayi City** (嘉義市立博物館; *jiāyì shìlì bówùguǎn*; Tues–Sun 9am–5pm; free) is a lavish, modern facility containing well-presented exhibitions on geology, fossils and art, labelled in Chinese only, but still the best place to view Chiayi's striking **stone monkeys** (*shíhóu*; second floor). Local sculptor Zhan Long started the fad in 1973, when he began to carve monkeys from fossilized rocks found in the Pachong River, and the sculptures have since become the city's most celebrated motif. The third floor is a good introduction to the city's most famous artist, **Chen Cheng-po** (1895–1947), who was killed during the 2-28 massacres in 1947. A statue of Chen sits outside the **Cultural Center** (文化中心; *wénhuà zhōngxīn*; Tues–Sun 9am–5pm; free), the older building opposite the museum at 275 Zongxiao Rd, home to a library and several galleries exhibiting the work of contemporary local artists. The most interesting part of the centre, however, lies in the basement: the **Koji Pottery Museum** (交趾陶館; *jiāozhìtáoguǎn*) is an excellent introduction to the ancient craft used extensively in temples to create detailed tableaux from famous Chinese stories or operas, and is crammed with stunning examples. The history of *koji* is described, as well as some of its most lauded practitioners such as Yeh Wang (1826–1887), a master craftsman born in Chiayi county. Kao Chi-ming's exquisite **dragon plate** is a must-see, created by Chiayi's most famous current *koji* artist.

Eating and drinking

The centre of Chiayi is packed with places to eat, with street stalls lining Renai Road just across from the train station. The city's main **night market** is on

Wenhua Road, with the busiest concentration of stalls south of Zhongshan Road and north of Xueyang Road. The city isn't known for its nightlife, but there are a few pubs, all serving Western meals and snack food.

Calgary Pub 卡加利美式餐飲 (*kǎjiālì měishì cānyǐn*) Lane 19, 351 Guohua St ☏05/227-0513. The town's main watering hole, attracting a mix of locals and expats, occupying a Japanese-era wooden building that's more than 90 years old. The cheap beers are complemented by burgers, pizzas and Mexican food. The pub is along a narrow lane off Linsen West Rd (at no. 224), just before Guohua St, and across the rail track. Mon–Thurs 9pm–4am, Fri–Sun 6pm–4am.

En Dian Cookies 恩典酥本舖 (*ēndiǎnsū běnpù*) 123 Minguo Rd ☏05/278-8990. "Square cookies" are a Chiayi specialty, and this more than 50-year-old tiny shop – now surrounded by parking lots – is the city's most famous place to buy them. The butter cookies are considered the most authentic, but chocolate is also good (small packets NT$45). Daily 9am–8pm.

Golden Eagle Pub & Restaurant 243 Qiming Rd ☏05/277-5277. Homely pub and restaurant with a British theme, close to Chiayi Park. The huge selection of over seventy beers complements the extensive menu of Western and Asian comfort food – the all-day breakfasts and burgers (NT$200 –300) are pretty good. Daily 5pm–2am.

Guo's Rice Stick Soup 郭家粿仔湯 (*guōjiā guǒzǐtāng*) 148 Wenhua Rd ☏05/225-6214. Totally delicious rice soup that's one of the best

treats in the city; don't be put off by the ingredients (slow-boiled pig intenstines, crisp pig stomach, preserved vegetables and leeks; NT$50). Daily 8.30am–5.30pm.

Lin Cong Ming Fish Head Casserole 林聰明沙鍋魚頭 (*lín cōngmíng shāguō yútóu*) 361 Zhongzheng Rd, between Wenhua and Guanghua rds ☏05/227-0661. The place to try rich and especially fragrant fish-head stew (NT$80), another local delicacy, crammed with chunks of giant silver carp, cabbage, mushrooms and bean curd; the secret is the broth, which is utterly adictive. Daily 4–10pm.

Penshui Turkey Rice 噴水火雞飯 (*pēnshuǐ huǒjīfàn*) 325 Zhongshan Rd ☏05/222-2433. The oldest restaurant serving Chiayi's signature specialty, small bowls of turkey rice (*huǒjīfàn*) for NT$40. The dish can be found all over the city, but this no-nonsense place is an old favourite with locals and tourists alike, centrally located near the Central Fountain (*pēnshuǐ*) roundabout. Daily 9am–9.30pm.

TK Food 老楊方塊酥 (*lǎoyáng fāngkuàisū*) 506 Zhongshan Rd ☏05/222-4619. Another place lauded for its sweet cookies since the 1970s (small bags for NT$40); just across from the train station so a lot more convenient if you can't make it to *En Dian* (though not quite as good). Daily 8.30am–9.30pm.

Listings

Banks Several banks with ATMs are clustered at the main roundabout on Zhongshan Rd. Citibank has a branch at 320 Chuiyang Rd (☏05/227-5100).

Car rental Car Plus (daily 8.30am–8.30pm; ☏0800/222-568, ❾www.car-plus.com.tw) or Easy-Rent (☏0800/024-550, ❾www.easyrent .com.tw) are both at the High-Speed Rail Station.

Hospital The Chiayi Christian Hospital (☏05/276-4994, ❾www.cych.org.tw) at 539 Zhongxiao Rd (Provincial Highway 1) has English-speaking doctors with walk-in clinics Mon–Sat.

Internet access Try the 24hr City Family (NT$20/hr), close to the train station at 337 Xingrong Rd, opposite the *Chiayi King Hotel*.

Pharmacies Watson's has branches at 379 Zhongshan Rd (daily 10am–11pm; ☏05/223-6952)

and 300 Renai Rd (daily 10am–10pm; ☏05/225-4776).

Post The main post office is at 107 Zhongshan Rd in the eastern part of the city, but there's a branch near the station at 647 Zhongzheng Rd.

Scooter rental You can rent scooters from shops on the corner of Renai, Zhongzheng and Zhongshan roads, just opposite the train station: try 168 Zhongzheng Rd (daily 6.30am–1.30am; ☏05/216-6689), which offers 125cc for NT$400 (24hr). It's relatively hassle-free for foreigners – usually all you'll need is a passport and any driving licence (they'll feel more comfortable if you give them a mobile number).

Taxi Lai Lai Taxi (☏05/228-8232); Meihua Taxi (☏05/224-7715).

Beigang

The otherwise unexceptional town of **BEIGANG** (北港; *běigǎng*), a short bus ride northwest of Chiayi (see box opposite), is worth a visit for the **Chaotian Temple**,

Moving on from Chiayi

Chiayi Airport only offers flights to Magong and Kinmen, both operated by Uni Air (☎05/286-2363). Regular **express trains** connect the train station to Taipei (NT$600), Taichung (NT$225), Tainan (NT$141) and Kaohsiung (NT$246).

From the central train station, you can catch the free bus (see p.216) to the **High-Speed Rail Station** by walking across the tracks via the footbridge (right at the exit), following Zhongming Road to Boai Road Section 2 and turning left: the bus stop (look for the "BRT" sign) is a short stroll ahead. Trains to Zuoying (Kaohsiung; NT$345) take around thirty minutes, while trains to Taipei take one hour fifteen minutes (NT$915).

By 2011 long-distance bus companies should have moved into the brand new **Transit Center of Chiayi City** (嘉義市先期交通轉運中心; *jiāyìshì xiānqí jiāotōng zhuǎnyùn zhōngxīn*), but check at the visitor centre in the train station to be sure; the new bus station is at the back of the train station, facing Boai Road Section 2 at the end of Zhongming Road. Kuo Kuang offers the cheapest rides to Taipei (daily 5am–11pm; NT$220–330) and Taichung (daily 6am–10pm; NT$165), while more luxurious buses are run by Ubus (NT$330 to Taipei) and Ho-Hsin (NT$470 to Taipei, NT$165 to Taichung and NT$260 to Kaohsiung). Buses depart every fifteen to thirty minutes.

The **Chiayi Transport Co Bus Station** (嘉義客運總站; *jiāyì kèyùn zǒngzhàn*) at 503 Zhongshan Road (between Xingrong Road and Xirong Street) has regular services (buses marked in English) to Guanziling Hot Springs (關仔嶺; *guānzǐlǐng*; daily 6am–9.40pm; every 30min; NT$81), Beigang (北港; *běigǎng*; daily 6am–10pm; NT$46; every 10–15min), Yanshui (every hr; NT$97 daily 6–8pm) and **Budai Port** (布袋港; *bùdàigǎng*; NT$114) – the latter terminates at the **Penghu ferry** (see p.339) terminal when boats are running (check before you get on). Buses to Budai depart at 8.10am, 9am and at irregular times thereafter – the journey can take up to ninety minutes. The bus stops at the High-Speed Rail Station around twenty to thirty minutes after leaving the centre. Chiayi is also is the starting point for the **Alishan Forest Railway**, though this was still **closed** at the time of writing thanks to Typhoon Morakot (see p.221). For information on getting to **Alishan**, see p.221.

178 Zhongshan Rd (朝天宮; *cháotiāngōng*), one of Taiwan's most significant religious sites. Dating back to 1694 (it's been expanded many times since then) to enshrine what many consider the country's most powerful Mazu image, the temple is one of the island's greatest **mother temples** (see p.403). As such, it's constantly filled with worshippers, making it arguably the best place in Taiwan to grasp the fundamental importance of Mazu to the Taiwanese, as well as featuring some of the most exuberant temple art on the island.

The most dramatic time to visit is during one of the weekends preceding **Mazu's birthday**, on the twenty-third day of the third lunar month, when hundreds of thousands of devotees besiege Beigang for the goddess's annual **inspection tour**; the image is paraded around town to a chaotic backdrop of fireworks, lion dances and stilt performers.

To get to the temple from Beigang bus station, turn right after you exit, take your first left and carry on for about 200m until you reach the rear of the temple.

Guanziling

Tucked away in the northeast corner of Tainan County but accessible from Chiayi, **GUANZILING** (關仔嶺; *guānzǐlǐng*) boasts beautiful scenery, unusual hot-spring spas, picturesque monasteries and a bizarre natural wonder. The Japanese started to develop the area in 1902 – the spring water is a rare type found in only two other places (Japan and Sicily). It contains alkali and iodine, has a light sulphuric smell and a greyish "muddy" colour.

Most of the spas and hotels are located within the upper and lower village on County Route 175, south of the junction with County Route 172, but apart from a few attractive **hiking trails** here, the real highlights of the area lie in the hills outside Guanziling within the **Siraya National Scenic Area** (西拉雅國家風景區; *xīlāyǎ guójiā fēngjǐngqū*; Ⓦ www.siraya-nsa.gov.tw). From the top of Guanziling upper village it's 4.5km to the **Water Fire Cave** (水火洞; *shuǐhuǒdòng*) – take the right-hand fork (Tainan Route 96) off Route 175. It's worth the effort to get here: the "cave" is more like a cleft in the hillside with a pool of bubbling spring water, and although it's not big, the flames smothering the rocks above the pool are a truly remarkable sight. The flames are fuelled by spontaneously igniting natural gas, shooting out of the earth. The stone carving just above it is the "Water Fire God".

Just under 2km further along Route 96 you should pass one of several Buddhist monasteries in the area: **Bi Yun Temple** (碧雲寺; *bìyúnsì*) occupies a stunning location beneath a craggy peak with great views of the plains below. About 3km from here, **Huoshan Daxian Temple** (火山大仙寺; *huǒshān dàxiānsì*) also serves as a busy monastery and is popular with tour groups: the three main halls are dedicated to various incarnations of Buddha with a couple of pagodas in the gardens outside. The complex sits on the hill just above the village of **Xiancaopu** (仙草舖; *xiāncǎopū*) and Route 172 where you can catch the bus back to Guanziling or Chiayi.

Practicalities

It's much easier to explore this part of Taiwan if you have a car or scooter – the latter are easy to rent in Tainan or Chiayi. With your own transport, you can see the most absorbing temples and Water Fire Cave in a half a day. If you want to walk, note that the route above, from Guanziling to Xiancaopu, is about 12km. The hike is scenic but much of it is uphill and the road gets busy at the weekends.

Buses from Chiayi (see box, p.219) pass through the **lower village** first before terminating in a car park at the start of the **upper village**. Hourly buses are supposed to head the other way from 6.25am but it's best to check the times in advance (ask your driver when you arrive, or get one of the hotels to check).

Guanziling's hot-spring spas all offer **accommodation** and places **to eat**, though it's usually possible to sample their spa facilities by paying day rates. The lower village is the original resort area developed by the Japanese: today it's a strip of slightly faded spas, restaurants and hotels that line the river at the bottom of the gorge. The *Jing Leh Hotel* (靜樂館; *jìnglèguǎn*; Ⓣ 06/682-2678; ④) at 17 Guanziling Village is the most historic place in town, established in 1902 with Japanese-style rooms and white-tiled spa bathrooms, located across the river at the bottom end of the lower village. The upper village is where you'll find more **restaurants** and better, more expensive hot-spring spas. The *Toong Mao Spa Resort* (統茂溫泉會館; *tǒngmào wēnquán huìguǎn*; Ⓣ 06/682-3456, Ⓦ www.toongmao.com.tw; ⑤) at 28 Guanziling Village is a modern behemoth, a short walk uphill from the bus terminus with smart, comfortable rooms. The public pools are open from 7am to 9.30pm ($250). The 🍴 *Mutsun Spring* (沐春溫泉養生會館; *mùchūn wēnquán yǎngshēng huìguǎn*; Ⓣ 06/682-3232; ⑦), just next door, is the most luxurious place in the village, a beautiful Japanese-style spa and restaurant with superb views of the valley below. Private spa rooms (two people) start at NT$1200 for an hour and a half on weekdays.

Alishan National Scenic Area

Stretching from the foothills of western Taiwan to the Yushan National Park, the extraordinarily diverse **ALISHAN NATIONAL SCENIC AREA** (阿里山國家 風景區; *ālǐshān guójiā fēngjǐngqū*) covers some 420 square kilometres of picturesque **tea plantations**, tranquil **homestays** and inviting **Tsou** aboriginal villages. The whole area took a real beating from **Typhoon Morakot** in 2009; **Provincial Highway 18**, the winding 70km road from Chiayi to Alishan, remained open but in a precarious state until mid-2010, and the spectacular **Alishan Forest Railway** is not expected to reopen until the end of 2011. The Tsou villages of Laiji and Shanmei were particularly hard hit, with the Danayigu River Ecological Park effectively destroyed.

Confusingly, there is no single mountain called Alishan; the actual peak that attracts the most sunrise viewers is named **Zhushan**, the centrepiece of the **Alishan Forest Recreation Area**, the region's main tourist hub and what most Taiwanese refer to as just "Alishan". Ruili and Fenqihu are traditionally stops on the railway line, but also accessible by road, while the other main attractions are close to Highway 18.

Ruili

Perched precipitously above a sheer cliff face and surrounded by tea plantations, the picturesque village of **RUILI** (瑞里; *ruìlǐ*) is a relaxing place to soak up the highland scenery while sipping cups of fragrant tea or roaming along hiking trails. Nature walks near the village link all the main scenic attractions, ranging from short paths to pristine waterfalls to longer historic trails leading to nearby towns. The **Ruitai Visitor Center** (瑞太遊客中心; *ruìtài yóukè zhōngxīn*; daily 8.30am–5pm; ☏05/250-1070) at 1 Ruili Village, northeast of the major concentration of homestays along the main Chiayi Route 122, can provide information on area hikes and has reliable English **maps** of several nearby villages. You'll also find the **Yuantan Visitor Centre** (圓潭遊客中心; *yuántán yóukè zhōngxīn*; daily

---

Getting to Alishan

Until the railway reopens, the only way to reach Alishan is by **bus** from **Chiayi** (see box, p.219). **Chiayi County Bus Station** (嘉義縣公共汽車站; *jiāyìxiàn gōnggòng qìchēzhàn*), to the right as you exit the front of the train station, has daily buses to **Alishan Forest Recreation Area** (6.10am, 7.40am, 8.10am, 8.40am, 9.10am, 10.10am, 12.10pm and 2.10pm; Fri–Sun also 9.40am and 10.40am; NT$221; 2hr 30min) via Xiding and Shizhuo. Other locations in the Alishan Scenic Area are served less frequently: **Fenqihu** (daily 7.10am and 3.10pm; NT$155), **Ruili** and **Ruifeng** (9.30am and 4.30pm; NT$189 and NT$200); and **Dabang** (11.10am and 5.10pm; NT$178).

From **Taipei**, Kuo Kuang runs buses from the West Bus Station (see p.103) on Friday & Saturday (March–Oct 8.45pm; Nov–Feb 9.45pm; NT$620; 6hr).

To travel between **Sun Moon Lake** (see p.200) and Alishan, take a bus to Shuili and switch to the Jiji Rail Line (around 1 train per hour; see p.197) – at Ershui you can catch trains to **Chiayi** (2/hr; 45min).

One of the scenic highlights of Taiwan, the **Alishan Forest Railway** (阿里山森林鐵 道; *ālǐshān sēnlín tiědào*) is an 86km narrow-gauge railway connecting Chiayi with Alishan Forest Recreation Area via Fenqihu and Jiaoliping, near Ruili. The line was severely damaged by Typhoon Morakot in 2009, and is not expected to reopen until the end of 2011 – if at all. Check the latest on the Alishan website (🌐www.ali-nsa.net) or at Chiayi train station.

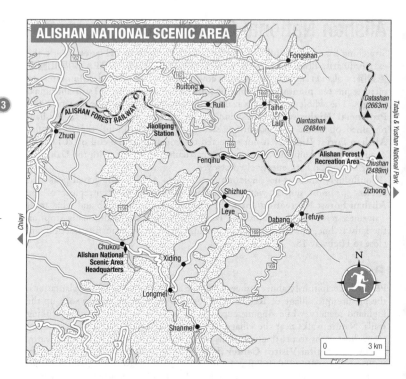

8.30am–5pm; ☏ 05/250-2026) and the **Yuantan Natural Ecological Park** (圓潭
自然生態園區; *yuántán zìrán shēngtàiyuán qū*) at Chiayi Route 122 km 23, which
has a café, exhibits on local flora and fauna and trails to the 200m **Yuantan Falls**
(雲潭瀑布; *yúntán pùbù*) at km 22 (which involve a stiff climb).

From March to June each year, the slopes around Ruili come alight at night,
when thousands of **fireflies** (*yínghuǒchóng*) put on a nightly performance
considered by many to be Taiwan's most magnificent.

Accommodation

The best places to stay are the village's superb **homestays**. In addition to offering
pick-ups from the bus or train station, most can prepare **home-cooked meals**
made from local ingredients. The *Clear Moon Guesthouse* (明月大船的家; *míngyuè
dàchuán de jiā*; ☏ 05/250-1626; ❹) on Route 122 at 48 Ruili Village, with rooms
surrounding a courtyard backed by an enormous family shrine, has friendly
owners who make their own plum wine and are keen to share it with guests. Their
main **weekday package** (NT$1200/person) includes one night's stay, pick-up,
three meals and an area tour, but you must call in advance to arrange this. More
upscale, the *Ren Sheng Holiday Resort* (瑞勝渡假木屋; *ruìshèng dùjiā mùwū*;
☏ 05/250-1011; ❻), 79 Ruili Village, is set in an attractive building and has
fragrant, Japanese-style wooden rooms. Prices include pick-up, but their delicious
meals cost extra. The best budget option is the *Ruoh–Lan Resort* (若蘭山莊; *ruòlán
shānzhuāng*; ☏ 05/250-1210; ❹) at 10 Ruili Village, Route 122 km 27.9, a
three-storey lodge with Western and Japanese-style rooms, some with balconies
commanding sweeping views of the valley below. The owners are particularly

proud of the local fireflies and arrange night viewing tours in season. Pick-up from Shizhuo costs NT$60, and meals range from NT$60 to NT$200.

Buses from Ruifang back to **Chiayi** via Ruili depart at 6am and 1pm daily (NT$189–200), but you'll need your own transport to make the most out of this area.

Fenqihu

Around 45km from Chiayi and 25km from Alishan by rail, and about 6.5km south of Ruili via a hiking trail, is **FENQIHU** (奮起湖; *fènqǐhú*), a former **train repair station** that makes a popular pit-stop on the way to Alishan. The **bus station** is just above "old street" and the rail tracks; buses to **Chiayi** leave Fenqihu at 9am and 5pm daily (NT$155), but the best way to get there is by train (see p.221 for details on getting to Fenqihu).

The compact village spills down the hillside immediately south of the train station and bus stop, its narrow "**old street**" (*fènqǐhú lǎojiē*) lined with curious **snack shops** and restaurants (see p.224). The **Fenqihu Garage** (奮起湖車庫; *fènqǐhú chēkù*), down the tracks from the station, houses a couple of American-made steam engines from the early twentieth century, while the **Exhibition Room of Culture & History of Fenqihu** (奮起湖文史陳列室啟用; *fènqǐhú wénshǐ chénlièshì qǐyòng*; daily 10am–4pm; free), further down the slope, houses some odd bits and pieces commemorating the village's past, housed in a nicely restored wooden house from the Japanese era.

Fenqihu's shorter **nature trails** have been upgraded with wooden boardwalks, steps and English-language signage; the **Logging Trail** (木馬棧道; *mùmǎzhàn dào*; 700m) and the **Fenqihu Walking Trail** (1.2km) offer bracing hikes through forests of bamboo with stupendous views.

The area's main hike is the energetic climb up **Datongshan** (大凍山; *dàtòngshān*; 1976m), which in clear weather offers extraordinary sunrise views. The trailhead is about 4km east of Fenqihu along Chiayi Route 155. Just past the trailhead, the path splits into two, with the right-hand fork leading to the **18 Arhats Cave** (十八羅漢洞; *shíbāluóhàn dòng*) – actually a sizeable sandstone rock house – just less than 2km further. The left-hand path winds to the top of Datongshan and is a moderate climb of 1.7km that takes about thirty minutes.

Accommodation

Most of Fenihu's **hotels** are just a short walk south of the train and bus stations, scattered along the lanes stemming out from the pedestrian-only "**old street**", itself accessible by the stairs just behind the station.

Arnold Janssen Activity Center 奮起湖楊生愛諾德活動中心 (*fènqǐhú yángshēng àinuòdé huódòng zhōngxīn*) 26 Fenqihu ☎05/256-1134. This Catholic hostel, down the hill from the train station, is Fenqihu's only real budget option. Dorm beds go for NT$250/person, and singles without attached bath can be had for NT$500. The Swiss sister who runs the place speaks excellent English and Mandarin and is extremely accommodating. Doubles are also available (❷).
Fenqihu Hotel 奮起湖大飯店 (*fènqǐhú dàfàndiàn*) 178 Fenqihu ☎05/256-1888. The town's best-known hotel, with a wide range of Japanese-style wooden-floored rooms, including some with traditional cedar tubs. It's famous for its

filling "railway lunchbox", and its gregarious owner knows the history of Fenqihu inside out. ❺
Yahu Hotel 雅湖山莊 (*yǎhú shānzhuāng*) 112 Fenqihu ☎05/256-1097. Located just off the far western end of the train platform, the cheap and cheerful *Yahu* has spartan but clean Japanese-style doubles and twins with large beds and TVs from NT$1200. There's also ten-person rooms with beds for NT$350/person. The owner sells aiyu jelly on "old street" during the day. ❸
Yeashow Hotel 雅琇山莊 (*yǎxiù shānzhuāng*) 159-1 Fenqihu ☎05/256-1336. Just down the steps to the left of Old Street, the shiny *Yeashow* has very friendly management and plain rooms that offer good value. ❹

Eating

Fenqihu's "old street" is the best place to eat in all Alishan, though many places tend to close or operate short hours mid-week; the best day to visit is Saturday. Local culinary delights such as **aiyu jelly** (*àiyùbīng*), made from a gel squeezed from fig seeds, the famous "**railway lunchbox**" (*tiělù biàndāng*), a compact arrangement of meat, boiled egg, rice and vegetables, and local **wasabi** (*shānkuí*) are all worth seeking out. Try also *Mary Store* (瑪莉商店; *mǎlì shāngdiàn*) at 143 Old Street, which sells special packet mixes of sweet ginger and longan teas (NT$200) – drink samples are handed out for free.

Aishan Aiyu Jelly 愛山屋野生愛玉店 (*àishānwū yěshēng àiyù diàn*) 139 Old St. This small stall at the end of "old street" features thirst quenching aiyu jelly drinks, made with freshly picked fruit from the mountains nearby (from NT$25). **Aiyu Uncle** 愛玉伯ㄟ厝 (*àiyù bó de cuò*). The most atmospheric place to sip tea and eat snacks in Fenqihu is this old teahouse tucked away in the narrow lanes below "old street". It's a little tough to find – if you can't find the signs (Chinese only), ask someone.

Dengshan Shitang 登山食堂 (*dēngshān shítáng*) 168 Old St ☏0923/223-993. The town's best-known maker of delicious *biàndāng*, with lunchboxes starting at NT$70 for a simple take-away version, to more fancy pots (NT$120–150) for sitting inside the wooden dining room (with free home-made soup). It's right by the station and features a unique ordering system, where you pay and receive change through slots, get an old train ticket in return and grab your food when the bell rings. **Fenqihu Hotel** 奮起湖大飯店 (*fènqíhú dàfàndiàn*) 178 Old St ☏05/256-1888. Famous producer of the ubiqitous lunchbox, a Japanese-inspired arrangement of meat, vegetables, boiled egg and white rice. Hawkers on the platform sell the boxes (NT$100) to tourists arriving on the train, or you can pick them up at the hotel, which now has a national franchise to sell its *biàndāng* through 7-Eleven.

Tian Mei Zhen 天美珍火車餅專賣店 (*tiānměizhēn huǒchēbǐng zhuānmàidiàn*) 142 Old St ☏05/256-1008. Established in 1943, this lauded cake-maker knocks out boxes of "train cakes" (*húhuǒchēbǐng*; pastries with train images embossed on the crust and fillings such as green bean, red bean and green tea sweetened with wild honey) for NT$120, and the more crumbly *gūzǎowèi hànbǐng* cakes for NT$100. Daily 8am–9pm.

Xiding

The village of **XIDING** (隙頂; *xìdǐng*), at around km 54 on Highway 18, is a great place to stay, with a growing number of **homestays** perched in the tea fields above the main road. The European-style *Alishan Season Star* (阿里山歐風民宿; *ālǐshān ōufēng mínsù*; ☏0960/091-683, ⊕ www.seasonstar.com.tw; ➐), 300m off Highway 18 at km 55.5, is one of the most luxurious, with spacious rooms (one has a loft with a spiral staircase), inspired by Neoclassical French interiors. The property faces a tea plantation and a bamboo grove, with sensational views of the mountains across the valley. Owner Gordon Fang speaks English and lays on more French inspiration for breakfast and afternoon snacks (included); dinner is extra. Plenty of decent hikes are close by, but again, you need your own transport to make the most of this.

Shizhuo and the Dingshizhuo Tea Terraces

Around 43km from Chiayi and 26km from Alishan on Highway 18, **SHIZHUO** (石棹; *shízhuǒ*) is an important junction, with Route 169 heading north to Fenqihu and south to Dabang. There's little to see in the village itself (though there are plenty of cheap canteens here). The **Dingshizhuo** (頂石棹; *dǐngshízhuǒ*) area, located above the highway at around 1450–1700m makes a better target, with enticing vistas of misty oolong tea farms and a large patch of lush forest – look for the turning at km 63.5.

There are over twenty **homestays** in the area, making it another great place to stay, and the tea is becoming a major attraction, with several places offering tastings and tours. There's a **visitor centre** (staffed at irregular times, but written information available 24hr; ℡05/256-2565) up here, which can advise on the latter.

Back on Highway 18, at km 65, just beyond the village, *Lauya Restaurant & Guesthouse* (神禾景觀餐廳民宿; *shénhé jǐnguān cāntīng mínsù*; ℡05/256-2341, Ⓦwww.lauya.com; ❺) is a fabulous place to stop if you have your own transport: a wooden chalet serving organic food, coffee (NT$100) and juices (try the pine juice for NT$150), with a stunning veranda high above the valley. Dishes include roast chicken (NT$280), hotpot (NT$350) and banana pie (NT$100). The guesthouse features homely all-wood rooms with decks overlooking the same view (they'll pick you up from Shizhuo bus station).

Dabang and Tefuye

Located south of Shizhuo via County Route 169, along the Zengwun River valley, **DABANG** (達邦; *dábāng*) is the closest thing the Tsou have to a capital and one of the best places to get a feel for contemporary Tsou life – it's a sleepy place during the week, full of colourful wooden and corrugated-iron cottages. There are a few local cafés and a couple of major streets, but the highlight is the large **Kuba Ta Tapangu** (*tapangu* means village) in the centre. With its red-cypress frame raised on stilts and its thatched roof, the *kuba* or sacred hall is a visual reminder of indigenous Taiwan's cultural links with the South Pacific. You can't go inside – only male members of the tribe can enter.

A few kilometres west of Dabang, the village of **TEFUYE** (特富野; *tèfùyě*) is about half the size and feels a lot more isolated, containing the second Tsou **kuba**, a couple of churches and some excellent trails. You can walk uphill from here to **Zizhong** (自忠; *zìzhōng*), 6.3km along the **Tefuye Old Trail** (特富野古道; *tèfùyě gǔdào*), lined with beautiful *hinoki* cypress trees and bamboo; you'll have to hike back or arrange a lift from Zizhong to Alishan; alternatively, it's a lot easier to walk down in the other direction.

Practicalities

Just two **buses** a day link **Chiayi** with Dabang (see p.221), with departures in the other direction at 2.10pm and 7.10pm (NT$178). To reach Tefuye from here you'll need to hike or have your own transport. For somewhere to **stay** in Dabang, *Keupana homestay* (給巴娜民宿; *gěibānà mínsù*; ℡05/251-1688; ❸) is a modern building surrounded by flowers and a *hufu* (wooden pavilion), just below the village centre on the road to Tefuye. In Tefuye, the *Tefuye Resort* (特富野山莊; *tèfùyě shānzhuāng*; ℡05/251-1513 or 0937/651265; ❺) can arrange guides for some of the longer hikes in the area (the owner is a former Tsou chief, and keeps a small museum of Tsou artefacts on site). The hotel is 2km beyond the village in an extremely quiet spot on the hillside – during the week you'll be the only person here. Rooms are basic but comfortable, with bathroom.

Alishan Forest Recreation Area

The **ALISHAN FOREST RECREATION AREA** (阿里山森林遊樂區; *ālīshān sēnlín yóulèqū*), at the terminus for both the Alishan Forest Railway and buses from Chiayi, is the National Scenic Area's premier attraction. Its pristine alpine forests are dotted with mostly easy walking paths and several scenic overlooks offering superb **views** of the surrounding mountains and the surreal "sea of clouds" sunrise. However, what attracts the most tourists to the Recreation Area are its **cherry trees**, which come into full bloom from mid-March to mid-April. During this period, the area is inundated with ten thousand visitors a day, completely choking walking trails and making accommodation scarce. If you visit during this season, it's advisable to come during the week, though hotel and food prices skyrocket for the entire period. The area is especially cherished by busloads of mainland Chinese tourists – the Taiwanese folk song *ālīshān de gūniáng* (*Alishan Girl*) dates back to 1949 and remains wildly popular amongst middle-aged Chinese (you'll probably hear them singing it).

Bear in mind that given the area's 2200m **altitude**, it can get cold here even in the height of summer, and afternoons tend to be quite chilly once the usual midday mists roll in.

Arrival, orientation and information

The Forest Recreation Area begins just beyond the turning for Tatajia and Yushan, at a 24hr **tollgate** (drivers NT$200 on weekends, NT$150 on weekdays; bus passengers NT$150). Around 300m further on, buses terminate at the main tourist centre, clustered around a sprawling car park and known simply as "Alishan", though technically this is **Zhongzheng Village** (中正村; *zhōngzhèngcūn*). Alishan Forest Railway **trains** (when running – see p.221) pull in just southwest and up from the car park. On the opposite side of the car park is the **visitor information centre** (daily 8.30am–5.30pm; ℡05/267-9917), with English-language exhibits on the area's main attractions as well as free English maps and brochures. Most of the other tourist amenities are also situated around the car park, including a **post office** (Mon–Fri 8am–noon & 1–4.30pm; ℡05/267-9970) with an **ATM**, although this only accepts Taiwan-issued cards, so bring plenty of cash if you don't have one of these. Up Zhushan Forest Road, to the east of Zhongzheng Village, is an area known as **Xianglin Village** (香林村; *xiānglín cūn*) where you'll find more upscale accommodation as well as the main hiking trails (see opposite); vehicles need special passes to drive beyond the gate on Zhushan Forest Road.

Accommodation

Most of the Forest Recreation Area's **hotels** are conveniently located in **Zhongzheng Village**, where you'll find a row of faceless mid-range establishments at the base of the hill behind the car park, along with a growing number of more appealing **homestays**. If you don't have a reservation – usually essential during peak times – your best bet is to head here and try your luck.

Alishan Catholic Hostel 阿里山天主教福若瑟服務中心 (*ālīshān tiānzhǔ jiàofú ruòsè fúwù zhōngxīn*) 57 Zhongshan Village ℡05/267-9602. The only budget accommodation in Alishan is down a narrow lane just after the tollgate on the left, in an area known as Zhongshan Village, which has four cheap-but-basic doubles and one dorm room (NT$400). ❸

Alishan Gou Hotel 阿里山閣大飯店 (*ālīshān gé dàfàndiàn*) 1 Xianglin Village ℡05/267-9611, ⓦwww.agh.com.tw. A stone's throw from

Zhaoping Station, this modern hotel boasts a terrace that's become a favoured spot for viewing the sea of clouds. Rooms are anonymous but comfortable, and its location makes for an easy early-morning stumble to catch the sunrise train; a shuttle bus also connects it with the bus station. ❻

Alishan House 阿里山賓館 (*ālīshān bīnguǎn*) 16 Xianglin Village ℡05/267-9811, ⓦwww .alishanhouse.com.tw. Also in Xianglin, a short walk or ride from the main tourist service centre, this the area's top hotel, set in a functional Japanese-era building with stylish rooms; if you have a reservation, the shuttle bus will pick you up at the bus station. **8**

Gau Shan Ching Hotel 高山青賓館 (*gāoshānqīng bīnguǎn*) 43 Zhongzheng Village ℡ 05/267-9988. Hotel with super-friendly management and clean, if slightly cramped, rooms that includes a Chinese breakfast in its rates. Though the staff have limited English, they can help you book bus tickets to Tatajia and Chiayi. **4**

Xin Xin Homestay 欣欣民宿 (*xīnxīn mínsù*) 24 Zhongzheng Village ℡ 05/267-9748. One of the newer homestays in Alishan, near the station, and generally a far better deal than most of the older hotels; cosy wooden cabin-like rooms, some with loft level, all en suite with TV – rates vary with room size and numbers of guests in a room from NT$1200 to NT$5500 (rates almost double at weekends and holidays). **4**

Zhushan and the "sea of clouds"

The most popular place to watch the sunrise and the famous "sea of clouds" (云海; *yúnhǎi*) is from the top of the 2489m **Zhushan** (祝山; *zhùshān*). The quickest way up is via the **Zhushan Sunrise Train** (祝山觀日火車; *zhùshān guānrì huǒchē*; NT$100 one-way, NT$150 return; 25min), which leaves well before dawn each morning from the main Alishan Forest Railway Station near the car park, stopping at **Zhaoping Station** (沼平車站; *zhǎopíng chēzhàn*) a few minutes later. The line was closed for a year after being pummelled by Typhoon Morakot; check the current departure times with your hotel staff, who can also arrange a wake-up call.

Despite the inevitable crowds, the carnival-like atmosphere on the train can be fun, although buying a return ticket is probably overdoing it: taking the train to the top and walking back along one of the area's forest paths is a more balanced option. For those wanting make their own way up, the peaceful **Zhushan Sunrise Trail** (祝山觀日步道; *zhùshān guānrì bùdào*) gently climbs through a beautiful old-growth cedar forest en route to the summit. The turnoff for the trail is on the side of the road between Zhongzheng and Xianglin villages, a few hundred metres before you get to Zhaoping Station; allow about an hour for the walk. There are no lights along the trail, so it's necessary to bring a torch.

Once at the **summit**, expect a barrage of Mandarin-only tourist information to be blasted through a screechy loudspeaker, while the first appearance of the sun will be signalled by the simultaneous clicking of thousands of camera shutters. Dozens of **food vendors** with pushcarts sell breakfast items ranging from boiled eggs to heated tins of coffee. If you're walking back from Zhushan and the weather is clear, the **Dui Gao Yue Forest Trail** (對高岳森林浴步道; *duìgāoyuè sēnlínyù bùdà*) – to the right at the first big bend in the road – offers a lovely detour through evergreen forest before it dead-ends at a **pavilion** overlooking the nearby valley. The path, which begins alongside the train tracks, is 1.65km one-way, starting from the bend in the road.

Alishan loop trails

For the less energetic there are several loop walks well signposted in English, offering a leisurely one- to two-hour hike through the thick forests that cover the slopes

Alishan's red cypress trees

While the area's cherry blossoms are indeed a moving sight, most of these trees ironically inhabit a still-visible cemetery of once-mighty **red cypresses**, logged by the occupying Japanese in the early twentieth century to be turned into thousands of smoothly lacquered **tea tables**. In place of these ancient giants, many of which were well over 2000 years old when they were felled, the Japanese planted an assortment of their cherished sakura cherry trees. Sadly, apart from taking perfunctory photos before a handful of celebrated cypress stumps, most Taiwanese tourists pay scant attention to them, instead rushing to admire the cherry blossoms in an unwitting salute to the Japanese colonial legacy.

around the resort area – depending on the season, the paths are littered with flowers and blossoms while a cluster of monuments reflects the Japanese impact on the area. You can also combine a walk with the **Divine Tree Line** (神木線; *shénmù xiàn*), another small-gauge train line that runs daily from the main station to the Sacred Tree Station (see below) at 9am, 10am, 11am, 3pm and 4pm (NT$50 one-way; NT$80 return).

The lower loop path begins on the road just beyond *Alishan House*: a short path on the left takes you to the main circuit. Walking clockwise you'll first pass the **Tree Spirit Monument** (樹靈塔; *shùlíngtǎ*), on your right, a Shinto shrine built by the Japanese in 1915 to appease the spirits of the decimated forests, and on the left the **High Mountain Museum** (高山博物館; *gāoshān bówùguǎn*; daily 8am–11am & 2–5pm; free), another Japanese building converted into a small display area for old woodworking machinery, examples of mountain flora and a collection of Tsou artefacts. Behind the tree monument you'll see the start of the **Giant Tree Trail** (600m), which cuts across the loop and down to the **Sacred Tree** (阿里山神木; *ālǐshān shénmù*), passing several ancient cypress trees that for some reason were spared the saw.

Carry on along the main path and you'll reach the **Ciyun Temple** (慈雲寺; *cíyún sì*; daily 7am–6pm; free), another Japanese shrine, built in 1919 and housing a bronze Sakyamuni Buddha given to Emperor Taisho by the king of Thailand one year before. More dubiously, the statue is said to be filled with gold dust. The path drops from here to the Sacred Tree Station and the other end of the Giant Tree Trail. Continue along the main path from here and you'll come to a small suspension bridge – carry on to return to *Alishan House* or cross it to reach **Shouzhen Temple** (受鎮宮; *shòuzhèn gōng*; daily 6am–6pm; free). Rebuilt in 1969 and surrounded by food stalls, this is biggest temple in the area and dedicated principally to the Supreme Emperor of the Dark Heaven. From here the **Alishan Trail** (阿里山遊覽步道; *ālǐshān yóulǎn bùdào*) is an easy walk through the **Magnolia Garden** (木蘭園; *mùlán yuán*) and past **Two Sisters Pond** (姊妹潭; *jiěmèitán*), named after two broken-hearted Tsou girls who drowned themselves here, before turning back to the *Alishan Gou Hotel* – there are several routes from here which cut through **Plum Tree Garden** (梅園; *méi yuán*) back to the main road and the village. This area was the site of the original Alishan settlement: after the great fire of 1976 development moved to the current site in Zhongzheng Village and the devastated area was converted into a park. In the late afternoon the terrace outside the hotel is the best place to view the sunset and sea of clouds over the valley.

Tatajia

Those wanting to get further into the mountains to watch the sunrise at **Tatajia** (塔塔加; *tǎtǎjiā*), just inside Yushan National Park, can book a slot on one of the pre-dawn **minibus tours** (3hr return trip; NT$300/person) that leave from hotels in Zhongzheng Village about an hour before sunrise each morning (3.45am in the summer).

Eating

You'll find plenty of **restaurants** in Zhongzheng Village, in the complex at the southern end of the car park. They invariably serve standard **Chinese fare**, from fried rice and noodles to basic stir fries, and you should be able to eat to your fill for under NT$200 even during peak season. At the southeastern end of the car park is a 24hr **convenience store** where you can buy drinks and snacks for your hikes.

The best place for a decent meal is *Alishan House* (see p.226), but a good choice in the main shopping area is *The Great Beauty of Rihchu* (日出有大美; *rìchū yǒudàměi*; daily 11.30am–2.30pm & 5.30–8.30pm; ☏05/267-9958), 30 Zhongzheng Village,

Moving on from Alishan

Buses to **Chiayi** (NT$221) depart at 9.10am, 11.10am, 1.10pm, 2.10pm, 3.10pm, 4.10pm, 4.40pm and 5.10pm (also 2.40pm and 3.40pm Fri–Sun). At the weekends, a bus also shuttles down to **Fenqihu** at 1.10pm, and Kuo Kuang runs to **Taipei** (12.30pm; NT$620). Buy tickets inside the 7-Eleven next to the bus stop. **Taxis** will try and charge NT$1600 to Chiayi, but late on a weekday afternoon you'll be able to bargain for much less. When the **Alishan Forest Railway** is reopened it should leave twice daily for the descent to Chiayi. For details on getting to **Yushan National Park** see p.230.

which has a cutesy theme, but lots of fine teas (NT$180) and superb **hotpots** with various meats, piled high with vegetables, pumpkin, bamboo shoots and dumplings (from NT$280–500). English menus available.

Yushan National Park

Taiwan's most untarnished breadth of backcountry, **YUSHAN NATIONAL PARK** (玉山國家公園; *yùshān guójiā gōngyuán*) is an archetypal mountain wilderness with a seemingly endless proliferation of 3000m peaks separated by yawning river valleys. The park is primarily known for the majestic **Yushan** (Jade Mountain) – at 3952m the tallest peak in northeast Asia. Climbing to the summit is an exhilarating experience, and not as challenging as it might sound.

Yushan National Park is by far Taiwan's largest, covering over three quarters of the country and accessible by road from three sides (the park is also, nominally at least, the homeland of the **Bunun** tribe, who remained semi-independent until they were brutally crushed by the Japanese in the 1920s). As such, its entry points and information centres are spread widely, making it seem like several different parks. If you're planning to climb Yushan, **Tatajia** (from Alishan/Chiayi) or **Dongpu** (from Sun Moon Lake) will be your gateway into the park: from Tatajia, the climb is easier and much more heavily trafficked, while the Dongpu approach

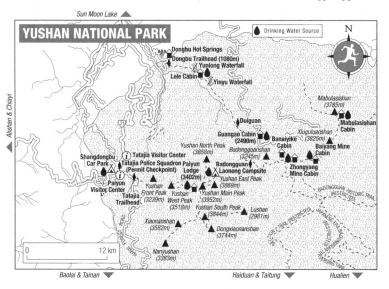

229

Getting to Yushan

Tatajia is just to the east of the immensely popular **Alishan Forest Recreation Area**, to which you can get public transport (see p.221); however, there is no public bus service from Alishan to the Tatajia entrance, and logistics can be tough without a car. You'll need to arrange a ride on one of the **hotel-run minibuses** (NT$300) that take tourists to see the sunrise at Tatajia Visitor Center each morning. It's a long hike to the trailhead from here (almost 4km), but some of the minibuses might be persuaded to shuttle you there for an extra charge of NT$150. You must arrange a return pick-up in advance (hard without a mobile phone), or you'll end up having to hitch or hike to the police post to beg for a lift back to Alishan. For considerably more money than the minibuses, you can hire your own driver in Alishan to take you past the police checkpoint to the trailhead and could also arrange a pick-up later that evening or the next day (ask at your hotel).

For **Dongpu**, buses leave from Shuili (1hr 10min) daily at 6am, 8am, 8.50am, 11.10am, 1pm, 2.30pm, 4pm and 5.10pm (NT$115).

is longer and more physically demanding. It was closed after Typhoon Morakot and at the time of writing had yet to reopen. The **Nanan** section of the park is covered on p.314. For the **southern section** see p.272.

Note that the main peak of Yushan was closed in September 2010 to allow for reconstruction of Paiyun Lodge – it should be open again by May 2011.

Information and permits

The **Yushan National Park Headquarters** and its main visitor centre (300 Zhongshan Rd Sec 1; 9am–4.30pm; ☎049/2773121, ⓦwww.ysnp.gov.tw) is located in Shuili (see p.199), near Sun Moon Lake, but the **Tatajia Visitor Center** (塔塔加遊客中心; *tǎtǎjiā yóukè zhōngxīn*; 9am–4.30pm, closed second and fourth Tues of every month; ☎049/270-2200), at the end of Highway 18, 19km from Alishan, has English maps, audio-visual presentations and an exhibition hall with information on the nearby mountains and endemic flora and fauna. The most convenient of all is the **Paiyun Visitor Center** (排雲遊客中心; *páiyún yóukè zhōngxīn*; daily 6.30am–4pm; ☎049/270-2228), 1km closer to Alishan, with a few displays and a five-minute safety video that all first-time climbers are officially required to watch.

You'll need to arrange a **national park entry permit** (入園; *rùyuán*) in advance to climb Yushan, but the park **website** has the application process clearly mapped out in English – you can do it all on-line as long as you can print out the permit (see p.37). Applications are supposed to be received **four months to 35 working days** before the proposed start date of your climb, though in practice they can often be approved within a few days. You also must reserve a bed at **Paiyun Lodge** (排雲山莊; *páiyún shānzhuāng*; NT$220; pay at the lodge), whether you plan to go up in one day or not. The real problem with Yushan is its popularity; only 102 people can be accepted by Paiyun Lodge, effectively making that the daily cut-off. The park holds a lottery for places if more applications are received. When the new lodge is completed in 2011 it may be able to hold more people.

Climbing Yushan from Tatajia

By far the easiest, most popular route up Yushan is from **TATAJIA** (塔塔加; *tǎtǎjiā*) along a well-maintained trail that is probably Taiwan's most famous hike. Though Taiwanese and even some aborigines will tell you it's an arduous two-day return climb, in reality a reasonably fit walker can make the 22km return journey from the **Tatajia Trailhead** (塔塔加登山口; *tǎtǎjiā dēngshānkǒu*) to the main peak in one long day – provided you get an early start.

Most of the minibuses from Alishan will drop you off near the **Tatajia Police Squadron** (塔塔加警察小隊; *tǎtǎjiā jǐngchá xiǎoduì*; ☏ 049/270-2203), next to the Paiyun Visitor Center, where you must pick up your **police permit** or **mountain entry permit** (入山; *rùshān*), in return for three copies of your hiking plan and route map and a copy of your passport, and you'll have to produce your national park entry permit you also have to watch the safety video at the visitor centre.

From here, you'll have to walk or hitch a ride to the trailhead, another 2.5km or so along Nanxi Forest Road, which will add about an hour to your journey each way. If you have your own vehicle, you can leave it in the **Shangdongpu** (上東埔; *shàngdōngpǔ*) **car park** below the police squadron on Highway 18, and either hike up the access road or try to get a lift with any hiking groups that are being driven to the trailhead.

From the Tatajia Trailhead (2610m) to the Paiyun Lodge (3402m) is an 8.5km walk of moderate intensity, with a fairly gradual ascent. If you reach the lodge quickly, you can stash your bag inside and make a speedy ascent of Yushan's **main peak** (玉山主峰; *yùshān zhǔfēng*), a steep 2.4km climb with an elevation gain of over 500m. Alternatively, you could first climb the lower 3518m **west peak** (玉山西峰; *yùshān xīfēng*) and return to the lodge for the night. Though it is hoped that the new lodge will be much improved when it opens in 2011, it's worth keeping in mind that the old lodge was an incongruously hectic and noisy place to stay. Most Taiwanese hikers set their alarms for around 2am to allow ample time to reach the summit before **sunrise**; but while sunrises from the top of Yushan can indeed be momentous, during busy periods you might consider sleeping in and waiting until the mobs start to descend – you'll have more chance of solitude at the top and spend less time waiting at bottlenecks along the trail.

Climbing Yushan from Dongpu

The climb of Yushan from the hot-springs village of **Dongpu** is one of Taiwan's most challenging – and thrilling – hikes, though the route was **severely damaged and closed** by Typhoon Morakot in 2009 and had yet to reopen at the time of writing. It is imperative to check with the national park authorities before attempting this route; the return journey is about 48km, with an elevation gain of nearly 3000m, and is suited to seasoned hill walkers with high fitness levels and heads for heights. The return journey takes the better part of three days to complete, with two overnight stays in the rustic **Guangao Cabin** (觀高山屋; *guāngāo shānwū*). You'll need to bring your own **sleeping bag** and foam or inflatable mattress, and apply for the necessary permits in advance (see opposite).

Yushan wildlife

Yushan National Park is revered by Taiwanese conservationists, who since its establishment in 1985 have worked tirelessly to protect its natural treasures. Sheltering six distinct vegetation zones, the park contains more than half of the island's endemic plant species, as well as some of Asia's rarest animal species. Chief among these is the elusive **Formosan Black Bear**, an omnivorous beast that mostly roams the foothills below 2000m. Far from being a threat, these bears are extremely rare and are seldom spotted by humans. Much more visible is the profusion of **deer species**, some of which can be seen by watchful trekkers, especially on the northern fringes of Yushan, near the beautiful high-altitude meadows of **Badongguan**. The most commonly seen of these is the diminutive **Formosan Reeve's Muntjac**, recognizable by its tan coat and stubby, single-pronged antlers.

Dongpu

Though many of the hotels in **DONGPU** (東埔; *dōngpǔ*) are slightly dated, with the hot-spring water piped into tiny tubs in attached bathrooms, there are a few with public indoor and outdoor bathing pools. Dongpu's top hotel – and one that is used to catering to Yushan climbers – is the ⚡ *Hotel Ti Lun* (帝綸溫泉飯店; *dìlún wēnqúan fàndiàn*; ☎049/270-2789, Ⓦ www.tilun.com.tw; ⑥) at 86 Kaigao Lane, the first hotel on the left as you enter the village from the bus stop. The *Ti Lun* has a wide range of rooms, from basic doubles to Japanese-style suites equipped with jacuzzis. Its outdoor **public bathing pools** have excellent views of the surrounding mountains and are an ideal place to watch the sun set. If you're climbing Yushan, the hotel has a safe **left-luggage room** where you can stash all of your extra gear.

Dongpu's main street, Kaigao Lane, is lined with small **restaurants** serving fresh **river trout** and mountain vegetables, though they generally cater to big groups.

Travel details

Trains

Changhua to: Chiayi (17 express daily; 50min); Kaohsiung (17 express daily; 2hr 15min); Taichung (17 express daily; 12min); Tainan (17 express daily; 1hr 35min).
Chiayi to: Changhua (17 express daily; 50min); Ershui (frequent; 50min); Kaohsiung (frequent High-Speed trains; 34min; 14 express daily; 1hr 15min); Taichung (frequent High-Speed trains; 25min; 14 express daily; 1hr 15min); Tainan (frequent High-Speed trains; 20min; 14 express daily; 40min); Taipei (frequent High-Speed trains; 1hr 15min; 16 express daily; 3hr 10min).
Ershui to: Chiayi (frequent; 50min); Jiji (8 daily; 30min); Kaohsiung (15 daily; 2hr 30min); Taichung (frequent; 45min); Tainan (15 daily; 1hr 45min).
Taichung to: Changhua (17 express daily; 10min); Chiayi (frequent High-Speed trains; 25min; 14 express daily; 1hr 15min); Ershui (frequent; 45min); Kaohsiung (frequent High-Speed trains; 1hr; 16 express daily; 2hr 30min); Tainan (frequent High-Speed trains; 45min; 16 express daily; 2hr); Taipei (frequent High-Speed trains; 1hr; 15 express daily; 2hr 5min).

Buses

With so many services operating in the region, some bus frequencies to major cities have not been included. Most inter-city buses leave every 30min, and services to Taichung and Taipei often run 24hr.
Changhua to: Lugang (30min); Taichung (30min); Taipei (2hr 15min).
Chiayi to: Alishan Forest Recreation Area (1hr 30min); Beigang (45min); Budai (1hr); Dabang (2hr); Guanziling (1hr); Kaohsiung (1hr); Tainan (30min); Taipei (3hr 30min).
Dongpu to: Shuili (8 daily; 1hr).
Lugang to: Changhua (30min); Taichung (1hr); Taipei (30min).
Puli to: Shuili (1hr); Sun Moon Lake (30min); Taichung (1hr); Taipei (3hr); Wushe (45min).
Sun Moon Lake to: Puli (30min); Shuili (30min); Taichung (2 daily; 2hr); Taipei (3hr 30min).
Taichung to: Changhua (30min); Chiayi (1hr 30min); Dajia (1hr); Kaohsiung (2hr 30min); Lugang (1hr); Puli (1hr); Tainan (2hr); Taipei (2hr); Sun Moon Lake (2 daily; 2hr).

Ferries

Budai to: Magong (summer only, 2 daily; 1hr).

Flights

Chiayi to: Kinmen (daily; 50min); Magong (2 daily; 30min).
Taichung to: Hualien (5 daily; 55min); Kinmen (10 daily; 55min); Magong (9 daily; 35min); Taitung (daily; 1hr 5min).

South Taiwan

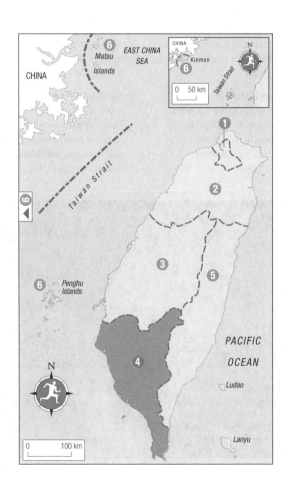

CHAPTER 4 # Highlights

* **Tainan** Taiwan's former capital is a city of historic but highly active temples, and home to some of the country's best street food. See p.235

* **Kaohsiung** Taiwan's second city is the vibrant and friendly capital of the south, with a smattering of historic sights and excellent seafood. See p.254

* **Foguangshan** Spend a day exploring the galleries, museums and elegant temples of this massive Buddhist monastery. See p.266

* **Southern Cross-Island Highway** Spectacular mountain road, linking Tainan to Taitung and cutting across the southern tip of Yushan National Park. See p.270

* **Little Liuqiu Island** Kick back and enjoy the alluring rock formations on this tranquil coral island. See p.274

* **Kenting National Park** Hire a car or scooter and explore Taiwan's southernmost national park, with pristine surf beaches and stunning coastal scenery. See p.278

▲ Spring Autumn Pavilion, Kaohsiung

South Taiwan

anguid, tropical **south Taiwan** is a world away from Taipei, a land of betel nut plantations, pineapple groves and sandy beaches. The southern plains are home to Taiwan's oldest Chinese settlements, a bastion of Taiwanese culture with a correspondingly high proportion of independence supporters – the counties of Tainan, Kaohsiung and Pingdong are Democratic Progressive Party (DPP) strongholds and the Taiwanese language is spoken everywhere in preference to Mandarin. The lush southern mountains, while not quite as dramatic as the central ranges, still offer plenty of gorgeous scenery, predominantly inhabited by the Bunun, Paiwan and Rukai tribes (see p.398) – although, sadly, they were hard hit by **Typhoon Morakot** in 2009, with eight Rukai and Paiwan villages effectively abandoned. Much of the region's exuberant culture is encapsulated in its **festivals**: many temples hold elaborate **boat-burning** ceremonies every three years, while the horizontal firework display at **Yanshui** is a chaotic but exhilarating event held over Chinese New Year.

Tainan is an essential stop on any tour of Taiwan. The former capital is crammed with ornate temples, engaging historical sights and some of the best snack food in the country. From here the **Southern Cross-Island Highway** snakes east across the mountains to Taitung, a dramatic and sometimes perilous route with incredibly scenic views; it cuts through the northern end of **Maolin National Scenic Area**, no less captivating, with the slate Rukai village of Duona and the thrilling mountain road up to Wutai, another Rukai village. (At the time of writing much of the Cross-Island Highway and Scenic Area is still inaccessible post-Morakot, but is expected to reopen in 2011.) **Kaohsiung** is the biggest city in the south, with a laid-back, friendly character, rapidly throwing off its grimy industrial image and close to the impressive monastery at **Foguangshan**. The narrow stub of land at the foot of Taiwan is dominated by **Kenting National Park**, with its somewhat overrated main resort but a wealth of less visited beaches and excellent surf easily accessible by scooter. The intriguing coral island of **Little Liuqiu** is just off the coast.

Tainan

Historic **TAINAN** (台南; *táinán*), just a few kilometres from the southwest coast, is a city of ancient monuments, delicious food and, above all, **temples**: there are more gods worshipped, and more festivals and rituals are observed in Tainan than in any other place in Taiwan. Much of this is a legacy of its former status as capital city, a title it enjoyed for more than two hundred years, and particularly of the seventeenth century, when it was the last independent outpost of China's **Ming dynasty**.

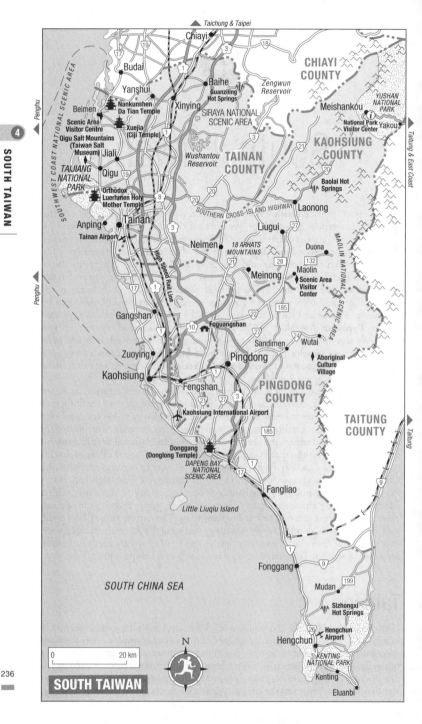

SOUTH TAIWAN

▲ Taichung & Taipei
Chiayi
CHIAYI COUNTY
Budai
YUSHAN NATIONAL PARK
Yanshui
Baihe
Guanziling Hot Springs
Zengwun Reservoir
Meishankou
Beimen
Nankunshen Da Tian Temple
Xinying
SIRAYA NATIONAL SCENIC AREA
National Park Visitor Center
Yakou
Scenic Area Visitor Centre
Xuejia (Ciji Temple)
KAOHSIUNG COUNTY
Qigu Salt Mountains (Taiwan Salt Museum)
Jiali
Wushantou Reservoir
TAINAN COUNTY
Qigu
TAIJIANG NATIONAL PARK
Baolai Hot Springs
Orthodox Luerhmen Holy Mother Temple
Laonong
Anping
Liugui
Duona
Tainan
Tainan Airport
Neimen
18 ARHATS MOUNTAINS
Maolin
Scenic Area Visitor Center
Meinong
SOUTHERN CROSS-ISLAND HIGHWAY
MAOLIN NATIONAL SCENIC AREA
Gangshan
Foguangshan
Sandimen
Wutai
Zuoying
Pingdong
Aboriginal Culture Village
Kaohsiung
Fengshan
PINGDONG COUNTY
TAITUNG COUNTY
Kaohsiung International Airport
Donggang (Donglong Temple)
DAPENG BAY NATIONAL SCENIC AREA
Fangliao
Little Liuqiu Island
SOUTH CHINA SEA
Fonggang
Mudan
Sizhongxi Hot Springs
Hengchun
Hengchun Airport
0   20 km
N
KENTING NATIONAL PARK
Kenting
Eluanbi

SOUTH TAIWAN

SOUTHWEST COAST NATIONAL SCENIC AREA

Penghu

High Speed Rail Line

Taitung & East Coast

Taitung

Some history

The ancestral home of the Siraya *píngpǔ* tribe, Tainan began its modern history with the **Dutch**, who established **Fort Zeelandia** in 1624 on a sand bar off the coast. At that time, the site of the modern city's western half was under water, part of a huge lagoon ringed by a chain of sandy islets. The Dutch called the area "Tayouan" and made it the capital of their colony (see Contexts p.383). In 1662, however, they surrendered to the vastly superior forces of Ming general Zheng Chenggong, also known as **Koxinga** (see box, p.245) after a nine-month siege. During the period of **Zheng family rule** that followed (1662–83) Tainan prospered, and many of its finest temples were constructed to befit its status as an independent Chinese kingdom. In 1664 one of the last descendants of the Ming royal family, the **Prince of Ningjing**, moved to the city. When the Zhengs surrendered to Chinese admiral Shi Lang in 1683, the city became known as **Taiwan-Fu** and was made prefectural capital of the island.

In 1823 a devastating storm led to the silting up of the lagoon, and **Anping** (the site of Fort Zeelandia) became permanently joined to the mainland. The Treaty of Beijing (1860) paved the way for a small community of foreign merchants to trade camphor, tea and opium in Anping, but after the Japanese occupied Taiwan in 1895 the sale of opium and camphor became a government franchise and, with the port silting up further, by 1911 most merchants had left. When Taiwan became a province in 1885, the city became known as **Tainan-Fu**, or "South Taiwan" and lost its capital status to Taipei. Today it is Taiwan's fourth-largest city, with a population of around 770,000.

Arrival

Tainan Airport (臺南機場; *táinán jīchǎng*) is 5km south of the city at 1002 Datong Rd, a short taxi (NT$200–250) or bus ride (NT$18) to the centre; most hotels will arrange a pick-up. **Tainan Train Station** (台南火車站; *táinán huǒchēzhàn*) is located on the eastern edge of the city centre and most **buses** terminate nearby. **Tainan High-Speed Rail Station** (高鐵台南站; *gāotiě táinánzhàn*) is located at 100 Gueiren Boulevard in **Gueiren** (歸仁; *guīrén*), 10km southeast of the centre, and connected to the city by three buses (free); take the **Tainan Park** (台南公園; *táinán gōngyuán*) bus to the train station downtown (daily 6.55am–11.55pm; every 20min; 30–40min). **Taxis** (around NT$500) are provided by Taiwan Fast-Link (☎0809/005-006), and you can also rent cars here (see p.250).

City transport

City buses (NT$18), run by **Kaohsiung Bus**, are relatively easy to use in Tainan, with English timetables at some bus stops, and bus announcements and electronic signs in English, although you are unlikely to need them within the old centre. The **main bus stations** line the roundabout on Chenggong Road across from the train station; from the south station you can pick up bus #2 to Anping and Fort Zeelandia, #5 to Tainan Airport and #14 to the Eternal Gold Castle; the bus to the High-Speed Rail Station normally departs from the north side. Special **free** bus #88 between Tainan Park and Anping, and #99 to Taijiang National Park, also run from here at weekends and holidays.

For trips outside the centre it's more convenient to take a **taxi** – the initial fare is NT$85 (use the meter). If you can't flag one down, there are usually plenty at the train station. For **bicycles** and **scooters**, see p.251 and p.252.

Information

The small **tourist office** (daily 9am–6pm; ☎06/229-0082, ⓦtour.tncg.gov.tw) next to the train station exit has a decent selection of English-language material. There's also a helpful **information centre** (Tues–Sun 8.30am–5.30pm) on the second floor of the **Old Tainan Forest Office** (台南山林事務所; *táinán shānlínshì wùsuǒ*) on Youai Street, across from the Confucius Temple. The city has opted to use *tōngyòng pīnyīn*, with streets marked in English and Chinese.

Accommodation

Tainan has plenty of **accommodation** conveniently located in the centre of the city, within walking distance or a short taxi ride from the station and most of the sights. The choice is improving at the top end, but there are still no hostels, and budget hotels are fairly uninispring.

Cambridge Hotel 劍橋大飯店 (*jiànqiáo dàfàndiàn*) 269 Minzu Rd Sec 2 ☎06/221-9966, ⓦwww.cambridge-hotel.com.tw. Solid mid-range hotel in the heart of Tainan, with clean, simply furnished standard rooms, cable TV, decent buffet breakfast and free internet access. Free self-serve laundry on the twelfth floor. ❺

Guang Hwa Hotel 光華大旅社 (*guānghuá dàlǔshè*) 155 Beimen Rd Sec 1 ☎06/226-3171. Tainan's best budget hotel, a short walk south of the station, with rooms from NT$980 and English-speakers on the front desk. All rooms have TV, and bathrooms come with a tub and hand-held shower. Extras include breakfast and free internet access, while YHA cardholders get a small discount. ❷

🏃 **JJ-W Hotel** 佳佳西市場旅店 (*jiājiā xīshìchǎng lǚdiàn*) 11 Jhengsing St ☎06/220-9866, ⓦwww.jj-whotel.com.tw. Fabulous boutique hotel, fusing traditional Chinese style with postmodernist design, luxury and sheer surrealism. Each room has a different design, loosely based on traditional Chinese themes: think lofts, old closets, flat-screen TVs, floor-to-ceiling windows, crazy Thai furniture and lots of glass and marble. ❼

La Plaza 天下大飯店 (*tiānxià dàfàndiàn*) 202 Chenggong Rd ☎06/229-0271, ⓦwww.laplaza .com.tw. This old hotel has been redesigned in elegant modern-Chinese style, with sleek fittings, Chinese art and grey stone bathrooms; the deluxe rooms are more like mini-suites. Facilities include free internet access, breakfast, gym and coin laundry. ❼

Shangri-La's Far Eastern Plaza Hotel 台南香格里拉遠東國際大飯店 (*táinán xiānggélǐlā yuǎndōng guójì dàfàndiàn*) 89 Dasyue W Rd ☎06/702-8888, ⓦwww.shangri-la.com. Tainan's top luxury hotel, tucked away above the FE21 shopping mall opposite the train station. Rooms are huge and typically lavish five-star style, but online deals can make this good value; the upper-level pool deck is an enticing extra. Huge breakfast buffet and free broadband internet access included. ❼

Tainan Teacher's Hostel aka Confucius Inn 教師會館 (*jiàoshī huìguǎn*) 4 Nanmen Rd ☎06/214-5588, ⓦwww.tainan-teachers-hostel .com.tw. Decent mid-range option in central Tainan, with rates starting around NT$1600 online for small but comfy en-suite doubles including basic breakfast. ❹

Taipung Suites 臺邦商旅 (*táibāng shānglǚ*) 199 Younghua 2nd St, Anping ☎06/293-1888, ⓦwww.taipungsuites.com.tw. Located near City Hall, between Anping and downtown, this plush boutique hotel is well worth the short taxi or bike ride into the centre, with a fabulous roof deck and stylish rooms with flat-screen TVs. There are discounts for singles and plenty of restaurants nearby. ❼

Tayih Landis 大億麗緻酒店 (*dàyì lìzhì jiǔdiàn*) 660 Simen Rd Sec 1 ☎06/213-5555, ⓦwww.tayihlandis.com.tw. Tainan's other top five-star hotel, its large rooms feature a contemporary minimalist style with flat-screen TVs and marble-clad bathrooms. The stylish gym (seventh floor) is at the foot of a large indoor atrium, and there's a spa, pool, hip lounge bar and choice of top-notch international restaurants. ❽

🏃 **Tayouan Bed & Breakfast** 台窩灣民居 (*táiwōwān mínjū*) 25 Guosheng Rd, Anping ☎06/228-4177, ⓦwww.tayouan.com.tw. Cute little B&B in a refurbished home, built in traditional Chinese style in 1947. Four small but cosy rooms are Japanese-style, with raised wooden platforms and simple futon mattresses. Bathrooms (three showers) and TV room are shared, breakfast included. Look for the sign opposite Kaitai Tianhou Temple. ❺

The City

The oldest and most absorbing parts of Tainan are Anping, on the west side of town by the sea, and the cultural zones in the heart of the old city; the latter were created specifically to make things easier for visitors, with city; information, signs and maps tailored to each zone and well marked in English. The **Chihkan, Dong-an Fang, Five Canals** and **Confucius Temple cultural zones** contain the richest concentration of sights – reckon on spending at least two days to do them justice.

Chihkan Tower, a collection of Qing dynasty pavilions in the northern section of the old city, is the best place to start. From here Tainan's most appealing **temples** are just short walks away, while the **Koxinga Shrine** and **Confucius Temple** provide a focus for the southern half of the old city. Historic **Anping**'s attractions are no less compact, located a brief taxi ride west of the centre.

Chihkan Cultural Zone

The **Chihkan Cultural Zone** (赤崁文化園區; *chìkǎn wénhuà yuánqū*) covers the northern part of the old city, home to some of Tainan's finest temples and **Chihkan Tower** (赤崁樓; *chìkǎnlóu*; daily 8.30am–9pm; NT\$50) at 212 Minzu Rd Sec 2 – a city landmark. This was the site of **Fort Provintia**, built by the Dutch in 1653, although very little remains of the original and today the site comprises two Fujian-style pavilions constructed in the nineteenth century. The fort was captured by Koxinga in 1661 prior to his siege of Fort Zeelandia. After the Dutch defeat the site was gradually abandoned and a temple was built on the ruins in 1875 (the first pavilion). Over the next ten years four more buildings were constructed here as part of a Qing dynasty educational and religious complex, although only three remain today.

The first thing you'll see on entering the grounds is the **statue** symbolizing the Dutch surrender. It says more about twentieth-century politics than real history: the Dutchman is far too short and dressed like a Spanish captain of the time – it was completed in the 1980s to draw attention to the Ming general's nationalist credentials (see box, p.245).

The base of the first pavilion is lined with **nine steles** sent to the city by Emperor Qianlong, praising the defeat of the Lin Shuangwen Rebellion of 1786–88 (see p.385). Originally a **Sea God Temple**, the first pavilion now houses a small exhibition (Chinese only) on Koxinga and the old Dutch fort. The pavilion beyond is the **Wenchang Pavilion**. The first floor houses an exhibition detailing the Qing civil service system, while upstairs contains a shrine to the fourth "Wenchang" or literature god, Kui Dou Xingjun (*kuídǒu xīngjūn*), said to aid those taking the old imperial civil service examinations. Like many Chinese deities he's supposed to have been a real person, and is said to have failed the examinations three times simply because the emperor was repulsed by his hideous looks – the poor scholar committed suicide and has been venerated ever since. Behind the pavilion on the left is all that remains of the **Peng Hu School**, built in 1886, while to the right are some redbrick foundations, all that remains of the **Dutch fort**.

Ten minutes' walk north of Chihkan Tower, **Kaiji Tianhou Temple** (開基天后宮; *kāijī tiānhòugōng*; daily 6am–9pm) is a real gem, well worth a short detour. This is the oldest temple to Mazu, goddess of the sea, in Tainan (there are seventeen in the city and nearly a thousand in Taiwan), established in 1662. The shrine is decorated with some fascinating artwork, such as the "barbarian" figures holding up the eaves of the temple corners, but the real highlight is the shrine to **Guanyin** at the back. This contains one of three celebrated images of the Bodhisattva in Tainan, the gold statue blackened with incense smoke over the years, her graceful pose capturing perfectly the ethos of Buddhist serenity embodied in this enlightenment being,

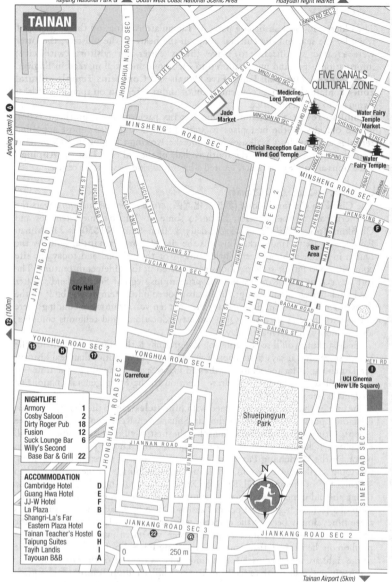

Taijiang National Park & ▲ South West Coast National Scenic Area　　　Huayuan Night Market ▲

TAINAN

4

SOUTH TAIWAN | Tainan

Anping (3km) & ◀

◀ (100m)

Tainan Airport (5km) ▼

FIVE CANALS
CULTURAL ZONE

Medicine
Lord Temple

Jade
Market

Water Fairy
Temple
Market

Official Reception Gate/
Wind God Temple

Water
Fairy
Temple

Bar
Area

City Hall

Carrefour

Shueipingyun
Park

UCI Cinema
(New Life Square)

NIGHTLIFE
Armory	1
Cosby Saloon	2
Dirty Roger Pub	18
Fusion	12
Suck Lounge Bar	6
Willy's Second Base Bar & Grill	22

ACCOMMODATION
Cambridge Hotel	D
Guang Hwa Hotel	E
JJ-W Hotel	F
La Plaza	B
Shangri-La's Far Eastern Plaza Hotel	C
Tainan Teacher's Hostel	G
Taipung Suites	H
Tayih Landis	I
Tayouan B&B	A

0　　250 m

N

associated with compassion. Walk up Chihkan Street and turn left at Chenggong Road, turn right at Zhiciang Street and the temple is at no. 12.

Official God of War Temple

The striking peach-coloured walls opposite Chihkan Tower belong to Tainan's **Official God of War Temple** (祀典武廟; *sìdiăn wǔmiào*; daily 6am–9pm) or, literally, the "Sacrificial Rites Martial Temple". The entrance is a short walk south

▲ *Chiayi & Siaobei Night Market (500m)*

GONGYUAN S. ROAD

GONGYUAN STREET

SIMEN ROAD SEC 3

CHICIAN STREET

BEIHUA STREET

BEIMEN ROAD

SIAODONG RD

CIANFONG ROAD

1

Kaiji Tianhou Temple

Kuo Kuang Bus Station

CHENGGONG ROAD

CHIHKAN CULTURAL ZONE

BEIJHONG STREET

Ubus Station

SIMEI STREET

CHIHKAN STREET

MINCIANG ST

OPEN ST

CHIYUN ST

BEIJHONG STREET

SITHA S STREET

Ho Hsin Bus Station

Tainan Train Station

DASYUEW RD

Official God of War Temple

3 **Chihkan Tower**

CHENGGONG RD

GONGYUAN ROAD

QUANCHENG RD

Tainan City Bus Station

FE 21 Department Store

i

Datianhou Temple

MINZU ROAD SEC 2

D

G

Scooter Hire

STONHA STREET SEC 3

4

5

Kaiji Guangong Temple **6**

Tainan Kuang Tsai Embroidery Shop

MINCYUAN ROAD SEC 2

Tainan Hospital ✚

QUANCHENG ST

JHONGSHAN ROAD

Singnan Bus Stop

E

Caves Bookstore

7-11 Stores & ATM (cash)

STIHSIAN ROAD

7

YONGFU RD SEC 2

LANE 225

9

LANE 239

8

FE21 Department Store & Vieshow Cinemas

More Cafe@

Shinkong Mitsukoshi Department Store

MINZU ROAD

WANCHONG ST

WIDES

BEIMEN ROAD

10

Citibank

STIMEI STREET

Tiantan

Catholic Church

WEIMIN STREET

JHONGJHENG ROAD

Jheng's Ancestral Shrine **11**

Tang De-Jhang Memorial Park

City God Temple

CINGNIAN ROAD

MINCYUAN ROAD

DONG-AN FANG CULTURAL ZONE

CHENGHUANG STREET

Chinatrust Bank

YOUAI STREET

National Museum of Taiwanese Literature

Old Tainan Forest office

i

Chin Wan Tze

Solaya

Books, Cultural Souvenirs of Taiwanese Heritage

Dongyue Temple

DONGMEN ROAD

Old Tainan Martial Arts Academy

Confucius Temple

FUJHONG STREET

13

FUCIAN ROAD SEC 1

14 **16** **G**

Lady Linshui Temple

KAISHAN ROAD

Koxinga Shrine & Museum

19

YONGFU RD SEC 1

JIANYE STREET

MINSHENG GREEN PARK CULTURAL ZONE

20

CONFUCIUS TEMPLE CULTURAL ZONE

Great South Gate

City Wall

SHUJIN STREET

NANMEN ROAD

JHONGYI ROAD SEC 1

WUFEI STREET

CIANJHONG STREET

21

Wufei Temple (Five Concubines Temple)

JIANKANG ROAD SEC 1

▼ *Kaohsiung*

High Speed Rail Station & Gueiren (10km) ▶

(100m) & Dadong Night Market (1.5km) ▶

(100m) & Dadong Night Market (1.5km) ▶

EATING AND DRINKING	
Ah-Xia Restaurant	9
Dream of Chrysanthemums	21
Fu Ji Meatballs	14
Geng Du Yuan	17
Go Dutch Café	10
Guohua St Sec 3	4
Hong's Noodles	5
Imma Bakery & Café	20
Lily Fruits	16
Narrow Door Café	13
Sen Maw Rice Food	3
Shantou Fish Noodles	7
Tu Hsiao Yueh (Slack Season Tan Tsai Noodles)	11
Water Drop Teahouse	15
Yong Ji Milkfish Balls	19
Zai Fa Hao	8

at 229 Yongfu Rd Sec 2. It is one of the city's most attractive temples, dedicated to god of war **Guan Di**, and significant because it originally served as the Prince of Ningjing's private gardens, built in 1665. He is said to have brought one of the images of the deity inside with him from China, but the temple was formally established in 1690, when it took on its current form. The **Main Hall** at the front of the complex contains the shrine to Guan Di, with an aged wooden tablet hanging from the beams above the entrance – carved in 1794, it reads 大丈夫

(*dàzhàngfū*) or "Great Man", an allusion to the fierce-looking god below. The **Rear Hall** contains tablets representing three generations of Guan Di's ancestors: on the left you'll see a small scroll inscribed with a bamboo engraving and poem said to have been penned by the general himself, although this is not the original – it's a rubbing from his tomb in China. To the left of here is a side hall containing another of Tainan's three captivating images of **Guanyin**, while around the back sits a plum tree said to have been planted by the Prince of Ningjing himself.

Datianhou Temple

Turn immediately right when you exit the Official God of War Temple into Lane 227, known as Fortune Tellers' Alley. It's a short walk from here to the front of **Datianhou Temple** (大天后宮; *dàtiānhòu gōng*; daily 5am–9pm), which stands on the location of the Prince of Ningjing's palace, built in 1664. Qing victor Shi Lang eventually converted the palace into a shrine, honouring the goddess he believed had delivered victory in 1683. The current buildings date from 1830.

The atmospheric **Main Hall** is packed with numerous Mazu deities, while the **stele** embedded in the wall to the right was commissioned in 1685 by Shi Lang to commemorate his triumph. The **dragon pillars** here are rare Ming originals from the time of Ningjing – this part of the temple is thought to have served as the private shrine where the last of the Mings would worship his illustrious ancestors. The **Rear Hall** is dedicated to Mazu's parents, previously serving as Ningjing's actual residence but more famous for its grisly association with his concubines – they're supposed to have hanged themselves from the beams above, after hearing of Shi Lang's victory. The shrine to the left of the main hall contains another exceptional **Guanyin** figure, this one black-faced and robed in gold, set, rather majestically, within an attractive grotto.

Tiantan Temple

Dating from 1854, **Tiantan Temple** (天壇; *tiāntán*; daily 5am–10pm) is one of Tainan's most important, around fifteen minutes' walk southeast of Datianhou Temple. Walk back to Yongfu Road and turn right; then turn left at Mincyuan Road; turn right when you come to Jhongyi Road and first left along narrow Lane 84. Despite the name ("Temple of Heaven"), the main building is a fairly typical south Fujian-style temple, with an elaborately carved facade and vivid dragons embellishing the double-eaved gable and hip roof of the Main Hall. The temple is primarily dedicated to the **Jade Emperor**, but operates more like a spiritual department store, with more deities and hosting more festivals than any other in Tainan.

The **Main Hall** is where the Jade Emperor is worshipped and, as is traditional, the god is symbolized by a tablet with his name on it – he's too powerful to be represented by a statue. The **Rear Hall** is crammed with smoke-stained deities: the shrine in the centre is dedicated to the San Guan Dadi, the three imperial officials of Taoism, overseeing heaven, earth and sea, but the hall's most animated occupants are the **fortune tellers** or "Red Head Masters", spirit mediums who are employed to communicate with the gods. Wearing white shirts and vivid red headgear, they usually perform rituals for a minimum donation of NT$100.

Five Canals Cultural Zone

The old merchant quarter west of Simen Road is known as the **Five Canals Cultural Zone** (五條港文化園區; *wǔtiáogǎng wénhuà yuánqū*). The quarter was established beyond the old city walls in the eighteenth century as traders tried to keep up with the retreating lagoon, although the canals are now long gone. Start at **Water Fairy Temple Market**, entering on the eastern side from Guohua Street, opposite Gonghua Street, and you should come to the tiny **Water Fairy Temple** (水仙宮; *shuǐxiāngōng*; daily 6am–9pm), surrounded by a sea of meat and vegetable stalls and dedicated to the five water lords of ancient Chinese tradition. Squeeze inside to view the intricately carved wooden beams and Chinese characters on the back of the pillars flanking the altar; uncovered in 2004, these etchings, which had been covered in plaster for hundreds of years, describe the origin of the temple.

Keep walking due west through the market and you'll emerge onto Haian Road; cross over, and look for narrow **Shennong Street** (神農街; *shénnóng jiē*) to the right. This is perhaps Tainan's most traditional and photogenic street, with ramshackle wooden houses and, at its western end, the **Medicine Lord Temple** (藥王廟; *yàowáng miào*; daily 5am–6pm). This small shrine, established in 1646, commemorates a doctor from the Tang dynasty: his statue sits in the Main Hall, flanked by two pages, one holding medical books, the other a bottle of medicine.

Confucius Temple Cultural Zone

The southern half of the old city falls within the **Confucius Temple Cultural Zone** (孔廟文化園區; *kǒngmiào wénhuà yuánqū*), littered with more temples and historic sights. The **Confucius Temple** (孔子廟; *kǒngzǐmiào*; daily 8.30am–5.30pm; ⓦconfucius.culture.tw) is Taiwan's oldest and most revered Confucian shrine, established in 1666 but rebuilt many times. With its pink and russet-red walls, classical architecture and languid tree-lined forecourt, it's one of the most charming structures in the city, laid out in traditional Confucian style. As you enter from Nanmen Road, the tower in the far right-hand corner is the **Wenchang Pavilion** (文昌閣; *wénchāng gé*; Sat & Sun 9am–noon & 1.30–5.30pm; free, maximum ten people at a time), a three-storey pagoda completed in 1715. You can clamber up the narrow stairs to see the simple shrines to Wenchang Dadi, the god of literature, on the second floor and Kui Dou Xingjun on the top floor. Nearby stands the **Hall of Edification** (明倫堂; *mínglúntáng*), a school for those preparing to take provincial-level exams in the Qing period. The central **Dacheng Hall** (大成殿; *dàchéngdiàn*; NT$25), with its distinctive double-eaved swallowtail roof, is at the heart of the complex. It's simply decorated inside, with just one tablet dedicated to Confucius, inscribed "Great Teacher Spirit Tablet". As is customary, on each side are tablets to his disciples, but what makes this temple unique are the twelve boards hanging from the beams, each beautifully inscribed by various emperors and leaders of Taiwan (see Contexts p.402). Qing dynasty Emperor Kangxi (ruled 1661 to 1722) wrote "Teacher of all Generations" on a black tablet directly above the main shrine; former Kuomintang (KMT) president Chiang Kai-shek wrote the blue tablet to the right of the main altar, while at the front right is the newest offering from current president of Taiwan Ma Ying-jeou (in black). The dark green eulogy from former DPP president Chen Shui-bian is on the front left.

Great South Gate and Wufei Temple

Fifteen minutes' walk south of the temple on Nanmen Road, the **Great South Gate** (大南門; *dànánmén*; daily 8–6pm; free) is the best remaining example of Tainan's old defences. The double gate was completed in 1835 to replace the former wooden stockade. Continue south along Nanmen Road and turn left at Wufei Street to reach the Temple of the Five Concubines, aka **Wufei Temple** (五妃廟; *wǔfēi miào*; daily 8.30am–9pm). Set in a peaceful park, it's dedicated to the five concubines of the Prince of Ningjing, who committed suicide rather than submit to the Qing dynasty in 1683. They were buried here, in what was once a cemetery outside the city walls – the burial mound is behind the temple. The tiny shrine a few metres to the left of the temple is known as the **Yi Ling Jun Shrine** (義靈君祠; *yìlíngjūn cí*) and commemorates the two eunuchs who also committed suicide. From here head up Cianjhong Street, turning right at the junction with Shulin Street, passing the best remaining section of Tainan's old **city wall**. Continue along Shulin Street east from here and you should emerge on Kaishan Road, just south of the Koxinga Shrine.

Koxinga Shrine

Dedicated to the Ming dynasty general still venerated on both sides of the Taiwan Strait, the **Koxinga Shrine** (延平郡王祠; *yánpíng jùnwáng cí*; daily 8am–6.30pm; free) sits in a small park at 125 Kaishan Rd. The shrine is to the right of the park entrance under the memorial arch, and fronted by a massive statue of the general atop a stallion, while the **Koxinga Museum** (daily 9am–5pm; free) is straight ahead. Koxinga died in Tainan in 1662, but his body was eventually returned to China. Local people set up a small shrine on this spot to remember him and an official shrine was built in 1874. The buildings you see today were rebuilt in northern Chinese style in 1963.

The side corridors are lined with tablets commemorating Ming dynasty officials and generals, while the main shrine, complete with a gracious statue of Koxinga surrounded by beautifully carved wood, sits in the centre. The **Rear Hall** contains shrines to Koxinga's Japanese mother (centre) and the Prince of Ningjing (right), while Koxinga's grandson Zheng Kezang is remembered on the left. The **museum** contains two floors of temporary exhibits, usually with a historical theme, although not always connected with Koxinga.

Lady Linshui Temple

Facing the park on the far side of Jianye Street, **Lady Linshui Temple** (臨水夫人廟; *línshuǐ fūrén miào*; daily 6am–8.30pm) is one of Tainan's most popular shrines, particularly with women. The temple was established in 1736 to worship the Birth Goddess, but in 1852, three female deities known as the "three ladies" (*sānnǎifūrén*) were added: Lady Linshui has since become the main deity, worshipped in the incredibly elaborate **Main Hall** and flanked by images of her 36 assistants, three for each month. Linshui is supposed to protect unborn children, babies and pregnant mothers – women often pray here for protection during childbirth.

Dong-an Fang Cultural Zone

A couple of absorbing temples lie to the north of the Koxinga Shrine in the **Dong-an Fang Cultural Zone** (東安坊文化園區; *dōngānfāng wénhuà yuánqū*), both associated with the Chinese underworld. From Kaishan Road follow Chenghuang Street for around 400m to Mincyuan Road and turn right: **Dongyue Temple** (東嶽殿;

The legacy of Koxinga

The life of Zheng Chenggong, traditionally known as **Koxinga** in the West (a bastardization of *guóxìngyé*, an official title given to him by one of the last Ming princes), is a complex mixture of historical fact, myth and politics. Born in 1624 in Japan to a pirate Chinese father and a Japanese mother, he was taken to Fujian in China when he was 7 and given a strict Confucian education. After the fall of the Ming dynasty in 1644, Fujian became the centre of **resistance** to the new Qing rulers and Koxinga rose rapidly through the ranks of the military, gaining honours from various Ming princes and becoming the leader of the entire resistance movement. In 1658 he was defeated in Nanjing, an event that led him to consider a tactical **retreat to Taiwan**, and in 1661 he led a sizeable fleet across the straits to remove the Dutch. Contrary to popular belief, the siege of Fort Zeelandia was characterized by a series of blunders, Koxinga's overwhelmingly superior forces taking nine months to oust the defenders. The general died a few months later in 1662, most likely from malaria and, although he was initially buried in Taiwan his body was taken back to China with his son in 1699. On the island he became known as *kāishān wáng*, "Open Mountain King", for his supposed role in developing infrastructure and opening up the country for Chinese immigrants, and is worshipped as a folk god – there are around 63 temples dedicated to him island-wide.

Today, Koxinga is eulogized not just in Taiwan but also in China (there's a huge statue of him gazing towards the island in Xiamen) for being the only Chinese general to inflict a major defeat on a colonial Western power. Those favouring **unification** claim he was the first to "take back" Taiwan, while Taiwan **independence activists** like to point out that Koxinga's family ruled an independent kingdom that had never been part of the Chinese empire. What's often forgotten in both cases is that Koxinga's brief war with the Dutch was a relatively minor footnote to his epic struggle with the Qing regime in Beijing.

dōngyuè diàn; daily 5.30am–9.30pm) is at no. 110 on the opposite side. Established in 1673, the temple is principally dedicated to the Great Emperor of East Mountain. He decides to which of the eighteen levels of hell to banish sinners, based on the City God's report, and holds court in the **Front Hall**. Dizang Wang occupies the **Middle Hall**, with lurid murals of hell on the walls, while the **Rear Hall**, permanently gloomy and always quiet, is the home of the "Great Emperor of Fengdu" (*fēngdū dàdì*), the deity that rules over hell itself.

Return to Chenghuang Street and continue to the junction with Cingnian Road and you should see the **City God Temple** (城隍廟; *chénghuáng miào*; daily 6am–5pm) on the other side at no. 133. Built in 1669, it's said to be the oldest City God Temple in Taiwan and one of the most traditional, the sombre black tablet hanging from the beams in the **First Hall** reading "Here You Come", meaning everyone will be judged in time. The City God uses an abacus to calculate individual misdeeds – you can see it behind you, hanging above the entrance. Also note the shackles and torture instruments on the back of main pillars here – supposed to be a deterrent to any mischief makers.

National Museum of Taiwanese Literature

Just north of the Confucius Temple on Nanmen Road, and a short walk west of the City God Temple, the **National Museum of Taiwanese Literature** (國家台灣文學館; *guójiā táiwān wénxuéguǎn*; Tues–Sun 10am–9pm; free; Ⓦ www.nmtl.gov.tw) occupies the former City Hall, a striking Neoclassical building built by the Japanese in 1916. It's been beautifully restored and now houses a small exhibition detailing the history of the building and a series of informative display rooms on the development of Taiwanese literature since the Japanese occupation. These are arranged historically and thematically, augmented with examples of prose translated into English (although most explanations are in Chinese); all the major authors are covered, with special sections on **Li Ang** (best-selling feminist writer) and pioneer **Lai He** (one of the first poets to write in Taiwanese).

Anping

Anping (安平; *ānpíng*) is the oldest part of Tainan, and indeed one of the oldest non-indigenous settlements in Taiwan: this is where the Dutch built their first fortress in 1624, and where Koxinga defeated them 38 years later, renaming the area after his hometown in China. It's 4km from Chihkan Tower, best reached via bus #2 (NT$18), #88 or #99 (both free; weekends only) or by taxi (NT$200), but you can also cycle along the Yanshui River.

Anping Fort and around

At the heart of Anping is **Anping Fort** (安平古堡; *ānpíng gǔbǎo*; daily: winter 8.30am–5.30pm, summer 8am–6pm; NT$50), the site of Fort Zeelandia, the first Dutch settlement in Taiwan (the main entrance is on Guosheng Rd, just off Guobao St). The only substantial Dutch remains are parts of the **outer wall** along the road in front of the fort – the imposing redbrick fortifications you see today were built by the Japanese. Check out the **Fort Zeelandia Museum** (熱蘭遮城博物館; *rèlán zhēchéng bówùguǎn*; across from the entrance), which traces the history of the fort and the Dutch presence here, as well as recounting recent archaeological digs. You can clamber up to the top of the fort, where there's a small exhibition room with models of the old fort and a copy of Koxinga's treaty with the Dutch (in Chinese). Bus #2 stops on Anping Road just outside.

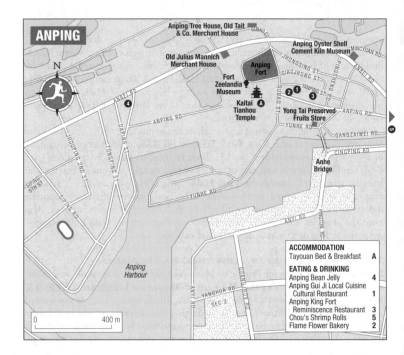

Just south of the fort at 33 Guosheng Rd, **Kaitai Tianhou Temple** (開台天后宮; *kāitái tiānhòugōng*; daily 5am–10pm) was established in 1668 but has been rebuilt many times, most recently in 1994. Its chief claim to fame is the senior Mazu deity inside (the large statue in the middle of the back row): this is said to be one of three images Koxinga brought with him from the holy Mazu shrine at Meizhou in China. Turn left at nearby Anping Road and left again at Gubao Street: the next junction should be narrow **Yanping Street** (延平街; *yánpíng jiē*), the oldest commercial thoroughfare in Taiwan, lined with tourist shops and snack food – it's the best place to eat in Anping (see p.248), although most of the stores are not as old as they seem. The exception is **Yong Tai Sing Preserved Fruits Store** (永泰興蜜餞行; *yǒng tàixīng mìjiànháng*; daily 10.30am–9pm) at no. 84, dating from the Qing dynasty and still producing sticky, sweet snacks (boxes from NT$150). The streets north of here are the best places to see Anping's **"sword lions"** (*ānpíng jiànshī*), elaborate hand-painted images, usually above the doors of tradional houses, of lions with swords in their mouths, thought to protect the occupants.

North Anping

North of the fort, the **Anping Oyster Shell Cement Kiln Museum** (安平蚵灰窯文化館; *ānpíngé huīyáo wénhuàguǎn*; Tues–Sun 9.30am–5pm; free) at 110 Anbei Rd is the only remaining example of what was once a booming industry in Anping: the production of "oyster ash", the key ingredient (along with sugar and sticky rice water) in cement used for building houses. The kiln and main buildings have been expertly restored, with English explanations. Bus #2 (daily), #99 and #88 (both free, weekends only), stop outside.

A twenty-minute walk west along Anbei Road, at 106 Gubao St (the same buses stop here), is the **Anping Tree House** (安平樹屋; *ānpíng shùwū*) and **Old Tait & Co Merchant House** (英商德記洋行; *yīngshāng déjì yángháng*; daily: summer 8am–6pm, winter 8.30am–5.30pm; NT$50). The Tree House is an abandoned warehouse that once belonged to the British *hong* (trading company), just behind an exhibition hall with displays on the Anping area. It is now engulfed by a massive banyan tree making it very picturesque. Other than a small room highlighting the local vegetation, there's not much inside the ruined interior, but walkways take you across the top towards the Yanshui River, where white egrets often feed. The Merchant House, next door, dates from 1867, and houses the excellent **Tayouan Early Settlers Life and Culture Museum**. Displays focus on the Dutch period in Tainan (1624–61), with hands-on exhibits and explanations in English. Upstairs is the rather tacky Taiwan Pioneer History Wax Museum. Not far from here, at 19 Lane 183 just south of Anbei Road, is the **Old Julius Mannich Merchant House** (東興洋行; *dōngxìng yángháng*; Sun–Thurs 10am–10pm, Fri & Sat 10am–midnight; free; ✆06/228-1000), the former premises of this German trading company, now mostly given over to a German-themed **café** which overlooks the water park; sip German beers (NT$110) or nibble sausages (NT$200) in the garden or inside the house itself.

Eternal Golden Castle and around

Around 3km south of Anping Fort at 3 Guangjhou Rd (NT$100 by taxi, or bus #14, #88 at weekends), the **Eternal Golden Castle** (億載金城; *yìzǎi jīnchéng*; daily 8.30am–5.30pm; NT$50) was commissioned by the Qing authorities in 1876. It was designed by French engineers, built with material from Fort Zeelandia and equipped with British cannons, although only one of the artillery pieces you see today is genuine, identified by the gun sight on the barrel in the northeast corner. The fortress saw action in the Sino-French and Japanese wars, but was abandoned during the Japanese occupation. Today, it has been well restored, with plenty of English labelling; clamber over the fortifications and take a trip in one of the pedal-powered "swanboats" (天鵝船; *tiānéchuán*) around the moat (NT$100 for 30min).

Eating

Tainan has a reputation for its traditional **Taiwanese** cuisine: many of its dishes are street favourites that are famous island-wide. *Dānzǐmiàn* (noodles with pork, egg and shrimp) is probably the best-known dish, created in 1895 by hawker Hong Yu Tou – the name recalls the shoulder poles he used to carry the noodles to market, while the brand he created, "Slack Season", is a reference to the slow season for fishermen (typically spring and summer typhoon season), when his noodles were a way to make food last; several shops claim to be descended from his original stall.

Coffin Bread (*guāncáibǎn*, literally "coffin board" in Chinese; hollowed-out thick toast filled with a creamy mix of vegetables and seafood) is another Tainan specialty, a dish concocted in the 1950s when US troops were stationed nearby, but the city's milkfish, eel noodles, oyster omelettes and shrimp rolls are equally renowned. For cheap Western food like burgers or fish and chips, Tainan's pubs are probably your best bet. None of Tainan's four traditional **night markets** is in the centre, although they are worth a visit to sample the city's traditional dishes, particularly coffin bread. **Huayuan Night Market** (花園夜市; *huāyuán yèshì*; Thurs, Sat & Sun) off Haian Road Section 3 and Hewei Road, is the biggest and one of the best in Taiwan.

Chihkan Cultural Zone

Ah-Xia Restaurant 阿霞飯店 (*āxiá fàndiàn*) 7 Lane 84, Jhongyi Rd Sec 2 ☏06/225-6789. Popular with locals, this venerable restaurant serves Chinese banquet-style food with lots of fish and crab on the menu, but is best experienced in a group (in order to sample a good range of dishes). Try the glutinous rice with crab, and assorted cold dishes – a complete set (ten dishes) will be at least NT$6000. Tues–Sun 11am–2.30pm & 4.30–9pm.

Guohua St Sec 3 國華街三段 (*guóhuájiē sānduàn*). South of the junction with Minzu Rd, this street is lined with famous stalls: on the corner at 19 Minzu Rd Sec 3 is *Jinde Spring Rolls* 金得春捲 (*jīndé chūnjuǎn*; daily 7.30am–6pm) with plump spring rolls (*lumpia*) for NT$30, and *Brother Yang Starfruit Juice* 楊哥楊桃湯 (*yánggē yángtáo tāng*) selling tangy starfruit juice next door (NT$10); on the other side, at 181 Guohua St is *A-Song Meat Buns* 阿松割包 (*ā-sōng gēbāo*) selling *guàbāo* (pork in bun with sate sauce, NT$60–80 for two); ask for lean meat (*shòuròu*). Open from 8am until they run out, usually around 5–6pm.

Hong's Noodles 洪芋頭擔仔麵 (*hóngyùtóu dānzǐmiàn*) 273 Simen Rd Sec 2 ☏06/288-1410. Tiny *dānzǐmiàn* shop with small seating area, cooking up excellent noodles with shrimp (NT$45) in the big pot by the door. The stall is named after the inventor of the noodles: the owner is his eldest grandson. Daily 9am–midnight.

Sen Maw Rice Food 森茂碗粿 (*sēnmào wǎnguǒ*) 228 Minzu Rd Sec 2 ☏06/214-3389. Appealing old Tainan diner, with wooden school desks for tables and antiques on the walls, including porcelain bowls signed by Taiwan celebrities. The main dish here is *wah gwui* (in Taiwanese), a tasty meat pudding with pork, egg and mushroom (NT$30). English menu. Daily 9am–9pm.

Shantou Fish Noodles 汕頭魚麵 (*shàntóu yúmiàn*) 158 Minsheng Rd Sec 1, between Simen and Yongfu roads ☏06/221-5997. Addictive hand-cut noodles served with fragrant fish balls (NT$30–40). Daily 10am–9pm. Grab some green tomatoes in special sauce or "eight treasures" (*bābāobīng tsuàbīng*) from *Bing Xiang* 冰鄉 (*bīngxiāng*) at no. 160 next door.

Zai Fa Hao 再發號 (*zàifāháo*) 71 Mincyuan Rd Sec 2 ☏06/222-3577. Best place to sample *zòngzi* (sticky rice wrapped in bamboo leaves), with tasty mushroom and fresh pork fillings served in an old, no-nonsense store (NT$50). Daily 9am–8.30pm.

Confucius Temple Cultural Zone

Dream of Chrysanthemums 夢東籬 (*mèngdōnglí*) 86 Cingjhong St ☏06/213-1090. Classical-style restaurant offering good-value *ramen* (noodles) a and a variety of Chinese and aboriginal dishes like betel nut chicken (NT$90–150), just north of Wufei Temple. Daily 10am–1am.

Fu Ji Meatballs 福記肉圓 (*fújì ròuyuán*) 215 Fucian Rd Sec 1 ℡06/215-7157. Close to *Lily Fruits* and opposite the Confucius Temple, this old shop sells delicious pork meatballs (*bah-wán*), in a glutinous rice wrapping – the slightly spicy sauce is delicious (NT$35 for two). No English menus. Daily 6.30am–6.30pm.

Go Dutch Café 18-1 Weimin St ℡06/209-3432. Chilled-out backpacker café with comfy sofas, free internet access and lots of secondhand books. Decent coffee, breakfasts, pasta and pizza on offer: from the train station cross the rail line via the underpass at Beimen Rd and Weimin St – the café is behind you next to *Malibu* pub. Wed–Mon 9am–3pm.

Lily Fruits 莉莉水果店 (*lìlì shuǐguǒ diàn*) 199 Fucian Rd Sec 1 ℡06/213-7522. Tainan's most famous *tsuàbīng* (shaved-ice) stall since 1947 (second generation), as well as an incredible range of fresh tropical fruits including guava, star fruit and mangoes served sliced, as juice, with soybean pudding or on ice (NT$30–50). Traditional red bean toppings also served along with indulgent banana and chocolate. Daily 11am–11pm.

Imma Bakery & Café 322 Shulin St Sec 2 ℡06/214-2102. This Israeli-Taiwanese bakery created quite a buzz when it opened in 2009, bringing real, freshly made bread, pies, baguettes, pastries and cookies to Tainan for the first time – the café section is a great place to sip Lavazza coffee. Wed–Mon 9am–10pm.

Narrow Door Café 窄門咖啡 (*zhǎimén kāfēi*) 2/F, 67 Nanmen Rd ℡06/211-0508. This lovely old Japanese-era house, with wooden floors and tables, is one of the most atmospheric cafés in town, with great views of the Confucius Temple; coffees/teas from NT$120, snacks and cakes from NT$60, with excellent Hakka spicy chicken for NT$280 and Hakka DIY *léichá* (cereal tea) for NT$150. Enter through the tiny passageway (a real squeeze at 38cm wide) at 67 Nanmen Rd – the name actually comes from an André Gide novel, though. English menu. Daily 11am–11.30pm.

Tu Hsiao Yueh (Slack Season Tan Tsai Noodles) 度小月擔仔麵 (*dùxiǎoyuè dānzǐmiàn*) 16 Jhongjheng Rd ℡06/223-1744. At the *dānzǐmiàn* store owned by the fourth generation of the founder's family and still bearing the name of his stall, the eponymous dish (NT$50) is cooked up on a traditional stove near the entrance – with low stools and wooden tables, it's a photogenic place. Also does classic grilled milkfish (NT$130), meatballs (NT$35) and braised duck eggs (NT$15). Tues–Sun 11.30am–10pm.

Yong Ji Milkfish Balls 永記虱目魚丸 (*yǒngjì shīmù yúwán*) 82 Kaishan Rd ℡06/222-3325.

This 85-year-old shop serves excellent *lǚròufàn* and fish-ball soup, and is justly lauded for its milkfish (*shīmùyú*) and sweet *hóngchá* (black tea). Note the early closing time. Daily 6.30am–1pm.

Yonghua Road

Geng Du Yuan 耕讀園 (*gēngdúyúan*) 23 Yonghua Rd Sec 2 ℡06/295-0099. A bit of a trek, but one of the most elegant classical teahouses of this Taichung chain, set in an atmospheric wooden building with cosy booths, goldfish pond and excellent pots of tea from NT$200, or NT$90 per person. Daily 10am–2am.

Water Drop Teahouse 滴水坊 (*dīshuǐfāng*) 168 Yonghua Rd Sec 2 ℡06/293-2188. Cheap, expertly prepared Buddhist vegetarian food, inside the Tainan branch of Foguanshan Monastery. Main dishes around NT$100, with plenty of fine teas. Tues–Sun 11am–8pm.

Anping

Anping Bean Jelly 安平豆花 (*ānpíng dòuhuā*) 433 Anbei Rd ℡06/391-5385. Spacious canteen-style place knocking out delicious soybean pudding, or *dòuhuā* (NT$30), for over fifty years: try it with lemon juice or red beans. The downside is location – it's a short taxi ride or a 20m walk from Anping Fort. Daily 9am–11pm.

Anping Gui Ji Local Cuisine Cultural Restaurant 安平貴記地方美食文化館 (*ānpíng guìjì dìfāng měishí wénhuàguǎn*) 93 Yanping St ℡06/222-9794. Rustic tables and tiny stools with simple menu of Tainan favourites including coffin bread (NT$50) and shrimp dumplings (NT$45); get a set (NT$100–160) for a taster of all the main dishes (including Chou's shrimp rolls; NT$50). English menu. Daily 11am–8pm.

Anping King Fort Reminiscence Restaurant 安平王城懷舊館 (*ānpíng wángchéng huáijiùguǎn*) 4 Lane 104, Yanping St ℡0931/838-553. Gorgeous old Chinese teahouse in the shade of a banyan tree, just off the main drag. Sip juices, coffees or teas (NT$40–60) or order pork fat rice and chicken leg in the garden or inside where old Chinese songs echo through the halls (live classical music Sat & Sun). No English. Wed–Mon 11am–8pm.

Chou's Shrimp Rolls 周氏蝦捲 (*zhōushì xiājuǎn*) 408 Anping Rd ℡06/280-1304. Tainan institution cooking up sublime shrimp rolls, lightly fried in batter tempura-style (NT$50 for two), and bowls of delicious noodles (NT$40). It has a fast-food-style system with two floors of seating and a posh restaurant on the third floor. Halfway to Anping from downtown: taxis should be NT$150 from the station. No English menu (photos only). Daily 10am–10pm.

Flame Flower Bakery 鳳凰花餅鋪 (*fènghuáng huābǐngpù*) 774 Anping Rd ☎06/220-8753. Cake shop with over 100 years of history (opened in 1895), most lauded for its *pèng bǐng*, sweet, round cakes made with egg and fried in sesame oil (NT$25). Daily 10am–10pm.

Drinking and nightlife

Tainan has plenty of bars and even a couple of decent nightclubs, although it tends to be quiet during the week. **Haian Road Section 2** (海安路二段; *hǎiānlù èrduàn*) between Minsheng and Fucian is the current nightlife district, lined with chilled out bars and cafés with open-air seating.

Armory 兵工廠 (*bīnggōng chǎng*) 82 Gongyuan S Rd ☎06/226-9520. Laid-back, two-floor pub with wooden floors, popular with expats and Taiwanese for its satellite TV (live sports events), live bands and dance nights. Bottled beer (from NT$100) and cocktails (NT$150) accompany a respectable menu of Chinese and Western comfort food. Daily 8pm–5am.

Cosby Saloon 1/F-20, 128 Gongyuan Rd (entrance at Lane 40, Chenggong Rd) ☎06/228-6332. Expat stalwart with a motorcycle theme, at the end of what's known as Pub Alley (it boasts several different watering holes to stumble between). *Cosby* is always good for beer, and is known for its juicy steaks and burgers, certainly the best NYC strip steak this side of Taipei. Daily 6pm–1.30am.

Dirty Roger Pub 141 Dongmen Rd Sec 1 ☎06/274-7003. The best thing about this pub, a Tainan institution, is the huge collection of records lining the walls – if you see something you'd like to hear, ask the owner and he's likely to put it on. There's table football upstairs. Daily 1pm–4am.

Fusion 483 Yonghua Rd Sec 2. Tainan's top dance club, with decent DJs and packed party nights: music is predominantly funky house, breakbeat or trance. Cover ranges NT$300–450. Mon & Wed–Sat 10pm–4am.

Suck Lounge Bar 92 Sinmei St ☎06/226-0045. Cosy lounge bar with comfy sofas, curtains and big TV screen, cocktails and beers. Look for the rusted doors and grey slate walls, just south of Mincyuan Rd. Daily 8pm–3am (4.30am Fri & Sat).

Willy's Second Base Bar & Grill 葳苙二壘酒吧 (*wēilì èrlěi jiǔbā*) 321 Jiankang Rd Sec 2 ☎06/291-1050. Slightly upmarket sports bar with free wi-fi, 1980s table-top video games, pool table upstairs and excellent food: pizzas, burgers and Tex-Mex classics. Shows all the major sports events on huge TV screen. Tues–Sun 7pm–3am.

Listings

Airlines China Airlines Rm A, 6/F, 358 Dongmen Rd Sec 1 ☎06/235-7861; EVA Air ☎06/222-6688; Far Eastern Air Transport ☎06/290-4419; TransAsia Airways ☎06/267-0367; Uni Air ☎06/260-2811.

Banks Most 7-Elevens have Chinatrust ATMs, and Citibank has a branch at 83 Yongfu Rd Sec 2 (☎06/226-2500).

Bicycle rental Tainan is fast developing a bicycle-path network, especially around Anping; you can rent bikes at the Koxinga Shrine, Chihkan Tower, Eternal Gold Castle, Anping Tree House and Anping Fort (daily 9am–5pm; NT$50/4hr), and drop them off at any of the above locations.

Books Caves Books 敦煌書局 (*dūnhuáng shūjú*) at 159 Beimen Rd Sec 1 (daily 10.30am–9.30pm) has a good selection of English-language books on the fourth floor; Books & Cultural Souvenirs of Taiwanese Heritage 台灣建築與文化資產出版社 (*táiwān jiànzhú yǔ wénhuà zīchǎn chūbǎnshè*) at 57 Nanmen Rd has some English books (Mon–Fri 2–9pm, Sat–Sun 10am–9pm), across from the Confucius Temple; Chin Wan Tze 金萬字 (*jīnwànzì*) at 6 Jhongyi Rd Sec 2 (nr Youai St) is a famous secondhand bookstore, with some books and magazines (such as *Time* and *National Geographic*) in English (Tues–Sun 10am–10pm).

Car Rental Car Plus (daily 8am–9.30pm; ☎0800/222-568 or 06/600-0006, Ⓦwww.car-plus.com.tw) or Hotai Leasing 和運租車 (*héyùn zūchē*; ☎0800/024-550 or 06/602-5599, Ⓦwww.easyrent.com.tw) are both at the High-Speed Rail Station. Car Plus also has an office in town at 115 Beimen Rd Sec 2 (☎06/223-5566).

Cinema Vieshow Cinemas 威秀影城 (*wēixiù yǐngchéng*) 8/F, 60 Gongyuan Rd (inside FE21 mall); Shin Kong Cineplex 新光影城 (*xīnguāng yǐngchéng*) 7/F, 658 Simen Rd Sec 1 (inside New Life Square).

Moving on from Tainan

Tainan Airport (℡06/260-1016) has regular **flights** to Kinmen and Magong via Uni Air, while express trains run along the west-coast line to Taipei (NT$738), Chiayi (NT$141) and Kaohsiung (NT$107) throughout the day. **High Speed Rail** services depart from the special station at Gueiren (see p.237). Free shuttles leave from the city bus station opposite the train station (daily 5.45–10.50am; every 20min; 30–40min). High-speed trains to Taipei cost NT$1145 and take 1hr 45min; Taichung is NT$550 and just 45min, but for Kaohsiung or Chiayi it's faster to take regular trains.

Most long-distance **buses** depart from offices on the left side of Beimen Road Section 3, north of the train station: Ho Hsin (℡06/227-0772) at no. 25 operates services to Taipei at regular 30min intervals (24hrNT; $380–600): Taichung (NT$110) and Chiayi (NT$160) buses leave from a second Ho Hsin office a few shops up the road at no. 49. Kuo Kuang at no. 43 also has Taichung (NT$100) and Taipei (NT$220) buses, while Ubus at no. 71 offers 24hr services to Taipei (NT$220) and Taichung (NT$100).

At least one bus every hour (daily 6.15am–8.40pm) departs the Singnan bus station at 182 Jhongshan Rd (℡06/222-3142) to the **Southwest Coast National Scenic Area**, including Nankunshen (NT$120) and Beimen (NT$112). For other destinations in Tainan county it's best to have your own transport. **Ferries** to Penghu no longer run from Tainan; you'll have to go via Budai (see p.339) or Kaohsiung (see p.254).

Hospital English-speaking staff and doctors can be found at National Cheng Kung University Hospital 成大醫院 (*chéngdà yīyuàn*) at 138 Shengli Rd (℡06/235-3535).

Internet access *More Café* at 129 Beimen Rd Sec 1, a short stroll from the station offers free wi-fi and two terminals (NT$25/hr). It's open 24hr and is a real café too (coffee NT$45).

Post The main post office is at 6 Chenggong Rd, not far from the train station.

Scooter Rental Try Chien Feng 前鋒機車出租 (*qiánfēng jīchēchūzū*) at 202 Cianfong Rd (daily 7am–10pm; ℡06/234-9722). You'll have to show a driving licence and passport. Take the underpass under the train station (just left of the exit) and as you emerge it's the shop opposite. Weekend prices are NT$450–600 (for a 50–125cc bike) for 24hr, but during the week you should pay around NT$250–350.

Shopping Beimen St 北門街 (*běiménjiē*), south of the train station is the city's computer bazaar, while the best department stores are FE21 Mega at 60 Gongyuan Rd and 210 Cianfong Rd, and the enormous New Life Square (Shinkong Mitsukoshi) at 658 Simen Rd Sec 1. There's even a 24hr Carrefour at 16 Jhonghua W Rd Sec 2. Tainan Kuang Tsai Embroidery Shop 光彩繡莊 (*guāngcǎi xiùzhuāng*) at 186-3 Yongfu Rd Sec 2 (opposite the Official God of War Temple), is full of brightly coloured fabrics used in temple festivals, clothing and puppets since 1941 – visitors are welcome to look around and take photos.

The southwest coast

Encompassing the flat, marshy stretch of coast between Tainan and the Hukou Wetlands in Yunlin county, the Taijiang National Park and **Southwest Coast National Scenic Area** (南濱海國家風景區; *nánbīnhǎi guójiā fēngjǐngqū*; Ⓦ www .swcoast-nsa.gov.tw) contain some of Taiwan's most important and oldest **religious sites**, remnants of a once thriving **salt industry** and hundreds of oyster farms which make for superb **seafood** and birdwatching.

Taijiang National Park

Taijiang National Park (台江國家公園; *táijiāng guójiā gōngyuán*; Ⓦ www.tjnp .gov.tw) is Taiwan's eighth national park and covers the coastline immediately north of Anping, from the south bank of the Yanshui River to Qingshan Fishing

Without a car, the best way to see the **national park**, which has around 30km of bike trails, is to rent a **bicycle** in Anping (p.250), or take a boat ride: pontoon **boats** depart from the Yanshui River, just across the bridge from Anping via a narrow lane on the right. Trips take in the main wetland areas, but you must book ahead (℡06/284-1709; NT$180 for 90min). You'll also need a car to make the most of the **scenic area**, but **Singnan Bus** near Tainan station (see p.251) runs a service to Nankunshen via Jiali, Xuejia and Beimen (the entire trip can take over two hours).

Harbour, overlapping with the Southwest Coast National Scenic Area at its northern end. The park is very much a work in progress – visit the temporary headquarters at 2 Chengping Rd, Anping (℡06/391-0000) or check the website for updates. It will be of most interest to ornithologists – the area is particularly noted for the endangered **black-faced spoonbill** (*hēimiàn pílù*) – although there is also plenty of history to explore. You can visit the **Salt Pan Ecological and Cultural Village** (鹽田生態文化村; *yántián shēngtài wénhuàcūn*; Mon–Fri 8am–5.30pm; free; bus #10 or #99 Sat & Sun) at 12 Lane 101, Dajhong St, which features salt-making demonstrations (NT$150), and the nearby **Taijiang Cetacean Museum** (台江鯨豚館; *táijiāng jīngtúnguǎn*; daily 8.30am–5.30pm; free), with two enormous sperm whale skeletons, a preserved whale heart (like a boulder) and whale testis (like a log) on display.

Not far from here is the phenomenal **Orthodox Luerhmen Holy Mother Temple** (正統鹿耳門聖母廟; *zhèngtǒng lùěrmén shèngmǔmiào*; daily 4am–9pm; bus #10), one of the largest temples in the world and certainly the biggest dedicated to Mazu.

Qigu Salt Mountains

The coastline north of Tainan is littered with salt pans, most abandoned after the industry collapsed in the 1990s. A few kilometres west of the town of **Qigu** (七股; *qīgǔ*) on County Route 176 you'll see the two pyramid towers of the **Taiwan Salt Museum** (台灣鹽博物館; *táiwānyán bówùguǎn*; Mon–Fri 9am–5pm, Sat & Sun 9am–5.30pm; NT$130; ⊚www.taiwan-salt.com.tw) and the famous salt mountains beyond. The museum has three floors of innovative displays covering the salt-making process and the history of the area, and even a mock Polish salt mine, but there are no English labels. The two **Qigu Salt Mountains** (七股鹽山; *qīgǔ yánshān*; daily 9am–6pm; NT$50, NT$100 with car; ℡06/780-0511; ⊚cigu .tybio.com.tw) comprise one sixty-thousand-ton, 20m-high pile, now dirty brown and scaled via a path cut into the rock-hard sodium crystals, and a slighly smaller mound of imported salt from Australia, pristine white and treated like snow by frolicking tourists. Although the area is a bit of a carnival at the weekends, with stalls selling surprisingly tasty **salt popsicles** in smoked plum, egg yolk and almond walnut flavours (NT$15), and even a pool where you can float, Dead Sea-like, in the brine, it's one of the most bizarre sights in Taiwan and worth the trek out. You'll need your own transport, or get a taxi from the bus station in **Jiali** (佳里; *jiālǐ*).

Ciji Temple

The small town of **XUEJIA** (學甲; *xuéjiǎ*) is the home of **Ciji Temple** (慈濟宮; *cíjì gōng*; daily 5am–10pm), noted for its exceptional artwork and great religious significance. Established in 1703, it is the oldest shrine to Baosheng Dadi (see p.406) in Taiwan. The most important deity in the **Main Hall** was brought to Taiwan by Koxinga in 1661 – it's said to be 800 years old, one of three originals made in China after the death of Baosheng in 1037 and now the only one in existence: it's the small statue in front of the biggest image, slightly to the right. The temple also contains over two hundred rare works of *koji*, some made by master Yeh Wang in the 1860s (see p.217) – the most important are encased in glass on the right side of the Main Hall. The temple is at 170 Jisheng Rd near Zhongzheng Road, a short walk from the bus station.

Beimen

The tiny village of **BEIMEN** (北門; *běimén*), 9km west of Xuejia, is the headquarters of the Scenic Area administration and visitor centre (daily 8.30am–5.30pm; ℡06/786-1000), where you can pick up maps and information. The Nankunshen bus stops in the centre of the village. Around 5km to the south, the village of Sanliaowan (三寮灣; *sānliáowān*) on County Route 174 is home to the informative **Wang Ye Culture Gallery** (王爺信仰文物館; *wángyé xìnyǎng wénwùguǎn*; daily 9am–5pm; NT$100; ℡06/785-0355), which contains some interesting exhibits and camphor models of *wángchuán* ("spirit ships"; labelled only in Chinese; see Contexts p.404). It's a twenty-minute walk from the nearest Tainan–Nankunshen bus stop.

Nankunshen

Three kilometres north of Beimen, in the equally small village of **NANKUNSHEN** (南鯤身; *nánkūnshēn*) lies the **Nankunshen Da Tian Temple** (南鯤身大天府; *nánkūnshēn dàtiānfǔ*; daily 5am–10pm). It's the most important shrine in southern Taiwan and the centre of Wang Ye worship (see Contexts p.404) on the island, heading an organization of around seven thousand branch temples. Established in 1662 and rebuilt on this site in 1817, the temple is dedicated to five senior Wang Ye gods: Li, Tsi, Wu, Chu and Fan, each with their own birthday and special annual festival attracting thousands of pilgrims (the biggest is on Lunar April 26 and 27). The original wooden statues of the gods are said to have arrived by unmanned boat, miraculously driven by the wind from China in the early seventeenth century and have since ensured the fishermen in the village abundant catches, good health and all-round prosperity.

Today the temple is part of a massive religious complex of halls, ponds and gardens, well worth exploring despite ongoing restoration, with the five gods housed in the **Main Hall** in the centre. If you get stuck here, *Kang Lang Villa* (槺榔懷古; *kānglàng huáigǔ*; ℡06/786-3711; ❺) is a pleasant place to stay the night: it's a guesthouse for pilgrims built in classical Fujian style with basic but comfortable

Yanshui beehive fireworks

An otherwise sleepy town, a short drive inland from Nankunshen, **YANSHUI** (鹽水 *yánshuǐ*) attracts thousands to its annual **firework festival** (鹽水蜂炮; *yánshuǐ fēngpào*) one of Taiwan's most famous. What makes this pyrotechnic display unique is that the fireworks – lodged in over two hundred walls or "beehives" the size of a truck – are fired horizontally into the crowds creating a cacophony of noise, fire and smoke throughout the night. Protective gear is essential if you want to participate but note that the crowds can be suffocating: around 300,000 people attend. The tradition began in 1885 when locals paraded an image of Guan Di around the town to ward off a cholera epidemic; their prayers were answered only after shooting off a ton of fireworks to "wake" the god. Each year during the Lantern Festival, usually in February, Guan Di is once again paraded around the town before the fiery climax. **Buses** from Chiayi Transport Co Bus Station to Yanshui depart 6am–8pm hourly (NT$97).

rooms. Unless it's a festival expect a quiet stay: there are no TVs and no breakfast, just the snack stalls in the village and around the temple.

Kaohsiung and around

Taiwan's second city, and one of the largest container ports in the world, **KAOHSIUNG** (高雄; *gāoxióng*) has undergone a dramatic metamorphosis in recent years, from polluted industrial centre of two million people to green city of lush parks, waterside cafés, art galleries and museums – all linked by a spanking new transport system.

The older districts of **Zuoying**, **Yancheng** and **Cijin Island** contain plenty of historic sights and traditional snack stalls, while modern Kaohsiung is best taken in with an evening stroll along the **Love River** or a visit to soaring **85 Sky Tower** close to its bustling **shopping districts**. To take a break from the city, hike up to the ridge of hills known as **Chaishan**, home of Kaohsiung's famously capricious troupe of monkeys.

Some history

The oldest parts of Kaohsiung are Cihou Village on **Cijin Island**, established in the early seventeenth century, and the suburb of **Zuoying**, created by Koxinga in the 1660s as county capital, a position it maintained until the late eighteenth century. Cihou, and the harbour as a whole, was known as Takau (or Takow), and remained a sleepy backwater until the port was opened up to foreign companies by the Treaty of Beijing in 1860, attracting merchants eager to exploit the south's growing export trade in sugar. Foreign trade had its dark side however: by the time the Japanese had assumed control of the city in 1895, a quarter of adult males in the south were addicted to opium. The Japanese imposed an Opium Monopoly in 1897, which effectively destroyed Western dominance of the sugar trade. They also began a major modernization programme, completing the harbour and docks in 1908 and opening the Takau Ironworks, Taiwan's first iron and steel mill, in 1919. Although the city was heavily bombed by US Air Force planes in 1945, the port was rebuilt and by the late 1970s Kaohsiung was Taiwan's premier industrial centre. In 1979 the **Kaohsiung Incident** was a defining moment in Taiwan's struggle for democracy (see box opposite), and today the city is a DPP stronghold.

Kaohsiung's **name** is worth explaining: Takau is thought to derive from a Makatau aboriginal word meaning "bamboo fence"; when this was transliterated into Chinese characters it read "beat the dog" (*dǎgǒu*), and in 1920 the Japanese changed the characters to the less offensive "Tall Hero", with the Japanese pronunciation "Takao". After 1949 the city became known by the Mandarin pronunciation of these characters.

Arrival

Kaohsiung International Airport (高雄國際航空站; *gāoxióng guójì hángkōng zhàn*) is a few kilometres south of the city centre, connected to the main train station via KMRT (NT$35) and by a regular bus service (every 15min; NT$12) or taxi (NT$250). The airport has international and domestic terminals, with several banks and ATM machines; the former also has a visitor information centre (daily 9am–12.30am; ☏07/805-7888) in the arrival hall, which can provide information on hotels, sights, and transport. Ho Hsin runs buses direct from the airport to Chiayi; change at the central bus station for other destinations. Buses to Taitung stop at the airport at 12.20am and 3.20am.

The Kaohsiung Incident

The **Kaohsiung Incident** (高雄事件; *gāoxióng shìjiàn*) of December 1979 was a political watershed, often regarded as the beginning of Taiwan's democratic revolution. Opposition to Taiwan's one-party state had been growing in the 1970s and, in an apparent concession, President Chiang Ching-kuo had agreed to hold legislative elections in 1979 – but at the last minute, he cancelled them. On Human Rights Day (Dec 10) a rally was organized in Kaohsiung in protest, the activists spurred on by the arrest the night before of two workers for *Meilidao* ("Formosa" in English), a clandestine publication that was a focus for dissidents. Things quickly got out of hand as police were brought in to disperse the crowds, and violent scuffles ensued. In the aftermath, almost every member of the unofficial opposition was arrested, culminating in the trial, in 1980, of the "**Kaohsiung Eight**" for sedition. Most were jailed for lengthy periods, but the trial was widely publicized and as a result the defendants garnered a great deal of sympathy, ultimately creating a wider base for democratic reform.

Today, the list of those involved reads like a "Who's Who" of Taiwanese politics, many becoming leaders of the **Tangwai** (*dāngwài*; Outside Party) movement and later the Democratic Progressive Party: Chen Shui-bian (president 2000–08) and Frank Hsieh (former Kaohsiung mayor and premier) were lawyers on the defence team, while Annette Lu (vice-president 2000–08), Lin Yi-hsiung (former leader of the DPP) and Shih Ming-teh (ex-DPP chairman and political activist) served five to ten years in jail. Although no one died during the incident, Lin's mother and twin 7-year-old daughters were murdered while he was in prison, a case that remains unsolved.

Kaohsiung Train Station (高雄火車站; *gāoxióng huǒchēzhàn*) is at the northern end of the city centre: the KMRT (metro) station entrance is just outside, allowing speedy connections to the rest of the city. City buses leave from the terminal outside where it's also easy to catch a taxi. Most long-distance **buses** terminate along Jianguo Road close to the train station (see p.265).

The **High-Speed Rail Station** (高鐵左營站; *gāotiě zuǒyíng zhàn*) is in the northern district of Zuoying at 105 Gaotie Rd, 5km north of downtown, but with easy access to the Zuoying KMRT station (NT$35 into the city) and the train station at **Xinzuoying** (新左營火車站; *xīnzuǒyíng huǒchēzhàn*). Taxis into the city will be around NT$200–250.

City transport

Kaohsiung's sights are scattered all over the city so you'll need to use public transport to get around; most streets are clearly marked in *tōngyòng pīnyīn* at junctions. The city **metro** or KMRT (高雄捷運; *gāoxióng jiéyùn*; Ⓦ www.krtco .com.tw) is the best way to get around, although it doesn't go everywhere. Two lines, **Red** and **Orange**, crisscross the city (meeting at Formosa Boulevard), from Gangshan in the north to the airport and Siaogang in the south, and from Sizihwan in the west to Daliao in the eastern suburbs. Buy single tokens (NT$20–60 depending on distance) from machines in the station. Sample fares from the train station are NT$25 to the High-Speed Rail Station, NT$20 to Sizihwan and NT$35 to the airport.

The **Kaohsiung City Bus Station** (高雄市公共汽車站; *gāoxióngshì gōnggòng qìchēzhàn*) is in front of the train station: timetables are in Chinese, but you can look for bus numbers and bilingual destinations on the front of the buses. Bus #248 (History Museum, Hamasen and Gushan Ferry Pier) and #100 (Liouhe Night Market, 85 Sky Tower and Sogo) depart from here. Fares are NT$12 (exact change required). **Taxis** are plentiful and reasonable: initial fare is NT$85. Driving isn't recommended within the city, but you can **rent cars** at the airport or High-Speed Rail Station to explore further afield (see p.265). Kaohsiung scooter operators only rent to those with a local licence.

Information

Kaohsiung has several **tourist offices** scattered around the city, with convenient branches in the train station (daily 10am–7pm; ☎07/236-2710), airport (daily 9am–12.30am; ☎07/805-7888), on the Love River at Hedong Road and Minsheng Road (inside the fish statue; daily 1–10pm; ☎07/221-0768) and at the High-Speed Rail Station (daily 9am–7pm; ☎07/588-0768). There are also branches on Cijin Island (see p.260) and at Lotus Lake (see p.261).

Accommodation

Kaohsiung has plenty of budget **hotels** around the train station and, for those with a bigger budget, a reasonable selection of mid-range options scattered across the newer downtown districts, all of which have wi-fi or broadband (ADSL) ports in the rooms and, for those without laptops, computer rooms where you can check email.

Around the station

Hotel Kindness 康橋商旅 (*kāngqiáo shānglǚ*) 44 Jianguo 3rd Rd ☎07/969-8899. Excellent budget option with branches all over the city; this one is near the train station. Rooms are small but modern, spotless and equipped with comfy doubles, flat-screen TVs, free wi-fi and a small desk. The bathrooms feature massage showers. Buffet breakfast included. ❹

Hotel New Image 喜悦商務大飯店 178 Cisian 2nd Rd ☎07/286-3033, ⓦwww.image-hotel.com. tw. Classical Chinese decor in the larger rooms adds a bit of character to this otherwise standard but comfortable mid-range option, not far from the station (with LCD TVs and breakfast included). It is worth upgrading to the Japanese-style rooms which have beds on wooden floors. ❻.

Hotel Skoal 世國商旅 (*shìguó shānglǚ*) 64 Minjhuheng Rd ☎07/287-6151, ⓦwww .skoalhotel.com.tw. Decent budget hotel, with basic rooms from NT$1600 – small but clean and modern. Includes breakfast, and within walking distance of the station. ❹

Union Hotel 國統大飯店 (*guótǒng dàfàndiàn*) 295 Jianguo 2nd Rd ☎07/235-0101, ⓦwww .unionhotel.tw. Popular option with travellers looking for somewhere cheap near the station, with doubles from NT$800 and twins NT$1000. English is spoken, but breakfast is not included and some rooms are showing their age. ❷

Downtown

Grand Hi-Lai Hotel 漢來大飯店 (*hànlái dàfàndiàn*) 266 Chenggong 1st Rd ☎07/216-1766, ⓦwww.grand-hilai.com.tw. Luxurious hotel offering rooms with Neoclassical decor and floors loaded with Chinese and Western *objets d'art*; don't miss the impressive collection of calligraphy on the eighth and tenth floors and *Lobster Bar* on the 45th. Located in Kaohsiung's third-highest building, the entrance is at the back. ❼

The Splendor 高雄金典酒店 (*gāoxióng jīndiǎn jiǔdiàn*) 1 Zihciang 3rd Rd ☎07/566-8000, ⓦwww.gfk.com.tw. The top luxury choice in the city, thanks to its deluxe rooms and magnificent views: the hotel occupies floors 37 to 79 of the 85 Sky Tower. There's also a ladies-only floor and a range of classy restaurants and bars – enjoy the sunset at *75 Lounge* on the 75th floor. The entrance is on Singuang Rd; check-in on the 39th floor. ❼

Urban Hotel 33 高雄商旅 (*gāoxióng shānglǚ*) 35 Minzu 2nd Rd ☎07/223-1333, ⓦwww.han-hsien.com.tw/urban. Not quite the flashy boutique hotel it aspires to be but the cheaper "elegance section" is comfortable enough. Upgrade to a "chic" room for smart, contemporary decor, free internet, kimono robes and an LCD screen. ❼

Yancheng and the Love River

Ambassador Hotel 國賓大飯店 (*guóbīn dàfàndiàn*) 202 Minsheng 2nd Rd ☎07/211-5211, ⓦwww.ambassadorhotel.com.tw. Kaohsiung's first five-star, offering luxurious rooms with views of the Love River. Discounts of up to forty percent can make this a good deal, especially given the location, although standard singles are a little small – and there are lots of tour groups here.

Free bikes and huge buffet breakfast are nice perks, but internet access is NT$200/24hr. **7**

Hotel Kingdom 華王大飯店 (*huáwáng dàfàndiàn*) 42 Wufu 4th Rd ☎07/551-8211, ⓦwww.hotelkingdom.com.tw. Comfortable if a little overpriced hotel with free internet and flat-screen TVs in all the rooms. Popular with upmarket tour groups, its location in the heart of the old pub district is excellent and conveniently close to the Love River. **7**

The City

Kaoshiung's best hotels, shops and restaurants are scattered around the downtown area, dominated by the colossal **85 Sky Tower**, the ideal place to get your bearings. You'll find a collection of historic sights in the older, western parts of the city; explore **Yancheng** and the **Love River**, before taking the ferry to **Cijin Island**. With more time, there's plenty to see on the slopes of **Gushan** to the west, and around **Lotus Lake** in **Zuoying** to the north.

85 Sky Tower

One of Taiwan's iconic buildings, the **85 Sky Tower** (高雄85大樓; *gāoxióng 85 dàlóu*) looms 347.5m over downtown Kaohsiung, its striking two-legged structure based on the Chinese character 高 (*gāo*), meaning tall – it was the tallest building in Taiwan from 1997 until 2003 when Taipei 101, also designed by C.Y. Lee, was completed. The 74th-floor viewing deck (daily 8am–midnight; NT$100) provides a mesmerizing panorama of the city and the harbour, especially at night. From the train station bus #100 passes the tower as it runs down Sanduo Road.

The Love River and Kaohsiung Harbour

The banks of **Kaohsiung Harbour** and **Love River** (愛河; *àihé*) on the western edge of the city centre have become spruced-up promenades in recent years, with the area between Jhongjheng and Wufu roads lined with open-air cafés and parks. The solar-powered "Love Boats" (愛之船; *àizhīchuán*; daily 4–11pm; every 15min; NT$80) that run up and down the river for twenty minutes between Kaohsiung and Jianguo bridges (with stops at the *Ambassador Hotel*, Renai Park and Music Center) are extremely popular at the weekends, but you can also take ferries from **Love Pier** (愛碼頭; *ài mǎtóu*) and the river mouth to Cijin Ferry Pier (旗津渡輪; *qíjīn dùlún*; Sat & Sun, hols 10am–8pm, every 40min, returning 10.20am–8.20pm; NT$20) or to Cijin Fishing Port (旗津漁港; *qíjīn yúgǎng*; Sat & Sun 11am–9pm; NT$150) further south, effectively making a tour of the harbour. At the fishing port you can see the fish market and wind-turbine park. Another option is to rent a bike and explore the bicycle paths that ring the harbour, along old rail tracks from Pier 1 to Pier 22, or along the Love River all the way to Lotus Lake (see p.264 for details of the **Kaohsiung City Public Bike** scheme).

Yancheng

The Love River marks the beginning of **Yancheng** (鹽埕; *yánchéng*) one of Kaohsiung's oldest neighbourhoods and crammed with some of its most traditional shopping streets, food stalls and temples. Bus #248 from the station follows Jhongjheng 4th Road to the river: get off on the western side, where the former City Hall at no. 272 has been converted into the **Kaohsiung Museum of History** (高雄市歷史博物館; *gāoxióngshì lìshǐ bówùguǎn*; Tues–Fri 9am–5pm, Sat–Sun 9am–9pm; free; ☎07/531-2560, ⓦw5.kcg.gov.tw/khm/). Much of the labelling is in Chinese, but English is gradually being added and it's worth a quick look. The first floor charts the history of the city and the old City Hall, while a special 2-28 Incident exhibition covers the bloody events of 1947 from a Kaohsiung perspective (see p.389). A short walk south along the riverbank, the **Kaohsiung Film Archive** (高雄市電影圖書館; *gāoxióngshì*

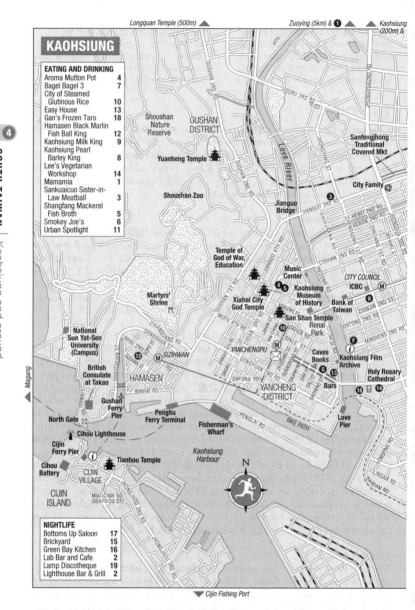

KAOHSIUNG

EATING AND DRINKING

Aroma Mutton Pot	4
Bagel Bagel 3	7
City of Steamed	
Glutinous Rice	10
Easy House	13
Gan's Frozen Taro	18
Hamasen Black Marlin	
Fish Ball King	12
Kaohsiung Milk King	9
Kaohsiung Pearl	
Barley King	8
Lee's Vegetarian	
Workshop	14
Mamamia	1
Sankuaicuo Sister-in-	
Law Meatball	3
Shangfang Mackerel	
Fish Broth	5
Smokey Joe's	6
Urban Spotlight	11

NIGHTLIFE

Bottoms Up Saloon	17
Brickyard	15
Green Bay Kitchen	16
Lab Bar and Cafe	2
Lamp Discotheque	19
Lighthouse Bar & Grill	2

GUSHAN DISTRICT

Shoushan Nature Reserve

Yuanheng Temple

Shoushan Zoo

Sanfengjhong Traditional Covered Mkt

City Family

Jianguo Bridge

Martyrs' Shrine

Temple of God of War, Education

Music Center

Xiahai City God Temple

Kaohsiung Museum of History

CITY COUNCIL

ICBC

Bank of Taiwan

San Shan Temple

Renai Park

National Sun Yat-Sen University (Campus)

SIZIHWAN

British Consulate at Takao

HAMASEN

YANCHENGPU

Caves Books

Kaohsiung Film Archive

Holy Rosary Cathedral

YANCHENG DISTRICT

Bars

Gushan Ferry Pier

North Gate

Penghu Ferry Terminal

Cihou Lighthouse

Cijin Ferry Pier

Fisherman's Wharf

Love Pier

BIKE PATH

Cihou Battery

Tianhou Temple

CIJIN VILLAGE

MIAOCIAN RD (SEAFOOD ST)

Kaohsiung Harbour

N

CIJIN ISLAND

Cijin Fishing Port

diànyǐng túshūguǎn; Tues–Sun 1.30–9.30pm; free) contains a library of almost 6000 Chinese and international films along with personal TVs for viewing them, all for free. You'll need to show your passport to gain temporary membership.

For a quick tour of the district's main temples head west along Sinle Street from the back of the Film Archive several blocks to Yancheng Street; turn right here and at no. 54 (across Daren Rd) you'll see **San Shan Temple** (三山國王廟; *sānshān guówáng miào*; daily 5.30am–10.30pm). Established in 1760 by Hakka immigrants

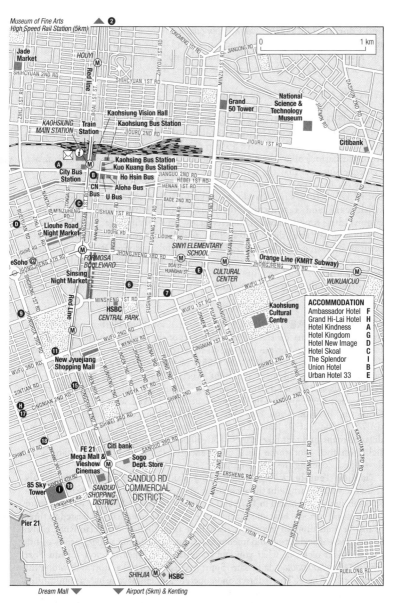

Map labels:

Museum of Fine Arts
High Speed Rail Station (5km)

Jade Market

HOUYI

Red line

SHIHCYUAN 2ND RD
SHIHCYUAN 1ST RD

TONGMENG 1ST RD

ZHOYOU RD

JIANGONG RD

MINZU 1ST RD

JIANGONG 2ND RD

DASHUN 2ND RD

JUEMIN RD

Kaohsiung Vision Hall

Grand 50 Tower

National Science & Technology Museum

KAOHSIUNG MAIN STATION

Train Station

Kaohsiung Bus Station

JIOURU 2ND RD

JIOURU 1ST RD

Citibank

City Bus Station

Kaohsiung Bus Station
Kuo Kuang Bus Station

Ho Hsin Bus

Aloha Bus

CN Bus

U Bus

JIANGUO 2ND RD

HEBEI 1ST RD

HENAN 1ST RD

BADE 2ND RD

DASHUN 3RD RD

NANTAI RD

JIANGUO 2ND RD

MINZUHENG RD

Liouhe Road Night Market

CISHAN 1ST RD

HANTIAN RD

LIOUHE RD

LIOUHE RD

eSoho

MINZU 1ST RD

SINGONG 1ST RD

JHONGSHAN RD

FUSHING 1ST RD

ZHONGZHENG RD

SINYI ELEMENTARY SCHOOL

SHANSYS ST

SHANGSIN

Orange Line (KMRT Subway)

JHONGZHENG 2ND RD

WUKUAICUO

FORMOSA BOULEVARD

Sinsing Night Market

Red Line

BOAI 1ST RD

HUANGHAI ST

CULTURAL CENTER

MINSHENG 1ST RD

HSBC CENTRAL PARK

WUFU 1ST RD

GUANGYA ST

FUJIAN ST

Kaohsiung Cultural Centre

WUFU 2ND RD

WENHAU RD

FUSING ST

JHONGHO 2ND RD

RENAI RD

CINGNIAN 1ST RD

MINCYUAN 1ST RD

SIHWEI 2ND RD

HEPING 1ST RD

ACCOMMODATION
Ambassador Hotel	F
Grand Hi-Lai Hotel	H
Hotel Kindness	A
Hotel Kingdom	G
Hotel New Image	D
Hotel Skoal	C
The Splendor	I
Union Hotel	B
Urban Hotel 33	E

New Jyuejiang Shopping Mall

WUFU 3RD RD

REN AIN 1ST

LINGYA 1ST RD

SIHWEI 3RD RD

SANDUO 2ND RD

SINTIAN RD

CINGNIAN 2ND RD

SIHWEI 4TH RD

FE 21
Mega Mall &
Vieshow Cinemas

Citi bank

SANDUO 3RD RD

Sogo Dept. Store

SANDUO RD COMMERCIAL DISTRICT

ERSHENG RD

KAISYUAN 3RD RD

85 Sky Tower

SANDUO 4TH RD

SANDUO SHOPPING DISTRICT

CINGUANG RD

MINCYUAN 2ND RD

GUANGHUA RD

HEPING 2ND RD

Pier 21

CHENGGONG 2ND RD

SANDUO 4TH RD

MINCYUAN 4TH RD

YISIN 1ST RD

SHIHJIA

HSBC

RUEILONG RD

Dream Mall

Airport (5km) & Kenting

0   1 km

---

and dedicated to the Three Mountain Kings, it's now the spiritual centre of Yancheng. From here head north along Yancheng Street, across Dagong Street and up the narrow shopping arcade (entrance at 28 Dagong St) to Fuye Road. Turn left, and just before Cisian 3rd Road on the left is the tiny but atmospheric **Xiahai City God Temple** (霞海城隍廟; *xiáhǎi chénghuáng miào*; daily 7.30am–9.30pm), with an extra-large statue of the deity in the Main Hall and *jian-nian* figures in the walls. At the end of Fuye Road, the imposing, multi-level **Temple of God of War**

259

and Education (文武聖殿; *wénwǔ shèngdiàn*; daily 5am–midnight), has its roots in the 1920s but is a 1950s construction: Guan Di, the god of war, is enshrined in the Main Hall, while Wenchang Dijun, the god of literature (third floor), and Confucius (fourth floor) are worshipped above.

British Consulate at Takao

Facing the ocean on the western side of the city, the **British Consulate at Takao** (打狗英國領事館; *dǎgǒu yīngguó lǐngshìguǎn*; daily 9am–midnight; free; ☎07/525-0271, ⓦwww.british-consulate.com.tw) occupies a strategic point high above Lianhai Road – it's a steep climb from the bus stop (take bus #99 from the station) up to the main entrance. Contrary to what you'll read on site, evidence suggests that the redbrick colonial mansion was built between 1878 and 1879, and served as a base from which the British could administer customs until 1895, before being abandoned in 1910. Today it functions principally as a swish **café** and **restaurant** (daily 11am–midnight) with outside tables commanding superb views of the city below, and serving beer, decent cocktails and of course, English-style tea. The small exhibition room inside contains paintings relating to the first British consul and zoologist **Robert Swinhoe**, and several of the Taiwanese animals named after him. Swinhoe established the first consulate in 1864 on Cijin Island, but left the area in 1866 and died before the current building was constructed.

Cijin Island

Cijin Island (旗津島; *qíjīndǎo*) lies between Kaohsiung Harbour and the sea, southwest of the city centre. It's the oldest part of the city, with plenty to keep you busy for half a day, but the best reason for a trip out here is to enjoy the views. Take the ferry from Love Pier (see p.257) or **Gushan Ferry Pier** (鼓山輪渡站; *gǔshān lúndùzhàn*; daily 6am–midnight, every 5–10min; NT$15; bikes free) – you can take bus #248 from the train station to the pier, which is located in **Hamasen**, an area first developed by the Japanese and now packed with harbourside cafés. Once on the island you can visit the information centre (daily 10am–7pm; ☎07/571-7442) at 10 Haian 2nd Rd near the terminal and post office for more detailed maps, and rent bikes for NT$30–50 per hour, but it's easy to visit the main sights on foot. For those with more energy, 15km of **bike trails** are being developed, covering the whole island.

Tianhou Temple (天后宮; *tiānhòu gōng*; daily 5.30am–10pm) is a short walk from the wharf: turn right then left along Miaocian Road. The temple is the oldest in Kaohsiung, established in 1673 and dedicated to Mazu. Note the *wángchuán* or "spirit ship", a model boat and shrine to the left of the main hall, dedicated to three Wang Ye gods thought to protect the village from disease. Miaocian Road is also known as **Seafood Street** and lined with restaurants offering a huge variety of fish and shellfish: pick out what you fancy and they'll cook it for you. **Cihou Fort** (旗後砲台; *qíhòu pàotái*; daily 8am–5pm; free) is on the hill a short walk along the lanes north of here. The redbrick and concrete gun emplacement was built in the 1870s and taken by the Japanese after a short but fierce gun battle in 1895. A path leads from the battery along the ridge to the **Cihou Lighthouse** (旗後燈塔; *qíhòu dēngtǎ*; Tues–Sun 9am–4pm; free) built in 1883 and still used today – the views from both sites are magnificent.

Shoushan Nature Park

The line of hills due west of the city centre forms the **Shoushan Nature Park** (壽山自然公園; *shòushān zìrán gōngyuán*) named after the peak of Shoushan (356m), a popular hiking spot. The southern end of the ridge is home to the Shoushan

Zoo, Martyrs' Shrine and Yuanheng Temple, a huge Buddhist monastery, while the northern section, known by the mountain's old name **Chaishan** (柴山; *cháishān*) is best known for its eight hundred or so **Taiwanese macaques** or rhesus monkeys, the densest such population in Taiwan. Although it's strictly forbidden to do so, people still feed them, with the result that the troupes can get aggressive. During the week it's far less crowded, but don't bring food, and keep a safe distance. The best way up is to take a taxi to the trail behind **Longquan Temple** (龍泉寺; *lóngquán sì*) on Lane 51 off Gushan 3rd Road – the stop for bus #245 is also a short walk from the entrance.

Kaohsiung Museum of Fine Arts

Located in **Neiweipi Cultural Park** (內惟埤文化園區; *nèiwéipí wénhuà yuánqū*) northwest of the train station, the **Kaohsiung Museum of Fine Arts** (高雄美術館; *gāoxióng měishùguǎn*; Tues–Sun 9am–5pm; free; ⓦ www.kmfa.gov.tw) houses a series of impressive modern art galleries, opened in 1994. Bus #205 stops at the Kaohsiung Municipal United Hospital (高雄市立聯合醫院; *gāoxióng shìlìliánhé yīyuàn*) nearby, and bus #73 runs from the High-Speed Rail Station. Inside there are four floors of galleries, enough to keep you busy for several hours: exhibits change every three months, but the emphasis is on modern Taiwanese painting, calligraphy and sculpture, particularly from the south of the country.

Zuoying and Lotus Lake

Founded in the seventeenth century, **Zuoying** (左營; *zuǒyíng*) is today a suburban district and the terminus of the High Speed Rail, 5km north of

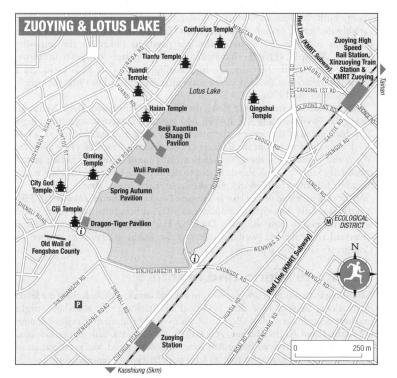

downtown. The main attraction is tranquil **Lotus Lake** (蓮花潭; *liánhuātán*) a relatively modest stretch of water roughly 1.5km long and 500m wide, but ringed by a handful of monuments, picturesque temples and pagodas. Trains to **Zuoying Station** (左營車站; *zuǒyíng chēzhàn*; don't go to Xinzuoying) depart from Kaohsiung Station every ten to twenty minutes (6min; NT$15). Cross the main road outside the station (ignoring the road signs to the lake) and walk straight up Shengli Road (勝利路; *shènglì lù*) – you'll see the water after about 500m. Alternatively, you can take bus #35 from the **Ecological District KMRT Station** (紅線生態園區站; *hóngxiàn shēngtài yuánqūzhàn*) or bike along the trail from the city; the lake itself is ringed by shady paths and bike trails, and you can rent bikes at Ecological District Station or the lake. Bus Red #55 also makes a loop around the lake sights from the High-Speed Rail Station (day ticket NT$55).

Little remains of old Zuoying, which once stood south of the lake, although the city wall is the best preserved in Taiwan. Known as the **Old Wall of Fengshan County** (鳳山舊城; *fēngshān jiùchéng*), it was completed in 1826 using bits of coral. You can see a section on Shengli Road, a few metres beyond the lake's southwestern corner and the **tourist office** (daily 10am–7pm; ☏07/588-2497) at 110 Shengli Rd, which provides decent English-language materials. From there you'll see the first pair of gaudy pagodas on the lake, the **Dragon–Tiger Pavilion** (龍虎塔; *lónghǔ tǎ*) knocked up in 1965 as an extension to **Ciji Temple** (慈濟宮; *cíjìgōng*) opposite. For good luck, enter through the dragon's mouth and exit via the tiger; inside are garish scenes of heaven and hell. A few metres ahead up the western shore along Liantan Road is the simply adorned **Spring Autumn Pavilion** (春秋閣; *chūnqiū gé*), two towers built in 1953 and fronted by a statue of Guanyin on top of a giant, garishly decorated dragon. **Wuli Pavilion** (五里亭; *wǔlǐtíng*) further out in the lake, was added in 1978, with all three pavilions linked to the imposing **Qiming Temple** (啟明堂; *qǐmíngtáng*; daily 4.30am–9.30pm) on shore, dedicated principally to Guan Di, but hosting an array of gods including a bearded Confucius at the back of the main altar. Established in 1909, the temple was rebuilt in the 1970s.

Four hundred metres further along the lake is the impressive **Beiji Xuantian Shang Di Pavilion** (北極玄天上帝廟; *běijí xuántiān shàngdì miào*) comprising a 22m-high statue of the Supreme Emperor of the Dark Heaven, reached via a pier lined with characters from the Chinese classic *Creation of the Gods* (*Feng Shen Yan Yi*). A short walk west along Yuandi Road is **Yuandi Temple** (元帝廟; *yuándì miào*; daily 5am–9.30pm), also dedicated to the Supreme Emperor, the chief image found by fishermen in 1758 and now displayed in the central altar.

At the northern end of the lake is Taiwan's largest **Confucius Temple** (孔子廟; *kǒngzǐmiào*; daily 9am–5pm), completed in 1977, although its status refers to the whole site rather than the main Dacheng Hall. The entrance to the central courtyard is on the left (western) side, but the Dacheng Hall is only open on Confucius's birthday (September 28).

Eating, drinking and nightlife

Kaohsiung is well supplied with places to **eat** and **drink**, although there are fewer international options here than in Taipei or Taichung. As elsewhere, **night markets** provide the widest selection of cheap snacks and meals: the most famous is **Liouhe Road Night Market** (六合路夜市; *liùhélù yèshì*; daily 5pm–midnight) on Liouhe Road between Jhongshan Road and Zihli Road, the proliferation of Japanese food stalls here reflecting its huge popularity with Japanese tourists.

Eating

Downtown

Bagel Bagel 3 貝果貝果之東西廚房 (*bèiguǒbèiguǒ zhī dōngxīchúfáng*) 158 Minsheng 1st Rd ☎07/222-3377. Located in the eastern side of downtown, deli and café with a variety of home-made bagels (NT$35) and cream cheeses (add NT$20), as well as decent sandwiches (NT$99), salads (from NT$100) and pastas (from NT$149). Outdoor and indoor seating. Daily 7am–10pm.

Gan's Frozen Taro 甘家老店冷凍芋 (*gānjiā lǎodiàn lěngdòngyù*) 113 Zihciang 3rd Rd. Tiny dessert store on a section of Zihciang Rd crammed with enticing night market stalls. Try the frozen taro (NT$30) – sweet relief on a sizzling hot day. Daily noon–midnight. No English.

Kaohsiung Milk King 高雄牛乳大王 (*gāoxióng niúrǔ dàwáng*) 65 Jhonghua 3rd Rd. Kaohsiung is renowned throughout Taiwan for papaya milk, popularized by this chain established in the 1960s. The canteen-style diner offers snacks and juices (NT$50–70) and the celebrated papaya drink for NT$60. English menu available. Daily 7am–11pm.

Kaohsiung Pearl Barley King 高雄薏仁大王 (*gāoxióng yìréndàwáng*) 449 Chenggong 1st Rd. Fifty-year-old store that produces sweet green bean desserts and barley drinks (NT$15–25) – traditional thirst quenchers especially welcome in the tropical heat. Not far from City Council KMRT Station. Daily 8am–10.30pm.

Lee's Vegetarian Workshop 李記素食工坊 (*lǐjì sùshí gōngfāng*) 145 Wufu 3rd Rd ☎07/282-6528 (look for "Vegetable Restaurant" sign in English). Solid vegetarian option just across the Love River from Yancheng, with English menus and set meals (including salad bar, bread, soup, drink and dessert) from NT$290 to NT$380. Mushrooms and yams feature. Daily 6.30–9.30am, 11.30am–2pm, 2.30–4pm & 5.30–9pm.

Mamamia 瑪瑪米亞餐廳 (*mǎmǎmǐyà cāntīng*) 2/F, 417 Longde Rd (near the Art Museum) ☎07/522-7300. Popular Italian eatery with locals and expats alike – reasonable at NT$300–400/dish (the pasta is recommended) with fun atmosphere and friendly service. Mon–Fri 11am–2pm & 5.30pm–midnight, Sat & Sun 11am–midnight.

Sankuaicuo Sister-in-Law Meatball 三塊厝肉圓嫂 (*sānkuàicuò ròuyuánsǎo*) 389 Jianguo 3rd Rd. Another traditional shop that will appeal to fans of Taiwanese food: the meatballs (NT$15 per order) here are unique, cooked with soy sauce and pork to make something closer to western stew and dumplings

than the glutinous variety elsewhere on the island. Daily 6.30am–6pm. No English.

Smokey Joe's 冒煙的喬 (*màoyān deqiáo*) 208 Jhongsiao 1st Rd. Decent Tex-Mex restaurant complete with adobe-style walls, long wooden tables and decor straight out of a Tijuana *cantina*. Lunch specials from NT$220. Daily 11am–2am.

Urban Spotlight 城市光廊 (*chéngshì guāngláng*) Intersection of Jhonghua and Wufu roads. Also known as the *Outdoor Café*, this is a great place to relax and people-watch at the south end of Jhongshan Park, open from early afternoon till midnight or later at weekends when it tends to get busier and features live music. Serves mostly cakes, light Western-style snacks, teas and coffees (from NT$70). Mon–Fri 1pm–2am, Sat–Sun 10am–3am.

Yancheng and Hamasen

Aroma Mutton Pot 味味香羊肉爐 (*wèiwèi xiāng yángròulú*) 100 Fuye Rd at Cisian 3rd Rd. This shop has been in business for over forty years and sells a combination of seafood and mutton hot-pots (NT$120–200), as well as a variety of other stir-fried dishes from NT$60. Daily 11am–2pm, 5pm–1am. No English.

City of Steamed Glutinous Rice 米糕城 (*mǐgāo chéng*) 107 Daren Rd. Cheap local shop that's over 50 years old, producing mouth-watering bowls of glutinous rice topped with pork or fish and cucumber (NT$30). Daily 9.30am–10.30pm. No English.

Easy House 寬心園 (*kuān xīn yuán*) 3 Hesi Rd ☎07/561-2631, ⓦwww.easyhouse.tw. Solid Chinese vegetarian chain, with sets ranging NT$210–260 and an excellent location right on the Love River. Daily 11.30am–9.30pm.

Hamasen Black Marlin Fish Ball King 哈瑪星旗魚丸大王 (*hāmǎxīng qíyúwán dàwáng*) 27 Gupo St (between Linhai Rd and Gushan St). This celebrated food stall is located in the forecourt of Da Tian Temple in Hamasen – locals reckon they serve the best fish-ball soup in the country – and it's a bargain at NT$30/bowl. It's a shop on the south side of the forecourt. Daily 10am–6pm. No English.

Shangfang Mackerel Fish Broth 尚芳鮀魚羹 (*shàngfāng tuó yúgēng*) 72 Fuye Rd. Tasty fried fish balls served with soup noodles in the heart of Yancheng's "temple street." Set lunches NT$90–110 or big bowls from NT$65. Daily 9.30am–7.30pm. No English.

Drinking and nightlife

Bottoms Up Saloon 236 Chenggong 1st Rd, at Cingnian 2nd Rd ☎07/269-3075; KMRT Central Park. Classic cocktail bar (try the signature martinis and superb mojitos from NT$160), doubling as an American sports bar with all the top events live on TV. The food and beer is excellent – think crab-cream-cheese dumplings and herbed T-bone pork chop (NT$350). Wed–Mon 5.30pm–2am.

Brickyard 紅磚地窖 (*hóngzhuān dì jiào*) B1, 507 Jhongshan 2nd Rd ☎07/215-0024, ⊛www.brickyard.com.tw; KMRT Central Park. Bar and live music venue, featuring everything from cutting-edge local rock and indie bands, to open-mic nights and DJs spinning house and electronica. Mon–Thurs & Sun 7pm–2am, Fri & Sat 7pm–6am.

Green Bay Kitchen 綠水彎河岸餐房 (*lùshuǐwān héàn cānfáng*) 97 Haibian Rd ☎07/251-9119; KMRT Yuchangpu. Cool bar and restaurant right on the Love River at Kaohsiung Bridge (Wufu 3rd Rd). Sit on the shady deck outside, enjoying the excellent views and food (they have Philly cheesesteak – a long bun with steak topped with onions and Cheez Wiz).

Lab Bar and Cafe 1 Minghua 1st Rd ☎07/559-0858; KMRT Kaohsiung Arena. Get a group and try the jugs of punch (NT$1000–1500) at this laid-back bar, plus fresh oysters, free wi-fi and whatever the owners feel like cooking up. Sat & Sun only 10am–midnight.

Lamp Discotheque 官方網站 (*guānfāng wǎngzhàn*) 42 Zihciang 3rd Rd ☎07/269-6527, ⊛www.lampdisco.com.tw; KMRT Sanduo Shopping District. The place to go for classic club nights and all-you-can drink deals; NT$500 weekdays and NT$600 Fri & Sat (women pay NT$100–200). Tues–Sun 10am–5pm.

Lighthouse Bar & Grill 燈塔外觀 (*dēngtǎ wàiguān*) 239 Fuguo Rd, Zuoying, in between Yucheng and Minghua 1st roads ☎07/559-2614, ⊛www.thelighthouse.com.tw; KMRT Kaohsiung Arena. Expat favourite, with decent beer, live Premier League and themed food nights: think Poutine (Tues), Indian curry (Wed) and daily drinks specials.

Wufu 4th Road 五福西路 (*wǔfú xīlù*); KMRT Yanchengpu. Traditional nightlife area in Yancheng, and still home to numerous pubs and restaurants, although these days it's looking a little tired and tends to be frequented by an older expat crowd. Plenty of cheap beer deals and happy hours from 6pm to 8pm however: *Night Owl* at no. 88 (☎07/532-0168) is a cosy place next to *Focus Pub* (also 88; daily 6.30pm–1.30am) with a popular happy hour, while friendly *Oxford* (just around the corner at 111 Dayi St ☎07/532-3595), is an expat stalwart (similar hours).

Shopping

Kaohsiung is second only to Taipei as a place to **shop**, with plenty of department stores as well as cheaper markets and gift shops.

Caves Books 敦煌書局 (*dūnhuáng shūjú*) 76 Wufu 4th Rd. Well-stocked bookshop with plenty of English magazines and books. Daily 10.30am–9.30pm.

Dream Mall 夢時代購物中心 (*mèngshídài gòuwùzhōngxīn*) 789 Jhonghua 5th Rd ☎07/973-3888, ⊛www.dreamall.com.tw. Bus #14, #36, #70, Red 12 or KMRT Kaisyuan. The city's latest shopping paradise, south of downtown, is the largest shopping mall in East Asia and home to the giant Kaohsiung Eye 高雄之眼 (*gāoxióng zhīyǎn*) ferris wheel.

Jade Market 高雄十全玉市場 (*gāoxióng shíquán yùshìchǎng*) 252 Shihcyuan Rd, at Zihli Rd ☎07/331-7199, ⊛www.kh-jademarket.com. Similar to Taichung's jade market, this vast hall is crammed with not just jade, but antique stalls selling statues and jewellery. Wed, Thurs & Sun 8am–3pm.

New Jyuejiang Shopping Mall 新堀江商場 (*xīnjuéjiāng shāngchǎng*) Lanes between Wenhang 2nd Rd and Renjhih St, just south of Wufu 2nd Rd. The narrow streets in this area are crammed with fashionable stalls, upmarket boutiques and coffeeshops, the best place to check out local street fashions. It's a bit like Taipei's Ximending.

Sanduo Road Commercial District 三多商圈 (*sānduō shāngquān*) Chief shopping zone in the modern, southeast side of downtown between Jhongshan and Wenheng roads, containing Sogo, FE21 Mega (which has *Cha For Tea* 11th floor), Eslite bookstore (17th floor) and Vieshow Cinemas) and Shinkong Mitsukoshi department stores; the alleys nearby are packed with clothes stores.

Sanfengjhong Traditional Covered Market 三鳳中街商圈 (*sānfèngzhōngjiē shānquānshāng quān*) Stretches from Zihli Rd to Jhonghua Rd, just north of Jianguo 3rd Rd and west of the train station, crammed with stalls selling all sorts of traditional Chinese snacks and dried foods.

Moving on from Kaohsiung

Kaohsiung International Airport has numerous daily **flights** to Taipei, mainland China and Magong (Penghu). You can also fly to Hualien, Kinmen and the southern Penghu Islands of Cimei and Wangan (see p.254 for airport transport).

From the train station there are frequent express **trains** north to Tainan, Taichung and Taipei, and across to Taitung on the east coast via the South Line, although the **High Speed Rail** services departing **Zuoying** station to the north, easily accessible by KMRT, are much faster to Taichung (46min; NT$670) and Taipei (1hr 36min; NT$1265).

Bus stations are clustered along Jianguo 2nd Road, just east of the downtown train station. To the left of the station exit on the corner of Jianguo and Jhongshan roads, **Kuo Kuang** offers 24hr services to **Taipei** (NT$400–520; 5hr) every thirty minutes, and **Taichung** every hour (5.40am–10pm; NT$200–300; 3hr). **Taitung** (NT$443) buses depart at 12.30am, 3am, 12.30pm and 5.30pm (4hr).

A little further to the left on Nanhua Street, **Kaohsiung Bus** (高雄客運; *gāoxióng kèyùn*; ☎07/746-2141, ⓦwww.ksbus.com.tw) has frequent services to **Donggang** (NT$91), **Foguangshan** (ten daily 6.20am–7.50pm; NT$80) and **Meinong** (7am–9pm; NT$124–147) as well as hourly buses to **Liugui** (daily 6.20am–8.20pm; NT$214) in the **Maolin National Scenic Area**; there is one daily bus at 6.05am to **Baolai** (3hr), but no further along the Southern Cross-Island Highway at the time of writing (see p.270). **CN Bus** (中南巴士; *zhōngnán bāshì*), a block closer to Jhongshan Road at the *Union Hotel*, runs frequent buses to **Donggang** (NT$91). Further along, **Ubus** departs from 263 Jianguo 2nd Rd to Taipei (24hr; NT$520) and Taichung (NT$300). Nearby **Ho Hsin** runs luxury buses to Taipei (NT$710), Chiayi (NT$260) and Taichung (NT$380).

Ferries to **Little Liuqiu Island** usually depart from **Love Pier** at 10am (Sat & Sun; ☎07/521-5838), returning at 4pm, but call ahead or check with any visitor centre to see if the service is still running.

To Kenting National Park

Kaohsiung Bus, Pingdong Bus (屏東客運; *píngdōng kèyùn* or just "Kenting Express"), CN Bus and Kuo Kuang now run combined services to **Kenting** (every 15–30min; 24hr); just take the first bus that comes along, as prices are all the same: Hengchun (NT$320), Nanwan (NT$340), Kenting Town (NT$355), Chuanfan Rock (NT$366), Shadao (NT$379) and Eluanbi (NT$384). You can catch them at the CN Bus or Kaohsiung Bus stations near the train station; they also leave the **High-Speed Rail Station** (Kenting Town NT$383) from bus stop no. 1, before heading into the city (the big Kenting resorts have shuttle buses at bus stop no. 2). Buses to Kenting from **Kaohsiung Airport** are less frequent, since most buses take Highway 88, which bypasses the airport.

To Penghu

The large **car ferry** to Magong on Penghu takes 4hr 30min (Tai Hua Ferry Co, ☎07/551-5823). Daily departures are 9am and 11pm; boats return at 9am and 4pm (basic seat NT$860, sleepers from NT$980). The terminal is in Hamasen district, off Binhai Road at Fisherman's Wharf, connected to the train station by bus #248.

Listings

Airlines Cathay Pacific Airways/Dragonair, 6/F, 21 Changhua 3rd Rd ☎02/2715-2333 (Taipei number); China Airlines, 81 Changhua 3rd Rd ☎07/282-6141; EVA Air 2-6 Jhongshan 4th Rd ☎07/795-9301; Mandarin Airlines ☎07/802-6868; Uni Airways ☎07/791-1000.

Banks/ATMs There are plenty of banks and ATMs in Kaohsiung, many located in 7-Elevens. HSBC has a branch at 111 Minsheng 1st Rd (Mon–Fri 9am–3.30pm; ☎07/963-8088) and at 6 Mincyuan 2nd Rd (same hrs; ☎07/337-7333; Shihja KMRT) while Citibank is at 502 Jiouru 1st Rd (Mon–Fri

9am–3.30pm; ☎07/391-6000), 111 Wufu 4th Rd (☎07/551-0361) and 472 Jhongshan 2nd Rd (☎07/261-8141).

Bicycle rental The Kaohsiung City Public Bike scheme (Mon–Fri 10am–9.30pm, Sat & Sun 9am–9.30pm; ☎07/973-1036, ⓦwww.c-bike .com.tw) allows you to rent a bicycle with a credit card from one location and drop it at another; bikes are located along subway lines and the Love River, with the major centre at Love Pier. You can pay NT$200 for a monthly membership and then NT$10 every 30min (free first 30min), or without membership it's NT$30 for the first 30min then NT$15 thereafter.

Car rental Car Plus (daily 8am–9.30pm; ☎0800/222-568 or 07/960-5008, ⓦwww .car-plus.com.tw) or Hotai Leasing 和運租車 (*héyùn zūchē*; ☎0800/024-550 or 07/963-0011, ⓦwww.easyrent.com.tw) are both at the Zuoying High-Speed Rail Station. Car Plus also has a desk at the airport (☎07/802-2148).

Cinema Vieshow Cinemas 威秀影城 (*wēixiù yǐngchéng*) is at 13/F, 21 Sanduo 4th Rd (inside FE21 Mega mall in the Sanduo Commercial District).

Hospital The Kaohsiung Medical University Chung-Ho Memorial Hospital 高雄醫學大學附設中和紀念醫院 (*gāoxióng yīxué dàxué fùshè zhōnghé jìniàn yīyuàn*) at 100 Zhiyou 1st Rd has outpatient clinics (☎07/320-8181; Mon–Fri 8.30am–noon, 2–5pm & 6–8.30pm).

Internet access City Family is at the junction of Jhonghua 3rd Rd and Jianguo 3rd Rd (NT$20/hr); eSoho is at the junction of Jhongjheng and Rueiyuan roads (NT$20/hr).

Left luggage Coin lockers are available at the train station and come in three sizes: NT$30, NT$120 or NT$150 for 24hr.

Post The post office at 2-2 Jianguo 3rd Rd is conveniently located to the right of train station exit (daily 8am–5pm).

Around Kaohsiung: Foguangshan Monastery

One of several wealthy Buddhist foundations established in Taiwan since the 1960s, **Foguangshan Monastery** (佛光山寺; *fóguāngshān sì*; daily 8.30am–10pm; museums and galleries Tues–Sun 8.30am–5pm; free; ☎07/656-1921) is a vast complex of grand temple architecture, giant statues and Buddhist art. Around 25km northeast of Kaohsiung, it's an absorbing day-trip from the city, with regular buses making it easy to reach (see box, p.265).

The monastery is the home of the Foguangshan International Buddhist Order, founded in 1967 by **Master Hsing Yun**, an enigmatic monk from China who has spent his life travelling and teaching his unique brand of "Humanistic Buddhism" (see p.418). Today Foguangshan is part monastery, with around three hundred monks and nuns, and part educational complex, with over a thousand students at its on-site university and high school campus.

Starting at the **Non Duality Gate** at the front of the monastery, take a look inside the **Foguangshan Treasury Museum** on the right, packed with Buddhist art, carvings and cultural relics. From here climb straight up the hill towards the stunning **main shrine** or "Great Hero Hall" – it contains three 7.8m-high Buddha statutes, beautifully cast in bronze and surrounded on all sides by a staggering 14,800 smaller Buddha images lit by tiny lights and displayed within an intricate latticework of carved wood. The latest grandiose addition to the site is the **Foguanshan Buddha Memorial Center**, with a colossal temple and 50m-high statue of the Buddha as its centrepiece (it's over 100m tall including the base). The hall houses the venerated **Buddha's tooth relic**, donated by a Tibetan monk in 1998. The other highlight is the 36m-high **statue of Amitabha Buddha** on the east side of the complex (an area known as "Great Buddha Land"). The iconic symbol of the monastery, it is approached by a road lined with 480 smaller statues. You'll hear the word *āmítuófó* everywhere you go: this is another name for Buddha, and has become a catch-all for thank you, bless you or hello.

Maolin National Scenic Area

Stretching over a sizeable expanse of the southern Taiwan hinterland, some 45km east of Kaohsiung, the **MAOLIN NATIONAL SCENIC AREA** (茂林國家風景區; *màolín guójiā fēngjǐngqū*) offers an enticing combination of mountain scenery and aboriginal cultures. Sadly, the area was badly affected by **Typhoon Morakot**, which struck the region in 2009 (35 people were killed in Liugui alone), and much of it will remain off limits to visitors for the life of this guide. The **Rukai aboriginal community** was especially hard hit; many settlements have now been relocated to safer areas. Virtually every concrete bridge in the area was destroyed and the famous **Duona Hot Springs** have been lost, buried by mounds of debris. **White-water rafting** at Laonong and Baolai has ceased indefinitely; note also that **paragliding** from Saijia Aviation Park is now only permitted through associations approved by Pingdong county authorities (see p.39). The **Scenic Area headquarters and visitor centre** at Maolin Village, as well as the visitor centre at Liugui, were both washed away by Morakot. A new visitor centre is planned near Maolin Village; check the website (Ⓦ www .maolin-nsa.gov.tw) for **information**. Assuming there are no other disasters, things should be much improved by 2012 and it's still worthwhile visiting the sections that remain open; the seldom-visited Rukai village of **Wutai** remains one of the highlights of the south.

Sandimen

Twenty-five kilometres east of Kaohsiung is **SANDIMEN** (三地門; *sāndìmén*), an aboriginal community nestled where the western plains meet the mountains, and the heartland of the Paiwan tribe (see p.397). While busloads of Taiwanese tourists come here to visit the rather commercial Taiwan Aboriginal Culture Park nearby (Ⓣ08/799-1219, Ⓦ www.maolin-nsa.gov.tw; Tues–Sun 8.30am–5pm; shows Tues–Sat 10.30am and 3pm), Sandimen is still a good place **to eat**: *Shan Zhong Tian* (山中天; *shānzhōngtiān* Ⓣ08/799-3440) is a justly popular place, set in an attractive wooden house with a large open terrace and serving aboriginal and Chinese dishes. It's on Provincial Highway 24 (10-1 Zhongzheng Road Sec 1) at the junction with Route 185.

Exploring Maolin Scenic Area

You'll get much more out of Maolin if you **rent a car** (see p.265). Public transport is sketchy at the best of times, and in the wake of Typhoon Morakot many bus services have been cancelled. Some areas are still accessible by bus, but once you get off you'll be limited to the immediate locale without your own wheels. Otherwise, join up with one of the hotels or homestays listed below, which will usually help with transport (picking you up from the nearest bus station, for example).

At the time of writing the daily **Kaohsiung Bus** (6.05am) to Meishankou (see p.265) is only running as far as **Liugui** and **Baolai** (3hr). Return buses leave Baolai at 1.25pm. Small buses also run between Liugui and Baolai (50min), departing at 10am, 2pm and 5pm and returning at 8am, noon, 4pm (Sat & Sun) and 6pm (Mon–Fri).

Pingdong (屏東; *píngdōng*) is connected to Kaohsiung by frequent **trains** (25min; express NT$48). The bus station is about a hundred metres to the left of the train station as you exit; there are regular **buses** from here to **Sandimen** (daily 6.30am–10.10pm; NT$77–85), but no buses to Duona, Maolin Village or Wutai at the time of writing.

Wutai

Sandimen is also the gateway to the spectacular 19km stretch of **Provincial Highway 24** leading to the remote Rukai village of **WUTAI** (霧台村; *wùtái cūn*). The area was devastated by Typhoon Morakot, and eight smaller communities beyond Wutai were evacuated; only Shenshan and Wutai itself remain. However it's well worth the effort to get here (a permit is no longer required) – the road winds through some truly amazing scenery, with steep roadside drop-offs framed by **rushing waterfalls** at almost every turn. And Wutai Village is a real treat, with Taiwan's most undiluted Rukai culture, stone-paved lanes and several friendly **homestays** (see p.398 for more on the Rukai).

Practicalities

Dugu (Du Huei-lan), the owner of *Dream House Guesthouse & Restaurant* (夢想之家民宿餐廳; *mèngxiǎng zhījiā mínsù cāntīng*; ⓣ08/790-2312, ⓦwww .dream-house.idv.tw; ⑤) at 38 Lane 5, can speak passable English and can arrange to pick up guests from Sandimen. Another safe bet is the *Salabo Leisure Village* (撒拉伯休閒山莊; *sālābó xiūxián shānzhuāng*; ⓣ08/790-2277 or 08/736-1962; ⑤) at 14–6 Shenshan Lane, in the tiny Rukai settlement of **Shenshan** (神山; *shénshān*) on the left-hand side of the road about 2km before you reach Wutai (just past the km 38 marker of Highway 24). In addition to arranging transport, both of these homestays can whip up traditional **Rukai meals** (packages available) if you reserve them several hours in advance; try the fresh, locally made **aiyu jelly**.

Meinong

Around 35km north of Sandimen and 40km northeast of Kaohsiung, **MEINONG** (美濃; *měinóng*) lies just outside the Scenic Area proper. The rural town, once a major tobacco-growing centre, is at the heart of **Hakka culture** in the south – ninety percent of its inhabitants claim Hakka ancestry and the majority still speak the traditional language. As with Beipu in the north (see p.155), Meinong is celebrated for its tasty **Hakka food**, but has the additional appeal of producing exquisite oil-paper **parasols** (油紙傘; *yóuzhǐsǎn*), although the traditional Chinese craft only took off here in the 1920s. Having your own transport is definitely an advantage here as things are spread out; renting a bike is a sensible option given the signposted network of **cycling trails** in the area – pick up a map from the Meinong Hakka Museum or any homestay.

Arrival and accommodation

Buses from Kaohsiung pull in at Meinong's small **bus station** in the centre of town, at the junction of Zhongshan and Zhongzheng roads. There are seven daily onward services to Liugui from here, but staying overnight in Meinong is a good idea, especially as many of the **homestays** in the area offer **bike rentals**. The best is *Renzi Homestay* (人字山莊 *rénzì shānzhuāng*; ⓣ07/682-2159 or ⓣ0912/199-926; ④) at 66-5 Minquan Rd, with comfortable rooms in a two-storey house in a tranquil area northeast of the centre. The owners speak some English, are very knowledgeable guides and will pick you up from the bus station. Bikes are NT$100 per day. Another good place, with free bicycle hire, is the *Shuangfeng Homestay* (雙峰民宿; *shuāngfēng mínsù*; ⓣ07/682-0839; ③) at 8 Shuangfeng St, a ten-minute walk from the bus station, with dorm beds for NT$250–300.

The Town

A short walk south of the bus station, **Yongan Street** (永安街; *yǒngān jiē* or "old street") runs under **Dongmen** (東門; *dōngmén*) or East Gate, a defensive work originally constructed in 1755 but rebuilt several times since. From here "old street" follows the course of the Shuang River, once an important trade route, although it's little more than a stream today. Further along, at no. 178, is **Lin Chun-Yu's House** (林春雨 林家夥房; *línjiā huǒfáng*) home of Meinong's richest family and much bigger than it looks from the street (it's still a private home). Opposite, at no. 177, the **Jinxing Blue Shirt Store** (錦興行藍衫店; *jǐnxīngháng lánshāndiàn*) was founded by master tailor Xie Jing Lai, who still makes traditional **blue Hakka clothes**; he turned 100 in 2009. Everything is made by hand and simple shirts or blouses cost NT$1000–1200.

Northeast of the town centre, just beyond Zhongzheng Lake on Minzu Road, lies the **Meinong Hakka Museum** (美濃客家文物館; *měinóng kèjiā wénwùguǎn*; Tues–Fri 9.30am–4.30pm; Sat–Sun 9am–5pm; NT$60), housing an interesting collection of exhibits, including a mock tobacco tower. Everything is labelled in Chinese only, but there are English leaflets.

To buy some of the famous umbrellas, visit **Meinong Prosperity Paper Umbrella Store** (美濃廣德興紙傘店; *měinóng guǎngdéxīng zhǐsǎndiàn*; ☏07/681-0451) at 362 Zhongshan Rd Sec 1, on the west side of town, where beautiful parasols cost NT$500–$2000. Nearby **Jing Zih Ting** (敬字亭; *jìng zì tíng*; ☏07/682-1325) at 339 Zhongshan Rd Sec 1 is also worth a look.

Just outside Meinong you can find two tourist centres with shops, souvenirs, food and yet more parasols. The most popular is **Meinong Folk Village** (美濃民俗村; *měinóng mínsú cūn*; daily 8am–6pm summer, 8am–5.30pm winter; free) at 80 Lane 421, Zhongshan Rd Sec 2, while south of Meinong, on Provincial Highway 28, **Yuan Xiang Yuan Cultural Village** (原鄉緣紙傘文化村; *yuánxiāngyuán zhǐsǎn wénhuàcūn*; Mon–Fri 8.30am–5.30pm, Sat–Sun 8.30am–6.30pm; free) at 147 Zhongxing Rd Sec 1, is a similar complex, with an excellent collection of Hakka artefacts on the second floor.

Eating

For **food**, try local Hakka specialities such as *bǎntiáo* (fried noodles), usually available at the two shopping complexes out of town (see above), or the atmospheric *Meinong Traditional Hakka Restaurant* (美濃古老文物客家菜; *měinóng gǔlǎo wénwù kèjiācài*) at 362-5 Zhongshan Rd, on the west side of town opposite Prosperity Paper Umbrella Store.

Maolin Recreation Area

The **MAOLIN RECREATION AREA** (茂林遊憩區; *màolín yóuqìqū*) covering the region around County Route 132, 45km north and 1hr drive from Kaohsiung, is a quiet haven of butterflies and waterfalls that makes a tranquil retreat from the rigours of urban Taiwan. In Maolin Village (茂林村; *màolín cūn*) itself, the only hotel-style **accommodation** is the *Fengshan Agricultural Activity Center* (鳳山市農會茂林會員活動中心; *fèngshānshì nónghuì màolín huìyuán huódòng zhōngxīn*; ☏07/680-1115, ⓦwww.fast.org.tw; ❹) at no. 16, across the road from Maolin Park; rooms here are basic but clean.

Purple Butterfly Valley

Over the road from Maolin Village is **Maolin Park** (茂林公園; *màolín gōngyuán*), in an area known as the **Purple Butterfly Valley** (紫蝶幽谷; *zǐdié yōugǔ*) – so named because it is a major sanctuary for four species of butterfly, one of which sports strikingly purple wings. Thousands of butterflies descend on the park every **winter**, from December to February, clinging to vegetation and at times carpeting the entire valley. The most arresting time to see the butterflies is at daybreak, when the rising sun wakes them and their wings begin to flutter en masse.

Duona

Winding County Route 132 climbs the 15km from Maolin Village to the Rukai village of **DUONA** (多納; *duōnà*), one of the last bastions of the traditional Rukai slate-slab houses. This area was hammered by Typhoon Morakot in 2009, with the **Duona High Suspension Bridge** (多納高吊橋; *duōnà gāo diàoqiáo*) one of the few bridges to survive; it yields sweeping views of the river valley. About 6km past the bridge is the village itself; time will tell if tourism here recovers from the loss of the hot springs that used to draw them in, but for travellers interested in a slice of Rukai life it's hard to beat. A friendly place to stay is the **Gumula Homestay** (古木拉民宿; *gǔmùlā mínsù*; ⊤07/680-1509; ❸) at no. 90, down a narrow road to the left of the main street in the middle of the village. Duona is a great place to try Rukai cuisine, with outdoor **barbecue stalls** serving up an assortment of meat grilled on smooth, fire-heated slate slabs. For a slightly more formal experience, try the *Dian Mi Restaurant* (甸咪餐廳; *diànmī cāntīng*) on the right-hand side of the main street just after the village entrance – you'll know it by the slate-slab grills out front.

On to Baolai

Heading into the far northern section of the Maolin National Scenic Area, picturesque Provincial Highway 28 cuts through some gorgeous scenery to the **Southern Cross-Island Highway** (Provincial Highway 20) at **Laonong** (荖濃; *lǎonóng*), and the hot-springs town of Baolai beyond.

Several kilometres before you reach **Liugui** (六龜; *liùguī*), look out for the **18 Arhats Mountains** (十八羅漢山; *shíbāluóhàn shān*) on the left, on the far side of the Laonong River. These are an extremely photogenic series of craggy, round-topped mountains nicknamed "Little Guilin" due to their resemblance to the world-famous karst mountains of Guilin in southern China.

Post-Morakot, **BAOLAI** (寶來; *bǎolái*) itself is best considered a refreshing pit-stop for anyone attempting the Southern Cross-Island Highway (see below); most of its public hot-spring areas were washed away and the only way to have a soak now is to stay in one of the **hot-spring hotels**. The *Fun Chen Resort Hotel* (芳晨溫泉渡假村; *fāngchén wēnquán dùjiàcūn*; ⊤07/688-1229, ⓦwww.phouse.com.tw; ❺) at 132 Zhongzheng Rd has spotless rooms and comfortable hot-spring pools in riverside cabins.

Southern Cross-Island Highway

The spectacular **SOUTHERN CROSS-ISLAND HIGHWAY** (南橫公路; *nánhéng gōnglù*) slices across south Taiwan in a dramatic traverse of the central mountains that leaves most travellers clutching the edge of their seats. Starting from the western coastal plains around Tainan, the highway climbs steadily to almost 2800m before dropping sharply down to the east coast, cutting through several distinct ecosystems as well as the southwestern fringe of **Yushan National Park** (see p.229). The road was severely damaged by **Typhoon Morakot** in 2009 however, and although it was open to small vehicles at the time of writing, the route remains precarious beyond the **Taoyuan Recreation Area**, north of Baolai, and is often closed completely in summer; ask at one of the Kaohsiung visitor centres before starting out.

Meishankou

Although the Southern Cross-Island Highway (aka Provincial Highway 20) actually links Tainan to Taitung, snaking through the mountains for 209km,

You'll need your own transport – preferably a **car** – to travel the highway in comfort, although with plenty of time it is possible to hitchhike the route. At the time of writing sections are still liable to closure post-Morakot – check at a visitor centre before you go. Travelling by **scooter** is also possible, although it can be uncomfortably cold and dangerous in wet weather.

Public transport is limited and highly dependent on weather and road conditions – always check ahead with visitor centres in Tainan or Kaohsiung before making plans. At the time of writing there are no direct buses from Tainan; the best place to start is **Kaohsiung**, from where **buses** (see p.265) run up the Laonong River Valley. As a result of Typhoon Morakot, however, at the time of writing the daily Kaohsiung Bus (6.05am) to Meishankou is only running as far as **Liugui** (六龜; *liùguī*) and **Baolai** (寶來; *bǎolái*), arriving 3hr later – which isn't much use if you want to get to the other side. Return buses leave Baolai at 1.25pm. Small buses also run between Liugui and Baolai (50min), departing at 10am, 2pm and 5pm and returning at 8am, noon, 4pm (Sat & Sun) and 6pm (Mon–Fri). For the latest, call the bus company (⊤07/746-2141) if you speak Chinese; otherwise ask at one of the visitor centres in Kaohsiung.

Things are not much better from **Taitung** (台東; *táidōng*) on the east coast (see p.315), where the Dingdong Mountain Bus Station has two daily buses to **Lidao** (利稻; *lìdào*; 6.20am & 1.05pm; NT$220) via **Wulu** (霧鹿; *wùlù*; NT$185).

Baolai (see opposite), around 85km from Tainan, is widely regarded as the highway's western gateway, as the road really starts to climb just beyond here. The southwestern entrance to Yushan National Park (see p.229), 25km from Baolai at **MEISHANKOU** (梅山口; *méishānkǒu*), survived Typhoon Morakot, but tourism has taken a massive hit and buses are unlikely to return for some time. The national park's **Meishankou Visitor Center** (梅山口遊客中心; *méishānkǒu yóukè zhōngxīn*; daily 9am–4.30pm, closed second Tues of each month; ⊤07/686-6181) at no. 44-5 Meishankou can provide you with the latest information on the route ahead.

Meishankou's only proper **hotel**, the *Meishan Youth Activity Center* (梅山青年活動中心; *méishān qīngnián huódòng zhōngxīn*; ⊤07/686-6166, ⓦmeishan.cyh .org.tw; ❸) at no. 55 (km 109.5) – on the left-hand side of the highway as you head east – occupies a scenic spot looking out onto nearby mountains and has spacious, comfortable double rooms. A Chinese breakfast is included in the room rate, and the hotel's restaurant also serves lunch and dinner (NT$120 per person). Just east of the visitor centre is a string of **restaurants** serving basic Chinese dishes and Bunun specialities such as roasted mountain pig (*shānzhū*; for around NT$150 for a small plate), although until the road is fully repaired most will remain closed.

Meishankou to Tianchi

For independent travellers without their own transport, the winding 25km section of road that climbs from Meishankou to **TIANCHI** (天池; *tiānchí*; 2280m) – gaining almost 1300m in elevation – presents a huge challenge at the best of times. This scenic stretch of road was especially battered by Typhoon Morakot and is often closed: it's imperative to check road conditions at a visitor centre or the *Meishan Youth Activity Center* (see above) before setting out.

If the road is open, after about 21km you'll reach **Zhongzhiguan** (中之關; *zhōngzhīguān*), the site of a police station during the Japanese occupation but now a rest area and the beginning of the 3.5km **Zhongzhiguan Trail** (中之關古道; *zhōngzhīguān gǔdào*). The trail runs through a tranquil forest and will help you avoid the road for the last few kilometres into Tianchi itself, essentially a roadside stop named after the tiny **alpine lake** nearby. At the time of writing there is nowhere open to stay or eat at Tianchi.

Tianchi to Yakou

From Tianchi, the road continues to climb for another 14km to its highest point, a roadside stop named **YAKOU** (埡口; *yǎkǒu*; 2772m) where there is an exceptional viewpoint and nearby lodging, although the latter is closed post-Morakot at the time of writing. This stretch of road is the Southern Cross-Island Highway at its most spectacular, and, accordingly, the trailheads to all four of the easily accessible 3000m peaks are located along this section – most of them should be open by 2011 (see p.230 for Yushan National Park permits).

The **Jinjing Bridge Trailhead** is only 4km past Tianchi near the km 139 marker, at 2380m. From here you can climb the area's tallest peak, the 3668m **Guanshan** (關山; *guānshān*) as well as nearby **Guhanuoxinshan** (庫哈諾辛山; *kùhānuòxīn shān*; 3115m), more easily tackled in a day. Along the trail is the **Guhanuoxin Cabin** (庫哈諾辛山屋; *kùhānuòxīn shānwū*), an enclosed shelter where you can stay overnight provided you have your own sleeping bag.

At the km 144 marker is the trailhead to **Daguanshan** (大關山; *dàguānshān*; 3222m) – it takes around 2 hours to reach the summit. Continuing along the cross-island highway from the trailhead the road climbs for just over 3km before entering the 600m-long **Daguanshan Tunnel** (大關山隧道; *dàguānshān suìdào*) at 2722m, the middle of which is very dark and somewhat dangerous to walk through given that there are no pavements – a torch is essential if you want to traverse it on foot. At the other end of the tunnel is Yakou, with a viewpoint on the right side of the road and a trailhead for the short-but-steep climb to **Guanshanlingshan** (關山嶺山; *guānshānlǐngshān*; 3176m) on the left – this is only major peak where **no permit** is required. On clear days, the **viewpoint** affords divine morning and evening vistas of the "sea of clouds".

A few hundred metres east along the road from here is a right-hand turn leading down the slope for about 1km to the China Youth Corps *Yakou Youth Hostel* (埡口山莊; *yǎkǒu shānzhuāng*; ☎07/686-6166), closed at the time of writing thanks to the parlous condition of the highway (the *Meishan Youth Activity Center* will know the latest).

Lidao

About 30km southeast of Yakou is **LIDAO** (利稻; *lìdào*) a laid-back Bunun village with a couple of welcoming homestays, worth an overnight stay for the glimpses it offers of genuine Bunun life – and the opportunity to try freshly prepared Bunun cuisine (see p.396).

Although Lidao is accessible by bus from Taitung, some adventurous travellers coming from the island's western side still **walk** the 30km stretch from Yakou, which is mostly downhill and can easily be done in a day – obviously this depends on current conditions.

Practicalities

The village's most agreeable accommodation option is the *Xian Feng Homestay* (賢鳳民宿; *xiánfèng mínsù*; ☎089/938-038; ❸) at 6-4 Lidao Village, while nearby at 3 Wenhua Rd is the friendly *Nanheng Lidao Yenong Homestay* (南橫利稻野農民宿; *nánhéng lìdào yěnóng mínsù*; ☎089/938-055; ❸), which has a few basic two- and four-person rooms but doesn't usually provide dinner unless a large group has reserved meals in advance. If you're stuck for food, the adjacent **Shenmao Store** at 6-3 Wenhua Rd (森茂商號; *sēnmào shānghào*; ☏089/938-095; 6am–9pm) has **drinks** and **snacks** such as instant noodles, and the owner also can prepare staples such as fried rice for NT$60 a plate.

Wulu

The last stop of significant interest along the highway is the tiny Bunun village of **WULU** (霧鹿; *wùlù*) known chiefly for its high-end hot-spring hotel, vertigo-inducing suspension bridge and world-famous local choir. The scenery between Lidao and Wulu is impressive, as the highway passes through the striking Wulu Canyon (霧鹿峽谷; *wùlù xiágǔ*); its sheer walls can be seen from the road's precipitous curves. Wulu's most popular place to stay is the pricey *Chief Spa Hotel* (天龍飯店; *tiānlóng fàndiàn*; ☏089/935-075, ⒲www.chiefspa .com.tw; ⑤), which has private hot-springs spas in the rooms but no public bathing pools. At weekends and public holidays, the hotel often hosts performances of the **Wulu Bunun Choir**, whose traditional songs – characterized by eight-part harmonies inspired by the sounds of nature – have attracted worldwide critical acclaim. Directly behind the hotel is the **Tianlong Suspension Bridge** (天龍吊橋; *tiānlóng diàoqiáo*), which crosses the Wulu Canyon at a dizzying height.

South from Kaohsiung

Along the busy coastal highway heading south from Kaohsiung to Kenting National Park are several worthwhile attractions, suitable as stopovers on an extended excursion to the island's tropical southern tip or as day-trips from Kaohsiung. Much of this region forms part of the **Dapeng Bay National Scenic Area** (大鵬灣國家風景區遊客中心; *dàpéngwān guójiā fēngjǐngqū yóukè zhōngxīn*; ⒲www.tbnsa.gov.tw), with the fishing town of **Donggang** boasting some of Taiwan's finest seafood and **Little Liuqiu Island** making for a relaxing retreat from city life. Just before the coastal highway reaches Kenting National Park, **Sizhongxi Hot Springs** and **County Route 199** make a worthwhile detour, offering interesting spas and beautiful countryside dotted with Paiwan villages.

Donggang

About an hour's bus ride south of Kaohsiung, **DONGGANG** (東港; *dōnggǎng*) is a frenetic fishing port traditionally known for its haul of the highly prized **Pacific bluefin tuna** (黑鮪魚; *hēiwěiyú*), whose soft underbelly yields the finest cuts of **sashimi**. The town's Bluefin Tuna Cultural Festival (held every May and June) attracts thousands of domestic tourists, although how long this will last is a controversial issue (at least outside Taiwan) – bluefin is an **endangered** species, with stocks at an all-time low (in 2010 Greenpeace added the fish to its seafood red list, and the tuna catch in Taiwan dropped 60 percent the same year). To fully appreciate the scale of the town's fish trade, visit the frenzied **Donggang Fish Market** (東港魚市場; *dōnggǎng yúshìchǎng*; 9.30am–noon, closed Fri and second Mon of each month) along the waterfront. Head northwest along Zhongshan Road (中山路; *zhōngshān lù*) until you reach Yanping Road (延平路; *yánpíng lù*), before Chaolong Road to the ferry; turn left here, cross the Fongyu Bridge and keep straight on for a few hundred metres until the road comes to a dead end in front of the market.

Donglong Temple

Framed with a majestic gold-plated archway, the **Donglong Temple** (東隆宮; *dōnglóng gōng*) at 21-1 Donglong St is the centre of Donggang religious life and attracts a continuous procession of worshippers – particularly fishermen – who pray for safety from the storms that frequently ravage the Taiwan Strait. The temple's most exalted deity is **Wen Hong**, a folk god who is part of Taiwan's vast pantheon of **protection deities** (see p.401).

To give thanks for the safe passage of their ancestors, local devotees stage the dramatic **Donggang King Boat Festival** (東港王船節; *dōnggǎng wángchuán jié*) here once every three years in October (next ceremony 2012). The climax of the festival is the burning of a large wooden vessel, filled with replicas of everyday items such as cars, clothing, houses and offerings of meat, in honour of Wen Hong.

To get here from the bus station on Zhongshan Road turn left at the junction with Guangfu Road (光復路; *guāngfù lù*), which in a few hundred metres crosses Donglong Street (東隆街; *dōnglóng jiē*; Route 128); turn left here and you'll soon see the gilded archway in front of the temple.

Practicalities

Buses from Kaohsiung (1hr) or Kenting (1hr 30min) drop passengers at the Pingdong Bus Company stops on Zhongshan Road, next to the 7-Eleven in the centre of town. Moving on, if you don't have correct change to pay the driver, buy tickets at the counter inside the store. To get to the **Little Liuqiu** ferry (see below), walk northwest along Zhongshan Road for about 1km until you reach Chaolong Road (朝隆路; *cháolóng lù*) just before the big bridge over the Donggang River; turn left here and a short walk ahead on the right you'll see the two ferry terminals.

One of the finest **restaurants** in town is *Dongsheng Restaurant* (東昇餐廳; *dōngshēng cāntīng*; ☎08/832-3112) at 66 Guangfu Rd Sec 2, one block north of Zhongshan Road, with exquisite seafood at reasonable prices. Those cynical about imminent bluefin tuna extinction (most of the diners here) will enjoy the sublime tuna sashimi, while the **Sakura shrimp** (櫻花蝦; *yīnghuāxiā*) is a delicious and far less guilt-laden treat. The shrimp is one of the town's "three marine treasures", along with the bluefin tuna and **oilfish roe** (烏魚子; *wūyúzǐ*), baked into delicate cakes that can be dipped in a garlic and radish sauce.

Little Liuqiu Island

The gem of the Dapeng Bay National Scenic Area, **Little Liuqiu Island** (小琉球; *xiǎo liúqiú*) makes for a convenient, relaxing retreat from the din of the west-coast cities. Composed of **coral**, the 4km-long, 2km-wide island is covered with curious rock formations and caves and offers seemingly endless sea views. Some visitors make it a long day-trip from Kaohsiung, but it's better to stay overnight and explore at leisure. There are plenty of hotels, restaurants and a seaside **camping area** that could easily win the accolade as Taiwan's finest.

Little Liuqiu's original aboriginal settlers were exterminated by the Dutch between 1636 and 1645, and it wasn't until the 1770s that Fujian fishermen began arriving, establishing small communities. Today, tourism competes with fishing as the island's biggest industry, but there is still plenty of fresh **seafood** to be had in the main village next to Baisha Port.

Accommodation

Liuqiu offers plenty of comfortable mid-range **accommodation**, ideal for short or overnight stays, much of it located close to the ferry at Baisha Port.

Athens 小琉球雅典民宿 (*xiǎoliúqiú yádiǎn mínsù*) 298-4 Sanmin Rd ☏ 08/861-3033, ⓦ www.athens.url.tw. Justly popular, modern place facing Baisha Harbour, with small brightly painted en-suite rooms and flat-screen TVs. Great deals on weekdays. ④

Coco Resort 椰林渡假村 (*yēlín dùjiàcūn*) 20-38 Minzu Rd ☏ 08/861-4368, ⓦ www.coco-resort.com.tw. A 20min walk up the main road from Baisha Port, the *Coco* boasts a tranquil location, with cosy whitewashed bungalows shaded by palm trees; rooms are fairly basic, but bathrooms are clean. ⑤

Liu-chiu Deluxe Resort Hotel 白龍宮休閒渡假旅館 (*báilónggōng xiūxián dùjiàlǚguǎn*) 272 Sanmin Rd ☏ 08/861-2536. Small hotel to the

LITTLE LIUQIU ISLAND

ACCOMMODATION
Athens	E
Coco Resort	B
Liu-chiu Deluxe Resort Hotel	C
Samaji Island Camping Resort	A
Shian Bin Ocean View Villa	D

RESTAURANTS
Dumplings God II	2
Flavour BBQ Store	1

Beauty Cave • Toll Gate
Vase Rock
ISLAND RING ROAD
Lingshan Temple
Visitor Information Center
MINZU ROAD
Baisha Port
Scooter Rental
Zhongao Beach
ZHONGHUA ROAD
ZHONGSHAN ROAD
ZHONGZHENG ROAD
Shanzhu Trench
Geban Beach
CORAL REEF PARK COASTAL TRAIL
ZHONGKENG ROAD
Biyun Temple
Jianshan
Old Banyan Tree
ISLAND RING ROAD
RENAI ROAD
Longxia Grotto
Black Ghost Cave
XINFU ROAD
White Lighthouse
Scooter Rental
Dafu Port
ZHONGAO ROAD
ISLAND RING ROAD
Guanyin Rock
Houshi Reef

N

0 — 500 m

Dongang

Dongang

right as you leave the ferry pier, with spotless, tiled-floor rooms with TVs, and fishing nets artfully draped from the ceiling. ❹

🏃 **Samaji Island Camping Resort** 沙馬基島露營渡假區 (*shāmǎjī dǎo lùyíng dùjiàqū*) ☏08/861-4880, ⊛www.samaji.com.tw. By far the most atmospheric option, set on a breezy oceanside knoll along the Island Ring Road about 3km from Baisha Port. Features several stylish cabins that sleep two, as well as numerous elevated wooden platforms for pitching tents (some with wooden rain shelters). Camping costs NT$200

per person (NT$300 weekends) if you have your own tent or NT$350 a head for tent/sleeping pad/bag rentals. With breakfast and a toiletry kit included in the price, it's a great deal. ❸

Shian Bin Ocean View Villa 賢濱山莊 (*xiánbīn shānzhuāng*) 206-1 Sanmin Rd ☏08/861-1230, ⊛www.8611230.com.tw. One of the cheapest places to stay, just up the flight of steps to the left as you leave the ferry pier. A short walk from Zhongao Beach, this tiny hotel has clean doubles and a very friendly owner, although no English is spoken. ❹

The Island

Liuqiu is best explored by **scooter** (see box opposite for rental details), with most road signs featuring English. Most of the sights are scattered alongside the **Island Ring Road**, a loop of around 13km that could also be walked in a full day.

Heading north from **Baisha** (白沙; *báishā*), the first feature you'll encounter is **Vase Rock** (花瓶石; *huāpíng shí*) a mushroom-shaped mound of eroded coral that has become the symbol of the island. Around 1km further along the ring road is **Beauty Cave** (美人洞; *měiréndòng*; NT$120 for Beauty Cave, Shanzhu Trench and Black Ghost Cave), a series of coral grottoes created by sea erosion – a paved shoreline pathway cuts through them. The next notable attraction, 2km along the road, is one of the island's best: **Shanzhu Trench** (山豬溝; *shānzhūgōu*) a narrow labyrinth of coral cliffs choked by overhanging tree roots, so named because mountain pigs are said to have roamed here once. For a closer look at the cliffs, stroll along the raised wooden walkway that loops inland from the ring road. Well into the "ditch" are some small rock houses where locals sought shelter during a US bombing raid towards the end of World War II.

Some of Liuqiu's best views can be had another 1km down the coast, at **Black Ghost Cave** (烏鬼洞; *wūguǐdòng*), a spectacular string of eroded seaside grottoes connected by a well-built pathway that offers sublime sea views. The views are tempered somewhat by the caves' macabre name, which stems from a massacre by the Dutch of local cave-dwelling aborigines (at times referred to simply as "dark people") in retaliation for the slaying of a few Dutch sailors (although the sign at the entrance incorrectly attributes the massacre to the English). A further 2.5km or so around the ring road, on the island's southwest coast, is a stretch of coral formations known as the **Houshi Reef** (厚石裙礁; *hòushí qúnjiāo*), which imaginative islanders liken to people and deities. Around 1km off the main road, up a hilly road to the left, is Liuqiu's odd little **White Lighthouse** (白燈塔; *báidēngtǎ*), just ten metres high and built by the Japanese during the occupation period – it tops the mountain of Jianshan, but there are sadly no views. On the way to the lighthouse is a short side road that leads to the impressive **Old Banyan Tree** (老榕樹; *lǎoróngshù*), which seems to strangle the diminutive shrine upon which it dwells.

If you're dying for a dip in the sea, about the only stretch of sand that isn't fringed with razor-sharp coral is **Zhongao Beach** (中澳海灘; *zhōngào hāitān*), 3.8km from Houshi Reef and just a few minutes' walk south of Baisha Port. From here there are fine night views of the lights of Kaohsiung.

Eating

Liuqiu is famed for its **seafood**, with plenty of low-key restaurants cramming the streets around Baisha Harbour. Alternatively, roast pork is the specialty at *Flavour BBQ Store* (香串串烤肉專賣店; *xiāngchuànchuàn kǎoròu zhānmàidiàn*;

Ⓣ08/861-1881) at 4 Zhongshan Rd, while *Dumplings God II* (餃神二代水餃; *jiǎoshén èrdài shuǐjiǎo*; daily 10.30am–2pm & 5–8.30pm; Ⓣ08/861-4444) knocks out bowls of tasty dumplings from NT$40.

Sizhongxi Hot Springs

Just north of Kenting National Park and 5.5km east of the coastal highway, hilly **SIZHONGXI HOT SPRINGS** (四重溪溫泉; *sìzhòngxī wēnquán*) is drenched in divine scenery and off-the-beaten-path attractions.

Sizhongxi's location in the foothills along Kenting National Park's northern fringe – the heartland of the **Paiwan aboriginal tribe** – also makes it an ideal base for exploring the many tribal villages along narrow **County Route 199**. You'll need your own transport to make the most of the area – indeed, with no public transport traversing this road, it remains delightfully underused.

Hot-spring resorts

There are several **hot-spring hotels** along County Route 199, but most of these are of the concrete-box variety, with spring water piped into large bathtubs in the rooms. More attractive options can be found near **Damei** (大梅; *dàméi*); take the left-hand turn at a small sign at the far end of Sizhongxi. About 1km down this road on the left is the gleaming *Fennel Resort* (茴鄉戀戀溫泉會館; *huíxiāng liànliàn wēnquán huiguǎn*; Ⓣ08/882-4900, Ⓦwww.fennel.com.tw; ❼), at 1-16 Damei Rd with spotless doubles, posh villas and outdoor **public bathing pools** (NT$280 per person).

An offbeat alternative is the *Dashan Hot Spring Spa & Farm* (大山溫泉農場; *dàshān wēnquán nóngchǎng*; Ⓣ08/882-5725; ❺) at 60-1 Damei Rd, with a modest **petting zoo** of horses and deer to complement its hot-spring pools. Its well-appointed cabins are clean and comfortable, and its outdoor public bathing pools (NT$200 per person) are in a relaxed setting. Drive to the far side of Damei and turn left on the dirt road leading up the hillside (marked with a sign in Chinese). After about a hundred metres the road forks – take the track to the left and you'll soon get to the hotel car park.

If you don't plan to stay overnight, a good option for a soak and a meal is the *Yuanxiang Hot Spring Restaurant* (緣鄉溫泉餐廳; *yuánxiāng wēnquán cāntīng*; daily 10am–10pm; Ⓣ08/882-4071) at 85 Wenquan Rd, the public complex on the left as you enter Sizhongxi Town. Here there are public pools (NT$200 per person) and private two-person rooms (NT$600 for 1hr 30min).

County Route 199

Winding northeast through the mountains beyond Sizhongxi, **County Route 199** is a fascinating attraction in its own right, a narrow paved road that crosses pristine **highland scenery** before sweeping down to the island's splendid southeastern seaboard. Along the way, it passes by Paiwan tribal villages that remain largely untouched by Taiwanese tourism, and it's possible to cross over to the east coast by car or scooter from Sizhongxi in about an hour and a half.

Around 5km east from Sizhongxi, the **Shimen Historic Battlefield** (石門古戰場; *shímén gǔzhàn chǎng*) is where, in 1874, a defiant group of Paiwan tribesmen defended themselves against a 3600-strong, Samurai-led expeditionary force of Japanese seeking reprisal for the 1871 **Mudan Incident** (see p.386). There is a stele here with an inscription commemorating the event. Just to the east is **Mudan** (牡丹; *mǔdān*) itself, an excellent place to try authentic Paiwan snacks, characterized by an astounding array of mountain vegetables. Even though Mudan – called "*shímén*" in Mandarin – has not been spoiled by tourism, there are a few shops where you can buy **handmade Paiwan crafts** for bargain prices.

Mudan B&B (牡丹民宿; *mǔdān mínsù* ☎ 08/883-1076 or 0935/845-213; ❹) at 1-8 Shimen Rd, offers simple rooms, meals and guide services.

Past the enormous **Shimen Reservoir** (石門水庫; *shímén shuǐkù*) the road climbs sharply into the mountains, offering fantastic views down to the plains below and running through several Paiwan villages. Gradually the road starts to descend to the east coast, where you can take the east-bound branch of County Route 199 through to Provincial Highway 26 East. From here you can travel south into Kenting National Park or north to Highway 9 and Taitung.

Kenting National Park

Straddling Taiwan's southern tip and bounded by sea on three sides, **KENTING NATIONAL PARK** (墾丁國家公園; *kěndīng guójiā gōngyuán*) attracts millions of visitors each year, lured by its warm tropical climate and magnificent white-sand beaches. The park covers most of the **Hengchun Peninsula**, which sits at the confluence of fault lines and tectonic plates. As a result, the peninsula has been pushed, pulled and twisted into a complex network of low-lying mountains, grassy meadows, steep cliffs, sand dunes and elaborate coral formations. Despite its remarkably varied natural scenery, much of it is overlooked by visitors, most of

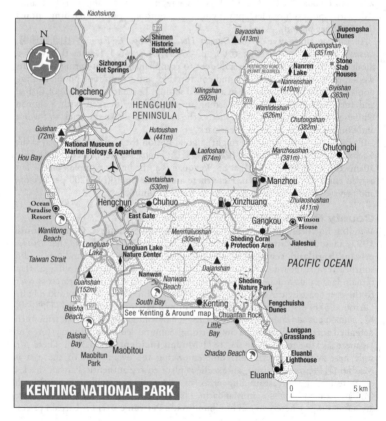

KENTING NATIONAL PARK

whom relish the amusement-park atmosphere of the main tourist area around **Kenting Town** and nearby **Nanwan**. With so many tourists clinging to these more developed spots, much of the park remains relatively quiet.

The park's **beaches** are definitely its biggest draw and, although the ones closest to Kenting Town and Nanwan are overrated (and often overcrowded), it's not hard to find your own stretch of fine white sand in a more secluded setting. While Kenting is no Ibiza, it can be entertaining at night and is also known as Taiwan's premier **surfing** destination (see box, p.281). Kenting's **busy season** starts in May and lasts through September, but weekends can be crazy year-round. To avoid the crowds visit midweek March to May, when it should be warm enough to lounge on the beach in relative peace.

Arrival and information

The nearest **airport** is at **Hengchun**, 10km north of Kenting Town, served by a handful of weekly flights from Taipei. Take a taxi (NT$250) or arrange a hotel pick-up if arriving here. Buses from **Kaohsiung** (see p.265) pass through Hengchun, Nanwan, Kenting Town and Chuanfan Rock, before terminating in Eluanbi. On the way back, you can normally hail these buses anywhere along the route, but look for the nearest bus stop sign to be safe. For routes from Taitung, see p.321. Some hotels can arrange **taxi** pick-ups from Kaohsiung (NT$1500, or NT$300–400/person; see "Accommodation", p.280).

The **Kenting National Park Visitor Center** (daily 8am–5pm; ☎08/886-1321; ⓦwww.ktnp.gov.tw) at 596 Kenting Rd, a few kilometres northwest of Kenting Town, has useful maps and brochures, and English-speaking staff are always on hand. There are also interesting exhibits on aboriginal culture and the area's geology. All of the 7-Elevens in Kenting Town have Chinatrust Commercial Bank **ATMs**.

Park transport

There is an infrequent **shuttle bus service** (NT$20–50) to various spots within the park from the Pingdong Bus hub in Hengchun (check the visitor centre for the timetable), but if you're sticking to the beaches it's easier to use the Kaohsiung–Kenting buses to hop along the coast: you should be able to pick up a ride anywhere between Nanwan and Eluanbi every thirty minutes (or less), 24 hours a day (just look for the nearest bus stop and flag them down). To Eluanbi, fares are NT$45 from Nanwan and N$30 from Kenting Town.

To see more of the park you have two choices: arrange a **tour** (usually by taxi; rates vary according to time and number of people) with your hotel, or **rent** your own transport. It's easier to rent a **car** in Kaohsiung (p.265), but plenty of places rent **scooters** in Kenting Town. While this was once easy for foreigners, thanks to a police crackdown most companies will now insist that you have a local or international driving licence. However some places will still rent with a foreign licence (they'll want to keep your passport as security): try **Sheng Li Zu Che** (勝利租車; *shènglì zūchē*; open 24hr; ☎08/886-1992) at 269 Kenting Rd, on the right just as you enter Kenting Town. Rates are typically NT$200/hr, NT$400/day or NT$600/24hr (for 125cc). If all else fails, your accommodation should be able to sort something out. **Taxis** tend to be very pricey unless arranged through your hotel.

Accommodation

Even on the busiest days it's possible to find **accommodation** in Kenting Town, although prices can double at weekends and holidays. Note that **rates** at the major resorts (which tend to be the only ones with English websites and English-speakers) have soared in recent years (NT$6000/night is common), so to save money you'll need to try the smaller local places on the main street. Below are average rates – add fifty percent for peak times.

Nanwan

Fudog Surf & Dive 福狗衝浪 (*fúgǒu chōnglàng*) 222 Nanwan Rd ☎09/8941-3258, ⊛www.fudogsurf.com.tw. The area's longest-running surf shop (see opposite), with two smart new doubles (NT$1700–2300) with ocean views and four-person suites (NT$2200–2800). ❺

Surf Pad 公寓 32 Linsan Lane ☎0930/996-905. Surf pad with style, opened in 2010 by a local surfer. Further up the hill behind Nanwan, it offers three designer rooms and a sun-deck with views of the ocean from on high; rates are NT$2100 Sept–May and NT$3000 June to Chinese New Year (for three people). All rooms come with flat-screen TVs, free wi-fi and DVD players. ❻

Kenting Town

Caesar Park Hotel 墾丁凱撒大飯店 (*kěndīng kǎisǎ dàfàndiàn*) 6 Kenting Rd ☎08/886-1888, ⊛www.caesarpark.com.tw. One of Kenting Town's top hotels, the *Caesar* is popular with families because of its child-oriented amenities, including free cots and a kids' play area. The plush rooms have a China-meets-Bali theme, and its restaurants are popular with non-guests. ❽

Catholic Kenting Student Activity Center 天主教墾丁學生活動中心 (*tiānzhǔjiāo kěndīng xuéshēng huódòng zhōngxīn*) 2 Wenhua Lane ☎08/886-1540. Clean, well-run hostel offering good value, with simple but affordable en-suite doubles. It's more relaxed than most of Taiwan's Catholic-run hostels – the gate remains open all night and drinking is allowed, provided guests behave respectfully. ❷

Château Beach Resort 夏都沙灘酒店 (*xiàdū shātān jiǔdiàn*) 451 Kenting Rd ☎08/886-2345, ⊛www.ktchateau.com.tw. On the northwestern edge of Kenting Town, this five-star luxury resort is the area's most exclusive hotel, controlling access to beautiful Dawan Beach. Rooms are spacious and stylish, many with fantastic views of the bay. The giant beachside pool has an adjoining bar. ❾

Hotel California 加州旅店 (*jiāzhōu lǚdiàn*) 40 Kenting Rd ☎08/886-1588, ⊛www.hotelca.idv.tw. Laid-back place run by local surfer A-Liao (who can set you up with boards and gear), with free internet (two terminals) and simple but spacious doubles for NT$1000–3000, depending on the season. ❸

Kenting Youth Activity Center 救國團墾丁青年活動中心 (*jiùguótuán kěndīng qīngnián huódòng zhōngxīn*) 17 Kenting Rd ☎08/886-1221, ⊛kenting.cyh.org.tw. Although this China Youth Corps-run hotel caters mostly to student groups and Taiwanese families, its unique design and location make it an interesting option. Built in the layout of a traditional Fujian village, it features elaborate facades and ornate roofs as well as clean, modern rooms. Tucked down a lane off the main strip, it's fairly quiet. ❹

Meei Shye Hotel 美協渡假旅館 (*měixié dùjiǎ lǚguǎn*) 126 Kenting Rd ☎08/886-1176. One of the cheapest hotels on the strip, with doubles for just NT$800 (weekdays/non-holidays); rooms lack style but are spotless and perfectly decent, with TVs, wooden floors and some with views.

Xiaowan Resort Hotel 小灣旅店 (*xiǎowān lǚdiàn*) 82 Kenting Rd ☎08/886-1015, ⊛uukt.idv.tw/inn/sw.htm. Boutique-like mini-hotel, with each room sporting its own funky, contemporary design and colour scheme, embedded flat-screen TVs and compact but stylish bathrooms. Off-season rates are a steal at NT$1300, but these can rise to over NT$3000 for the cheapest double at peak times. ❹

Chuanfan Rock

Whale Shark Coast Hotel 鯨鯊海岸 (*jīngshā hǎiàn*) 606 Chuanfan Rd ☎08/885-1606, ⊛www.whale-coast.idv.tw. Three spotless and spacious seaview rooms, with large terraces, and two cheaper non-seaview doubles that start at NT$1500, rising to NT$3000 in peak season. ❺

Ya Ke Beach Resort 亞哥之家 (*yàgē zhījiā*) 690 Chuanfan Rd ☎08/885-1788, ⊛www.yake.idv.tw. The village's best deal is near the 7-Eleven, its stylish doubles with sea-view balconies and breakfast included. There is no English sign for the hotel and the owners speak little English, but they're friendly and are happy to rent basic snorkelling equipment at a discount. ❺

Yanshou Hotel 岩手旅店 (*yánshǒu lǚdiàn*) 678 Chuanfan Rd ☎08/885-1360. Gets the award for craziest facade, with a remodelled exterior that resembles the mouth of a cave. Rooms inside are super hip, though, with sleek contemporary design, funky sunken tubs and wooden floors, most with balconies overlooking the ocean. Rates start at just NT$1500, rising to NT$4500 at peak times. ❻

Eluanbi

Sand 沙點民宿 (*shādiǎn mínsù*) 230 Shadao Rd ⊕08/885-1107, ⓦwww.sand.com.tw. On the left-hand side of the road as you enter Eluanbi from Chuanfan Rock, this elegantly designed boutique hotel combines stone-slab minimalism with all the amenities of a five-star resort. With only eleven rooms – seven of them doubles – reservations are recommended. Rates start at NT$2000 off-season. ❻

The west coast

Ocean Paradise Resort 海境渡假民宿 (*hǎijìng dùjià mínsù*) 2-4 Hongchai Rd (Pingdong Route 153) ⊕08/886-9638, ⓦwww .oceanparadise.com.tw. Fabulous hill top hotel, best place to splurge if you can afford it, though you'll need wheels to get here. Rooms feature crisp black and white decor, LCD TVs and wi-fi, and rates include breakfast and afternoon tea; prices start at NT$4200 for weekdays off-season, rising to NT$6800. ❼

Exploring the park

Amazing **natural attractions** are scattered throughout Kenting National Park, but without your own transport you'll be confined to the busy main strip between **Nanwan** and **Eluanbi**, with **Kenting Town** itself at the heart of the beach scene. **Dajianshan** makes an easy excusion, while a longer day-trip might take in the intriguing coastal coral formations at **Jialeshui**, natural gas fires at **Chuhuo** and the idyllic white-sand beach at **Baisha**, on the park's far southwest fringe – one of the finest places to watch the sunset.

Nanwan

The first beach area heading south from Hengchun on Provincial Highway 26 is **NANWAN** (南灣; *nánwān*), about 6km northwest of Kenting Town, a busy strip of small hotels and **surf shops**. Parking costs NT$20 for scooters and NT$40 for cars; the beach itself is free. Nanwan is slightly less frantic than Kenting Town, with well-priced small hotels (see opposite).

In search of southern surf

Kenting has become synonymous with **surfing** in the Taiwanese psyche, as the typically gentle beach breaks along the southern coast are ideal for beginners; the season generally peaks in the **summer** months, although operators here can also organize surf trips to Taitung (where it's best in winter; see p.315).

Kenting's most popular surfing spot is **Nanwan**. The waves here are chronically soft and subject to close-outs, but they are good for beginners to practise their paddling and take-offs – and the handful of surf shops have no shortage of **longboards** for rent and also offer lessons and accommodation. **Fudog Surf** (see opposite), owned by American expat Sammy Hawkins, offers surf lessons (2hr) including board rental, at NT$1000 for hotel guests and NT$800 thereafter (NT$1800 for one-on-one), surfboard rentals for NT$600 per day and bodyboards for NT$200 per day. In Kenting Town itself, the **Kenting Surf Shop** (墾丁衝浪店; *kěndīng chonglàngdiàn*; daily 10am–10pm; ⊕08/886-2076, ⓦkentingsurfshop.com.tw) at 21 Kenting Rd offers hostel rooms and surf wear and boards to sell.

For slightly more consistent surf, drive around the coast road to the park's Pacific side, where the shallow bay and river mouth near **Jialeshui** can dish up some sweet barrels. The black-sand beach here is a nice place to camp, but if you're tentless there's a friendly surfers' hostel about 200m up the road. The homely *Winson House* at 244 Chashan Rd (周文生衝浪教學會館; *zhōuwénshēng chōnglàng jiāoxué huìguǎn*; ⊕08/880-1053, ⓦwww.tbay.com.tw; ❸), run by one of Taiwan's best-known surfers, has communal **dorm beds** (NT$400/person) and eleven rooms that sleep four to six people from NT$1200. The hostel also rents **surfboards** (NT$800/day), **bodyboards** (NT$500/day) and wetsuits (NT$200/day). **Lessons** are NT$2000 for one day. Kaohsiung pick-ups start at NT$3000 for one person.

Kenting Town

Undoubtedly the park's nerve centre, **Kenting Town** (墾丁; *kěndīng*) has by far the widest range of hotels, restaurants, shops and bars, and during peak seasons it becomes a lively party town. The main drag, Kenting Road (墾丁路; *kěndīnglù*) is packed with **clubs** and **discos** pumping out music at night, and **food stalls** serving a dizzying array of "little eats" line the road in the evenings. There are also myriad **souvenir stands** and shops, selling everything from earthy bead necklaces to Kenting T-shirts and trendy swimwear. Unfortunately, the beach scene lags behind all this: access to most of the longest stretch of sand, **Dawan Beach** (大灣海灘; *dàwān hǎitān*), is controlled by *Château Beach Resort* and open to guests only. Things may be changing: check for the latest at places like Fudog Surf (p.280).

The only beach in Kenting Town easily accessed by the public is the much smaller **Xiaowan Beach** (小灣海灘; *xiǎowān hǎitān*), directly across Kenting Road from the *Caesar Park Hotel*. At weekends and in summer this beach suffers from chronic overcrowding and the shallow part of the bay is a complete free-for-all of swimmers, surfers and snorkellers. The biggest danger comes from **jet-skis** that rip through the water, often coming dangerously close to bathers. The huge rock on the west side of the bay is part of **Frog Rock Marine Park** (青蛙石海洋公園; *qīngwāshí hǎiyáng gōngyuán*; NT$50/scooter, NT$100/car) accessed via the lane to *Kenting Youth Activity Center*. Here you can clamber around the outcrop, which looks a bit like a giant frog, and the ancient lava flows crumpled along the nearby promontory.

Inland loop: Dajianshan to Chuanfan Rock

The entrance to the park's main inland area is through the archway on the north side of the main intersection at Kenting Town's western edge. From the archway, a solitary road climbs northeast, with **Dajianshan** (大尖山; *dàjiānshān*; 318m) in constant view on the left. About 4.5km up the winding road a car park signals the entrance to the **Kenting Forest Recreation Area** (墾丁森林公園;

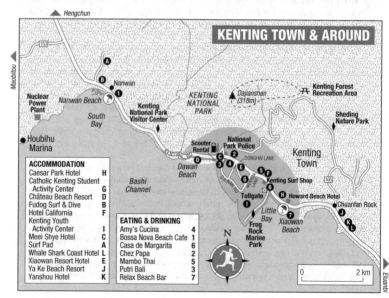

KENTING TOWN & AROUND

ACCOMMODATION

Caesar Park Hotel	H
Catholic Kenting Student Activity Center	G
Château Beach Resort	D
Fudog Surf & Dive	B
Hotel California	F
Kenting Youth Activity Center	I
Meei Shye Hotel	C
Surf Pad	A
Whale Shark Coast Hotel	L
Xiaowan Resort Hotel	E
Ya Ke Beach Resort	J
Yanshou Hotel	K

EATING & DRINKING

Amy's Cucina	4
Bossa Nova Beach Cafe	1
Casa de Margarita	6
Chez Papa	2
Mambo Thai	5
Putri Bali	3
Relax Beach Bar	7

Dive Kenting

Kenting is better known for its surf than its **diving**, but the latter is fast improving thanks to better conservation and fishing regulations. Highlights include the Flower Garden and Maobitou sites, just offshore, with an incredible spread of soft corals, and Chuanfan Rock, where you can see blue spotted rays. Boat dives can access richer sites; contact Canadian expat John Boo (℡091/338-8065, ⊛www.udive .com.tw), who runs two-dive packages from NT$2400, and also a cheap hostel (NT$400–500/person).

kěndīng sēnlín gōngyuán; daily 8am–5.30pm; NT$150; parking NT$50/cars, NT$20/scooters), a 435-hectare maze of trails, ranging from short nature walks to two more challenging hikes to the top of Dajianshan. While these hikes afford unfettered views of the entire park, the trails are often closed due to landslips and the peak is currently closed to tourists, so enquire at the national park visitor centre before setting out. The area is also renowned for its cave-like formations and lush botanical gardens, including the **Valley of the Hanging Banyans**, which slices through a succession of limestone cliffs covered in hanging banyan tree roots.

Just southeast along the same road, the **Sheding Nature Park** (社頂公園; *shědīng gōngyuán*; daily 8am–5pm; free; parking NT$40/car, NT$10/scooter) also features a web of hiking trails, through valleys of inland coral reef, limestone caves and grasslands. The park hosts legions of colourful butterflies as well as chirping cicadas for much of the year. From here the road circles down the mountain towards the shore, yielding clear views of the coastline around Chuanfan Rock.

Chuanfan Rock

A few kilometres south of Kenting Town, **Chuanfan Rock** (船帆石; *chuánfān shí*) is a comparatively laid-back cluster of hotels and restaurants looking out over an arresting stretch of coral-lined coast. A few hundred metres west of the hotel strip is a beach, while directly across from the main hotels is the village's namesake, a massive slab of eroded coral jutting from the water in a formation said to resemble a **Chinese junk sail** (*chuánfān*). The reef that encircles this tower of coral is home to an astonishing array of **tropical fish** and has become a popular **snorkelling** spot (rent equipment at the nearby hotels; see p.280), although the jet-skis that encroach on this area from their base at the nearby beach can make it a slightly unnerving pastime.

Shadao Beach and Eluanbi

Heading southeast from Chuanfan Rock on the coast road you'll pass pristine **Shadao Beach** (砂島海灘; *shādǎo hǎitān*), composed almost entirely of sand from seashells, coral and marine microorganisms known as foraminifers. The beach is protected and off-limits, but there is an adjacent exhibition hall with a **viewing platform**. The coast road continues to **ELUANBI** (鵝鑾鼻; *éluánbí*), 7km from Kenting Town, Taiwan's southernmost village. The area's defining landmark is the **Eluanbi Lighthouse** (鵝鑾鼻燈塔; *éluánbí dēngtǎ*; Tues–Sun 9am–4pm; free), first erected in 1882 and rebuilt in 1947 after being bombed by the US Air Force; the views are well worth the short stroll up the hill. The 21.4m lighthouse is the centrepiece of **Eluanbi Park** (鵝鑾鼻公園; *éluánbí gōngyuán*; Tues–Sun: Nov–March 7am–5.30pm, April–Oct 6.30am–6.30pm; NT$40; parking NT$10/scooter, NT$40/car), just off the main road and popular with tour buses.

The east coast

From Eluanbi Highway 26 curves sharply north, clinging to the **cliffs** and **dunes** along the park's Pacific shoreline. Along the way are numerous viewpoints where you can pull off the road and admire the scenery. Carry on until the road forks at **Gangkou** (港口; *gǎngkǒu*) and turn right to reach **Jialeshui** (佳樂水; *jiālèshuǐ*), a string of fantastic **coral formations** which locals liken to an array of animal shapes.

For a taste of the park's remote, **hilly northeast**, return to Gangkou and head northwest along County Route 200 for 4.4km before turning right towards the village of **Manzhou** (滿州; *mǎnzhōu*); from here the road passes sleepy Paiwan hamlets, far removed from the tourist hordes in Kenting Town.

Around 12km beyond Manzhou, and just outside of the national park boundary, are the shimmering **Jiupengsha Dunes** (九棚砂; *jiǔpéngshā*); from here, you'll need to go back the way you came, head north to make an even bigger loop on County Route 199 (see p.277) or drive due south along the bumpy old **coastal track** that runs directly back to Jialeshui. This road is technically off-limits to tourists, but the rule is not enforced and it makes for an exciting detour (be sure you have plenty of petrol).

Chuhuo and Hengchun

County Route 200 runs around 14km west from Gangkou to the **natural gas fires** at **Chuhuo Special Scenic Area** (出火特別景觀區; *chūhuǒ tèbié jǐngguān qū*; free), just before Hengchun. Caused by methane escaping through fissures in the mudstone, the fires are a bizarre sight, although rather phoney-looking as they are ringed off by a shallow fence – tourists sometimes cook eggs on the fires. Although they're more impressive at night, you can usually see them during the day (best in spring and winter dry seasons). Just west of Chuhuo, on the outskirts of the busy but otherwise uninteresting town of **HENGCHUN** (恆春; *héngchūn*), the **East Gate** (東門; *dōngmén*) is a well-preserved section of an imperial Chinese city wall built in the 1870s.

The west coast

The major draw for tourists in the northwest corner of the national park is the futuristic **National Museum of Marine Biology and Aquarium** (國立海洋生物博物館; *guólì hǎiyáng shēngwù bówùguǎn*; daily: April–Nov Mon–Fri 9am–6pm, Sat & Sun 8am–6pm; Dec–March 9am–5pm; NT$450; Ⓦ www.nmmba.gov.tw), just off Highway 26 on Pingdong Route 153, a lavish facility containing marine displays, a water park and huge fish tanks with an 81m underwater moving track (the park shuttle bus stops here).

Spring Scream

The US has Spring Break, but Taiwan has Spring Scream. For the country's growing legions of rock music fans, Kenting Town has become the site of one of Taiwan's biggest annual rock festivals – **Spring Scream** (春天吶喊; *chūntiān nàhǎn*; Ⓦ www .springscream.com) – held every April since 1995. Popular with Taiwanese and expatriates alike, this five-day event showcases both international and home-grown talent and is consistently the country's biggest gathering of foreigners, with expats from all corners of the island converging on Kenting Town for days of unbridled indulgence. Book accommodation way in advance or prepare to crash on the beach. Expect to pay around NT$1500 for an all-event pass, or NT$600–900 for single days. The venue changes, but all the most recent festivals have been held at the Eluanbi Lighthouse.

South on Route 153 is the park's largely untrammelled southwest corner, ringed with alluring and often empty **beaches**. Follow the signs for **Maobitou Park** (貓鼻頭公園; *máobítóu gōngyuán*; daily 8am–5pm; free; parking NT$10/scooter, NT$40/car), another patch of eroded coastal coral formations with a small **visitor centre** (daily 8am–noon & 1–5pm) and fabulous views across to Nanwan and Kenting Town.

The real highlight of this area – and indeed of the park as a whole – is the glorious 400m-long white-sand beach at **Baisha Bay** (白沙灣; *báishāwān*). Unlike beaches closer to Kenting Town, which are perennially packed, Baisha looks and feels like the quintessential tropical beach, with glistening sands seeming to melt into the turquoise sea – **sunsets** here are truly outstanding.

Eating and drinking

In addition to the many **food stalls** along Kenting Road (evenings only), there are numerous **restaurants** specializing in a broad range of cuisine in Kenting Town, including Western-style establishments serving favourites such as **pizza** and **pasta**. **Thai food** is a current craze, although it's not particularly authentic. For cheap Taiwanese seafood, head to the Hengchun Fishery Association Building (恆春漁會大樓吃海鮮; *héngchūn yúhuì dàlóuchī hǎixiān*; daily 11am–9pm) on the road to Maobitou, where numerous stalls serve huge plates of sashimi for NT$100.

Nanwan

Bossa Nova Beach Cafe 巴沙諾瓦 (*bāshānuòwǎ*) 100 Nanwan Rd ☏08/889-7137. Beautifully decorated restaurant that offers a spread of tasty Malaysian food (now that the former owner and chef at *Warung Didi*, below, is here, not to mention the standout views of the bay. The house specialty – hot and spicy chicken with Thai sauce – is delicious, as is the spicy shrimp coconut curry (main dishes NT$200–300). Daily 11am–2pm & 5–10pm.

Kenting Town

Amy's Cucina 酒吧餐廳 (*jiǔbā cāntīng*) 131-1 Kenting Rd ☏08/886-1977. This Kenting stalwart, a redbrick, Italian-style eatery, serves up some of Kenting Town's tastiest pizza and pasta. Reckon on NT$350/person for a full meal.
Casa de Margarita 瑪格利特餐廳 (*mǎgélìtè cāntīng*) 21-3 Kenting Rd ☏08/886-1679. Inviting bar owned by English expat, with bright interiors and wicker chairs to fit the Mexican theme, excellent cocktails and decent Mexican-style food (breakfast NT$200). Daily 9am–10pm.
Chez Papa 爸爸的家 (*bàbàdejiā*) 142 Kenting Rd ☏08/889-1464 (opposite *Amy's*). Cosy restaurant owned by French expat and Taiwanese wife, knocking out some of the best

(large) pizzas on the island; the house specials are margherita (NT$220), calamari and four seasons (both NT$280), but there's a huge variety of flavours. Also does sublime paella. Daily 11am–1am.
Mambo Thai 曼波 泰式料理 (*mànpō tàishì liàolǐ*) 46 Kenting Rd ☏08/886-2878. Cut above the other Thai restaurants on the strip – the owner pays regular visits to Thailand to hone his skills. Portions small and expensive (NT$180–200), but very tasty and quite authentic. Daily 11am–3pm & 5–11pm.
Putri Bali 峇里公主 (*kělǐ gōngzhǔ*) 273 Kenting Rd ☏08/885-6885. Plush southeast Asian place at the north end of the village, which also does Balinese-themed rooms (❺). Opt for the good-value set lunches and dinners (from NT$680) or order from the menu (NT$180–200/dish). Daily 11am–2.30pm & 5–11pm.

Xiaowan

Relax Beach Bar Xiaowan Beach. This chilled-out place sits on a wooden deck right on the beach – the only real beach bar in Kenting, owned by *Caesar Park* and perfect for sunset drinks. Walk down the wooden steps to the beach. Daily 10am–midnight, live bands 9–11pm.

Travel details

Trains

Fangliao to: Kaohsiung (5 express daily; 1hr 10min); Taitung (3 express daily; 1hr 20min).
Kaohsiung to: Fangliao (5 express daily; 1hr 10min); Pingdong (9 express daily; 20min); Taichung (frequent High-Speed trains; 46min; 14 express daily; 2hr 30min); Tainan (frequent High-Speed trains; 15min; 17 express daily; 30min); Taipei (frequent High-Speed trains; 2hr; 15 express daily; 4hr 30min); Taitung (5 express daily; 2hr).
Tainan to: Chiayi (frequent High-Speed trains; 18min; 14 express daily; 40min); Kaohsiung (frequent High-Speed trains; 15min; 17 express daily; 30min); Taichung (frequent High-Speed trains; 43min; 14 express daily; 2hr); Taipei (frequent High-Speed trains; 1hr 33min; 15 express daily; 4hr).

Buses

With so many services operating in the region, inter-city bus frequencies have not been included.

Most buses leave every 30min, and services to Kenting, Taichung and Taipei often run 24hr.
Kaohsiung to: Baolai (1 daily; 3hr 30min); Donggang (1hr); Foguangshan (40min); Kenting (2hr); Meinong (1hr); Taichung (2hr 40min); Taipei (5hr); Taitung (3–4hr).
Kenting to: Kaohsiung (frequent; 2hr).
Pingdong to: Maolin (frequent; 1hr); Sandimen (every 20min; 1hr).
Tainan to: Kaohsiung (40min); Nankunshen (hourly; 2hr); Taichung (2hr); Taipei (4hr 30min); Xuejia (hourly; 1hr);.

Flights

Hengchun to: Taipei (3 weekly; 1hr 10min).
Kaohsiung to: Hualien (3 or 4 daily; 45min); Kinmen (5 daily; 55min); Magong (19 daily; 35min); Qimei (2 daily; 20min); Taipei (20 daily; 50min); Wangan (2 weekly; 25min).
Tainan to: Kinmen (2 daily; 50min); Magong (4 daily; 25min).

5

The east coast

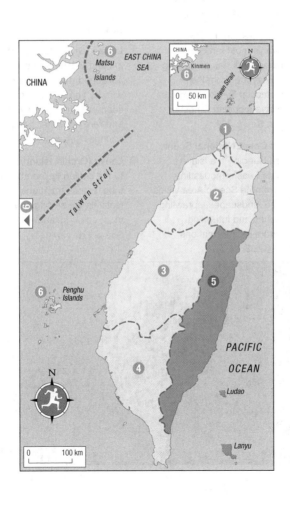

CHAPTER 5

Highlights

✱ **Hualien** The east coast's largest city retains a relaxed holiday feel, with some delicious specialities and a wide range of hotels, making it a convenient base for Taroko National Park. See p.289

✱ **Taroko National Park** Taiwan's most famous national park has something for everyone, from the spectacular Taroko Gorge to the awe-inspiring Qingshui Cliffs. See p.299

✱ **East Coast National Scenic Area** Hugging the island's isolated eastern coastline, this remote Scenic Area yields varied landscapes, sprawling beaches and intriguing offshore rock formations. See p.308

✱ **East Rift Valley National Scenic Area** Another Scenic area, this one encompassing an inviting valley of hot springs and outdoor recreation areas, including popular whitewater raftingand paragliding spots. See p.312

✱ **Ludao (Green Island)** This ancient volcanic island attracts droves of tourists with its verdant coastal scenery, superb snorkelling and rare saltwater hot springs. See p.322

✱ **Lanyu (Orchid Island)** Home to the seafaring Tao aboriginal tribe, whose traditional festivals are among Taiwan's most colourful and exotic. See p.328

▲ The beautiful Qingshui Cliffs

5

The east coast

Nowhere in Taiwan shatters the myth of the island as an industrial wasteland more resolutely than its pristine **east coast**, cut off from the country's crowded west and north by the cloud-piercing central ranges. While the region is best known for the awe-inspiring **Taroko Gorge** – the centrepiece of **Taroko National Park** – it encompasses a broad array of geological wonders. The plunging **Qingshui Cliffs** in the north of Taroko National Park are among Asia's most magnificent, while the **East Coast and East Rift Valley national scenic areas** are defined by picturesque landscapes and outdoor activities: hiking, surfing, snorkelling, diving, and **whitewater rafting**on rivers such as the Xiuguluan. The main cities of **Hualien** and **Taitung** are fairly slow-paced and well equipped for tourism, with numerous companies offering tours of nearby attractions. And just off the coast of Taitung are two exotic Pacific islands, both easily accessed by air and sea and fringed with coral suitable for snorkelling and diving. The closer, **Ludao** (Green Island), was a centre of exile for political prisoners during the White Terror of the 1950s, while the less touristy **Lanyu** (Orchid Island) is home to the Tao people – by far the most isolated of Taiwan's aboriginal tribes.

The region is visibly marked by ethnic diversity, with Taiwan's densest concentration of **indigenous peoples**: seven officially recognized tribes are represented here, and their relative isolation has enabled them to preserve many of their traditional beliefs, languages and practices. The stretch between the cities of Hualien and Taitung is the heartland of the **Ami**, and scattered throughout are villages of the Atayal, Bunun, Paiwan, Puyuma, Rukai, Sakizaya and Tao people (see Contexts p.395). Visiting the area during a **festival** period – the busiest of which is in July and August – gives a fascinating glimpse into a seldom seen side of Taiwan.

Hualien

The biggest city on the east coast, **HUALIEN** (花蓮; *huālián*) sits on a mountain-fringed plain 26km south of Taroko Gorge, making an ideal base for expeditions to Taroko National Park. It is also one of the world's major producers of **marble**, and elegant stonework is used liberally all over the city to adorn temples, pavements, the airport and even the train station. The relatively large number of tourists passing through give Hualien a laid-back, holiday-town atmosphere, with a growing number of pleasant teahouses and attractive restaurants where you can try delicious local specialities, as well as a handful of absorbing temples and an inexpensive stone market.

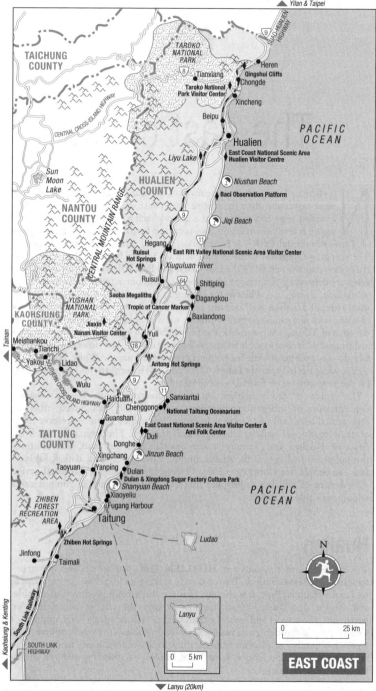

▲ *Yilan & Taipei*

TAICHUNG
COUNTY

*TAROKO
NATIONAL
PARK*

8 ● Tianxiang

Heren
Qingshui Cliffs
Chongde

**Taroko National
Park Visitor Center**

Xincheng

● Beipu

CENTRAL CROSS-ISLAND HIGHWAY

*PACIFIC
OCEAN*

Hualien

Liyu Lake

**East Coast National Scenic Area
Hualien Visitor Centre**

Sun
Moon
Lake

*HUALIEN
COUNTY*

Niushan Beach

Baci Observation Platform

NANTOU
COUNTY

9

Jiqi Beach

CENTRAL MOUNTAIN RANGE

● Hegang
**Ruisui
Hot Springs**

11

East Rift Valley National Scenic Area Visitor Center

Xiuguluan River

● Ruisui

64 ● Shitiping

Saoba Megaliths

*YUSHAN
NATIONAL
PARK*

● Dagangkou

Tropic of Cancer Marker

● Baxiandong

KAOHSIUNG
COUNTY

Jiaxin
Nanan Visitor Center

● Yuli

Meishankou

18

● Tianchi

Yakou ●
● Lidao

Antong Hot Springs

● Wulu

9

SOUTHERN CROSS-ISLAND HIGHWAY

● Haiduan

11 **Sanxiantai**

● Chenggong

National Taitung Oceanarium

● Guanshan

**East Coast National Scenic Area Visitor Center &
Ami Folk Center**

TAITUNG
COUNTY

● Donghe   Duli

Xingchang

Taoyuan ●

Yanping

Jinzun Beach

● Dulan

Dulan & Xingdong Sugar Factory Culture Park

Shanyuan Beach

Xiaoyeliu

*PACIFIC
OCEAN*

*ZHIBEN
FOREST
RECREATION
AREA*

Fugang Harbour

Taitung

Ludao

Zhiben Hot Springs

Jinfong ●

● Taimali

N

Lanyu

0   25 km

0   5 km

EAST COAST

◀ *Kaohsiung & Kenting*

South Link Railway

SOUTH LINK
HIGHWAY

290

▼ *Lanyu (20km)*

◀ Tainan

Some history

Hualien has a relatively short history, making it something of a frontier town: **Chinese settlers** from Danshui established the first village in 1851, but conflicts with various aboriginal tribes, including a fierce battle with the **Sakizaya**, resulted in the colony being abandoned twice and only in the 1890s did a permanent settlement take hold. The **Japanese** had a strong impact here, the region becoming an immigration zone for poor Japanese families during the occupation era, but Hualien remained a remote place for much of the twentieth century: it wasn't until the 1920s that the Japanese hacked out a road to replace the old track up the coast to Suao; the Central Cross-Island Highway was completed in 1960; and the rail line from Taipei opened in 1980. Today Hualien is a city of 110,000, unique in having almost equal numbers of Hakka, Hoklo, mainlander and aboriginal citizens: the last group are primarily Atayal and Ami.

Arrival

Hualien Airport (花蓮機場; *huālián jīchǎng*) is 6km north of the city, equipped with a **tourist office** (daily 8am–9.30pm; ℡03/821-0625), ATM and **car rental** desks (IWS Rent-a-Car ℡0800/008414) in the arrival hall. The **airport bus** into downtown (via the *Astar* and *Parkview*) operates around 14 times daily (8.30am–7pm; NT$38), while tour buses to Taroko also stop here twice a day – ask athe tourist office for details. A **taxi** into the city should cost around NT$200–250.

Hualien's **train station** (花蓮火車站; *huālián huǒchēzhàn*) lies just over 2km northwest of downtown. There are **lockers** just outside (NT$100/day, maximum six days), while **ATM** machines can be found in the ticket hall. **Taxis** are around NT$150 for trips downtown from here (for **scooters** see p.298), while buses charge around NT$25.

Hualien Bus Company services from Taroko and Taitung stop just outside the station, while **Dingdong Bus Company** has a small stop a few shops down from the visitor centre (see below), in front of a restaurant. Note that most other Hualien Bus Company services terminate in the smaller **downtown bus station** ("old" or "main" station) at the end of Zhongshan Road, closer to the shops, bars and restaurants.

Information and tours

The **visitor centre** (旅遊服務中心; *lǚyóu fúwù zhōngxīn*; daily 8am–10pm; ℡03/836-0634, Ⓦtour-hualien.hl.gov.tw) in front of the train station is well stocked with English-language material and helpful English-speakers. The Tourism Bureau sponsors "Taiwan Bus" **tours** of the east coast, Taroko National Park and the East Rift Valley, operated by local tour company Merry Travel Service (549-2 Zhongshan Rd; ℡03/835-5447), departing from the airport and visitor centre daily (from around NT$988). You can also ask about **whale-watching** tours (April–Oct; six times daily 6am–3.30pm; NT$1000) at the visitor centre and most hotels. **Huadong** (花東鯨世界; *huādōng jīngshìjiè*; ℡03/823-8000, Ⓦwww.huadong .com.tw) is the main operator.

Note that Hualien street signs still feature the old MPS2 *pīnyīn* system; Zhongshan Road is commonly labelled "Jung-Shan Road", for example. Smaller signs on buildings feature *tōngyòng pīnyīn*.

Accommodation

Accommodation is plentiful in Hualien, although, as elsewhere in Taiwan, **budget hotels** are harder to find. Apart from a couple of decent options closer to downtown, the cheapest hotels tend to be close to the train station in the north-western part of the city, which is convenient if you're passing through or hiring a scooter, but a bit dead. The harbour area north of the Meilun River contains several **top-class hotels**, but, once again, transport is a pain and you'll spend a lot on taxis if you stay here. **Mid-range hotels** offer the best value in Hualien, with a host of new and comfortable places scattered all over town.

Train station area

Amigos Hostel 阿美客國際青年民宿 (ā měikè guójì qīngnián mínsù) 68 Guolian 2nd Rd ☏03/836-2756, ⓦwww.amigoshostel.tw. Clean, friendly hostel 5min walk from the train station, with eight-, ten- and sixteen-person dorms for NT$450 per person, free wi-fi and shared kitchen; the owners can sort out all sorts of tours and activities. ❶

Chan Tai Hotel 仟台大飯店 (qiāntái dàfàndiàn) 83-1 Guolian 1st Rd ☏03/833-0121. Convenient budget option, across from the more expensive *Green Hotel* opposite the train station. Rooms are plain but adequate. ❷

Charming City Hotel 花蓮香城大飯店 (huālián xiāngchéng dàfàndiàn) 19 Guoshing 2nd St ☏03/835-3355, ⓦwww.city-hotel.com.tw. Hualien's first boutique hotel, with stylish rooms and a blend of contemporary Asian and Art Deco themes. Discount schemes can bring the cost under NT$2000, and it's within sight of the train station. ❻

Green Hotel 青葉綠地飯店 (qīngyè lǜdìfàndiàn) 83 Guolian 1st Rd ☏03/833-0186, ⓦwww.greenhotels.com.tw The old *Chin Yeh* has been given a thorough makeover by the Green Hotel chain, making this a convenient and comfy mid-range option, just across from the station. ❹

Mistro Homestay 密絲朵民宿 (mìsīduǒ mínsù) 104-1 Guomin 8th St ☏03/826-1512, ⓦwww.mistro.com.tw. Cute and cosy B&B in a modern home, with smart, stylish en-suite doubles equipped with flat-screen TVs and a friendly English-speaking owner, Claire, who will help organize tours and tickets. ❹

Downtown

Azure Hotel 藍天麗池飯店 (lántiān lìchí fàndiàn) 590 Zhongzheng Rd ☏03/833-6686, ⓦwww.azurehotel.com.tw. Elegant hotel popular with well-heeled tourists, though the 45 percent discounts available online make it good value midweek. The compact rooms are stylishly furnished, with marble-clad bathrooms and great views of the city from the large French windows. Free internet. ❼

C'est Jeune Hotel 花蓮喜臻藝術精品飯店 (huālián xǐzhēn yìshù jīngpǐn fàndiàn) 122 Zhongfu Rd ☏03/833-2889, ⓦwww.cj-hotel.com. Comfortable mid-range option a short walk from the Golden Triangle. Rooms are small but have been given boutique touches: stylish modern bathrooms, and free breakfast delivered to your room. Internet and bikes available. ❹

Formosa Backpackers Hostel 青年民宿 (qīngnián mínsù) 206 Jianguo Rd ☏03/835-2515, ⓦformosabackpackershostel .webs.com. Excellent modern hostel with friendly English-speaking owners who can set you up with tours, surf groups, kayaking, whale-watching and car/scooter rentals. The marble-floored dorm is modern and spotlessly clean. Extras include free wi-fi, tea and coffee, a shared kitchen and free pick-up from airport, train or bus stations if you call ahead. Dorm beds are NT$420, and there's a Japanese futon double room for NT$1100–1200. The location isn't bad, a short walk from downtown and the bars on Linsen Rd. ❸

Maya Hotel 瑪亞旅店 (mǎyǎ lǚdiàn) 516 Fujian St ☏03/832-6171. Budget hotel with a Bali-meets-China theme. It's an old building, but rooms are relatively cheap and have been attractively refurbished. ❷

Quality Inn 花蓮馥麗生活旅店 (huālián fùlì shēnghuó lǚdiàn) 46-1 Sanmin St ☏03/832-0000. This plush new branch of the chain hotel delivers all the standard comforts, with sleek contemporary rooms with large flat-screen TVs, daily fresh fruit and free tea and biscuits all day in in the lobby. Free wi-fi, though connection is poor on some floors. Worth shelling out for the executive rooms (❽) on the top floor, for the views, space and extra tranquility. ❼

Wuzhou Hotel 五洲商務旅館 (wǔzhōu shāngwù lǚguàn) 84 Zhongshan Rd ☏03/833-2292, ⓦwww.wzhotel.com.tw. This small hotel at the end of Zhongshan Rd, with a smart stone facade and great-value discounts mid-week (NT$1800), offers traditional modern Chinese interiors and good-value two-bed and three-bed rooms. ❹

North of the Meilun River

Ola Hotel 洄瀾客棧 (huílán kèzhàn) 11 Haian Rd ☏03/822-7188, ⓦwww.ola.com.tw. Bright hotel overlooking a palm-fringed section of the seafront, though views of the ocean are obstructed somewhat by the cement-loading port in front. Rooms are disappointingly plain considering the Surrealist theme in the lobby and café, but the free bike hire is handy for the Coastal Bike Trail opposite. ⑥

Parkview Hotel 美侖大飯店 (*měilún dàfàndiàn*) 1-1 Linyuan Rd ☏03/822-2111, ⓦwww.parkview-hotel.com. Still Hualien's top

luxury hotel, with all the extras including pool, spa, landscaped gardens and tennis courts. Rooms standard five-star comfort. There's a free shuttle bus from the airport, but otherwise it's a trek from downtown. The lavish buffets and *shabu-shabu* restaurant on site are the most convenient dining options. ⑧

The City

Zhongshan Road connects the relatively sleepy train station area to **downtown Hualien**, home to most of the city's bars, restaurants and shops. The best place to pick up locally produced marble is **Stone Art Street** (石藝大街; *shíyì dàjiē*; Mon–Sat 2–10.30pm, Sun 10am–10.30pm), towards its southern end. The "street" is in fact a large compound of market stalls selling cheap marble carvings and statues, fossilized coral and wood, and precious stone and jade jewellery, at the junction of Boai Street and 326 Chongqing Rd. Touristy **dance shows** are held here every evening (8.10–9.10pm; free) by local Ami people. This once shabby part of downtown is being slowly transformed by the **Hualien Railway Cultural Park** (花蓮鐵道文化園區; *huālián tiědào wénhuà yuánqū*; Tues–Sat 8.30–noon & 1.30–5pm; free ☏03/833-8061), a series of wooden Japanese-era buildings now serving as galleries for exhibits on the original East Coast Line Railway. The exhibits (labelled in Chinese only) are nothing special, but the buildings have been beautifully restored: the best examples are the old police station on Chongqing Road next to the bus station, and the collection of timber administrative buildings at Fuding Road and Fujian Street, built in 1910, where you can still smell the rich scent of cedarwood.

Return to Zhongshan Road and walk east along Huagang St to reach **Dongjingchan Temple** (東淨禪寺; *dōngjìng chánsì*; daily 5am–5pm), a tranquil Buddhist shrine. The entrance is at 48 Wuquan St, just to the left of the junction with Huagang Street. The main hall contains three golden Buddha statues, several massive **geodes** (rocks with quartz cavities) – and is plastered with local marble, making it unusually opulent (take off your shoes to go inside).

Hualien's **Golden Triangle** commercial district is formed by Zhongshan, Zhongzheng and Zhonghua roads just north of here. This is where most of the city's famous *muaji* (麻糬; *máshū* – *muaji* is Taiwanese), stores are located, selling the cakes made of sticky, glutinous rice and stuffed with sweet fillings: at 142 Zhongshan Rd at Zhonghua Road is one of many bright yellow **Zeng Ji** (曾記; *zēng jì*) *muaji* stores, probably the most popular brand in town (the original is at 4 Minguo Rd). The cakes here (NT$10–20) are always fresh and best eaten within two days (try the peanut or sesame fillings, or the frozen ice cream version).

Further along at 144 Zhonghua Rd, the **Hualien Creative & Cultural Park** (花蓮創意文化園區; *huālián chuàngyì wénhuà yuánqū*; Tues–Sun 10am–8pm, 9.30pm Fri & Sat; free) is another collection of handsome wooden buildings, which once served as the Hualien Brewery, built by the Japanese in 1920; today it houses gallery space for temporary art shows.

Sheng An Temple and Cihui Temple

Around 2km west of the Golden Triangle, along Zhonghua Road, are the most important Taoist temples in Hualien, regarded as the "Lourdes of Asia" for their power to heal the sick. They can be a little tricky to find: turn right off Zhonghua Road by the canal along Cihui (Tsz Huei) 1st Street then first right at Sheng An 2nd Street (marked by a large stele): turn left along Cihui (Tsz Huei) 3rd Street after around 200m, and you'll reach **Sheng An Temple** (勝安宮; *shèngān gōng*; daily

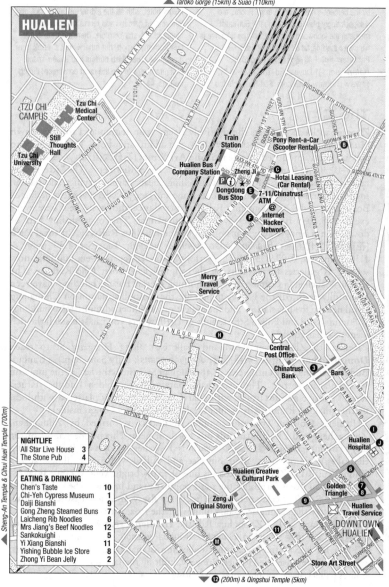

HUALIEN

Taroko Gorge (15km) & Suao (110km)

Tzu Chi Campus
Tzu Chi Medical Center
Still Thoughts Hall
Tzu Chi University

Train Station
Pony Rent-a-Car (Scooter Rental)
Hualien Bus Company Station
Zheng Ji
Hotai Leasing (Car Rental)
Dongdong Bus Stop
7-11/Chinatrust ATM
Internet Hacker Network

Merry Travel Service

Central Post Office
Chinatrust Bank
Bars

Hualien Hospital

Hualien Creative & Cultural Park
Zeng Ji (Original Store)
Golden Triangle
Hualien Travel Service
DOWNTOWN HUALIEN

Stone Art Street

(200m) & Qingshui Temple (5km)

NIGHTLIFE
All Star Live House   3
The Stone Pub   4

EATING & DRINKING
Chen's Taste   10
Chi-Yeh Cypress Museum   1
Daiji Bianshi   9
Gong Zheng Steamed Buns   7
Laicheng Rib Noodles   6
Mrs Jiang's Beef Noodles 12
Sankokuighi   5
Yi Xiang Bianshi   11
Yishing Bubble Ice Store   8
Zhong Yi Bean Jelly   2

Sheng-An Temple & Cihui Huei Temple (700m)

4am–9.30pm). A modern, garish building completed in 1950, it's dedicated to the chief Taoist goddess **Queen Mother of the West** (*wángmǔ niángniáng*) and significant because in 1949 the goddess is supposed to have spoken on this spot through the body of a young man in a trance. **Cihui Temple** (慈惠堂; *cíhuìtáng*; daily 5.30am–9.30pm) next door is dedicated to the same goddess, but this shrine belongs to another sect and here she's known as *jīnmǔ niángniáng* ("Golden

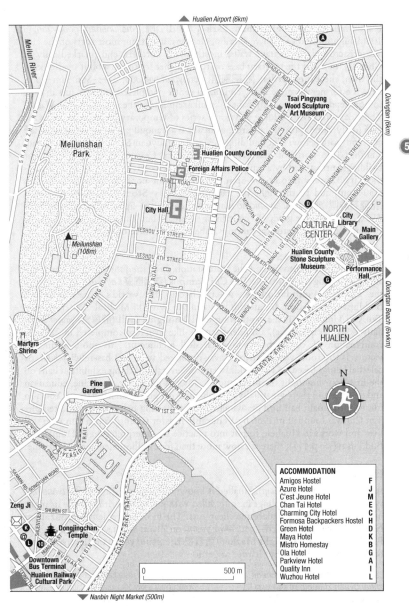

Mother"). Though it looks older and is far more alluring (the main hall is inlaid with marble), it was consecrated at the same time as Sheng An and completed in 1963.

North of the Meilun River

The area northeast of downtown across the Meilun River is a sleepy, modern district containing the city government buildings, hotels and a handful of sights.

It's dominated by **Meilunshan Park** (美崙山公園; *měilúnshān gōngyúan*) a 108m-high mound of lush vegetation, clearly visible from most parts of the city and crisscrossed by pleasant trails, mostly at its northern end (marked only in Chinese), to avoid the military base on top. Further south, on a bluff overlooking the river, the **Pine Garden** (松園別館; *sōngyuán biéguǎn*; Tues–Sun 9am–6pm; free) is a former Japanese Navy command centre completed in 1944, just in time to host send-off parties for Japanese kamikaze pilots at the end of World War II. These days the main building serves as a series of temporary art galleries while the **café** (daily 9am–8pm) in the gardens outside is a tranquil place to contemplate the city and port below. The building lies at 26 Shuiyuan St off Zhongmei Road. Another 1km north of here, Hualien's **Cultural Center** is a complex of four buildings surrounded by a sculpture park near the coast: facing Minquan Road is the **City Library** (Mon 6.30–8pm, Tues–Sun 9am–noon & 1.30–5pm, Fri also 6.30–8pm) and to the right the **Hualien County Stone Sculpture Museum** (花蓮石雕博物館; *huālián shídiāo bówùguǎn*; daily 9am–5pm; NT$20; ☎03/822-7121, ⓦstone.hccc.gov.tw), containing a small but intriguing collection of contemporary and historical carvings (labelled in Chinese only).

Tzu Chi Campus

Northwest of downtown and the train station, near the junction of Zhongshan and Zhongyang roads, sits the **Tzu Chi Campus** (慈濟園區; *cíjì yúanqū*), home of the **Tzu Chi Foundation** (ⓦwww.tzuchi.org), the world's largest charitable Buddhist organization. Located in between the Tzu Chi Medical Center and the Tzu Chi University is the captivating **Still Thoughts Hall** (靜思堂; *jìngsī táng*; daily 8.30am–5pm; free), a modern temple-like structure completed in 2001. A combination of contemporary and classical architecture, its most distinctive feature is the roof, with its triple eaves decorated with 362 bas-relief *fēitiān*, or celestial beings based on the Buddhist sutras. Several absorbing exhibition halls on the first floor highlight the foundation's activities in charity, medicine, education and culture, and there are usually English-speaking guides on hand (free). You also can visit the main hall upstairs which acts as a meeting hall rather than a temple. Tzu Chi was founded in 1966 by **Venerable Master Cheng Yen**, a nun who still lives and works in Hualien, to put into practice her interpretation of Humanistic Buddhism (see p.417); there are now more than four million members worldwide.

Eating

In addition to *máshǔ* (*muaji*), Hualien is known throughout Taiwan for *biǎnshí*, a type of wanton or dumplings in soup, filled with pork and shrimp, while its night markets are also a good place for cheap eats. The most convenient is **Gouzaiwei Night Market** (溝仔尾夜市; *gōuzǎiwěi yèshì*) on Ziyou Street south of Zhonghua Road, while **Nanbin Night Market** (南濱夜市; *nánbīn yèshì*) on the coast south of downtown is bigger but harder to get to.

Chen's Taste 陳記狀元粥舖 (*chénjì zhuàngyuán zhōupù*) 10 Xuanyuan Rd ☎03/833-3864. Congee specialist, set in a gorgeous old Japanese-era wooden house, with kitchen up front and tranquil dining room at the back. Various congees (fish, pork, vegetables) from NT$70, as well as smaller Cantonese snacks and teas. Daily 11am–9pm.

Chi-Yeh Cypress Museum 奇業檜木館 (*qíyè kuàimù guǎn*) 106 Zhongmei Rd ☎03/836-2577, ⓦwww.chi-yeh.com.tw. Not a museum, but an attractive Chinese restaurant, teahouse and woodcarving showroom in an old Japanese-style wooden house. No English, but menus have photographs of the main dishes and sets (NT$250–300). Daily 10am–2pm & 5–10pm.

Daiji Bianshi 戴記扁食店 (*dàijì biǎnshí diàn*) 120 Zhonghua Rd ☎03/835-0667. One of Hualien's most celebrated *biǎnshí* dumpling shops, a no-nonsense local canteen with a special recipe handed down within the Dai family from the Japanese era (NT$60). Daily 7.30am–12.30am.

Gong Zheng Steamed Buns 公正包子店 (*gōngzhèng bāozi diàn*) 199-2 Zhongshan Rd. Justly famous pork bun (*bāozi*) and dumpling place, with tables spilling out onto the road, steamers piled high on tables and women lined up making pork dumplings with super-human speed (NT$30–35 for/ six). Expect long queues at meal times. Open 24hr.

Laicheng Rib Noodles 來成排骨麵 (*láichéng páigǔmiàn*) 544 Zhongzheng Rd. No-fuss diner serving delicious bowls of noodles with a fried pork chop in soup, topped with green onions and pieces of leek (NT$60). Daily 10.30am–10pm.

Mrs Jiang's Beef Noodles 江太太牛肉麵店 (*jiāng tàitai níuròumiàn diàn*) 128 Zhongzheng Rd. Made famous by visits of late president Chiang Ching-kuo, this traditional place with wooden tables cooks up big bowls of sumptuous beef noodles (NT$70); the soup is spicy and delicious, though the meat might be a little fatty for some. Mrs Jang's son now runs the place but the matriarch still totters around at lunchtime. Daily 11am–2pm & 5–9pm.

Sankokuighi 三國一休閒餐廳 (*sānguóyī xiūxián cāntīng*) 536-1 Heping Rd ⓣ03/831-1902. Modern, stylish restaurant specializing in local sunfish or manbo (*mànpō yú*); special set meals are NT$600, and you can also try manbo tofu (NT$100), deep-fried manbo (NT$488), manbo sashimi (NT$500) and plenty of other seafood dishes (NT$200–300) to go with it. Daily 11am–2pm & 5–9pm.

Yi Xiang Bianshi 液香扁食店 (*yìxiāng biǎnshí diàn*) 42 Xinyi St. The most famous biǎnshí shop in Hualien, another one patronized by Chiang Ching-kuo and established more than seventy years ago. Bowls of the tasty dumplings get dished out automatically when you sit down (NT$60). Daily 9am–9.30pm; closes 2–3 days every month, some days between 1.30–4.30pm.

Yishing Bubble Ice Store 一心泡泡冰 (*yīxīn pàopàobīng*) 16 Zhonghua Rd. Downtown favourite with local students thanks to the huge bowls of ice cream and shaved ice (NT$40), with all the usual taro and bean toppings.

Zhong Yi Bean Jelly 中一豆花 (*zhōngyī dòuhuā*) 2 Minquan 5th St ⓣ03/834-3303. Popular local eatery not far from the *Astar Hotel*, specializing in *dòuhuā*, a tasty soybean dessert mixed with syrup and peanuts (NT$30). It's especially delicious with lemon juice in the summer. Daily 10am–11.30pm.

Drinking

Hualien has a number of atmospheric places to sip coffee or tea, but its **nightlife** is fairly subdued. **Linsen Road** between Zhongshan and Mingli roads is lined with several pubs and lounge bars, but it's likely to be very quiet during the week, and bars rarely open before 7 or 8pm. The *All Star Live House* (歐斯達; *ōusīdá*) at 403 Linsen Rd (daily 9pm–4am) is a friendly bar, with happy hour till 9.30pm, live bands and a menu of reasonable snack food. The *Stone Pub* (石頭族樂園; *shítóuzú lèyuán* daily 11am–1am; ⓣ03/833-1103) on Haian Road and Minquan 4th Street is a laid-back bar on the seafront framed by two banyan trees and offering various beers, tea and snacks. It's best to go later in the evening when the traffic on Haian Road has thinned out, and the cement port lights below seem far more exotic.

Listings

Airlines Mandarin Airlines (ⓣ03/826-8785); TransAsia Airways (ⓣ03/826-1365).

Banks There are plenty of banks in Hualien and most 7-Elevens have Chinatrust ATMs inside.

Bicycle rental Hualien's popular Coastal Bike Trail runs from Nanbin Park in the south to Qixingtan Beach 15.8km to the north, and is a pleasant way to travel between the two places. Rent bikes at your hotel or shops along the coast – you'll find a couple on the stretch south of the Meilun River or 793 Bike, 341 Zhongming Rd (ⓣ0933/537-793).

Car Rental You can rent cars from Hotai Leasing (和運租車; *héyùn zūchē*) at 69 Guolian 1st Rd (ⓣ03/831-5500, ⓦwww.easyrent.com.tw) near the station or at the airport (see p.291).

Hospital Hualien Hospital (ⓣ03/532-2352) has walk-in clinics Mon–Fri at 600 Zhongzheng Rd, near the *Azure Hotel*.

Internet Most hotels offer free internet access: if not try Internet Hacker Network (24hr; NT$20/hr) at 39 Guolian 2nd Rd, a short walk from the station. Downtown, try the cafe at 102 Zhongshan Rd (24hr; NT$20/hr).

Flights connect Hualien Airport with Kaohsiung and Taipei (see "Travel details" p.334). Hualien is a major stop on the Eastern Line with regular **express train** services to Taipei (NT$441), Yilan (N$225), Fulong (NT$314), Ruisui (NT$144) and Taitung (NT$346).

Hualien Bus Company runs just one bus a day to **Taitung** (台東; *táidōng*; NT$514) along the coast at 10.20am, via Baxiandong (NT$237), Chenggong (NT$345), Duli (NT$375), Donghe (NT$396) and Dulan (NT$435). Six other buses go as far as Chenggong. Buses along the **East Rift Valley** sometimes go as far as Fuli (NT$335) via Ruisui (NT$199), Yuli (NT$269) and Antong (NT$286) – at any of these towns you can pick up onward buses to Taitung – but most services only get as far as Guangfu, much closer to Hualien.

A few stores down from the Hualien Bus Company and train stations, **Dingdong Bus Company** offers three daily services to Taitung (NT$495) via the coast road (4.10am, 1.10pm, 2.20pm): the restaurant next to the bus stand sells tickets from 10am.

Most visitors to **Taroko Gorge** (太魯閣; *tàilǔgé*) take a **tour** (see p.302) or rent a **scooter** or car in Hualien (p.297). Hualien Bus (☎03/833-3468) also serves the gorge: **buses** for Taroko Village (NT$86) at the park entrance and not far from the Taroko National Park visitor centre run most frequently, almost every hour between 5.30am and 9.30pm from the train station (and downtown bus station 10min later).

Buses all the way to **Tianxiang** (天祥; *tiānxiáng*; 1hr 30min; NT$172), via Changchun Shrine (NT$104), leave Hualien at 6.30am, 8.40am, 10.50am and 1.50pm. Note that only the 10.50am and 1.50pm buses stop right outside the visitor centre (otherwise you'll have to walk up from the road). There's just one bus to **Lishan** (梨山; *líshān*) daily at 8.40am (5hr; NT$447), via Wenshan (NT$153), Luoshao (NT$189) and Dayuling (大禹嶺; *dàyùlǐng*; NT$326), plus an extra service to Luoshao at 6.30am.

Taxis and touts around the train station will offer to drive you on a short round-trip tour of **Taroko Gorge**: expect to pay NT$2000–2500 (per car). One-way fares as far as Tianxiang are usually NT$1500. Though Hualien buses to **Chongde** (崇德; *chóngdé*; NT$103) do travel a short way along the coast road to the north, the best way to see the **Qingshui Cliffs** is to drive yourself or take a tour.

Post The main post office is at 92 Zhongshan Rd (daily 9am–5pm).

Scooter rental Try the shops across from the train station: a good option is Pony Rent-A-Car Group (小馬租車集團; *xiǎomǎ zūchē jítuán*; 81 Guolian 1st Rd) to the left of the *Green Hotel*: in theory you need a driving licence but a passport or photo ID usually does the trick. It's NT$500/day for 125cc (NT$400 for 50cc).

Around Hualien

Before heading to Taroko Gorge, it's worth taking a day to explore **Qixingtan Beach** to the north and **Qingxiu Temple** further south. It's best to have your own transport here.

Qixingtan Beach

Around 6km north of Hualien, **Qixingtan Beach** (七星潭; *qīxīngtán*) is a popular hangout for locals, although it's a shingle beach and sits next to a major airforce base. There are a couple of attractive parks at its northern end, however, and though it's not a popular place to swim, it's at the end of the coastal bike trail and the site of an annual **manbo** or sunfish festival (April/May).

The southern section of the beach borders Qixingtan Village, which has several cafés on the seafront and **Chihsingtan Katsuo Museum** (七星柴魚博物館; *qīxīng cháiyú bówùguǎn*; daily 9am–8pm; free; ⓦwww.katsuo.com.tw) on the main road. *Katsuo* is a Japanese word for dried, fermented and smoked skipjack tuna, sliced into thin flakes and a staple of Japanese cooking. Today Qixingtan's old *katsuo* processing factory has been reborn as a working tourist attraction, and the museum has three floors of displays on the history of the fish and the local area, plus fish tanks, housed in an atmospheric wooden storehouse. Labels are in Chinese only, but it's worth sampling the product via steaming bowls of noodles (NT$50) or fishballs (NT$90) served at the *Manbo Wave* **café** on site. Japanese chefs smoke the tuna over straw-fed flames (NT$150 for seared tuna sashimi).

   Bus #105 runs from the Hualien train station to Qixingtan via the downtown bus station (10min later) and the Cultural Center, but only seven times a day (5.50am, 7.20am, 9.30am, 11.20am, 1.10pm, 3.30pm & 6.30pm).

Qingxiu Temple

Around 5km southwest of Hualien, close to the town of Jian (吉安; *jí'ān*), **Qingxiu Temple** (慶修院; *qìngxiūyùan*; Tues–Sun 9am–noon, 2–5pm) is Taiwan's best-preserved and most beautiful Japanese Buddhist temple, tangible evidence of the strong Japanese presence here before World War II. It was built in 1917 to serve as the spiritual centre for immigrants from Kyushu, mostly poor farmers who were relocated as part of a controversial government scheme begun in 1909. Derelict for many years, the complex was skilfully restored in 2003: the wooden Main Hall is surrounded by a garden containing 88 statues, representing the equivalent number of "distresses" in human life and recalling Kyushu's 88 Shingon temples. The temple is at 345 Zhongxing Rd, 1km off Zhongyang Road.

Taroko National Park

Framed by sheer seaside cliffs and majestic inland mountain peaks, **TAROKO NATIONAL PARK** (太魯閣國家公園; *tàilǚgé guójiā gōngyuán*) is Taiwan's most diverse national park and one of the island's top tourist destinations. The amazingly narrow **Taroko Gorge** (太魯閣峽谷; *tàilǚgé xiágǔ*) is the park's namesake and main attraction for good reason: stretching some 20km, with marble walls that soar several hundred metres above the **Liwu River** (立霧溪; *lìwù qī*) the canyon offers some of Taiwan's most awe-inspiring scenery, from crystal-clear waterfalls plunging down the rock faces to ethereal canvasses of ferns swaying gracefully in the wind as they hang from hairline cracks in the stone. Walking through some sections of the gorge is akin to stepping into an ancient Chinese scroll painting, with water cutting fantastic formations across the marble-cake cliffs and lushly vegetated outcrops draped in heavy bouquets of mist. Alongside the winding road through the canyon are several easy **hiking trails**, providing superb vantage points for some of the most spectacular features and giving a greater sense of scale. Though the gorge is Taroko's claim to fame – and the main tourist magnet – it comprises only a small part of the park, which also has some of Taiwan's most challenging mountain climbs, including rugged **Qilai Ridge** and the revered **Nanhushan**. Another of the park's finest attractions are the **Qingshui Cliffs**, which plummet dramatically into the Pacific Ocean along the park's northeastern boundary and are accessible only by the Suao-Hualien Highway (Highway 9).

   The park is named after the **Truku (Taroko) aboriginal tribe** (see Contexts p.399). Though the Truku, traditionally known for their hunting prowess and weaving skills, once populated many river valleys within the park's current boundaries, few remain today. Most of those still living inside the park are located in Buluowan and the Bamboo Village. As with all parks in Taiwan, extreme weather

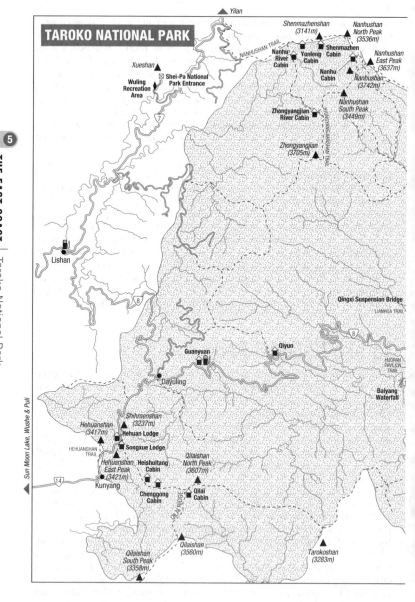

has an inordinate impact – Typhoon Morakot hammered Taroko in 2009, and much will remain closed into 2011.

Information

The **Taroko National Park Headquarters and Visitor Center** (太魯閣國家公園遊客中心; *tàilǔgé guójiā gōngyuán yóukè zhōngxīn*; 8.30am–4.45pm, closed second

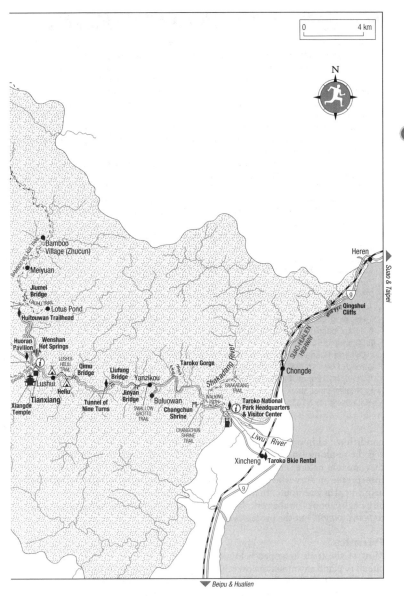

Mon of each month and Lunar New Year's Eve; ☎03/862-1100, ⓦwww.taroko
.gov.tw) are located just inside the main entrance, and most public buses will let
you off on the main road just below it (a 700m walk); only the 10.50am and
1.50pm buses from Hualien drop off outside. Allow for 45 minutes by scooter
from the Hualien train station.

If you're planning to spend some time in the park, it's well worth stopping here
to gather free **maps** and brochures, as well as to find out about the latest **trail**

Taroko National Park can be reached from several directions, making it one of Taiwan's most accessible wilderness areas. While it can easily be entered – and even traversed – by **public buses**, to cross the entire park you'll need to plan your onward route carefully to ensure you make your connections. For maximum flexibility, **renting a car** – or a scooter for the hardy – would be ideal, allowing you to see much more. Those wishing to truly explore the area – including its remote west – could easily spend several days here.

Most visitors approach Taroko from **Hualien** (see p.298), but you could also drive or take the bus from **Lishan** (see p.214); there is only one bus a day, at 3pm, arriving at Tianxiang at 6.30pm (and Hualien at 8pm). From **Sun Moon Lake** and Puli the route takes you into the western side of the park at **Hehuanshan**, but unless you coordinate with the Lishan bus, you'll need your own transport (see p.211).

The only **public transport** in the park is provided by the **Hualien buses** that ply the main gorge. Buses to **Tianxiang** (1hr 30min) leave Hualien main station at 6.30am, 8.40am, 10.50am and 1.50pm, but only the latter two drive up to the visitor centre entrance (1hr). The first two buses pass the main road near the visitor centre at around 7.30am and 9.40am respectively; these are the only buses that pass the upper trailheads beyond Tianxiang, and only the 9.40am bus goes all the way to **Lishan** (this stops in Tianxiang at 10.10am and reaches Lishan at around 1.40pm). From the visitor centre, these buses charge NT$55 to Tianxiang and NT$49 to the Tunnel of Nine Turns. The buses that depart directly from the centre at 11.50am and 2.50pm also stop at **Buluowan** and charge NT$71 for Tianxiang and NT$65 for the Tunnel of Nine Turns. Always double-check times at the visitor centre.

Heading back, buses leave Tianxiang for Hualien at 9.10am, 2pm, 4.40pm and 6.30pm, passing the visitor centre at 9.40am, 2.50pm, 5.30pm and 7pm (only the 2.50pm and 5.30pm buses stop at the entrance).

Cycling is another option, but you'll need to make reservations in Chinese from Taroko Bike (太魯閣峽谷自行車; *tàilǔgé xiágǔ zìxíngchē*; @Luicelu@gmail.com, ⊤0955/712726) at **Xincheng** (新城; *xīnchéng*) train station (with good connections to Hualien), just outside the park. Reserve in advance via email (Chinese only). Mr Lu rents bikes for NT$150/hr or NT$350/8hr.

conditions: although the park's trails are well maintained, heavy seasonal rains and the resulting landslips result in frequent closures, so it's important to ensure they are safe before setting out. There is always at least one **English-speaking interpreter** on duty who can brief you on trail conditions, bus schedules and even help you plan your route. In the centre is a café and **souvenir shop** where you can buy English books on the park. Note that the park is gradually converting signage to *hànyǔ pīnyīn*, but the process is unlikely to be complete for several years.

Permits

Most of the trails described below can be walked without permits, but if you intend to climb any mountain over 3000m, you need to apply for a **national park entry permit** (入園; *rùyuán*) and the **mountain entry permit** (入山; *rùshān*). Both are free and the process (with all the forms) is clearly explained in English on the park website (@www.taroko.gov.tw; see also p.37), which also gives details of current trail conditions. Applications need to be received via mail or in person at least seven days and not more than two months before the scheduled departure date. Due to the technical difficulty of the climbs (and potential risks involved), solo hikers will find it almost impossible to get a permit for peaks such as Qilaishan and Nanhushan (see p.307). However experienced climbers will have a better chance of success if they apply in person, allowing them to fully explain their plans to park officials. Generally, you're more likely to get a permit if there are at least two in your group. You can get the mountain permit for the **Dali-Datong Trail** (see p.304) on the spot, at the police station next to the visitor centre (with the correct form and ID).

Accommodation

Most park **accommodation** is located in Tianxiang, but hotels tend to fill up quickly at weekends, public holidays or during the summer high season, so if you visit during one of these times, be sure to book a room in advance. There are no **campsites** in Tianxiang itself, but just a few kilometres to the east are two places where you can camp, provided you have your own tent.

Heliu Campsite 合流營地 (héliú yíngdì) ☏03/869-1359. Located at the end of the 2km Lushui-Heliu Trail (see p.305), this normally tranquil site has calming views of the Liwu River. It is equipped with clean showers, toilets and elevated wooden platforms for tents (NT$200/pitch). At the other end of the trail, the campsite at *Lushui* (綠水營地; lùshuǐ yíngdì) is a bit more primitive, but it is free and its shielded location is even more serene. From here it's only about 2km to Tianxiang. Buses from Hualien can drop you off at either campsite, but you must let the driver know in advance.

Leader Village Taroko 立德布洛灣山月村 (lìdé bùluòwān shānyuècūn) 231-1 Fushi Village (Highway 8 km 180) ☏03/861-0111, ⓦwww.leaderhotel.com. Magnificent location, 8km from the park entrance and 2km off the main highway in the mountains, this is a great option if you have a car and/or money to spare, with stand-alone aboriginal-style cabins, simply but beautifully finished in wood, and stylish bathrooms. Free wi-fi and a fine restaurant on site. It's all a bit pricey considering the basic room standard, however. Pick-up from Xincheng train station is NT$100/person, or NT$200 from Hualien. ❼

Silks Place Taroko 太魯閣晶英酒店 (tàilǔgé jīngyīng jiǔdiàn) 18 Tianxiang ☏03/869-1155, ⓦtaroko.silksplace.com.tw. The park's only five-star hotel, with spacious rooms, marble bathrooms, a gorgeous pool, spa, bar and two pricey restaurants; the Japanese and Riverview rooms are definitely worth the extra cash. ❽

Tianxiang Catholic Inn 天祥天主堂來賓宿舍 (tiānxiáng tiānzhǔtáng láibīnsùshè) 33 Tianxiang ☏03/869-1122. Taroko's only budget option, with clean doubles – some with balconies overlooking the valley – and no-frills dorm beds for NT$300/head. ❸

Tianxiang Youth Activity Center 天祥青年活動中心 (tiānxiáng qīngnián húodòng zhōngxīn) 30 Tianxiang ☏03/869-1111, ⓦtienhsiang.cyh.org.tw. Excellent value, perched on the hill at the village's western edge, just past the *Catholic Inn*. The centre has a wide range of rooms and prices, starting from spotless rooms (NT$650/person for single-sex six-person dorms) to tasteful Japanese-style doubles (NT$4000) and double rooms (NT$1800–3000). Room rates include a Chinese-style breakfast, and the restaurant also serves lunch and dinner. Inside the hotel complex is a souvenir shop, a snack bar serving decent coffee and a very handy coin-operated washing machine and dryer. ❹

The national park

Most tour buses whip through Taroko Gorge to **Tianxiang** (the best place to stay and eat), briefly stopping at the main sights along **Provincial Highway 8** before speeding back to Hualien, but to appreciate the national park you need to get **hiking**. There are at least half a dozen good **trails** in the gorge; several of these are short and relatively flat, while a few of them are more challenging, with steep hill sections and trailside drop-offs. These are **often closed** due to landslip damage, so ask for updated conditions at the visitor centre near the main entrance before you get started. With more time (and hiking experience), the park contains some of Taiwan's most enticing peaks further to the west, while the awe-inspiring Qingshui Cliffs mark where the mountains fall dramatically into the Pacific.

Shakadang Trail

One of Taroko's easiest walks, the mostly flat **Shakadang Trail** (砂卡礑步道; *shākǎdàng bùdào*) hugs the bank of the bubbling Shakadang River, filled with translucent pools and time-worn boulders. To get to the **trailhead**, walk west from the park headquarters, through the tunnel with a pedestrian walkway (870m). Just after you exit the tunnel, there is a set of stairs on the right; descend these to the river's edge and you're at the start of the trail. The path sticks to the river for 4.4km, passing a small Truku village that has been all but abandoned. At the 4.4km point, the trail climbs to another former Truku village; from here, it's about 1.5km to the trailhead for the **Dali-Datong Trail** (大禮大同步道; *dàlǐ dàtóng bùdào*), which leads to a pair of far-flung Truku villages. However, the trail climbs steeply, with many switchbacks, and a mountain entry permit (but not the park entry permit) is required to venture beyond the 4.4km marker; this is the only permit in Taroko that's relatively easy to get (see p.302). Allow about three hours for the return hike on the Shakadang Trail.

Changchun Shrine Trail

Another easy walk, the scenic **Changchun Shrine Trail** (長春祠步道; *chāngchūn cí bùdào*) is only 1.4km from one end to the other, and can be started from the car park that overlooks the shrine itself or from Highway 8 about 2.3km from the park visitor centre. Coming from the centre, the trail starts under an arch to the left of the main road, and if you go in this direction there is slightly less climbing involved. After crossing a suspension bridge there is a short climb before you reach the ageing **Changuang Temple**, a Chan (Zen) Buddhist monastery with commanding views of the river. From here, the trail skirts the edge of a cliff before descending a steep flight of stone steps to the rear of the dignified **Changchun Shrine**, which straddles an elegant cascade – fitting location for a memorial dedicated to the 225-odd workers who perished while battling to build the Central Cross-Island Highway. The shrine is one of the park's most recognizable landmarks, and, as such, is a requisite stop for all tour buses, whose passengers pile out throughout the day to make the short walk from the car park for a perfunctory photo shoot. If you start your hike from the car park, you'll have to huff up the steep steps behind the shrine to complete the loop.

Buluowan

Once a cradle of Truku civilization, **BULUOWAN** (布洛灣; *bùluòwān*), 5km on from the Changchun Shrine, is now a tiny tourist village devoted primarily to the preservation – and sale – of the tribe's **traditional arts**. The small community of Truku here makes a living producing handmade crafts, which are on display in the **Taroko Handicrafts Exhibition Room** (太魯閣手工藝展覽室; *tàilǔgé shǒugōngyì zhǎnlǎnshì*; 9am–4.30pm, closed first and third Mon of each month). This is a good place to see women giving demonstrations of traditional loom weaving, while the men are engaged mostly in bamboo and rattan basket weaving. The village is about 2km off Highway 8 and is accessed via a steep, curvy road.

Swallow Grotto Trail

The tiny **Swallow Grotto Trail** (燕子口步道; *yànzikǒu bùdào*), another 1.4km along the highway from the Buluowan turning, runs 480m from the "Yanzihkou" stop on the highway, along the Liwu River gorge and main road to the Jinheng Bridge. It's an easy but dramatic stroll along the steep sides of the river; the grottoes on the cliff face that gives the trail its name are created by erosion as the river or groundwater rises out of the rock. There's a small snack shop at **Jinheng Park** (靳珩公園; *jìnhéng gōngyuán*) near the bridge, and a viewpoint of the **Indian**

Festivals of Taiwan

Festivals are a vivid expression of Taiwanese identity, a way to reaffirm cultural roots. The major Chinese festivals arrived with the earliest settlers, ancient traditions that have assumed a vigorous, distinctive character on the island. Celebrations such as the Lantern Festival mark the passing of the seasons, while others are held to honour the vast pantheon of Chinese gods, both Taoist and Buddhist. Taiwan's indigenous tribes still hold festivals with animist roots, passed down for hundreds of generations. For information on dates see pp.33–35.

Religious festivals

The **birthdays** of Chinese gods are celebrated with boisterous parades, with deities carried on palanquins to the accompaniment of traditional music, firecrackers, lion dances and opera singers. The birthdays of the Taipei **City God** (June) and **Baosheng Dadi** (March/April) tend to be the most colourful, while **Mazu's Birthday** (April) is the most fervently commemorated; the **Dajia Mazu Pilgrimage** is one of the world's largest religious festivals. **Confucius's Birthday** on September 28 is marked by a one-hour ceremony in Taipei that begins at 6am, an elaborate combination of bright costumes, strictly observed rituals and ancient music, considered by many to be the most authentic Confucian ceremony on the planet – the attendance of the current direct descendant of Confucius (79th generation) adds legitimacy.

Taipei City God Festival ▲

Lantern Festival, Yilan ▼

Heavenly lanterns and beehive fireworks

The **Lantern Festival** marks the end of the Chinese New Year, with decorative paper lanterns (usually depicting the upcoming year's zodiac animal) in temples and homes symbolizing hope for a bright future. The most spectacular celebration is held southwest of Chiayi, where **Yanshui Beehive Fireworks**, lodged in over two hundred walls or "beehives" the size of a truck, are fired into the crowds that pack the town, creating a cacophony of noise, fire and smoke throughout the night. The **Pingxi Heavenly Lantern Festival** culminates in elegant **sky lanterns** released en masse into the night sky, creating one of Taiwan's most mesmerizing sights.

Yanshui Beehive Fireworks ▼

Dragon Boat Festival

The **Dragon Boat Festival**, held on Lunar May 5 (usually June), is marked by **dragon boat races** and eating *zòngzi*, balls of rice wrapped in bamboo leaves. The races commemorate a futile attempt to save an ancient Chinese folk hero from drowning, over two thousand years ago. Unique races take place in **Erlong**, near Yilan, which are much smaller and more intimate than other events: the Erlong rowers stand or kneel in their boats, and rhythm is maintained by banging gongs rather than drums.

Ghost Festival

The **Ghost Festival** is held in Lunar July (the actual dates change every year), a time Chinese believe that spirits of the dead roam the world and must be appeased with offerings of food and prayers. **Keelung** hosts Taiwan's biggest celebration, with events held throughout the month; on Lunar July 14, **water lanterns**, thought to guide the souls of those that have drowned to salvation, are released into the harbour after a huge parade of floats, marching bands, traditional martial arts performers and musicians.

Hakka Yimin

The **Hakka Yimin Festival**, held during Ghost Month, is unique to Taiwan, a commemoration of Hakka warriors killed in the eighteenth century. Today it's infamous for the "**God Pigs**", giant hogs fed to gargantuan proportions, slaughtered, then displayed over special metal frames and arranged in front of Yimin Temple near Hsinchu on the morning of the festival. Every year the event is criticized by those who say that the ritual is extremely cruel (see p.155).

▲ Dragon boat race

▼ Temple lit up for Keelung's Ghost Festival

The Big Three

The three most important holidays in Taiwan are **Chinese New Year**, the **Dragon Boat Festival** (see previous page) and the **Mid-Autumn Festival**. Festivals tend to follow the **lunar calendar**, with families gathering on Lunar New Year's Eve for a lavish reunion dinner and exchange of "lucky money". During the Mid-Autumn Festival (Lunar August 15) families gather outdoors to gaze at the moon, eat mooncakes (rich pastries stuffed with red bean paste and egg yolk) and, increasingly, to share a barbecue. Many Chinese would add Qingming or the **Tomb Sweeping Festival** to this list, the day when families visit ancestral graves – in Taiwan it's officially celebrated on the anniversary of Chiang Kai-shek's death, April 5.

Aboriginal celebrations

Dragon dance ▲

Aboriginal dancing ▼

Many Aboriginal tribes hold **harvest festivals**, usually in the summer, while others mark important rites of passage. Rituals are enacted by clan elders and embody animist traditions that seek to balance the tribe's relationship with the natural and spirit worlds, usually accompanied by singing, dancing and communal feasts. The **Tsou Mayasvi Festival**, hosted annually in rotation by Tefuye and Dabang villages in February, was traditionally a celebration of warriors returning from battle, the main ceremony a series of dances culminating in the slaughter of a wild boar. **Paiwan** and **Ami** villages celebrate their harvest festivals individually with communal dancing, races, tugs-of-war and arrow-shooting, while the **Puyuma coming-of-age festival** is marked by bouts of wrestling. The **Thao** open their harvest festival at the end of summer with "**pestle music**" created by large pestles being thumped onto wooden blocks.

Chieftain's Rock (a hunk of marble that resembles a human profile with a headdress of grassy vines). A new road tunnel will divert traffic away from the trail (until it's completed the trail runs along the road).

Tunnel of Nine Turns Trail

Just under 4km along the highway from Swallow Grotto, the **Tunnel of Nine Turns Trail** (九曲洞步道; *jiǔqūdòng bùdào*) is the park's **premier hike**, following a stretch of the original road through the narrowest part of the gorge and providing unparalleled view points of the smoothly **sculpted marble** with its ornate patterns and the precipitous canyon walls. The wide 1.9km path has been cut into the cliff and much of it is sheltered by a cave-like overhang; note, however, that this is another trail frequently **closed** after heavy rain, typhoons and earthquakes. Check the visitor centre for the latest.

Heading west, the path starts on the left-hand side of the main road, and can easily be walked in a half-hour. **Buses** from Hualien will let you off here if you tell the driver in advance, but once you reach the other end of the trail you'll still have to find onward transport; **taxis** congregate here at times, but in their absence you'll either have to walk, hitch or wait for the next public bus that comes through the gorge.

Lushui–Heliu Trail

The mostly flat **Lushui–Heliu Trail** (綠水合流步道; *lùshuǐ héliú bùdào*) runs for 2km above a cliff overlooking the highway, offering clear views of the Liwu River. Just outside Lushui the trail winds through the remnants of an old **camphor forest**, with some ageing specimens of this valuable tree visible from the path. The walk takes just over half an hour and can be started from either Heliu or Lushui, both of which have free public **campsites** (see p.303). In Lushui, which is only 2km from Tianxiang, there is a **snack bar** where you can buy drinks. The **trailhead** at Heliu is only a couple of kilometres from the western end of the Tunnel of Nine Turns Trail (where you exit the tunnel), so if it's early enough in the day you could walk along the main road to get here; alternatively, a taxi can get you here in a few minutes.

Tianxiang

The tiny tourist village of **TIANXIANG** (天祥; *tiānxiáng*), 19km from the visitor centre, somehow manages to accommodate most of the overnight visitors to Taroko National Park while remaining remarkably free of tacky overdevelopment. There is little to do in Tianxiang itself, but it makes a convenient base for exploring the park's main trails. Everything is within easy walking distance from the **bus stop**,

Directly across the main road from the bus stop is the town **post office** (Mon–Fri 8.30am–noon & 1–3.30pm), which sells postcards and can handle international parcels. A short walk up the hill opposite takes you to the **Tianxiang Visitor Center** (daily 9am–4pm, closed second and fourth Mon of each month), where you can pick up free maps and brochures on park trails, but it's seldom staffed with English-speakers. Near Tianxiang's eastern entrance, on a hillside reached by the **Pudu Bridge** (普渡橋; *pǔdù qiáo*), is the **Xiangde Temple** (祥德寺; *xiángdé sì*), a Buddhist place of worship run by a handful of resident monks. Near the temple is a giant whitewashed statue of Guanyin (see p.404) and a graceful **pagoda** that visitors can climb for fine views of the surrounding valley.

Eating

Tianxiang is the best place to stay and the only place to **eat** in the park, with a clutch of overpriced Chinese **buffet restaurants** located next to the bus station – at these you simply fill your plate with what you want and the staff will weigh it, charge you and then stick your food in the microwave before serving it. Next to the post office is a small café run by the park, serving instant noodles (*pào miàn*) and coffee, while the restaurant in *Tianxiang Youth Activity Center* (see p.303) serves three decent meals a day for about NT$180. For a real blow-out head to *Silks Place* (see p.303), which offers a mountainous Western-style buffet at the *Wellesley Restaurant* (daily noon–9.30pm; lunch NT$715, dinner NT$880), or go for Chinese food at *Mei Yuan Restaurant* (daily noon–2.30pm & 6–9.30pm).

Huoran Pavilion Trail

The 1.9km walk from Tianxiang along the **Huoran Pavilion Trail** (豁然亭步道; *huòrántíng bùdào*) was still **closed** in late 2010 thanks to serious rockslide damage, so check the latest at the visitor centre or on the park website (it's unlikely to reopen before 2012). Hike it if you can – when the weather is clear, the **views** of the valley from the top (450m gain) are superb. Allow at least an hour for the climb.

Baiyang Waterfall Trail

This beautiful trail leads to the **Baiyang Waterfall** (白楊瀑布步道; *báiyáng pùbù bùdào*), which turns into a raging torrent during periods of heavy rain and can be quite a sight to behold. This is another trail **closed** at the time of writing, due to landslides that blocked the access tunnel entrance in 2009; the park hopes to have it open again by the end of 2011 (check before setting out).

To get to the trailhead, walk westbound along the main road from Tianxiang for 860m until you see a long **tunnel** on the left; walk through this 380m tunnel and carry on for another 2km, through a few shorter tunnels, to reach the waterfall. Cross the bridge leading to the **wooden platform** for direct views of the falls. Beyond here the trail ends at the **Shuiliandong** ("Water Curtain Tunnels") – so named because water drips from their roofs. However they have been closed ever since the 921 Earthquake (see p.183) dangerously weakened the rocks around them. The hike from Tianxiang to the falls and back takes about two hours.

Wenshan Hot Springs

Situated in the middle of the Dasha River, **Wenshan Hot Springs** (文山溫泉; *wénshān wēnquán*) have been officially closed to visitors after one death and four serious injuries in 2005. Locals and some visitors still slip under the metal gate, but at the time of writing the site had been severely damaged by rockslides and it is not advisable to enter. In any case, given that it is illegal, and that if you get caught you'll be fined NT$1500 (locals might dodge this, but you won't), it's not worth the risk. Check at the tourist centre for the latest (plans have been floated to pipe the hot water up to a safer roadside bathhouse). The springs are just off the main highway about 2.5km west of Tianxiang, on the right-hand side.

Lianhua Trail

The **Lianhua Trail** (蓮花池步道; *liánhuāchí bùdào*) is a little harder to reach than the others in the area, but is certainly worth the effort. The **Huitouwan Trailhead** (迴頭灣登山口; *huítóuwān dēngshānkǒu*), which marks the beginning of the path, is about 5km west of Tianxiang along Highway 8, by a hairpin bend behind the bus stop (km 163.4). To walk here along the main highway, you'll have to pass through a handful of dark tunnels, so a torch is essential. The trail is exciting from the onset, as the beginning has been cut into the rocky face of a towering cliff overlooking the Dasha River, and there are sheer drop-offs all along this stretch. Carry on for about 1km, crossing the **Qingxi Suspension Bridge** (清溪吊橋; *qīngxī diàoqiáo*; after 400m), until you reach the **Jiumei Suspension Bridge**

(九梅吊橋; *jiǔméi diàoqiáo*). Cross the bridge, turn right and start the steep ascent up the dirt path, where the earth has been secured by wooden planks embedded into the ground. Beyond this stage, the trail follows a winding, grassy road up the hill for several hundred metres before flattening out for the final stretch to the Lotus Pond, which is covered in green algae – the walk is mainly notable for the **lush forests** along the way. From the Jiumei Bridge it's about a 7.4km (3hr) round-trip to the pond, so allow ample time to complete the return journey and still walk the 5km stretch of road back into Tianxiang before it gets dark.

Note that the 12.4km trail to **Meiyuan** (梅園; *méiyuán* or Plum Orchard) and **Zhucun** (竹村; *zhúcūn* or Bamboo Village), which follows the river from the Jiumei Bridge, is expected to remain closed until at least 2012.

Qilaishan

The jagged saw-tooth protrusion known as **Qilaishan** (奇萊山; *qíláishān*), not far from the park's southwestern entrance near **Hehuanshan** (合歡山; *héhuānshān*; see p.214) is one of Taroko's most striking features and represents one of Taiwan's most challenging climbs. Narrow, craggy **Qilai Ridge** connects the main summit to several outstanding peaks, with steep drops on both sides, making it an exhilarating and sometimes dangerous climb. While the **trail** that runs over the ridgeline is well marked and in good condition, with no serious technical sections requiring the use of ropes, several climbers have fallen to their deaths over the years after losing their footing in thick mists, while typhoon-force **winds** have actually blown a few people off. In light of these risks, park officials are conservative in issuing the **permits** required to climb legally in this area (see p.302), and the best strategy is to join a group (see p.303).

The main **trailhead** is just inside the park's southwest entrance on the road to Puli (Provincial Highway 14A), near the **Hehuan Lodge** (合歡山莊; *héhuān shānzhuāng*; ☎049/280-2732), which offers information but can no longer provide accommodation. Instead, you can stay at the pricey **Songxue Lodge** (松雪樓; *sōngxuělóu*; ☎049/280-3393; ●) just across the road, 100m from *Hehuan Lodge*. There are several **cabins** along the trail, but most groups try to make it to the **Qilai Cabin** (奇萊山屋; *qílái shānwū*) for the first night so they can get an early start on the ridge and **Qilai North Peak** (奇萊被峰; *qílái bèifēng*), the highest on Qilaishan at 3607m. After negotiating the ridge, the majority of climbers return to Qilai Cabin for a second night before descending to the road on the third day. The safest time to climb here is in late **autumn**, when the summer typhoons have ceased and the weather is drier and less windy.

Nanhushan

Tucked away in Taroko's remote northwest corner is **Nanhushan** (南湖山; *nánhúshān*), Taiwan's fifth-tallest peak at 3742m and the favourite of most Taiwanese climbers. Despite its reputation, it's very seldom scaled due to its isolation and inherent technical difficulties, although seasoned climbers are unlikely to find it overly challenging. Like the Qilai Ridge, the biggest obstacle here is the **harsh weather**, as Nanhushan is pelted with strong winds, rain or snow for an average of about two hundred days a year, making some key sections of the trail arduous. Winter is a popular time to climb Nanhushan, although this is only for experienced climbers and, at the bare minimum, **crampons** are essential for the higher regions.

Park officials are extremely cautious about issuing **permits** for Nanhushan, and as with Qilaishan, you are better off joining a group (see p.303). The mountain can be reached from the north and south, but the more common route – and the one that starts closer to the peaks – is from the **north**, via a trailhead just off Provincial Highway 7 between Yilan and Lishan.

The staggering **Qingshui Cliffs** (清水斷崖; *qīngshuǐ duànyái*), located along a precarious stretch of the **Suao–Hualien Highway** (Highway 9) just inside the park's northeastern boundary, are among the east coast's most awe-inspiring attractions. Spanning a 21km section of the coastline between the hamlets of Chongde (崇德; *chóngdé*) and Heren (和仁; *hérén*), these sheer cliffs plunge straight into the turquoise waters of the Pacific Ocean – in places from heights of almost a thousand metres. Today, the coastal highway is heavily trafficked, with endless convoys of trucks spewing exhaust into the air and making it a perilous journey for cyclists, motorcyclists and motorists alike. The series of long **tunnels** carved straight through the cliffs is an engineering marvel, with each tunnel opening up to another invigorating view of more bluffs and sea.

Unfortunately for visitors, there are no public buses between Suao and Hualien, so the only way to see the cliffs is to rent your own transport. Cars and scooters can easily be rented in Hualien (see p.297), from where it's about an hour's drive to the cliffs. If you drive yourself, especially if you go by **scooter**, it's wise to leave early in the morning so you can make the return trip before the traffic starts to pick up around 9am. Just past the 176km marker is a car park (at the entrance of the Chongde Tunnel, about 12km from the park headquarters), with some of the best views of the cliffs.

East Coast National Scenic Area

Just to the south of Hualien is a crossroads, giving a choice of two routes south to **Taitung** running either side of the Coastal Mountain Range. Provincial Highway 11 hugs the Pacific through the heart of the **East Coast National Scenic Area** (東部海岸國家風景區; *dōngbù hǎiàn guójiā fēngjǐngqū*), prime aboriginal territory, scattered with idyllic fishing villages, rice paddies, herds of water buffalo and some of the best **surf breaks** in Taiwan. Buses ply the highway, and with careful planning (and pick-ups from your accommodation) you can visit the main spots on public transport, but to make the most of the area you need your own transport. If you're visiting in late summer and hope to witness some of the many aboriginal **festivals** held each July and August, private transport is essential – indeed, one of the joys of coming at this time is whipping from one festival to another on a **scooter**, soaking up the boundless seascapes along the way. The Scenic Area's **Hualien Visitor Center** (花蓮遊客服務中心; *huālián yóukè fúwù zhōngxīn*; daily 9am–5pm ☎03/867-1326; ⓦwww.eastcoast-nsa.gov.tw) lies just off the highway a few kilometres south of Hualien, with information and displays on the region.

Niushan Beach and Jiqi Beach

South of Hualien along Highway 11 are two of the area's finest beaches. The first, about 30km from Hualien, is **Niushan Beach** (牛山海岸; *niúshān hǎiàn*) a secluded stretch of sand that comes to a dead end at rounded Cow Mountain. Unlike some of the other east coast beaches, this one remains undeveloped and is an ideal spot to relax and enjoy some solitude. At times the swell is suitable for **surfing**, although experienced surfers are only likely to be challenged here during a tropical storm. To get here, you'll need your own transport – given its proximity to Hualien, it makes for an excellent day-trip by scooter or car.

About 10km further south, enveloping a bay surrounded by leafy hills, is the three-kilometre-long **Jiqi Beach** (磯崎海濱; *jīqí hǎibīn*) which is considerably more developed than Niushan and can get crowded in summer, when there are lifeguards on duty. The beach, near the 37km marker of Highway 11, is equipped with toilets, shower facilities and elevated wooden platforms for **camping**, although you're advised to bring your own tent. The water in the sheltered bay is considerably calmer than that of many other east coast beaches, making it a favoured **swimming** spot. Another interesting feature of this beach is the changing colour of the sand: during the lower tides of summer, it's mostly a dusty golden colour, while the higher tides of winter churn up dark stones and sand from the seabed, giving the beach a dark grey hue. About halfway between the Niushan and Jiqi beaches, near the 32km marker, is the **Baqi Observation Platform** (芭崎瞭望台; *bāqí liàowàng tái*) which commands a panoramic view of the coast to the south.

Shitiping and Dagangkou

Another 30km or so to the south, near the 66km marker, is **Shitiping** (石梯坪; *shítīpíng*), a 1km-long stretch of volcanic rock that has been eroded into terraces and other curious formations. The surrounding area is popular for **fishing**, and the **Shitiping Visitor Center** (石梯坪遊客服務中心; *shítīpíng yóukè fúwù zhōngxīn*; daily 9am–5pm; ☎03/878-1452) has exhibits on local marine life and other natural resources. A circular walkway allows visitors to inspect the rock formations more closely, and there are raised wooden platforms for camping – again, bringing your own tent is advisable.

Just south of Shitiping is **Dagangkou** (大港口; *dàgǎngkǒu*), which lies by the enormous estuary of the Xiuguluan River. Here, Hualien Route 64, more commonly known as the **Ruigang Highway** (瑞港公路; *ruìgǎng gōnglù*) cuts across the coastal mountains, following the Xiuguluan River for 22.5km to Ruisui, the starting point for whitewater raftingtrips (see p.314). This scenic road offers frequent glimpses into the gorge below, but there is no bus service so it's only possible by private transport – it makes for an excellent scooter or bicycle ride. Carrying on down the coast, just south of Dagangkou, a towering **white monolith** (北迴歸線標誌; *běihuí guīxiàn biāozhì*) shaped like a sundial marks the point where Highway 11 crosses the **Tropic of Cancer**.

Baxiandong

A few kilometres further south, near the km 78 marker, are the **Baxiandong** (八仙洞; *bāxiāndòng*), a collection of more than a dozen **caves** carved into the 150m-high coastal cliffs and one of Taiwan's most important archeological sites. In 1968, a number of **Stone Age artefacts** such as tools made of animal bones and stone were found in some of the caves, giving evidence of the **Changpin Culture** (named after the present-day Changbin; 長濱; *chángbīn*). Some of the artefacts date back thirty thousand years, placing the culture in the Palaeolithic period and making these hunter-gatherers the earliest people known to have inhabited Taiwan.

Today, most of the caves have been turned into Buddhist and Taoist shrines and filled with scores of religious deities. Wooden walkways with steps leading up the cliff face link the caves, and from the highest ones there are outstanding sea views. At the entrance (free) is the **Baxiandong Visitor Center** (八仙洞遊客服務中心; *bāxiāndòng yóukè fúwù zhōngxīn*; daily 9am–5pm; ☎089/881-418), which has some basic information in English about the caves and the artefacts they have yielded. All of the **buses** that travel between Hualien and Taitung stop just outside the car park (cars NT$40, scooters free).

Sanxiantai

South of Baxiandong, the road crosses a flat plain, passing by several unusual rock formations along the coastline. By far the most famous of these is the **Sanxiantai**

(三仙台; *sānxiāntái*), a series of small islets crowned with three rocky outcroppings named after a trio of legendary Taoist sages who, according to local lore, once visited the area. The turnoff, near the 112km marker, leads to a car park (cars NT$40) and a lengthy footbridge with eight arches spanning the shallow water that separates the islets from the mainland. Though the bridge tends to be packed with Taiwanese tour groups on weekends and during the summer, it's worth crossing it to reach the **boardwalks** that skirt the islets, thereby leaving the crowds behind. Much of this area is surrounded by coral reef, sheltering an amazing array of tropical fish and making for some of the east coast's best **snorkelling**. However, there is nowhere nearby to rent equipment, so you'll need to bring your own, and it's a good idea to stay close to the coastline. Beside the car park is the **Sanxiantai Visitor Center** (三仙台遊客服務中心; *sānxiāntái yóukè fúwù zhōngxīn*; daily 9am–5pm; ☎089/850-785), which has English-language exhibits on local geology and marine life.

Chenggong

Just south of Sanxiantai, near the 117km signpost, is the sizeable fishing town of **CHENGGONG** (成功; *chénggōng*) which boasts one of Taiwan's liveliest **fish markets** and some of the freshest seafood anywhere on the island. Inhabited by a mix of Chinese, Ami and members of the officially unrecognized *píngpǔ* Siraya tribe (see p.395), Chenggong has a population of about twenty thousand, making it the largest coastal settlement between Hualien and Taitung. Every afternoon at about 3pm, the local fishermen return to the town's Xingang Fishing Port to unload and sell the day's catch. These entertaining **auctions**, usually in full swing before 4pm, are a highlight of a visit here, with swarthy, betel-nut-chewing auctioneers rattling off prices in a maelstrom of Mandarin and Taiwanese, while weather-beaten fishmongers hack up the catch. One of the best times to visit is during the **swordfish** season in October and November, when scores of the pointy-proboscis fish are put on auction each day. Next to the fishing dock is a small market with a variety of local fish specialities, the most famous of which are the delicious dried tuna fish shavings (*cháiyú*). Just up the hill behind the market is the **National Taitung Oceanarium** (國立台東海洋生物展覽館; *guólì táidōng hǎiyángshēngwù zhǎnlǎnguǎn*; Sun–Fri 8.30am–6pm & Sat 8.30am–8.30pm; NT$200; ☎089/854-702), with several aquariums containing rare species of mullet, shark and skate. Highway 11 runs through the middle of Chenggong, and alongside the road are several small **restaurants** that serve up some of Taiwan's tastiest seafood for lunch and dinner.

Duli

About 12km south of Chenggong, near the Ami village of **DULI** (都歷; *dūlì*) is the **East Coast National Scenic Area Headquarters and Visitor Center** (都歷處本部遊客中心; *dūlìzhù běnbù yóukè zhōngxīn*; daily 9am–5pm; ☎089/841-520), which has a broad overview of the east coast's main attractions. The headquarters, near the 129km marker, include the sprawling **Ami Folk Center** (阿美族民俗中心; *āměizú mínsú zhōngxīn*; 9am–5pm, closed Tues; free, donations suggested), an open-air museum with reconstructions of historic Ami buildings and daily dance performances at around 2pm. The centre, managed by Taitung county's Aborigine Social Welfare Commission, also has a variety of traditional Ami handicrafts for sale.

Donghe

Don't be surprised if you see long queues of tourists in the otherwise sleepy Ami village of **DONGHE** (東河; *dōnghé*), 4km or so south of Duli; it has become famous island-wide for **Donghe** *baozi* (東河包子; *dōnghé bāozi*), exquisitely steamed buns with juicy pork and vegetable fillings (NT$18). Two rival shops claim to be the original and face each other across the highway, but both are pretty good. Donghe is also a top-notch **surf** destination (see box, p.312), although the grey-sand beach at **Jinzun Recreation Area** (金樽休憩區; *jīnzūn xiūqìqū*), a couple of kilometres south of the village, is a pleasant pit-stop for all, with a tranquil café overlooking the waves at the 136.5km mark. *Tropical Surf* (熱帶低氣壓民宿; *rèdài dīqìyā mínsù*; ☎089/896-738, Ⓦwww.easttaiwan-surf.com; ❸) at 99 South Donghe Rd is a comfy modern guesthouse targeted at surfers, with a variety of rooms, ranging from NT$1400 with a shared bathroom to NT$3600 for en-suite four-person rooms. LCD TVs and breakfast included; Taitung pick-ups from NT$1000 and surf lessons from NT$1200.

Dulan

Another 10km south, **DULAN** (都蘭; *dūlán*) is one of the largest Ami settlements on the coast. It's also a burgeoning surf centre (although **Dulan Beach** is a pleasant spot for just lounging) and some exceptional B&Bs make it the perfect place to stay a night or two. The town's primary attraction is the **Xindong Sugar Factory Culture Park** (新東糖廠文化園區; *xīndōng tángchǎng wénhuà yuánqū*), formerly the **Dulan Sugar Factory** (都蘭紅糖文化藝術館; *dūlán hóngtáng wénhuà yìshùguǎn*; Tues–Sun 10am–5pm, & Sat from 8pm most nights; ☎089/531-212), at 61 Dulan Village, 1930s sugar plant converted into a popular art centre and **café** (都蘭糖廠咖啡屋; *dūlán tángchǎng kāfēiwū*), on the north side of town on Highway 11; the Saturday night **live music** shows here are worth checking out, usually featuring local Ami talent.

For **accommodation**, the best deal is *Taitung Sea Art Hostel* (台東海之藝民宿; *táidōng hǎizhīyì mínsù*; ☎0935/061-578, Ⓔdreamboat6166@yahoo.com.tw; ❷) at 71 Neighbourhood 13, Lane 5, surrounded by lush forest and beautifully decorated by the artist owners. Rates start at NT$500; add NT$100 for breakfast and NT$250 for dinner. The owners will pick you up from the bus station in Dulan for NT$150, or Taitung for NT$500. For a step up in comfort, try the *Moon Rise Inn* (台東月昇都蘭民宿; *táidōng yuèshēng dōulán mínsù*; ☎089/531-065, Ⓦwww .moonriseinn.com; ❺) at 30-3 Xinshe, off Highway 11 at the 146.5km mark.

Shanyuan Beach

Just north of Taitung, near the 158km signpost, is **Shanyuan Beach** (杉原灣; *shānyuán wān*) one of the east coast's most picturesque. Sadly, at the time of writing the beach was officially closed due to a dispute over the construction of a resort hotel, although you can still access the sand by walking 100m north from the closed car park, and wandering down a narrow lane to a temple across from the beach. Check at any visitor centre for the latest situation.

Xiaoyeliu

About 6km south of Shanyuan, and marking the southernmost point of the East Coast National Scenic Area, is **Xiaoyeliu** (小野柳; *xiǎoyěliǔ*; daily 8.30am–5pm; free), a smaller version of the fanciful geological marvel Yeliu (see p.130) in northern Taiwan. Known for its surreal coastal **rock formations**, composed of a rare mix of sandstone and shale that is easily eroded by wind and waves, it also offers a very attractive accommodation alternative to the hotels of Taitung – one of Taiwan's most charming **campsites**, perched on a grassy plateau overlooking the sea. With elevated wooden platforms (Sun–Thurs NT$300; Fri–Sat NT$500;

Taitung's secret surf spots

Taiwan's strongest and most consistent **surf** can be found along the 50km stretch of coastline north of Taitung. Most of the best spots are shielded from the road by small villages, keeping them the closely guarded secrets of a hardcore handful of expat surfers living in Taitung. It's best to arrange your own transport so you can explore the coast at your leisure.

The closest to Taitung, and the easiest for novice surfers, is near **Dulan**. To get to this sandy beach, which has small but consistent waves, cross the bridge just north of Dulan and turn east on the third lane to your right. A couple of kilometres further up the road, just north of the village of **Xingchang** (興昌; *xīngchāng*) are the area's top summer breaks. Just past the village, when the coastal road starts to veer eastwards, you'll see a statue of a giant custard apple alongside the road – the first right after this leads to the beach. At the northern end is reef, while the southern end is mostly sandy. Another kilometre or so to the north, near the **141.5km marker**, there is a narrow lane leading down to the shore, where you'll find two howling breaks: one left and one right (be prepared to kick out early because there are loads of rocks close to shore); if you reach Longchang Village (隆昌; *lóngchāng*), then you've gone too far north. For some pure beach action, head north another 5km until you reach the popular **Jinzun Beach** (see p.311), 3km of fine dark sand with some usually rideable waves close to shore. Be careful of paddling too far out, as the seabed drops off sharply here and there is a formidable riptide. Finally, if you're an experienced surfer and are here in winter or just before a typhoon, you won't want to miss the **Donghe River mouth** – the turn off is just north of Donghe (with several surfer-friendly hostels; see p.310) before you reach the Donghe Bridge. Though there are rocks on either side of the estuary, if you have some groundswell from a tropical storm you should get some lovely river-mouth barrels.

🕾089/281-938), attached barbecue pits and toilet and hot shower facilities (NT$20/15min), this breezy campsite is vastly underused, and you might have it all to yourself even in the height of summer (you need to bring your own tent). Register and pay at the **Xiaoyeliu Visitor Center** (小野柳遊客服務中心; *xiǎoyěliŭ yóukè fúwù zhōngxīn*; daily 9am–5pm; 🕾089/281-530), next to the car park (cars NT$40, scooters NT$15). Behind the visitor centre are walkways leading to the rock formations, which have been given names such as "tofu rock," "mushroom rock" and "honeycomb rock". By the car park is a shelter that houses souvenir stalls and snack shops selling instant noodles and drinks.

East Rift Valley National Scenic Area

Heading southwest from Hualien, Provincial Highway 9 cuts through the **East Rift Valley National Scenic Area** (花東縱谷國家風景區; *huādōng zònggǔ guójiā fēngjǐngqū*) a haven of hot springs sandwiched between the Coastal Mountain Range and the eastern fringe of the central ranges. The valley's other claim to fame is **whitewater rafting** on the Xiuguluan River, but the valley also provides access to **Yushan National Park** and the **Southern Cross-Island Highway**. The main **visitor centre** (daily 9am–5pm; 🕾03/887-5306, ⓦwww.erv-nsa.gov.tw) is at 168 Xinghe Rd Sec 2 (County Route 193), in Hegang Village near Ruisui, but you'll need your own transport to get there.

The **train** from Hualien to Taitung passes through the valley, but many of the main sights aren't near train stations – although at some stations (Ruisui for example), you can also **rent bikes**. Likewise, while both the Dingdong and Hualien **bus** companies have daily services through the valley, stopping at most towns, many of the sights are along side roads that are hard to get to by local buses. Given this, if you want to visit several places it's much more convenient to arrange private transport (**taxis** will charge around NT$2500/day) – or even a specialized tour – in Hualien (see p.298).

Ruisui Hot Springs

About 4km northwest of the Ruisui train station are the **Ruisui Hot Springs** (瑞穗溫泉; *ruìsuì wēnquán*), carbonated, iron-rich spring water with a yellow tint and an average temperature of 48°C; it's said to be effective in treating rheumatism and some skin rashes. Some Taiwanese also believe that if women bathe regularly in this type of water it will increase their chances of bearing a male child, hence the large number of newlyweds who come here to soak. In 1919 the Japanese developed the springs into a resort, with a hotel and public bathing areas; this hotel, now known as the *Ruisui Hot Springs Villa* (瑞穗溫泉山莊; *ruìsuì wēnquán shānzhuāng*; ☏03/887-2170, ⓦwww.js-hotspring.com.tw; ⑥), at 23 Hongye Village has added an open-air bathing pool and this, as well as the other public pools are open to non-guests (daily 7.30am–11pm; NT$150). To get here from the train station, rent a bike or take a taxi and tell the driver you're going to the "outer hot springs" (*wài wēnquán*). About 2km further northwest is another Japanese-developed hot-springs resort, the *Hongye Hot Springs Hotel* (紅葉溫泉旅社; *hóngyè wēnquán lǚshè*; ☏03/887-2176, ⓦhong-ye.hotel.com.tw; NT$120 for non-guests; ⑤) at 188 Hongye Village, which has clear, odourless alkaline water with an average temperature of 47°C. Here, the spring water is pumped into private bathhouses. If you take a taxi, ask the driver for the "inner hot springs" (*nèi wēnquán*).

Saoba Megaliths

Back on Highway 9, about 2km south of the Ruisui train station, the **Saoba Megaliths** (掃叭石柱; *sǎobā shízhù*) stand alongside the road. The pair of 2m-high stone columns are thought by archeologists to be remnants of the Beinan civilization that thrived in the valley some five thousand years ago. According to local legend, however, they are actually the incarnations of incestuous twins who tried to escape the wrath of their tribe and were turned to stone. Nearby, a white monolith shaped like a sundial denotes the point where the valley road crosses the **Tropic of Cancer**; there is an identical marker along the coast road.

Good-value accommodation can be found at *Saobading Homestay* (掃叭頂民宿; *sǎobādǐng mínsù*; ☏0910/552-019 or 03/887-1378, ⓦwww.netete.com/saba; ④), 211 Wuhe Village (舞鶴; *wǔhè*), not far from the stones off Highway 9 at the 276.8km mark, with well-equipped neat doubles, amiable hosts and renowned food, including their "hitting the wall" dumplings (*zhuàngqiáng shuǐjiǎo*).

Antong Hot Springs

The **Antong Hot Springs** (安通溫泉; *āntōng wēnquán*), about 8km southeast of **Yuli** (玉里; *yùlǐ*), a major stop on the Hualien–Taitung train line, were discovered by loggers in 1904 in the Antong Creek. The springs still well up in the stream at temperatures ranging from 60 to 66°C and can be enjoyed by bathers for free. Though the water is clear, it smells strongly of hydrogen sulphide. The part of the stream that's best for bathing is below the Japanese-style *Antong Hot Spring Hotel* at 36 Wenquan Rd (安通溫泉大飯店; *āntōng wēnquán dàfàndiàn*; ☏03/888-6108, ⓦwww.an-tong.com.tw; ⑤), which has doubles with private baths. All trains through the valley stop at Yuli Station, from where you can get a taxi (NT$300)

Rafting the Xiuguluan

The **Xiuguluan River** (秀姑巒溪; *xiùgūluán xī*) is Taiwan's premier whitewater rafting spot and, for many, a wet and wild trip down it is the highlight of their visit to the East Rift Valley. Running 104km from its source near Xiuguluan Mountain to the Pacific estuary at Dagangkou, it's eastern Taiwan's longest river, and the main 24km rafting route can be an exciting run for amateurs after prolonged rains or a typhoon. But the best bit is definitely the scenery – the river cuts through a **deep gorge** in the coastal mountains and is surrounded by steep vertical cliffs in many places, with your raft providing an unparalleled perspective on the immensity of it all.

Depending on the water level, the trip usually takes three to four hours, including a lunch break at the Ami village of **Qimei** (七美; *qíměi*) and by the end you'll be soaking wet. Though the **rafting season** depends mostly on the level of rainfall, it generally runs from **early April to late October**. Most trips start at the town of **Ruisui** (瑞穗; *ruìsuì*) about halfway between Hualien and Taitung on Highway 9. All trains running through the East Rift Valley stop here. Though most travel agents in Hualien can arrange rafting trips, including return transport, equipment rental and lunch, for about NT$1000 per person, they usually only charge about NT$750 if you have your own transport to and from Ruisui. It's also possible to arrange trips in Ruisui itself, and near the main start point at the Ruisui Bridge is the **Ruisui Rafting Service Center** (瑞穗泛舟服務中心; *ruìsuì fànzhōu fúwù zhōngxīn*; April–Oct 9am–5pm; closed Nov–March; ☎03/887-5400), 215 Zhongshan Rd Sec 3 where there are several private rafting operators. However, most of them have branches or representation in Hualien (see p.291), and unless you're with a group of six or more people it can be time-consuming to arrange a trip here, as individual travellers may have to wait to join a Taiwanese group. If you take the train from Hualien to Ruisui, it's complicated to get from the train station to the rafting service centre by bus, so you're better off taking a taxi for the four-kilometre ride. Both the Dingdong and Hualien bus companies that ply this route from Hualien make stops at Ruisui, but you'll have to take a local bus to get from town to the rafting centre, and again it might be easier to take a taxi.

to the springs (Antong Station is now closed). The Dingdong and Hualien buses will get you closer to the resort, as they stop a short walk from the springs.

Yushan National Park: the eastern corridor

Immediately south of Yuli, just past the 294km marker of Highway 9, is the turnoff to scenic Highway 18, which winds its way to the eastern entrance of **Yushan National Park** (玉山國家公園; *yùshān guójiā gōngyuán*; Ⓦ www.ysnp .gov.tw; see p.229). This peaceful, little-visited fringe of the park is a worthwhile detour for those with private transport. About 8km from the turnoff is the **Nanan Visitor Center** (南安遊客中心; *nánān yóukè zhōngxīn*; 9am–4.30pm; closed second Tues each month; ☎03/888-7560), where you can get English information and detailed trail maps for this section of the park. Around 2km on, the **Nanan Waterfall** (南安瀑布; *nánān pùbù*) is a thin but impressive seven-storey cascade, with pools big enough for a dip at the base. Another 4km ahead, the road ends at a trailhead for the **Walami Trail** (瓦拉米古道; *wǎlāmǐ gǔdào*), which can be hiked without a mountain permit. Less than 2km up the trail is the magnificent **Shanfeng Waterfall** (山風瀑布; *shānfēng pùbù*), which plunges below a suspension bridge. Some 3km further on is **Jiaxin** (佳心; *jiāxīn*), an overlook with fine views of the valley to the east – the return trip to Jiaxin takes about half a day, but if you want to linger you can camp here, provided you have your own tent. If you wish to walk the entire 14km to **Walami** (瓦拉米; *wǎlāmǐ*), at 1060m above sea level, it's possible to stay overnight in a solar-heated shelter there and make a two-day trip of it, but you should first ask at the visitor centre to ensure there is enough space, as the shelter only holds 24 people and is popular with hiking clubs.

South to Taitung

Back on Highway 9, about 30km south of the turnoff to the Nanan Visitor Center, is **Haiduan** (海端; *hǎiduān*), near the eastern entrance to the stunning **Southern Cross-Island Highway** (南橫公路; *nánhéng gōnglù*; see p.270). A few kilometres south of here is the old logging town of **Guanshan** (關山; *guānshān*) now best known for the scenic 12km **bicycle path** that loops around the city. Rent bikes at the Giant store at Guanshan Station (daily 9am–6pm, closed Thurs; from NT$150/day; ☎089/814-391).

Near the southern end of the East Rift Valley, about 18km north of Taitung, is a small road that heads west to **Yanping** (延平; *yánpíng*) near which is the idyllic **Bunun** village of **Taoyuan** (桃源; *táoyuán*) offering a genuine glimpse of the tribe's culture and heritage (see p.396). If you have your own transport, this is a fascinating side-trip, whether you just stop to sample some authentic Bunun cuisine, or camp, or stay overnight in the village's hostel, which has several well-kept **cabins** (❸). Cradled near the confluence of the coastal and central mountains, the village is a relaxing retreat overlooking a tributary of the Beinan River and at weekends the tribe puts on one of the most authentic aboriginal song and dance shows in Taiwan at the **Bunun Tribe Cultural Park** (布農部落文化園區; *bùnóng bùluò wénhuà yuánqū*; Sat & Sun 10.30am & 2pm; free). The park contains over a hundred pieces of locally made sculpture (daily 9am–5pm; ☎089/561-211) and a spacious **craft workshop** where you can watch traditional handicrafts being made.

Taitung

Stretched across an open plain between lush mountains and the Pacific, **TAITUNG** (台東; *táidōng*) is an essential base for exploring Taiwan's rugged east coast and the dreamy Pacific islands of **Ludao** and **Lanyu**. With a population of 110,000 – including significant numbers of the Ami, Bunun, Rukai, Paiwan, Puyuma and Tao tribes – it has the laid-back feel of a place half its size, though there's nothing much to see in the city itself other than the excellent **National Museum of Prehistory**. Just to the south are the immensely popular **Zhiben Hot Springs**, with a range of resorts to suit most budgets, and the adjacent Zhiben Forest Recreation Area, which offers some leisurely hiking options.

Arrival and city transport

Taitung Airport (台東機場; *táidōng jīchǎng*) is about 7km northeast of the city centre and has a **visitor information centre** (daily 9am–5pm; ☎089/362-472), an ATM and a **car rental** counter in the arrivals hall. The **airport bus** to the old train station downtown operates irregularly from the terminal (7.55am–7.35pm; NT$23); **taxis** will charge at least NT$200.

Taitung's **train station**, known as the new train station (新火車站; *xīnhuǒchēzhàn*), is about 6km northeast of the centre; the old station (舊火車站; *jiùhuǒchēzhàn*), located in the city centre, is no longer in use. **Buses** run irregularly (15 min; NT$23) from the bus station just outside the new train station (turn right as you exit) to the **Dingdong Inland Bus Station** (鼎東客運山線站; *dǐngdōng kèyùn shānxiànzhàn*) downtown, passing all the cheap hotels on Zhongshan Road.

You can also pick up **long-distance buses** that run to the **Dingdong Coastal Bus Station** (鼎東客運海線站; *dīngdōng kèyùn hǎixiànzhàn*) from the same place, and onwards up the coast (there's a timetable on the road next to the bus station). **Taxis** from the new station to the old station, or to anywhere in the downtown area, usually cost NT$200 – drivers generally prefer to charge a flat rate rather than use the meter, but for trips within the city you can insist on the latter. The meter starts at NT$100 and goes up in increments of NT$5, rarely topping NT$120 for most journeys. If you're heading directly to **Fugang Harbour** (富岡漁港; *fùgāng yúgǎng*) for the **Lanyu/Ludao ferries**, take a taxi (NT$300).

It's tough for foreigners to rent **scooters** in Taitung (residents should be OK with an ARC and local licence), but you can rent **cars** (with an international driving licence) at the airport or from **Car Plus** (602 Lane 101, Yanwan Rd; ☏089/227-979), near the train station. Alternatively, renting **bikes** is a viable option (several hotels offer them to guests for free).

Information

There are convenient **visitor information centres** inside the new train station (daily 9am–5pm; ☏089/238-231 or 089/357-131) and in the old train station downtown (daily 9am–5pm; ☏089/359-085); both have an assortment of English-language brochures and maps of the area, including the offshore islands and sights along the east coast, but you are more likely to find English speakers at the new train station. The best place to exchange foreign currency is the **Bank of Taiwan** (台灣銀行; *táiwān yínháng*) at 313 Zhongshan Rd, which also has an **ATM** that recognizes most international debit and credit cards. A few of the downtown 7-Elevens have Chinatrust Commercial Bank ATMs. The **post office** is at the junction of Datong and Xinsheng roads, near the bus station. Most hotels have some sort of **internet** access; you can also try **E Internet** (NT$15/hr; 24hr) at 279 Guangming Rd, near the Old Station.

Accommodation

Taitung remains a firm favourite of Taiwanese tourists during summer holidays, as well as growing busloads of Chinese mainlanders year-round – so there is ample **budget accommodation**, mainly along Zhongshan Road as you head northeast (into town) from the old train station. The rooms at these tend to be small and dingy, but staff at some will help you book **ferry tickets** to Ludao and Lanyu and can arrange transport to the ferry pier at nearby Fugang. Outside the city centre, but closer to the New Station and the airport, are a couple of **mid-range options**, as well as a gleaming **five-star hotel**.

Formosan Naruwan Hotel & Resort 娜路灣大酒店 (*nàlùwān dàjiǔdiàn*) 66 Lianhang Rd ☏089/239-666, ⊛ www.naruwan-hotel.com.tw. Located in the city's northwest, a short taxi ride from the airport and New Station, this five-star hotel has lavish, airy rooms with all the usual amenities. Included in the complex are restaurants, a nightclub, a shopping area, a spa and massage centre and a saltwater swimming pool. ❼

Fuyuan Hotel 富源大飯店 (*fùyuán dàfàndiàn*) 72 Wenhua St ☏089/331-136, ⊛ www.fyhotel .myweb.hinet.net. Tucked away in a tiny lane just off Zhongshan Road, this is the best of the older budget hotels downtown, with bright, spotless rooms with cable TV that are marginally cheaper than the more tatty hotels nearby. The friendly managers speak very basic English but can nonetheless help you book ferry tickets to Ludao and Lanyu for no additional fee. ❷

🏃 **Kindness Hotel** 康橋商旅 (*kāngqiáo shānglǚ*) 16 Lane 209, Zhongxing Rd Sec 1 ☏089/229-226, ⊛ www.kindness-hotel.com.tw. Excellent mid-range option, with smart, comfy rooms, cable TV, free bikes and free wi-fi, laundry and internet computers. Breakfast buffet included, as well as "midnight danzi noodles" from 10pm. The only downside is the location; you'll need to use the bikes or take taxis (NT$120 downtown). ❺

Oia Café & Guesthouse 台東伊亞咖啡民宿 (*táidōng yīyǎ kāfēi mínsù*) 11 Alley 62, Lane 76, Zhengqi N Rd ☎089/333-010, Ⓦwww.oiacafe.com. Just three plush rooms set in a modern two-storey house with a vaguely Mediterranean theme (red-tile bathrooms, small balconies and wrought-iron beds); the café serves great coffee, tea, beef stew and chicken curry (from N$150). Free bikes. ❻

Taitung Aboriginal Culture Hotel 原住民文化會館 (*yuánzhùmín wénhuà huìguǎn*) 10 Zhongshan Rd ☎089/340-605, Ⓦwww.tac-hotel .com.tw. Run by friendly local aborigines of various tribes, this hotel makes up with ambience for its slightly inconvenient location about 1km north of the city centre. The large Japanese-style rooms are kept immaculately clean and offer great value for money. ❸

Taitung Jilin International YH 台東吉林YH國際青年旅舍民宿 (*táidōng jílín YH guójì qīngnián lǚshè mínsù*) 27 Lane 2, Jilin Rd Sec 1 ☎089/232-322, Ⓦttjiyh.myweb.hinet.net. Cheapest beds in town, with YH members paying just NT$499 (NT$450 second night) for shared-dorm bunks in a clean and friendly place that's more like a home than a hostel (non-members pay NT$599). Doubles from NT$1200. Free bikes, free

wi-fi, but the catch is the location, 5km from downtown and the train station (only 4km from Fugang). ❶

Taitung Traveler Hotel 台東旅行家商務會館 (*táidōng lǚxíngjiā shānwù huìguǎn*) 42 Anqing St ☎089/326-456, Ⓦtravelerhotel.com.tw. Solid budget option in the heart of town, close to the bus stations, with small but comfy doubles and Japanese-style rooms; rates start at NT$980 on weekdays, but rise to over NT$3000 on holidays. Computer for free internet access in the lobby, or connections in the room. Free bikes too. The *Taitung Traveler Hostel* (台東旅行家青年住宿會館; *táidōng lǚxíngjiā qīngnián zhùsù huìguǎn*) section offers mixed-dorm beds for NT$750 per person and NT$800 for en-suite private rooms. ❷

U-Dive 2 Taitung Hostel Fugang Harbour ☎0972/065-479, Ⓦwww.udive.com.tw. A cosy hostel next to the ferry pier, and the best place to stay if you want to focus on dive trips and the offshore islands. Dorm bunks are NT$350 (NT$400) weekends, but rates-lower the longer you stay. Doubles start at NT$800. The owners will pick you up from the train or bus station and airport for NT$250–300, offer discounted ferry tickets to Lanyu and Ludao and rent bikes for NT$300–400/day. ❷

The City

Downtown Taitung offers little in the way of conventional sights, but there are a few pleasant spots to occupy some spare time. **Liyushan Park** (鯉魚山公園; *lǐyúshān gōngyuán*), less than 1km northwest of the old train station, is crisscrossed with concrete walking paths, some with steps leading up to the spine of 75m-high Liyushan itself. A path along the backbone of the hill leads to several lookout points offering 360-degree panoramas of the city, and is an ideal place to catch Taitung's cooling afternoon breezes. At the base of the hill, and accessible via several paths, is the imposing **Longfong Temple** (龍鳳寶玉塔; *lóngfèng bǎoyùtǎ*), a Buddhist sanctuary popular with both worshippers and the retirees who practise tai chi (*tàijí*) in its courtyard every morning. In the complex is a multistorey pagoda which visitors are allowed to climb.

Covering Taitung's southeastern flank is the sprawling **Seaside Park** (海濱公園; *hǎibīn gōngyuán*), with commanding views of the coastline. The park, about 2km east of the old train station, is filled with aboriginal sculptures and woodcarvings, and is sliced by the 20km **cycle path** that loops around peaceful **Pipa Lake** (琵琶湖; *pípá hú*) and links up with the adjacent **Black Forest Park** (台東森林公園; *táidōng sēnlín gōngyuán*) before making a circuit of downtown Taitung.

National Museum of Prehistory

One of Taiwan's best museums, the **National Museum of Prehistory** (國立台灣史前文化博物館; *guólì táiwān shǐqián wénhuà bówùguǎn*; Tues–Sun 9am–5pm, last entry 4.40pm; NT$80; Ⓦwww.nmp.gov.tw) was created primarily to house the fascinating hoard of Neolithic artefacts dug up from the Beinan Culture Park (see p.319) around 7km away. The museum also provides a thorough introduction to Taiwan's rich prehistory as a whole, and information on all its major archeological

CENTRAL TAITUNG

Hualien via East Coast Highway, Fugang Harbour, C & D

B (200m)

D & Hualien via East Rift Valley

(1.5km), New Train Station, Taitung Airport, Beinan Culture Park & National Museum of Prehistory

Zhiben Hot Springs

Beinan River

Black Forest Park

Pipa Lake

Seaside Park

Siwei Road Night Market

Tianhou Temple

Chinatrust (ATM)

Taiwan Cooperative Bank

Chinatrust Commercial Bank

Taitung Hospital

Bank of Taiwan

Foreign Affairs Police

Carrefour

Fruit Market

Central Market

Dingdong Inland Bus Station

Kuo-Kuang Bus Station

E Internet

Dingdong Coastal Bus Station

Old Train Station

Longfong Temple

Liyushan Park

Liyushan (75m)

Streets and roads: MATENGSHENG BLVD, GUANGGUO STREET, HANGGUO STREET, JINSCHENG ROAD, SIWEI ROAD, BADOSANG ROAD, BENAI STREET, GUANGDONG STREET, TONGLE ST, DIHUA ROAD, GUANGMING ROAD, BENDE E ROAD, GUANGXING ROAD, CHENGGONG ROAD, ZHONGXIAO ROAD, DATONG ROAD, HEPING ROAD, ZHENGQI ROAD, NANHAI ROAD, OUTER RING ROAD, PINGDENG ROAD, XINGSHENG ROAD, XINYI ROAD, FUXING ROAD, LIEHUA ROAD, ZHENGHUA ROAD, ZHONGHUA ROAD, GUILIN N. RD, FENGGLO RD., ZHENGCI ROAD, BOM ROAD, LAKING ROAD, WUCHENG STREET, ZHONGSHAN ROAD, NEW STATION ROAD, ANNING STREET, GENGSHENG ROAD, ZHONGZHENG ROAD, ZHONGHUA ROAD, HANGZHOU STREET, NINGBO STREET, ZHEJIANG ROAD, CHUANGGUANG ROAD, LUOYANG ST., XINGSHENG ROAD, HANGGUI ST

ACCOMMODATION

Formosan Naruwan Hotel & Resort	E
Fuyuan Hotel	G
Kindness Hotel	A
Oia Café & Guesthouse	F
Taitung Aboriginal Culture Hotel	B
Taitung Jilin International YH	D
Taitung Traveler Hotel	H
U-Dive 2 Taitung Hostel	C

EATING & DRINKING

A-Mei's Sugar Apple Cakes	9
Beinan Pig's Blood Soup	2
Chi Li Po	10
Hongfan Qu (Sitting Bull)	4
Kasa Café	6
Lin Chou Doufu	7
Mibanai	1
Old Taidong Noodles	8
Who's Club & Lounge	5
Xiao Jia Meatballs	3

0 _____ 200 m

sites via two core permanent exhibitions: the **Natural History of Taiwan** and **Taiwan's Prehistory**. The large, futuristic halls combine contemporary design and technology with a fascinating collection of exhibits, models and dioramas to present each section in English and Chinese. The first exhibition explains the geological and ecological development of the island over millions of years, while the second takes a chronological journey from the first known humans in Taiwan (Tsochen Man, between twenty and thirty thousand years ago) to the early Iron Age, two thousand years ago. The exquisite **jade** ornaments and **pottery** taken from the Beinan site have their own exhibition areas, but the most startling finds are the distinctive **stone coffins** and moon-shaped **stone pillars**, the latter reminiscent of the stone circles of northwest Europe. The museum also has an exhibition on the **Indigenous Peoples of Taiwan**, charting the development of Taiwan's aboriginal tribes and how they may relate to the island's prehistoric peoples.

The museum is inconveniently located around 8km west of the city centre, but well worth the trip: you can either take a train to Kangle (康樂; *kānglè*; 8 daily; 5min; NT$11) and walk (15min), or take a taxi (around NT$200). Alternatively there are three buses daily (7.40am, 11.10am & 4.20pm; 20min; NT$23) to the museum from the Dingdong Coastal Bus Station.

Beinan Cultural Park

Once the location of a flourishing Neolithic community, **Beinan Cultural Park** (卑南文化公園; *bēinán wénhuà gōngyuán*; free) is a major archeological site with a series of landscaped open spaces, containing another absorbing exhibition hall managed by the Museum of Prehistory. The Japanese began working here in the 1940s, but most excavation was carried out in the 1990s, and today it's the largest and most productive archeological site in Taiwan, yielding more than twenty thousand artefacts (mostly pottery) and 1600 slate coffins. The park's informative **visitor centre** (Tues–Sun 9am–5pm; NT$30) contains a sunken area displaying the **coffins** and an exhibition dedicated to the people that once lived here, between 1500 and 300 BC. Archeologists have been able to surmise an astonishing amount about this community of hunters and farmers, although there is still disagreement over whether they were the ancestors of any of today's aboriginal tribes: the local Puyuma people call themselves "Beinan", but some anthropologists think the Paiwan or the Ami are more likely to be related to the prehistoric Beinan culture.

Elsewhere in the park, the two-level **observation deck** offers fine views over the area, while the **stone pillar** or standing stone is the only artefact left in its original location – archeologists think this may have marked the centre of the village. The houses that once stood here were made of schist and wood, with roofs of bamboo and straw and an average size of 69 square metres. Each had an attached storehouse, but communal granaries were also scattered around the village. You'll need a vivid imagination to picture any of this today however, as nothing remains above ground, though it's usually possible to observe archeologists working on sections of the grounds. The park is at the back of the New Station in the northern suburbs of Taitung – just follow the road round (right as you exit) and under the bridge (10min).

Eating

Taitung has an eclectic assortment of eating options, many of them visible at the myriad roadside food stalls throughout the city. Every Sunday night, the whole of Siwei Road between Zhonghua and Guangfu roads is blocked off for the lively **Siwei Road Night Market** (四維路夜市; *sìwéilù yèshì*) where you can find all of Taitung's specialty dishes. One of the most popular treats, but not one for the finicky, is **pigs' blood soup** (豬血湯; *zhūxiětāng*), a thick broth filled with diced cubes of congealed pig's blood. Taitung is also known for its amazing variety of **fruit**, the most famous of which is the **custard apple** (釋迦; *shìjiā*). The best place to find it is along **"Fruit Market"** (水果市場; *shuǐguǒ shìchǎng*), the long stretch of Zhengqi Road between Zhongshan and Boai roads. For self-catering, Carrefour has a branch at 200 Zhengqi Rd.

A-Mei's Sugar Apple Cakes 阿美釋迦形象館 (*āměi shìjiā xíngxiàng guǎn*) 65 Xinsheng Rd, at Anqing St ☎089/353-509. Visit this store to buy locally made custard apple cakes and fish products (NT$120–150/box). Daily 9am–10pm.

Beinan Pig's Blood Soup 卑南豬血湯 (*bēinán zhūxiětāng*) 117 Chuanguang Rd ☎089/324-472. No-frills place famous in Taitung for pig's blood soup (NT$70), a tasty concoction that tastes a lot better than it sounds. No English. Daily 9.30am–7pm.

Chi Li Po 七里坡 (*qīlǐpō*) 2 Datong Rd ☎089/325-777. Bright, modern restaurant serving Korean hotpot (from NT$199) and *bibimbap* or stone pot rice (NT$170–270), as well as pasta (NT$155) and Chinese staples such as steamed fish (NT$190). One of the few places near the ocean and the cycle path – good for a coffee or beer (no English signs, but English menu available). Daily 10am–2am.

Lin Chou Doufu 林臭豆腐 (*lín chòudòufǔ*) 130 Zhengqi Rd, between Fujian and Guangdong roads ☎089/334-637. This tiny shop is legendary with locals, as much for its eccentric owner as for its unique stinky tofu. As if

to underscore the pungency of his deep-fried tofu (NT$35 for small portion, NT$100 for large), which is made from green beans rather than the usual soya, the owner wears camouflage fatigues and a gas mask when preparing food for customers. Daily 3.30–11.30pm.

Mibanai 米巴奈 (*mǐbānài*) 470 Chuanguang Rd at Renai Rd ☎089/220-336. Touristy aboriginal restaurant aimed squarely at groups and ostensibly Ami-themed (the staff wear traditional dress), but not bad as a basic introduction; the betel-nut salad, corn wrapped in bacon and salty wood-fired pork are delicious. Daily 11.30am–2pm & 5–10pm.

Old Taidong Noodles 老台東米台目 (*lǎotáidōng mǐtáimù*) 134 Zhengqi Rd ☎089/348-952. Beloved noodle shop (right next to Lin Chou Doufu), knocking out big bowls of aromatic soup noodles with tea eggs for NT$40 since 1955. No English. Daily 11.30am–11.30pm.

Xiao Jia Meatballs 蕭家肉圓 (*xiāojiā ròuyuán*) 177 Zhonghua Rd Sec 1, at Siwei Rd ☎089/327-316. Small shop that opens in the afternoons only, selling the local version of *bah-oân* or meatballs of delicately fried glutinous rice with a pork filling (NT$35/bowl). Daily 2–5.30pm.

Drinking

Though Taitung tends to be fairly sedate at night, there are a few interesting options for both a quiet drink and a late-night dance. The town's hippest **bar** is *Hongfan Qu* (紅番區; *hóngfānqū*, aka *Sitting Bull*; daily 9pm–5am; ☎089/347-200) at 74 Wenhua St, next to the *Fuyuan Hotel* just off Zhongshan Road. Run by some clued-up young aboriginal entrepreneurs and decorated with posters and off-the-wall photos of indigenous folk heroes from the American West, it's a good place to get a feel for the cultural revival that's taking place among the urbanized aborigines of Taiwan's southeast. It also has upbeat music and bottled beer starting from NT$150. If you fancy a boogie, the top spot is *Who's Club & Lounge* (胡氏餐廳; *húshì cāntīng*; daily 8pm–5am; ☎089/320-618) at 323 Zhonghua Rd, which tends to feature live bands from the Philippines and cabaret-type dance shows; it can be fun in a group. For less kitsch and cheaper drinks, try *Kasa Café* at 102 Heping St (usually 5pm–2am), just off Datong Road near the post office, a casual place that also serves coffee, barbecue ribs and nachos and has internet access.

Around Taitung: Zhiben Hot Springs

The **Zhiben Hot Springs** (知本溫泉; *zhīběn wēnquán*), in a long river valley about 20km southwest of Taitung, are among the finest in Taiwan. Developed into a resort by the Japanese in the early twentieth century, their **sulphur**

Uni Air (℡089/362-625) and Mandarin Airlines (℡089/362-669) operate regular **flights** from Taitung Airport (⑩www.tta.gov.tw) to Taipei (Songshan) throughout the day.

Taitung has regular **express train** services to **Hualien** (NT$346) and **Taipei** (NT$786), and several **slower trains** to towns in the **East Rift Valley** (Guanshan NT$33–71; Antong NT$70–150; Ruisui NT$95–203). There are also several express trains daily to **Kaohsiung** (2hr 20min; NT$364) via **Fangliao** (NT$105–225). To get to **Kenting**, take the train to Fangliao and catch one of the regular buses south from Kaohsiung (p.265).

The **Dingdong Coastal Bus Station** (℡089/333-443) at Zhongshan and Xinsheng roads has regular services to destinations along the coastal Provincial Highway 11. There are three buses daily to Hualien (6.10am, 8.30am & 12.40pm; NT$496), while several buses a day make a trip to **Chenggong** (1hr; NT$151); it's possible to take one of these and catch one of the several Chenggong–Hualien buses for the remainder of the journey to Hualien. Some of these buses also pass the **New Station** (NT$23), and around twelve buses make the run to the **airport** daily (7.25am–5.30pm; NT$23).

To the east of the Old Station, the **Kuo Kuang Bus Station** (國光客運站; *guóguāng kèyùnzhàn*) at 94 Xinsheng Road now only provides a bus service to Kaohsiung (6am, 12.30pm, 5.30pm & 10.30pm; 4hr; NT$443) via Fangliao (NT$320).

The **Dingdong Inland Bus Station** at Fuxing Road and Anqing Street has frequent buses to points on Provincial Highway 9 in the **East Rift Valley**, including **Guanshan** (NT$110), as well as two daily to **Lidao** (6.20am & 1.05pm; NT$220) via **Wulu** (NT$185); this is now the furthest you can get on the **Southern Cross-Island Highway** (see p.270) by public transport. It also runs twelve buses daily to **Zhiben Hot Springs** (6am–6.25pm; NT$48) and the Forest Recreation Area beyond (NT$63).

For **Ludao** (**Green Island**) and **Lanyu** see p.323.

---

carbonate waters are believed to be some of the island's most therapeutic, effective in treating everything from arthritis to intestinal disorders (the colourless, odourless spring water is drinkable). Though in its early days bathers soaked in the riverbeds where the springs emerged, today all of the natural springs have been tapped and are pumped into the proliferation of luxury hotels that line the valley entrance. Despite this, the area retains considerable charm, and further inland the development starts to diminish, as do the crowds. At the end of the main Longquan Road – which cuts straight through the valley – is the tranquil **Zhiben National Forest Recreation Area**, which has attractive scenery and several easy walking paths. While renting a car or scooter will give you much more flexibility, it's also fairly easy to reach Zhiben by **bus** from Taitung (see above).

Hot-spring hotels

As you enter the valley you're likely to be greeted by a welcoming party of indigenous people on scooters, entreating you to stay at their hot-springs hotels. Most of these places are near the highway turnoff, an overdeveloped area of faceless high-rises. If you're after is a quiet soak, you'll do better going to the far end of the valley, near the entrance to the serene Zhiben National Forest Recreation Area, where there are several more down-to-earth options. If you don't plan to stay overnight, it's possible to soak in some of the hotels' **public pools** for a nominal fee. Zhiben isn't really known for its places to **eat**, so it's best to stick to the resort hotels.

Hotel Royal Chihpen 知本老爺大酒店 (*zhīběn lǎoyé dàjiǔdiàn*) 113 Lane 23, Longquan Rd ☏089/510-666, ⓦwww .hotel-royal-chihpen.com.tw. Zhiben's poshest hotel, with 183 rooms equipped with private jacuzzis. Occupying the side of a hill just off the main Longquan Rd, the complex includes a swimming pool, recreation area, putting greens, an archery range and an outdoor stage where touristy Puyuma dance performances are held nightly. Non-guests can soak in the public bathing pools for as long as they want for NT$350. ❽

Hoya Hot Springs Resort & Spa 知本富野渡假村 (*zhīběn fùyě dùjiǎcūn*) 16 Longquan Rd ☏089/510-510, ⓦwww.hoyaresort.com.tw. A five-star option close to the river valley entrance, with sleek, modern rooms and an attractive spa (private rooms NT$900/hr), within walking distance of the main stretch of overpriced Chinese restaurants. ❼

Ming Chuan Hotel 明泉旅遊山莊 (*míngquán lǚyóu shānzhuāng*) 265 Lane 2, Longquan Rd ☏089/513-996. A cheap and cheerful option, on the hill directly across from the Forest Recreation Area entrance. Facilities are basic but clean, with a small outdoor bathing pool, and some of the motel-style rooms and private cabins look out onto the valley's beautiful scenery, including the spectacular waterfall that comes crashing down behind the suspension bridge. Price includes breakfast at the riverside café below the hotel. ❸

Rainbow Resort 泓泉溫泉渡假村 (*hóngquán wēnquán dùjiǎcūn*) 1 Lane 139, Longquan Rd ☏089/510-150, ⓦwww.rainbow-hotel.com.tw. Reasonable mid-range option located up a hilly lane above Longquan Rd, with sweeping views of the river valley. Rooms are comfy but nothing special; price includes breakfast. ❺

Songquan Holiday Hotel 松泉渡假山莊 (*sōngquán dùjiā shānzhuāng*) 135 Lane 6, Longquan Rd ☏089/510-073. Small, family-run hotel with basic but attractive rooms offering excellent value (from NT$1200 weekdays). Located up a very steep lane, about 100m off the main road. Breakfast costs an extra NT$50. ❸

Temple and forest trails

In addition to hot springs, the valley has a few other worthwhile attractions, both man-made and natural. Sharing a hillside with the *Hotel Royal Chihpen*, up Lane 23 just off Longquan Road, the peaceful **Qingjue Temple** (清覺寺; *qīngjuési*) houses a pair of exquisite **Buddha statues**: one carved of white jade from Myanmar and the other a bronze image from Thailand. There is a small monastery nearby, and its monks frequently meditate inside the temple.

The highlight of the valley is where the road ends and the **Zhiben National Forest Recreation Area** (知本森林遊樂區; *zhīběn sēnlín yóulèqū*; July–Sept 8am–6pm, Oct–June 7am–5pm; NT$100) begins. The area is accessed by the **Forest-view Suspension Bridge** (觀林吊橋; *guānlín diàoqiáo*), which looks out onto a magnificent multi-tiered **waterfall**. At the tollgate you can get an English-language brochure with information and a basic map of the trails, all of which are well marked and easy to follow. The **Banyan Shaded Trail** (榕蔭步道; *róngyīn bùdào*), a leisurely walk of just over 2km, remains cool even in summer, sheltered as it is by old-growth forest – including seventeen 100-year-old banyans. In some sections, **Taiwanese macaques** can be seen leaping from tree to tree.

Ludao (Green Island)

A verdant Pacific gem about 33km east of Taitung, **LUDAO** (綠島; *lǜdǎo*) flourishes with tropical vegetation inland and a jaw-dropping abundance of colourful **marine life** amid the nourishing coral that skirts most of its shoreline. Its beauty and relative accessibility – a twelve-minute flight or fifty-minute ferry ride from Taitung – have made it an immensely popular tourist destination, with a holiday atmosphere starkly at odds with its recent history as Taiwan's principal place of exile for political prisoners. Site of the notorious **Ludao Lodge**, where tens of thousands were held without proper trials and routinely tortured during the

White Terror period (see p.390), the island is now equally well known for some of Taiwan's finest **snorkelling** and **diving**. It also boasts the atmospheric **Zhaori Hot Springs**, one of only two known natural **saltwater hot springs** in the world (the other is near Mount Vesuvius in southern Italy).

Given its small size – an eighteen-kilometre surfaced road loops round it – Ludao can easily be explored by scooter or taxi, and many Taiwanese opt to fly in for a day-trip before returning to Taitung for the night. It gets very crowded during the **summer holidays**, and especially at weekends, when tourist numbers easily dwarf the island's summer population of just over two thousand. In contrast, during the

Getting to Ludao and Lanyu

Daily Air Corp (booking ☎089/362-485, airport ☎089/362-676, ⓦwww.dailyair.com .tw) is the only airline with **flights** from Taitung to **Ludao** (8.20am, 12.15pm & 4.10pm; 15min; NT$1028 one-way) and **Lanyu** (8.50am, 9.40am, 10.35am, 1pm, 2.30pm, 3.35pm; 25min; NT$1345 one-way). Phone reservations are advisable, but the schedule is always dependent on the weather – call the morning you depart. Flights return from Ludao at 9.05am, 12.50am and 4.45pm; from Lanyu at 9.35am, 10.25am, 11.20am, 1.45pm, 3.20pm and 4.25pm – more flights are added at peak times.

There are regular **ferry services** (☎089/281-047) to both islands from the fishing village of **Fugang** (富岡; *fùgǎng*), a few kilometres north of Taitung, accessible by **taxi** (NT$300) or **Dingdong Bus** (NT$23): take any one of the coastal buses north, but make sure the driver knows you're getting off at Fugang. The port is around half a kilometre from the village bus stop on Songjiang Road (just off Highway 11). On the way back, buses depart 6.43am to 9.43pm (at least once every hour) from the same stop; you can also catch buses up the coast (6.30am–9.50pm).

Ferry times depend largely on the season and the weather; rough water, heavy rain or storms can adversely affect schedules, and services outside the busy summer season (June–Sept) are drastically cut back. It's always best to reserve in advance; you can call direct (Chinese only) or get an agent or hotel in Taitung to do it for you.

At **Taitung train station** (opposite the information desk), **Pony Travel Service** (daily 9am–5.30pm; ☎089/229-198, English spoken at ☎0910/892-553) offers inclusive packages that are not bad value: for around NT$2400 you get free shuttle to Fugang, return ferry, scooter rental, insurance, entry into the hot springs and one night in the *Toong Hsiang Hotel* (ⓦwww.toonghsiang.com.tw) with breakfast.

At the **Fugang ferry terminal** itself, three companies – Uranus (天王星號; *tiānwáng xīnghào*; ☎089/281-617); Farnlin (凱旋客輪, *kǎixuán kèlún*, ☎089/281-047) and Golden Star (金星客輪, *jīnxīng kèlún*; ☎089/281-477) sell tickets (same prices), but visit the handy **East Island** (綠島專業娛樂網站; *lüdǎo zhuānyè yúlè wǎngzhàn*; ☎089/280-282, ⓦwww.eastisland.com.tw) desk just outside, where English is spoken: they sell tickets and can also arrange package deals (NT$2400). These deals generally require a minimum of two people. **Green Island Adventures** (☎0972/065-479, ⓦwww.greenislandadventures.com) is another reputable operator.

Ferries to **Ludao** (NT$460 one-way, NT$920 return; 40min) generally depart Mon–Fri at 9.30am, 1.30pm & 3.30pm, returning at 10.30am, 2.30pm & 4.30pm. At weekends (and most of the summer) boats tend to run every 2hr from 7.30am to 8pm, returning from 9.30am to 9pm, but always check in advance. For **Lanyu** (NT$1000 one-way, NT$2000 return; 3hr), ferries usually depart once a day at 7.30am, heading back at 3.30am; June–Sept there should be extra services.

Travelling between Lanyu and Ludao is possible (NT$920 one-way; 2hr), but, again, ferries are more frequent June–Sept; outside this period ferries only run two or three times a week (10am, 3.30pm, twice weekly from Ludao at 8.30am). In general it's best to take a ferry to Lanyu first, then go back via Ludao, though the boats can be smaller and the crossing a lot rougher on this section.

winter months, there is a sharp decline in the number of visitors, and ferries and flights are prone to last-minute cancellations due to inclement weather. If you come during this time, you're likely to have the island mostly to yourself, but many tourist facilities are closed and it's hard to arrange snorkelling trips unless you've brought your own kit.

Some history

Archeological evidence suggests that humans inhabited Ludao as long ago as 1000 BC. According to aboriginal myth, it was known as *Sanasai*, and the Ami, Kavalan and Ketagalan tribes believe their ancestors used it as a land bridge for migration. The first **Han Chinese** immigrants arrived in the early 1800s and named it *Huoshaodao* (火燒島; *huǒshāodǎo*) or "Fire-burned Island", in reference to the fires that locals would light to help guide fishing boats to shore (the island's highest point, at 281m, is still named Huoshaoshan). In the early 1930s, the occupying Japanese built processing plants for dried fish, which was shipped to Japan. By the 1970s, the raising of **Sika deer**, prized commercially for their antlers, had become a boom industry, and at one point there were more of these diminutive creatures than people. Though this industry has been in decline on Ludao since 1986, there are still plenty to be seen, and today they are something of a tourist attraction. In the main village of Nanliao, some hotel and restaurant owners keep them as pets, sadly tied up for photo opportunities.

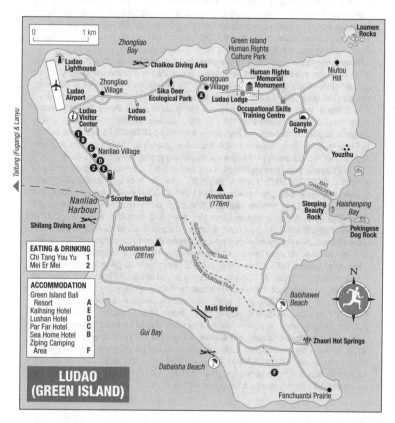

Arrival, transport and information

Ludao Airport (綠島機場; *lǜdǎojīchǎng*; ☏089/671-261) is less than 1km north of Nanliao Village (南寮村; *nánliáocūn*), the island's main tourist centre. In summer, touts will greet you, offering deals including accommodation, food, scooter rental and snorkelling trips. The same is true if you arrive by ferry at **Nanliao Harbour** (南寮漁港; *nánliáo yúgǎng*), about 1km south of the village. These all-in-one arrangements can be good value, the downside being that you get the luck of the draw, and you might wind up with a dingy room and find yourself being shunted around on an overcrowded snorkelling trip the next day.

For greater freedom, it's best to rent a **scooter** from one of the many rental shops near the ferry pier, or from one of the airport touts, and set about looking for a room on your own. Scooters usually cost about NT$300 per day (or NT$400 for 24hr), not including petrol, but the price can jump on summer weekends, when they can often be completely rented out; package deals (see above) usually include scooter rental. You can also **rent cars** (NT$1200/3hr; NT$1500/24hr; add NT$300 at weekends) and **bikes** (NT$200/day) from the same shops. A whirlwind **taxi tour** around the island, with perfunctory stops at the main sights, will cost a minimum of NT$750, more at crowded weekends.

The **Ludao Visitor Center** (綠島遊客服務中心; *lǜdǎo yóukè fúwù zhōngxīn*; daily 8.30am–5.30pm; ☏089/672-026), across the road from the airport and just north of Nanliao Village, has crude maps and some English-language information. The staff can arrange snorkelling and diving trips and also make reservations for the excellent **campsite** near the island's southern tip (see p.326). In addition, you can also buy a multi-use **bus ticket** (NT$100) here that allows you unlimited rides for a three-day period on the **public bus** that makes a circuit around the loop every thirty minutes or so (daily 7am–6pm). There are thirteen bus stops around the island – roughly one for every kilometre.

Accommodation

The bulk of **accommodation** on Ludao is concentrated in congested Nanliao Village, which teems with Taiwanese tourists all summer, especially at weekends, when most hotels here are fully booked. A more relaxed alternative to Nanliao is **Gongguan Village** (公館村; *gōngguǎncūn*), in the north of the island, where there are a handful of small hotels near one of the top snorkelling and diving spots. Off-peak season (cheapest) is November to March.

Nanliao Village

Kaihsing Hotel 凱薪飯店 (*kǎixīn fàndiàn*) 102–12 Nanliao Village ☏089/672-033, ⓦkaihsing.okgo.tw. Ludao's biggest – and busiest – hotel, catering mostly to domestic tour groups; rooms are comfortable and modern, with wooden floors and bright colours. Discounts are routinely given in winter. ❺

Lushan Hotel 綠山飯店 (*lǜshān fàndiàn*) 102–6 Nanliao Village ☏089/672-243, ⓦlushan-hotel.okgo.tw. Next door to the *Kaihsing*, the *Lushan* offers a range of clean doubles, twins and triples and some Japanese-style dorm rooms with tatami mats, ideal for groups of young people. ❹

Par Far Hotel 雙發渡假飯店 (*shuāngfā dùjià fàndiàn*) 146 Nanliao Village ☏089/672-552, ⓦwww.lcf.com.tw. Bright, spotlessly clean rooms – some with superb sea views. Given the great location, the *Par Far* is often fully booked, so if you want to stay here you should have your hotel in Taitung call to make a reservation (the affable woman who runs it doesn't speak English). ❺

Sea Home Hotel 海洋之家渡假村 (*hǎiyáng zhījiā dùjiǎcūn*) 39 Nanliao Village ☏089/672-515, ⓦwww.ocean-resort.com.tw. Immaculate, breezy rooms with sea views, but a little pricey and the management is reluctant to discount in summer; breakfast is included, though, and in winter sizeable discounts can be had. ❻

Gongguan Village

Green Island Bali Resort 綠島峇里會館 (*lǜdǎo kēlǐ huìguǎn*) 2–10 Gongguan Village ☏089/235-365; ⓦgreenisland-bali.hotel.com.tw. Upmarket resort-style hotel, with a pleasing (though not very authentic) Balinese theme; some rooms do feature wood and wicker furniture, and the most expensive rooms have stunning views of coastal rock formations, but you are paying a hefty premium for location (breakfast and TV come with every room). **⑥**

Southern island

Ziping Camping Area 紫坪露營區 (*zǐpíng lùyíng qū*) ⏆089/672-027. This shady southern island campsite, between Zhaori Hot Springs and Dabaisha Beach, is the only place where you can pitch a tent (on grass or elevated wooden platforms). At the time of writing the site was still under construction, but it should be open sometime in 2011. Check prices and make reservations at the visitor centre, where staff can also direct you to a private vendor if you need to rent tents, sleeping bags and foam mattresses.

The island

A good place to start (or end) a tour is the 33m-tall **Ludao Lighthouse** (綠島燈塔; *lǜdǎo dēngtǎ*) on the island's northwest corner and one of its most prominent landmarks. Accessible via a side road from Zhongliao Village (中寮村; *zhōngliáo cūn*), it's an especially dramatic place to watch the sunset. It was built in 1938, a year after the US cruise liner SS *President Hoover* ran aground on an offshore reef, prompting villagers to stage a valiant rescue effort. In gratitude, the US Government financed the construction of the lighthouse, which sustained serious damage during World War II a few years later.

Heading east along the ring road at km 3 you'll see the turning to the **Sika Deer Ecological Park** (梅花鹿生態園區; *méihuālù shēngtài yuánqū*), one of the best places to see the famous island wildlife, but come early to avoid the crowds (and have the best chance of seeing the deer). Along the main ring road further east are three former **prisons** that have come to symbolize the White Terror period of martial law (see box opposite).

In the island's northeast corner is **Niutou Hill** (牛頭山; *niútóushān*), a rock at the edge of a grassy plateau which offers fabulous views of the coastline. Just south of here at km 6 is **Guanyin Cave** (觀音洞; *guānyīn dòng*), a water-eroded limestone opening containing several stalactites and stalagmites: one of the latter is said to resemble Guanyin, the goddess of mercy, and is wrapped accordingly in a flaming red robe. Legend has it that during the Qing dynasty a fisherman in peril was led safely to shore near here by a mysterious light emanating from the cliffs. The area was then searched by locals, who found the stalagmite and likened it to Guanyin sitting on a lotus. South of the cave, a steep, winding road leads down to an extraordinary stretch of wave-beaten coral coastline, surrounded by towering crags just offshore. The sheltered, sandy area just inland at km 7 is an abandoned aboriginal settlement known as **Youzihu** (柚子湖; *yòuzihú*), where several derelict **old dwellings** are slowly succumbing to the encroaching vegetation. The area is one of the island's most atmospheric and, largely hidden from view of the main road, it remains refreshingly free of the student-driven scooter armadas that race round the island. Further south along the main road at km 8 is the **Xiao Changcheng** or Little Great Wall (小長城步道; *xiǎochángchéng bùdào*), a short path tracing the spine of a hill to a lookout point, and indeed bearing some resemblance to a stretch of the Great Wall winding towards a guard tower. It's a quick walk to the lookout point, from where there are truly majestic views of the shoreline to both north and south. Jutting out of Haishenping Bay (海參坪; *hǎishēnpíng*) to the south are two giant **rock formations** named Sleeping Beauty Rock and Pekingese Dog Rock (哈巴狗與睡美人岩; *hābāgǒu yǔ shuìměirén yán*).

Carry on south and you'll come to the trailheads of two footpaths that eventually link up and lead over the hills in the island's centre before dropping down behind Nanliao Village on the west side. The first is the **Guoshan**

Remembering the White Terror

In the minds of many Taiwanese, especially the elderly, Ludao's natural beauty is overshadowed by its brutal past as the primary place of imprisonment, torture and execution during the country's **White Terror** (白色恐怖; *báisè kǒngbù*; see Contexts p.390). Although in the late 1940s and early 1950s it was mostly targeted at those suspected of being **Communist spies** for the mainland, eventually students, intellectuals and professionals accused of criticizing the government were rounded up, tortured and interrogated before being imprisoned or executed. During this time, more than ninety thousand people were arrested in Taiwan and at least half were put to death. From 1951 until the end of martial law in 1987, more than twenty thousand political prisoners were shipped to Ludao, where they were held in the notorious Green Island Reform and Re-education Prison or **Ludao Lodge** (綠島山莊; *lǜdǎo shānzhuāng*), just east of Gongguan Village (the current buildings date from 1972). Here, inmates were routinely tortured and often confined to damp underground bunkers where they were eaten alive by mosquitoes. Some were held for more than thirty years before being freed, and an estimated one thousand were executed here. The prison, dubbed "Oasis Villa" in Chinese in the 1970s (in extreme irony) is now part of the **Green Island Human Rights Culture Park** (綠島人權文化園區; *lǜdǎo rénquán wénhuà yuánqū*; daily: May–Sept 8am–6pm, Oct–April 8.30am–5pm; free; ☎089/671-095), with a small **visitor centre** recounting the history of the site through films and displays, and the **Human Rights Monument** (人權紀念碑; *rénquán jìniàn bēi*). The words on the graceful stele, by writer Bo Yang, who spent twelve years in prison here, read: "During that era, how many mothers have cried through the night for their children imprisoned here?" To the west of Ludao Lodge, between Gongguan and Zhongliao villages, is the **Ludao Prison** (綠島監獄; *lǜdǎo jiānyù*), a maximum-security complex built in 1971 to hold Taiwan's most dangerous convicts, including some of the island's infamous organized-crime bosses (it's off limits to the public).

Historic Trail (過山古道; *guòshān gǔdào*) at km 11, a short but quiet walk of less than 2km that runs into the maintenance road leading north to Nanliao Village. The second, the **Guoshan Mountain Trail** (過山步道; *guòshān bùdào*; 1.84km) begins a little further south at km 13 and skirts the eastern flank of 281m Huoshaoshan (火燒山; *huǒshāoshān*), the now-extinct volcano whose eruption created the island. However, the mountaintop has a military radar installation and is strictly off limits. This trail also meets up with the maintenance road heading north to Nanliao.

Zhaori Hot Springs

Near Ludao's southern tip are the **Zhaori Hot Springs** (朝日溫泉; *zhāorì wēnquán*; May–Sept open 24hr, Oct–April 8am–midnight; NT$200; ☎089/671-133), which rank as one of the world's most unusual hot-springs areas. The saltwater hot springs are created by a rare phenomenon: the tide carries seawater into coral crevices, where it's funneled deep underground, heated geothermically and pressurized back to the earth's surface. Here, it has been harnessed into three circular **seawater bathing pools**, each with different temperatures that allow you to adjust gradually to the hottest one: the range is typically 53–93°C, and once you get too hot you can clamber into the sea to cool down. During the scorching-hot summer, when a daytime soak would be anathema to most, the pools are open 24 hours, allowing you to come for a late-night dip and stay through to the **sunrise**, as the waves crash against the surrounding tidal flats. Just inside the entrance are changing facilities and an open-air spa pool with several gushing **massage showers**.

Green Island snorkelling and diving

Snorkelling (trips from NT$300) is a highlight of Green Island, ringed as it is by remarkably intact coral that teems with tropical fish. The sheer diversity of marine life here easily rivals or surpasses many better-known snorkelling areas in southeast Asia, making it a real treat if you can manage to avoid the summer weekend crowds. If you plan to snorkel, it's recommended that you bring your own kit: mask, snorkel and neoprene booties (to protect your feet from sharp coral) should be sufficient. However, at times **jellyfish** can be a problem, in which case you can easily **rent a wetsuit** from one of the many snorkelling and diving operators in Nanliao and Gongguan villages. The best spots are close to shore and an easy wade out and, unless you're a weak swimmer or are uncomfortable in the ocean, it's best to avoid the **organized snorkelling trips** arranged by local operators. Such outings will entail a group of several dozen people, clad in life vests and linked together by a rope forming a line across the shallow water with each participant waiting for a turn to look through the hole of a ring buoy at whatever fish might be swimming by at that moment. Even if you only rent equipment from these operators, they may try to insist that you adhere to their safety protocol – it's best to tell them up front that you want to rent some gear and make your own way. The cautious nature of these local outings has left the coral incredibly well preserved.

The best-known snorkelling spots are Chaikou and Shilang (石朗潛水區; *shíláng qiánshuǐ qū*), both of which have gentle currents and are very safe. The stretch of reef near **Dabaisha Beach** (大白沙潛水區; *dàbáishā qiánshuǐ qū*) in the southwest also has excellent snorkelling, but as currents here are less predictable it's better suited to strong swimmers and scuba divers. The most easygoing operators are near Gongguan Village, not far from the **Chaikou Diving Area** (柴口潛水區; *cháikǒu qiánshuǐ qū*). One operator specializing in diving trips off the coast of Ludao is Green Island Diving (ⓦwww.greenislanddiving.com), which runs **hammerhead-shark**-spotting excursions off the island's southern tip from January to March of each year. For scuba instruction, reputable operators include John Boo (ⓣ09/1338-8065; ⓦwww.udive.com.tw) and Taichung-based *Taiwan Scuba* (ⓣ09/2381-8469; ⓦwww.taiwanscuba.com), which offers **PADI certification** courses from NT$15,000.

Eating

Both Nanliao and Gongguan villages are filled with **seafood restaurants**, although some cater mainly to large tour groups, making it difficult for independent travellers to order specific items. At the northwestern end of Gongguan Village are a couple of open-air **barbecue restaurants** with festive atmospheres and plenty of grilled seafood: in summer, these places draw the party crowd, especially university students putting away their share of Taiwan Beer. The restaurant most amenable to foreigners is *Chi Tang You Yu* (池塘有魚; *chítáng yǒuyú*; noon–2pm & 6pm–midnight) at 150 Nanliao Village, which serves up tasty seafood and has a relaxing seafront patio on the first floor. The most popular dish here is the garlic octopus (*suàn xiang zhāngyú*). A great spot for a light **breakfast** of egg pancakes (*dàn bǐng*) is *Mei Er Mei* (美而美; *měiérměi*; 5am–noon) at 103–1 Nanliao Village, which has a breezy upstairs balcony with splendid sea views.

Lanyu (Orchid Island)

Jutting sharply out of the sea some 91km southeast of Taitung, **LANYU** (蘭嶼; *lányǔ*), is one of Taiwan's most precious places. This volcanic island consists of a green-velvet mountain surrounded by a flat, narrow strip of alluvial plain, which stretches into some of the most unspoilt **coral reef** in all of Asia. In addition to its astounding natural allure, Lanyu is the sole domain of Taiwan's purest aboriginal tribe: the seafaring **Tao** or "Dawu" (see Contexts p.399), whose isolation has allowed them to preserve much of their traditional heritage. Despite all this – and the fact that it's fairly easy to reach for most of the year – remarkably few travellers make it to Lanyu, but those who do find themselves enchanted by its many charms, and some consider it the most memorable part of their travels in Taiwan. Much of the appeal is its sheer simplicity: apart from a budding seasonal tourism business, there is no industry on the island and it remains blessedly free of development. There are few tourist sites per se, with the main attractions being the rich tropical scenery, the Tao villages with their signature **semi-subterranean houses** and some of the world's most underrated **snorkelling**. Even in the height of summer, when nearby Ludao is choked with tourists, Lanyu is quiet and peaceful, a place to relax and absorb its timeless rhythms. For **getting here**, see box, p.323.

Some history
Lanyu's history has long been defined by its remoteness, with its native Tao inhabitants left mostly to themselves for the better part of eight hundred years. Traditionally a peaceful seagoing people with strong cultural and linguistic links to the Philippines' **Bantan Islands**, the Tao's relations with outsiders were mainly limited to small-scale trade with Taiwan's **Ami tribe** until their initial contact with Dutch colonists in the early seventeenth century. The tribe has for centuries made its livelihood from **fishing** and taro farming, gradually adding millet and sweet potatoes to the crops they have cultivated along the thin belts of fertile land between the mountains and the sea. Though there were infrequent conflicts between villages, the tribe as a whole maintained its cohesion through social conventions, particularly its strict code of **taboos**: many of these related to

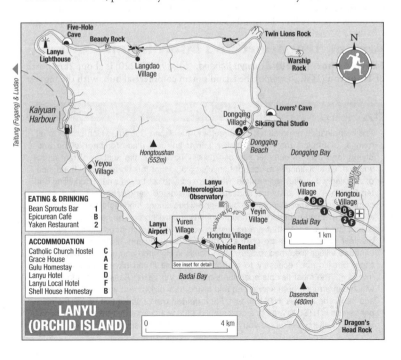

EATING & DRINKING

Bean Sprouts Bar	1
Epicurean Café	B
Yaken Restaurant	2

ACCOMMODATION

Catholic Church Hostel	C
Grace House	A
Gulu Homestay	E
Lanyu Hotel	D
Lanyu Local Hotel	F
Shell House Homestay	B

LANYU (ORCHID ISLAND)

respect for life and protection of nature, which helped ensure a sustainable supply of the resources necessary for their survival.

During the **Japanese** colonial period, the occupiers were intrigued with Tao culture and did little to influence it, although an error by a Japanese anthropologist led to the misnaming of the tribe as the "**Yami**" (which merely means "people") – a name that stuck until recent years. Things began to change for the Tao after the Kuomintang (KMT) seized power, when boatloads of Han Chinese were sent to the island in an attempt to Sinicize the tribe. Although the Tao fiercely resisted the campaign, intermarriages did take place, blurring once-clear lines of ancestry. In 1966, the KMT banned the Tao's traditional **homes** and had them demolished and replaced with concrete buildings. However, the shoddy construction and above-ground design of these structures made them vulnerable to the formidable typhoons that hit the island each year, and many were destroyed, forcing the government to lift the ban in 1980.

Despite the government's assimilation efforts, the Tao have been more successful than any other Taiwanese aboriginal group in preserving their old ways of life, and time-honoured customs are still routinely observed. A few villages consist almost exclusively of the stone **semi-underground dwellings** (地下屋; *dìxiàwū*), and some elderly men still wear traditional **loincloths**, although the number is rapidly diminishing. The rite of handing down massive **silver helmets** from father to son is still observed, although the younger generation is losing interest in this custom and the art of silversmithing is in danger of dying out. One conventional practice that looks set to stay is the building of handmade **wooden canoes**, intricately carved and colourfully painted vessels. Still, modernization is taking its toll, with Lanyu's estimated three-thousand-strong Tao population dwindling fast as young men forsake silver helmets and loincloths in favour of baseball caps and blue jeans and leave the island in search of greater economic prospects. Another threat, and one that has catapulted Lanyu into the international news headlines over the years, is the presence of 98,000 barrels of low-level **nuclear waste** that the Taiwan Power Company has stored on the island's southern tip since 1982 (see Contexts p.399).

Arrival, transport and information

Lanyu Airport (蘭嶼機場; *lányǔ jīchǎng*; ☎089/732-220) is about 2km north of **Hongtou** (紅頭; *hóngtóu*) the island's main commercial hub, with the biggest

Orchid Island snorkelling and diving

The combination of untainted coral reef and the Japan Current, which brings in all manner of tropical marine life, makes Lanyu an ideal place for **snorkelling** and **diving**, and even in summer you can usually have an entire section of reef all to yourself. One distinctive aspect of Lanyu's coral is that it is home to an abundance of amazingly beautiful **sea snakes**, which are easy to spot even when snorkelling but tend to keep their distance and are not considered very dangerous. The most common snake sports zebra-like black-and-white stripes, and sighting one of these is an exhilarating experience. Though superb snorkelling can be had all around the island, the two spots that are easiest to access and which consistently have the greatest variety of fish are on the northern shore, between Twin Lions Rock and Langdao Village (see map, p.329). Most hotels in Hongtou can arrange **snorkelling trips**, but it's not necessary to participate in these if you have rented your own transport. The most flexible operator is based at the *Yaken Restaurant* (see p.333), which can arrange both snorkelling and diving trips or just rent you a mask, snorkel and neoprene booties (NT$150/day). For a **guided trip** of about two hours, the cost per person is NT$600 without a boat and NT$800 with a boat that takes you to some fantastic outlying reef where you're virtually guaranteed to spot sea snakes.

choice of hotels and restaurants. In summer, you're likely to be greeted by touts offering you accommodation and scooter rental: most are friendly and will give you a lift into Hongtou, although chances are they'll drop you off at their homestay. Expect a similar reception if you arrive by ferry at **Kaiyuan Harbour** (開元港; *kāiyuán gǎng*), several kilometres north of Hongtou. Though the touts here might seem off-putting, keep in mind that scooters are seldom available for rent at either the airport or harbour, and if you decline their services you could wind up on a long, hot walk into the village.

The **vehicle rental** shop is alongside the main road, just below the *Lanyu Hotel*. **Scooters** cost NT$500 per day: however, if you agree to rent a scooter for three days or more, the price should be NT$400 a day, payable in advance. Make sure there's enough fuel in the tank to at least get you to the island's only petrol station, next to the harbour. While a scooter is ideal for a sunny summer day, if you're visiting in winter or during a rainy spell you might consider the more comfortable option of renting a **car** for about NT$1500 a day. A few **bicycles** are also available for rent here (NT$150/day), and these make for a pleasant way to tour around the mostly flat 37km paved road that loops round the island. There are no taxis, but a **bus** makes four daily loops round the island, starting from **Yeyou** (椰油村; *yéyóu cūn*) about 2km south of the harbour. The bus stops at all villages – and basically anywhere as long as you ask the driver in advance. If you want to flag it down you'll need to make your intentions fairly obvious. Many villagers depend on this bus, and though it's not a particularly quick or convenient way to get around, it's a great way to rub elbows with the locals.

Given Lanyu's undeveloped nature, there is no tourist office, but some hotels can provide you with basic maps.

Accommodation

Lanyu's major villages all have ample **accommodation**, but the places best suited for independent travellers are in Hongtou and the adjacent Yuren (漁人村; *yúrén cūn*), while quaint Dongqing on the island's sparsely populated east side has a cosy **homestay** offering delicious home-cooked meals.

Hongtou

Gulu Homestay 古魯民宿 (*gǔlǔ mínsù*) 80 Hongtou ☎089/732-584. This tiny homestay has two bright, well-kept rooms with double beds and a shared bathroom, as well as two larger rooms for six and eight people (NT$500–600/person), which offer some of the best value on the island. ❹

Lanyu Hotel 蘭嶼別館 (*lányǔ biéguǎn*) 45 Hongtou ☎089/731-611. Overpriced concrete box catering mostly to Taiwanese tour groups, but an acceptable option if everything else is full. Guests can order breakfast (NT$100), lunch (NT$200) and dinner (NT$200) in advance. It also conducts bus tours round the island (minimum of eight people) for NT$300 a head, and snorkelling outings from NT$400 per person. ❻

Lanyu Local Hotel 蘭嶼民宿 (*lányǔ mínsù*) ☎089/732-669. Directly across the main road from the hospital, this homestay offers

half a dozen rooms, including a large, bright dormitory (NT$500/bed). Guests can make themselves at home on the rooftop patio, which has sweeping ocean views. ❷

Yuren

Catholic Church Hostel 天主堂 (*tiānzhǔtáng*). In the centre of the village, Lanyu's cheapest accommodation is also its most spartan, with only thin mattresses on the floor of its three basement rooms (shared bathroom and kitchen facilities). To stay here, ask anyone in the village for the church's caretaker. NT$200 per person.

Shell House Homestay 貝殼屋民宿 (*bèikéwū mínsù*) 77 Yuren ☎089/732-554. Adjoining the *Epicurean Café* and run by the same family, this homestay has six rooms and can hold up to twenty people; reservations are recommended in summer. ❷

Dongqing

Grace House 蘭嶼恩典之家 (*lányǔ ēndiǎn zhījiā*) 69 Dongqing ⊕089/732-885. Immaculate homestay run by the family of the village's Presbyterian minister, a hospitable Tao man who speaks excellent Mandarin and English. A true homestay, rooms are in the family house, with a/c on the first floor and a breezy six-person rooms

upstairs. Guests here can share traditional, home-cooked Tao meals with the family, though you must let them know in advance. If you make a reservation, the owner's son can give you a lift from the airport or ferry pier; alternatively, rent a scooter in Hongtou and drive here yourself. Note that alcohol and cigarettes are prohibited, and there is a 10pm curfew. ❷

The island

Lanyu is mostly devoid of designated tourist sights, and one of the best things to do is to simply take a scooter or bicycle round the island (37km), stopping at your leisure to swim, snorkel or just soak up the captivating coastal scenery. The surrounding igneous rock has been sculpted by wind and water into curious formations, the best known of which is **Dragon's Head Rock** (龍頭岩; *lóngtóu yán*) at Lanyu's southeastern tip.

One of the most exciting things to do is to take a ride over the winding **mountain road** (5.7km) that connects **Hongtou** and **Yeyin** villages, with each bend offering a new perspective on the coastline far below. Near the top of the pass is a turnoff to an extremely steep bit of road that leads to the **Lanyu Meteorological Observatory** (蘭嶼氣象觀測站; *lányǔ qìxiàng guāncèzhàn*) which commands astounding views of Dongqing Bay to the east: sunrises here are truly spectacular. Intriguing **Yeyin** (野銀部落; *yěyín bùluò*) aka **Ivalino**, is the only community on the island that still has more **semi-underground homes** than modern structures. These dwellings, dug into the earth, fortified with low walls of wood or stone and covered with thatched roofs, still withstand the test of the typhoons that rip through the Pacific each year. Close to many homes are **sitting platforms** with thatched roofs, where villagers while away balmy afternoons chatting, playing cards, chewing betel nut – and, for the men, often drinking copious amounts of alcohol. The village is strikingly photogenic, but be careful if people wander into your viewfinder, as many Tao don't want their likenesses captured on film and you could find yourself becoming decidedly unwelcome.

A few kilometres north of Yeyin is the dazzling **Dongqing Bay** (東清灣; *dōngqīng wān*) with fine white sand and some of Lanyu's safest swimming. Nearby is Dongqing itself (東清; *dōngqīng*), with its inviting homestay and one of Taiwan's oddest art studios: the **Sikang Chai Studio** (希岡菜工作室; *xīgāngcài gōngzuòshì*; ⊕089/732-793) at 38 Dongqing Village, inside a weather-beaten waterfront shack adorned with a motley array of ornaments, has a curious selection of Tao-influenced **woodcarvings** and sculpture, many with maritime themes. The owner, a young Tao fisherman-cum-artist who renders his Chinese name as "Sikang Chai", should be happy to show you around his shop, which is closed most mornings while the artist is out fishing. If you'd like to buy some original art, it's best to come in the afternoon; if the studio is locked up, ask in the village for the owner by name. In front of the village along the waterfront is Lanyu's largest collection of traditional **wooden canoes**, each exquisitely carved and painted in red and white.

Continuing on to the north coast of the island, the road passes more of those distinctive stone configurations: **Warship Rock** (軍艦岩; *jūnjiàn yán*), **Twin Lions Rock** (雙獅岩; *shuāngshī yán*) and **Beauty Rock** (玉女岩; *yùnǚ yán*). Just past Beauty Rock is the **Five-Hole Cave** (五孔洞; *wǔkǒngdòng*), a series of five grottoes eroded into petrified coral. The Tao once called these grottoes the "Home of Evil Spirits" and forbade women and children to come here. In between Twin Lions

Lanyu's colourful festivals

Every year, Lanyu's villages are swept up in traditional **festivals**, considered by many to be the most colourful and exotic in Taiwan, and certainly the most profound and vivid expressions of the enduring Tao identity. The three major events are listed below.

The **Flying-Fish Festival** (蘭嶼飛魚季; *lányǔ fēiyújì*) which takes place every spring – usually in March – just before the flying-fish (*fēiyú*) season begins, is essentially a coming-of-age ceremony for young Tao males that also is viewed as the harbinger of a plentiful summer flying-fish catch. During the festival, young men dressed in loincloths, steel helmets and breastplates chant for the return of the flying fish before they paddle out to sea in their canoes. The flying fish is an important figure in Tao mythology, and historically it was felt that the more flying fish a young man could catch, the greater his merit to a would-be bride.

The **Millet Harvest Festival**, usually held in mid-June, is a vibrant extravaganza highlighted by an ancient dance performed by the men and the surreal **hair dance** of long-haired Tao women. The latter, which entails the synchronized, dervish-like whirling of long locks of hair by women in a circle, is an unforgettable sight.

Boat-launching festivals are much harder to track down, as they are only held when a village has finished building a handmade canoe, and the completion dates for these are always very rough estimates (but are usually in the warmer months). However, if your visit coincides with the launch of a new canoe, you're in for a real treat. The ornate vessels are built through a painstaking process of binding 27 separate pieces of wood together without a single nail, which typically takes two to three years to complete. Once a canoe has been built, intricately carved and painted in red, white and black, villagers hold a monumental **feast** in preparation for the ceremonial launch. Once everyone has finished eating, the canoes are carried down to the sea, where the men perform an elaborate dance in the water before paddling out into the open ocean.

Rock and Beauty Rock is **Langdao** (朗島; *lǎngdǎo*), another idyllic Tao community with numerous semi-underground houses and handmade wooden canoes.

Eating and drinking

Several simple **restaurants** and **bars** can be found in Hongtou and Yuren, where you can sample traditional Tao fare and fresh seafood or simply usher in a summer evening with a cold beer. However, some of these establishments close during the winter. The east coast village of Dongqing (東清; *dōngqīng*) hosts a daily night market (which opens in the late afternoon most days), where you can buy cheap grilled fish, barbecued pork and other snacks. The island's most outstanding restaurant is the ♨ *Epicurean Café* (無餓不坐; *wúèbúzuò*; March–Oct: Fri–Mon 10am–1pm & 6–11pm, Tues–Thurs 6–11pm; ☏089/731-623) at 77 Yuren Village. The Tao food here is excellent (lots of fish and taro root), and the patio upstairs is a relaxing spot for an after-dinner beverage. The best place for **breakfast** (and open year-round), is the friendly *Yaken Restaurant* (Yaken 茶坊; *yaken cháfāng*; daily 6am–7pm; ☏089/731-635) at 38 Hongtou Village, just across from the post office. In addition to delicious dumplings, steamed buns and egg pancakes, they also do Western-style breakfasts such as omelettes with toast and bacon or ham. For lunch, they prepare passable hamburgers and spaghetti. Locals flock here throughout the day for their **iced milk tea**. The owners are very helpful and can arrange scooter rental as well as snorkelling. Another great place for breakfast, lunch or **evening drinks** is the open-air seaside *Bean Sprouts Bar* (荳芽菜酒吧; *dòuyácài jiǔbā*; April–mid Oct daily 8am–midnight; ☏0921/486-110), perched above the beach in front of Badai Bay midway between Yuren and Hongtou villages. This bar, with comfortable **hammocks** strung up alongside it, has a wide selection of **cocktails** and bottled beers, as well as coffee and tea.

Travel details

Flights

Hualien to: Kaohsiung (1 daily; 55min); Taipei (6 daily; 40min).
Taitung to: Lanyu (6 daily; 25min); Ludao (3 daily; 15min); Taichung (4 daily; 1hr 10min); Taipei (7–9 daily; 50min).

Trains

Hualien to: Fulong (5 express daily; 2hr); Luodong (14 express daily; 1hr 20min); Taipei (14 express daily; 2hr 50min); Taitung (9 express daily; 2hr 40min).
Taitung to: Fangliao (4 daily; 1hr 40min); Hualien (9 express daily; 2hr 40min); Kaohsiung (5 daily; 2hr 45min); Pingdong (4 daily; 2hr 20min); Taipei (6 daily; 5hr 45min).

Buses

Hualien to: Lishan (1 daily; 5hr); Taitung (4 daily; 3hr); Taroko Village (frequent; 30min); Tianxiang (4 daily; 1hr 30min).
Taitung to: Chenggong (12 daily; 1hr); Fangliao (4 daily; 3hr); Hualien (4 daily; 3hr); Kaohsiung (4 daily; 4hr); Lidao (2 daily; 2hr); Wulu (2 daily; 1hr 30min) Zhiben (12 daily; 40min).
Tianxiang to: Dayuling (1 daily; 2hr); Hualien (4 daily; 1hr 30min); Lishan (1 daily; 2hr 45min).

Ferries

Taitung (Fugang Harbour) to: Ludao (every 2hr in summer; 40min); Lanyu (every 2hr in summer; 2hr 20min).

6

The Taiwan Strait Islands

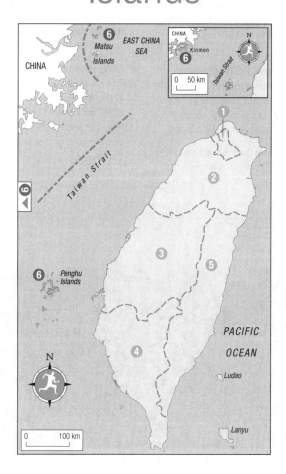

CHAPTER 6 Highlights

* **Magong** The capital of the Penghu Islands is a laid-back, historic town with plenty of sights and snack food specialities. See p.342

* **North Sea Islands (Penghu Archipelago)** Snorkel in the turquoise waters surrounding Xianjiao and Mudou islets. See p.349

* **Wangan Island (Penghu Archipelago)** Spend the night on this tiny islet, the annual nesting site of the endangered green sea turtle. See p.351

* **Kinmen** Just a few kilometres from China, this former battleground features extensive tunnels, war museums, ancestral halls and unique hybrid architecture. See p.353

* **Beigan (Matsu Islands)** Stroll secluded beaches, sample superb seafood and stay the night in Qinbi Village. See p.374

* **Dongyin (Matsu Islands)** The most dramatic scenery in the Matsu Islands, with sheer cliffs plunging to the sea, capped by the lonely Dongyong Lighthouse. See p.377

▲ Basalt columns, Penghu Islands

6

The Taiwan Strait Islands

The **TAIWAN STRAIT ISLANDS**, sprinkled across the windswept channel that separates Taiwan from the People's Republic of China, hold endless fascination for travellers and Chinese history buffs. With enormous geopolitical significance that far transcends their tiny size, the islands to this day form a natural buffer between the two versions of China.

Closest to the main island of Taiwan, the **Penghu Archipelago** is littered with ruins from the Dutch colonial period as well as successive Chinese regimes, and boasts some of Asia's most magnificent **golden-sand beaches** and unspoilt coral reefs. In the warmer months, regular commuter ferries allow for easy island-hopping here, opening up possibilities for a variety of watersports, from the region's most underrated **snorkelling** and diving to some of the world's most celebrated **windsurfing**. In addition, the curious **basalt columns** that buttress the sheer cliffs of many of Penghu's islands give them a mysterious, primordial dimension and make them eminently photogenic.

Kinmen and the **Matsu Islands**, huddled just off the mainland Chinese coast, were once among the world's most austere **Cold War flashpoints** but are now becoming the main bridges for closer ties between Taiwan and the People's Republic. Despite the damage caused to these islands by heavy PRC bombardment in the 1950s and 60s, many historic monuments and relics remain largely intact, testifying to their prolific histories and strategic importance as maritime trading entrepôts. Kinmen, an island of extensive tunnels and imposing military installations, boasts especially well-preserved Ming dynasty structures and entire villages of hybrid Chinese-European houses.

The Penghu Islands

The windswept **PENGHU ISLANDS** (澎湖群島; *pénghú qúndǎo*) are considered national treasures by the Taiwanese, who invariably gush over their epic histories, striking topography, searing heat and, perhaps most of all, the brilliant fine-sand **beaches** that attract legions of holidaymakers every summer. Situated in the south of the strait, the sprawling archipelago stretches some 60km north to south and 40km east to west, encompassing 64 islands – only twenty of which are

inhabited. The major population centres are on the **main islands** of **Penghu** (the largest island and the archipelago's namesake), **Baisha** and **Xi** – the large landmasses that comprise the island chain's heart. Sprinkled to the north and south of here are distinct groups of islets known as the **North Sea Islands** and the **South Sea Islands**, accessible by ferries operating from two separate hubs on Penghu, whose main town of **Magong** is the primary entry and exit point for most tourists.

During the March–October **summer** tourist season, the Penghu Islands are eminently accessible by air and sea from Taiwan's major west coast cities – provided there are no typhoons. In **winter**, transport connections are cut back dramatically as domestic demand dwindles due to strong winds and colder weather. **Magong** is the main arrival point, but the biggest of the South Sea Islands – **Wangan** and **Qimei** – both have airports that receive flights from Kaohsiung (and on to Magong).

By air

In the busy season, Magong can be reached by air daily from Taipei, Taichung, Chiayi, Tainan and Kaohsiung, with services running from about 7am to mid-afternoon. **Flights** take 30–50 minutes and prices range from around NT$1200 to NT$2000. The airlines operating from each city are:

Chiayi: Uni Air ☏05/286-2363.

Kaohsiung: Daily Air ☏07/803-1759; TransAsia Airways ☏07/805-7861; Uni Air ☏07/791-1000.

Magong: Daily Air ☏06/922-1838; Mandarin Airlines ☏06/922-8688; TransAsia Airways ☏06/922-8866; Uni Air ☏06/922-8986.

Taichung: Mandarin Airlines ☏04/2615-5088; Uni Air ☏04/2615-5199.

Tainan: Uni Air ☏06/260-2811.

Wangan: Daily Air ☏06/999-1009.

By sea

Ferries to Magong are considerably cheaper than flying and are convenient, with daily services from Budai (west of Chiayi) and Kaohsiung during the busy summer months.

The **fastest option** in terms of sea-travel time is **All Star** (滿天星; *mǎntiānxīng*; ☏05/347-0948 or ☏06/926-9721 in Penghu), a fast ferry that runs from **Budai** (布袋, *bùdài*; connected to Chiayi by bus, see below) to Magong daily from mid-March to early October (1hr 30min; NT$1000 one-way or NT$1950 return). It usually departs at 10am, returning at 4.30pm (with more services in the peak summer months), but always check in advance. **First Today Ferry** (今一之星; *jīnyīzhīxīng*, ☏06/926-9191) runs a similar service from the same terminal. You need to bring your passport and preferably a mobile phone with you. If you speak Chinese, you can call ahead to make a reservation and pay on arrival.

Most of the fast ferries do not run from late October to the end of February. However the Taiwanline **Taihua Ferry** (台華輪; *táihuá lún*) from **Kaohsiung** to Magong (5hr; NT$860; ☏07/561-5313) and from Magong back to Kaohsiung (4hr 30min; NT$819; ☏06/926-4087), has a year-round service, although in winter it makes only four to five trips per week. Although the sailing time is longer than from Budai, the Taihua Ferry is much larger – holding more than a thousand people, plus vehicles – so the ride is also much smoother.

To reach Budai Port from **Taipei** you can take the High Speed Rail to Chiayi in just 1hr 25min, and transfer to a Chiayi Transport Company bus just outside the High Speed Rail Station at 8.30am, 9.20am and every hour thereafter till 7.20pm – the journey can take up to 90min. Heading back, buses usually meet ferries at Budai, with the last bus to Chiayi (NT$114) at 6.30pm.

Moving on

In between the main ferry piers in Magong is the **Magong Harbor Passenger Terminal** (馬公港務大樓; *mǎgōng gǎngwù dàlóu*), where you can buy return ferry tickets to mainland Taiwan in advance on the ground floor. On the right side as you enter are the desks for First Today ferries to Budai and the Taiwanline Taihua Ferry to Kaohsiung (open daily 8.30–11.30am & 1.30–4.30pm). Just to the left of the entrance is All Star's office (daily 8am–6pm; ☏06/926-9721) for Budai.

The Penghu Islands are continually buffeted by strong **northeasterly winds**, which have weathered away their rock foundations, creating some of their biggest attractions – the magnificent **basalt mesas** that rise sharply from the sea in astonishing arrays of temple-like columns. The winds also make Penghu a major centre for **windsurfing**, particularly in winter, when Magong hosts one of the sport's premier international competitions. The islands are also havens for other **watersports** such as sailing, sea kayaking, fishing and snorkelling.

Rounding out Penghu's appeal is the rich assortment of historic sites scattered throughout the chain, and unusual local snacks such as dried squid, brown sugar cakes and peanut candy. You'll need at least a week to see everything.

Some history

Archaeological evidence suggests that the first settlements in Penghu were not formed until the early twelfth century. In 1281, shortly after the **Mongols** conquered China and founded the Yuan dynasty, they set up an official garrison to govern the islands.

During the late Ming period, Penghu's population began to rise dramatically as droves of **Fujianese** fled the political and military upheaval on the mainland. The **Dutch** set up a temporary base in 1604, but the Ming government expelled them under threat of force. After failing to seize other outposts in the South China Sea, the Dutch returned in 1622, reoccupied the main island of Penghu and built a fort near Magong. In response, Ming forces attacked in 1624 and, after eight months of fighting, the Dutch signed a treaty that actually allowed them to build outposts on the main island of Taiwan in exchange for leaving Penghu.

In 1661, when Ming loyalist **Koxinga** was en route to Taiwan (see p.245), he used Penghu as a base, and a garrison was later established here. But his family's rule over the islands was short-lived: Qing-dynasty admiral **Shi Lang** seized Penghu in a naval battle in 1683. Just over two hundred years later, in 1884, the **French** briefly occupied Penghu, but their rule was also cut short when the Qing ceded the islands to **Japan** in the 1895 Sino-Japanese Treaty of Shimonoseki. Just over fifty years later, the archipelago again fell into Chinese hands, when the **Nationalists** seized it during their retreat from the mainland.

Following the lifting of martial law in 1987, Taiwanese began to visit and the archipelago was officially designated a **national scenic area** in 1995. Though development of Penghu has been decidedly low-key until now, the local government has been pushing to build a slew of giant five-star resorts and casinos to attract more international (read mainland Chinese) tourists. The plan was quashed, in its current form at least, by a referendum held in 2009 (56 percent of residents voted against the casinos).

Arrival

Magong Airport (馬公機場; *mǎgōng jīchǎng*; ☎06/922-8188) is about 8km east of Magong itself. There is an **airport bus** (30min; NT$23) which makes trips downtown at irregular times each day (six via the Penghu Visitor Center; see opposite), from 7.10am to 6.55pm, but the service isn't timed with arrivals from major cities (most buses run in the morning). If you have booked accommodation, some hotels include an **airport pick-up service** in the price; otherwise, take a **taxi**, which should cost about NT$300 to the town centre.

If you arrive by **ferry**, most of the hotels are a short walk from the pier in Magong; alternatively, some will offer to pick you up if you've reserved.

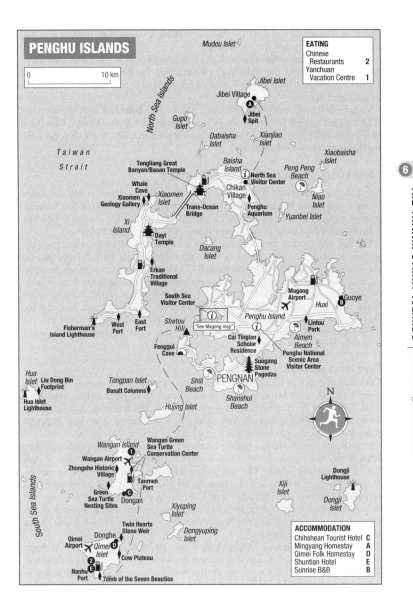

PENGHU ISLANDS

Mudou Islet

EATING
Chinese
  Restaurants   2
Yanchuan
  Vacation Centre   1

0   10 km

North Sea Islands

Jibei Islet

Jibei Village

A

Jibei
Spit

Gupo
Islet

Dabaisha
Islet

Xianjiao
Islet

Xiaobaisha
Islet

T a i w a n

S t r a i t

Tongliang Great
Banyan/Baoan Temple

Baisha
Island

Peng Peng
Beach

North Sea
Visitor Center

Whale
Cave

Chikan
Village

Niao
Islet

Xiaomen
Geology Gallery

Xiaomen
Islet

Trans-Ocean
Bridge

Penghu
Aquarium

Yuanbei Islet

*Xi
Island*

Dayi
Temple

*Dacang
Islet*

Erkan
Traditional
Village

South Sea
Visitor Center

Magong
Airport

Guoye

Huxi

B

Shetou
Hill

Penghu Island

"See Magong map"

Lintou
Park

Fisherman's
Island Lighthouse

West
Fort

East
Fort

Cai Tinglan
Scholar
Residence

*Aimen
Beach*

Fenggui
Cave

Penghu National
Scenic Area
Visitor Center

*Hua
Islet* Liu Dong Bin
Footprint

Tongpan Islet

Basalt Columns

*Shili
Beach*

Suogang
Stone
Pagodas

PENGNAN

Hua Islet
Lighthouse

Hujing Islet

*Shanshui
Beach*

N

Wangan Island

Wangan Green
Sea Turtle
Conservation Center

1

Wangan Airport

Zhongshe Historic
Village

Tanmen
Port

*Dongji
Lighthouse*

*Xiji
Islet*

Green
Sea Turtle
Nesting Sites

C

Dongan

*Xiyuping
Islet*

*Dongji
Islet*

South Sea Islands

Twin Hearts
Stone Weir

*Dongyuping
Islet*

Qimei
Airport

Donghe

D

*Qimei
Islet*

Cow Plateau

ACCOMMODATION
Chihshean Tourist Hotel   C
Mingyang Homestay   A
Qimei Folk Homestay   D
Shuntian Hotel   E
Sunrise B&B   B

2 **E**

Nanhu
Port Tomb of the Seven Beauties

THE TAIWAN STRAIT ISLANDS | The Penghu Islands

6

Information

Penghu has no convenient visitor centre if you are arriving by ferry or plane. Tour buses, however, pull in at the **Penghu Visitor Center** (澎湖遊客中心; *pénghú yóukè zhōngxīn*; daily 8am–5.30pm; ☎06/921-6521, ⓦ www.penghu-nsa.gov.tw) at 171 Guanghua St, halfway between the airport and Magong; if you have transport (taxis charge around NT$150 from the ferry pier) this is an excellent place to visit before you head out to the islands. In addition to maps and information, there are interesting exhibits on Penghu culture, geology and marine life, but English-speakers are not always on hand.

The closest **visitor information desk** (daily: April–Sept 6.30am–6.30pm, Oct–March 7am–5pm), to the main ferry pier is inside the South Sea Islands Visitor Center (see below), though you'll need to speak Chinese to make the most of the help offered here.

Magong is the only place in the Penghu Islands with **banking** services, but most ATMs do not accept foreign cards, so bring plenty of cash with you. The Bank of Taiwan at 24 Renai Rd is your best bet for foreign cards; it also has the only **foreign–currency exchange** desk.

Getting around the islands

For transport purposes, the archipelago is divided into three parts: the **main islands** of Penghu, Baisha and Xi, connected by bridges; the **North Sea Islands**, reached by ferry from the North Sea Visitor Center on Baisha; and the **South Sea Islands**, served by ferry from the South Sea Visitor Center in Magong.

The bad news is that the main islands are set up primarily for tour bus groups – getting around on your own can be tough. The islands have limited **public transport**, with infrequent **bus** services (NT$23–51) tailored to locals rather than tourists. Getting around by **taxi** can be expensive; negotiate rates in advance (most trips in Magong should be NT$100–150). A full-day tour of the main islands is likely to cost around NT$3500, more at peak times. While taxis can be useful for shorter trips to and from the airport (NT$300), or from Magong to the North Sea Visitor Center (NT$450), you'll really need to rent a **car** or **scooter** if you want to see the main sights outside Magong (see below).

Car and scooter rental

Cars and **scooters** are the most convenient way to get around the main islands, but many rental shops in Magong refuse to rent them to foreigners unless they have a valid Taiwanese driving licence and an ARC (see p.23); officially, if you have an **international driving licence** you should be OK. Rental shops can be found along Zhongzheng, Zhonghua and Renai roads in central Magong.

Some **hotels** are also happy to help overseas guests **rent scooters**, although they often prefer you to take a tiny 50cc contraption that is considerably slower than the 125cc standard-bearer. The staff at the *Zhongxin Hotel* (see p.344) in central Magong can help arrange a rental from an affiliated shop down the street if you plan to stay in their hotel for a few days. Similarly, the *Sunrise B&B* in Guoye can help guests rent scooters (see p.348). In such a case, the rental shop owner will still want to see some sort of driving licence and will require you to leave some form of **identification** as a deposit.

If you do rent a scooter, it's best to keep it for a few days, as you can use it to get to the North and South Sea visitor centres and leave it in the nearby car parks if you plan to stay overnight on one of the outlying islands. As scooter rental is generally NT$250/$350 per day for 50cc/125cc machines, this works out cheaper than taking taxis (even accounting for NT$70 or so for petrol).

Magong

Penghu Island (澎湖本島; *pénghú běndǎo*) is home to the archipelago's biggest town, **MAGONG** (馬公; *mǎgōng*), which is also the major transport hub with an abundance of hotels, restaurants and **historic monuments**. The downtown area itself is easy to navigate on foot: you can duck into the narrow lanes that traverse the old centre without fear of getting lost.

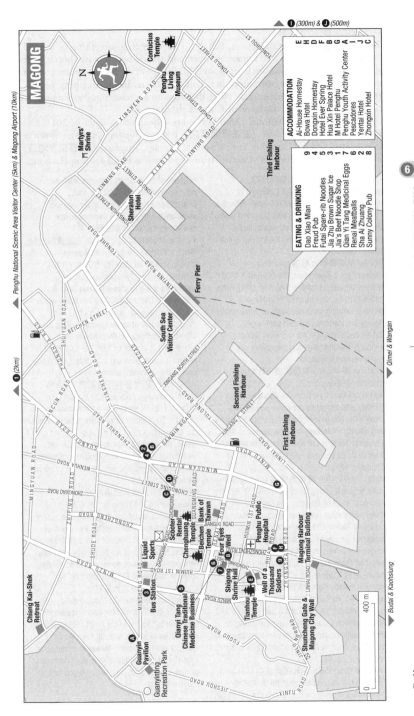

Penghu National Scenic Area Visitor Center (5km) & Magong Airport (10km) ▲

▲ ① (2km)

▲ ● ① (300m) & ⑩ (500m)

Confucius Temple

Penghu Living Museum

Martyrs' Shrine

Sheraton Hotel

Third Fishing Harbour

Ferry Pier

South Sea Visitor Center

Second Fishing Harbour

First Fishing Harbour

Chiang Kai-Shek Retreat

Guanyin Pavilion

Guanyinting Recreation Park

Liquid Sports

Scooter Rental Business

Qianyi Tang Chinese Traditional Medicine Business

Bus Station

Chenghuang Temple

Beichen Bank of Temple Taiwan

Four Eyes Well

Well of a Thousand Soldiers

Shigong Shrine Hall

Tianhou Temple

Shuncheng Gate & Magong City Wall

Penghu Public Hospital

Magong Harbour Terminal Building

▼ Budai & Kaohsiung

▼ Qimei & Wangan

ACCOMMODATION	
Ai-House Homestay	E
Bowa Hotel	H
Dongxin Homestay	D
Hotel Ever Spring	F
Hua Xin Palace Hotel	B
M Hotel Penghu	G
Penghu Youth Activity Center	A
Pescadores	I
Yentai Hotel	J
Zhongxin Hotel	C

EATING & DRINKING	
Dao Xiao Mian	9
Freud Pub	4
Futai Spare-rib Noodles	5
Jia Zhu Brown Sugar Ice	3
Jia's Beef Noodle Shop	1
Qian Yi Tang Medicinal Eggs	7
Renai Meatballs	6
Sha Ai Zhuang	2
Sunny Colony Pub	8

400 m

0

THE TAIWAN STRAIT ISLANDS

6

343

Accommodation

Thanks to government incentives, Penghu is experiencing something of a hotel boom, with more than 150 homestays open and several new five star hotels built since 2008. Most of these are in or around Magong, but rooms can become scarce during the June to August school break. If you come during this busy period, **reservations** are recommended. Note that few hotels have signs in English or *pīnyīn*, so look out for the relevant Chinese characters.

Magong's first international chain hotels are scheduled to open in 2011: the *Four Points Penghu Hotel* (澎湖福朋酒店; *pénghú fúpéng jiǔdiàn*; Ⓦwww .fourpoints-penghu.com.tw) and adjacent *Sheraton Penghu* (澎湖喜來登酒店; *pénghú xǐláidēng jiǔdiàn*) on Xintian Road opposite the Third Fishing Harbour.

Ai-House Homestay 澎湖愛鄉民宿 (*pénghú àixiāng mínsù*) 14 Zhengyi St (near Tianhou Temple) Ⓣ06/927-9296. Friendly homestay in great location, with basic but clean rooms, some with shared bathrooms, and a pleasant balcony overlooking the temple. Some English spoken. ❸

Bowa Hotel 寶華大飯店 (*bǎohuá dàfàndiàn*) 2 Zhongzheng Rd Ⓣ06/927-4881, Ⓦwww.bowahotel.com.tw. The pick of the older hotels in town, a short stroll from Magong Harbour, offering good discounts on week nights. Rooms are bland but modern with large flat-screen TVs, while the sea-view rooms, although considerably more expensive, are highly recommended. ❹

Dongxin Homestay 東信民宿 (*dōngxìn mínsù*) 12 Zhongxing Rd Ⓣ06/927-9123. Just down the street from the *Zhongxin Hotel* (below), and owned by the same person, this small hotel has several Japanese-style rooms for only slightly more than the basic rooms at the *Zhongxin*. There is not always an attendant at the front desk, so you may need to enquire at the *Zhongxin*. ❷

Hotel Ever Spring 長春大飯店 (*chángchūn dàfàndiàn*) 6 Zhongzheng Rd Ⓣ06/927-3336. Also near Magong Harbour, and one of downtown's more upmarket options, featuring gleaming rooms with internet access. With breakfast included in the room rate, it's reasonably priced, even during the height of summer. There are several rooms with harbour views, all at a higher price. ❻

Hua Xin Palace Hotel 華馨大飯店 (*huáxīn dàfàndiàn*) 40 Sanmin Rd Ⓣ06/926-4911. While hardly a palace, the *Hua Xin* is a decent option and offers significant discounts on most week nights, even in summer; rooms are smarter than they look from the outside, with modern furnishings and flat-screen TVs. ❹

🏊 **M Hotel Penghu** 和田大飯店 (*hétián dàfàndiàn*) 2 Minquan Rd Ⓣ06/926-3936, Ⓦwww.mhoteltw.com. This small but stylish boutique offers a variety of rooms with chic, minimalist furnishings, LCD TVs and English-speaking staff that can arrange just about anything. Free wi-fi throughout, and spa and restaurant on site. ❼

Penghu Youth Activity Center 澎湖青年活動中心 (*pénghú qīngnián huódòng zhōngxīn*) 11 Jieshou Rd Ⓣ06/927-1124, Ⓦpenghu.cyh.org.tw. Located near the waterfront along peaceful Jieshou Road is this comfortable China Youth Corp-run hotel, which has fifteen spacious en-suite doubles with TV and a variety of larger rooms catering to different-sized groups. From Nov to Jan, prices are cut almost by half. The location is perfect if you're planning to windsurf in the bay next to the Guanyin Pavilion. ❺

Pescadores 百世多麗花園酒店 (*bǎishì duōlì huāyuán jiǔdiàn*) 420 Xindian Rd Ⓣ06/921-9399, Ⓦwww.pescadoresresort .com.tw. The biggest resort-style hotel in Penghu (so far) can be lots of fun if you get a good deal online; plush rooms face a giant atrium with wavy walls, and come with opulent furnishings and extremely enticing sunken marble baths with a view. ❼

Yentai Hotel 元泰大飯店 (*yuántài dàfàndiàn*) 477 Xindian Rd Ⓣ06/921-1111, Ⓦwww.yentai-hotel.com.tw. One of the best of the new generation of large luxury resorts in Penghu, slightly reminiscent of a posh mainland Chinese resort. Rooms are beautifully decorated with polished wooden floors and contemporary takes on traditional Chinese furniture. ❽

Zhongxin Hotel 中信大旅社 (*zhōngxìn dàlǚshè*) 12 Zhongxing Rd Ⓣ06/927-9250. One of the best budget options, conveniently located in the heart of Magong with some of the cheapest rates in town. As a result, it can fill up with Taiwanese students, so enquire early in the day to raise your chances of getting a room. Staff here can help you rent a scooter. ❷

The town

Starting your tour at Magong's most important historic and religious site, the **Tianhou Temple** (天后宮; *tiānhòu gōng*; daily 5am–8pm), will take you to the city's oldest quarter. The name "Magong" actually derives from the Chinese nickname for the temple, dedicated to **Mazu**. Originally a small shrine erected by **Fujianese fishermen** at the end of the sixteenth century, the exact date of its inception is disputed: the earliest date for which there is archaeological evidence of the temple's existence is 1604, the year in which a **stone stele** announcing the eviction order served on the Dutch by the Ming court was engraved. This stele, unearthed in 1919, bears the weathered twelve-character inscription of Ming general **Shen You-rong**'s arrogant demand for the Dutch "red-haired barbarians" to leave the island without a fight. The original stele (now badly faded) is reverently maintained in a special chamber at the rear right-hand side of the temple. While the stele proves that the temple existed at this site before the Dutch arrived, the structure itself has undergone numerous renovations. In 1922, during the Japanese occupation, a distinguished mainland Chinese artisan was hired to oversee the engraving of the present-day structure's elaborate wooden beams – the Chinese artistry, coupled with the Japanese influence, led to the elegant fusion of styles that makes this one of Taiwan's most visually captivating temples.

Down the narrow lane to the right of the Tianhou Temple, then almost immediately to the right, is the so-called **Well of a Thousand Soldiers** (萬軍井; *wànjūnjǐng*), with a modern concrete exterior that belies the story behind it. When Qing general **Shi Lang** arrived on Penghu in 1683, his troops were not immediately welcomed by the locals, who refused to share their limited water. Studying the landscape, the crafty general discovered a water source at this spot and, making a display of praying to Mazu for water, he stuck his sword in the ground here, ordering troops to dig for water, which they found almost immediately. The well has long since gone dry. A few feet further down the lane and to the left is the **Shigong Shrine** (施公祠; *shīgōng cí*), rebuilt here in the 1940s after the original, built in honour of Shi Lang in the 1680s, was demolished by the Japanese.

Follow the lane as it veers left and you will shortly run into the pedestrian-only **Zhongyang Street** (中央街; *zhōngyāng jiē*), Magong's oldest and now a busy hive of craft shops. At the head of the street is a tiny square, the centrepiece of which is the **Four Eyes Well** (四眼井; *sìyǎnjǐng*), said to have been dug as early as the fifteenth century. Locals believe there is a "Well Mother God" inside, and many come here to pray every month.

On the square behind the well is the **Qianyi Tang Chinese Traditional Medicine Shop**, 42 Zhongyang St (乾益堂藥行; *qiányìtáng yàoháng*; daily 7am–9pm), a historic building filled with aromatic medicinal herbs since 1918 (try the great snack stall here; see p.346).

Guanyin Pavilion

A short walk northwest of Zhongyang Street, on Jieshou Road, is the **Guanyin Pavilion** (觀音亭; *guānyīntíng*; daily 5am–8pm), a small but graceful temple dedicated to **Guanyin**, the Bodhisattva associated with compassion, dating from 1696. Although the temple structure itself has been levelled twice during respective wars with the French and the Japanese, the **old bell** inside is original. In front of the temple is the expansive **Guanyinting Recreation Park** (觀音亭親水遊憩區; *guānyīntíng qīnshuǐ yóuqìqū*), located along a bay that is one of the world's best windsurfing spots.

Penghu Living Museum and Confucius Temple

Magong's latest attraction is the lavish **Penghu Living Museum** (澎湖生活博物館; *pénghú shēnghuó bówùguǎn*; Fri–Wed 10am–5pm; NT$80; ☏06/921-0405, ⓦwww.phlm.nat.gov.tw) at 327 Xinsheng Rd, a vast multistorey celebration of Penghu history and culture. Inside you'll find multimedia exhibits and videos, a huge scale model of Wangan Village and displays on early migrations to Penghu from China, folk belief, everyday life and the modern history of the islands. Labels are in English, but all the explanations are in Chinese only. You can walk here in around 20 minutes from the ferry pier, or take a taxi for NT$120.

Next to the museum is the austere **Confucius Temple** (孔廟; *kǒngmiào*; daily, courtyard open 24hr). This site originally housed the **Wenshi School**, built by the Qing in 1766 as Penghu's only centre of higher learning. The school was converted into a Confucius temple during the Japanese occupation. Access to the main courtyard is via a pathway to the right of the temple.

Eating and drinking

Magong is renowned for its **culinary specialities**, ranging from fresh seafood and dried squid to signature noodle dishes and **brown-sugar cake** (黑糖糕; *hēitánggāo*), **peanut candy** (花生糖; *huāshēngtáng*) and **seaweed cake** (海苔酥; *hǎitāisū*), sold in shops all over town. There are a number of small outdoor **night markets** where you can sample cheap local food, while upmarket **seafood restaurants** specialize in several-course meals for large parties. Among the seafood delights that Penghu is most famous for are steamed grouper, raw lobster, abalone and "five-flavour" balloonfish (*cìhétún*).

Dao Xiao Mian 刀削麵 (*dāoxiāomiàn*) 30 Zhongshan Rd. Penghu's most famous noodle joint has no name; it's a tiny, unassuming place identified by its main dish, *dāoxiāo miàn* ("knife-cut noodles"), shaved out in thick, wide slabs and fried with pork and bean sprouts (NT$65/plate). Fri–Wed 9.30am–6.30pm.

Freud Pub 弗洛伊得酒吧 (*fúluòyīde jiǔbā*) 2-1 Xinsheng Rd ☏06/926-4166. One of Magong's longest-running bars, with by far the city's most extensive drinks list (a huge selection of whiskies/white liquors and a range of imported bottled beers costing NT$180–220). Taiwan Beer is just NT$90, basic cocktails are NT$180, and the house special "Absolutely Drunk" (NT$300) – mixed with five different spirits – would suit a college punch party. Daily 6pm–2am.

Futai Spare-rib Noodles 福台排骨麵 (*fútáipáigǔ miàn*) 30 Minzu Rd at Gongming Rd ☏06/927-3397. Another popular no-frills noodle place, this one specializing in delicious spaghetti-like noodles topped with fragrant chunks of pork off the bone (from NT$90 per bowl). Daily 11am–9pm.

Jia Zhu Brown Sugar Ice 家竹黑砂糖冰 (*jiāzhú hēishātáng bīng*) 27 Fuguo Rd ☏06/927-6722. Magong's best-known ice dessert shop continues to serve up its specialty eight-flavour delight, with all the "little treasures" hand made on site (think taro balls, red and green beans, fresh mango). Choose six toppings with brown sugar sauce on top (NT$40–50). Daily 9.30am–midnight.

Jia's Beef Noodle Shop 賈老闆紅燒牛肉麵專賣店 (*jiǎlǎobǎn hóngshāo niúròumiàn zhuānmàidiàn*) ☏06/927-9737 Siwei Rd, outside National Penghu Institute of Technology. Students line up at this no-fuss place for the Sichuan-style spicy braised beef noodles, a fragrant dish with chilli sauce and large chunks of meat (from NT$70). Daily 11am–9pm.

Qian Yi Tang Medicinal Eggs 乾益堂藥膳蛋 (*qiányìtáng yàoshàndàn*) 42 Zhongyang St. This stall's main product is a lot tastier than it sounds, with eggs (NT$10) and tofu (NT$5) boiled in a rich, aromatic broth – it also sells refreshing herbal teas (NT$35). Just in front of the Traditional Medicine Shop (p.345). Daily 9am–5pm.

Renai Meatballs 仁愛小吃 (*rénài xiǎochī*) 73-1 Renai Rd. This tiny place is famous for its Taiwanese meatballs, wrapped in a glutinous coating (NT$40 for two), and is usually packed with student tourists. Daily 3–9pm.

Sha Ai Zhuang 傻愛莊 (*shǎ ài zhuāng*) 14 Xinsheng Rd ☏06/926-3693. This restaurant and teahouse, in a renovated house that originally belonged to Penghu's first county chief, has great atmosphere. The interior is lavishly decorated with local crafts and the menu features items such as "cactus noodles" (NT$200; only in summer) and "coral pancakes" (made with carrot, egg and sugar; NT$65). There is an extensive list of freshly squeezed juices from NT$120, and cocktails start at NT$180. Daily 10am–midnight.

Sunny Colony Pub 陽光殖民地酒吧 (*yángguāng zhímíndì jiǔbā*) 4 Lane 3, Zhongzheng Rd ☎06/927-8710. Tucked away down narrow Lane 3, with an English sign visible from Zhongzheng Road, is this popular bar, with dim lighting, comfortable seating and loud, upbeat music. Daily 6pm–2am.

Pengnan

Winding south and then west from Magong along a narrow peninsula, the area of Penghu Island known as **PENGNAN** (澎南地區; *péngnán dìqū*) is packed with historic sites and also boasts some of the archipelago's finest scenery. Head east out of town along Guanghua Street and turn south at the junction of Highway 201 to find the **Cai Tinglan Scholar Residence** (蔡廷蘭進士第; *càitínglán jìnshìdì*), the ruined house of Penghu's only *jìnshì*, or scholar, during the Qing dynasty. Built in 1846, the house is a popular sight despite its dilapidated state, thanks to the fame of its former owner (in Taiwan at least). Nearby, the well-maintained Cai Family Shrine (蔡氏祠堂; *càishì cítáng*) has a statue of the official in the courtyard.

A few kilometres further south on Highway 201 is the small fishing village of **Suogang**, whose twin centrepieces are the two 11m **Suogang Stone Pagodas** (鎖港子午寶塔; *suǒgǎng zǐwǔ bǎotǎ*), pyramid-shaped towers believed to drive away evil spirits and provide protection during natural disasters. The pagodas, one called the "north tower" and the other the "south tower", are in separate locations around the village so you may need to ask someone to point you in the right direction.

About 2km southwest of Suogang is the popular **Shanshui Beach** (山水沙灘; *shānshuǐ shātān*) with fine sand, clear water and a gentle break that is suitable for surfing in winter (see box above). Continue westbound on Highway 201 until you reach the **Fenggui Cave** (風櫃洞; *fēngguì dòng*), actually a wave-carved hole in the rock that comprises a natural chute through which water rushes at high tide, often creating a spectacular plume. Head back east until you see the sign for **Shetou Hill** (蛇頭山; *shétóu shān*), and turn left to climb to this once heavily fortified point. Here in 1622 the Dutch built Penghu's first Western-style fort. A short path leads to a few remnants of the structure, but these are far overshadowed by the splendid views across the bay to Magong.

Huxi

The central and eastern sections of Penghu Island comprise an area known as **HUXI** (湖西; *húxī*), a broad swath of flat land filled with farmland, parks and the beautiful **Aimen Beach** (隘門沙灘; *àimén shātān*), accessed via a short road that branches to the south from Highway 204. The bay here is ideal for swimming and a variety of watersports, and there are toilet and shower facilities. Just east of here is **Lintou Park** (林投公園; *líntóu gōngyuán*), the only place in the archipelago where trees grow in abundance. A path leads through the park to a long stretch of beach that links up with Aimen to the west. At the edge of this beach is a **granite stele** with an inscription commemorating the landing here in 1895 of the Japanese navy.

On the east coast (ideal for sunrise viewing), right on the beach in the village of **Guoye** (果葉; *guǒyè*), a tranquil alternative to Magong, the 🧍 *Sunrise B&B* (菓葉觀日樓; *guǒyèguān rìlóu*; ☏06/992-0818, Ⓦwww.sunrisebb.idv.tw; ④) has genuine single rooms that start at NT$1200 and doubles from NT$1600. The homestay is a modern building with a balcony, 12km from Magong, but the owners will pick you up from the airport (free) and can help you rent a scooter or car. Free bicycles, internet and breakfast included.

Baisha Island

Directly north of Penghu Island, and connected by two short bridges, is the island of **BAISHA** (白沙島; *báishā dǎo*), best known for the **Penghu Aquarium** (澎湖水族館; *pénghú shuǐzúguǎn*; daily 9am–5pm; NT$200; ☏06/993-3006) at 58 Qitou Village (歧頭村; *qítóu cūn*). The aquarium provides an overview of the archipelago's abundant marine life; its main highlight is the underwater tunnel that allows visitors to watch fish swim overhead.

To the west along Highway 203 is the **Tongliang Great Banyan** (通梁古榕; *tōngliáng gǔróng*), whose enormous roots form a magnificent canopy that stretches some 660m above and beyond the entrance to the **Baoan Temple** (保安宮; *bǎoāngōng*; daily 5.30am–6pm). More than 300 years old, the sprawling tree is one of Asia's biggest temple-bound banyans and far overshadows the temple itself. The shops nearby are famed for their **"purple ice" treats** (*xiānrénzhǎn bīng*) made from cactus fruit; *Yi Jia* (易家仙人掌冰; *yìjiā xiānrénzhǎn bīng*) at 191-2 Tongliang Village is one of the most famous.

Xi Island

Southwest of Baisha, and linked to it by the 2.5km Trans-Ocean Bridge (澎湖跨海大橋; *pénghú kuàhǎi dàqiáo*), is **XI ISLAND** (西嶼; *xīyǔ*), with enough attractions to keep you busy for a full day. Just after the bridge, a turnoff to the right leads to the tiny islet of **Xiaomen** (小門嶼; *xiǎoményǔ*) where you'll find the **Whale Cave** (鯨魚洞; *jīngyúdòng*), a basalt cliff whose underbelly has been worn by waves into a noteworthy arch – prompting imaginative locals to liken the formation to a beached whale. Nearby is the **Xiaomen Geology Gallery** (小門地質館; *xiǎomén dìzhíguǎn*; daily 8am–5.30pm; free; ☏06/998-2988), at 11–12 Xiaomen Village with exhibits on the island's predominant geological features.

Further south down Highway 203 is the **Erkan Traditional Village** (二崁聚落; *èrkàn jùluò*), a mostly crumbling compound of old houses with basalt foundations and coral walls, the oldest dating back to 1690. Although many of the buildings are in a state of profound disrepair, some of them have been renovated and are still inhabited.

Closer to the island's southern tip are two **Qing-dynasty forts**, completed in 1887. The smaller of the two, the **East Fort** (東嶼古堡; *dōngyǔ gǔbǎo*), is accessed via a narrow track just beyond Neian Village – the path turns to dirt before you reach the whitewashed battlement, which lies in the middle of a partially restricted military zone. It's possible to wander inside here, as there is no entry gate to the compound. The much larger **West Fort** (西嶼西台; *xīyǔ xītái*) daily: summer 7am–7pm, winter 8am–5.30pm; NT$30), 278 Waian Village, a bit further southwest along Highway 203, is easier to find and captures most of the tourist traffic. The walls were made of a mixture of mud, black-sugar water and glutinous rice.

At the island's southern tip, next to a military base, is the **Fisherman's Island Lighthouse** (西嶼燈塔; *xīyǔ dēngtǎ*; Tues–Sun 9am–4pm; free). Originally constructed in 1779, the seven-storey structure was rebuilt in its current Western style in 1875. The lookout point from the edge of the grassy plateau next to the lighthouse is a serene place to watch the sunset.

The North Sea Islands

The smattering of tiny islets in the north of the archipelago, known collectively as the **NORTH SEA ISLANDS** (北海遊憩系統; *běihǎi yóuqì xìtǒng*) have broad appeal, with white-sand beaches, basalt formations and some of Taiwan's top snorkelling spots.

Peng Peng Beach

Idyllic **Peng Peng Beach** (澎澎灘; *péngpéng tān*) is actually a stretch of glistening offshore **sand bars** between Yuanbei Island and nearby Niao Islet. The water here is remarkably clear, making it prime **snorkelling** territory. Most of the multi-islet boat tours include a stop here, mooring offshore while you wade or swim to the beach. The area also is becoming a favoured destination for sea kayakers who paddle over from Baisha or Huxi. In summer, about three-quarters of the beach is made off limits to visitors in order to protect nesting terns, leaving only the northeast tip open for tourist activity.

Xianjiao

Surrounded by spectacular **coral reef** and rich in marine life, **Xianjiao** (險礁嶼; *xiǎnjiāoyǔ*), is another favoured snorkelling and diving location. In addition, the blinding **white-sand beaches** here are probably the archipelago's most stunning. Some boats starting from the visitor centre will stop here en route to Jibei to allow passengers to swim, snorkel or participate in a range of other watersports. The operator with the sign "Ming Yang Co" (名揚; *míngyáng*; ☎06/993-2362) specializes in watersports tours to Xianjiao and Jibei. A return ticket to both islets is NT$500, including use of snorkelling equipment.

Jibei

The largest and most popular islet, **Jibei** (吉貝嶼; *jíbèiyǔ*), is covered in golden-sand beaches and is home to the spectacular **Jibei Spit** (吉貝沙嘴; *jíbèi shāzuǐ*), a mini-peninsula of sand that stretches out into the teal-blue waters for almost 1.5km. Fortunately, most tourists tend to congregate on the beach to the right – where watersports activity is concentrated – leaving the spit itself refreshingly devoid of people. It's located a few kilometres west of the ferry pier.

North Sea ferries

The departure point for the North Sea Islands is the **North Sea Visitor Center** (北海遊客中心; *běihǎi yóukè zhōngxīn*; daily 6.30am–5.30pm; ☎06/993-3082), on the waterfront near Chikan Village (赤崁村; *chìkǎn cūn*) on Baisha. At the centre you can get maps and information, and in summer there are numerous **ferries** to all the main islands. Most of these are run by private operators who offer **multi-stop tours**, usually including the option of snorkelling or other watersports such as sea kayaking and jet-skiing. Prices for these tours range from NT$300 for single-island trips to over NT$1000 for multi-island excursions including watersports activities. The range of options and schedules can be confusing, and few of the operators speak English, so it's best to approach first the main **information desk** (at the far end of the hall to the left of the entrance) and tell the staff there where you'd like to go.

Accommodation on Jibei is not cheap in summer, but the homestays that stay open in winter offer discounts of up to half-price. About halfway between the ferry pier and the Jibei Spit is the *Mingyang Homestay* (名揚山莊; *míngyáng shānzhuāng*; ☎06/991-1113; ❹), 182 Jibei Village, with about a dozen cabins with double beds from NT$1700. It fills up quickly in summer so it's best to call in advance. The section of Jibei Village to the right as you leave the ferry pier has several small **restaurants** with reasonably priced Chinese dishes as well as local seafood specialities. Return ferry tickets to Jibei cost NT$300, and the trip takes about fifteen minutes. The small **Jibei Visitor Center** (吉貝遊客中心; *jíbèi yóukè zhōngxīn*; daily 8am–5.30pm; ☎06/991-1487) stands next to the ferry pier and can help with accommodation.

Mudou and Gupo Islet

The archipelago's northernmost islet, 7km north of Jibei, tiny **Mudou** (目斗嶼; *mùdǒuyǔ*) is dominated by a towering 40m-high lighthouse built in 1921. It's a remarkably photogenic spot, but thanks to heavy storms in recent years the nearby reefs that once proved so enticing have been severely damaged. Local operators now visit **Gupo Islet** (姑婆嶼; *gūpóyǔ*) instead, another basalt outcrop ringed by stunning coral gardens and a silver anchovy fish breeding ground (it's also known for the huge laver or seaweed beds on the north side). One company that specializes in snorkelling trips to Gupo is the Baisha Sea Tourist Center (白沙海上遊樂中心; *báishā hǎishàng yóulè zhōngxīn*; ☎06/993-2626), which offers a range of trips and packages in summer. A full-day outing starts at NT$1500, including snorkelling gear and lunch.

The South Sea Islands

Dozens of landmasses comprise what are known as the **SOUTH SEA ISLANDS** (南海遊憩系統; *nánhǎi yóuqì xìtǒng*), but only five are regularly accessible by public or private ferries. While there are some notable historic sites on these islands, the overwhelming focus of most is on the natural environment, particularly the curious **basalt formations** that decorate their fringes.

Tongpan

About fifteen minutes by boat from Magong, the tiny inhabited islet of **TONGPAN** (桶盤嶼; *tǒngpányǔ*) is best known for the vertical cliffs of symmetrical **basalt columns** that surround it. Most boats only stop here for

---

South Sea ferries

Ferries to these islands leave from the **South Sea Visitor Center** (南海遊客中心; *nánhǎi yóukè zhōngxīn*; daily 6.30am–5.30pm; ☎06/926-4738), at 25 Xinying Rd in Magong. Here a couple of private operators offer a variety of tours; weather permitting, these sail daily to Tongpan, Hujing, Wangan and Qimei for around NT$700, leaving at 7.30–8.30am and returning in mid-afternoon – the boats make very short stops at each island. For NT$500 you can visit the first three islands only (skipping Qimei), while NT$350 covers just Tongpan and Hujing. Try to buy tickets in advance.

Otherwise, to stay longer you need to take the **public ferry**, giving you the option of staying overnight. The ferry departs daily at 9am, arriving at Wangan at 9.45am (NT$278); it departs Wangan at around 10.05am and heads to Qimei (NT$443 from Magong). The boat leaves Qimei at 1.40pm to arrive at Wangan at 2.25pm; it then leaves Wangan at 2.40pm for arrival in Magong at 3.25pm.

40–50 minutes – if you follow the tour guides assigned to most boats, they'll take you to some of the islet's finest columns in this time. The **Fuhai Temple** (福海宮; *fúhǎigōng*), located near the pier, is dedicated primarily to the pestilence god Wen Wang Ye (see Contexts p.402) and is the archipelago's most popular shrine.

Hujing

Just southeast of Tongpan is **Hujing** (虎井嶼; *hǔjǐngyǔ*), also known for its towering mesas of **basalt columns** but with the added attraction of **Japanese military tunnels** from World War II. The most visually striking – and accessible – of these columns line the road that leads up the hill to the west. Follow the road to the right of the pier to reach **Xishan Park** (西山公園; *xīshān gōngyuán*), home to a line-up of imposing basalt columns to the left of the road. If you look closely here you can see the openings of tunnels dug by Japanese soldiers. At the top of the hill is a viewpoint looking out over the sea and a few tunnel entrances concealed in concrete buildings.

Multi-island boat tours usually stop here for less than an hour, so if you want to have a good look around you'll need to get motorized transport. Most Taiwanese tourists get shuffled onto a **minivan** for an additional cost of NT$150, but you can also rent one of the many **scooters** lined up near the pier for NT$200.

Wangan

The archipelago's fourth-largest island, **WANGAN** (望安島; *wàngān dǎo*), is one of the highlights of a visit to the Penghu Islands, with secluded beaches, one of Taiwan's best-preserved traditional fishing villages and the chain's only nesting sites for the endangered **green sea turtle**. As with other islands, the best way to get around here is by scooter, especially if you want to see all the main sights.

One of the island's biggest treats is the captivating **Zhongshe Historic Village** (中社古厝; *zhōngshè gǔcuò*) on the west side. Written records of the village date back about two hundred years, but locals claim it was first established about three hundred years ago. Although there is a small, ageing population, most of the houses have long since been abandoned, leaving the tiled roofs and coral walls to collapse. The upside of this neglect is that the village has retained its original dynastic layout, giving it a timeless aura. Just north of the village is **Tiantai Hill** (天台山; *tiāntáishān*; 53m), an excellent spot for a panoramic view of the island. On top of the hill is "God's Footprint" (仙腳印; *xiānjiǎoyìn*) where, according to legend, **the footprint of Lu Dong Bin** – one of the most renowned of China's "Eight Immortals" – is said to be embedded. According to the tale, the footprint was left after Lu stopped to relieve himself while walking through the Taiwan Strait. His other footprint is allegedly on top of a cliff on the east side of nearby Hua Islet (花嶼; *huāyǔ*).

About one kilometre north of the ferry pier is the **Wangan Green Sea Turtle Conservation Center** (望安綠蠵龜觀光保育中心; *wàngān lùxīguī guāngguāng bǎoyù zhōngxīn*; daily 8.30am–5.30pm; free; ☎06/999-7368), a museum with exhibits on all marine turtles endemic to the region. Wangan's beaches are the only nesting sites in Penghu where green sea turtles return regularly to lay eggs, and the museum is mostly geared towards educating visitors about the importance of not disturbing them. The turtles usually mate in March and April and typically crawl onto Wangan's **southwestern beaches** in May and June to lay eggs. If you're visiting during this time, or even later in the summer, there's a chance you could see them. However, access to these beaches is often restricted during this period.

It's possible to **fly** between **Wangan Airport** (望安機場; *wàngān jīchǎng*; ✆06/999-1806) and Kaohsiung. Daily Air (see p.339) offers one-way flights from Kaohsiung (35min; around NT$2000) in a small propeller-driven plane on Tuesday and Friday mornings (returning a few minutes later).

   Multi-island boat tours starting from the South Sea Visitor Center call here for up to two hours as part of their circuits, but to really gain an appreciation of the island it's best to stay overnight. Rent a **scooter**, as the sights are spread out (NT$200/2hr or NT$350/day, including a full tank of fuel; no driving licence required). The other option is to join a group of Taiwanese tourists on a whirlwind **minivan tour** for NT$150 per person.

   A great place to stay on Wangan is the *Chihshean Tourist Hotel* (致仙屋海景民宿; *zhìxiānwū hǎijǐng mínsù*; ✆06/999-1413; ❹), 24 Dongan Village, which has spotless blond-wood chalets in a variety of sizes from doubles up (all en-suite with TVs).

Qimei

One of the best-known islets, **QIMEI** (七美嶼; *qīměiyǔ*, also "Cimei"), has some of the area's most stunning scenery, with **steep cliffs** plunging down to craggy coastlines. Despite its relative isolation, it gets swamped with domestic tourists in summer and the giant tour buses and legions of scooter-revving students greatly disrupt the tranquillity. Qimei means "Seven Beauties" and relates to a legend about seven Ming dynasty maidens who were attacked by Japanese pirates while doing laundry at a well. Rather than surrender their chastity they jumped to their deaths inside the well, which was later filled and covered with a tomb in their honour. Shortly afterwards, seven trees began to grow around the site. The **Tomb of the Seven Beauties** (七美人塚; *qīměi rénzhǒng*; daily 8am–5pm; NT$30) is a mandatory stop for Taiwanese tourists, and it's worth a visit just to observe some of the rituals that take place here. Carry on around the islet's hilly east coast until you get to the **Cow Plateau** (牛母坪; *niúmǔpíng*), a beautiful stretch of grassland looking out onto some of the Penghu Islands' best coastal scenery.

   Located at the base of a cliff on the islet's northeast corner is the **Twin Hearts Stone Weir** (雙心石滬; *shuāngxīn shíhù*), a traditional **fish trap** made of stones piled into the shape of two large hearts. Although the archipelago is covered in stone weirs, this one is the most famous and now sees far more tourists trampling over it than fish.

Daily Air (see p.339) has two **flights** daily (30min; NT$1800 one-way) on propeller-driven aircraft from Kaohsiung to **Qimei Airport** (七美機場; *qīměi jīchǎng*; ✆06-9971256) in summer; you can also fly to and from Magong daily with the same airline.

   Multi-island ferry tours starting from the South Sea Visitor Center make Qimei their last port of call before returning to Magong, usually allowing passengers an insufficient hour and a half to look around. If you want to soak up the scenery you'll need to spend the night at one of the hotels near the ferry pier, but if time doesn't allow for that it's best to rent a **scooter** for a quick spin round the island (NT$200/2hr, NT$350/day, including petrol). Alternatively, you can board a **bus** (NT$150) for a dizzying tour in Mandarin and Taiwanese.

   The best **accommodation** on Qimei is the *Qimei Folk Homestay* (七美風情民宿; *qīměi fēngqíng mínsù*; ✆06-997-1271; ❸) at 5 Donghu Village, with shared dorm beds from NT$300 and comfy doubles for NT$1200. A cheaper and more convenient option closer to the pier is the *Shuntian Hotel* (順天旅社; *shùntiān lǚshè*; ✆06/997-1888; ❷), 18 Nangang Village, with budget doubles from NT$600, beds in seven-person dorms for NT$300 and the reasonable *Qimei Fishing Village Restaurant* (七美漁村餐廳; *qīmĕi yúcūn cāntīng*) on the first floor. There's also free internet access for guests. There are a handful of basic Chinese restaurants directly in front of the pier.

Kinmen

The islands of **KINMEN** (金門; *jīnmén*), huddled just over 2km off the mainland Chinese coast, are among Taiwan's most fascinating travel destinations, with a wealth of historic, cultural and culinary delights rolled into one of the most heavily fortified places on earth. Once the front line in the struggle between Mao Zedong's Communists and Chiang Kai-shek's Nationalists, the main islands of Kinmen and **Lieyu** are seemingly impregnable fortresses. Indeed, if you're looking for a **beach**, think again; the superstitious Chinese fear of the sea is still much in evidence here, and beaches remain underdeveloped or littered with rusting iron spikes. Yet within this harsh exterior, and in between myriad military sites, some of Taiwan's most emblematic culture thrives, largely undiluted by outside forces and the encroachment of modernism.

Kinmen is home to an impressive concentration of historic structures, from Ming-dynasty memorial arches and Qing-inspired burial mounds to "**Western-style houses**" (*yánglóu*), actually European-Fujianese hybrid structures built by prosperous Kinmen natives who made their fortunes in southeast Asia. Scattered all over the island are Kinmen's signature folk icons, the most common of which are the intriguing stone **wind-lion god statues** (風獅爺; *fēngshīyé*) that for centuries have watched over the island's villages and are believed to protect them from the ravages of heavy winds and storms.

In 1995, much of the island became Taiwan's sixth **national park** – the only one dedicated to the preservation of historic monuments and battlefield memorials. Many once-important **military sites** have been decommissioned and are now open to the public, giving tangible insights into the grim reality that for Kinmen's hardy residents has only recently begun to brighten.

Some history

Though archaeological evidence suggests that Kinmen was inhabited as long as 6500 years ago, it was not until 317 AD that the first traceable ancestors of contemporary **Kinmen clans** moved to the island to escape turmoil in central China. This settlement was on a small scale however, and the island remained a cultural backwater until the Tang dynasty, when the ancestors of twelve clans, led by **Chen Yuan**, arrived to breed and raise horses in 803. The horse-breeding efforts met with limited success, and much of Kinmen's development over the next few centuries consisted in the establishment of **oyster farms**. In 1297, a **salt mine** was set up to supply the mainland. In the following centuries the island became a popular hiding place for Chinese and Japanese **pirates**. In the 1640s, the Ming loyalist general **Koxinga** (see p.245) occupied the island and used it while preparing his navy to fight against the Qing forces that had overrun China. During his reign, many of the island's indigenous trees were felled for use in shipbuilding, leaving much of Kinmen barren and subject to the severe winds that dominate the Taiwan Strait.

After the **Opium War** in 1842, when the nearby city of Xiamen became one of China's five **treaty ports**, many Kinmen residents began travelling to southeast Asia via Xiamen to do business, in the process amassing considerable wealth, which they used to build lavish, European-inspired houses back home. But when the

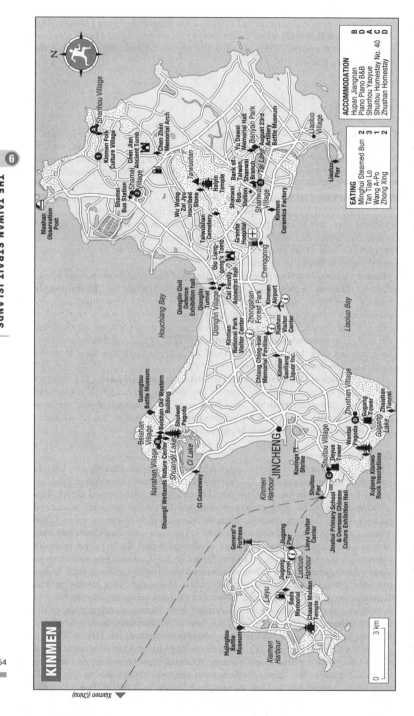

KINMEN

N

ACCOMMODATION

Hupan Jiangnan	B
Piano Piano B&B	D
Shamou Yaoyue	A
Shuitou Homestay No. 40	C
Zhushan Homestay	D

EATING

Minghui Steamed Bun	2
Tan Tian Lo	3
Wang A-Po	1
Zhong Xing	2

Shamou Village

Mashan Observation Post

A Kinmen Folk Culture Village

Chen Zhen Memorial Arch

Shamei Chen Jian Ancient Tomb

Shamei Bus Station

Shamei Village

Taiwushan

Wu Wang Zai Jyu Inscribed Stone

Haiyin Temple

Yu Dawei Memorial Hall

Banyan Park

August 23rd Artillery Battle Museum

Liaoluo Village

Taiwushan Cemetery

Shanwai: Bank of Taiwan, bus station, Shanwai branch

Shanwai Village

Bu Liang-gong's Tomb

Granite Hospital

Kinen Ceramics Factory

Liaoluo Pier

Qionglin Civil Defence Exhibition hall

Qionglin Village

Qionglin Tunnel

Cai Family Ancestral Hall

Chenggong

Houchiang Bay

Kinmen National Park Visitor Center

Chiang Ching-kuo Memorial Pavilion

Zhongshan Forest Park

Rushan Visitor Center

Kinmen Airport

Liaoluo Bay

Kinmen Gaoliang Liquor Inc.

Guningtou Battle Museum

Beishan Village

Beishan Old Western Building

Shuiwei Pagoda

Nanshan Village

Shuangli Wetlands Nature Center

Shuangli Lake

Ci Lake

Ci Causeway

Zhushan Village

Gugang Tower

Wentai Pagoda

Zhaishan Tunnel

Gugang Lake

JINCHENG

Koxinga Shrine

Shuitou Village

Deyue Tower

Kinmen Harbour

Shuitou Pier

Xujiang Xiaowo Rock Inscriptions

General's Fortress

Lieyu

Jiugong Tunnel

Jiugong Pier

Lieyu Visitor Center

Luocuo Harbour

Jinshui Primary School & Overseas Chinese Culture Exhibition Hall

Hujingtou Battle Museum

Bada Memorial

Chaste Maiden Temple

Xiamen Harbour

0   3 km

Sino-Japanese War broke out in 1937, **Japanese forces** immediately seized the island and occupied it for eight years, bringing to an end its most prosperous period. In 1949, Kinmen bore the brunt of another invasion force, this time from Chiang Kai-shek's retreating **Nationalist army**, which used the island as the front line in its preparations to recover mainland China from Mao Zedong's Communists. On August 23, 1958, the Communists launched a brutal **artillery attack** on Kinmen, firing almost 475,000 shells in 44 consecutive days of bombing. The shelling continued intermittently for the next twenty years. Since the lifting of **martial law** in 1987, Kinmen has undergone a small-scale renaissance, with promising economic ties to mainland China being forged, setting the stage for a new period of growth and development.

Orientation

There are fifteen islands in the Kinmen Archipelago, with twelve under Taiwanese administration and three under mainland Chinese control. Only the two biggest – Kinmen and Lieyu – are inhabited by civilians and open to visitors. The main island, Kinmen, is shaped like a dumbbell, spanning only 3km from north to south in its centre and as much as 15km from north to south in its eastern portion. From east to west it's about 20km. Most visitors make the main commercial hub of **Jincheng** their first stop, as the majority of hotels, restaurants and shops are located here, but there are plenty of enticing **homestays** across the island. Given the sheer number of sights – and the fact

---

Getting to Kinmen

From Taiwan

The only way to get to Kinmen from Taiwan is to **fly**. There are **daily flights** throughout the year from five west coast cities. Return tickets typically cost between NT$3200 and NT$3500, with one-way fares starting from NT$2000. **Uni Air** (☏082/324-481) flies to Kinmen from Chiayi, Kaohsiung, Taichung, Tainan and Taipei; **TransAsia Airways** (☏082/321-502) from Kaohsiung and Taipei; and **Mandarin Airlines** (☏082/328-000) from Taichung and Taipei.

From China

Foreigners can now take the ferry between **Xiamen** (厦门; *xiàmén*) in Fujian, China, and Kinmen. Going into Taiwan is relatively straightforward, but going the other way most travellers will need a Chinese visa – which cannot be acquired directly in Taiwan (see p.19). All Xiamen ferries arrive at Kinmen's **Shuitou Pier** (水頭碼頭; *shuǐtóu mǎtóu*), where you'll find a **visitor information centre** (daily 8am–6pm; ☏082/322-124) that usually has English-speakers and renminbi (Chinese currency) exchange counters (but no ATMs). **Taxis** between Shuitou and Jincheng charge NT$200; **bus** #7 is NT$12.

Assuming you have a Chinese visa, it's possible to take the ferry to Xiamen, an express bus from Xiamen to Fuzhou and then another ferry to Matsu (see p.370), from where you can fly or take a ferry back to Taiwan main island. Ferries depart Shuitou for Xiamen at 9am, 11am, 1pm, 2pm, 4pm and 5.30pm and cost around NT$750; heading back you'll pay around Rmb160. Several companies share the route and prices are all the same.

In Xiamen, there are two ferry terminals: **Wutong Port** (五通码头; *wǔtōng mǎtóu*) is around 30 minutes from Kinmen and just 15 minutes by taxi from **Xiamen Airport** (shuttle buses connect the port with downtown), while ferries also run to the more central **Dongdu International Ferry Terminal** (东渡国际轮码头; *dōngdù guójì yóulún mǎtóu*) in around 1 hour.

6

THE TAIWAN STRAIT ISLANDS | Kinmen

355

that they are spread out across the island – seeing them all might prove to be a stretch, especially if your time is limited. By renting a **scooter** or car, you could probably take in most of the main attractions in about five days; double that if you're relying on public buses.

Arrival

Kinmen Airport (金門機場; *jīnmén jīchǎng*) is located just over 4km from the centre of Jincheng. Near the main exit is a **visitor information centre** (daily 8am–6pm; ☎082/329-354), with a formidable array of English **maps** and brochures on Kinmen's main attractions. Just to the left is an **ICBC ATM**, which accepts most international cards apart from American Express or Visa (bring plenty of cash if you use these cards). There is also a **post office** (Mon–Fri 8am–noon & 1–4.30pm). There are plenty of **taxis**, which can take you to the centre of Jincheng for about NT$250. Alternatively, take **bus #3** (16 times daily, 6am–7.50pm; 25min; NT$12 one-way), but note that it also runs in the opposite direction to the village of Shanwai, so make sure Jincheng or Shuitou is displayed on the front. For the **ferry** from China, see box, p.355.

Transport

The most convenient way to get around the island is by **scooter** (NT$400–500/ day), provided you can produce a valid international driving licence; renters are fairly strict about enforcing this rule. Try **Xin Jing Ye Scooter Rentals** (新敬業機車; *xīnjìngyè jīchē*; daily 8am–9pm; ☎082/322-658) at 1 Huandao 4th Road Sec 1, immediately south of the roundabout between Minsheng Road and Wangdu West Road in Jincheng. **Cars**, oddly enough, seem easier to rent with just any national driving licence, although they are more expensive (from NT$1600/ day); try **San De Rental Cars** (三德租車; *sāndé zūchē*) at 28 Yu Village, Jinhu (☎082/332-252), which will usually deliver the car to you. Note that most hotels will help you rent scooters or cars.

Travelling the island by public **bus** is possible, but painfully slow and requires careful planning to get to the main sights. **Jincheng Bus Station** (金城車站; *jīnchéng chēzhàn*) at Minsheng and Chubu East roads has regular **bus services** to Shanwai (NT$24) and Shamei (NT$24), the next-biggest villages and near several worthwhile attractions; fares start at NT$12 and rise to NT$24 for longer distances.

Kinmen's system of **tour buses** is an easier way to go; tickets are NT$160/ 24hr. Short stops at sights along the way are programmed into the schedule, although each route tends to operate just one service a day. There are four main loop routes: A (Old Kinmen Town and Zhushan; 8.30am; 3hr 30min) and B (Guningtou; 1.30pm; 3hr 52min) run from Jicheng Bus Station, while C (Taiwushan, Jinshan; 8.30am; 3hr 32min) and D (Banyan Park; 1.30pm; 3hr 13min) run from Shanwai.

Kinmen National Park (金門國家公園; *jīnmén guójiā gōngyuán*) provides **bicycle rentals** (free) at Shuangli Wetlands Nature Center, Zhaishan Tunnel, Jinshui Elementary School and Lieyu Visitor Center; you usually have to return the bike the same day (8.30am to 3–4.30pm) and leave some form of photo ID.

Information

The most convenient **information centre** is at the airport (see above). You won't learn much more at the **Kinmen National Park Visitor Center** (金門國家公園遊客中心; *jīnmén guójiā gōngyuán yóukè zhōngxīn*; daily 8.30am–5pm; ☎082/313-100), in the centre of the island at Zhongshan Forest Park (p.363).

The **Kinmen Post Office** at (4 Minsheng Rd); Mon–Fri 7.30am–5pm, Sat 8–11.30am, closed Sun) is across the street from the main bus station in Jincheng. Although there are **ATMs** scattered across the island, many will not accept international cards, although MasterCard would be your best bet. The most reliable one on Kinmen is an unassuming 24 hour dispenser for **Land Bank**, located across Minsheng Road from the main bus station in Jincheng, between the Catholic Church and 7-Eleven. The other safe bet is the 24 hour ATM at Jincheng's main **Bank of Taiwan branch** at 162 Minquan Rd (Mon–Fri 9am–3.30pm, closed Sat & Sun), which is the only place on the island where you can change foreign currency and traveller's cheques.

Internet access should be provided by your hotel; otherwise you can buy a week's subscription to the island's wi-fi service for NT$100 (NT$350/month); visit *Wireless Kinmen* (金門無線島; *jīnmén wúxiàndǎo*) on the third floor above the bus station in Jincheng (☎082/322-676; www.km-airnet.net). Failing that, try the *Powernet* gaming centre opposite the same bus station (24hr; NT$20/hr).

Accommodation

The vast majority of Kinmen's traditional **hotel** accommodation is concentrated in the bustling commercial district of Jincheng. Although this is the most convenient place to stay on the island, the hotels here lack character, and for a bit more charm and atmosphere it's well worth opting for one of the growing number of family-run **homestays** (Ⓦguesthouse.kmnp.gov.tw); you'll find more than ten in Shuitou.

Jincheng

Hai-Fu Hotel & Suites 海福商務飯店 (*hǎifú shāngwù fàndiàn*) 85 Mincquan Rd, Jincheng ☎082/322-538. One of Jincheng's higher-end options, with plush, contemporary-style rooms with cable TV, given a thorough makeover in 2009. Prices include breakfast, and hotel staff will pick you up at the airport or ferry pier if you make arrangements in advance. ❹

Hong Fu Hotel 宏福大飯店 (*hóngfú dàfàndiàn*) 169 Minzu Rd, Jincheng ☎082/326-768. Conveniently located close to Juguang Rd, Jincheng's historic artery, but the rooms are nothing special, and those overlooking busy Minzu Rd tend to be noisy day and night; if you stay here, ask for a room away from the road. ❹

Around Kinmen island

Hupan Jiangnan 湖畔江南 (*húpàn jiāngnán*) 5-6 Nanshan Village ☎082/373-978 or 0939/725883. Great option in a restored traditional house not far from the Shuangli Wetlands Nature Center in the heart of Nanshan. Rooms are small but cosy and crammed with old Chinese furniture (and local TV). Prices start at NT$1000 and include breakfast. The owner can arrange scooter rentals and free transfers to and from the airport. ❸

Piano Piano B&B 慢漫民宿 (*mànmàn mínsù*) 75 Zhushan Village ☎082/372-866. Very classy homestay, with rates starting at NT$2000. The

traditional-style home and rooms are similar to other places (antique beds, tiled floors and peaceful courtyard), but the comfort level is slightly higher here, with extras like CD players, Tiffany lamps and a soporific roof deck.

🏃 **Shanhou Yaoyue** 山后遙月 (*shānhòu yáoyuè*) aka *Kinmen B&B*, 45 Shanhou Village ☎082/353-745 or 0929/121-008. Fabulous homestay with five guest rooms surrounding the main hall of a traditional-style family home. The building is new, but the tiled floors and Chinese calligraphy are very authentic; rooms feature a small living area with flat-screen TV, modern bathrooms and cosy bedroom with Chinese dressers. Room rates include a filling Chinese breakfast, and the helpful owners (who speak good English) can help arrange scooter/car rental and will let you use one of their bicycles for free (taxis are around NT$320 from the airport). Free wi-fi. ❸

Shuitou Homestay No. 40 (Shuitiaogetou) 水頭 40號民宿 (水調歌頭) *shuǐtóu 40hào mínsù* (*shuǐdiàogētóu*) 40 Shuitou Village ☎082/322-389. Solid, characterful option in beautiful but homestay-heavy Shuitou Village. Rooms all have wood beams and tiled floors in a traditional house, some with lofts. Rates start at NT$1200, free bikes and breakfast included. ❸

🏃 **Zhushan Homestay No. 82 (Lexis Inn)** 珠山82號民宿 (來喜樓), *zhūshān*

357

82hào mínsù (*láixǐ lóu*) 82 Zhushan Village ☎ 0928/121-649. Renovated in 2010, this handsome two-storey *yánglóu* was built in 1928 by a Chinese merchant who earned his fortune in the Philippines; the interiors are classical Chinese (the bathrooms are modern), with fine, carved rosewood beds, attractive common areas and a tranquil balcony for chilling out. ❸

Jincheng and around

The core of **JINCHENG** (金城; *jīnchéng*), Kinmen's only major town, is a labyrinth of narrow lanes and alleys, twisting their way through a hodgepodge of curious old houses and an amazing assortment of tiny temples and shrines. Most of the best-known attractions are situated around Juguang Road and quaint Mofan Street, both of which have some superb little restaurants.

The old centre

The present design of **Mofan Street** (模範街; *mófàn jiē*) dates back to 1925, when forty brick buildings were erected in the Western-influenced style popular at that time, with arches lining the entranceways. This enchanting little street now houses the hippest of Kinmen's teahouses-cum-bars (see p.360). Framing the main intersection of nearby Juguang Road is **Qiu Liang-gong's Maternal Chastity**

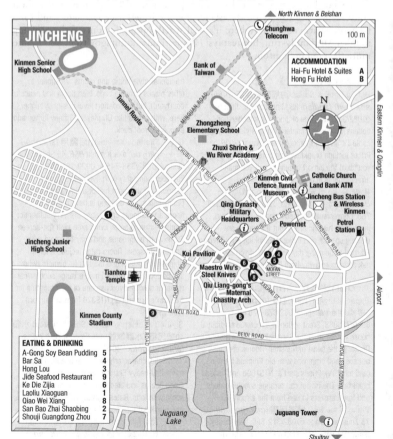

Arch (邱良功母節孝坊; *qiūliánggōng mǔjié xiàofāng*), the largest surviving monumental archway in Taiwan. **Qiu Liang-gong**, a Kinmen native who rose through the Qing military ranks to become commander-in-chief of the navy stationed in China's Zhejiang province, ordered the imposing, intricately carved arch built in 1812 as a tribute to his mother's devotion to his father – she refused to remarry during the 28 years between her husband's death and hers. A few minutes' walk from here is the two-storey **Kui Pavilion** (奎閣; *kuígé*), originally built in the 1830s. The pavilion is tricky to find: to get here from the memorial arch, walk northwest along Juguang Road for about a hundred metres, until you reach 27 Juguang Rd Sec 2 on the left-hand side. Here, a narrow alley runs for about twenty metres before intersecting another small lane – keep to the right for another thirty metres or so and you'll come to the pavilion.

Opposite the alley to the pavilion, on the other side of Juguang Road, is a small square that ends with the **Qing Dynasty Military Headquarters** (清金門鎮總兵署; *qīng jīnmén zhènzǒng bīngshǔ*; daily 10am–10pm; free), a large complex of traditional Chinese halls dating back to 1682. The compound now serves as a history museum for the island, focusing on the Qing period and particularly this building's role in its military past (with English labels). Inside you'll also find another **visitor information centre** (☏082/371-717), usually with English-speakers.

Kinmen Civil Defence Tunnel Museum

Just above the bus station on the east side of town (5min walk from the Qing complex), the **Kinmen Civil Defence Tunnel Museum** (金城民防坑道; *jīnchéng mínfáng kēngdào*; daily 10am–9.30pm; free) provides an overview of the island's "combat villages" and the tunnel that was dug under Jincheng in 1978. At 1285m, it's the longest you can walk through and the most evocative of Kinmen's military past, although you must join the guided tours that depart every hour and take around forty minutes. You emerge at the Kinmen Senior High School (see map opposite) on the northwestern side of town, although there are a couple of emergency exits along the way. You must walk back along the surface from here. The museum also contains another **visitor information centre** (same times).

Juguang Tower

On Jincheng's southeastern fringe, overlooking nearby Juguang Lake, is the 16m **Juguang Tower** (莒光樓; *jǔguānglóu*; daily 8am–10pm; free), built in 1953 in the style of a **classical Chinese palace tower** to honour Nationalist soldiers. On the first floor is yet another **visitor information centre** (same hours), as well as bilingual displays introducing the key themes in Kinmen's history and culture. On the second floor is a particularly enlightening exhibit on Jincheng's City Gods and related festivals, while the third and final storey offers more Kinmen history, as well as fine views of Juguang Lake, the outskirts of Jincheng and the hazy towers of Xiamen beyond. Buses #3 and #6 stop just outside the tower.

Eating and drinking

Decent restaurants are hard to find in Kinmen outside Jincheng, which thankfully is packed with delightful places **to eat** – the area between central Juguang Road and Mofan Street is teeming with **food stalls** and tiny **restaurants**. Among Kinmen's most famous **specialities** are the handmade thin noodles (*miànxiàn*) that can be seen drying on racks all over town and so-called *guǎngdōng zhōu*, a local approximation of Cantonese congee. Street-side shops sell locally made hard "tribute candies" (*gòngtáng*) by the bucketful, including the popular **peanut candy** made from a mix of malt and peanuts grown on the island. And while

Jincheng has a distinct lack of **nightlife** – with an atmosphere like a curfew after dark – a couple of the trendier joints on Mofan Street can get lively, usually after enough of their curious **cocktails** made with Kinmen *gāoliáng* (sorghum liquor) have been consumed.

A-Gong Soy Bean Pudding 阿公ㄟ豆花 (*āgōng de dòuhuā*) 15 Mofan St ☎082/325-870. Huge bowls of shaved ice (*tsua bing*) with six toppings for NT$40, as well as creamy *dòuhuā* (soybean pudding); they also do Japanese-style octopus balls (NT$40).

Bar Sa 吧薩串烤餐廳 (*bāsà chuànkǎo cāntīng*) 13 Mofan St ☎082/372-305. This tiny teahouse-cum-restaurant doubles as a low-key drinking establishment, serving up its own cocktails (NT$120) made from *gāoliáng* and a variety of fruit juices. Nominally open 11am to 11pm, but often open evenings only.

Hong Lou 戀戀紅樓 (*liànliàn hónglóu*) 22-24 Mofan St (look for the Mao poster) ☎082/312-606. Another trendy teahouse-bar-restaurant decorated with an eclectic array of local artefacts, from old movie posters to mainland Communist kitsch. Occasionally local folk artists perform animated acoustic sets in the evening, and the regulars enjoy being able to write and draw on the walls. Daily 10am–11pm (sometimes closes in the afternoon).

Jide Seafood Restaurant 記德海鮮餐廳 (*jìdé hǎixiān cāntīng*) 253 Minzu Rd ☎082/324-461. Favoured by locals for its fresh seafood but with a wide selection of dishes, from fried rice and noodles to aboriginal staples and well-known mainland Chinese recipes with a Kinmen twist. Most dishes start from about NT$150. Daily 11am–2pm & 6pm–midnight.

Ke Dia Zijia 蚵嗲之家 (*kēdiā zhījiā*) 59 Juguang Rd Sec 1 ☎082/322-210. Just behind Qiu Liang-gong's arch is this immensely popular snack stall, which sells everything from deep-fried oyster fritters (NT$25) to scrumptious sweet balls

(NT$12) filled with pastes made of green bean, red bean and peanuts. Daily 2.30–7pm.

Laoliu Xiaoguan 老六小館 (*lǎoliù xiǎoguǎn*) 65 Minquan Rd ☎082/324-068. "Old Six" is a friendly family-run eatery specializing in seafood, although it caters more to groups sitting at its round tables than individual travellers – try the fish hotpot (NT$450) that can feed up to six. Daily 11am–2pm & 5–9pm.

Qiao Wei Xiang 巧味香小吃店 (*qiǎowèixiāng xiǎo chī diàn*) 39 Juguang Rd Sec 1 ☎082/327-652. The best place in Jincheng to try handmade glass noodles, served in big, steaming bowls of soup with fresh oysters (*ké cài miàn xiàn*). It's conveniently located, clean and offers bowls of the noodle (NT$60) without the chopped pig intestine that crops up in most of the town's other *miàn xiàn* diners. Daily 8am–1pm.

San Bao Zhai Shaobing 三寶齋燒餅店 (*sānbǎozhāi shāobǐngdiàn*) 10 Mofan St. Literally small hole-in-the wall, selling delicious, freshly baked buns with sweet bean or taro fillings (*shāobǐng*) for just NT$15.

Shouji Guangdong Zhou 壽記廣東粥 (*shòujì guǎngdōng zhōu*) 50 Juguang Rd Sec 1 ☎082/327-878. Kinmen's most famous breakfast spot, specializing in the local version of Cantonese congee, served in huge bowls (NT$60) and usually eaten with fried bread sticks (*yóutiáo*). The family-run establishment has been in business for almost ninety years, and the owners are proud of their congee-making heritage, which began when some of their clan emigrated to southern Guangdong province. Daily 7am–12.30pm.

Shuitou

Southwest of Jincheng, along the road that leads to the Shuitou pier, lies the enchanting village of **SHUITOU** (水頭; *shuǐtóu*), home of traditional southern Fujianese houses and Kinmen's best-preserved *yánglóu*, the European-Fujianese hybrid homes that have become one of the island's hallmarks. Ever since moneyed Shuitou emigrés began returning to the village in the 1920s and 30s and started building elaborate houses inspired by the colonial architecture of Malaysia and Singapore, Kinmen residents have had a saying: "Just because you're as rich as a Shuitou person doesn't mean you'll be able to build a house as beautiful as a Shuitou house." A leisurely stroll (English signs and maps dot the village) will give you a close-up view of some of their painstakingly detailed ornamentation. Tour buses and numerous homestays haven't really spoilt it – for the time being.

Getting an edge on the enemy

By far the most unique of Kinmen souvenirs – and the most telling of its recent history – is the amazing range of **cutlery** forged and fashioned from melted-down **artillery encasements** left over from mainland attacks. With more than 970,000 shells having pounded Kinmen over a twenty-year period, there is a seemingly endless supply of raw materials, and industrious locals have learnt how to make a living from designing **knives**, meat cleavers, axes and even swords from the spent casings.

Although you'll find the cutlery for sale in shops all over Jincheng, usually starting at about NT$900 for a basic knife or meat cleaver, the creations of **Maestro Wu's Steel Knives** (金合利鋼刀; *jīn hé lì gāng dāo*) are widely considered the finest; pen-knives are NT$900, with up to NT$2200 for the best cleavers. Founder Wu Chao Hsi, son of an iron caster who learned tool-making techniques in Xiamen during the Qing dynasty, carried on the family tradition with Allied bomb shells in World War II, and continued during the years of mainland bombardment, transforming the exploded casings into magnificent instruments (after 1958 he used mostly propaganda shells that only partly broke up). His business continues to thrive under third-generation Wu Tseng-dong, drawing on Japanese designs, with outlets all over Kinmen and a glitzy **showroom** on a small square just off Juguang Road (51 Wujiang St ☏82/373-977), just outside the Qing Dynasty Military Headquarters (see p.359), and a **store** at 21 Mofan St. The showroom is a good place to buy the cutlery, and staff can arrange tours of their **workshops**.

Start at **Jinshui Primary School** (金水學校; *jīnshuǐ xuéxiào*; daily 9am–5pm; free), a handsome *yánglóu* structure completed in 1932, south of the main road next to a small car park. Today it contains a series of bilingual exhibits highlighting Kinmen emigration, the subsequent remittance system and development of local school systems. Most of the predominantly male immigrants went to Singapore and Malaysia in several waves starting in the 1860s, migrations that generated huge cashflows back to China, funded elaborate construction projects and even fed cultural changes.

Behind the school lies the village's best-known landmark, the 11m-high **Deyue Tower** (得月樓; *déyuè lóu*; daily 8.30am–5pm; free) built in the 1930s by businessman Huang Huei-huang to protect his estate from burglary. Essentially a glorified gun emplacement, the four-storey tower has no staircase, with each floor connected to the next by a removable wooden ladder. You can't go inside the tower, but the "false house" (another deterrent) and stately **Huang Residence** next door have been turned into a series of absorbing display rooms, this time focusing specifically on the culture of Chinese immigrants to Indonesia and Malaysia. The nearby Chinese-style home containing the **Overseas Chinese Culture Exhibition Hall** (僑鄉文化展示館; *qiáoxiāng wénhuà zhǎnshìguǎn*; daily 8.30am–5pm; free) completes the picture, with exhibits charting the cultural impact of the overseas Chinese, from architecture and fashion, to language and cuisine.

From here you can simply wander the narrow streets, lined with traditional swallowtail houses; the largest is the **Youtang Villa** (酉堂別業; *yǒutáng biéyè*), built in 1766 by Huang Jun, the head of the village's founding Huang clan and still privately owned. It's the one that fronts the small fishpond, north of Deyue Tower. **Bus** #7 from Jincheng stops just outside the village.

Wentai Pagoda

Southeast of Shuitou, signposted down a narrow lane off the main road, is the serene stone **Wentai Pagoda** (文台寶塔; *wéntái bǎotǎ*) built in 1387 and one of Taiwan's oldest surviving relics. The only one of Kinmen's three ancient stone towers still in existence, the solid granite structure sits atop an enormous boulder above the car park, cutting a solitary figure above the surrounding trees. The stone tower may well have been a marker for heavenly worship, as characters carved on the northeast side of its third level state: "the star of literature shines high in the sky." Underneath these characters is a time-worn relief of **Wenchang Dijun** (known as the god of literature; see Contexts p.405) kicking a vessel said to resemble the Big Dipper. However, Kinmen historians say the pagoda's main function was to serve as a navigational marker for ships plying the nearby shallow waters. About 50m west of the pagoda are the **Xujiang Xiaowo Rock Inscriptions** (虛江嘯臥碣群; *xūjiānxiàowò jiéqún*) overlooking the sea (and the grimy old Kinmen Distillery next door). According to legend, they were carved into the rock face in honour of **Ming general Xujiang**, who was said to enjoy the sea views from this spot. The characters read: "Xujiang shouts while lying here."

Zhaishan Tunnels

Just southeast of the Wentai Pagoda is **Gugang Lake** (古崗湖), where signposts lead to the **Zhaishan Tunnels** (翟山坑道; *zháishān kēngdào*; daily 8.30am–5pm; free), another man-made defensive structure completed in 1966. These are unique: a wide, cave-like passage runs down to a cavernous U-shaped water tunnel, with both ends filtering into the sea (now blocked by gates). This could safely shelter up to 42 **supply boats** during intensive artillery attacks, becoming a crucial lifeline for the island. You can wander to the end and back, although there's not much to do except wonder at the effort that went into such a thing. **Bus** #6 from Jincheng stops just outside Gugang Lake and the tunnels.

The northwest peninsula

Once brutally scarred by war, Kinmen's **northwestern tip** has made a remarkable recovery in the last twenty years, although look closer and you'll still see signs of destruction. The area's best-known attraction is the fort-like **Guningtou Battle Museum** (古寧頭戰史館; *gǔníngtóu zhànshǐguǎn*; daily 8.30am–5pm; free), located near the beachfront that was the site of the most crucial Nationalist victory of the entire Chinese civil war. After a series of crushing defeats and retreats, it was here, in October 1949, that Chiang Kai-shek's troops finally stopped Mao's Communists, and ensured the KMT's survival; after three days of savage fighting, a ragtag invasion force of more than ten thousand Communist soldiers were routed, with just nine hundred remaining soldiers surrendering on the beach. In total, more than fifteen thousand soldiers from both sides were killed. The museum's collection consists primarily of a dozen enormous **oil paintings** depicting the battle's defining moments, in graphic and understandably biased detail – you are unlikely to see mainland Chinese tourists at this museum. **Buses** #10, #11 and #26 stop in a car park near the museum entrance.

Beishan and Nanshan

Near the centre of nearby **Beishan** (北山; *běishān*) is the **Beishan Old Western Building** (北山古洋樓; *běishān gǔyánglóu*), a bullet-hole-riddled *yánglóu* that has become a symbol of the Nationalist victory at Guningtou. Seized early in the conflict by the Communists, who turned it into a **command post**, it was eventually recaptured by the Nationalists after a series of vicious battles. Although there's little to see here but a few crumbling old walls, it's an important point of pilgrimage for patriotic Taiwanese. There is no English sign marking the building.

Beishan itself is still inhabited and after a long recovery effort is worth a quick look, with many traditional homes. **Buses** #10 and #11 stop at the village bus shelter, which has a handy map inside.

Just to the southwest, alongside the road between Beishan and Nanshan villages, is the **Shuiwei Pagoda** (水尾塔; *shuǐwěitǎ*), a quadrilateral granite tower erected in 1695 upon the recommendation of a geomancer who predicted it would help stem the **flooding**. The pagoda faces **Shuangli Lake**, on the left-hand side of the road as you head towards **Nanshan** (南山; *nánshān*). Opposite, about 100m up the small lane leading to the national park's administrative centre, is one of Kinmen's most celebrated **wind-lion god statues**.

On the other side of Shuangli Lake is the **Shuangli Wetlands Nature Center** (雙鯉溼地自然中心; *shuānglǐ shīdì zìrán zhōngxīn*; daily 8.30am–5pm; free), a two-storey facility with exhibits (some in English) on local flora and fauna, with particular emphasis on some of the more than 250 species of **migratory birds** that stop at Shuangli and Ci lakes throughout the year. The best period for birdwatching is from November to March. Buses #10 and #11 also stop near here. Nearby **Ci Lake** (慈湖; *cíhú*), which until 1950 connected the villages to the sea, is Kinmen's best all-round birdwatching spot, and the **Ci Causeway** is the best place to see the now rusting (and effectively redundant) rows of anti-amphibious landing spikes that once lined all the beaches of Kinmen.

Kinmen Gaoliang Liquor Inc

Kinmen's most famous product is its fiery **Kinmen gaoliang liquor**, made here from local sorghum (*gāoliáng*) since 1953 and most commonly available in 38- or 58-proof incarnations. Shops all over Jincheng sell the liquor in ornate ceramic bottles, but you can also visit the shiny headquarters of **Kinmen Gaoliang Liquor Inc** (金門酒廠; *jīnmén jiǔchǎng*; ☏082/325-628, Ⓦwww.kkl .com.tw) at 1 Taoyuan Rd, not far from the airport and Zhongshan Forest Park. **Guided tours** of the distillery and small museum are available (Mon–Fri 8am– noon & 1–5.30pm; free), but usually only in Chinese; the **shop** (where you can buy and taste the various liquors on sale) is open Mon–Fri 8am–noon & 1–5.30pm, Sat & Sun 8am–noon & 1–4.30pm. A huge *gāoliáng* bottle on the main road marks the entrance.

Zhongshan Forest Park

The **Zhongshan Forest Park** (中山紀念林; *zhōngshān jìnniàn lín*) in the centre of the island, is a peaceful evergreen forest lined with paved pathways for short nature walks. Access is via the Kinmen Park Visitor Center at the northern end (see p.356), or the **Rushan Visitor Center** (乳山遊客中心; *rǔshān yóukè zhōngxīn*: daily 8.30am–5pm) at the south, which contains displays on the park's flora and fauna, as well as a preserved dolphin, half cut-away. Nearby, the **Chiang Ching-kuo Memorial Pavilion** (蔣經國紀念館; *jiǎngjīngguó jìniànguǎn*; daily 8.30am–5pm; free) commemorates the son of Chiang Kai-shek, who commanded troops on Kinmen and eventually succeeded his father as president. Inside the pavilion is a bust of the younger Chiang, as well as displays of items from his wardrobe and key utensils from his personal **grooming kit**, including such essentials as razors, a comb, hair cream and a bottle of his favourite cologne. Exhibition halls on either side chronicle Chiang's life, and his involvement with Kinmen in English and Chinese, although this is predictably flattering stuff. **Bus #1** from Jincheng stops outside the national park visitor centre.

Qionglin

Northeast of Zhongshan Forest Park is the fascinating village of **QIONGLIN** (瓊林村; *qiónglín*) renowned equally for its ancestral halls and its extensive network of tunnels.

Entering the village from the north, the main square fronts the old Farmers' Association Hall, spruced up and converted into the **Qionglin Civil Defence Exhibition Hall** (瓊林民防館; *qiónglín mínfángguǎn*; daily 8.30am–5pm; free), a remarkable record of Kinmen's organization of "combat villages" and the incredible paranoia and restrictions that governed local lives until 1992: no swimming, no kites, no radios, a nightly curfew and restricted travel included (English labels). Next door is an example of that era; the **Qionglin Tunnel** (瓊林坑道; *qióng lín kēngdào*; daily 8am–noon & 1–6pm; NT$10) was hacked out by the villagers in the 1970s, a shallow, narrow passage that winds under the houses for several hundred metres. Just as you think it's never going to end, you emerge at the northern end of the village, opposite an impressive wind-lion god standing guard. It is a short walk back to the car park from here, but you can detour into the warren of Qionglin's crumbling Chinese homes, predominantly inhabited by the scholarly **Cai clan**, and its seven **ancestral halls** (*cítáng*). The grandest of these is the **Cai Family Ancestral Hall** (蔡氏祠堂; *càishì cítáng*), its ancient interior embellished with intricate woodcarvings and large lanterns looming from the ceiling (usually open during daylight hours).

Taiwushan

The hilly terrain east of Qionglin gives rise to **Taiwushan** (太武山; *tàiwǔshān*), or Taiwu Mountain, which at 253m is Kinmen's highest peak and a popular walking area, with several worthwhile attractions.

The car park at the foot of the mountain sits at a graceful stone bridge spanning lily ponds leading to a **martyrs' shrine**, behind which is the enormous **Taiwushan Cemetery** (太武山公墓; *tàiwǔshān gōngmù*) filled with thousands of headstones of Nationalist soldiers – army bases still circle the site. On the left side of the cemetery, a road cuts through the army base to the **Taiwushan Footpath**, a 3.5km paved pedestrian-only road leading to the mountaintop.

Just over 1km up the path is the famous **Wu Wang Zai Ju Inscribed Stone** (毋忘在莒勒石; *wúwàngzàijǔ lèshí*), a massive smooth-faced outcrop inscribed with the four characters of Chiang Kai-shek's oft-recited rallying cry to reclaim the Chinese mainland. The slogan, which literally means "Forget Not the Time in Chu", refers to the ancient military achievement of **General Tian Dan**, who retreated to the territory of Chu to regroup and train his troops before recovering their former territory of Qi during the Zhou dynasty. Chiang ordered the characters inscribed in the stone in 1952, exhorting civilians and soldiers alike to be inspired by Tian Dan's historic example.

Further up the footpath is the **Haiyin Temple** (海印寺; *hǎiyìnsì*), which was originally built near the top of Taiwushan during the Song dynasty, between 1265 and 1274. At first it was a Taoist shrine, but during Ming-dynasty renovations the Taoist statuary was replaced with Buddha images. The temple was destroyed during the August 23 Artillery Battle in 1958 and a new one was built in the current location. From here you can continue to follow the footpath as it descends to Taiwushan's northeastern base or retrace your steps to the entrance near the cemetery.

Shanwai

Kinmen's second-largest settlement, **SHANWAI** (山外; *shānwài*) is mostly populated with young soldiers and is mainly useful to tourists as a transport hub, with a **bus station** in the centre offering services to nearby attractions. There's a small **visitor centre** (daily 9am–6pm) in the bus station and plenty of taxis outside. With numerous **restaurants**, it's also a convenient place to stop for lunch or dinner. Tan Tian Lo (談天樓; *tántiānlóu*) at 3 Fuxing Rd serves superb savoury and sweet sesame dumplings with shaved ice (NT$60–80), while *Lucky Star* (滿天星; *mǎntiānxīng*) at 47 Fuxing Rd offers a wider range of tasty Chinese dishes. There are plenty of bakeries and teashops along the main road near the bus station and 7-Eleven.

Just east of Shanwai is **Tai Lake** (太湖; *tàihú*) a recreation area favoured by locals and an important breeding ground for cormorants and ospreys. On the lake's northeastern side is the **Banyan Park** (榕園; *róng yuán*), containing several historical attractions, notably the **August 23 Artillery Battle Museum** (八二三 戰史館; *bāèrsān zhànshǐguǎn*; daily 8.30am–5pm; free), which chronicles the crippling battle that began on the eve of August 23, 1958, when Communist forces launched an artillery attack against Kinmen and Lieyu that lasted 44 days, firing almost 475,000 shells and destroying 2649 buildings. The museum provides an excellent overview of the bombardment and its aftermath, including fascinating exhibits about the prolonged **propaganda war** between the two sides. Most of the displays have English captions, and there is a variety of black-and-white photos and video footage from the period.

Shamei and the Mashan Observation Post

The village of **SHAMEI** (沙美; *shāměi*), in the northern section of the island, is primarily another transportation hub and a place to grab a snack. ✻ *Minghui Steamed Bun* (明惠饅頭; *mínghuì mántóu*; ☎082/352-922) at 48 Bohai Rd, is famed for its crumbly, tasty meat and sweet *shāobǐng* (NT$12), and well worth seeking out. Look out also for *Zhong Xing* (中興; *zhōngxīng*) at the end of the road, which knocks out addictive *baozi* and mantóu for just NT$7 per order.

About 3km north of Shamei, right on the island's northeasterly tip, is the **Mashan Observation Post** (馬山觀測站; *mǎshān guāncèzhàn*; daily 8am–6pm; free), a once heavily fortified station from which Taiwanese troops still keep tabs on the mainland. Up from the car park, follow the sunken road to the observation post entrance (the road on the left is still used by the military). Once inside turn right (left is for washrooms) for the 174m-long tunnel leading to a concrete bunker offering clear views of some inhabited **mainland Chinese islands** less than 2km away. Inside the pillbox are high-powered binoculars that can give you close-up views of the islands and at the weekends, boatloads of gawking mainland tourists. No buses go this far, so if you don't have your own transport (or miss the daily tour bus), you'll need to catch a taxi in Shamei.

Shanhou: Kinmen Folk Culture Village

Some 5km southeast of the Mashan Observation Post is the **Kinmen Folk Culture Village** (金門民俗文化村; *jīnmén mínsú wénhuà cūn*; daily 24hr; shops 8.30am–5pm; free), a spectacularly photogenic compound of well-preserved **southern Fujian-style houses** on the edge of **SHANHOU** (山后; *shānhòu*) Village. The compound contains sixteen traditional houses, plus the **Wang Ancestral Hall** (王氏宗祠; *wángshì zōngcí*) and the **Haizhu Hall** (海珠堂; *hǎizhūtáng*), a traditional private school, all interconnected and aligned in perfect symmetry, accessible via a neatly organized network of narrow lanes. It was built by members of the wealthy **Wang clan**, overseas merchants who made their fortunes in Japan. The entire complex took more than twenty years to build and was completed in 1900. Most of the family homes are still privately owned, although some have been converted into shops, with a simple snack place at the front (no. 64); 🥢 *Wang A-Po* (王阿婆小吃店; *wáng ā-pó xiǎochī diàn*; ☏082/35238) is famed throughout Kinmen for its delicious oyster omelettes (NT$60).

You can go inside the **Wang Ancestral Hall** (the main building at the front to the right), where displays (labelled in English) shed some light on the history of the village and Wang family, and also the **Marriage Custom Exhibition Hall** behind it, the only house you can actually wander around. Inside you'll find basic displays on Chinese marriage customs and more Wang memorabilia. The village of Shanhou itself is a tranquil, traditional place, home to a fabulous homestay (see p.357). Buses #25 and #31 from Shamei stop at the entrance gate.

Lieyu (Little Kinmen)

Commonly known as "Xiao Jinmen" (Little Kinmen), **LIEYU** (烈嶼; *lièyǔ*) – the small island just west of Kinmen – was relentlessly shelled by the PRC for decades and today it is Kinmen at its most surreal. The island's regeneration has produced tranquil cycle paths, swaths of bucolic wheatfields and largely rebuilt traditional villages, yet the military remains firmly entrenched here – sometimes metres from the tourists – and the island bristles with landmines (but all public areas are perfectly safe).

Lieyu is easy to reach, with **ferries** leaving from Shuitou Pier every half-hour (daily 7am–6pm; 15min; NT$60). Bus #7 runs from Jincheng to Shuitou Pier (the Lieyu ferry is along the pier behind the large China ferry terminal). All ferries will allow you to bring a **bicycle** (free) or **scooter** (an extra NT$50) on board, although you can also **rent bikes** for free on arrival – highly recommended, as the island's most attractive asset is the blissfully traffic- (and tour bus-) free 18km **cycle path** that circles the coast. **Buses** do run across the island (NT$12–15), but are not that practical for sightseeing.

Upon arrival at **Jiugong Pier** you can get detailed maps of the island at the tiny **visitor information centre** (daily 8am–6pm). Walk up the hill behind the centre to find the entrance to the **Jiugong Tunnel** (九宮坑道; *jiǔgōng kēngdào*; daily 8.30am–5.30pm; free), commonly referred to as the "Siwei Tunnel". Blasted into solid granite in the 1960s to transport and shelter personnel and rations, it was hacked out in a double-T configuration, with four exits to the sea and five connecting tunnels leading to piers. You can walk through the main 790m cavern-like tunnel to **Luocuo Harbour** (羅厝漁港; *luócuò yúgǎng*), on the other side, but it's easier to come back the same way than continue on foot.

A bit further up the hill from the main tunnel entrance is the **Lieyu Visitor Center** (烈嶼遊客中心; *lièyǔ yóukè zhōngxīn* daily 8.30am–5pm; ☏082/364-401), with a small display area in Chinese, a coffee shop and souvenir stand. Near the entrance is the park's **bicycle stand** (8am–noon & 1–5pm; bring ID/passport); the island bike trail starts just above the visitor centre.

As you head north on this trail, the first attraction you'll encounter is the **General's Fortress** (將軍堡; *jiāngjūnbǎo*), an abandoned command outpost situated on a lonely stretch of golden-sand beach. Further around the loop on the island's northwestern corner is the **Hujingtou Battle Museum** (湖井頭戰史館; *hújǐngtóu zhànshǐguǎn*; daily 8.30am–5.30pm; free), essentially a lookout post with unparalleled views of the ever-expanding mainland Chinese city of **Xiamen**. The museum itself (English labels) commemorates the local Lieyu Regiment and its role in the defence of tiny Dadan and Erhan islets, as well as recordings of troops and videos of current special forces training (mainly bare-chested exercises on the beach).

The Matsu Islands

Poised tantalizingly close to the coast of mainland China's Fujian province, the **MATSU ISLANDS** (馬祖列島; *mǎzǔ lièdǎo*) are second only to Kinmen in their proximity to the PRC – a fact that explains the formidable displays of **military force** on most of them. The archipelago is geographically, historically and culturally distinct from mainland Taiwan. Its inhabitants' ancestors originally migrated from **northern Fujian**, and here more than anywhere else their traditional ways of life are preserved. In addition to upholding their fishing heritage, most of the islanders speak the **Minbei dialect**, commonly referred to in English as the "Fuzhou" dialect – it's markedly different from the "Minnan" (southern Fujian) dialect that's predominantly spoken throughout Taiwan.

Although the archipelago comprises nineteen islands and islets, only six of them are accessible to tourists, each with a distinct flavour and appeal. While the main island and tourist centre, **Nangan**, has the greatest variety of attractions, the less crowded **Beigan** has the best beaches and examples of northern Fujianese architecture. Hilly **Dongyin** and **Xiyin** – which are connected by a causeway – feature the most striking topography, and the sister islands of **Dongju** and **Xiju** are brimming with historic landmarks. In fair weather, all the islands can easily be reached via **ferries** originating at Nangan, but you should allow at least a week if you want to visit all of them at a leisurely pace. Given the distance required to travel here from mainland Taiwan, it makes sense to take your time and soak up the atmosphere at each one.

Although the entire archipelago is named "Matsu", locals and Taiwanese tourists routinely refer to the biggest, most visited island of Nangan as "Matsu" as well: according to legend, the Chinese goddess **Mazu**'s dead body washed ashore on one of its beaches.

The **best period to visit** is from late May to September, as warm weather and clear visibility allow for regular flights and ferry services. The islands are shrouded in thick fog from March to early May and battered by heavy winds in winter, making air and sea connections highly erratic and visits far less enjoyable at these times.

Some history

The Matsu Islands were first settled in the mid-1300s, when **fishermen** from China's Fujian province used them for shelter during stormy weather and eventually set up permanent bases. The heaviest migration took place in the 1600s, when boatloads of mostly northern Fujianese refugees began arriving in the wake of the **Manchu invasions** from northeastern China. Throughout much of the Qing dynasty the islands were plagued by **piracy**, with periodic raids forcing many settlers at least temporarily to abandon their homes. Unlike the rest of Taiwan, the Matsu Islands were never colonized by the Japanese, and they remained sleepy fishing outposts until 1949, when the retreating **Nationalists** seized them along with Kinmen and built numerous military installations to fend off advances by mainland Communists. In August 1954, the Nationalist government sent 15,000 troops to Matsu, instigating an artillery bombardment by the Communists. The shelling continued steadily until 1956, when the US supplied the Nationalists with sophisticated weaponry that effectively countered the Communist offensive, and the bombing continued only sporadically until August 1958, when the Communists resumed a massive artillery attack on the island and threatened to

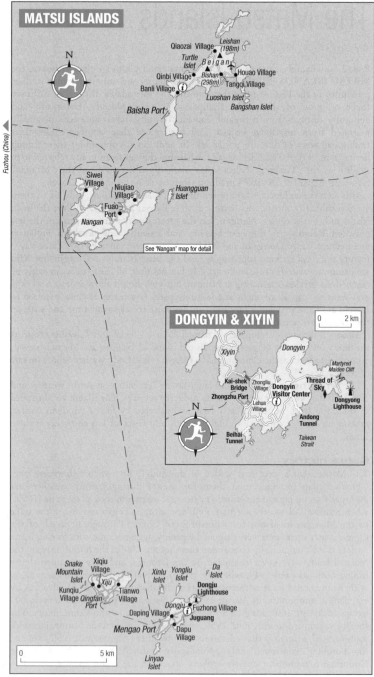

MATSU ISLANDS

N

Qiaozai Village
Leishan (198m)

Turtle Islet
Beigan

Qinbi Village
Bishan (298m)
Houao Village

Banli Village (i)
Tangqi Village

Luoshan Islet
Bangshan Islet

Baisha Port

Siwei Village

Niujiao Village
Huangguan Islet

Fuao Port

Nangan

See 'Nangan' map for detail

DONGYIN & XIYIN

0   2 km

Xiyin
Dongyin

Martyred Maiden Cliff

Kai-shek Bridge
Zhongliu Village
Dongyin Visitor Center (i)
Thread of Sky

Zhongzhu Port
Lehua Village
Dongyong Lighthouse

Andong Tunnel

Beihai Tunnel
Taiwan Strait

N

Snake Mountain Islet
Xiqiu Village
Xinlu Islet
Yongliu Islet
Da Islet

Xiju

Kunqiu Village
Qingfan Port
Tianwo Village
Dongju (i)
Dongju Lighthouse
Fuzhong Village

Daping Village
Juguang

Mengao Port
Dapu Village

Linyao Islet

0   5 km

invade. The US responded by deploying its **Seventh Fleet** to the Taiwan Strait, providing naval aircraft that enabled the Nationalists to establish control of the region's airspace. In October 1958, Communist Party Chairman **Mao Zedong** proposed a deal: if US warships stayed away from the mainland coastline, the Communists would only bomb the strait islands on odd-numbered days. The offer was rejected at first, but two years later the Americans and Taiwanese agreed and the alternate-day shelling continued until 1978.

Martial law wasn't lifted on Matsu until 1987, but since then the military presence has been gradually scaled back and local businesses have increasingly turned towards **tourism**. In recognition of the islands' unique history and culture, the archipelago was designated the **Matsu National Scenic Area** in 1999. In 2001 Matsu (and Kinmen) received an economic boost with the implementation of the **Three Small Links** agreement, which allows local residents to engage in limited direct travel and trade with mainland China.

Nangan

The largest of the Matsu Islands, **NANGAN** (南竿; *nángān*) is the administrative and cultural centre and captures the vast majority of the area's tourist traffic. Nangan has a wide range of sights, from former **military installations** that have been opened to the public to restored **traditional stone houses** and one of Taiwan's most famous distilleries. It's also a place of legend, where the earthly body of the goddess **Mazu** is reputed to have washed ashore.

Arrival

Whether you arrive by ferry at **Fuao Port** (福澳港; *fúàogǎng*) or by air at **Nangan Airport** (南竿機場; *nángān jīchǎng*) – both on Nangan's eastern end – you'll find plenty of **taxis** waiting. Taxis have meters (starting fare NT$100, then NT$5 every 250m), but also have a fixed-rate schedule to main destinations: from the airport to Fuao Port is NT$100, while to Matsu Village is NT$200. Taxis are also an option for sightseeing, with whirlwind island **tours** starting at about NT$500 an hour, or NT$1500 for a half-day.

If you want to stay at one of the interesting homestays in one of the island's villages your best option is to rent a **car** or **scooter**. Scooter **rentals** are widely available for about NT$500–600 a day (NT$300/half-day), although most companies insisting on an international driving licence for overseas visitors. At the ferry terminal try *Ren Wo Xing Motorcycle Rental* (任我行出租機車; *rènwǒxíng chūzūjīchē*; ☏0911/289-968 or 0932/070-998). Near the airport, at 72 Jieshou Village, *Langjian Motorcycle Rental* (良健機車行; *liángjiàn jīchēháng*; ☏0836/22577) is a reliable option.

Nangan also has two **bus** lines, one that hugs the coast (via the distillery and Tianhou Temple) and the mountain line, both originating at Jieshou (介壽; *jièshòu*) Bus Station (NT$15 all trips); these are not particularly frequent, though, and a scooter is much more convenient.

Information

The **Matsu National Scenic Area Visitor Center** (馬祖國家風景區管理處; *mǎzǔ guójiā fēngjǐngqū guǎnlǐchù*; daily 8am–5.30pm; ☏0836/25630, ⓦwww .matsu-nsa.gov.tw) is in Renai Village in the south of the island; it's off to the left before the entrance to the Beihai Tunnel complex, about a fifteen-minute scooter ride from either the airport or ferry pier. As it has few exhibits and no English maps, however, your time would be better spent visiting the **Matsu Folklore Culture Museum** at 135 Qingshui Village (see p.372), which is also closer to Fuao Port and the airport.

The Matsu Islands are among Taiwan's most remote destinations, but with time and planning they may well be a highlight of your trip.

By sea

The **ferry** is a fun if time-consuming way to get to the islands, and is the only means of transport to Dongyin. The waters of the Taiwan Strait can be rough, but the ferry is large, so risk of seasickness is minimal. There is one ferry to **Matsu** (daily except Tues), departing from the northern port of **Keelung** (see p.134) every night at 9.50pm; on odd days it sails first to **Nangan**, arriving at around 8am (10hr), before departing for **Dongyin** at 9.30am (2hr) on the way back to Keelung (departing Dongyin at 11am and arriving at Keelung around 6pm). On even days the order is reversed, and the boat stops at Dongyin first (8hr) before heading on to Nangan at around 6am. It's worth noting, however, that in winter and during the March–May foggy season this ferry is often cancelled, so it's only a reliable means of transport from June to September. Services are operated by **Shinhwa Navigation** (新華航業公司; *xīnhuá hángyè gōngsī*; 3/F, 6 Zhongshan Rd ☏ 02/2423-2423) on the ship *Taima*. Their offices are on the second floor of the West Passenger Terminal in Keelung. To get there, turn left as you exit the Keelung train station and walk straight for a few hundred metres – the building is directly in front of the road where it begins to veer left. It's best to reserve your **ticket** at least one day in advance, but same-day purchases are possible (7.30–9pm only). You'll need to show your **passport** when reserving and paying for your ticket (steerage from NT$350, dorm beds NT$630-1000, quad NT$1000–1575, twins from NT$1890), as well as before you board the boat. During summer, reservations also can be made by **phone** three days in advance (Keelung ☏ 02/2424-6868 ext 2, Nangan ☏ 0836/26655, Dongyin ☏ 0836/77555), but only in Chinese, and you also must fax the office a photocopy of your passport. In Dongyin, buy your ticket between 2pm and 5pm the day before departure from the *Laoye Hotel*.

By air

Flying is a more reliable option, although during the March–May foggy season flights are also frequently cancelled. **Uni Air** (Taipei ☏ 02/2518-5166, Nangan ☏ 0836/26511,

---

It's a good idea to bring enough **money** for your entire stay in the Matsu Islands, as there is only one bank with an **ATM** that accepts international credit cards: the **Bank of Taiwan**, 257 Jieshou Village, on the steep hill that heads northwest out of the settlement. It's also possible to change money here.

Accommodation

Although there are about a dozen villages on Nangan, most of the attractive **accommodation** options are concentrated in only a few of them. If you arrive by ferry, there are a handful of fairly run-down old **hotels** in Fuao Village, a few minutes' walk from the pier. These establishments charge a premium due to their proximity to the port, and you'll do better at one of the atmospheric **homestays** in either **Jinsha** (津沙; *jīnshā*) or **Niujiao** (牛角; *niújiǎo*).

Coast of the Dawn 日光海岸 (*rìguāng hǎiàn*) 6 Renai Village ☏ 0836/26666. Along the main road to the east of Renai Village, Nangan's swankiest abode features modern, chic rooms overlooking the Beihai Tunnel entrance and the coastline beyond. Price includes breakfast, and dinner is available in the hotel restaurant. ❺
Hailanghua Inn 海浪花客棧 (*hǎilànghuā kèzhàn*) 64 Renai Village ☏ 0836/22568. Smart

eighteen-room hotel, immediately to the south of the village's Tianhou Shrine, with six good-value sea-view rooms and scooter rental. ❹
Jinsha Culture Village 津沙文化村 (*jīnshā wénhuàcūn*) 71 Jinsha Village ☏ 0836/26189. By far the best deal on Nangan, featuring several rooms in beautifully restored traditional houses scattered throughout idyllic Jinsha. The office and excellent restaurant are

Ⓦ www.uniair.com.tw) has seven return flights daily between **Taipei** (**Songshan**) and **Nangan** (6.50am–5.20pm; NT$1962). Uni Air (Taichung ☏04/2615-5199, Beigan ☏0836/56578) also has one flight daily from **Taichung** to **Nangan** (11.10am; NT$2336) and three flights daily from **Taipei** to **Beigan** (9.20am–6.50pm; NT$1962).

If you have plenty of cash, check out the spectacular **helicopter service** (Oct–March Mon, Wed & Fri 12.40pm) between Nangan and Dongyin (NT$3000) and Nangan and Dongju (NT$2000); there is a minumum passenger requirement of four people (usually Matsu residents; call ☏0836/23500 for information).

From China

Ferries (90min) between **Fuzhou** (福州; *fúzhōu*) in China and **Nangan** are now open to foreigners (many Taiwanese use this as a cheap short-cut between Taiwan and the mainland). Leaving Fuzhou's Mawei Port (马尾; *máwěi*), ferries depart at 9.15am (arriving in Nangan at 10.45am) and 2pm (arriving at 3.30pm). Ferries usually depart from Nangan at 9.40am to arrive at Mawei at 11.10am, and 2pm to arrive at 3.30pm. Buy tickets at an agent such as Sanlin (☏0836/23868). You can also buy special tickets that cover the whole trip between Fuzhou and Keelung (see above) from around NT$1300.

Inter-island ferries

Unfortunately, it isn't possible to hop directly from one island to another, as all **local ferries** originate from Nangan's **Fuao Port**. This means you'll have to return to Nangan after visiting each island to catch a ferry to another one. The only exception is that most of the ferries from Nangan to **Dongju** call at nearby **Xiju** along the way, so it's possible to alight at Xiju and then catch an onward ferry later to Dongju. While there are usually daily ferries from Nangan to the other islands from June to August, weather permitting, at other times of year schedules can be cut back considerably. For local ferry information, check the "Arrival and accommodation" section under each island.

---

tucked into an alley – turn left at the far end of the village and you'll see it to the left. If you don't mind climbing steps, ask for the rooms on the hilltop to the right as you enter Jinsha – all have aromatic wooden interiors, some command sweeping bay views, and one has an attached balcony. ❹
Night on the Cape Homestay 夜宿海角民宿 (*yèsù hǎijiǎo mínsù*) 143 Niujiao Village ☏0836/26125. Not far from the airport, in Niujiao Village, is Nangan's first restored-house homestay, renovated with an eye for aesthetics. As a result, it's popular with trendy young Taiwanese tourists in search of a slice of history, and its handful of rooms (from NT$1400), can fill up quickly so it's a

good idea to call in advance. Follow the English sign to *Grandma's Eatery*, a restaurant with the same owner, to ask about rooms. ❸
Shen Nong Resort 神農山莊 (*shénnóng shānzhuāng*) 84-2 Qingshui Village ☏0836/26333). Alongside the main road, roughly halfway between Fuao and Renai villages – and close to the island's petrol station – the multi-storey Shen Nong is good value, with actual prices that are exactly half of the listed rates. Although a bit sterile, its rooms are big, clean and comfortable, and some offer broad views of the island. However, the nearby military firing range can be very distracting. ❹

The island

The sights on Nangan are spread out, so it's best to visit all the attractions in each area while working your way round the island in order to avoid backtracking. Starting from **Fuao Village** (福澳村; *fúào cūn*), for example, a convenient **circuit** would be to head southwest on the main road before making a clockwise loop around Nangan's sight-filled western half.

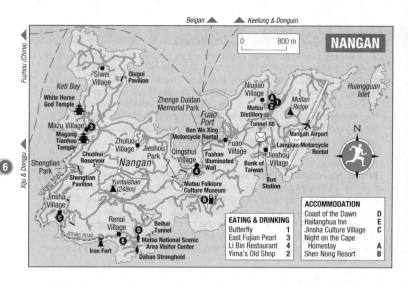

Zhenge Daidan Memorial Park

Once dedicated to Chiang Kai-shek, the pleasant (and renamed) **Zhenge Daidan Memorial Park** (枕戈待旦紀念公園; *zhěngē dàidàn jìniàn gōngyuán*) lies on the hilltop just outside Fuao, along the road heading southwest. Just across the main road is the rather forlorn-looking symbol of the unfulfilled aspirations of the KMT, the **Fushan Illuminated Wall** (福山照壁; *fúshān zhàobì*). The imposing whitewashed wall is emblazoned with four giant red characters that comprise an old idiom meaning "sleep with one's sword ready". The characters were inscribed on the orders of the Generalissimo himself during a 1958 inspection of Nangan.

Matsu Folklore Culture Museum

Continue southwest along the main road until you reach Qingshui (清水; *qīngshuǐ*), then take the left-hand road through the village to get to the multi-storey **Matsu Folklore Culture Museum** (民俗文物館; *mínsú wénwùguǎn*; 9am–5pm, closed Mon; free), which gives a better introduction to the Matsu Islands than all of the national scenic area visitor centres combined. The exhibits on the first floor have explanations in Chinese, English and even Spanish, but those on the upper floors are only labelled in Chinese.

Renai Village and around

Further southwest, around Nangan's most southerly point near **RENAI VILLAGE** (仁愛村; *rénàicūn*), are the island's major decommissioned **military sites**, all of which are now being promoted as tourist attractions. East of the village is the 700m **Beihai Tunnel** (北海坑道; *běihǎi kēngdào*; daily 9am–5pm; free), built as a shelter for military vessels and ammunition. Getting to the tunnel entrance is a bit daunting, as you must turn left through a **checkpoint** manned by heavily armed soldiers – this is one of only three checkpoints in the Matsu Islands that tourists are allowed to pass. A few hundred metres south of the tunnel is the **Dahan Stronghold** (大漢據點; *dàhàn jùdiǎn*; daily 9am–5pm; free), a decommissioned labyrinth of underground fortifications, completed in 1976, that lead through a granite hill to some abandoned gun emplacements overlooking the ocean. It's worth the short walk for the sea views alone.

Just west of Renai Village, on the scenic road that winds along the coast, is the so-called **Iron Fort** (鐵堡; *tiěbǎo*; daily 24hr; free), a former **bunker** carved into a rocky coral outcrop that once served Matsu's amphibious forces. Inside are living quarters and plenty of strategically placed sniper points.

Coastal road: from Renai Village to Mazu Village

The scenic **coastal road** that runs between Renai and Mazu villages is a worthwhile attraction in its own right, yielding sweeping sea views and making for a superb walk or scooter ride. About halfway between the two villages is lovely **JINSHA** (津沙; *jīnshā*), a living museum of traditional northern **Fujianese stone houses**, many of which have been restored to their original grandeur. In addition to its aesthetically pleasing architecture, the village surrounds a beautiful rocky bay, is filled with gregarious locals and boasts Nangan's finest **homestay** (see p.370). Despite all of its charm, Jinsha's isolation at the base of a steep hill has kept it well off the main tourist circuit.

A few kilometres beyond Jinsha is the 10-hectare **Shengtian Park** (勝天公園; *shèngtiān gōngyuán*), which features Nangan's most remarkable seaside scenery. In the middle of the park, next to the **Chushui Reservoir** (儲水澳水庫; *chúshuǐào shuǐkù*), is the tastefully designed **Shengtian Pavilion** (勝天亭; *shèngtiān tíng*), a Song-dynasty-style structure built by the military in 1990. With its graceful flying eaves and natural hues, the pavilion blends in with the natural surroundings and is a relaxing place to enjoy some solitude.

A couple of kilometres further along the coastal road is the intersection with the main road, which drops sharply to the left to enter **MAZU VILLAGE** (馬祖村; *mǎzǔcūn*), home of the nationally famous **Magang Tianhou Temple** (馬港天后宮; *mǎgǎng tiānhòu gōng*; daily 24hr). According to one local legend, the earthly body of the Chinese goddess **Mazu** washed ashore on the adjacent beach, now dominated by a garish display of naval landing craft. The villagers are said to have recovered Mazu's body and buried it in the **stone coffin** embedded in the temple floor directly in front of the altar. Some locals say it now holds only the clothes recovered from Mazu's body, while others maintain it actually contains the remains of Mazu's drowned father. Regardless of the coffin's contents, one thing everyone agrees on is that it's the only part of the temple with historic significance: while the building itself was first constructed at the end of the Qing dynasty on the site of a much smaller shrine, it has been renovated and expanded several times since then. Despite this, locals claim the coffin is still lying in its original location. Given the site's historic import, it's a requisite stop for Taiwanese tourists and draws a steady stream of worshippers.

Just north of Mazu Village, on the road that leads to **Siwei** (四維; *sìwéi*), the tiny **White Horse God Temple** (白馬文武大王廟; *báimǎ wénwǔ dàwángmiào*; daily 24hr) is devoted to two Qing-dynasty generals whose bodies floated ashore at nearby Keti Bay in the late 1800s. Villagers buried the bodies and, shortly after they were interred, one of the generals reputedly instructed the villagers through a spirit medium to build a temple in his honour. Locals believe that the temple deity now provides protection for boats in the bay, as a mysterious warning light is said to flash across the water every time a storm is approaching. If you double back to Mazu Village and then drive southeast on the main road you'll pass **Yuntaishan** (雲台山; *yúntáishān*), the island's highest point at 248m and a favoured place to watch the sun set. From the top, there are unparalleled views of Nangan and nearby islands and, accordingly, there is an active **military observation post** bristling with soldiers. Tourists are welcome to photograph the scenery to the north, but if you turn your camera towards the guard station you're likely to have your camera confiscated and you might even get arrested.

Matsu Distillery and Tunnel 88

On Nangan's northeast corner is the well-known **Matsu Distillery** (馬祖酒廠; *mǎzǔ jiǔchǎng*; Mon–Fri 8.30–11.30am & 1–5pm, Sat–Sun 3–5pm), a fitting place to cap off a long day of sightseeing. Here you can sample some of Matsu's fiery **gaoliang sorghum liquor** as well as the milder *lǎojiǔ*, a traditional rice spirit. Although there is no actual distillery tour, samples are usually provided in the exhibition room and shop inside. Nearby **Tunnel 88** (八八坑; *bābā kēng*) is a former air-raid shelter completed in 1974, now used for the fermentation and storage of the strong-smelling spirits. The 273m tunnel, the entrance to which is lined with giant decorative jars, is usually locked up during the week (when you have to make an appointment to join a tour at 9.30am, 10.30am, 2.30pm & 4.30pm; free), but it is usually open on weekends (Sat–Sun 3–5pm). Both the distillery and tunnel are near the roundabout at the entrance to Niujiao Village.

Eating and drinking

Nangan is an outstanding place for **eating**, with inexpensive restaurants in many villages offering authentic **northern Fujian cuisine**.

Butterfly 依嬷的店 (*yīmā dediàn*) 72-1 Niujiao Village ℡0836/26125. Although there is a shortage of bars on Nangan, this is good place for a drink or meal, down the hill and directly across the street from *Yima's Old Shop*. It serves a respectable selection of cocktails and bottled beers in another converted stone house; for a snack try the *mǎzǔ hànbǎo* (aka *jiguāng bǐng*, or buns that look a bit like bagels). Daily 11.30am–2.30pm & 5.30–9.30pm.

East Fujian Pearl 閩東之珠餐廳 (*mǐndōng zhīzhū cāntīng*) 22 Mazu Village ℡0836/22900). One of the best places to sample Fujianese dishes and especially seafood. The house specialty is the "Buddha's hand" clams (*chǎofó shǒu*), so named because the prongs on their shells are althought to resemble the fingers of the Buddha. Cooked with a healthy dose of *lǎojiǔ*, this dish exemplifies the red-marinated cooking style for which Matsu is famous. Be sure to ask for a

demonstration of how to open the shells before you begin your meal. Daily 10am–2pm & 5–9pm.

Li Bin Restaurant 儷儐飲食店 (*libīn yīnshídiàn*) 107 Qingshui Village ℡0836/25198. This small, unpretentious canteen is a favourite of locals and soldiers, who flock here in the evenings for fresh seafood and the house specialty – big, juicy dumplings. Meals here are cheap and portions are generous.

Yima's Old Shop 依嬷老店 (*yīmā lǎodiàn*) 143 Niujiao Village ℡0836/26016. Homely option in an atmospheric and wonderfully restored Fujian-style stone house. The emphasis here is fittingly on traditional northern Fujian dishes, with red-marinated seafood taking centre stage. The fish-ball soup is a favourite of the crowds of Taiwanese tourists that converge on the place for dinner. It's also a popular drinking hangout, particularly for those with a taste for *lǎojiǔ*. Daily 10am–2pm & 5–10pm.

Beigan

The archipelago's second-largest island, **BEIGAN** (北竿; *běigān*) has charming villages and superb scenery, including several **secluded beaches** with dramatic mountain backdrops. Beigan once boasted the Matsu Islands' only airport and was the nerve centre for tourism, but since the 2003 opening of the Nangan Airport it has become sleepy even by comparison with its bucolic neighbour to the south. although some tourists still fly to Beigan from Taipei, many arrive by ferry from Nangan and spend a night in a rustic village homestay.

Arrival and information

Beigan is easy to reach by **passenger ferry** from Nangan's Fuao Port. In summer these leave every hour, on the hour (daily 7am–5.10pm; 20min; NT$110 one-way; ℡0836/22193), calling at Beigan's **Baisha Port** (白沙港; *báishāgǎng*). Note that sometimes there are no taxis waiting near the pier (and scooter rental isn't possible here), so you may have to walk until a ride comes along or wait for up to an hour for Beigan's one **bus** (just flag it down; NT$15) to stop at the port on its circuit around the island. It's also easy and safe to **hitch** a ride with any locals that pass by. If you manage to catch a **taxi**, it should cost about NT$100 to get to **Tangqi** (塘岐; *tángqí*), where most of Beigan's hotels and restaurants are – and where you can rent a **scooter** for NT$500 per day (no licence required, helmets mandatory). A scooter is critical if you wish to stay in one of the restored stone-house hotels, as they are on the island's north side, separated from Tangqi by a steep hill. A scooter also is the most convenient means for sightseeing, but if you can find a taxi the driver might be willing to give you a two-hour tour for about NT$1000.

The main advantage of arriving by air from Taipei is that **Beigan Airport** (北竿 機場; *běigān jīchǎng*) is located next to Tangqi and a very short walk from the town's main hotels. Along the road from Baisha Port to Tangqi, just behind Banli Beach, is the small **Beigan Visitor Center** (北竿遊客中心; *běigān yóukè zhōngxīn*; daily 8am–5pm).

Accommodation

Your choice of **accommodation** is limited to the uninspiring but convenient hotels in Tangqi or one of the two traditional stone-house homestays in captivating Qinbi Village, on Beigan's north side.

Tangqi

Beihai'an Hotel 北海岸飯店 (*běihǎiàn fàndiàn*) 240 Tangqi Village ☎0836/55036. Features modern rooms, most Japanese-style with raised wooden platforms and roll-up beds (most also have flat-screen TVs and sea views), from NT$1900. Free broadband internet access. ❹

Biyuntian Holiday Village 碧雲天渡假村 (*bìyúntiān dùjiàcūn*) 255 Tanqi Village ☎0836/55461. Just down the street from the *Beihai'an*, the *Biyuntian* also has all of its rooms equipped with TVs and broadband internet access – rooms are plain but spotlessly clean, modern and bright. ❹

Taijiang Hotel 台江大飯店 (*táijiāng dàfàndiàn*) 200 Tangqi Village ☎0836/55256. While the *Taijiang* has seen better days, its price includes breakfast and a pick-up from the ferry pier for those with reservations – making it one way to overcome the shortage of transport from Baisha Port. Rooms have TV, tile floors and adequate but old-fashioned decor. ❸

Qinbi

Qinbi Holiday Village 芹壁休閒渡假村 (*qínbì xiūxián dùjiàcūn*) 49 Qinbi Village ☎0836/55456. One of Taiwan's most distinctive accommodation options, and Matsu's most interesting place to stay, perched on a terrace in the midst of the village. Rooms occupy restored old stone houses, which are rustic but clean, with comfy beds and traditional windows that frame splendid views of the ocean. Rates are good value on weekdays and during the off-season. Ask at the attached *Café Chin Be* (see p.377), which serves excellent meals on a relaxing veranda. ❸

Qinbi Mediterranean B&B 芹壁地中海民宿 (*qínbì dìzhōnghǎi mínsù*) 54 Qinbi Village ☎0836/56611. Unlike the *Qinbi Holiday Village*, the collection of buildings that make up this B&B are rustic with stone walls and wood floors, but the rooms are actually modern, with a variety of sizes and single/double beds. Ask at the adjoining *Chin-Bi Village Café* if you want to stay here. The B&B also offers pick-ups from the airport or ferry pier if you have a reservation. ❸

The island

Starting from Baisha Port and heading northeast, the first stretch of sand you'll encounter is beautiful **Banli Beach** (坂里沙灘; *bǎnlǐshātān*), at the edge of Banli Village. Some enterprising locals offer **jet-ski** and **quad bike** rentals, but there are usually only takers at weekends in summer. There are shower and toilet facilities here. At the southwest end of the beach is a tiny **Tianhou Temple** (天后宮; *tiānhòugōng*), dedicated to Mazu.

Heading east from Tangqi, which has hotels, restaurants and food shops but little in the way of tourist attractions, continue along the main road, past the airport, until you reach **Tanghoudao Beach** (塘后道沙灘; *tánghòudào shātān*), a long spit of sand that forms a natural causeway between Tangqi and Houao to the east. The bay here is considerably calmer than the one at Banli Beach, and it's Beigan's favoured swimming spot.

Houao and the War & Peace Memorial Park

HOUAO (后澳; *hòuào*) is a small fishing community with some beautifully restored stone-slab houses and is a nice place for a stroll, especially around dusk, when elderly villagers typically come out to socialize. Behind the village, up the steep road heading southeast, the **War & Peace Memorial Park** is built around a handful of decommissioned army outposts, designed to commemorate Beigan's recent military history. The centrepiece is the **War & Peace Memorial Park Exhibition Center** (戰爭和平紀念公園主題館; *zhànzhēng hépíng jìniàn gōngyuán zhǔtíguǎn*; daily 8.30–11.30am & 1.30–5pm; free), a spanking new museum chronicling the troubled modern history of the islands, from 1949 to the present, through films, exhibits and multimedia displays.

Qiaozai and Qinbi

Nestled in the island's northwest corner is the village of **QIAOZAI** (橋仔; *qiáozǎi*), so named because of the many small bridges that span the gullies carrying runoff from nearby **Leishan** (雷山; *léishān*). While most villages in Matsu were settled by northern Fujianese, Qiaozai is unique in that it was founded by fishermen from the southern part of the province. Once Beigan's biggest, most affluent village, these days it's not much more than a laid-back fishing settlement, although it is noted for having more **temples** than any other village in the Matsu Islands.

To the west of Qiaozai along the main road is the unmistakable village of **QINBI** (芹壁; *qínbì*), with terrace upon terrace of two-storey **stone houses** tumbling down a hillside to the sea – arguably the archipelago's most picturesque community. Spending a night in one of Qinbi's rustic **homestays** (see p.375) is highly recommended, but even if you don't stay here it's definitely worth a stroll through its narrow lanes and up its steep steps. If time permits, a short swim across the shallow water to **Turtle Islet** (龜島; *guīdǎo*) – a granite outcrop in the middle of the bay – yields unrivalled views of the village as well as of the sea to the north.

Bishan

For a bird's-eye view of Beigan's eastern half, nearby **Bishan** (壁山; *bìshān*) – at 298m the Matsu Islands' highest hill – is the place to go. Near the top is an **observation point** looking out over Tangqi and Houao villages, as well as the airport, making a perfect place to watch the small planes make their precarious landings. You can drive a scooter up the road or walk to the top along the challenging stone-stepped path that starts behind Tangqi.

Eating

Beigan is an excellent place to try fresh **seafood** at reasonable prices. The island is most famous for its **fish noodles** (*yúmiàn*), made from corn starch and pressed fish such as eel and drum. To see the noodles being hand made and dried in the sun, stop by *A-Po's Fish Noodles* (阿婆魚麵; *āpó yúmiàn*; daily 9am–5pm; ☎0836/56359), at 168 Zhongshan Rd in Tangqi. This unassuming little shop is run by a friendly old woman who is happy to give demonstrations. You can buy a bag of the noodles here for only NT$80. If you want to try a hot bowl of these noodles, the best place in Tangqi is the *Hong Xing Ping Seafood Restaurant* (鴻星平海鮮樓; *hóngxīngpíng hǎixiānlóu*; daily 11.30am–2pm & 5–8pm; ☎0836/55426) at 242 Zhongzheng Rd. At lunchtime it can be crowded with Taiwanese tourists making day-trips from Nangan.

Just across the street from the airport exit is the spartan *Meihua Canyin* (梅花餐飲; *méihuā cānyǐn*; daily 10am–1.30am; ☎0836/55518), at 272 Zhongshan Rd, which caters to local soldiers with cheap noodle and rice dishes starting from NT$50.

On the island's north side is one of Beigan's best places to eat, *Café Chin Be* (芹壁咖啡廳; *qínbì kāfēitīng*; daily 10am–9pm; ☎0836/55456), at 49 Qinbi Village. The fish noodles here are fresh and tasty, and you can enjoy them on a veranda looking out onto Turtle Islet and the sea.

Dongyin and Xiyin

Matsu's most visually compelling islands are **DONGYIN** (東引; *dōngyǐn*) and **XIYIN** (西引; *xīyǐn*), two hilly tracts of land connected by a causeway at the archipelago's northernmost point. Characterized by sheer **granite cliffs** that plunge dramatically to the sea, the scenery here is sublime – especially on the larger island of Dongyin, where most of the sights and all of the tourist amenities are located. Dongyin also has some standout historical sites, such as the solitary **Dongyong Lighthouse** that dominates the island's far eastern tip.

Due to their isolation, the islands get comparatively few tourists and locals tend to go well out of their way to make them comfortable. And, although both islands are still heavily militarized, even the soldiers are exceedingly friendly to the few visitors who make it here.

Arrival and information

The easiest way to get here from mainland Taiwan is on the **Keelung ferry**, which stops at Dongyin's **Zhongzhu Harbour** (中柱港; *zhōngzhùgǎng*; see p.370) on even-numbered days. If you want to get here from Nangan, your only option is to take the Keelung ferry at 9.30am (odd-numbered days only; buy tickets at Fuao Harbour 7–8.30am). Tickets cost NT$350, and the boat usually arrives around 11.30am. In winter you also have the option of taking the **helicopter** from Nangan (see p.371). There is no public transport on the islands, so you'll probably need to rent a **scooter** or hire a **taxi** for sightseeing – walking is a possibility, but Dongyin is several kilometres in width and it would take the better part of a day to see the main sights on foot.

There are no scooter rentals at Zhongzhu Harbour, but it's possible to rent them in the nearby villages of **Lehua**, **Nanao** or **Zhongliu**, all of which are clustered together on the hill that rises from the harbour and are a short walk or taxi ride from the pier. Some hotels in the villages will rent scooters for NT$500 a day without needing to see any identification.

The **Dongyin Visitor Center** (東引遊客中心; *dōngyǐn yóukè zhōngxīn*; daily 8am–noon & 1.30–5.30pm), 160–1 Lehua Village, has interesting English-captioned exhibits on the islands' history.

Accommodation

All of Dongyin's **accommodation** is centred in the villages of Lehua, Nanao and Zhongliu, and consists of standard but affordable hotels whose management will often book onward ferry tickets for you without charging commission.

The *Lao Yue Hotel*, 29 Lehua Village (老爺大飯店; *lǎoyé dàfàndiàn*; ☎0836/77168; ❸), has small, clean rooms with TVs, some with views onto the harbour. Further up the hill, the *Mingjian Star Hotel*, 66 Zhongliu Village (明建星大飯店; *míngjiànxīng dàfàndiàn*; ☎0836/77180; ❷), has basic rooms from NT$900, some with computers and free internet. Near the post office, the *Xinhua Hotel*, 46 Lehua Village (昕華飯店; *xīnhuá fàndiàn*; ☎0836/77600; ❸), is great value and has a restaurant and free internet café – it's a short walk from here to the ferry pier. Comfy but with less style is the *Yingbin Hotel*, 78 Lehua Village (盈賓休閒旅館; *yíngbīn xiūxián lǚguǎn*; ☎0836/76336; ❸), with rooms from NT$1200.

Dongyin

Most of **DONGYIN**'s sights are situated along the main road that winds east of the three villages, but one – the **Beihai Tunnel** (北海坑道; *běihǎi kēngdào*) – is located to the south of Zhongzhu Harbour and accessed by a paved road leading south from the visitor centre. Built in the 1970s to provide refuge for small naval vessels during rough seas and artillery attacks from mainland China, the tunnel is only 193m in length, but still worth a visit. Hollowed out with only hand tools and blasting powder, it was opened to tourists in 2000, when eight **bronze statues** of tunnel builders were erected at the deep end in memory of those who died building it. The tunnel was **closed** for renovation at the time of writing – check at the visitor centre for the latest.

About 1km east of the visitor centre, the much larger **Andong Tunnel** (安東坑道; *āndōng kēngdào*; daily 8am–5.30pm; free) cuts through the heart of a hill before ending up at vertical **cliffs** on Dongyin's southern coast. The 640m tunnel, once housed soldiers and military equipment, contains old barracks, ammunition depots and even a pen where pigs were raised to feed the troops. The return walk to the cliffs takes about an hour.

A few kilometres northeast of the Andong Tunnel along the main road is one of Dongyin's most celebrated examples of eroded coastline – the so-called **Thread of Sky** (一線天; *yíxiàntiān*; daily 24hr; free) a vertical, narrow crevice between two sharply angled cliff faces that yields only a fragmentary glimpse of the sea beyond. Listening to the waves crashing against the rocks here is obligatory for Taiwanese tourists: the four-character **inscription** on the cliff means "hearing waves at the crevice of heaven". You have to sign in before being escorted to the viewpoint.

A bit further along the main road, on the left-hand side as you head east, is another evocative section of coastline known alternately as **Suicide Cliff** or **Martyred Maiden Cliff** (烈女義坑; *liènǚ yìkēng*), as according to legend a young woman leapt to her death here during the Qing dynasty to escape from pirates. You can walk out to the edge of this sea-eroded cliff, which plunges more than 100m to the rocks below – a guardrail is in place to prevent falls.

Crowning the island's far eastern tip is the highlight of a visit to Dongyin – the **Dongyong Lighthouse** (東湧燈塔; *dōngyǒng dēngtǎ*; daily 24hr; free), built by **British engineers** in 1902. A path leads up to the lighthouse, and you can wander around the former residential buildings to the rear. From this vantage point, the lighthouse seems to jut out into the sea.

Eating

Dongyin's best **eating** places are down-to-earth and serve up mostly northern Chinese specialities. For dinner, try *Zhen Shan Mei* (珍膳美餐廳; *zhēnshànměi cāntīng*; daily 2–9pm; ☎0836/77289), 93 Lehua Village, whose friendly owner learn how to make dumplings in Beijing. The most popular place for breakfast is *Maiweideng* (麥味登早餐; *màiwèidēng zǎocān*; daily 6am–3pm; ☎0836-77255), 123 Zhongliu Village, which has morning goodies ranging from steamed buns and fried bread sticks to rice porridge and hot soy milk.

Dongju and Xiju

At the southernmost point of the Matsu Islands are **DONGJU** and **XIJU**, originally called "East Dog" and "West Dog" because they were said to resemble canines when viewed from the sea. The islands, whose names mean "East Chu" and "West Chu", were symbolic of Chiang's ambitions to reclaim the mainland.

Both islands are laid-back, with ample accommodation and restaurants, and easily accessible by ferry from Nangan. In good weather, and especially during the busy summer tourist season, there are **ferries** each day from Nangan's Fuao Port at

7am, 11am and 2.30pm (NT$200); on odd months (May, July and so on) to Xiju first (50min) then Dongju (another 15min), and even months to Dongju first then Xiju (same times). There are four daily sailings between the two islands (NT$80): 7.30am, 10am, 2pm and 5.10pm (Xiju to Dongju) and 7.50am, 10.20am, 2.20pm and 5.30pm (Dongju to Xiju). In winter you can also take the **helicopter** from Nangan (see p.371).

Dongju

The larger of the two islands, **DONGJU** (東莒; *dōngjǔ*) can be covered on foot in several hours. With few trees, however, it gets scorching hot in summer, so it's easier to rent a **scooter** for a day (NT$500, no identification required) and enjoy the handful of sights at your leisure. Scooters can be rented at **Daping Village** (大坪村; *dàpíng cūn*) where all the **hotels** and **restaurants** are. The village is about 1km from **Mengao Port** (猛沃港; *měngwògǎng*) where the ferry arrives, so you could walk there or take a **taxi** (NT$100). Some hotels have a **pick-up service** for guests with reservations.

The island

A good place to start a tour of the island is the **Juguang Visitor Center** (莒光遊客中心; *jǔguāng yóukè zhōngxīn*; daily 8am–5.30pm) at 1 Fuzheng Village, about a fifteen-minute walk northeast of Daping. Here you can pick up an English map of Dongju and Xiju, and there are English-captioned **exhibits** on local culture and flora and fauna. Just past the visitor centre on the left as you head northeast is **Fuzheng Beach** (福正海灘; *fúzhèng hǎitān*), which during low tide is a popular place for Taiwanese to collect mussels and **limpets** – the latter recognizable by their distinctive oval-shaped shells. Carry on to the island's northeast tip, where the **Dongju Lighthouse** (東莒島燈塔; *dōngjǔdǎo dēngtǎ*) stands atop a small hill. It was built by the British in 1872 to help with the navigation of ships trading with China in the wake of the Opium Wars.

Near the island's southwest corner is the village of **DAPU** (大埔; *dàpǔ*), an abandoned fishing settlement that has been completely restored. The **stone buildings** essentially comprise an open-air museum and lack the character of some of the archipelago's inhabited communities. Yet the village is located on an isolated, rocky promontory and makes for quite a sight when viewed from a distance. Further south, at Dongju's southern tip, is the **Dapu Stone Inscription** (大埔石刻; *dàpǔ shíkè*), a rare tablet with a 42-character engraving commemorating the capture of pirates by a Ming-dynasty general in 1617. Below the pavilion built around the tablet is a set of steps leading gently to the sea. This spot, another prime shellfish-gathering area, is a favourite place to watch the sunset.

Practicalities

All of Dongju's **accommodation** and **restaurants** are in Daping Village. The *Chuanlao Homestay* (船老大民宿; *chuánlǎodà mínsù*; ☎0836/88022; ❸) at no. 55-1 has big, comfortable doubles in a modern building; **scooters** can be rented here. In the north of the village, at no. 5, is the *Hongjing Hostel* (鴻景山莊; *hóngjǐng shānzhuāng*; ☎0836/88033; ❸), another modern building with clean, airy rooms from NT$1200 and the island's most comfy beds. The *Remember Minsu* (Remember 民宿; *Remember mínsù*; ☎0836/88030; ❸) at no. 21 has four breezy rooms with beautiful wooden ceilings – reservations are recommended, and a pick-up at the pier is included in the price. To stay here, ask at the adjacent *Zhao Bu Dao Restaurant* (找不到客棧; *zhǎobúdào kèzhàn*; ☎0836/88030), which opens for lunch and dinner whenever tourists are around. Its **seafood** and **tofu dishes** are excellent.

Xiju

The smallest of the Matsu Islands, **XIJU** (西莒; *xījǔ*) today is but a shadow of its former self, its once bustling **Qingfan Port** (青帆港; *qīngfángǎng*) now serving a slow trickle of tourists. Xiju has long been a pivotal **command post** and has absorbed more than its share of artillery fire from mainland China. It continues to be of immense strategic importance, and a strong military presence remains. The island's heyday was during the **Korean War**, when the Western Enterprise Co – a CIA front – stationed spies here, ushering in Western goods and decadence. Qingfan Village (青帆村; *qīnfáncūn*) was flooded with bars, ballrooms and brothels, earning it the nickname "**Little Hong Kong**".

The best thing to do is take a **walk** around the island, which can easily be covered in a few hours. On its northeast corner is **Caipuwo** (菜埔沃; *càipǔwò*), once the favoured place for villagers to gather **laver** (edible seaweed).

Practicalities

Ferries from Nangan arrive at Qingfan Port, a few minutes' walk from Qingfan Village. Most of the **hotels** are located in **Tianwo** (田沃; *tiānwō*), over the hill to the northeast of Qingfan, which has the island's only places to eat; if you stay in Tianwo, you'll need to walk to Qingfan for meals. Although it's hardly worth getting a **scooter**, they can be rented in Qingfan (NT$300 half-day, NT$500 full day).

The nicest place to stay in Tianwo is the *Friendship Hotel* (友誼山莊; *yǒuyí shānzhuāng*; ☏0836/89107; ❷) at no. 67, where there are bright, clean rooms from NT$900; the owner speaks a little English. At no. 68-3, is the *Haijing Holiday Village* (海景渡假村; *hǎijǐng dùjiàcūn*; ☏0836/88125; ❷), a decent budget choice with basic rooms. On the first floor are a few computers with **internet** access.

Across from the post office in Qingfan Village, at no. 23 is the *Flowers Café* (花兒音樂咖啡餐坊; *huāér yīnyuè kāfēi cānfāng*;; ☏0836/89265; ❸), a **homestay** with four spotless rooms. There is an attached **restaurant** and **café** which serves good coffee.

Travel details

The number of air and sea connections to the major islands of the Taiwan Strait can vary significantly throughout the year, and the frequencies below are what can be expected in the busy March–October season.

Flights
Chiayi to: Kinmen (1 daily; 50min); Magong (2 daily; 30min).
Kaohsiung to: Kinmen (6 daily; 55min); Magong (13–15 daily; 35min); Wangan (twice weekly; 35min) Qimei (1–2 daily; 35min).
Magong to: Qimei (1 daily; 15min).
Taichung to: Kinmen (9 daily; 55min); Magong (5–7 daily; 35min); Nangan (1 daily; 1hr 5min).
Tainan to: Kinmen (2 daily; 50min); Magong (3–4 daily; 30min).
Taipei to: Beigan (3 daily; 50min); Kinmen (11–16 daily; 55min); Magong (9–13 daily; 55min); Nangan (7 daily; 50min).

Ferries
Budai to: Magong (1 daily, mid-March to early October; 1hr).
Kaohsiung to: Magong (1 daily in summer, 4–5 weekly in winter; 5hr).
Keelung to: Dongyin (1 nightly, June–Sept; 8hr); Nangan (1 nightly, June–Sept; 10hr).
Nangan to: Beigan (hourly in summer; 20min); Dongju (several daily in summer; 1hr); Dongyin (3–4 weekly, June–Sept; 2hr 30min); Keelung (1 daily, June–Sept; 10hr); Xiju (several daily in summer; 50min).
Xiju to: Dongju (six daily in summer; 15min).

Contexts

Contexts

A brief history of Taiwan

Taiwan has an exceptionally short recorded history by Asian standards, starting with the arrival of the Dutch in 1624. Though the Taiwanese have a long tradition of rebellion and resistance, they've rarely been masters of their own fate – what ex-president Lee Teng-hui calls the "Taiwanese Sadness"; in addition to the Dutch, the island has been occupied by the Spanish, mainland Chinese, Japanese and briefly the French.

Early history

Humans have inhabited Taiwan for thousands of years, arriving in a series of migrations from mainland Asia; the simple bone, horn and stone implements found on the east coast and dating from 30,000 to 50,000 years ago represent the **Changpin Culture**, Taiwan's first, while **Tsochen Man**, who lived between 20,000 and 30,000 years ago, is the earliest remains of a human found in Taiwan. The **Shisanhang** people were the last of these prehistoric cultures and the only one to possess iron-smelting capabilities, flourishing from 200 to 1500 AD. By this time the indigenous tribes recognized today were well established, having been in Taiwan for at least four thousand years, and the first temporary **Chinese settlements** were starting to emerge, with small groups of fishermen and pirates thought to have arrived sometime in the sixteenth century. Though vague references are made to the island in Chinese sources from the Sui dynasty (581–618 AD), and an official party on their way to the Ryukyu Islands made a brief landing in 1292, it was regarded as a wild, uninhabitable place and largely ignored by mainland China.

The Dutch

The **Dutch East India Company** had established a base in Indonesia in 1619, and occupied **Penghu** in 1622. In 1624 the Chinese attacked and, in the subsequent truce, agreed that the Dutch could have Taiwan if they abandoned Penghu (though whether this means the Ming dynasty regarded Taiwan as part of its territory is still debated).

The Dutch made a base at **Anping** (near Tainan), where they found a small group of Chinese settlers, and well-established indigenous tribes. As Dutch rule

The beautiful island

Portuguese sailors, passing Taiwan on their way to Japan in the sixteenth century, named it **Ihla Formosa**, "the beautiful island". In the West, Taiwan was referred to as Formosa until the 1950s, and the name is still used by companies, hotels and museums today. The origin of the Chinese word **Taiwan** is less clear, though Ming-dynasty negotiators used the name in their treaty with the Dutch in 1624. It seems likely that it stems from the aboriginal word "Taiyan", which meant alien, or from early Chinese references to the island as "Dayuan", pronounced "Dai Wan" in Fujianese. Since 1949 its official name has been the **"Republic of China"**, but locals rarely use this in practice.

Who are the Taiwanese?

Around 98 percent of Taiwanese citizens today claim descent from Han Chinese immigrants from mainland China. Over eighty percent of immigrants came from Quanzhou and Zhangzhou prefectures in Fujian province: the descendants of these people form the Taiwanese or **Hoklo** (*hō-ló* in Taiwanese) majority today, around seventy percent of the country. Taiwan's smaller **Hakka** (*kèjiārén*) population hails from Guangdong province, migrating in the early eighteenth century, and now forming fifteen percent of the population. Taiwan's "mainlanders" (*wàishēngrén*) came with Chiang Kai-shek in 1949, political migrants from the eastern provinces of Zhejiang and Jiangsu, but including people from almost every major region in China – they now represent around thirteen percent. Though Taiwan's **indigenous population** (*yuánzhùmín*) is officially just two percent of the total, it's worth remembering that very few Chinese women crossed the Taiwan Strait in the early years of colonization, and that in reality most Hoklo Chinese have some aboriginal blood – as this will almost certainly be on the mother's side it's rarely recognized. Some studies suggest that up to sixty percent of Taiwanese have aboriginal genes.

spread across the island, many of the latter were converted to Christianity, but relations were often hostile: in 1629 the aborigines at Madou massacred some Dutch soldiers, resulting in a brutal punitive campaign between 1635 and 1636 which brought much of the southern plains under Dutch control. Farming was developed on a large scale for the first time, but the greatest Dutch legacy was **Chinese immigration**: the Dutch needed Chinese labour and settlers to build a successful colony, offering land (to rent, not to buy) to farmers who made the voyage across the Taiwan Strait. When the Dutch arrived in 1624, they estimated only one thousand to 1500 Chinese were living on the island, but 38 years later the figure had increased to over fifty thousand. These farmers had to pay a five to ten percent levy on profits, a head tax and sales tax on commodities like butter and alcohol. These high taxes and resentment of Dutch authority led to a series of **rebellions**, notably in 1652, when a plot by local leader **Guo Huai-yi** was exposed before he had time to properly organize his force of sixteen thousand, and at least four thousand were killed by an army of Dutch and aboriginal warriors.

The Spanish

Spain had carved out a profitable colony in the Philippines in the 1560s, and the Spanish were eager to expand their trade with Japan; Taiwan seemed perfectly located midway along the sea routes, and in 1626 they occupied **Heping Island** near modern-day Keelung and built Fort San Salvador. In 1628 a second base at **Danshui** was established, Fort Santo Domingo, but the Spanish had a fairly miserable time in Taiwan. The local aborigines proved impossible to subdue, the wet tropical climate was debilitating and profits from deer hides and the sulphur trade meagre. In the 1630s the Dutch launched a series of violent assaults on the Spanish forts, and with Japan now closed to foreign trade the whole venture seemed pointless. In 1638 Danshui was abandoned and in 1642 the Dutch occupied Heping Island, forcing the Spanish back to Manila.

The Zheng dynasty

In 1661 Chinese general **Zheng Chenggong**, also known as Koxinga, attacked the Dutch capital at Tainan with 25,000 men as part of a strategic retreat from mainland China. He'd been fighting a civil war on behalf of the Ming dynasty, which had been toppled by the Manchurian Qing dynasty in 1644 (see box, p.245). After a nine-month siege, he secured the Dutch surrender in February 1662, kicking them off the island and establishing an independent Chinese state that included Penghu (known as the "Kingdom of Tungning" or *dōngníng wángguó*).

Koxinga died later that year, but his son, **Zheng Jing**, ruled until 1681. Tainan was developed as an imperial capital, Dutch land was privatized and Chinese-style taxation, administration, education and finance were introduced. The Chinese population continued to expand, reaching around 100,000 in the 1680s, but after Zheng Jing's death, fighting between his sons, **Zheng Kezang** and **Zheng Keshuang**, weakened the kingdom. In 1683 the Qing regime in China decided to bring the Zhengs to heel. **Admiral Shi Lang** led the Qing navy to a devastating victory in Penghu, and by the time he reached Tainan, Keshuang, who had won the leadership struggle with his brother, had no stomach for a fight. The Zheng kingdom was handed over without further bloodshed, the "King" being pensioned off to a small palace in Beijing.

The Qing era

At first, Qing Emperor Kangxi wanted to force Taiwan's Chinese inhabitants back to the mainland and abandon the island. Shi Lang managed to persuade him that it was worth keeping, primarily as a defensive measure, but also to develop its potentially rich resources, and in 1684 Taiwan was officially admitted into the **Chinese empire** as a prefecture of Fujian province. Taiwan, or at least the part of it inhabited by Chinese farmers, was ruled by the Qing for another 212 years.

Early Qing rule

From the start, the Qing administration segregated the aboriginal and Chinese sectors of the island, banning interracial marriages and limiting contact. Despite travel restrictions, illegal immigration flourished. The growing Taiwanese population became resentful of corrupt officials, who typically served three to five years in a place they considered the end of the earth and ripe for plunder. Morale within the relative tiny militia kept on the island was low and it's no surprise there were 159 major incidents of civil disturbance during the Qing era, several of them serious rebellions against imperial authority.

Rebellion

Rebellion in the early years of Qing rule was motivated primarily by political factors, while economic grievances became more important in the nineteenth century. In the most serious cases, troops from the mainland were required for the Qing to regain control, an expensive undertaking that exasperated the emperors. In the **Zhu Yi-gui Rebellion** of 1721, when Zhu (a duck farmer) managed to occupy Tainan and declare himself king, a mainland army only restored order six months later. Taiwan's most serious insurgency was the

Lin Shuangwen Rebellion of 1786–88, when Lin's "Heaven and Earth Society" mobilized tens of thousands in an attempt to overthrow the government and reinstate the Ming dynasty – Lin ruled Taiwan for over a year, and was finally defeated by a combination of mainland, Hakka and aboriginal troops.

Between 1780 and 1860 Taiwan underwent an **agricultural revolution** as more land was cultivated for rice and sugar cane, but tensions grew between the now increasingly large immigrant communities – the Qing era saw hundreds of bitter fights and brawls between Chinese settlers, some of them, like those in Taipei and Keelung in the 1850s, resulting in scores dead.

The Nineteenth Century: Taiwan opens up

In the nineteenth century the Qing dynasty was weakened by a series of external crises, all of which affected Taiwan. In 1841 the British shelled Keelung during the **First Opium War**, and in 1860 the **Treaty of Beijing** forced China to open its ports to foreign trade: in Taiwan, only Anping and Danshui were included, but in the 1860s the list was expanded to include the deeper harbours at Keelung and Takao (now Kaohsiung). These ports subsequently attracted a mix of missionaries such as **George Mackay** (see box, p.113), and merchants and officials, many of them British – the latter administered customs and represented the other Western nations, including the US from 1875. In 1868 the Qing monopoly on **camphor** was abolished, and this, along with a huge upsurge in **sugar** and **tea production** (the latter encouraged by entrepreneurial Englishman **John Dodd**), created a boom in exports in the 1870s, dominated by the foreign *hongs* or trading companies.

The Mudan Incident

The **Japanese**, modernizing incredibly fast after the Meiji Restoration in 1868, were eager to match the West in every way, including imperialist ambition. Taiwan, as one of the closest territories to Japan, was a natural target. In 1871 a ship from the Japanese-held Ryukyu Islands ran aground near the southern tip of Taiwan. The 66 survivors stumbled on the **Paiwan** village of **Mudan**; traditional accounts suggest the sailors were mistaken as enemies and 54 sailors were beheaded in the melee that followed. After the survivors finally returned to Japan, their government spent the next three years demanding the Qing regime take action – the Qing claimed that the Paiwan were beyond their jurisdiction. In 1874 the Japanese took matters into their own hands, sending a punitive force to Taiwan, resulting in a series of bloody encounters and **massacres** in several Paiwan villages. The Qing government deployed an army to Taiwan from the mainland, but war was narrowly avoided: instead the Chinese paid the Japanese compensation for the dead men and expenses for the operation. The attack shocked the Qing into a review of their Taiwan policy, with Imperial Commissioner **Shen Baozhen** initiating a building programme of forts around the island (1874–75), reversing the immigration policy to boost the Chinese population and proposing the establishment of Taipei.

The Sino-French War and provincial status

In 1884 Taiwan became involved in another war, this time a conflict between China and France over Vietnam. French troops raided the Danshui area, and managed to occupy Keelung for over six months. The general credited with holding them back was **Liu Mingchuan**, regarded as hero in Taiwan and more recently in China, where he's buried in Hefei and is one of only a handful of Qing officials rehabilitated by the Communist Party. After the war, in 1885, Taiwan was finally given **provincial status**, and Liu was appointed its first governor. Liu began the modernization of the island in earnest, building rail lines, developing coal mines and improving infrastructure. However, he was less successful in pacifying the mountain tribes and, after forty military missions and heavy Chinese casualties, Taiwan's wild hinterland remained virtually independent. After he was replaced in 1891 by Shao You-lian, attempts to modernize were stymied and momentum was lost.

The Sino-Japanese War and the Taiwan Republic

In 1894 China became embroiled in a war with Japan over the sovereignty of Korea. Though none of the fighting took place near Taiwan, China's defeat in 1895 led to the **Treaty of Shimonoseki**, a humbling agreement in which the Qing regime agreed to hand over Taiwan and Penghu to the Japanese. Shocked by the abandonment of the island, a group of wealthy and educated Chinese in Taiwan pressed the recently appointed governor, **Tang Jing-song**, into declaring an independent **Taiwan Republic** on May 15, 1895. Tang was made president and a cabinet was appointed; the new nation even had a flag and stamps printed. Japan had no intention of letting its first colony slip away that easily however, and landed a force of twelve thousand men on the north of the island on May 29. Lacking the stomach for a fight, the regime collapsed almost immediately, Tang fleeing back to the mainland ten days after his inauguration. After overcoming the Republic's army with relative ease, the Japanese marched into Taipei on June 7, beginning the period of **Japanese occupation**.

The Japanese occupation

The **Japanese** ruled Taiwan for fifty years, a period of colonial exploitation but also of unparalleled economic development: by the time the KMT took control in 1945, Taiwan was a model economy, far more modernized than China. In recent years the period has been undergoing a thorough reassessment: under Chiang Kai-shek (as in China today), children were taught that Japan was a wicked, imperialist power, but many older Taiwanese compare the Japanese favourably with what they see as the equally alien and cruel KMT regime. Though it's certainly true that Japanese rule could be beneficial and even enlightened, especially in the 1920s and early 1930s, Taiwan was developed primarily to benefit Japan – it's also the case that the initial occupation was fiercely resisted, and violently imposed.

The Japanese invasion and Taiwanese resistance

The Japanese army took five months to suppress formal resistance to their occupation (Tainan surrendered on October 21), a violent campaign in which fourteen thousand Taiwanese died, but it took another seven years before they mopped up smaller bands of guerrillas or "bandits". Resistance was fiercest in Yunlin and Chiayi, and for the first time Chinese fought with aborigines in numbers.

In 1898 the appointment of **Governor Kodama Gentaro** and his chief administrator **Goto Shinpei** signalled a change in tactic and the imposition of "bandit laws" (which expanded the definition of what included banditry, made relatives of rebels equally guilty and imposed severe punishment for all those accused) – 32,000 Taiwanese were punished under this authoritarian piece of legislation. With the massacre of famed rebel leader **Lin Shao Mao** and his army in 1902, guerrilla resistance was effectively wiped out. During the 1920s there was a series of attempts to petition the colonial government for a Taiwanese assembly, without success, and the **Taiwan Cultural Association**, formed in 1921, organized large-scale events to encourage a sense of identity in the face of continued Japanization. The Japanese increasingly cracked down on left-wing movements after 1931, and after full-scale war broke out in China in 1937, all popular organizations were banned.

Economic development

Kodama and Goto instituted an ambitious programme of **economic development**, building factories, harbours, rail lines, highways and bridges, as well as introducing medical schools and hospitals. They also established a central **Bank of Taiwan** in 1899, stabilizing the currency, and encouraged the development of rice and sugar exports to Japan – the European *hongs* were gradually forced out. Kodama was governor until 1906, but development continued: the appointment of **Den Kenjiro** in 1919, Taiwan's first civilian governor-general, ushered in a period of relatively enlightened colonial government that lasted until 1936, when militarism started to dominate Japanese politics.

The Wushe Incident and aboriginal resistance

The Japanese were the first rulers of Taiwan to undertake a comprehensive study of the mountain-dwelling aborigines, but also to demand their complete subjugation – in order to exploit Taiwan's rich **lumber** and **camphor** resources, they had to control the mountains. After a series of military campaigns (1911–14), when Bunun and Atayal areas were especially hard hit, policemen were stationed in every village and a school system established, making Japanese compulsory for all aboriginal children. Such policies angered tribal leaders, and in October 1930 a misunderstanding at a wedding provided the spark for an **Atayal** uprising led by **Chief Mona Rudao** at **Wushe** in central Taiwan. The local school – which was holding a sports day – was attacked, the Atayal warriors slaughtering 132 Japanese men, women and children (and two Chinese by mistake). Japanese reaction was swift: an army of 2700 was sent, along with trackers from rival Atayal clans, to hunt down the rebels, a campaign which took fifty days, involved aerial bombing and poison gas and left around 644 Atayal dead – Chief Mona Rudao, along with almost three hundred other warriors, opted to hang himself rather than surrender. In the aftermath most of the local villages were wiped out, the Japanese offering bounties to other Atayal warriors to mop up resistance, leading to further massacres of those who surrendered. Rudao's body was taken to Taipei and only given a formal burial in 1981 – a special NT$20 coin was minted in his honour in 2001.

World War II

War between China and Japan from July 1937 meant that Japanization in Taiwan was intensified, traditional Chinese customs banned and Chinese writing suppressed. To feed the Japanese war machine, Taiwan was transformed into a giant military-industrial base, a policy that created an economic boom. While fighting in China continued, Japan attacked the US at **Pearl Harbor** in 1941, marking the official start of **World War II** in Asia.

Initially the war left Taiwan physically untouched, but between 1942 and 1944, an estimated six thousand Taiwanese volunteered to fight for the Japanese, including 1800 members of the aboriginal **Takasago Volunteers** (see box opposite). In 1944 a

In 1974 the discovery of a man in the Indonesian jungle, described as "the last Japanese soldier from World War II" made headlines around the world. In fact, the soldier was an **Ami tribesman** from Taiwan called Suniyon, who had joined the **Takasago Volunteers** in 1943. Recruitment of indigenous tribesmen into the Imperial Army was largely covered up after the war, but between four thousand and eight thousand men are thought to have fought and almost half were killed. After the Wushe Incident, the Japanese regarded aboriginal warriors as excellent fighters, and ironically many volunteers came from the Atayal region, devastated by the Japanese. After the war many of them were enshrined with Shinto ritual at the Yasukuni Shrine in Tokyo (along with over 27,000 other Taiwanese) without family consent, and many Taiwanese aborigines still visit Japan to protest.

further 22,000 Taiwanese were conscripted and by the war's end an estimated 200,000 personnel were involved in war-related activities, including over seven hundred "**comfort women**" forced to serve as sex slaves. In total, around thirty thousand Taiwanese died. The island was also home to fifteen **Allied Prisoner of War camps**, including the notorious **Kinkaseki** (see box, p.138). Heavy US bombing destroyed Keelung and Kaohsiung harbours and many other parts of the island between 1944 and 1945, but when the Japanese surrendered in August 1945, Taiwan was still occupied – the last governor, Ando Rikichi, committed suicide soon after.

Return of mainland rule and the 2-28 Incident

According to the terms of the **1943 Cairo Declaration** agreed (but not signed) by Franklin Roosevelt, Winston Churchill and Chiang Kai-shek, Taiwan was returned to China after Japan's surrender in 1945, though the mainland had changed dramatically since it handed the island to Japan in 1895. The Qing dynasty had been overthrown by revolutionaries led by **Sun Yat-sen**, creating the **Republic of China** in 1911 and the Chinese Nationalist Party in 1912, commonly known as the **Kuomintang** (KMT). The KMT held power in China, on and off, for the next twenty years, and from the 1920s was led by **Generalissimo Chiang Kai-shek**. The party had been involved in a fierce civil war with the rival Communist forces of Mao Zedong since 1927, only briefly put on hold during the struggle with the Japanese, and when **Chen Yi** was appointed the Chinese governor of Taiwan in 1945, he promptly began stripping Taiwan of all its industrial wealth in order to bolster the KMT's renewed campaign against the Communists. Methods were often brutal and the Taiwanese quickly came to resent the brusque and corrupt officials sent to replace the Japanese. Meanwhile, the 480,000 Japanese inhabitants of Taiwan, many of whom had been born on the island, were told to leave by April 1946 – the KMT confiscated all Japanese real estate and property left behind.

The 2-28 Incident

The **2-28 Incident** began in Taipei on February 27, 1947, when a local vendor selling smuggled cigarettes was roughed up by KMT government officials – in the ensuing fracas a bystander was shot and killed. The next day, a large crowd gathered outside the local police station to protest, and fearing attack, the police opened fire, killing more civilians. Protests, strikes, riots and school closures spread across the island until March 8, when reinforcements from the mainland arrived to restore order in a bloody crackdown that took at least 28,000 lives (estimates vary wildly) and initiated forty years of martial law known as "White Terror". During this period, all discussion of the massacre was banned, and today it's still the source of heated debate among Taiwanese, especially the elderly, many of whom regard the KMT as murderers. No one has ever been charged over the incident, though Chen Yi was recalled to China in disgrace, and Chiang later had him executed.

The Republic of China: the Kuomintang and martial law

In 1949 the Communists finally defeated Chiang's Nationalist forces, and the remnants of his army retreated across the Taiwan Strait – almost two million "mainlanders" arriving in Taiwan to establish the last outpost of the **Republic of China**. Chiang Kai-shek became president in 1950, a post he held until his death in 1975. During martial law, opposition parties and the Taiwanese language were banned, mainlanders dominated positions of authority and Chiang had statues of himself built in every town. Although the economy began to flourish in the late 1970s (see box opposite), resources in the early part of KMT rule were primarily earmarked for defence and stockpiled for an eventual invasion of China. In reality, Taiwan's independence, as today, was made possible solely by **US support**. The conflict against Communism in Korea and later Vietnam ensured that US administrations backed Chiang's anti-communist KMT as an important ally – President

The Chiang dynasty

Chiang Kai-shek and his descendants have had a greater impact on modern Taiwan than any other family. Chiang ruled the island for 26 years, though its his activities in China pre-1949 that appear most colourful to outsiders and the focus of most biographies. Born in Zhejiang province in 1887 and trained as a soldier, he worked his way up to the position of general and then leader of the KMT in the 1920s, in part due to his wife's (**Soong Mei-ling** aka Madam Chiang) connections and links to the Shanghai mob. By the time of his flight to Taiwan in 1949, his position as Generalissimo was unchallenged. After his death in 1975 and a brief but fruitless attempt at influencing politics, Madam Chiang moved to the US, dying in New York in 2004 at the age of 106. Chiang's only son **Chiang Ching-kuo** (by his first wife – he had no children with Mei-ling) was president between 1978 and his own death in 1988. Ching-kuo married Russian-born **Faina Epatcheva Vahaleva** (1916–2004, known as Chiang Fang-liang) in 1935, but their three sons died shortly after Ching-kuo and only their daughter is still alive, living in the US. In the early 1990s, Chiang Kai-shek's adopted son **Chiang Wei-kuo** briefly mounted a political challenge to Lee Teng-hui, but the Chiang family was falling out of favour and he died in 1997. That wasn't the end of the Chiangs however. Ching-kuo also had two illegitimate sons: one of them, **John Chiang**, who used his mother's family name Chang until March 2005, is now the family's unofficial political heir in Taiwan, serving as a member of the Legislative Yuan since 2002. Meanwhile, **Demos Chiang**, a grandson of Chiang Ching-kuo, has become a bit of a celebrity in Taiwan, dating actresses and starting a successful brand-marketing company (DEM Inc).

The Taiwan Miracle

Perhaps the greatest achievement of KMT rule was economic reform, laying the foundations of what became known as the **Taiwan Miracle** – the rise from developing nation status to one of the top twenty largest economies in the world in the early twenty-first century. **Land reform** in the 1950s was a crucial first step, resulting in the opening up of new land to farmers and increased agricultural yields and incomes. From 1951 to 1964, the US supplied Taiwan with around US$1.5 billion in non-military aid, much of this channelled to infrastructure projects and investment in the **textile industry**, Taiwan's first big export success story.

Education was another factor, with the KMT building new schools and universities in the 1950s. In the 1960s, the government initiated an aggressive export-oriented strategy: liberalizing the financial system and setting up a stock market, increasing manufacturing and creating export-processing zones (Kaohsiung was the first in Asia). Between 1960 and 1970 Taiwan became the world's fastest-growing economy, averaging 9.7 percent GNP growth a year. In the 1980s, Taiwan began to produce high-quality electronics, especially **semiconductors** and **computers**, and though it has few recognizable domestic brands (Acer and BenQ the obvious exceptions), chances are that your PC or laptop contains components made by Taiwanese companies – however, all of their production factories are now in mainland China where Taiwan is the largest investor. Today the service sector accounts for around two thirds of GDP, while agriculture accounts for just 1.86 percent and industry around thirty percent.

Truman sent the Seventh Fleet to patrol the Taiwan Strait in the 1950s and stationed troops in Taiwan, but despite a vicious Communist assault (see p.355) on **Kinmen** and **Matsu** in 1954 (which was repulsed by Taiwanese troops), and the heavy bombardments of 1958, major conflict was avoided. In 1951 Japan signed the **Treaty of San Francisco** with the Allies, formally ending World War II and officially giving up sovereignty over Taiwan, but without specifying whom to – a fudge which provides plenty of bitter debate today. Independence activists want the date of the treaty – September 8 – to become **Taiwan's Independence Day**.

Withdrawal from the United Nations

Taiwan became increasingly isolated in the 1970s. Mao Zedong's People's Republic of China (PRC) was finally admitted to the United Nations in 1971, but rather than share a seat, Chiang's Republic of China **withdrew**, a move which was to have serious implications in the years to follow. In 1972 President Nixon made his historic visit to China, and in December 1978 the unthinkable happened – President Carter switched US recognition to the PRC, severing formal relations with Taiwan. Much of the world has since followed suit. Though the **Taiwan Relations Act** ensured the US would still supply the island with weapons, US troops left and with the reconquest of China now impossible, the KMT began to commit more resources to infrastructure and economic development, creating one of the world's most dynamic economies.

Democracy

After Chiang Kai-shek's death in 1975, the now largely forgotten **Yen Chia-ken** became president, but in 1978 Chiang's son, **Chiang Ching-kuo** took over and ruled till his own demise in 1988. Chiang Ching-kuo was a complex figure, presiding over a period of unprecedented economic growth and eventual political liberalization in Taiwan, while remaining dedicated to KMT hegemony and the goal of reunifying China.

Opposition to one-party rule and KMT corruption (dubbed "**Black Gold**" because of notorious links with local mafia) grew in the 1970s. The **Tangwai** (*dāngwài*), or "outside the party" movement, involved students and academics at first, almost all of them Taiwanese; members started by contesting local elections, but government oppression led to the 1979 **Kaohsiung Incident**, now regarded as a landmark in Taiwan's democracy movement (see box, p.255), and the trial of the "Kaohsiung Eight" which garnered much public sympathy. Between 1980 and 1985 however, progress was limited: the Chiang regime continued to crack down on dissent, though informal opposition grew. In September 1986 the leaders of the Tangwai movement illegally established the **Democratic Progressive Party** (DPP). In response, President Chiang lifted martial law in July 1987 and press restrictions were removed in January 1988. Much of this was due to US pressure, but with growing opposition inside Taiwan, Chiang seems to have genuinely accepted the need for change.

KMT chairman **Lee Teng-hui** became Taiwan's first native-born president in 1988, ushering in a period of reform and the end of formal hostilities with China in 1991. **Student demonstrations** in Taipei in 1990 led to more democratic concessions, and though the DPP made gains in the Legislative Yuan, Taiwan's **first free presidential election** in 1996 was won by KMT incumbent Lee. This despite intimidation from China, which tested missiles close to the island to mark its disapproval of Lee's growing independence sympathies. Though now retired from government, Lee remains an enigmatic and active figure, despised by many in China and even Taiwan – once a KMT loyalist, he's now the spiritual father of the independence movement and an outspoken critic of China.

In 2000, in a landmark election, the KMT lost power for the first time in almost fifty years: **Chen Shui-bian** of the DPP, a lawyer by training who earned his political stripes defending dissidents after the Kaohsiung Incident, became president with 39.3 percent of the vote, beating independent and ex-KMT member James Soong (36.84 percent) and KMT candidate Lien Chan (23.1 percent). The peaceful change of regime was vindication of how far Taiwan had come – the world's first Chinese democracy, while a little rough around the edges, was largely created by the Taiwanese themselves in a dramatic rebuttal to pundits who claimed democracy was alien to "Asian Values".

Taiwan today: the struggle for political identity

Since the election of 2000 Taiwan's **struggle for political identity** has become the primary issue of the day. While ordinary Taiwanese and especially the youth have continued to develop a very recognizable identity in terms of music, pop culture, food, fashion and art, Taiwan's status in the world remains unclear, its **relationship with China** its most challenging problem. The China debate reflects a very real and passionate **divide** across Taiwanese society, although you're unlikely to see much expression of this on the streets. Around 75 percent of Taiwanese remain in favour of what's called the "**status quo**" (see box opposite), while ten percent favour reunification and fifteen percent formal independence. Given this, most politicians support the status quo position,

Taiwan's existence depends largely on the concept of **"One China"**, but what does this actually mean? Taiwanese officials (mostly KMT) claim that there is "one China controlled by two governments". The Communist Party in China believes there is one China controlled by one government (them), and that this includes the actual territory of Taiwan, its **"renegade province"**. This poses a thorny problem for the international community: no nation wants to upset China, but at the same time it would be extremely hypocritical for the West to turn its back on a flourishing democracy. The solution since the 1950s has been to focus on semantics: that only one country can call itself China. As long as Taiwan calls itself the "Republic of China", nations can simply refuse to recognize it by invoking the One China policy.

It seems like a good compromise: Taiwan goes unrecognized in much of the world, its athletes at the Olympics compete under the embarrassing designation "Chinese Taipei", and it has no representation at the UN, but it remains de facto independent. Even better, China has indicated it is content to maintain this status quo, and therefore the de facto independence of Taiwan (though of course this would never be admitted publicly), as long as Taiwan keeps the door open for eventual reunification.

If Taiwan were to abandon the concept of it being an alternative China, drop the "Republic of China" moniker and become the "Republic of Taiwan" instead, China would threaten to invade, and the world would have to choose between upsetting an up-and-coming superpower or turning its collective back on a new democracy. Not surprisingly, the international community is focused on maintaining the **status quo** at all costs.

Up to the 1970s, most nations tended to recognize Taiwan as the real China. Though the Communists took control of mainland China in 1949, Chiang Kai-shek and the KMT maintained the belief that they were the legitimate government of all China, a claim that looked increasingly delusional by the 1970s. After the People's Republic of China joined the UN in 1971 and Taiwan withdrew (see p.391), the situation changed; following the example of the US in 1978, most nations began to switch official recognition to the PRC.

Only a tiny rump remains. Today Taiwan, in its official guise as the Republic of China, and bolstered by considerable sums of financial aid, is recognized as the "real" China by only 23 states (as of December 2010): Belize, Burkina Faso, Dominican Republic, El Salvador, Gambia, Guatemala, Haiti, Honduras, Kiribati, Marshall Islands, Nauru, Nicaragua, Palau, Panama, Paraguay, St Kitts and Nevis, St Lucia, St Vincent and the Grenadines, São Tomé and Príncipe, Solomon Islands, Swaziland, Tuvalu and the Vatican City.

masking a fundamental division between many KMT and DPP supporters: the real issue remains **unification** versus **formal independence**.

The return of the KMT

Taiwan's highly adversarial political parties are drawn into two informal alliances, broadly reflecting their positions on China: the **pan-green** (which has no relation to the Green parties of the West), including the DPP, pro-independence Taiwan Solidarity Union and the minor Taiwan Independence Party; and the **pan-blue coalition**, comprising the KMT, the People First Party, led by James Soong, and the marginal New Party. Many pan-blues believe that Taiwan ought to be, at some stage, united with the mainland, while independence-minded pan-green members want a truly sovereign nation and membership of the UN.

In 2004 Chen Shui-bian won re-election by just thirty thousand votes (50.3 percent), after an **assassination attempt** that many opposition members believe was staged. Chen's presidency hit rock-bottom in 2006, after corruption allegations involving his close aides as well as family members led to widespread calls for his resignation – in 2009 Chen himself was given a life sentence for corruption (reduced somewhat in 2010). In 2008 **Ma Ying-jeou** of the KMT won the presidential election in a landslide, and as of 2010 the opposition DPP held only 33 seats out of 113 in the Legislative Yuan. Ma has been following a conciliatory China policy ever since his victory; **Economic Cooperation Framework Agreement** talks began in 2010, which would unify the two countries economically. Despite fears that this would inevitably lead to political unification, Ma and the KMT argue that Taiwan has no choice.

Taiwan's indigenous peoples

More commonly known as **aborigines**, or *yuánzhùmín* ("original inhabitants") in Chinese, Taiwan's **indigenous peoples** represent just two percent of the island's 23 million people. Things have improved over the last ten years, but Taiwan's indigenous population still suffers discrimination and remains very much at the bottom of the country's economic and social ladders.

Taiwan's indigenous tribes form part of the **Austronesian** cultural and linguistic family. The **origins** of Taiwan's aborigines are still fiercely debated, though most agree that they are descendants of Neolithic peoples that have inhabited the island for thousands of years. The most radical theory, and the one currently in favour in Taiwan, claims that the island is in fact **the homeland of all Austronesian people** – that migrations from Taiwan would eventually, over thousands of years, colonize the entire Pacific. The formation of the **Alliance of Taiwan Aborigines** in 1984 marked the formal beginning of the indigenous political movement, and a cabinet-level **Council of Indigenous Peoples** was established in 1996 to oversee aboriginal affairs (currently headed by Sun Ta-chuan, a Puyuma). In 2001 the Ministry of Education added **aboriginal classes** to the schools language curriculum (in aboriginal areas), but in practice lesson time is limited and the incentives to learn poor. In 2005 the **Indigenous Television Network**, a 24-hour cable TV station (with programmes in Mandarin and aboriginal languages) dedicated to aboriginal news, documentaries and entertainment was launched, one of the requirements of the Aboriginal Education Law (2000).

One of the key differences between the aboriginal population and the Chinese today is religion: thanks to an aggressive missionary effort, the indigenous population is now almost completely **Christian** (mostly Presbyterian); a proliferation of churches and a Christian graveyard are easy ways to tell if you are in an aboriginal village.

The Tribes

As of December 2010, there were fourteen **official indigenous tribes** in Taiwan: the Ami, Atayal, Bunun, Kevalan, Paiwan, Puyuma, Rukai, Saisiyat, Sakizaya, Sediq, Tao, Thao, Truku (Taroko) and Tsou. Being recognized as an official tribe brings public recognition and government subsidies for community projects, but the process has been highly controversial and is based largely on simplistic classifications established by Japanese anthropologists in the 1920s.

During the Qing era, aborigines were classified as either *shēng fān*, "raw" or uncivilized barbarians who inhabited the mountains, or *shóu fān*, "cooked" or civilized tribes that lived on the plains and generally paid taxes. Although most aborigines primarily associated themselves with their village and locale, in the 1920s the Japanese grouped the *shēng fān* into nine core "mountain" tribes. The plains aborigines were referred to collectively as *píngpǔ*: until very recently these people were considered totally assimilated by the Han Chinese and even today many Taiwanese will tell you that there are no *píngpǔ* left on the island – quite untrue. The reason for this is that most *píngpǔ* tribes have yet to gain official recognition as distinct ethnic groups, partly because they have ceased to speak tribal languages and maintain limited cultural traditions. This has been changing: in addition to the acknowledgement of *pingpŭ* tribes (like the Kevalan), those regarded as subgroups of larger "mountain" tribes are becoming recognized as distinct communities (the Thao were once considered part of the Tsou, the Truku part of the Atayal). The **Ketagalan**, **Makatau** and **Pazeh**, supposedly extinct *pingpŭ* tribes, are currently pushing for official recognition. Depending on how you classify them, there are at least seven officially unrecognized *pingpŭ* tribes: Babuza, Hoanya, Ketagalan (which includes the Basay, Luilang and Trobiawan clans), Papora, Pazeh, Siraya (including the Makatau), and Taokas (Dougai).

The fourteen official tribes are usually distinguished by traditional dress, rituals and exotic customs such as headhunting that have long died out, and though you will see bright costumes, singing and dancing at festivals, little of this has much bearing on contemporary aboriginal life.

Ami

The **Ami** (阿美族; *āmĕizú*) are Taiwan's **largest tribe** with around 170,000 members, concentrated along the east coast between Hualien and Taitung. The **Harvest Festival**, known as *Ilisin*, is the most important Ami event, usually taking place in July or August and marking New Year: each village holds its own celebration, lasting from one to seven days. Although Taitung city contains the largest concentration of Ami people, there are numerous Ami villages along the east coast and East Rift Valley, notably **Dulan** (see p.311). Its annual **Art Festival** (October) acts as a magnet for traditional performers. The Ami are particularly well known for their **musical** traditions, producing Mandopop star Van Fan and alternative rocker Chang Chen-yue – more familiar to Western audiences, New Age dance project Enigma sampled an Ami performance group singing the traditional "Song of Joy" (without their permission) on their 1993 single "**Return to Innocence**", which was later used to promote the 1996 Atlanta Olympics. The Ami singers sued the group and reached an out-of-court settlement in 1998.

Atayal

The **Atayal** (泰雅; *tàiyă*) is the second largest tribe (81,000) and the most widely spread, inhabiting the mountainous northern half of Taiwan. Despite their geographical dispersion, the Atayal have offered the most resistance to colonization over the years, gaining a reputation as fierce fighters after the 1930 Wushe Incident (see p.388). In 1999 the Atayal began opposing the creation of the **Makao National Park** as it threatened local land rights, with vociferous Independent Legislator **May Chin** (a former actress), whose mother was Atayal, one of those against it (as of 2010 protests against the proposed park were ongoing). The Atayal are best known in Taiwan however, for their quality **weaving** and the tradition of **facial tattoos**, particularly on women: the practice was banned by the Japanese in 1913 and died out in the 1920s – the few remaining elders with tattoos live in the **Taian** area. Other important Atayal centres are **Fuxing**, **Smangus**, **Wulai**, **Baling** and **Wushe**.

Bunun

The **Bunun** (布農; *bùnóng*) occupy the central mountains of Taiwan and are another widely dispersed tribe of around fifty thousand, divided into six clans. High mountain dwellers with a reputation for being formidable hunters and skilled guides, the Bunun were the last tribe to be suppressed by the Japanese. Their most important celebration is the **Ear-shooting Festival** held in April or May, traditionally a test of archery skills designed to mark the coming of age of men in the tribe and to pray for a good millet harvest – traditionally hunted animals (usually deer) are used as target practice. The Bunun are also known for the haunting **Pasibutbut**, eight-octave harmonies that sound a bit like humming, first recorded by the Japanese in 1943.

The Bunun have also been active players in the campaign for aboriginal rights: the **Bunun Culture and Education Foundation** was established in 1995 in **Yenping**, Taitung county, while in 1987 the destruction of ancient Bunun graves by a hotel contractor in **Dongpu** sparked the "Return Our Land" campaign – since the 1970s the village has also clashed with Yushan National Park over water and land rights. **Luona** in Nantou county and **Haiduan** (Taitung county) are also large Bunun communities, but the village of **Hongye** is the best known in Taiwan: this was the home of a Little League baseball team whose defeat of a side from Wakayama (Japan) in 1968 thrilled the nation (though the Japanese team were not the world champions as is still sometimes claimed). As with many other tribes, one of the most visibly recognizable Bunun in Taiwan is a popular singer, **Wang Hong-en**, though another tribe member, **Topas Tamapima**, became a noted writer in the 1980s, and his novel *The Last Hunter* is highly acclaimed.

Kavalan

The 1100 **Kavalan** (噶瑪蘭族; *gámǎlánzú*) became Taiwan's eleventh indigenous tribe in 2002 (the first *píngpǔ* tribe to be given such status), after a ten-year campaign and the strong support of former premier Yu Shyi-kun. Originally from Yilan county, where legend has it they drove the Atayal into the mountains, most Kavalan migrated south along the east coast in the nineteenth century and developed cultural ties with the Ami. Today their largest settlement is **Xinshe** near Fongbin in Hualien county.

Paiwan

The **Paiwan** (排灣; *páiwān*; 85,000), inhabiting the far south of Taiwan in Pingdong and Taitung counties, have managed to retain a strong cultural and linguistic identity. The Paiwan call themselves the "descendants of the paipushe snake" and the snake, associated with their ancestors, is a common symbol among the tribe and eating it is banned. Major Paiwan settlements include **Sandimen**, **Taiwu** and **Mudan**, but their villages are also spread throughout the Hengchun Peninsula and Kenting National Park – many still use slate or **slab-stone houses**. The most important Paiwan **festival** is **Masaru**, which is an end-of-year celebration rather than a harvest festival, taking place in individual villages between July and November. The Paiwan are renowned **woodcarvers** but have also produced some talented writers: **Chen Ying-hsiung**'s collection of short stories *Traces of Dreams in Foreign Lands* (1971), is considered Taiwan's first piece of aboriginal literature, while blind poet **Monaneng** has been publishing since 1984. Writer **Sakinu Ahronglong**, whose *Mountain Pig, Flying Fox, Sakinu* was a big hit in Taiwan, also starred in a film adaptation of his book *The Sage Hunter* in 2005, which won plaudits in the US. He opened Taiwan's first traditional hunting school in November 2005. Other Paiwan celebrities include the rock band **Power Station**, famous Asia-wide in the late 1990s, and female pop singer **Dai Ai-ling**.

Puyuma

Inhabiting the plains around Taitung city, the 11,000 **Puyuma** (卑南族; known as **Beinan** or *bēinánzú* in Chinese, after the district in which most of them live), are traditionally divided into two main subgroups with different origin myths: the **Nanwang** group are "born from bamboo" while the **Zhiben** group are "born from stone". The tribe is further divided into eight villages, traditionally independent and ruled by a chief – villages often fought among each other, the Puyuma developing a tradition for Spartan-like training of young men in community halls known as **parakwan**. The tribe's most important festival, the **Mangamangaya**, or "Monkey Ritual", grew out of this warrior tradition, marking the coming of age of male teenagers and involving wrestling and hunting monkeys – today the monkeys are made of straw. Puyuma singer **A-mei** (Chang Hui-mei) has become one of the island's most successful pop stars, while **Samingad** is becoming equally famous for singing in Puyuma as well as Mandarin.

Rukai

The 12,000-strong **Rukai** (魯凱族; *lǔkǎizú*) tribe is loosely divided into three groups: **Taitung** (east), **Wutai** (west) and those inhabiting the **Maolin National Scenic Area**. The tribe, like the Paiwan, is noted for its striking slate houses in villages such as **Duona** – the Rukai also traditionally cook food on stone slabs. In 1990 the **Return to Kochapongan Movement** was established to rebuild traditional stone houses in an abandoned mountain village (with no roads), evolving into a symbol of the Rukai's determination to maintain their culture (events are now held at **Kochapongan**, also known as Old Haocha, twice a year).

Saisiyat

The **Saisiyat** (賽夏; *sàixià*), numbering around 5600, are based in the **Lion's Head Mountain** region and comprise a Northern Branch (**Wufong**) and a Southern Branch (**Nanzhuang** and **Shitan** in Miaoli), each with its own dialect. Given the size of the tribe and its proximity to larger Atayal and Hakka populations, the struggle to maintain Saisiyat culture is particularly hard. The **"Ritual of the Short Black People"**, held by both clans every ten years, with a smaller version every two, has become their most powerful expression of identity. The ceremony commemorates a legendary tribe of black pygmies, called *taai*, or "short people", that once lived in harmony with the Saisiyat. Things changed after some of the *taai* sexually molested Saisiyat women – the whole tribe was exterminated. The ritual is meant to appease their spirits, many anthropologists suggesting the story might be based on true events, and that the *taai* may represent peoples that inhabited Taiwan before the aborigines.

Sakizaya

The **Sakizaya** (撒奇萊雅族; *saqíláiyǎzú*) were once considered part of the Ami, but became the thirteenth officially recognized tribe in January 2007. The tribe has around 355 registered members, having been long absorbed by the Ami tribe after a devastating military campaign against the Qing in 1878. Estimated actual tribe numbers range from 5000 to 10,000.

Sediq

The **Sediq** (also Seediq; 賽德克族; *sàidékèzú*), once considered part of the Atayal, were officially recognized as Taiwan's fourteenth indigenous group in 2008 with around 9700 members (living primarily in Nantou and Hualien counties).

Tao

The 3500 **Tao** or **Dawu** (達悟族; *dáwùzú*; previously known as the Yami) retain the strongest identity of any tribe in Taiwan, mainly because of their relative isolation. The only seagoing tribe, they inhabit **Lanyu** (Orchid Island) off the southeast coast, their language more closely related to that of the Philippines than to the aboriginal languages of mainland Taiwan. The most iconic expression of that identity is the Tao wooden canoe, hand-carved and richly decorated but serving a mostly ceremonial purpose today. The Tao's traditional dress is also very distinctive, the men wearing loincloths and striking steel helmets, generally worn now only at celebrations like the **Flying Fish Festival** in March/April. The Tao's traditional underground houses, protection against the fierce Pacific weather, are also becoming rare.

It's not as tranquil as it seems on Orchid Island, however; in 1982 the state-owned Taiwan Power Company (Taipower) duped the Tao into building a **nuclear waste storage site** on Lanyu in return for more jobs. The Tao have campaigned long, and so far unsuccessfully, to have the waste removed: some fear the containers are leaking. Taipower plans to transport them off the island by 2016, and is desperately seeking an alternative dump overseas – North Korea appears the most likely destination.

Thao

Sun Moon Lake is the ancestral home of the Thao (邵族; *shàozú*), **Taiwan's smallest aboriginal tribe**, with around 647 members. One of the most important Thao legends tells that a chief known as Paidabo stumbled upon Sun Moon Lake after an exhausting chase of a large **white deer** – Paidabo was so impressed he ordered the whole tribe, originally located near Alishan, to move here, and today you'll see symbols of the white deer everywhere. Many fear the Thao will become completely assimilated by the Chinese, with only a handful of "pure" Thao still living and fluent in the Thao language. However, the destruction wrought by the 921 Earthquake (see box, p.183) led to a re-examination of government policy and a greater focus on preserving Thao culture: in 2000 Lalu Island was renamed to reflect Thao tradition, and its sacred shores protected (only Thao are allowed on the island), while in 2001 the Thao became Taiwan's tenth official aboriginal tribe (previously they had been regarded as a subgroup of the Tsou).

The most popular Thao festival is the **Harvest** or **Moon Festival** held Lunar August 1–15, marking the start of the Thao new year. On the last day of Lunar July, in the Sun Moon Lake village of Itashao, local Thao pound huge wooden pestles on stone mortars to call the tribe together – the thumping sound created, or **pestle music**, is one of the festival's chief attractions.

Truku

In 2004, after an eight-year campaign, the 24,000 **Truku** (太魯閣族; *tàilǔgézú*; also sometimes romanized as Taroko) were officially recognized as the twelfth indigenous ethnic group in Taiwan, though not without controversy. The Truku were formerly part of the Sediq subgroup of the Atayal tribe, and the seven thousand Sediq from Nantou that remain are unhappy at what they feel is an unnecessary split. As the name suggests, the tribe once inhabited the area around **Taroko Gorge** (Taroko means "lookout on a hillside") though the largest settlements today lie outside the national park at Sioulin, Wanrong and Jhousi in Hualien county. The tribe is most noted for suffering one of the worst abuses of **land rights** in Taiwan; between 1973 and 1995 **Asia Cement** leased land from the tribe, but when the lease expired, it said it had documents proving all claim to it had been surrendered. The tribe denies this, and feeling the company has done little for the community, wants it removed. Even after a court found in favour of the Truku, Asia Cement refused to budge and nothing has been done by the government since – the local Land Reclamation Committee continues its protests. The case has larger implications for traditional land rights across the island, and raised the disturbing possibility that a major Taiwanese company forged important documents (vociferously denied by Asia Cement).

Tsou

The Tsou (鄒; *zōu*) are usually divided into a northern group, centred on the **Alishan National Scenic Area**, and a southern tribe found in **Kaohsiung county**, with around 6500 people claiming Tsou ancestry altogether. There are only two Tsou **hosas** (also called *dashe*), which means "major village": Dabang and Tefuye, both in Alishan. Each *hosa* has a hereditary chief or *peogsi* who still has limited authority over the villagers. Only these villages contain a **kuba**, the traditional, male-only meeting house which lies at the centre of all Tsou festivals and rituals. Other villages have smaller structures known as **hufu** that have similar functions but are less important.

By far the most interesting Tsou festival to watch, the **Mayasvi Festival** is hosted annually in rotation by Tefuye and Dabang villages in February: traditionally a celebration of warriors returning from battle, the rituals give thanks to the god of war and god of heaven.

Religion in Taiwan

Religious belief is apparent everywhere you look in Taiwan: in addition to literally thousands of temples, almost every home and store has a shrine, taxi drivers hang icons inside their cars, and small altars laden with offerings or braziers burning "ghost money" stand on pavements outside shops and offices. Popular religious practice, often described as "**folk religion**", is usually lumped together with **Taoism** to distinguish it from the clearly identifiable **Buddhist** and **Confucian** traditions, and while it's true that Taoist concepts are important, popular "folk religion" is really a blend of ancient animist beliefs with all three traditions. As a result, Taiwan has a broad pantheon of gods and goddesses that include Buddhist and Taoist deities, as well as famous historical figures.

The beliefs outlined below are subscribed to by the vast majority of Taiwanese, but there are many other faiths practised on the island. Since the 1950s there has been a **Buddhist revival** in Taiwan, with several monasteries advancing a purer form of teaching and practice, and strict adherents (there are around four million) dismissing the Buddhist deities in older folk temples as childish superstition. **Christianity** is the next most popular, with over one million believers (mostly Protestant), followed by **I-kuan Tao** with 850,000 followers, a mixture of various religions, but with a fundamentally Chinese character and roots in Qing-dynasty China. It's now primarily a Taiwanese faith after suppression on the mainland. There are also around fifty thousand Taiwanese **Muslims**.

Core beliefs

Ancestor worship lies at the heart of Taiwanese (and traditional Chinese) belief, based on the hazy boundary between the human and spirit worlds. Worship of ancestors, by offering incense, food or spirit money at family or clan shrines, is imperative to ensure a peaceful afterlife. After death, everyone is said to pass through a series of supernatural courts (where a period in hell might be prescribed for wrongdoing). The deceased then become either **ancestral spirits** or "**hungry ghosts**", uncared for by their families and destined to haunt the living (these are the unfortunates appeased in "Ghost Month"). If worshipping certain individuals over the years proves particularly efficacious, these eventually become elevated to the status of **god** (Mazu and Guan Di are the best examples), joining the vast pantheon of folk and Taoist deities. Gods live in an alternative reality, with an administration modelled on the old imperial bureaucracy, with their own courts and a strict system of hierarchy. The supreme deity is the **Jade Emperor** or the Lord of Heaven. Worship of **gods** is slightly different from that of ancestors as the latter (and ghosts) are spirits that must be appeased or looked after, while gods are worshipped in exchange for protection, specific types of help or general good fortune (usually in the form of wealth). Note that although almost all Taiwanese subscribe to the concept of ghostly afterlife, people describing themselves as Buddhists will normally believe in reincarnation.

The three teachings

The three teachings of Confucianism, Taoism and Buddhism have been a foundation for Chinese religious belief for centuries.

Confucianism

More philosophy than religion, **Confucianism** is associated with **Kong Zi** (551–479 BC), known as "Confucius" in the West, a real scholar and teacher who lived during the Warring States period in modern Shandong, China. Confucius taught that if people behaved according to a strict code of moral and social values, society would be transformed and happiness achieved – discussion of gods and spiritualism is unimportant, though Confucian temples were created later in order to commemorate the great sage and perform important rituals. His sayings, collected in the *Analects*, along with the five ancient Confucian Classics, became the basis for Chinese imperial examinations until the end of the Qing dynasty, and the emphasis on virtuous rulers, strict hierarchy and education has influenced Chinese thought ever since. Confucianism, along with its temples, was completely abandoned in mainland China after 1949, but thrives in Taiwan, and the official 79th descendant of Confucius, Kung Tsui-chang *(kǒng chuícháng)* is the Sacrificial Official to Confucius in Taipei.

Taoism

Taoism (or "Daoism"), stems from the philosophy laid out in the *Tao Te Ching*, attributed to quasi-historical monk **Lao Zi** (a contemporary of Confucius), and the later teachings of **Zhuang Zi**. "Tao" means "the way" and, in contrast to the humanistic ethos of Confucianism, Taoism emphasizes man's need to connect with the natural universe in order to lead a fulfilling life, replacing greed with harmony in nature.

Contemplative, spiritual and abstruse, **philosophical Taoism** is often differentiated from the more superstitious **religious Taoism**: the latter is closer to the "folk religion" practised in most of Taiwan, with its vast pantheon of gods and goddesses. Taoist thought is closely linked to practices such as fengshui, and the concepts of *yin* and *yang*, as well as many common daily rituals.

Buddhism

Buddhism is essentially a way of life, based on the teachings of Indian prince Siddhartha Gautama (563–483 BC), who attained enlightenment in 528 BC and was thereafter known as the Buddha or "enlightened one". The **Four Noble Truths** stand at the core of his teachings: the truth about *duhkha* (usually translated as "suffering"); the truth of how suffering in life arises; the truth that giving up desire will eliminate suffering; and that the eightfold path is a practical way to achieve this goal. **Enlightenment** (or *nirvana*) means to escape the endless cycle of rebirth and therefore suffering. A few hundred years after Buddha's death, his followers divided into two schools: **Theravada** (which thrives in Sri Lanka and southeast Asia) and **Mahayana**, the interpretation most prevalent in northeast Asia and Taiwan today. Mahayana Buddhism, and particularly the form that developed in China (where it mixed with Taoist and Confucian thought), differs primarily in its belief that there are multiple Buddhas (that the historical Buddha, known as **Sakyamuni**, is just one of a series of past and future enlightened ones); and that there are **Bodhisattvas**, enlightened beings that have chosen continued rebirth in order to end the suffering of others (**Guanyin** is the most common in Taiwan – see p.404).

Buddhism in Taiwan

Taiwan is one of the world's great strongholds of Buddhism. The two main forms practised today are **Pure Land** and the meditative **Chan** (or Zen), though most Buddhist organizations on the island tend to blend aspects of the two. Buddhist **monasteries** developed in Taiwan during the Japanese occupation, and since the

1960s have blossomed, giving the island one of the highest monastic populations in Asia. As Taiwan has grown richer, it's become a pioneer for what's known as **Humanistic Buddhism** and its attempt to accommodate modern capitalism: accepting that becoming a monk isn't practical for most people, the emphasis is on blending daily life with Buddhist tenets, and particularly on performing charity and good works. Other than Sakyamuni, the most common Buddhas represented in Taiwan are **Amitabha** (the Buddha of Boundless Light, who oversees the "Pure Land", a paradise attainable by prayer recitation), and the **Medicine Buddha** (*yàoshīfó* in Chinese), a past Buddha famed for his healing abilities and usually portrayed holding a medicine ball or pagoda. The three are often arranged together in temples as a trinity, with Sakyamuni in the middle. The **Maitreya Buddha**, known as *mílèfó* in Chinese, is portrayed as a fat, happy monk, an image that commemorates a past incarnation as a quasi-historical Chinese monk. Though he's still technically a Bodhisattva, *mílèfó* is expected to return as the next future Buddha, and is worshipped as such.

The Taoist pantheon

Most Taiwanese worship a mixture of Taoist and Buddhist **deities**, though this blurring of faiths would be considered wholly Taoist or "folk religion" by strict Buddhists today. The following is an introduction to the most common gods, though there are literally hundreds, often within the same temple. See p.32 for the relevant festival days (usually described as "birthdays" in English) for each one.

Mazu

Mazu (媽祖; *māzǔ*), also known as the Queen of Heaven (天后; *tiānhòu*), is the most important deity in Taiwan. Regarded as the **goddess of the sea**, it's not hard to work out why she became so important in Taiwan, an island nation that was in large part dependent on fishing and immigration by sea in its early history. Like many deities in Taiwan, Mazu has historical roots in Fujian province, the ancestral home of most Taiwanese. Her popularity can also be explained by her perceived ability to grant the wishes of her believers, most evident in the tremendous wealth of Mazu temples, and their attraction of celebrities, politicians and huge donations. The historical Mazu was a woman called **Lin Mo-niang**, who was born around 960 AD on Meizhou Island off the Fujian coast. As a teenager, she's said to have been taught the mysteries of the Tao by a priest, and thereafter began a life of selfless charity, guiding ships into harbour and saving seafarers from drowning. This culminated in the dramatic rescue of her father or brothers while in a trance (some stories say her father was lost after Lin was disturbed mid-trance). She died at the age of 28, and was later deified, being awarded the title "Queen of Heaven" in the Qing dynasty.

Statues of Mazu are usually identifiable by her mortarboard-like headdress, fronted with beads. She is usually flanked by statues of "**Ears That Hear on the Wind**" (*shùnfēngěr*) and "**Thousand-Mile Eyes**" (*qiānlǐyǎn*), two demons that fell in love with her (she never married), and whom she converted to the Tao, now serving as trusted guardians with special powers indicated by their names.

Mazu's birthday is one of the country's most exuberant and intense festivals, while the **Dajia Mazu Pilgrimage** (see p.403), has its roots in the practice of "spirit division". This is essentially a system of hierarchy, where "mother" temples, containing ancient or revered Mazu deities, provide new statues or relics to smaller "branch" temples (the system also applies to other deities). Traditionally these subsidiary temples return their deities to the mother temple every year at the time of Mazu's birthday, to enhance their spiritual power. The highest-ranking temple is undoubtedly the shrine on **Meizhou Island** in Fujian, but the problems start when trying to identify Taiwan's most senior place of worship: almost every major temple claims it's the "first" or "oldest" and many hold precious deities from Meizhou. Rivalries are fierce and disputes can become very heated. Today, the most popular contenders are in Beigang (see p.218), Dajia (see p.188), Xingang and the Tainan area (see p.247).

Guanyin

Though a Buddhist Bodhisattva, **Guanyin** (觀音; *guānyīn*) is worshipped in Taoist temples throughout Taiwan, and even where she's the main deity in a nominally Buddhist temple, practice tends to follow popular Taoism rather than orthodox Buddhism. Guanyin was originally worshipped as a male Indian Bodhisattva called Avalokitesvara, who represented the ideal of compassion, able to relieve suffering and grant children: the deity began to be depicted as a female during the twelfth century in China, and she's now known as the **goddess of mercy**. She's normally depicted as an elegant lady, robed in white and, being associated with **vegetarianism**, her image also adorns many vegetarian restaurants.

Wang Ye

Wang Ye (王爺; *wángyé*) gods are incredibly popular throughout Taiwan, but particularly in the south where they equal Mazu in importance. The name Wang Ye, or "pestilence gods", is an umbrella term for around 360 different deities: there are reckoned to be around 106 to 132 individual family names for each (Chi, Chu, Fan, Li, Su, Wen and Wu are the most common), and they are thought to have originally been diseased spirits, now honoured in an attempt to ward off plague and disease. The tradition migrated to Taiwan from Fujian and is linked to the practice of burning "spirit ships", or *wángchuán*: model boats loaded with Wang Ye gods, set alight, and launched into the ocean in an attempt to expel disease/bad luck. Taiwan's chief Wang Ye temple is in **Nankunshen** (see p.252), north of Tainan – pestilence gods rarely appear in temples on their own, and are usually represented in groups of three, five or seven.

Guan Di

Red-faced **Guan Di** (關帝; *guāndì*, or just *guāngōng*), is one of the most admired deities in Taiwan, with over three hundred temples and numerous shrines in homes and shops. He's usually described as the **god of war**, but this is misleading. He was originally more like a patron of chivalrous warriors, and is today worshipped by executives, police, restaurant owners, rebels and criminal gangs, as well as being revered as a god of wealth and literature by the public in general. His appeal derives from being one of the most respected characters in the Chinese classic the *Romance of the Three Kingdoms*, loosely based on the historical events of the Three Kingdoms period (206–220 AD). Known then as **Guan Yu**, the general was one of the **three oath brothers** (the main characters in the saga), and noted for his extreme bravery and loyalty. Apart from the red face, he's usually depicted with a long, flowing beard and a Chinese halberd in his hands. Buddhists claim Guan Di was taught Buddhism by a great master on the night of his death, and as a result swore to protect the *dharma* (Buddhist teachings) – he's often seen in Buddhist temples where he's known as *qíelán*.

Earth God

The **Earth God**, known as *Tudi Gong* (土地公; *tŭdìgōng*, or *fúdé zhèngshén* in Chinese), is traditionally one of the most important in the Chinese pantheon, though as Taiwan has modernized his popularity has waned. His main task in the Jade Emperor's administration is to keep a register of births and deaths and govern the local area in his charge, usually a village or parts of a town (towns traditionally had five Earth God shrines for north, south, east, west and central districts), though he's more associated with agriculture and probably evolved from ancient harvest rituals. In his secondary role as a god of wealth, shopkeepers erect temporary altars on the roadside to make offerings to him twice a month. Earth God shrines are usually very small but ubiquitous, found literally all over the island. He's normally represented by a statue of a cheerful old man, dressed in yellow robes with a long white beard and a stick in his right hand. Tucked away under his altar is usually an effigy of the **Tiger God**, thought to be his servant and ridden by the Earth God on his spiritual "inspection tours" of the locale.

City God

Every major city in Taiwan has a **City God** (城隍; *chénghuáng*), which protects the inhabitants and, like the Earth God, acts as a registrar of all births and deaths in the area. He also keeps account of the citizens' moral behaviour, and it's his report after death which will determine punishment in the courts of the underworld – it's usual to find a giant abacus somewhere in his temple, as well as graphic images of hell. Though the City God tradition is thought to have evolved from nature worship, and his role is the same in every city, each deity tends to double as an incarnation of a famous local figure, meaning his birthday is celebrated on different days. In Taiwan, many City God temples are branches of mainland counterparts, usually in Fujian.

In temples, the City God usually appears flanked by a large entourage of smaller statues, representing officials in his administration; there are military and civilian branches, the latter with six departments. The most famous officials, and prominent at festivals, are **General Xie** (*bāyé*) and **General Fan** (*qīyé*), charged with capturing evil spirits.

Wenchang Dijun

Known as the **god of literature** or culture, **Wenchang Dijun** (文昌帝君; *wénchāng dìjūn*) is portrayed today as a particularly honest court official; legend has it that the Jade Emperor made him head of all officials on earth, including all appointments through examinations. With the imperial system long gone, today he's popular with students (and their parents) preparing for school and university exams. Wenchang Dijun is one of **five culture gods** or *wŭ wénchāng*: *kuí xīngjūn*, *zhūyī*, *guāndì* and *lǚ dòngbīn*, one of the Eight Immortals.

Qingshui Zushi

A quasi-historical figure, popular in North Taiwan, **Qingshui Zushi** (清水祖師; *qīngshuǐ zŭshī*) is another deity that originated in Fujian. There are several legends concerning his life: some portray him as a Fujianese monk, while others claim he was Chen Zhao-ying, born in Kaifeng during the Song Dynasty (960–1128). Awarded a local government post in recognition of his wisdom and munificence, he later established a shrine at Qingshui rock near Anxi in Fujian where he spent his retirement – after his death people began to worship him as the "Divine Progenitor of Qingshui" and he became one of the guardian gods of the county ("Zushi" is an honorific title meaning "ancestor and teacher of the people"). His most famous temple is in Sanxia (see p.118), outside Taipei.

Baosheng Dadi

Baosheng Dadi (保生大帝; *bǎoshēng dàdì*) or the "Great Emperor who Preserves Life" is known as a god of medicine or healing, and is another deity based on a historical figure. Wu Tao was born in Tongan (in Fujian) in 979 AD, and led a selfless life helping and curing sick people. Villagers began to worship Wu after his death in 1037, claiming that this was very efficacious in times of epidemic, and he soon became part of a popular Fujianese cult that was brought to Taiwan in the seventeenth century – his formal title was awarded by an emperor in the Ming dynasty. Today there are over two hundred temples dedicated to him island-wide – Ciji Temple in Xuejia (see p.252) is the oldest.

Jade Emperor

The **Jade Emperor** (玉皇; *yùhuáng*), or "Heavenly Grandfather" (天公; *tiāngōng*), is the chief Taoist deity (though not the most revered), and the head of the celestial government that was thought to mirror that of imperial China. Traditionally, he could only be worshipped by the living emperor and was symbolized by a tablet rather than an image (as in Tainan, see p.243). In Taiwan today he's been absorbed into the pantheon of folk deities, with important temples in Daxi and Taichung. Often depicted sitting on a throne, his face obscured by strings of pearls hanging from his hat (a bit like Mazu), he usually holds a piece of jade in his hands as a symbol of authority.

Queen Mother of the West

The highest ranking female deity, the **Queen Mother of the West** (西王母; *xīwángmǔ*) is often portrayed as the **Jade Emperor's wife** and known by a confusing number of alternate names in Chinese; *Wangmu Niangniang* (王母娘娘; *wángmǔ niángniáng*), Golden Mother (金母; *jīnmǔ*) and *Laomu* (老母; *lǎomǔ*) among them. She's said to live in the Kunlun Mountains in China's far west, and guards the "Peaches of Immortality" which only ripen every 3600 years – eating at the banquet she holds in honour of this event confers immortality. She's regarded as a particularly liberated female figure in the male-dominated pantheon, and is subsequently popular with women; she's also a protector against epidemics and a symbol of longevity. Hualien is the centre of her cult in Taiwan (see p.294).

Birth Goddess

The **Birth Goddess** (注生娘娘; *zhùshēng niángniáng*) is a popular subsidiary deity in many temples, worshipped primarily by pregnant women, or those hoping to get pregnant. She's also thought to be able to determine the sex of a child and protect mothers during pregnancy and the birth itself, as well as being a guardian of children up to the age of 16. At many shrines she is flanked by the **Twelve Maternal Ancestors**, lesser deities that are thought to help the Birth Goddess deliver children, one for each month of the year. Legend suggests she's based on a historical figure from the Tang dynasty, but there's little evidence to back this up. In many respects she's similar to the deity **Lady Linshui** (臨水夫人; *línshuǐ fūrén*), also guardian of children and childbirth.

Matchmaker

The Old Man Under the Moon (月下老人; *yuèxià lǎorén*), better known as the **Matchmaker** (媒人; *méirén*), is the Chinese version of Cupid and one of the more fashionable of the minor deities in Taiwan today. Like a modern dating agency, he uses a list supplied by Lady Linshui to match ideal partners at birth, tying them together by an invisible red thread. Fate ought to bring these couples together later in life, but just to make sure, offerings are made to the Matchmaker (he's usually represented by an old man with a long white beard); single men and women buy "matrimonial thread" from the temple, keeping it close to them until their predetermined partner is found.

Dizang Wang

Dizang Wang (地藏王; *dìzàngwáng*), otherwise known as the Buddhist Bodhisattva Ksitigarbha, is misleadingly called the **King of Hell** in English. Though portrayed as a monk in Chinese tradition, legend has it that Dizang Wang was originally a girl, heartbroken at the death of her mother who had been disrespectful of Buddhist teachings and had gone to hell. Through intense prayer and meditation her daughter managed to assume enough merit to ensure her mother's release, but in the process glimpsed all the suffering in the underworld and vowed to empty hell before becoming a Buddha. Though from the Buddhist pantheon, Dizang Wang is now portrayed as a man and worshipped in many Taoist temples (see Chiayi, p.217).

Temples

Most folk or **Taoist temples** (*miào* or *gōng*) in Taiwan feature south Fujianese architecture dating from the Qing dynasty, which is when most of them were established. Such temples are always built according to the principles of fengshui, a geomantic practice concerned with the balancing of *qì*, or cosmic energy, in the natural world. Note that the temple establishment date rarely refers to the building you'll see today: early shrines were built solely from wood, and in addition to damage caused by Taiwan's harsh typhoon- and earthquake-prone environment, it's typical for temple followers to rebuild them every few generations. As a simple rule, the more paintings or visual decoration inside the temple, as opposed to calligraphy, the older it is; Qing-dynasty Taiwan was mostly illiterate. Note that in this guide, directions (right and left), are provided assuming the reader is facing the temple: in Chinese it's normal to describe the sides of the temple as if looking outwards, from the point of view of god or goddess inside.

Exterior

Taiwanese temples tend to have similar gable-and-hip-style **roof** structures, often with double eaves, and usually decorated with colourful dragons and *jiǎnnián* figures (literally "cut and stick"), made from pieces of coloured glass. Older temples usually have *koji* figures outside and inside the temple: these are hand-sculpted pottery figurines, usually making up vivid tableaux from Chinese legends – the craft is traditionally Chiayi-based (see p.217). **Stone lions** (*shīshī*) guard the temple entrance: the left is female, the right male, primarily decorative symbols of nobility and royalty. Always **enter** at the side entrance to the right of the main gate, and exit on the other side. The right side is more important in fengshui terms (being *yang*), and is usually adorned with paintings or images of **dragons** (*lóng*), while **tigers** (*hǔ*) appear on the opposite (*yin*) side. Dragons are immensely powerful creatures in Chinese mythology, emblems of the emperor and symbols of fertility.

Interior

Most temples are laid out as a series of halls and courtyards: the main gate, or **entrance hall**, leads to a **front hall** or a small courtyard facing the **main hall** in which the chief deity is enshrined. There is sometimes a **rear hall** beyond this, and often numerous shrines tucked away all over the site. Every temple has at least two **Door Gods** (*ménshén*) painted on the main doors, usually selected from a group of around twenty different historical figures. The most common are Tang-dynasty generals Qin Shu-bao and Yu-chi Jing-de, whose protection of the emperor against an evil dragon spirit was so effective even their painted images seemed to scare it away. The ceilings above the entrance hall are usually incredibly elaborate. Known as **algal wells**, they are supposed to trick demons into thinking the temple is underwater, and therefore impermeable to fire. Though they serve as enigmatic decoration today, the paintings inside temples once had a dual purpose – they can be hard to decipher without a guide, but the images are loaded with practical advice ranging from what to wear inside and how to pray, to when to have children.

The chief deity is worshipped at the main **altar**, usually represented by several statues (in some temples there are numerous images of the same god). Different **statues** can represent different incarnations of the god, and can have different uses: the oldest, most venerated effigy rarely leaves the protected casing of the altar, but others will be used for festivals and inspection tours (when the god "inspects" the local area as part of a boisterous parade). Towards the back or sides of the temple you're likely to see towers of tiny lights, known as *guāngmíng*: believers pay the temple to have their name inscribed under one of these lights for a set period, in the hope their generosity will be rewarded by the chief deity.

Traditional **Buddhist temples** (*sì*) are similarly designed, but usually feature statues of the **Four Heavenly Kings** (風調雨順; *fēngtiáo yǔshùn*) at the entrance, protecting the main images of Buddha inside and depictions of the eighteen *arhats* (*luóhàn*) along the walls: these are Buddhist saints respected for their great wisdom and power. Newer Buddhist temples in Taiwan tend to be less gaudy than Taoist or popular shrines, and often form a part of monasteries or nunneries. **Confucian Temples** (*kǒngmiào*) have a fairly standardized layout of halls and courtyards, the most notable difference being the absence of deities – Confucius is commemorated with a **tablet** (see p.78 for the best example of a Confucian temple).

Rituals

The most common form of *bàibài* (worship) in temples is to make a series of bows before the image of the deity, hands together before the chest – usually, **incense sticks** (*xiāng*) are held, the smoke symbolizing prayers floating to heaven. Believers ask for the deity's help for a specific problem, or just general good fortune, and it's also normal to give thanks to the deity for previous help. You'll often see people buying bundles of incense at the temple entrance, before making a circuit of all the main shrines and deities inside. Once *bàibài* is complete, incense is placed in the large **censer**, usually facing the main hall. In addition, the tables in front of the main altars are often covered in **offerings**, usually food (especially types of fruit, which often have symbolic meaning), incense and **joss** money or "gold paper" (*jīnzhǐ*), all intended to help convey the sincerity and loyalty of the worshipper. In order to pass into the spiritual realm, the money must be burnt – you'll see people throwing piles of it into the large chimney-like furnaces that stand in courtyards or outside the temple.

Various forms of **divination** or fortune-telling are practised in traditional Taiwanese folk religion, and you're likely to see several versions of this in temples. The most common is the use of *zhíjiǎo* (pronounced *buǎ-buēi* in Taiwanese) or **throwing blocks**, also known as "moon blocks" on account of their crescent shape. Worshippers use these to ascertain the gods' answer to a specific question. If one lands flat-side up and the other the opposite, this is taken to be positive – this needs to happen three times in a row for the believer to be sure the deity is in agreement. If any other combination comes up before the third positive, the believer must start all over again. If both blocks fall round side up, this is taken as a negative, while both landing round side down is the "laughing" response, meaning that you must rephrase the question.

Drawing lots (*chōuqiān*) is also popular. These are the thin bamboo strips lodged into a cylindrical container, each marked with a number. This corresponds to a piece of paper (usually contained in numbered drawers nearby) that contains an obscure saying or poem, a piece of ancient wisdom that usually requires an expert to interpret. Temples are also the best place to see **spirit mediums** or *jītóng* (*dáng-gī* in Taiwanese), men who become possessed by a deity while in a trance (they usually specialize in just one), and thus can deliver far more effective oracles or responses to petitioners' queries. These men usually work in temples, but are not attached to them, being independent and free to work wherever they choose.

Arts and culture

Taiwanese **culture** is rooted in millennia of Chinese tradition, art and philosophy, but much of what is considered "Taiwanese" today emerged relatively recently, during the Japanese occupation. The Taiwanese contemporary arts scene is a dynamic blend of Western, Japanese, indigenous, Fujianese and northern Chinese influences, much of it tied to the search for a separate identity, at its most intense since the 1980s.

Visual arts

Generally recognized as the "father of modern Taiwanese art", **Kinichiro Ishikawa** (1871–1945) was one of many Japanese painters that came to Taiwan to paint and teach. In the 1920s and 30s, artists such as **Chen Cheng-po** (1895–1947) and **Yang San-lang** (1907–95), who had been pupils of Ishikawa and studied European oil painting in Japan, particularly French Impressionism, created the first **Nativist** movement, characterized by the depiction of typically Taiwanese images and scenes. Chen grew up in Chiayi, and his work captures the essence of rural south Taiwan and its languid street life: the oil painting *Streets of Chiayi* (1926) was the first by a Taiwanese painter to be exhibited at the Imperial Art Expo in Japan. Yang's contrast of light and colour is heavily reminiscent of Monet, his natural landscapes and scenes containing a nostalgic, plaintive quality.

After World War II, there was renewed interest in traditional Chinese painting, but by the 1960s disillusionment with conservative styles had precipitated a move towards abstract Western art; **Lee Chun-shan** (1911–84) and **Liu Kuo-sung** (b.1932) were the most important and innovative painters of the period. Lee was an avant-garde pioneer, maintaining a reclusive existence in Changhua.

In the 1970s, **Nativism** (also known this time as the "Native Soil Movement") was revived, partly as a rejection of the Western-inspired art of the 1960s. **Hung Tung** (1920–87) became one its most celebrated exponents, noted for his use of vivid colours and imaginative interpretation of Buddhist themes, Chinese myth and traditional historical drama. The movement also incorporated sculptors such as **Ju Ming** (see p.129) and his teacher **Yu Yu Yang**, who had studied in Japan.

The 1980s was a transitional period in art terms, mirroring the political upheavals that led to the ending of martial law in 1987. The most significant figures were **Yang Mao-lin** and **Wu Tien-chang**, both of whom dealt with social and political issues in their work. Wu became famous for his *Portraits of the Emperors* (completed in 1990), large caricatures of Mao Zedong, Deng Xiaoping, Chiang Kai-shek and Chiang Ching-kuo, but turned to photography in the 1990s and now uses digital imagery to blend flat and 3D graphics. Yang's *Made in Taiwan* series is a more subtle approach to Taiwanese history, blending a diversity of images such as aboriginal peoples, references to the Dutch period and domestic fruits and vegetables.

In the 1990s, influenced by Postmodernism and the growth in art galleries and museums, art in Taiwan blossomed in several different directions: the Nativist movement continued to evolve, and multimedia, particularly photography, video and installation art became more mainstream. **Lee Ming-sheng** is one of the most influential proponents of a mixed media approach, while **Chen Chieh-jen's** work has been exhibited all over the world, best known for his shocking photographic images such as *A Way Going to an Insane City* (1999).

Taiwan also has a strong tradition of **art photography**: Chang Tsai, Deng Nan-guang and Lee Ming-diao are known as the "Three Swordsmen of Taiwanese Photography", their work documenting the island's development in the postwar period – Tsai is particularly lauded for his portraits of folk festivals and aboriginal people.

Music

Traditional Chinese music was brought to Taiwan with immigrants from the mainland, most audibly in the form of **folk music** played at celebrations, festivals and temples, but in recent years there has been a revival of the more complex traditions of Chinese **classical music**, particularly *nánguǎn*. **Contemporary** pop, rock and hip-hop are also important elements of modern Taiwanese identity.

Traditional music

Traditional Chinese music comes in many different styles, but in Taiwan it's usual to divide the whole field into two groups: *běiguǎn* ("northern music"), a fast-tempo music that commonly accompanies operas and traditional puppet shows, and *nánguǎn*, which originated in Fujian and has a more delicate and soothing sound, traditionally far more popular in Taiwan. The **Han–Tang Yuefu Music Ensemble** (漢唐樂府; *hàntáng yuèfǔ*; ℡02/2725-2008, Ⓦ www.hantang .com.tw) is a Taiwanese cultural icon, founded in 1983 by famous performer Chen Mei-o to preserve *nánguǎn*.

In addition, there are several professional Chinese music orchestras in Taiwan: the **Kaohsiung City Chinese Orchestra** (高雄市國樂團; *gāoxióngshì guóyuètuán*); the **National Chinese Orchestra** (國家國樂團; *guójiā guóyuètuán*), based at the National Theater in Taipei; Ⓦ 192.192.14.59), and the **Taipei Chinese Orchestra** (臺北市立國樂團; *táiběi shìlì guóyuètuán*; Ⓦ english.tco.taipei.gov.tw), based at Zhongshan Hall in Taipei.

Contemporary music

Taiwan is home to some of the biggest **Mandopop** (Mandarin Chinese pop music) stars in the world. The undisputed queen of Chinese pop was (and some would say still is), **Teresa Teng** (*dèng lìjūn*) whose tragic early death in 1995 was mourned throughout Asia. Often compared to Karen Carpenter, she influenced a generation

---

U-Theatre

Laoquan Mountain, shrouded in lush vegetation south of Taipei, is the home of esoteric drum and performance troupe **U-Theatre** (優人神鼓; *yōurén shéngǔ*; ℡02/2938-8188), one of Taiwan's most famous and reclusive artistic groups. Not a conventional theatre troupe, the group is lauded internationally for its traditional **drumming** performances, often combined with powerful movement and dance, as well as traditional gongs and singing. Established in 1988 by Taiwan's most famous actress at the time, **Liu Ruo-yu**, U-Theatre comprises a group of ascetic performers that take their training very seriously. They spend up to two years creating new performances, often with a premiere at their outdoor mountain theatre, where the performers meet each day to practise martial arts, drumming and meditation. A U-Theatre production can be an incredibly powerful, hypnotic experience.

of singers, and dominated pop music in the region throughout the 1970s and 1980s. **Jay Chou** has been the undisputed king of Taiwan and Chinese pop since 2001 (even gracing the cover of *Time* magazine), while Chang Hui-mei, aka **A-Mei**, remains one of Asia's favourite female singers. There's plenty of other stars however, as the island has a seemingly endless production line of singers/models/ actresses, epitomized by cutesy **Jolin Tsai**, the "little queen of pop".

Though pop certainly dominates, Taiwan also has a vibrant **rock** scene and a growing **hip-hop** culture. A small but well-attended network of live venues supports an eclectic **indie rock** and **alternative music** scene, with Mayday, 1976, Sodagreen and Tizzy Bac leading players. **Rock festivals** have become an important part of the scene in recent years: the largest are Ho Hai Yan in Fulong (see p.143), Spring Scream in Kenting (see p.284), and the Formoz Festival in Taipei. The **Golden Melody Awards** are Taiwan's version of the Grammies, held every June at the Taipei Arena.

Dance

Taiwan's **modern dance** groups are world class, noted for their creative fusion of Western and Chinese traditions. **Liu Feng-shueh** is credited with bringing modern dance to Taiwan in the 1960s, creating the **Neoclassic Dance Company** (新古典 舞團; *xīngǔdiǎn wǔtuán*; Ⓦ www.neo.org.tw) in 1976, and still choreographing shows today. The best-known group internationally is **Cloud Gate Dance Theatre** (雲門舞集; *yúnmén wǔjí*; ☎ 02/2712-2102, Ⓦ www.cloudgate.org .tw), another Taiwanese cultural treasure. Established in 1973 by **Lin Hwai-min**, who studied in New York under Martha Graham, one of America's most famous dancers, the troupe fuses classical Asian traditions such as t'ai chi with modern dance – the result is hauntingly beautiful. One of the best known of the newer companies is the **Taipei Dance Circle** (光環舞集舞蹈團; *guānghuán wǔjí wǔdàotuán*; ☎ 02/8972-0061, Ⓦ www.taipei-dance-circle.com.tw), established in 1984 by Liu Shao-lu (a Cloud Gate founder) and Yang Wan-rung.

Opera

Traditional Chinese opera is thriving in Taiwan. The most famous form is **Beijing Opera** (performed in Mandarin), though **Taiwanese Opera** (performed in Taiwanese) is just as popular. **Hakka Opera**, which is based on traditional tea-farming folk songs and originally developed in China's Jiangxi province, has made a comeback in Taiwan in recent years, while the more obscure **Kun Opera** (from Jiangsu province), best known for the mammoth opera *Peony Pavilion*, and **Beiguan Opera** styles are also performed on the island.

Opera is actually a mix of acrobatics, music, singing, stylized movements and dialogue, still performed on outdoor stages at festivals or in front of temples, as well as in formal indoor theatres. In either case you won't need to understand Chinese to appreciate what's going on, since most operas are visually stunning, elaborately costumed affairs.

Opera basics

The following primarily applies to Beijing Opera, though other styles more or less follow the same principles. Traditionally, operas have four types of lead characters. The *shēng* (male lead), who can be old, young or a soldier; the *dàn* (female); the *jìng*, usually a male character with a painted face (see below); and the *chǒu* (male clown). The **painted face of** the *jìng* characters each has a meaning: red symbolizes loyalty; black signifies bravery or determination; white means treacherous or sly; and blue or green signifies a violent temper. **Clothing** is similarly colour-coded: yellow robes are worn by the imperial family, red by high officials, black by the short-tempered, brown by the elderly and green by the virtuous.

Sets are very basic: the same table and chairs are normally used throughout, operas relying on the ability of the actors and a strong imagination. **Props** are also used simply and symbolically (a single oar can represent a boat). Live **music** is an important part of any production, the action complemented by traditional instruments such as the *sānxián*, a three-stringed lute, the *pípá*, a four-stringed lute, the *dòngxiāo*, a flute, and the *suǒnà*, a trumpet-shaped bamboo horn.

Opera companies

The **National Guoguang Opera Company** (國光劇團; *guóguāng jùtuán*; ☏ 02/2938-3567, ⊛ www.kk.gov.tw) is the foremost exponent of Beijing Opera in Taiwan and regularly performs in Taipei, though it often tours smaller villages or suburbs during festivals and holidays. Tainan-based **Ming Hwa Yuan Arts & Cultural Group** (明華園戲劇總團; *mínghuáyuán xìjù zǒngtuán*; ☏ 02/2772-9398, ⊛ www.twopera.com) was established in 1929 by opera star Chen Ming-chi, and is now the most respected name in Taiwanese Opera, still run by the Chen family. The **Holo Taiwanese Opera Troupe** (河洛歌仔戲團; *héluò gēzǎixìtuán*; ☏ 02/2581-3029) is primarily known in Taiwan for its acclaimed work on television, but it also performs on stage all over the world. The **Rom-shing Hakka Teapicker Opera Troupe** (榮興客家採茶劇團, *róngxīng kèjiā cǎichá jùtuán*; ☏ 037/725-099) is one of the best Hakka Opera companies, usually performing outdoors in small venues, festivals and temples across the island.

Film

Taiwan has a strong tradition of **film-making** dating back to the Japanese occupation, but these days the local movie industry knocks out little more than a dozen popular and high-quality art-house films per year; revenues are minuscule (just two percent of the domestic box office) compared to output from nearby Hong Kong, and light years away from the far more popular Hollywood-produced blockbusters. Taiwanese movie stars often double as pop singers, frequently working on both sides of the Taiwan Strait. Their profile beyond the Chinese-speaking world is limited, though respected actress **Sylvia Chang** has appeared in films such as *Red Violin* and **Shu Qi** appeared in Hollywood action flick *The Transporter* in 2002 and *New York, I Love You* in 2009. Taiwanese **directors** are generally better known internationally, **Ang Lee** being the most famous.

The **Golden Horse Film Awards**, held annually in November or December, is Taiwan's version of the Oscars, honouring film throughout the Chinese-speaking world, but often dominated by Hong Kong movies and actors.

The New Taiwanese Cinema

Between the 1950s and early 1980s, Taiwan's domestic film industry was dominated by romantic melodramas and martial arts epics. In 1982 the movie *In Our Time* broke with tradition by depicting gritty social change in Taiwan over three generations, and is generally regarded as the birth of the **New Wave Movement**. **Hou Hsiao-hsien** and **Edward Yang** (both born in mainland China) are the best known of what is sometimes called the first generation of Taiwanese directors. Hou was one of three directors of the ground-breaking *Sandwich Man* (1983), a dramatization of three short stories written by Huang Chun-ming, examining the disintegration of Taiwanese rural life in the 1950s and 60s; this theme, with particular focus on adolescent male characters, dominated Hou's subsequent movies. His most famous film is *City of Sadness* (1989), which was the first to allude to the 2-28 Incident (see p.389). *The Puppet Master* (1993), which followed the life of Li Tien-lu, a master puppeteer, and *Café Lumiere* (2003), a tribute to Japanese film-maker Ozu Yasujiro, were both well received by critics. *Three Times* (2005), which blends three stories set in three different time periods and sees a return to familiar Hou themes, was nominated for the Palme d'Or at Cannes. His last movie was also a critical success, a French production called *The Flight of the Red Balloon* starring Juliette Binoche, released in 2007.

In contrast, Yang tends to focus on female characters, the newly emerging middle class and urban society. Yang is best known for *Taipei Story* (1985) and especially *Yi Yi* (2000), a three-hour epic depicting a troubled year in the life of a Taipei family that won him the best director award at Cannes.

The Second New Wave

The most famous of the "**second generation**" of New Taiwanese cinema directors is undoubtedly **Ang Lee**, Oscar-winning director of *Crouching Tiger, Hidden Dragon* (2000) and *Brokeback Mountain* (2005). In 2007 *Lust, Caution* earned him a second Golden Lion (*Brokeback Mountain* was his first). He's respected locally for his immensely entertaining *Wedding Banquet* (1993), which highlighted the dilemmas facing gay Chinese men, and *Eat Drink Man Woman* (1994) set in contemporary Taipei. His latest project is a film version of the Booker Prize-winning novel *Life of Pi* (2012).

Often considered part of the New Taiwanese film movement, despite being born and raised in Kuching, Malaysia, **Tsai Ming-liang** settled in Taipei in 1977 and has become one of the country's most acclaimed directors. A successful TV film-maker, Tsai made his jump to the big screen in 1992 with *Rebels of the Neon God*, the story of a high-school dropout who becomes involved with organized crime. Tsai's films are highly stylized and thought-provoking, though the lack of dialogue, confusing plots and focus on dysfunctional families, inebriation and delinquency make them hard to watch and strictly art-house material. *Vive l'Amour* (1994) won the Golden Lion, while *Goodbye, Dragon Inn* (2003) and the sexually explicit *Wayward Cloud* (2005) were received less kindly by critics. His French film, *Face* (2009), was nominated for the Palme d'Or at Cannes Film Festival.

Chiayi-born **Sylvia Chang** is sometimes regarded as part of this group (though she's also been acting for over thirty years), and is one of Taiwan's few female Chinese directors. Her *20, 30, 40* (2004) is an entertaining portrayal of the lives of three women in modern Taipei, and she's also the star of the cross-cultural comedy *American Fusion* (2005).

The Seventh Graders

The New Wave directors, while critically acclaimed overseas, were gradually seen as elitist and obscure in Taiwan, turning audiences away from even mainstream domestic movies. The hopes of Taiwan's film industry now rest with the island's younger directors. Referred to as the "**seventh-grade generation**" (a reference to the 1980s, the seventh decade after the 1911 Revolution), many were still university students when they started making movies. **Chen Yin-jung** scored a big hit in 2004 with *Formula 17*, a frank and humorous exploration of gay life in Taipei, and in 2009 contributed one of eight segments for *Taipei24H*. **Leon Dai**'s *Twenty-Something Taipei* (2002) also focused on youth, sex and modern Taipei, with the director going on to sweep the 2009 Golden Horse Awards for his *No Puedo Vivir Sin Ti* ("*Cannot Live Without You*"). **Alex Yang** is another talented member of the group, his *Taipei 21* (2003) and 2005 romantic campus comedy *My Fair Laddy* receiving much international acclaim despite being shot on a shoestring and having limited release domestically.

Books

aiwan has a rich literary tradition that dates back over a century, and a dynamic contemporary scene which is a fusion of all the island's multicultural elements. The problem is that very little of this is translated into English, in part a reflection of Taiwan's low profile on the international stage. Seminal figures such as **Lai He** (regarded as the father of Taiwanese literature), and Hakka pioneer **Chung Li-ho**, as well as modern writers such as **Li Ang** (one of Taiwan's top female authors), are rarely translated.

In other areas, apart from a fairly dry ensemble of books analysing Taiwan's economic success, there's a dearth of material on the island, though you'll find plenty on Chinese culture in general. Expats have started writing guides to fill the gaps, usually published by local houses, and those interested in **Buddhism** will find a voluminous amount of English-language material knocked out by the island's premier monasteries. Books marked with 🏃 are particularly recommended.

Fiction

🏃 **Chang Ta-chun** *Wild Kids*. Two novellas (in one book) from the 1990s popular literature icon, exposing the frustrations of Taiwanese youth and the darker side of Taipei in the 1980s. Chang's unpretentious style, with dashes of black humour, works well in translation.

Chu T'ien-wen *Notes of a Desolate Man*. A thoughtful study of a Taiwanese gay man reflecting on his life and loves as his friend lies dying of AIDS in the 1990s, by turns erotic, morose and humorous. Chu is one of Taiwan's best contemporary female writers.

Hsiao Li-hung *A Thousand Moons on a Thousand Rivers*. A captivating tale of love, betrayal and complex family relationships in a traditional south Taiwan town in the 1970s, from one of Taiwan's pre-eminent female writers.

Huang Chun-ming *The Taste of Apples*. Collection of nine compelling short stories, portraying the poverty and disintegration of traditional Taiwanese rural life in the face of rampant modernization. Penned by the doyen of the Nativist movement in the 1970s.

Indigenous Writers of Taiwan *An Anthology of Stories, Essays and Poems*. The first collection of indigenous literature in English, with contributions from writers such Topas Tamapima (*The Last Hunter*), Sakinu (*Wind Walker*) and Moaneng (*Five Poems*), providing an enlightening perspective on the state of aboriginal culture in modern Taiwan.

Li Ang *The Butcher's Wife and Other Stories*. This short novel from Taiwan's best-known female writer shocked the island in 1983 with its powerful critique of traditional Chinese society and fearless portrayal of superstition, violence and abuse of women.

Li Qiao *Wintry Night*. Vivid historical saga, following the lives of the Peng family from the 1890s to the end of World War II, Hakka settlers battling the elements, corrupt officials, aboriginal tribes and the Japanese.

Pai Hsien-yung *Crystal Boys* and *Taipei People*. *Crystal Boys* is still regarded as a ground-breaking classic, a tragic love story and evocative depiction of Taiwan's gay community in the repressive 1960s and 1970s. *Taipei People* is a fascinating collection of short stories, examining life in the post-1949 capital.

Wang Chen-ho *Rose, Rose I Love You.* One of Taiwan's most outrageous comic novels, this irreverent satire follows the citizens of Hualien as they prepare for a boatload of US soldiers on R&R. The result is hilarious, though Wang's subtle word plays are difficult to appreciate in translation.

🏃 **Wang Wen-hsing** *Family Catastrophe.* The publication of this Modernist classic caused a sensation in 1972, with its subtle but powerful depiction of the unravelling of a traditional Chinese family.

Wu Zhuoliu *Asia's Orphan.* Wu was one of Taiwan's leading literary figures in the 1940s and 1950s; this masterpiece spans the entire period of Japanese occupation, an allegory of colonial rule and Taiwan's disillusion with Chinese nationalism.

History and politics

Macabe Keliher *Out of China* and *Small Sea Travel Diaries.* This Taipei-based writer has knocked out a decent translation of Chinese official Yu Yonghe's diary of his trip to Taiwan in 1697, a fascinating account of the island at the time. *Out of China* is an easy-to-read companion volume, enhancing the journal with history, anecdote and useful background.

George Mackay *From Far Formosa.* Part autobiography, part history of the island, Mackay's original work of 1896 has been republished in Taipei. The Canadian missionary's observations are a fascinating insight into 1880s Taiwan, as well as the often chauvinistic attitudes dominant in the West at that time.

Jonathan Manthorpe *Forbidden Nation: A History of Taiwan.* A well-written and comprehensive new history of the island.

🏃 **Denny Roy** *Taiwan A Political History.* Roy's crisp history of Taiwan is a good introduction, though its primary focus is political events post-1949.

Jay Taylor *The Generalissimo's Son: Chiang Ching-kuo and the Revolutions in China and Taiwan.* Long-overdue study of Chiang Kai-shek's son and successor, one of Taiwan's most complex figures who oversaw its transition from martial law to nascent democracy.

Shih-shan Henry Tsai *Lee Teng-hui and Taiwan's Quest for Identity.* Biography of former President Lee Teng-hui, the primary figure in the island's political transformation over the past two decades.

Religion

🏃 **Mark Caltonhill** *Private Prayers and Public Parades.* Accessible introduction to Taiwan's eclectic religious practices, especially focusing on its Taoist and folk traditions and customs. The author is an English long-time resident of Taiwan.

Dharma Master Cheng Yen *Still Thoughts I & II.* These books contain a series of thought-provoking quotations derived from the numerous speeches and talks of Taiwan's senior female Buddhist master, the founder of the Tzu Chi Foundation.

Confucius *The Analects.* Modern translation of this classic collection of Confucius's sayings, compiled by his pupils after his death in 479 BC and still one of the most important texts in Chinese philosophy.

Venerable Master Hsing Yun *Humanistic Buddhism: A Blueprint for Life*. The founder of Foguangshan Monastery is one of Taiwan's most prolific Buddhist writers and teachers of Chan Buddhism. This book outlines the principles of Humanistic Buddhism and how it can be applied to daily life.

Lao Zi *Tao Te Ching*. The collection of laconic, esoteric sayings that provides the philosophical basis for Taoism, attributed to the sixth-century BC Chinese mystic.

Chan Master Sheng Yen *Zen Wisdom* and *Hoofprint of the Ox*. The founder of Dharma Drum Mountain monastery has written numerous books on Chan (or Zen) Buddhism and these two works are the best introductions. *Zen Wisdom* is structured as a series of questions and answers, while *Hoofprint* follows a more traditional essay-type structure.

Miscellaneous

Menno Goedhart *The Real Taiwan and the Dutch*. Part history, part travel guide and written by the long-time Dutch envoy to Taiwan (who plans to settle here after he retires), this book provides a readable and fascinating insight into areas of the island rarely visited by foreigners, and especially its aboriginal and Dutch heritage.

Richard Saunders *Taipei Day Trips 1 and 2*. Written by another long-term English expat, these two books are handy for anyone contemplating an extended stay in the Taipei area, especially for those interested in hiking. Usually on sale in local bookshops for NT$400, along with his comprehensive guide to Yangmingshan (NT$500).

Yeh Yueh-yu and Darrell Davis *Taiwan Film Directors: A Treasure Island*. Insightful study of Taiwan's New Cinema via four of its most famous directors: Hou Hsiao-hsien, Ang Lee, Edward Yang and Tsai Ming-liang.

Language

Language

Language

The official language of Taiwan is the same as China, **Mandarin Chinese**, commonly referred to as *guóyǔ* ("national language") on the island and *pǔtōnghuà* ("common speech") across the Taiwan Strait. Though there are some differences in word use, pronunciation and slang, Chinese spoken on the mainland is indistinguishable from that used in Taiwan. The major divergence comes with **written Chinese**: Taiwan (like Hong Kong) uses **traditional characters**, while China follows the simplified system devised in the 1950s.

Mandarin Chinese is a relative newcomer to the island however: before 1945 very few people ever spoke the language in Taiwan. Although everyone learns Mandarin these days, **Taiwanese** (*táiyǔ*) was once the dominant tongue, and is still widely spoken as a first language. In much of south Taiwan you'll hear nothing else, though even here everyone but the very elderly will be able to understand Mandarin (though they'll try, optimistically, to converse with you in Taiwanese if they can). Taiwanese is a form of **Fujianese** (*mǐnnán yǔ*), which originated in southern Fujian province in China and is similar to the Hokkien spoken by other Fujianese communities in southeast Asia. Part of the same Sino-Tibetan family and usually described as a dialect of Chinese on the mainland, Taiwanese is in fact a totally different language, with its own dialects, seven tones, unique vocabulary and distinct philology. In the nineteenth century, missionaries developed a written form of Taiwanese known as *péh-ōe-jī*, using Roman letters, but otherwise Taiwanese can be written with the same Chinese characters as Mandarin. **Hakka** (*kèjiāhuà*) is still spoken in Taiwan (see p.154), though along with numerous **aboriginal languages** on the island, it faces an uphill struggle for survival. Given Taiwan's history and current economic and cultural ties with the country, it's no surprise many Taiwanese can also speak **Japanese** quite well. The following section focuses exclusively on **Mandarin Chinese**.

Pronunciation and pinyin

The main distinguishing characteristic of Chinese languages is that they are **tonal**: each word must be pronounced not only with the right sound, but also the right tone. Mandarin has four tones, and in order to be understood it's vital to get these as accurate as possible. The **pinyin system**, a way of writing Chinese using the Roman alphabet, is the best way to learn the correct tones, represented by **accents** above each syllable.

In China, where *pīnyīn* is taught in schools, the system is widely used, but most Taiwanese have never seen or used pinyin. Schools on the island still use *zhùyīn* or **bopomofo** to teach children pronunciation, a system of symbols that looks much the same as characters. As a result, Chinese characters on street signs, buildings or in restaurants are rarely translated. Where *pīnyīn* is used, Taiwan's notorious penchant for using a hodgepodge of different systems often adds to the confusion. Mainland China uses *hànyǔ pīnyīn*, favoured throughout most of the world by Chinese speakers and students. Since the 2008 election, this system is finally being introduced throughout Taiwan (replacing *tōngyòng pīnyīn*, created in Taiwan in 1998 and favoured by the former DPP government), though it's still only used extensively in Taipei, Taichung and Hsinchu. These two systems have largely replaced nineteenth-century **Wade Giles** and **MPS2** (another Taiwanese script used in the 1980s), though you might still see vestiges of these in places – the names of Taiwan's major cities retain their basic Wade-Giles forms (for example "Kaohsiung" would be "*Gāoxióng*" in *hànyǔ pīnyīn*). The Chinese terms in this section have been given in both characters and *hànyǔ pīnyīn*, to reflect the predominant global trend. In the main body text the approach has been to use the system most visible in each locale: *hànyǔ* is now considered the default, in line with government policy.

The tones

First or "High" tone (usually described as flat or level) is represented by a (¯) added to the vowel: *ā ē ī ō ū ǖ*

Second or rising tone (as when expressing surprise) is represented by an acute accent (´): *á é í ó ú ǘ*

Third or "falling-rising" tone is represented by (ˇ): *ǎ ě ǐ ǒ ǔ ǚ*

Fourth or falling tone is represented by a grave accent (`): *à è ì ò ù ǜ*.

The so-called "fifth tone" or **neutral tone** is just represented by a normal vowel without any accent mark. In practice however, you'll need to take some lessons (or at least listen to a native speaker) if you're serious about coming to grips with spoken Chinese.

Useful words and expressions

Note that all the words below are Mandarin Chinese terms, expressed in Chinese characters, *hànyǔ pīnyīn* and the English equivalent.

Basics

Hello	你好	*nǐ hǎo*
Good morning	早!	*zǎo!*
Thank you	謝謝	*xiè xiè*
You're welcome	不客氣	*búkèqì*
Sorry	對不起	*duìbúqǐ*
No problem	沒關係	*méi guānxì*
Goodbye	再見	*zài jiàn*
I	我	*wǒ*
You	你	*nǐ*
He	他	*tā*
She	她	*tā*
We	我們	*wǒmén*
You (plural)	你們	*nǐmén*
They	他們	*tāmén*
Mr	先生	*xiānshēng*
Mrs	太太	*tàitài*
Miss	小姐	*xiǎo jiě*

| Toilet (men) | 男廁所 | *nán cèsuǒ* |
| Toilet (women) | 女廁所 | *nǚ cèsuǒ* |

Useful phrases

I want	我要	*wǒ yào*
I don't want	我不要	*wǒ bú yào*
Have	有	*yǒu*
Have not	沒有	*méiyǒu*
I don't speak Chinese	我不會説中文	*wǒ bú huì shuō zhōngwén*
Can you speak English?	你會説英語嗎?	*nǐ huì shuō yīngyǔ mā?*
Please speak slowly	請慢慢説	*qǐng màn màn shuō*
I understand	我聽得懂	*wǒ tīngdedǒng*
I don't understand	我聽不懂	*wǒ tīngbùdǒng*
What does this mean?	這是甚麼意思?	*zhè shì shènme yìsī?*
What's your name?	你叫什麼名字?	*nǐ jiào shénme míngzì?*
My name is…	我的名字是	*wǒ de míngzì shì...*

Countries

What country are you from?	你是哪國家的人?	*nǐ shì nǎ guójiā de rén?*
Australia	澳洲	*àozhōu*
Canada	加拿大	*jiānádà*
China	中國	*zhōngguó*
England	英國	*yīngguó*
Hong Kong	香港	*xiānggǎng*
Ireland	愛爾蘭	*àiěrlán*
Japan	日本	*rì běn*
Macau	澳門	*àomén*
Malaysia	馬來西亞	*mǎlái xīyǎ*
New Zealand	紐西蘭	*niüxīlán*
Scotland	蘇格蘭	*sūgélán*
Singapore	新加坡	*xīnjiāpō*
South Africa	南非	*nánfēi*
Taiwan	台灣	*táiwān*
United States	美國	*měiguó*
Wales	威爾士	*wēiěrshì*

Numbers

Zero	零	*líng*
One	一	*yī*
Two	二/兩	*èr/liǎng*
Three	三	*sān*
Four	四	*sì*
Five	五	*wǔ*
Six	六	*liù*
Seven	七	*qī*
Eight	八	*bā*

Nine	九	jiǔ
Ten	十	shí
Eleven	十一	shíyī
Twelve	十二	shíèr
Twenty	二十	èrshí
Twenty-one	二十一	èrshíyī
One hundred	一百	yībǎi
Two hundred	二百	èrbǎi
One thousand	一千	yīqiān
Ten thousand	一萬	yīwàn
One hundred thousand	十萬	shíwàn
One million	一百萬	yībǎiwàn
One hundred million	一億	yīyì
One billion	十億	shíyì

Time

Now	現在	xiànzài
Today	今天	jīntiān
Morning	早上	zǎoshàng
Afternoon	下午	xiàwǔ
Evening	晚上	wǎnshàng
Tomorrow	明天	míngtiān
Yesterday	昨天	zuótiān
Week/month/year	星期/月/年	xīngqī/yuè/nián
Monday	星期一	xīngqī yī
Tuesday	星期二	xīngqī èr
Wednesday	星期三	xīngqī sān
Thursday	星期四	xīngqī sì
Friday	星期五	xīngqī wǔ
Saturday	星期六	xīngqī liù
Sunday	星期天	xīngqī tiān
What's the time?	幾點了?	jǐ diǎn le?
6 o'clock	六點	liù diǎn
6.20	六點二十	liù diǎn èrshí
6.30	六點半	liù diǎn bàn

Getting around

Map	地圖	dìtú
I want to go to…	我要去…	wǒ yào qù…
When does it leave?	幾點開車?	jǐ diǎn kāi chē?
When does it arrive?	幾點到?	jǐ diǎn dào?
How long does the journey take?	旅途需要多久?	lǚ tú xū yào duō jiǔ?
Airport	飛機場	fēijīchǎng
Dock/pier	碼頭	mǎtóu
Taxi	計程車	jì chéng chē

Directions

Where is…?	…在那裡?	…zài nǎ lǐ?
Go straight on	直走	zhí zǒu
Turn right	轉右	zhuǎn yòu
Turn left	轉左	zhuǎn zuǒ
North	北	běi
South	南	nán
East	東	dōng
West	西	xī
Road	路	lù
Street	街	jiē
Section	段	dùan
Number 12	十二號	shí èr hào
Lane	巷	xiàng
Alley	弄	nòng

By train

Train	火車	huǒchē
Train station	火車站	huǒchē zhàn
Left luggage office	寄存處	jìcúnchù
Ticket office	售票處	shòupiàochù
Ticket	票	piào
Taiwan High Speed Rail	台灣高速鐵路	táiwān gāosù tiělù
Platform	站台	zhàntái
Underground/subway	捷運	jiéyùn

By bus

Bus	公車	gōngchē
Bus station	公車站	gōngchē zhàn
Regional bus station	客運站	kèyùn zhàn
When is the next bus?	下一班車幾點開?	xià yí bān chē jǐ diǎn kāi?
Does this bus go to…?	這輛車到…嗎?	zhè liàng chē dào…ma?
Please tell me where to get off	請告訴我在哪裡下車	qǐng gàosù wǒ zài nǎlǐ xià chē

By car/scooter

Car	汽車	qìchē
Bicycle	腳踏車	jiǎotàchē
Motor scooter	摩托車	mótuōchē
I want to rent…	我想租	wǒ xiǎngzū
How much is it per hour/day?	一小時/一天 多少錢?	yí xiǎo shí/yí tiān, duō shǎo qián?

Places

Beach	海濱	hǎibīn
Bookshop	書店	shūdiàn
Buddhist temple	寺	sì

Cave	洞	*dòng*
Church	教堂	*jiāotáng*
City	市	*shì*
Farm	農場	*nóngchǎng*
Harbour/port	港	*gǎng*
Hot spring	溫泉	*wēnquán*
Island	島	*dǎo*
Lake	湖	*hú*
Laundry	洗衣店	*xǐyīdiàn*
Library	圖書館	*túshūguǎn*
Lighthouse	燈塔	*dēngtǎ*
Market	市場	*shìchǎng*
Mountain	山	*shān*
Museum	博物館	*bówùguǎn*
Park	公園	*gōngyuán*
River	河	*hé*
Stadium	體育場	*tǐyùchǎng*
Temple	廟	*miào*
Waterfall	瀑布	*pùbù*

Accommodation

Hotel	飯店/旅館	*fàndiàn/ lǚguǎn*
Homestay	民宿	*mínsù*
How much for a room?	一晚多少?	*yī wǎn duō shǎo?*
Can I have a look at the room?	能不能看一下?	*néng bù néng kàn yí xià?*
Single room	單人房	*dānrénfáng*
Twin room	雙人房	*shuāngrénfáng*
Passport	護照	*hùzhào*
Key	鑰匙	*yàochí*

Shopping and money

How much is it?	多少錢?	*duōshǎo qián?*
It's too expensive	太貴了	*tài guì le*
Do you accept credit cards?	可不可以用信用卡?	*kěbúkěyǐ yòngxìnyòngkǎ*
NT$1	一塊	*yí kuài*
US$1	一塊美金	*yí kuài měijīn*
£1	一個英磅	*yí gè yīngbàng*
Change money	換錢	*huàn qián*
Chinatrust Commercial Bank	中國信託銀行	*zhōngguó xìntuō yín háng*
Bank	銀行	*yínháng*
ATM	提款機	*tíkuǎnjī*

Communications

| Post office | 郵局 | *yóujú* |
| Envelope | 信封 | *xìnfēng* |

Stamp	郵票	*yóupiào*
Airmail	航空信	*hángkōng xìn*
Telephone	電話	*diànhuà*
Reverse charges/collect call	對方付錢電話	*duìfāngfùqián diànhuà*
Fax	傳真	*chuánzhēn*
Telephone card	電話卡	*diànhuàkǎ*
Internet café	網吧	*wǎngbā*

Health

Hospital	醫院	*yīyuàn*
Pharmacy	藥店	*yàodiàn*
Medicine	藥	*yào*
Chinese Medicine	中藥	*zhōng yào*
Diarrhoea	腹瀉	*fùxiè*
Vomit	嘔吐	*ǒutù*
Fever	發燒	*fāshāo*
I'm ill	我生病了	*wǒ shēngbìng le*
I've got flu	我感冒了	*wǒ gǎnmào le*
I'm (not) allergic to…	我(不)對過敏…	*wǒ (bù) duì… guòmǐn*
Antibiotics	抗生素	*kàngshēngsù*
Condom	避孕套	*bìyùntào*
Mosquito coil	蚊香	*wénxiāng*

Food and drink

General

Beerhouse	啤酒屋	*píjiǔ wū*
Bill/cheque	買單	*mǎidān*
Chopsticks	筷子	*kuàizi*
Ice	冰	*bīng*
Knife and fork	刀叉	*dāochā*
Lunchbox	便當	*biàndàng*
Market	市場	*shìchǎng*
Menu	菜單	*càidān*
Night market	夜市	*yèshì*
Restaurant	餐廳	*cāntīng*
Snacks ("little eats")	小吃	*xiǎo chī*
Spoon	勺子	*sháozi*
Supermarket	超級市場	*chāojí shìchǎng*
Taiwan buffet/self-service caféteria	自助餐	*zìzhù cān*
Take-away	帶走	*dàizǒu*
Teahouse	茶館	*cháguǎn*
How much is that?	多少錢?	*duōshǎo qián?*
I'm a vegetarian	我是吃素的	*wǒ shì chīsù de*
I don't eat (meat)	我不吃 (肉)	*wǒ bù chī (ròu)*

| I would like | 我想要 | *wǒ xiǎng yào* |
| Not spicy | 不辣 | *bùlà* |

Aiyu jelly drink	愛玉凍飲	*àiyù dòngyǐn*
Beer	啤酒	*píjiǔ*
Coffee	咖啡	*kāfēi*
Fruit juice	果汁	*guǒzhī*
Gaoliang	高粱酒	*gāoliáng jiǔ*
Milk	牛奶	*niúnǎi*
Papaya milk	木瓜牛奶	*mùguā niúnǎi*
Red wine	紅酒	*hóng jiǔ*
Rice wine	米酒	*mǐjiǔ*
Shaohsing wine	紹興酒	*shàoxīng jiǔ*
Starfruit juice	楊桃汁	*yángtáozhī*
Sugar cane juice	甘蔗汁	*gānzhèzhī*
Taiwan Beer	台灣啤酒	*táiwān píjiǔ*
Tea	茶	*chá*
Baozhong tea	包種茶	*bāozhǒng chá*
Black tea	紅茶	*hóng chá*
Bubble tea	泡沫紅茶	*pàomò hóng chá*
Dongding oolong	凍頂烏龍	*dòngdǐng wūlóng*
Fruit tea	水果茶	*shuǐguǒ chá*
Green tea	綠茶	*lù chá*
Iron Guanyin tea	鐵觀音茶	*tiěguānyīn chá*
Jasmine tea	茉莉花茶	*mòlìhuā chá*
Oolong tea	烏龍茶	*wūlóng chá*
Oriental Beauty tea	東方美人茶	*dōngfāng měirén chá*
Pearl milk tea	珍珠奶茶	*zhēnzhū nǎichá*
White wine	白酒	*bái jiǔ*
Wine	酒	*jiǔ*
Yoghurt	酸奶	*suānnǎi*

Beef	牛肉	*niúròu*
Bread	麵包	*miànbāo*
Chicken	雞	*jī*
Chilli	辣椒	*làjiāo*
Crab	螃蟹	*pángxiè*
Duck	鴨子	*yāzi*
Eel	鰻魚	*mán yú*
Egg	雞蛋	*jīdàn*
Fish	魚	*yú*
Garlic	蒜	*suàn*
Ginger	薑	*jiāng*
Green bean	綠豆	*lù dòu*
Lamb	羊肉	*yángròu*

MSG	味精	wèijīng
Mushroom	香菇	xiānggū
Noodles	麵	miàn
Oyster	蠔	háo
Pork	豬肉	zhūròu
Prawn/shrimp	蝦	xiā
Red bean	紅豆	hóngdòu
Rice (uncooked)	米	mǐ
Rice (steamed)	白飯	báifàn
Rice (fried)	炒飯	chǎofàn
Salt	鹽	yán
Soup	湯	tāng
Soy sauce	醬油	jiàngyóu
Squid	魷魚	yóuyú
Sugar	糖	táng
Tofu	豆腐	dòufǔ
Vegetables	菜	cài

Fruit

Fruit	水果	shuǐguǒ
Apple	蘋果	píngguǒ
Banana	香蕉	xiāngjiāo
Cherry	櫻桃	yīngtáo
Coconut	椰子	yēzi
Durian	榴蓮	liúlián
Grape	葡萄	pútáo
Guava	芭樂	bālè
Honeydew melon	哈密瓜	hāmìguā
Kiwi fruit	奇異果	qíyìguǒ
Longan	龍眼	lóngyǎn
Lychee	荔枝	lìzhī
Mango	芒果	mángguǒ
Orange (tangerine)	橘子	júzi
Papaya	木瓜	mùguā
Peach	桃子	táozi
Pear	梨子	lízi
Persimmon	柿子	shìzi
Pineapple	鳳梨	fènglí
Plum	李子	lǐzi
Pomelo	柚子	yòuzi
Watermelon	西瓜	xīguā

Breakfast

Clay oven roll	燒餅	shāobǐng
Congee	稀飯	xīfàn
Dough fritter	油條	yóutiáo
Egg pancake	蛋餅	dànbǐng

Soybean milk	豆漿	*dòujiāng*
Spring onion pancake	蔥油餅	*cōngyóubǐng*
Steamed bread	饅頭	*mántóu*
Steamed bun	包子	*bāozi*

Everyday dishes/snacks

Baked sweet potatoes	烤蕃薯	*kǎo fānshǔ*
Beef noodles	牛肉麵	*niúròu miàn*
Boiled dumplings	水餃	*shuǐjiǎo*
Braised pork rice	滷肉飯	*lǔròufàn*
Fish balls	魚丸	*yúwán*
Fried dumplings	鍋貼	*guōtiē*
Fuzhou beef pepper pies	福州牛肉胡椒餅	*fúzhōu niúròu húijiāo bǐng*
Hot and sour soup	酸辣湯	*suānlàtāng*
Knife-cut noodles	刀削麵	*dāoxiāo miàn*
Lu wei	蘆薈	*lú huì*
Oyster omelette	蚵仔煎	*é a jiān*
Rice dumplings	粽子	*zòngzi*
Rice noodles	米粉	*mǐfěn*
Sanbei	三杯	*sānbēi*
Sesame paste noodles	麻醬麵	*májiàng miàn*
Shaved ice (dessert)	刨冰 (礤冰)	*bàobīng* (*tsuàbīng* in Taiwanese)
Spring roll	潤餅	*rùnbǐng*
Soybean pudding	豆花	*dòuhuā*
Steamed dumplings	小籠包	*xiǎolóng bāo*
Steamed meat buns	肉包子	*ròubāozi*
Steamed vegetable buns	素菜包子	*sùcài bāozi*
Stinky tofu	臭豆腐	*chòu dòufǔ*
Tea eggs	茶葉蛋	*cháyè dàn*

Local specialities

Brown-sugar cake (Penghu)	黑糖糕	*hēitánggāo*
Coffin bread (Tainan)	棺材板	*guāncáibǎn*
Danzi noodles (Tainan)	擔仔麵	*dān zǐ miàn*
Deep-fried meat cakes (Hsinchu)	竹塹餅	*zhúqiàn bǐng*
Dumplings in soup (Hualien)	扁食	*biǎnshí*
Green bean cakes (Keelung)	綠豆沙餅	*lǜdòushā bǐng*
"Little pastry wrapped in big pastry" (Taipei)	大餅包小餅	*dà bǐng bāo xiǎo bǐng*
Mashu (Hualien)	麻薯	*máshǔ*
Meatballs (Changhua/Hsinchu)	貢丸	*gòngwán*
Milkfish (south Taiwan)	虱目魚	*shīmù yú*
Ox-tongue cake (Lugang)	牛舌餅	*niúshé bǐng*
Phoenix-eye cakes (Lugang)	鳳眼糕	*fèngyǎngāo*

Rice dumplings (Shihmen)	肉粽	ròuzòng
Rice powder tea (Lugang)	麵茶	miàn chá
Shrimp monkeys (Lugang)	蝦猴	xiāhóu
Shrimp rolls (Tainan)	蝦捲	xiājuǎn
Square cookies (Chiayi)	方塊酥	fāngkuàisū
Suncakes (Taichung)	太陽餅	tàiyáng bǐng
Taro balls (Jiufen)	芋丸	yùwán
Turkey rice (Chiayi)	火雞肉飯	huǒjīròu fàn
Wah gwei (Tainan)	碗粿	wah gwei (Taiwanese)

Hakka specialities

Bamboo shoots	竹筍	zhúsǔn
Ban tiao	板條	bǎntiáo
Braised stuffed tofu	釀豆腐	niàng dóufù
Fried pork intestines with ginger	生薑炒豬腸	shēngjiāng chǎozhūcháng
Hakka mashu	客家蔴薯	kèjiā máshǔ
Lei cha (cereal tea)	擂茶	léichá
Wild lotus	蓮	lián

Aboriginal specialities

Bamboo rice	竹筒飯	zhútǒngfàn
Betel nut chicken	檳榔雞	bīnlángjī
Millet wine	小米酒	xiǎo mǐjiǔ
Mountain pig (boar)	山豬	shānzhū

Regional Chinese cuisine

Beijing duck	北京烤鴨	běijīng kǎoyā
Buddha jumps over the wall (Fujianese)	佛跳牆	fótiàoqiáng
Chicken with peanuts (Sichuan)	宮保雞丁	gōngbǎo jīdīng
Dim sum (Cantonese)	點心	diǎnxīn
Drunken chicken (Shanghai)	醉雞	zuìjī
Hotpot (Sichuan)	火鍋	huóguō
Mapo doufu (Shanghai)	麻婆豆腐	mápó dòufù
Songren yumi (Shanghai)	鬆軟玉米	sōngrén yùmǐ
Yellow croaker (Shanghai)	黃魚	huángyú

Japanese cuisine

Japanese curry rice	日本咖哩飯	rìběn kālǐfàn
Ramen	拉麵	lāmiàn
Sashimi	生魚片	shēngyúpiàn
Shabu shabu	涮涮鍋	shuànshuàn guō
Sushi	壽司	shòusī
Teppanyaki	鐵板燒	tiěbǎnshāo

Glossary

Aborigines Common English name for Taiwan's indigenous population.

Amitofu 阿彌陀佛 (*āmítuófó*) Greeting used by Buddhist monks, a reference to Buddha.

ARC Alien Resident Certificate.

Arhat Buddhist saint.

Austronesian Cultural and linguistic family that stretches across the Asia-Pacific region, and includes Taiwan's indigenous population.

Betel nut Seed of the betel palm, also known as areca nut, and used extensively in Taiwan as a stimulant, chewed but not swallowed.

Betel nut beauty 檳榔西施 (*bīnláng xīshī*) Used to describe the scantily dressed young women who sell betel nut from glass booths along roadsides island-wide. *Xīshī* was a legendary beauty in ancient China.

Black Gold Term used to describe the KMT's links with local mafia and endemic corruption during the martial law period.

Bodhisattva Buddhist who has attained enlightenment, but who has chosen not to leave the cycle of birth and death (*samsara*) until all other beings are enlightened. Worshipped as a god or goddess.

Camphor Tree containing camphor crystals that produce aromatic oil. Used for its scent, as an embalming fluid and in medicines, especially in the nineteenth century.

Daizi 袋子 (*dàizi*) Bag. Supermarkets and convenience stores will ask if you want to buy one (you don't get them for free in environment-friendly Taiwan).

Dalu 大陸 (*dàlù*) Common term for mainland China, formally known as *zhōngguó*.

Democratic Progressive Party (DPP) 民主進步黨 (*mínzhǔ jìnbù dǎng*) Taiwan's first opposition party when it was established in 1986, winning the presidency under Chen Shui-bian in 2000 and 2004 (see p.392).

Executive Yuan The prime minister's cabinet.

Fo 佛 (*fó*) Buddha.

Formosa Name given to Taiwan by Portuguese sailors in the sixteenth century, and used in the West to describe the island until the 1950s.

Fujian Southeastern province in China, ancestral home of seventy percent of Taiwan's population.

Fuxing 復興 (*fùxīng*) Revival. Common street name.

Hakka 客家人 (*kèjiā ren*) Chinese ethnic group and language.

Han Chinese Used to describe all the Chinese ethnic groups (including Taiwanese, Hakka and mainlanders), as distinct from Taiwan's Austronesian indigenous population.

Hanyu Pinyin 漢語拼音 (*hànyǔ pīnyīn*) System of transliterating Chinese script into roman characters favoured by mainland China and Taiwan's KMT.

Heping 和平 (*hépíng*) Peace. Common street name.

Hoklo See under "Taiwanese".

Homestay 民宿 (*mínsù*) Private hotel, usually supplying bed and breakfast and often located in a family home.

Jianguo 建國 (*jiànguó*). "National founding" or "to found a nation". Common street name.

KTV Karaoke TV. Usually refers to lavish karaoke centres with private rooms, drinks and food.

Kuomintang (KMT) 國民黨 (*guómíndǎng*) Chinese Nationalist Party, established in 1912 in China, and led by Chiang Kai-shek from the 1920s. Defeated by Mao Zedong's Communist Party in China's civil war, and based in Taiwan from 1949 where it held power until 2000, and from 2008 onwards (see p.393).

Legislative Yuan Taiwan's parliament.

Mainlanders 外省人 (*wàishēngrén*) Term used to describe the Chinese who fled to

Taiwan from the mainland in the wake of the Communist victory in 1949. Resented by younger generations who feel the term suggests they are less Taiwanese.

Mandarin Chinese English name for the official language of China and Taiwan, where it's called *pǔtōnghuà* ("common speech") and *guóyǔ* ("national language") respectively. Originally based on the Beijing dialect (spoken by "mandarins", or imperial government officials).

Mandopop Slang for Mandarin Chinese pop music. Cantopop refers to music from Hong Kong (Cantonese language).

Meiguoren 美國人 (*měiguórén*) American, but often applied to all foreigners in Taiwan.

Ming dynasty Imperial family that overthrew the Mongolian Yuan dynasty and ruled China from 1368 to 1644, when China was seized by the Manchurian Qing dynasty.

Minquan 民權 (*mínquán*) Second of Sun Yat-sen's "Three Principles of the People", meaning "people power" or democracy. Common street name.

Minsheng 民生 (*mínshēng*) Third of Sun Yat-sen's "Three Principles of the People", meaning "the people's welfare" or "government for the people", and equated with socialism in China. Common street name.

Minzu 民族 (*mínzú*) First of Sun Yat-sen's "Three Principles of the People", loosely translated as "nationalism", or freedom from imperial domination. Common street name.

Oolong 烏龍 (*wūlóng*) Type of semi-fermented tea, as opposed to black tea (fully fermented) and green tea (unfermented).

Pingpu 平埔 (*píngpǔ*) Umbrella term used to describe the indigenous peoples that traditionally lived on the plains rather than the mountains.

PRC 中華人民共和國 (*zhōnghuá rénmín gònghéguó*) People's Republic of China. Official name for mainland China.

Qing dynasty Last imperial family to rule China (1644–1911), a Manchurian dynasty that overthrew the Ming and was in turn replaced by Sun Yat-sen's Nationalist Party.

Renai 仁愛 (*rénài*) "Beneficence". Common street name.

Republic of China (ROC) 中華民國 (*zhōnghuá mínguó*). Taiwan's official name.

Sakyamuni Name given to the historical Buddha.

Shophouse Chinese-style house, long and narrow, with a store in the front and living quarters at the back.

Stele Freestanding stone tablet carved with Chinese characters.

Sutra Sacred Buddhist text.

Taiwanese Commonly used to describe the ethnically Fujianese Chinese in Taiwan, and the language they speak. The term "Hoklo" is preferred officially, as technically all citizens on the island are Taiwanese.

Takasago Former Japanese colonial name for Taiwan, meaning "the country of high mountains".

Tongyong Pinyin 通用拼音 (*tōngyòng pīnyīn*) System of transliterating Chinese script into roman characters favoured by Taiwan's former DPP government, devised by a Taiwanese professor in 1998.

Wade Giles Antiquated system of transliterating Chinese script into roman characters, formerly used in Taiwan and still the preferred method of writing names for many of its citizens.

Waiguoren 外國人(*wàiguórén*) Foreigner (literally "someone outside their own country"). Foreigners are also sometimes called *laowai* (老外; *lǎowài*), literally "old foreigner".

Xinsheng 新生 (*xīnshēng*) "New life" or "new born". Common street name.

Xinyi 信義 (*xìnyì*) Honesty. Common street name.

Yuanzhumin 原住民 (*yuánzhùmín*) Official Chinese name for Taiwan's indigenous tribes, meaning "original inhabitants".

Zhongshan 中山 (*zhōngshān*) Chinese name for Sun Yat-sen. Common street name.

Zhongxiao 忠孝 (*zhōngxiào*) "Loyalty and filial piety". Common street name.

Zhongzheng 中正 (*zhōngzhèng*) Chinese name for Chiang Kai-shek. Common street name.

Small print and

Index

A Rough Guide to Rough Guides

Published in 1982, the first Rough Guide – to Greece – was a student scheme that became a publishing phenomenon. Mark Ellingham, a recent graduate in English from Bristol University, had been travelling in Greece the previous summer and couldn't find the right guidebook. With a small group of friends he wrote his own guide, combining a highly contemporary, journalistic style with a thoroughly practical approach to travellers' needs.

The immediate success of the book spawned a series that rapidly covered dozens of destinations. And, in addition to impecunious backpackers, Rough Guides soon acquired a much broader and older readership that relished the guides' wit and inquisitiveness as much as their enthusiastic, critical approach and value-for-money ethos.

These days, Rough Guides include recommendations from shoestring to luxury and cover more than 200 destinations around the globe, including almost every country in the Americas and Europe, more than half of Africa and most of Asia and Australasia. Our ever-growing team of authors and photographers is spread all over the world, particularly in Europe, the US and Australia.

In the early 1990s, Rough Guides branched out of travel, with the publication of Rough Guides to World Music, Classical Music and the Internet. All three have become benchmark titles in their fields, spearheading the publication of a wide range of books under the Rough Guide name.

Including the travel series, Rough Guides now number more than 350 titles, covering: phrasebooks, waterproof maps, music guides from Opera to Heavy Metal, reference works as diverse as Conspiracy Theories and Shakespeare, and popular culture books from iPods to Poker. Rough Guides also produce a series of more than 120 World Music CDs in partnership with World Music Network.

Visit www.roughguides.com to see our latest publications.

Rough Guide credits

Text editor: Emma Gibbs
Layout: Ankur Guha
Cartography: Rajesh Chhibber
Picture editor: Mark Thomas
Production: Rebecca Short
Proofreaders: Jennifer Speake, Grace Pai
Cover design: Nicole Newman, Dan May
Photographer: Brice Minnigh
Editorial: London Andy Turner, Keith Drew, Edward Aves, Alice Park, Lucy White, Jo Kirby, James Smart, Natasha Foges, Róisín Cameron, James Rice, Emma Beatson, Kathryn Lane, Monica Woods, Mani Ramaswamy, Harry Wilson, Lucy Cowie, Alison Roberts, Lara Kavanagh, Eleanor Aldridge, Ian Blenkinsop, Joe Staines, Matthew Milton, Tracy Hopkins; **Delhi** Madhavi Singh, Jalpreen Kaur Chhatwal, Jubbi Francis
Design & Pictures: London Scott Stickland, Dan May, Diana Jarvis, Nicole Newman,

Sarah Cummins, Emily Taylor; **Delhi** Umesh Aggarwal, Ajay Verma, Jessica Subramanian, Pradeep Thapliyal, Sachin Tanwar, Anita Singh, Nikhil Agarwal, Sachin Gupta
Production: Liz Cherry, Louise Daly, Erika Pepe
Cartography: London Ed Wright, Katie Lloyd-Jones; **Delhi** Ashutosh Bharti, Rajesh Mishra, Animesh Pathak, Jasbir Sandhu, Swati Handoo, Deshpal Dabas, Lokamata Sahu
Marketing, Publicity & roughguides.com: Liz Statham
Digital Travel Publisher: Peter Buckley
Reference Director: Andrew Lockett
Operations Coordinator: Becky Doyle
Publishing Director (Travel): Clare Currie
Commercial Manager: Gino Magnotta
Managing Director: John Duhigg

Publishing information

This second edition published April 2011 by

Rough Guides Ltd,
80 Strand, London WC2R 0RL
11, Community Centre, Panchsheel Park, New Delhi 110017, India
Distributed by the Penguin Group

Penguin Books Ltd,
80 Strand, London WC2R 0RL

Penguin Group (USA)
375 Hudson Street, NY 10014, USA

Penguin Group (Australia)
250 Camberwell Road, Camberwell, Victoria 3124, Australia

Penguin Group (NZ)
67 Apollo Drive, Mairangi Bay, Auckland 1310, New Zealand

Rough Guides is represented in Canada by Tourmaline Editions Inc. 662 King Street West, Suite 304, Toronto, Ontario M5V 1M7

Cover concept by Peter Dyer.

Typeset in Bembo and Helvetica to an original design by Henry Iles.

Printed in Singapore
© Stephen Keeling and Brice Minnigh
Maps © Rough Guides
No part of this book may be reproduced in any form without permission from the publisher except for the quotation of brief passages in reviews.
448pp includes index
A catalogue record for this book is available from the British Library
ISBN: 978-1-84836-657-2

The publishers and authors have done their best to ensure the accuracy and currency of all the information in **The Rough Guide to Taiwan**, however, they can accept no responsibility for any loss, injury, or inconvenience sustained by any traveller as a result of information or advice contained in the guide.

1   3   5   7   9   8   6   4   2

Help us update

We've gone to a lot of effort to ensure that the second edition of **The Rough Guide to Taiwan** is accurate and up-to-date. However, things change – places get "discovered", opening hours are notoriously fickle, restaurants and rooms raise prices or lower standards. If you feel we've got it wrong or left something out, we'd like to know, and if you can remember the address, the price, the hours, the phone number, so much the better.

Please send your comments with the subject line "**Rough Guide Taiwan Update**" to ©mail @uk.roughguides.com. We'll credit all contributions and send a copy of the next edition (or any other Rough Guide if you prefer) for the very best emails.

Find more travel information, connect with fellow travellers and book your trip on ⓦwww.roughguides.com

Acknowledgements

Stephen Keeling: Thanks to Cheng Ying-Huei at the Tourism Bureau, Mary Leung for the tips, Connie Wu for translation advice, Pan Shu-Han at Sun Moon Lake, Sammy Hawkins in Kenting, Lucille Sun for being so generous in Checheng, Ariel Lee for her help in Alishan, Kuang-Ying Lafei Huang at Taijiang National Park, Liu Chun-chi at the National Palace Museum, Megan Jefferies, Joey and Roland in Kinmen, Seven in Penghu, Lily Lee in Taitung, Wen Ching Ching in Kaohsiung, Tsan Drese at Shei-Pa National Park, Ken Huang and Liao Xiu Yue in Maolin, Liu Yi-Pin and her team in Tainan, Kenny Wang, Holly He Mei-ying in Taichung, Sandra Yu Chen-yi at Taroko National Park, Katherine Huang at Yushan National Park, Anne Wang in Hsinchu and Rick Yu Chen-che in Matsu.

Extra special thanks is due to Maurice Ngo for his tips and generosity in Taipei, Elisa Lu for her continued support and sage advice, and Tim Hsu Ting-fa for going far above and beyond the call of duty; Emma Gibbs did a great job in London (thanks also to Harry Wilson, Mark Thomas and Georgina Palffy), while as always, none of this would be possible without the support of Tiffany Wu.

Readers' letters

Thanks to all the readers who have taken the time to write in with comments and suggestions (and apologies if we've inadvertently omitted or misspelt anyone's name):

James Clark, Alice Huang, A.G. Klei and Ruth Campbell-Page, Tim.

ROUGH GUIDES

SMALL PRINT

Photo credits

Index

Map entries are in colour.

Map symbols

-----	International boundary		🏠	Mountain refuge/lodge
--- ---	Chapter division boundary		♦	Place of interest
▬▬▬	Highway		@	Internet access
═══	Major road		ⓘ	Information office
═══	Minor road		⊠	Post office
▬▬▬	Pedestrianized street		☏	Phone office
───	Unpaved road		⊞	Hospital
▬▬▬	Railway line		⛽	Petrol station
- - - - -	Path		♦	Museum
— —	Ferry route		🏛	Monument
───	River/coast		∴	Ruin
───	Wall		🗼	Lighthouse
—Ⓜ—	Metro station & line		🏰	Fortress
– Ⓜ –	Metro station & line		■	Tower
	(under construction)		⊙	Statue
●- - -●	Cable car & station		⊠	Gate
	Cliff		‿	Bridge
	Rocks		⌂	Observatory
	Crater		⚔	Battlefield
	Mountain range		⅛	Picnic area
▲	Peak		🏖	Beach
⌂	Cave		✂	Snorkelling/diving area
	Waterfall		🏯	Monastery
	Surf area		🎋	Chinese temple
	Spring		▲	Hindu temple
☽	Sand dune		🕌	Mosque
	Banyan tree		🛕	Buddhist temple
∩	Arch		♦	Pagoda
⚓	River boat/ferry		🏮	Shrine
★	Bus stop		⊞	Church
🅿	Parking		▬	Building
✈	Airport		▢	Market
✈	Airport-domestic		⬭	Stadium
◉	Accommodation		⊞	Christian cemetery
▣	Restaurant/bar			Park
⚠	Campsite			Beach

So now we've told you about the things not to miss, the best places to stay, the top restaurants, the liveliest bars and the most spectacular sights, it only seems fair to tell you about the best travel insurance around

WorldNomads.com
keep travelling safely

Recommended by Rough Guides